CW00429600

The
INTERNATIONAL CRITICAL COMMENTARY
on the Holy Scriptures of the Old and New Testaments

GENERAL EDITORS

G. I. DAVIES, F.B.A.

Professor of Old Testament Studies in the University of Cambridge
Fellow of Fitzwilliam College

AND

G. N. STANTON, HON. D.D.

Emeritus Lady Margaret's Professor of Divinity, University of Cambridge
Former Fellow of Fitzwilliam College

CONSULTING EDITORS

J. A. EMERTON, F.B.A.

Emeritus Regius Professor of Hebrew in the University of Cambridge
Fellow of St John's College, Cambridge
Honorary Canon of St George's Cathedral, Jerusalem

AND

C. E. B. CRANFIELD, F.B.A.

Emeritus Professor of Theology in the University of Durham

FORMERLY UNDER THE EDITORSHIP OF

S. R. DRIVER
A. PLUMMER
C. A. BRIGGS

JOHN 1–4

A CRITICAL AND EXEGETICAL COMMENTARY

ON

JOHN 1–4

BY

JOHN F. McHUGH

taught in the Faculty of Theology in the University of Durham
and served as a member of the Pontifical Biblical Commission

edited by Graham N. Stanton

t&t clark

T&T Clark International
A Continuum Imprint

The Tower Building
11 York Road
London SE1 7NX

80 Maiden Lane,
New York, NY 10038
USA

www.tandtclark.com

British Library Cataloguing-in-publication Data
A catalogue record for this book is available at the British Library

ISBN: 0-567-03158-6
ISBN: 978-0-567-03158-7

The NewJerusalem and GraecaII fonts used to print this work are available from Linguist's Software, Inc., PO Box 580, Edmonds, WA 98020-0580 USA. Tel (425) 775-1130. www.linguistsoftware.com

Typeset and copy-edited by Forthcoming Publications Ltd
www.forthcomingpublications.com

Printed and bound in Great Britain by MPG Books Ltd., Bodmin, Cornwall

CONTENTS

GENERAL EDITORS' PREFACE

Much scholarly work has been done on the Bible since the publication of the first volumes of the International Critical Commentary in the 1890s. New linguistic, textual, historical and archaeological evidence has become available, and there have been changes and developments in methods of study. In the twenty-first century there will be as great a need as ever, and perhaps a greater need, for the kind of commentary that the International Critical Commentary seeks to supply. The series has long had a special place among works in English on the Bible, because it has sought to bring together all the relevant aids to exegesis, linguistic and textual no less than archaeological, historical, literary and theological, to help the reader to understand the meaning of the books of the Old and New Testaments. In the confidence that such a series meets a need, the publishers and the editors are commissioning new commentaries on all the books of the Bible. The work of preparing a commentary on such a scale cannot but be slow, and developments in the past half-century have made the commentator's task yet more difficult than before, but it is hoped that the remaining volumes will appear without too great intervals between them. No attempt has been made to secure a uniform theological or critical approach to the problems of the various books, and scholars have been selected for their scholarship and not for their adherence to any school of thought. It is hoped that the new volumes will attain the high standards set in the past, and that they will make a significant contribution to the understanding of the books of the Bible.

G. I. D.
G. N. S.

PREFACE

John McHugh was surely one of the most learned and able New Testament scholars of the latter part of the twentieth century and the first years of the twenty-first. For some years a member of the Pontifical Biblical Commission, he had a worldwide reputation. The great wealth of his learning was matched by penetrating insight, originality and clarity of mind. He was, I think, exceptionally well prepared to undertake the especially formidable task of writing a full-scale commentary on St John's Gospel. It is a matter of profound regret that he did not live to complete it.

John was a splendid colleague, who could always be relied on to give wise counsel. Always generous in his readiness to assist other scholars, he sometimes allowed his altruism to hold up the progress of his own work. He was greatly appreciated by the students who heard his lectures, and those who had tutorials with him were specially privileged.

In addition to his knowledge of the Bible, of Rabbinic writings and of the Qumran texts, he had a wonderful familiarity with classical Greek and Latin literature, with mediaeval Latin, and with a wide range of English and other literatures. He was fluent in a number of European languages. He had a notable feeling for language, which is reflected in the clarity and felicitousness of his own English style.

John McHugh had a keen realization of the need for theologians to be concerned about politics. He was always well informed about current affairs, and cared deeply for justice and compassion. He was, for example, deeply concerned about the injustices suffered by the Palestinians since 1948, though he was never forgetful of the sufferings of the Jews in the 1930s and 1940s or lacking in compassion for them.

He was a wonderful friend and a shining example of what it means to be a faithful Christian pastor.

Charles Cranfield

INTRODUCTION

Introductions to commentaries on biblical books have nearly always set out the author's views on the authorship, sources, setting, and textual tradition of the writing about to be considered. Now and again, a commentator will explain that while the extended Introduction precedes the exegesis, this was the last part of the commentary to be written.

At the time of his sudden death on 3 February 2006 at Alnwick, Northumberland, Dr John McHugh left a largely complete commentary on the first four chapters of John's Gospel. He had not written the Introduction to his planned ICC commentary on the whole of John's Gospel. Several years ago in discussion with me (as General Editor of the New Testament ICC commentaries) he explained that it would not be possible to draft the Introduction until he had completed at least half the planned two volume commentary. I fully concurred.

Dr McHugh's views on the topics usually considered in an Introduction would have been of considerable interest to many readers. In a few places in the commentary which follows it is possible to glimpse the ways he would have tackled disputed questions concerning the origin and structure of this Gospel, and its relationship to other early Christian writings. Alas, the notes he left did not allow me to include a summary of his views with any confidence.

The sub-divisions adopted and the titles given to the main sections and sub-sections of John 1–4 are striking. They presuppose particular ways of construing the text and will certainly stimulate many readers to further thought. For example, along with many commentators, Dr McHugh confines the Prologue to John 1.1-18. Verses 19 to 51 of ch. 1 are not read as 'a second Prologue', but as the first section of the evangelist's presentation of 'The First Week' in the 'ministry' of Jesus which runs from 1.19 to 2.12.

In notes Dr McHugh left he carefully compares his own plans for the topics to be discussed in his Introduction with the Introductions to the major modern commentaries. While it is a pity that there is no traditional Introduction to this commentary, there is a sense in which its absence may be an advantage. We have no option but to consider carefully with Dr McHugh the text, the text, and nothing but the text. This commentary focuses sharply on precisely what the evangelist wrote. The exegesis is not pre-determined by theories about the origin, social and religious setting of this Gospel. Dr McHugh would certainly have accepted the old adage that the evangelist is the finest commentator on this Gospel.

John McHugh gave an intriguing foretaste of his views on many passages in the later chapters in John's Gospel in his article, '"In Him was Life": John's Gospel and the Parting of the Ways', in ed. James D. G. Dunn, *Jews and Christians: The Parting of the Ways A.D. 70 to 135*, WUNT 66, Tübingen 1992, 123-58. There he tackled a topic which continues to attract comment and debate: the extent to which John's Gospel is anti-Jewish. He insisted that the Fourth Gospel cannot be called polemically anti-Jewish. 'There is certainly a powerful and deep stream of apologetic directed towards those of the Jewish faith who might wish to understand how the new Christians looked at Jesus, but hostility in principle seems too strong a word' (p. 158).

Dr McHugh had been working on his ICC commentary for many years. From time to time he sent his drafts on sections of the text to me. So I have known for a long time that we could anticipate an outstanding, fresh reading of John's Gospel. Dr McHugh also sought comments on his drafts from his friends and former colleagues in the Department of Theology at Durham University, Professors Kingsley Barrett and Charles Cranfield. They both shared my conviction that since Dr Mc Hugh's draft on chs. 1 to 4 was quite distinctive and almost complete, we should try to secure its publication.

My predecessor as General Editor of the series, Professor Charles Cranfield, first invited Dr McHugh to write the ICC commentary on John's Gospel. His warm commendation of the commentary and his appreciation of Dr McHugh as scholar, colleague, and teacher have been printed as a Preface on p. ix. Professor Barrett, himself the author of one of the most influential commentaries on John's Gospel published in the twentieth century, writes as follows:

> To be asked to add a note to what Professor Cranfield has written in his Preface is a great privilege. It can only be a word of whole-hearted agreement. Nothing he has said is exaggerated. Dr McHugh's sudden death was not only a deep personal sorrow but a grievous academic loss. He was in every way—in languages, in history, in theology, in philosophy—qualified to write a great commentary on the Gospel of St John, and had begun, in the four chapters we have, to write such a commentary. Completed it would have stood beside those of Augustine, of Hoskyns (also incomplete at the author's death), and of Bultmann. It is left to another generation to complete the task.

It remains for me to add a word about the commentary which follows. Following his retirement from his Durham University post, for several years Dr McHugh undertook some parish duties while he continued to work on his commentary. I am certain that he conveyed in sermons and homilies to his parishioners some of his theological reflections on John's Gospel. How fortunate his parishioners were! When ill health forced early retirement from his parish responsibilities, he pressed ahead as he was able with his scholarly work.

In his correspondence with me, Dr McHugh mentioned that once he had completed his exegesis of the whole Gospel, he intended to add some further theological comments to the drafts. He also mentioned that he intended to interact more fully with at least some of the secondary literature. I readily agreed, anxious that he should press ahead with his invaluable exegesis.

As far as possible I have refrained from modifying the material which John left. The bibliographies are the major exception. I have drawn on John's own bibliographies and added references to some of the more recent secondary literature. I hope the bibliographies will assist readers who wish to consult some of the enormous secondary literature. I doubt whether any individual can now master it all! I am responsible for the present arrangement of the bibliographies and of the supplementary material in the fourteen excursuses.

I am very grateful to Mr Damian McHugh, John's brother, for making available to me not only computer disks and printouts, but also John's impressive collection of offprints and his bibliographical and other notes. The enthusiasm and support of Mr Haaris Naqvi of T&T Clark International has been much appreciated, as has the meticulous copy editing of Dr Duncan Burns of Forthcoming Publications Ltd.

Graham Stanton
Epiphany 2009

ABBREVIATIONS

General

α	Aquila
ca.	circa; about
cf.	consult the commentary (or commentaries) on that verse
ed(s).	editor(s), edited by
ellipsis	words in incomplete sentence
et al.	*et alii* (and others)
ETr	English translation
EV	English versions
FS	Festschrift, essays published to honour a friend and / or colleague
HB	Hebrew Bible
HT	Hebrew text
κτλ	και τα λοιπα = etc.
LXX	Septuagint
MT	Massoretic text
NF	Neue Folge
pace	with due deference to
sc	*scilicet*; that is to say, namely
slav	Slavonic version
s.v.	*sub voce*; under the word, look up the word
s.v.l.	*si vera lectio*; if this is the correct reading
TR	Textus Receptus
vid.	*vide*; see, consult

Journals, Series, and Works of Reference

AB	Anchor Bible
ABD	*Anchor Bible Dictionary*, 6 vols., New York, 1992
Abel	F.-M. Abel, *Grammaire du greq biblique*, Paris, 1927
Altaner	B. W. Altaner, *Patrology*, Freiburg, 1960
ANRW	eds. H. Temporini and W. Haase, *Aufstieg und Niedergang der römischen Welt: Geschichte und Kultur Roms im Spiegel der neueren Forschung*, Berlin, 1972–

ANT	ed. J. K. Elliott, *The Apocryphal New Testament*, Oxford, 1993
AOFG	C. F. Burney, *The Aramaic Origin of the Fourth Gospel*, Oxford, 1922
ASTI	*Annual of the Swedish Theological Institute*
AtBib	L. H. Grollenberg, *Atlas of the Bible*, ETr, London, 1956
BAG	W. Bauer, W. F. Arndt and F. W. Gingrich, *A Greek–English Lexicon of the New Testament and Other Early Christian Literature*, Chicago/Cambridge, 1957
BDAG	W. Bauer, F. W. Danker, W. F. Arndt and F. W. Gingrich, *A Greek–English Lexicon of the New Testament and Other Early Christian Literature*, Chicago/Cambridge, 2000
BDB	F. Brown, S. R. Driver and C. A. Briggs, *A Hebrew and English Lexicon of the Old Testament*, Oxford, 1906
BDF	F. Blass, A. Debrunner and R. W. Funk, *A Greek Grammar of the New Testament and Other Early Christian Literature*, ETr, Chicago, 1961
Ben	references to the seventeenth- to eighteenth-century Benedictine (Maurist) editions of the Fathers (convenient, since all later editions such as *PL PG SC* cite them with this abbreviation)
BETL	Bibliotheca ephemeridum theologicarum lovaniensium
BHS	*Biblia Hebraica Stuttgartensia*, editio funditus renovata, Stuttgart, 1967–77. The Massoretic text (MT) is cited according to this edition
BJ	*Bible de Jérusalem*
BJRL	*Bulletin of the John Rylands Library*
B-L	M. E. Boismard and A. Lamouille, *Un évangile pré-johannique.* [Includes the text of the homilies of Saint John Chrysostom which contain citations of John's Gospel, in Greek with French translation.] Études Bibliques 17, 18, 24, 25, 28, 29, Paris, 1993–96
BZ	*Biblische Zeitschrift*
CBQ	*Catholic Biblical Quarterly*
CBQMS	Catholic Biblical Quarterly Monograph Series
CCSG	Corpus Christianorum, series Graeca, Turnhout, 1977–
CCSL	Corpus Christianorum, series Latina, Turnhout, 1967–
CH	Corpus Hermeticum
Chilton	B. Chilton, *The Isaiah Targum: Introduction, Translation, Apparatus, and Notes*, Edinburgh, 1987
CSCO	Corpus scriptorum christianorum orientalium, Paris, 1903
CSEL	Corpus scriptorum ecclesiasticorum latinorum, Vienna, 1886–

DACL	eds. F. Cabrol and H. Leclercq *Dictionnaire d'archéologie chrétienne et de liturgie*, I–XV, 1903–53
DBS	eds. L. Pirot and A. Robert, *Dictionnaire de la Bible, Supplément*, Paris, 1928–
DCH	ed. D. J. A. Clines, *The Dictionary of Classical Hebrew*, Sheffield, 1993–
CGPAT	A. D. Denis, *Concordance greque des pseudépigraphes d'ancient testament*, Paris, 1987
DS	H. Denziger and E. Schönmetzer, *Enchiridion symbolorum*
DSSE	G. Vermes, *The Dead Sea Scrolls in English*, Harmondsworth, 2nd ed., 1975
EDNT	eds. H. Balz and H. Schneider, *Exegetical Dictionary of the New Testament*, 3 vols., Grand Rapids, 1990–93 (German original, 1978–83)
EstBibl	*Estudios Bíblicos*
ETL	*Epheremides Theologicae Lovanienses*, 1924–
EvTh	*Evangelische Theologie*
ExpTimes	*Expository Times*
GANT	M. Zerwick, *A Grammatical Analysis of the New Testament*, trans. and ed. by M. Grosvenor, Rome, 1974–79
GCS	Die griechischen christlichen Schriftsteller der ersten drei Jahrhunderte, 1897–
GGNT	A. T. Robertson, *A Grammar of the Greek New Testament*, London, 1914
Goodwin	W. G. Goodwin, *Syntax of the Moods and Tenses of the Greek Verb*, London, 1890
HALAT	eds. W. Baumgartner et al., *Hebräisches und aramäisches Lexicon zum Alten Testament*, 5 vols., Leiden, 1967–95
HALOT	eds. L. Koehler et al., *Hebrew and Aramaic Lexicon of the Old Testament*, ETr, 2 vols., Leiden, 2000
HDB	*Hastings Dictionary of the Bible*
HDCG	ed. J. Hastings, *Dictionary of Christ and the Gospels*, 2 vols., Edinburgh, 1906–1908
HJ	*Heythrop Journal*
HR	E. Hatch and H. A. Redpath, *A Concordance to the Septuagint and other Greek Versions of the OT*, 2 vols. and supplement, Oxford, 1892–1906
HTR	*Harvard Theological Review*
IBNTG	C. F. D. Moule, *An Idiom Book of New Testament Greek*, Cambridge, 1953
ICC	International Critical Commentary
Jastrow	M. J. Jastrow, *Dictionary of the Targumim*, London, 1903
JB	Jerusalem Bible, 1966
JB^{mg}	marginal note to JB

JBL	*Journal of Biblical Literature*
JG	E. A. Abbott, *Johannine Grammar*, London, 1906
JSNTSup	Journal for the Study of New Testament, Supplement Series
JSNT	*Journal for the Study of the New Testament*
JSOTSup	Journal for the Study of the Old Testament, Supplement Series
JTS	*Journal of Theological Studies*
JV	E. A. Abbott, *Johannine Vocabulary*, London, 1905
KBR	L. Koehler, W. Baumgartner and M. E. J. Richardson, *The Hebrew and Aramaic Lexicon of the Old Testament*, 2 vols., Leiden, 2001
LAB	*Liber Antiquitatum Biblicarum* of Pseudo-Philo
LHVT	ed. F. Zorell, *Lexicon Hebraicum Veteris Testamenti*, Rome, 1940–84
Loeb	Loeb Classical Library
LSJ	H. G. Liddell, R. Scott and H. S. Jones, *A Greek–English Lexicon*, Oxford, 9th ed., 1925–40
LXX	ed. Alfred Rahlfs, *Septuaginta*, 2 vols., Stuttgart, 1935
Neofiti	Martin McNamara's translations, introductions and apparatus to *Codex Neofiti: Genesis, Exodus, Numbers, Leviticus*, 4 vols., Edinburgh, 1992–95
MHT	J. H. Moulton, W. F. Howard and N. Turner, *A Grammar of New Testament Greek*, Edinburgh: I by J. H. Moulton (1906); II by W. F. Howard (1929): III and IV by Nigel Turner (1963 and 1976)
MM	J. H. Moulton and G. Milligan, *The Vocabulary of the Greek New Testament illustrated from the Papyri and Other Non-Literary Sources*, London, 1930
NA[26]	eds. Kurt Aland, Matthew Black, Carlo M. Martini, Bruce M. Metzger and Allen Wikgren, *Novum Testamentum Graece post Nestle communiter*, Stuttgart, 26th ed., 1979
NA[27]	eds. Barbara and Kurt Aland, Johannes Karavido-poulos, Carlo Martini and Bruce M. Metzger, *Novum Testamentum Graece post Nestle communiter*, Stuttgart, 27th ed., 1993
NAB	New American Bible, 1970
NIV	New International Version, 1995
NIV[mg]	marginal note to NIV
NJB	New Jerusalem Bible, 1985
NovT	*Novum Testamentum*
NovTSup	Novum Testamentum, Supplement Series
NRSV	New Revised Standard Version, 1989
NRSV[mg]	marginal note to NRSV
NTA	eds. E. Hennecke and W. Schneemelcher, *The New Testament Apocrypha*, 2 vols., London, 1963–65

NTD	Das Neue Testament Deutsch
NtlAbh	Neutestamentliche Abhandlungen
NTVoc	F. Neirynck, F. Van Segbroeck and H. Leclerc, *New Testament Vocabulary*, BETL 65, Louvain, 1984
OTP	ed. J. H. Charlesworth, *The Old Testament Pseudepigrapha*, 2 vols., London/New York, 1983–85
PG	ed. J.-P. Migne, *Patrologia Graeca*, 162 vols., Paris, 1857–66
PGL	ed. G. W. H. Lampe, *A Patristic Greek Lexicon*, Oxford, 1961
PL	ed. J.-P. Migne, *Patrologia Latina*, 217 vols., Paris, 1844–64
Quasten	J. Quasten, *Patrology*, 3 vols., Utrecht, 1966
RB	*Revue Biblique*
REB	The Revised English Bible, Cambridge, 1989
RHE	*Revue d'histoire ecclésiastique*
RHPR	*Revue d'histoire et de philosophie religieuses*
RScPhT	*Revue des sciences philosophiques et théologiques*
RSR	*Recherches des science religieuse*, 1910–
RSV	Revised Standard Version, 1946
RThom	*Revue Thomist*
RTP	*Revue de théologie et de philosophie*
RV	Revised Version, 1884
RV^mg	marginal note to RV
SB	H. L. Strack and P. Billerbeck, *Kommentar aus Talmud und Midrasch*, 6 vols., Munich, 1922–61
SBLDS	Society of Biblical Literature Dissertation Series
SBLSS	Society of Biblical Literature Symposium Series
SC	*Sources chrétiennes*
ScEs	*Science et esprit*
Schürer	Emil Schürer, *The History of the Jewish People in the Age of Jesus Christ (175 BC AD 135)*, rev. and ed. by G. Vermes et al., 4 vols., Edinburgh, 1973–87
SEÅ	*Svensk exegetisk årsbok*
SMTNTG	E. de W. Burton, *Syntax of the Moods and Tenses in New Testament Greek*, London, 2nd ed., 1893
SNTSMS	Society for New Testament Studies Monograph Series
SNTU	*Studien zum Neuen Testament und seiner Umwelt*
TB	*Theologische Berichte*
TCGNT	*A Textual Commentary on the Greek New Testament*, Bruce M. Metzger, Stuttgart, 1971; 2nd ed., 1994
TDOT	eds. G. J. Botterweck et al., *Theological Dictionary of the Old Testament*, Grand Rapids, 1974–
Thayer	J. H. Thayer, *A Greek–English Lexicon of the New Testament*, ed. C. L. W. Grimm, Edinburgh, 1888
ThHKNT	Theologischer Handkommentar zum Neuen Testament

TLG	*Thesaurus Linguae Graecae* CD Rom #*D*, Irvine, 1992; cf. *Thesaurus Linguae Graecae. Canon of Greek Authors and Works*, eds. L. Berkowitz et al., Oxford, 1990
TR	*Theologische Rundschau*
TWNT	eds. G. Kittel and G. Friedrich, *Theologisches Wörterbuch zum Neuen Testament*, 11 vols., Stuttgart, 1933–37
UBS	United Bible Societies' *Greek New Testament*
UBS³	United Bible Societies' *Greek New Testament*, 3rd ed., 1975
VD	*Verbum Domini*
Vg	Biblia Sacra iuxta Vulgatam versionem recensuit Robertus Weber, 2 vols., Stuttgart, 1969
VL	Vetus Latina: Die Reste der altlateinischen Bibel, 1949–
WA	M. Luther, *Kritische Gesamtausgabe* (= Weimar Ausgabe), 1883–1983
Wettstein	J. J. Wettstein, *Novum Testamentum Graecum*, 2 vols., Graz, 1962 (1751–52)
WTJ	*Westminster Theological Journal*
WUNT	Wissenschaftliche Untersuchungen zum Neuen Testament
ZDPV	*Zeitschrift des deutschen Palästinavereins*
Zerwick–Smith	M. Smith, *Biblical Greek: Illustrated by Examples*, ed. J. Smith, Rome, 1963
ZNW	*Zeitschrift für die neutestamentliche Wissenschaft*

BIBLIOGRAPHY

The bibliography that follows is divided into five major sections, and gives full references for literature cited in the footnotes in abbreviated form:

In a category of its own for research on John's Gospel is:
   eds. U. Schnelle et al., *Neuer Wettstein: Texte zum Neuen Testament aus Griechentum und Hellenismus*, Band 1/2 Texte zum Johannesevangelium, Berlin, 2001.

I. THE GREEK TEXT OF JOHN'S GOSPEL

Aland, B., et al., *Novum Testamentum Graece*, Stuttgart, 27th ed., 1993 (= NA[27]). [26th ed., 1979 = NA[26]]

Aland, K., et al., *The Greek New Testament*, United Bible Societies, New York/London, 3rd ed., 1975 (= UBS[3]). In the 4th ed. of 1994, the Greek text is unchanged; the apparatus has been revised.

Comfort, P. W., 'The Greek Text of the Gospel of John according to the Early Papyri', *NTS* 36 (1990), 625-29.

Elliott, J. K., *A Bibliography of Greek New Testament Manuscripts*, Cambridge, 2nd ed., 2000.

Elliott, W. J., and D. C. Parker, *The New Testament in Greek. IV. The Gospel according to St John: The Papyri*, Leiden, 1995.

Metzger, B. M., *A Textual Commentary on the Greek New Testament: A Companion Volume to the United Bible Societies' Greek New Testament*, Stuttgart, 1971; 2nd ed., 1994 (= *TCGNT*).

Schmid, U. B., with W. J. Elliott and D. C. Parker, *The New Testament in Greek*. IV. *The Gospel according to St John: The Majuscules*, Leiden, 2007.

Tischendorf, Constantin von, *Novum Testamentum Graece*. Editio octava maior, 2 vols., Leipzig, 1869–72; vol. 3, ed. C. R. Gregory, Leipzig, 1894.

Vogels, H. J., ed. *Novum Testamentum Graece et Latine*. Dusseldorf, 1922.

II. SURVEYS AND LISTS OF MONOGRAPHS AND ARTICLES

Becker, J., 'Aus der Literatur zum Johannesevangelium (1978–1980)', *TR* 47 (1982), 279-301, 305-47.

—'Das Johannesevangelium im Streit der Methoden (1980–1984)', *TR* 51 (1986), 1-78.

Haenchen E., 'Aus der Literatur zum Johannesevangelium 1929–1956', *TR* NS (1955), 295-335.

Haldimann, K., and H. Weder, 'Aus der Literatur zum Johannesevangelium 1985–1994', *TR* 67 (2002), 328-48, 425-56; 69 (2004), 75-115; 71 (2006), 91-113.

Kealy, S. P., *John's Gospel and the History of Biblical Interpretation*, 2 vols., Lewiston/Queenston/Lampeter, 2002.

Kysar, R., 'The Fourth Gospel. A Report on Recent Research', in eds. H. Temporini and W. Haase, *Aufstieg und Niedergang der römischen Welt: Geschichte und Kultur Roms im Spiegel der neueren Forschung*, II.25.3, Berlin/New York, 1985, 2389-480.

—'The Gospel of John in Current Research', *RSR* 9 (1983), 314-23.

Malatesta, E., *St John's Gospel, 1920–1965: A Cumulative and Classified Bibliography of Books and Periodical Literature on the Fourth Gospel*, Rome, 1967.

Mills, W. E., *The Gospel of John*, Bibliographies for Biblical Research, New Testament Series 4, Lewiston/Queenston/Lampeter, 1995.

Rábanos, E. R., and D. Muñoz León, *Bibliografía Joánica: Evangelo, Cartas y Apocalipsis 1960–1986*, Bibliotheca Hispana Biblica 14, Madrid, 1990.

Sloyan, G. S., *What are They Saying about John?* Johannine Scholarship 1965–2005, rev. ed., New York, 2006.

Smalley S. S., 'The Johannine Literature: A Sample of Recent Studies in English', *Theology* 103 (2000), 13-28.

Thyen, H., 'Aus der Literatur zum Johannesevangelium', *TR* 39 (1974–75), 1-69, 222-52, 289-330; 42 (1977), 211-70; 43 (1978), 329-59; 44 (1979), 97-134; 47 (1982), 279-301.

Van Belle, G., *Johannine Bibliography 1966–1985*, BETL 82, Leuven, 1988.

Wagner, G., *An Exegetical Bibliography of the New Testament: John and 1, 2, 3 John*, Macon, GA, 1987.

Three journals regularly list new books and articles:

Elenchus of Biblical Bibliography, Rome.
Internationale Zeitschriftenschau für Bibelwissenschaften und Grenzgebieten, ed. Bernhard Lang, Düsseldorf.
New Testament Abstracts, Cambridge, MA.

III. COMMENTARIES

Barclay, W., *The Gospel of John*, 2 vols., Edinburgh, 1956.
Barrett, C. K., *The Gospel according to St John*, London, 2nd ed., 1978.
Bauer, W., *Das Johannesevangelium*, Tübingen, 2nd ed., 1925.
Becker, J., *Das Evangelium des Johannes*, 2 vols., Gütersloh, 1979, 1981.
Bengel, J. A., *Gnomon Novi Testamenti*, Tübingen, first of many editions, 1742.
Bernard, J. H., *The Gospel according to St John*, ed. A. H. Mc Neile, ICC, 2 vols., London, 1928.
Boismard, M.-E., and A. Lamouille, *L'Évangile de Jean*, Paris, 1977.
Brodie, T. L., *The Gospel according to John: A Literary and Theological Commentary*, Oxford, 1993.
Brown, R. E. *The Gospel according to John*, 2 vols., New York, 1966–70.
Bruce, F. F., *The Gospel of John*, Basingstoke, 1983.
Büchsel, F., *Das Evangeliums nach Johannes*, NTD 4, Göttingen, 1949.
Bultmann, R., *The Gospel of John*, ETr, Oxford, 1971.
Burge, G. M., *John*, NIV Application Commentary, Grand Rapids, 2000.
Calvin, J., *The Gospel according to St John*, 2 vols., 1553; ETr, London, 1959.
Carson, D. A., *The Gospel according to John*, Leicester/Grand Rapids, 1991.
Dietzfelbinger, C., *Das Evangelium nach Johannes*, Züricher Bibelkommentare, 2 vols., Zürich, 2001.
Dodd, C. H., *The Interpretation of the Fourth Gospel*, Cambridge, 1953.
Edwards, M., *John*, Blackwell Bible Commentaries, Oxford, 2004.
Ellis, P. F., *The Genius of John: A Composition-Critical Commentary on the Fourth Gospel*, Collegeville, 1984.
Gnilka, J., *Johannesevangelium*, Würzburg, 1983.
Godet, F., *Commentary on the Gospel of St John*, 3 vols., Edinburgh, 1899–1900.
Grundmann, W., *Das Evangelium nach Johannes*, Berlin, 1968.
Haenchen, E., *Das Johannesevangelium*, ed. U. Busse, Tübingen, 1980; ETr, Hermeneia, 2 vols., Philadelphia, 1984.
Holtzmann, H. J., *Evangelium, Briefe und Offenbarung des Johannes*, 3rd ed., Tübingen, 1908.
Hoskyns, E. C., *The Fourth Gospel*, ed. F. N. Davey, London, 1947.
Howard, W. F., *The Gospel according to John*, Interpreter's Bible 8, Nashville and New York, 1952.
Keener, C. S., *The Gospel of John*, 2 vols., Peabody, 2003.

Köstenberger, A. J., *John*, Grand Rapids, 2004.
Kruse, C. G., *The Gospel according to John*, Tyndale New Testament Commentaries, Grand Rapids/Cambridge, 2004.
Lagrange, M. J., *Évangile selon St John*, Paris, 1948.
Lightfoot, R. H., *St John's Gospel: A Commentary*, ed. C. F. Evans, Oxford, 1956.
Lincoln, A. T., *The Gospel according to Saint John*, Black's New Testament Commentaries, London, 2005.
Lindars, B., *The Gospel of John*, London, 1972.
Loisy, A., *Le quatrième évangile*, Paris, 2nd ed., 1921.
Macgregor, G. H. C., *The Gospel of John*, London, 1928.
Maldonatus (Juan de Maldonado), *Commentaria in Quattuor Evangelia*, Pont-à-Mousson, 1596–97; see the edition by J. M. Raich, 2 vols., Mainz, 1874.
Marrow, S. B., *The Gospel of John: A Reading*, New York, 1995.
Marsh, J., *Saint John*, Harmondsworth, 1968.
Michaels, J., *John*, New International Biblical Commentary 4, Peabody, 1989.
Moloney, F. J., *The Gospel of John*, Sacra Pagina 4, Collegeville, 1998.
Neyrey, J. H., *The Gospel of John*, New Cambridge Bible Commentary, Cambridge, 2007.
Odeberg, H., *The Fourth Gospel Interpreted in its Relation to Contemporaneous Religious Currents in Palestine and the Hellenistic-Oriental World*, Uppsala, 1929; repr. Amsterdam, 1968.
Ridderbos, H., *The Gospel of John: A Theological Commentary*, ETr, Grand Rapids, 1997.
Sanders, J. N., and B. A. Mastin, *The Gospel according to St John*, London, 1968.
Schenke, L., *Johannes. Kommentar*, Düsseldorf, 1998.
Schlatter, A., *Der Evangelist Johannes*, Stuttgart, 4th ed., 1977.
Schnackenburg, R., *The Gospel according to St John*, 3 vols., London, 1968, 1980, 1982.
Schneider, J., *Das Evangelium nach Johannes*, NTD 4, Göttingen, 1972.
Schnelle, U., *Das Evangelium nach Johannes*, ThHKNT, Leipzig, 1998.
Schulz, Siegfried, *Das Evangelium nach Johannes*, NTD 4, Göttingen, 1972.
Smith, D. M., *John*, Abingdon New Testament Commentaries, Nashville, 1999.
Stibbe, Mark W. G., *John*, Sheffield, 1993.
Talbert, C. H., *Reading John, A Literary and Theological Commentary on the Fourth Gospel and the Johannine Epistles*, Macon, GA, rev. ed., 2005.
Thyen, H., *Das Johannesevangelium*, Handbuch zum Neue Testament 6, Tübingen, 2005.
Wellhausen, J., *Das Evangelium Johannes*, Berlin, 1908.
Wengst, K., *Das Johannesevangelium.* Theologischer Kommentar zum Neuen Testament 4/1, 2 vols., Stuttgart/Berlin/Cologne, 2000, 2001.
Westcott, B. F., *The Gospel according to St John*, 2 vols., London, 1908.

Whiteacre, R. A., *John*, Downers Grove/Leicester, 1999.
Wilckens, U., *Das Evangeliums nach Johannes*, NTD 4, Göttingen, 1998.
Witherington, B., III, *John's Wisdom: A Commentary on the Fourth Gospel*, Louisville, 1995.
Zahn, T., *Das Evangelium des Johannes ausgelegt*, Leipzig, 5th ed., 1921.

IV. GENERAL BIBLIOGRAPHY

Anderson, P. N., *The Christology of the Fourth Gospel, its Unity and Disunity in the Light of John 6*, WUNT 2.78, Tübingen, 1996.
—*The Fourth Gospel and the Quest for Jesus*, London/New York, 2006.
Ashton, J. A., ed., *The Interpretation of John*, London, 1986; 2nd ed., Edinburgh, 1997.
—*Studying John: Approaches to the Fourth Gospel*, Oxford, 1994; 2nd ed., 2007.
—*Understanding the Fourth Gospel*, Oxford, 1991.
Attridge, H. W., 'Genre Bending in the Fourth Gospel', *JBL* 121 (2002), 3-21.
Barrett, C. K., *Essays on John*, London, 1982.
—*The Gospel of John and Judaism*, London, 1975.
Bauckham, R. J., 'Historiographical Characteristics of the Gospel of John', *NTS* 53 (2007), 17-36.
Beattie, D., and M. MacNamara, *The Aramaic Bible*, JSOTSup 166, Sheffield, 1994.
Becker, J., 'Die Hoffnung auf ewiges Leben im Johannesevangelium', *ZNW* 91 (2000), 192-211.
—*Johanneisches Christentum: Seine Geschichte und Theologie im Uberblick*, Tübingen, 2004.
Berger, K., *Die Amen-Worte Jesus. Eine Untersuchung zum Problem der Legitimation in Apokalyptischer Rede*, BZNW 39, Berlin, 1970.
—*Im Anfang war Johannes. Datierung und Theologie des vierten Evangeliums*, 2nd ed., 2003.
Beutler, J., *Studien zu den johanneischen Schriften*, Stuttgart, 1998.
Bienaimé, G., *Moise et le don de l'eau dans la tradition juive ancienne: Targum et midrash*, Analecta Biblica 98, Rome, 1984.
Bieringer, R., et al. eds., *Anti-Judaism and the Fourth Gospel: Papers of the Leuven Colloquium 2000*, Assen, 2001.
Bittner, W. J., *Jesu Zeichen im Johannesevangelium. Die Messias-Erkenntnis im Johannesevangelium vor ihrem jüdischen Hintergrund*, WUNT 2.26, Tübingen, 1987.
Blank, J., *Krisis. Untersuchungen zur johanneischen Christologie und Eschatologie*, Freiburg, 1964.
Boismard, M. E., *Critique textuelle ou critique littéraire*, Cahiers de la Revue Biblique 40, Paris, 1998.
—'Le disciple que Jésus aimait d'après Jn 21.1ss et 1.35ss', *RB* 105 (1998), 76-80.

—*Moise ou Jésus. Essai de christologie johannique*, BETL 94, Leuven, 1988.

Borgen, P., 'God's Agent in the Fourth Gospel', in ed. J. Neusner, *Religions in Antiquity*, FS E. R. Goodenough, Leiden, 1968, 137-48.

Brant, J.-A. A., *Dialogue and Drama: Elements of Greek Tragedy in the Fourth Gospel*, Peabody, 2004.

Braun, F.-M., *Jean le Théologien*, Études Bibliques, 4 vols., 1959–72.

Brown, R. E., *The Community of the Beloved Disciple*, New York, 1979.

—*An Introduction to the Gospel of John*, ed. F. J. Moloney, New York, 2003.

Brown, T. G., *Spirit in the Writings of John: Johannine Pneumatology in Social-Scientific Perspective*, London, 2003.

Bühner, J. A., *Der Gesandte und sein Weg im 4. Evangelium*, WUNT 2.2 Tübingen, 1977.

Bultmann, R., *New Testament Theology*, ETr, 2 vols., London, 1952.

Burge, G. M., *The Anointed Community: The Holy Spirit in the Johannine Tradition*, Grand Rapids, 1987.

Busse, U., *Das Johannesevangelium. Bildlichkeit, Diskurs und Ritual. Mit einer Bibliographie über den Zeitraum 1986–1998*, BETL 162, Leuven, 2002.

Campbell, J. C., *Kinship Relations in the Gospel of John*, CBQMS 41, Washington, DC, 2007.

Casey, M., *Is John's Gospel True?* London, 1996.

Collins, R. F., 'From John to the Beloved Disciple: An Essay on Johannine Characters', *Interpretation* 49 (1995), 359-69.

Coloe, M. L., *God Dwells with Us: Temple Symbolism in the Fourth Gospel*, Collegeville, 2001.

Colwell, E. C., *The Greek of the Fourth Gospel: A Study of the Aramaisms in the Light of Hellenistic Greek*. Chicago/Cambridge, 1931.

Conway, C. N., 'Speaking through Ambiguity: Minor Characters in the Fourth Gospel', *Biblical Interpretation* 10 (2002), 324-41.

Coppens, J., *La relève apocalpytique III: Les logia du fils de l'homme dans l'évangile johannique*, Leuven, 1981.

Counet, P. C., 'Het messias geheim in Johannes: Analyse van het impliciete gebod tot zwijgen', *Tijdschrift voor Theologie* 43 (2001), 253-79.

Cullmann, O., *The Johannine Circle*, London, 1975.

—*Heil als Geschichte*, Tübingen, 1965; ETr, *Salvation in History*, London, 1967.

Culpepper, R. A., *Anatomy of the Fourth Gospel: A Study in Literary Design*, Philadelphia, 1983.

—*Johannine Literature*, Sheffield New Testament Guides, Sheffield, 2000.

—*John, the Son of Zebedee: The Life of a Legend*, Edinburgh, 2nd ed., 2000.

—'The Plot of John's Story of Jesus', *Interpretation* 49 (1995), 347-58.

Culpepper, R. A., and C. C. Black, eds., *Exploring the Gospel of John*, FS D. Moody Smith, Louisville, 1996.

Dalman, G., *Grammatik des jüdisch-palästinischen Aramaisch*, Leipzig, 1894.

—*Sacred Sites and Ways*, ETr, London, 1935.
—*The Words of Jesus*, ETr, London, 1902.
Davies, M., *Rhetoric and Reference in the Fourth Gospel*, JSNTSup 69, Sheffield, 1992.
De Jonge, M., ed., *L'Évangile de Jean. Sources, redaction, théologie*, BETL 44, Louvain, 1977.
De la Potterie, I., *La Verité dans Saint Jean*, 2 vols., Rome, 1977.
Diefenbach, Manfred, *Der Konflikt Jesus mit den "Juden". Eine Versuch zur Lösung der johanneischen Antijudäismus-Diskussion mit Hilfe des antiken Handlungsverständnisses*, Münster, 2002.
Dodd, C. H., *Historical Tradition in the Fourth Gospel*, Cambridge, 1963.
—*The Interpretation of the Fourth Gospel*, Cambridge, 1953.
Elliott, J. K., *The Apocryphal New Testament: A Collection of Apocryphal Christian Literature in an English Translation*, Oxford, 1993.
Elowsky, J. C., ed., *John 1–10*, Ancient Christian Commentary on Scripture: New Testament 4a, Downers Grove, 2006.
Ensor, Peter W., *Jesus and his "Works": The Johannine Sayings in Historical Perspective*, WUNT 2.85, Tübingen, 1996.
Forestell, J. T., *The Word of the Cross: Salvation as Revelation in the Fourth Gospel*, Rome, 1974.
Fortna, R. T., *The Fourth Gospel and its Predecessor: From Narrative Source to Present Gospel*, Edinburgh, 1989.
—*The Gospel of Signs: A Reconstruction of the Narrative Source Underlying the Fourth Gospel*, Cambridge, 1970.
Fortna, R. T., and T. Thatcher, eds., *Jesus in Johannine Tradition*, Louisville, 2001.
Frey, J., *Die johanneische Eschatologie*, I, WUNT 96, Tübingen, 1997; II, WUNT 110, 1998; III, WUNT 117, 2000.
Frey, J., et al. eds., *Imagery in the Gospel of John: Terms, Forms, Themes, and Theology of Johannine Language*, WUNT 200, Tübingen, 2006.
Frey, J., and U. Schnelle, eds., *Kontexte des Johannesevangelium: Das vierte Evangelium in religions- und traditionsgeschichtliche Perspektive*, WUNT 175, Tübingen, 2004.
Grässer, E., 'Die antijüdische Polemik im Johannesevangelium', *NTS* 11 (1964), 74-90.
Hägerland, T., 'John's Gospel: A Two-Level Drama?', *JSNT* 25 (2003), 309-22.
Hakola, R., *Identity Matters: John, the Jews and Jewishness*, Leiden, 2005.
Hanson, A. T., *The Prophetic Gospel: A Study of St John and the Old Testament*, Edinburgh, 1991.
Harnack, A. von, 'Das "Wir" in den Johanneischen Schriften', *Sitzungsberichte der Preussischen Akademie der Wissenschaften zu Berlin* (1923), 96-113.
Harnack-Ehrung: Beiträge zur Kirchengeschichte, FS A. Harnack, Leipzig, 1921.
Harvey, A. E., *Jesus on Trial: A Study in the Fourth Gospel*, London, 1976.
Hayward, R., *Divine Name and Presence: The Memra*, Totowa, NJ, 1981.
Hengel, M., *The Johannine Question*, London, 1989.

Hill, C. E., *The Johannine Corpus in the Early Church*, Oxford/New York, 2004.

Hofius, O., and H.-C. Kammler, *Johannesstudien. Untersuchungen zur Theologie des vierten Evangeliums*, WUNT 88, Tübingen, 1996.

Howard, W. F., *The Fourth Gospel in Recent Criticism and Interpretation*, rev. and ed. C. K. Barrett, London, 1955.

Jeremias, J., *The Eucharistic Words of Jesus*, ETr, London, 1966.

—*Jerusalem in the Time of Jesus*, ETr, London, 3rd ed., 1966.

—*The Prayers of Jesus*, ETr, London, 1967.

Käsemann, E., *The Testament of Jesus according to John 17*, ETr, London, 1968.

Kim, S., *The 'Son of Man' as the Son of God*, WUNT 30, Tübingen, 1983.

Köstenberger, A. J., *The Missions of Jesus and the Disciples according to the Fourth Gospel*, Grand Rapids, 1998.

Kysar, R., *The Fourth Evangelist and His Gospel*, Minneapolis, 1975.

—*Voyages with John: Charting the Fourth Gospel*, Waco, 2005.

Larsson, T., *God in the Fourth Gospel: A Hermeneutical Study of the History of Interpretations*, Coniectanea Biblica, New Testament Series 35, Stockholm, 2001.

Lee, D. A., *The Symbolic Narratives of the Fourth Gospel: The Interplay of Form and Meaning*, JSNTSup 95, Sheffield, 1994.

Léon-Dufour, X., 'Towards a Symbolic Understanding of the Fourth Gospel', *NTS* 27 (1981), 439-56.

Lewis, F. W., *Disarrangements in the Fourth Gospel*, Cambridge, 1910.

Lierman, J., ed., *Challenging Perspectives on the Gospel of John*, WUNT 2.219, Tübingen, 2006.

Lieu, J. M., 'The Mother of the Son in the Fourth Gospel', *JBL* 117 (1998), 61-77.

—'Temple and Synagogue in John', *NTS* 45 (1999), 51-69.

Lincoln, A. T., 'The Beloved Disciple as Eyewitness and the Fourth Gospel as Witness', *JSNT* 85 (2002), 3-26.

—*Truth on Trial: The Lawsuit Motif in the Fourth Gospel*, Peabody, 2000.

Lindars, B., *Behind the Fourth Gospel*, London, 1971.

—*Essays on John*, ed. C. M. Tuckett, Leuven, 1992.

Lingad, C. G., *The Problems of Jewish Christians in the Johannine Community*, Rome, 2001.

Maccini, R. G., *Her Testimony is True*, JSNTSup 125, Sheffield, 1996.

Malina, Bruce J., *The Gospel of John in Socio-Linguistic Perspective*, ed. H. Waetjen, Berkeley, 1985.

Martyn, J. L., *History and Theology in the Fourth Gospel*, Nashville, 2nd ed., 1979.

McGrath, J. F., *John's Apologetic Christology. Legitimation and Development in Johannine Christology*, SNTSMS 111, Cambridge, 2001.

McHugh, J., '"In Him was Life": John's Gospel and the Parting of the Ways', in ed. J. D. G. Dunn, *Jews and Christians: The Parting of the Ways AD 70 to 135*, WUNT 66, Tübingen, 1992, 123-58.

—*The Mother of Jesus in the New Testament*, London, 1975.

Meeks, W. A., 'The Man from Heaven in Johannine Sectarianism', *JBL* 91 (1972), 44-72.

—*The Prophet-King, Moses Traditions and the Johannine Christology*, Leiden, 1967.

Menken, M. J. J., 'Observations on the Significance of the Old Testament in the Fourth Gospel', *Neotestamentica* 33 (1999), 125-43.

Metzner, R., *Das Verständnis der Sünde im Johannesevangelium*, WUNT 122, Tübingen, 2000.

Miranda, J., *Der Vater, der mich gesandt hat*, Bern/Frankfurt am Main, 1972.

Moloney, F. J., 'The Fourth Gospel and the Jesus of History', *NTS* 46 (2000), 42-58.

—*The Gospel of John: Text and Context*, Biblical Interpretation 72, Boston/ Leiden, 2005.

—'Raymond Brown's New *Introduction to the Gospel of John*: A Presentation—and Some Questions', *CBQ* 65 (2003), 1-21.

Motyer, S., 'Method in Fourth Gospel Studies: A Way Out of the Impasse?', *JSNT* 66 (1997), 27-44.

—*Your Father the Devil? A New Approach to John and 'the Jews'*, Carlisle, 1997.

Moule, C. F. D., 'The Individualism of the Fourth Gospel', *NovT* 5 (1962), 171-90.

Mussner, Franz, *ZWH: Die Anschauung vom "Leben" im vierten Evangelium, unter Berücksichtigung der Johannesbriefe*. Munich, 1952.

Mutschler, B., *Das Corpus Johanneum bei Irenaeus von Lyon*, WUNT 189, Tübingen, 2006.

Neirynck, F., 'The Question of John and the Synoptics: D. Moody Smith 1992–1999', *ETL* 76 (2000), 122-32.

Ng, W.-Y., *Water Symbolism in John: An Eschatological Interpretation*, Studies in Biblical Interpretation 15, New York/Bern, 2001.

Nissen, J., and S. Pedersen, eds. *New Readings in John. Literary and Theological Perspectives: Essays from the Scandinavian Conference on the Fourth Gospel in Aarhus 1997*, JSNTSup 182, Sheffield, 1999.

Obermann, A., *Die christologische Erfüllung der Schrift im Johannesevangelium, Eine Untersuchung zur johanneischen Hermeneutik anhand der Schriftzitate*, WUNT 2.83, Tübingen, 1996.

Okure, T., *The Johannine Approach to Mission: A Contextual Study of John 4.1-42*, WUNT 2.31, Tübingen, 1988.

Olsson, B., *Structure and Meaning in the Fourth Gospel: A Text-Linguistic Analysis of John 2:1-11 and John 4:1-43*, Lund, 1974.

Pagels, E. H., 'Exegesis of Genesis 1 in the Gospels of Thomas and John', *JBL* 118 (1999), 477-96.

Painter, J., *The Quest for the Messiah: The History, Literature and Theology of the Johannine Community*, Edinburgh, 1991.

Pancaro, S., *The Law in the Fourth Gospel*, Leiden, 1975.

Rese, M., 'Das Selbstzeugnis des Johannesevangelium über seinen Verfasser', *ETL* 72 (1996), 75-111.

Salier, W. H., *The Rhetorical Impact of the Semeia in the Gospel of John*, WUNT 186, Tübingen, 2004.

Sanders, J. N., *The Fourth Gospel and the Early Church*, Cambridge, 1943.

Schneiders, S. M., *Written that You May Believe: Encountering Jesus in the Fourth Gospel*, New York, 1999.

Schnelle, U., *Antidocetic Christology in the Gospel of John: An Investigation of the Place of the Fourth Gospel in the Johannine School*, ETr, Minneapolis, 1992.

Scholtissek, K., 'Eine Renaissance des Evangeliums nach Johannes. Aktuelle Perspektiven der exegetische Forschung', *Theologische Revue* 97 (2001), 267-88.

Schröder, J.-M., *Das eschatologische Israel im Johannesevangelium. Eine Untersuchung der johanneischen Israel-Konzeption in Joh 2–4 und Joh 6*, Tübingen/Basel, 2003.

Schweizer, E., *EGO EIMI. Die religionsgeschichtliche Herkunft und theologische Bedeutung der johanneischen Bildreden*, Göttingen, 1939, 2nd ed., 1964.

Segovia, F. F., ed., *"What is John?" Readers and Readings of the Fourth Gospel*, SBLSS 7, Atlanta, 1996.

Smalley, S. S., *John: Evangelist and Interpreter*, Exeter, 1978; 2nd ed., 1998.

Smith, D. M., *Johannine Christianity: Essays on its Setting, Sources, and Theology*, Colombia, 1984.

—*John among the Gospels*, 2nd ed., Columbia, 2001.

—*The Theology of the Gospel of John*, Cambridge, 1994.

Söding, T., '"Was kann aus Nazareth schon Gutes kommen?" (Joh 1,46). Die Bedeutung des Judenseins Jesu im Johannesevangelium', *NTS* 46 (2000), 21-41.

Staley, J. L., *The Print's First Kiss: A Rhetorical Investigation of the Implied Reader in the Fourth Gospel*, SBLDS 82, Atlanta, 1988.

Stibbe, M. W. G., *John as Storyteller: Narrative Criticism and the Fourth Gospel*, SNTSMS 73, Cambridge, 1992.

Stibbe, M. W. G., ed., *The Gospel of John as Literature*, Leiden, 1993.

Teeple, H. M., *The Literary Origin of the Gospel of John*, Evanston, 1974.

Thompson, M. M. T., *The Incarnate Word: Perspectives on Jesus in the Fourth Gospel*, Peabody, 1993.

Thüsing, W., *Die Erhöhung und Verherrlichung Jesu im Johannesevangelium*, Ntl Abh., 21, Münster, 1960; 3rd ed., 1979.

Tolmie, D. F., 'The Characterization of God in the Fourth Gospel', *JSNT* 69 (1998), 57-75.

Van Belle, G., et al. eds., *Theology and Christology in the Fourth Gospel: Essays by the Members of the SNTS Johannine Writings Seminar*, BETL 184, Leuven, 2005.

Wahlde, U. C. von, '"The Jews" in the Gospel of John: Fifteen Years of Research (1983–1998)', *ETL* 76 (2000), 30-55.

Watt, Jan G. van der, 'Ethics and Ethos in the Gospel according to John', *ZNW* 97 (2006), 147-76.

Westermann, C., *Das Johannesevangelium aus der Sicht des Alten Testament*, Stuttgart, 1994.
Williams, C. H., *'I am He': The Interpretation of ʾANI HU in Jewish and Early Christian Literature*, WUNT 2.113, Tübingen, 2000.
Wrede, W., *Charakter und Tendenz des Johannesevangeliums*, Tübingen, 1903.

V. BIBLIOGRAPHY FOR SUB-SECTIONS OF JOHN 1–4

(i) The Prologue: 1.1-18

Aland, K., 'Eine Untersuchung zu Joh:13.4', *ZNW* 59 (1968), 174-209.
Barrett, C. K., 'The Prologue of St John's Gospel', in *New Testament Essays*, London, 1972, 28-42.
Bindemann, W., 'Der Johannesprolog: Ein Versuch, ihn zu verstehen', *NovT* 37 (1995), 330-54.
Boismard, M.-E., *Le Prologue de Saint Jean*, Paris, 1953.
Borgen, P., '"Logos was the True Light": Contributions to the Interpretation of the Prologue of John', *NovT* 14 (1972), 115-30.
—'Observations on the Targumic Character of the Prologue of John', *NTS* 16 (169–70), 288-95.
Boyarin, D., 'The Gospel of the *Memra: Jewish Binitarianism and the Prologue to John*', *HTR* 94 (2001), 243-84.
Büchsel, F., μονογενη, *TWNT* IV (1942), 745-50.
Calloud, J., 'Quartrième Évangile: Le témoinage de Jean (I)', *Sémiotique et Bible* 100 (2000), 25-49.
Cryer, C., 'The Prologue of the Fourth Gospel', *ExpTimes* 32 (1920–21), 440-43.
Culpepper, R. A., 'The Pivot of John's Gospel', *NTS* 27 (1980–81), 1-31.
Dahms, J. V., 'The Johannine Use of Monogenes Reconsidered', *NTS* 29 (1983), 222-32.
De Jonge, M., ed., *L'Évangile de Jean: Sources, redaction, théologie*, BETL 44, Louvain, 1977.
De la Potterie, I., '"C'est lui qui a ouvert la voie" La finale du prologue johannique', *Biblica* 69 (1988), 340-70.
—'Structure du Prologue de Saint Jean', *NTS* 30 (1984), 354-81.
Demke, C., 'Der sogennante Logos Hymnus in Johanneische Prolog', *ZNW* 58 (1967), 45-68.
Dyroff, A., 'Zum Prolog des Johannesevangelium', in eds. T. Klauser and A. Rücker, *Pisciculi: Studien zur religion und kultur des altertums*, FS F. J. Dölger, Münster, 1939, 86-93.
Grappe, C., 'Jean 1,14(-8) dans son contexte et à la lumiere de la littérature intertestamentaire', *RHPR* 80 (2000), 153-69.
Harris, E. A., *Prologue and Gospel: The Theology of the Fourth Evangelist*, JSNTSup 107, Sheffield, 1994.
Harris, J. R., *The Origin of the Prologue to St John's Gospel*, Cambridge, 1917.

Hofius, O., 'Struktur und Gedankengang des Logos-Hymnus in Joh 1–18', *ZNW* 78 (1987), 1-25.

Hooker, M. D., 'The Johannine Prologue and the Messianic Secret', *NTS* 21 (1974–75), 40-58.

—'John the Baptist and the Johannine Prologue', *NTS* 16 (1969–70), 354-58.

Jeremias J., 'The Revealing Word', in *The Central Message of the New Testament*, ETr, London, 1965, 71-90.

Käsemann, E., 'The Structure and Purpose of the Prologue to St John's Gospel', in *New Testament Questions of Today*, ETr, London, 1969, 138-67.

Marrow, S. B., 'Κοσμος in John', *CBQ* 64 (2002), 90-102.

McGillivray, D., 'The Prologue of the Fourth Gospel', *ExpTimes* 32 (1920–21), 281-82.

Merwe, D. G. van der, 'The Historical and Theological Significance of John the Baptist as He is Portrayed in John 1', *Neotestamentica* 33 (1999), 267-92.

Miller, E. L., '"In the Beginning": A Christological Transparency', *NTS* 45 (1999), 587-92.

Pendrick, G., 'Μονογενης', *NTS* 41 (1995), 587-600.

Phillips, P. M., *The Prologue of the Fourth Gospel: A Sequential Reading*, Library of New Testament Studies 294, London/New York, 2006.

Richter, G., 'Die Fleischwerdung des Logos im Johannes-Evangelium', *NovT* 13 (1971), 81-126; 14 (1972), 257-76.

Robinson, J. A. T., 'The Relation of the Prologue to the Gospel of St John', *NTS* 9 (1962–63), 120-29.

Sanders, J. T., *The New Testament Christological Hymns*, SNTSMS 15, Cambridge, 1971, 29-57.

Spicq, C., 'Le Siracide et la structure littéraire du prologue de s. Jean', *Mémorial Lagrange*, Paris, 1940, 183-95.

Stolle, V., 'Jesus Christus, der göttliche Exeget (Joh 1,18). Zur theologischen Standortbestimmung neutestamentliche Exegese', *ZNW* 97 (2006), 64-87.

Sys, J., ed., *Prologue de Jean*, Lille, 2001.

Theobald, M., 'Le prologue johannique (Jean 1,1–18) et ses "lecteurs implicates"', *RSR* 82 (1995), 193-216.

Tobin, T. H., 'The Prologue of John and Hellenistic Jewish Speculation', *CBQ* 52 (1990), 252-69.

Voorwinde, S., 'John's Prologue: Beyond Some Impasses of Twentieth Century Scholarship', *WTJ* 64 (2002), 15-44.

Waetjen, W., 'Λόγος πρὸς τὸν Θεόν and the Objectivation of Truth in the Prologue of the Fourth Gospel', *CBQ* 63 (2001), 265-86.

Yamauchi, E. M., 'Jewish Gnosticism, the Prologue of John, Mandaean Parallels and the Trimorphic Protennoia', in eds. R. van den Broek and M. J. Vermaseren, *Studies in Gnosticism and Hellenistic Religions*, FS G. Quispel, Leiden, 1981, 467-97.

Zumstein, J., 'Le prologue, seuil du quartrième évangile', *RSR* 83 (1995), 217-39.

(ii) The Witness of John the Baptist: 1.19-34
Bammel, E., 'The Baptist in Early Christian Tradition', *NTS* 18 (1971–72), 95-128.
Barrett, C. K., 'The Lamb of God', *NTS* 1 (1954–55), 210-18.
Bennema, C., 'Spirit–Baptism in the Fourth Gospel: A Messianic Reading of John 1,33', *Biblica* 84 (2003), 35-60.
Berger, K., 'Zum traditionsgeschichtlichen Hintergrund christologischer Hoheitstitel', *NTS* 17 (1970–71), 391-425.
Bloch, R., 'Quelques aspects de la figure de Moïse dans la tradition rabbinique', in *Moïse, l'homme de l'Alliance*, Paris, 1955, 93-167.
Bockmuehl, M. N. A., 'Das Verb φανερόω im Neue Testament', *BZ* 32 (1988), 87-99.
Chevallier, M.-A., *Souffle de Dieu: Le Saint-Esprit dans le Nouveau Testament*, Paris, 1978, 11-80.
Coppens, J., *La relève apocalyptique du messianisme royal II: Le Fils de l'homme vétéro- et intertestamentaire*, BETL 61, Leuven, 1983.
De Jonge, M., 'Jesus as Prophet and King in the Fourth Gospel', in *Jesus: Stranger from Heaven and Son of God*, Missoula, 1977, 49-76.
—'Jewish Expectations about the "Messiah" according to the Fourth Gospel', in *Jesus: Stranger from Heaven and Son of God*, Missoula, 1977, 77-116.
Goedt, M. de, 'Un schème de révélation dans le 4e Evangile (Jn 1.29-34; 1.35-39; 19.24b-27)', *NTS* 8 (1961–62), 142-50.
Iersel, B. M. F. van, 'Tradition und Redaktion in Joh 1, 19–36', *NovT* 5 (1962), 245-67.
Keck, L. E., 'The Spirit and the Dove', *NTS* 17 (1970–71), 41-67.
Müller, P.-G., φανερόω, *EDNT* III 413-14.
Murphy-O'Connor, J., 'John the Baptist and Jesus: History and Hypotheses', *NTS* 36 (1990), 359-74.
Proulx P., and L. Alonso-Schökel, 'Las Sandalias del Mesías Esposo', *Biblica* 59 (1978), 1-37.
Riesner, R., *Bethanien jenseits des Jordan. Topographie und Theologie im Johannes-Evangelium*, Giessen/Basel, 2002.
Segalla, G., '"In Betania...aldilà del Giordano" (Gv 1,28)', *Studia Patavina* 49 (2002), 201-26.
Wink, W., *John the Baptist in the Gospel Tradition*, SNTSMS 7, Cambridge, 1968.

(iii) The Calling and Testimony of the First Disciples: 1.35-51
Betz, O., '"Kann denn aus Nazareth etwas Gutes kommen?" Zur Verwendung von Jesaja Kap.11 in Johannes Kap. 1', in eds. H. Gese and H. P. Rüger, *Wort und Geschichte*, FS K. Elliger, Neukirchen, 1973, 9-16.
Clarke, E. G., 'Jacob's Dream at Bethel as Interpreted in the Targums and the New Testament', *Studies in Religion: Sciences Religieuses* 4 (1975), 367-77.
Hill, C. E., 'The Identity of John's Nathanael', *JSNT* 67 (1997), 45-61.
Jeremias, J., 'Die Berufung des Nathanael (Jo 1, 45-51)', *Angelos* 3 (1928), 2-5.

Koester, C. R., 'Messianic Exegesis and the Call of Nathanael (John 1.45-51)', *JSNT* 39 (1990), 23-34.

Kuhn, H.-J., *Christologie und Wunder: Untersuchungen zu Joh 1.35-51*, Biblische Untersuchungen 18, Regensburg, 1988.

Michel, O., 'Der aufsteigende und herabsteigende Gesandte [Jn 1.51]', in ed. W. C. Weinrich, *The New Testament Age*, FS Bo Reicke, Macon, GA, 1984, II 335-61.

Nicklas, T., '"Unter dem Feigenbaum". Die Rolle des Lesers im Dialog zwischen Jesus und Natanael (Joh 1,46-50)', *NTS* 46 (2000), 193-203.

Rowland, C., 'John 1.51, Jewish Apocalyptic and Targumic Tradition', *NTS* 30 (1984), 498-507.

Schreiber, S., 'Die Jüngerberufungsszene Joh 1, 43-51 als literarische Einheit', *SNTU* 23 (1998), 5-28.

Tovey, D., 'Stone of Witness and Stone of Revelation: An Exploration of Inter-textual Resonance in John 1:35-51', *Colloquium* 38 (2006), 41-58.

(iv) The Son of Man: 1.51 and 3.13, 14

Borgen, P., 'Some Jewish Exegetical Traditions as Background for Son of Man Sayings in John's Gospel', in M. de Jonge, *L'Evangile de Jean*, BETL 44, Louvain, 1977, 243-58.

Burkett, D., 'The Nontitular Son of Man: A History and Critique', *NTS* 40 (1994), 504-21.

—*The Son of Man in the Gospel of John*, JSNTSup 56, Sheffield, 1991.

Coppens, J., *La relève apocalpytique III: Les logia du fils de l'homme dans l'évangile johannique*, Leuven, 1981.

Moloney, Francis J., *The Johannine Son of Man*, Biblioteca di scienze religiose 14; Libreria Ateneo Salesiano, Rome, 1976; 2nd ed., 1978.

O'Neill, J. C., 'Son of Man, Stone of Blood (John 1:51)', *NovT* 45 (2003), 374-81.

Painter, J., 'The Enigmatic Johannine Son of Man', in eds. F. van Segbroeck et al., *The Four Gospels 1992*, FS Neirynck, Leuven, 1992.

Pamment, M., 'The Son of Man in the Fourth Gospel', *JTS* 36 (1985), 56-66.

Ruckstuhl, E., 'Abstieg und Erhöhung des johanneischen Menschensohns', in eds. R. Pesch et al., *Jesus und der Menschensohn*, FS A. Vögtle, Freiburg, 1975, 314-41.

—'Die johanneische Menschensohnforschung 1957–1969', *TB* 1 (1972), 171-284.

Schnackenburg, R., 'Der Menschensohn im Johannesevangelium', *NTS* 11 (1964–65), 123-37.

Schulz, Siegfried, *Untersuchungen zur Menschensohn-Christologie im Johannesevangelium*, Göttingen, 1957.

Smalley, S. S., 'Johannes 1.51 und die Einleitung zum vierten Evangelium', in eds. R. Pesch et al., *Jesus und der Menschensohn*, FS A. Vögtle, Freiburg, 1975, 300-314.

—'The Johannine Son of Man Sayings', *NTS* 15 (1968–69), 278-301.

(v) The Wedding at Cana in Galilee: John 2.1-12

Betz, O., 'Das Problem des Wunders bei Flavius Josephus im Vergleich zum Wunderproblem bei den Rabbinen und im Johannesevangelium', in eds. O. Betz et al., *Josephus-Studien*, FS O. Michel, Göttingen, 1974, 23-44.

Boismard, M.-E., 'Rapport entre foi et miracles dans l'Evangile de Jean', *ETL* 58 (1982), 357-64.

Braun, F. M., 'Le baptême d'après le quatrième Evangile', *RThom* 48 (1948), 347-93.

Cerfaux, L., 'Les miracles, signes messianiques et ouevres de Dieu selon l'Evangile de S. Jean', in *L'attente du Messie*, Bruges, 1958, 131-38.

Charlier, J. P., *Signes et prodiges: Les miracles dans l'évangile*, Paris, 1987.

Cullmann, O., *Urchristentum und Gottesdienst*, Zürisch, 4th ed., 1962; ETr *Early Christian Worship*, London, 1953.

Deines, Roland, *Jüdische Steingefässe und pharisäische Frömmigkeit: Ein archäologisch-historischer Beitrag zum Verständnis von Joh 2,6 und der jüdischen Reinheitshalacha zur Zeit Jesu*, WUNT 2.52, Tübingen, 1993.

Dillon, R. J., 'Wisdom Tradition and Sacramental Retrospect in the Cana Account', *CBQ* 24 (1962), 268-96.

Feuillet, A., 'Les épousailles du Messie. La Mère de Jésus et l'Eglise dans le Quatrième Evangile', in *RThom* 86 (1986), 357-91, 536-75.

—'L'heure de Jésus et le signe de Cana', *ETL* 36 (1960), 5-22 = *Etudes johanniques*, Paris, 1962, 11-35: ETr *Johannine Studies*, New York, 1956, 17-37.

—'La signification fondamentale du premier miracle de Cana (Jn 2.1-22) et le symbolisme johannique', *RThom* 65 (1965), 517-35.

Formesyn R., 'Le sèmeion johannique et le sèmeion hellénistique', *ETL* 38 (1962), 856-94.

Hengel, M., 'The Interpretation of the Wine Miracle at Cana: John 2.1-11', in eds. L. D. Hurst and N. T. Wright, *The Glory of Christ in the New Testament*, FS in Memory of G. B. Caird, Oxford, 1987, 83-112.

Herrojo, Julián, *Cana de Galilea y su localización: Un examen critico de las Fuentes*, Cahiers de la Revue Biblique 45, Paris, 1999.

Johns, L. L., and D. B. Miller, 'The Signs as Witnesses in the Fourth Gospel: Reexamining the Evidence', *CBQ* 56 (1994), 519-35.

Kopp, C., *Das Kana des Evangeliums*, Köln, 1940.

Lindars, B., 'Two Parables in John [Jn 2.10; 3.29]', *NTS* 16 (1969–70), 318-29, reprinted in ed. C. M. Tuckett, *Essays on John*, Leuven, 1992.

Linnemann, E., 'Die Hochzeit zu Kana und Dionysos', *NTS* 20 (1973–74), 408-18.

Little, E., *Echoes of the Old Testament in the Wine of Cana in Galilee and the Multiplication of the Loaves and Fish: Towards an Appreciation*. Cahiers de la Revue biblique 41, Paris, 1998.

Lohse, E., 'Miracles in the Fourth Gospel', in eds. M. Hooker and C. Hickling, *What about the New Testament?*, FS C. F. Evans, London, 1975, 64-75.

Lütgehetmann, W., *Die Hochzeit von Kana (Joh. 2.1-11): Zur Ursprung und Deutung einer Wundererzählung im Rahmen johanneischer Redaktionsgeschichte*, Biblische Untersuchungen 20, Regensburg, 1990.

Martin, T. W., 'Assessing the Johannine Epithet "the Mother of Jesus"',
    CBQ 60 (1998), 63-73.
Michl, J., 'Bemerkungen zu Joh. 2.4', *Biblica* 36 (1955), 492-509.
Nicol, W., *The Semeia in the Fourth Gospel: Tradition and Redaction*,
    NovTSup 32, Leiden, 1972.
Olsson, B., *Structure and Meaning in the Fourth Gospel: A Text-Linguistic
    Analysis of John 2.1-11 and 4.1-42*, Lund, 1974.
O'Neill, J. C., 'Jesus' Reply to his Mother at Cana of Galilee (John 2:4)',
    Irish Biblical Studies 23 (2001), 28-35.
Phillips, T. E., '"The Third Fifth Day?" John 2:1 in Context', *ExpTimes* 115
    (2004), 328-31.
Richardson, P., 'What has Cana to do with Capernaum?', *NTS* 48 (2002),
    314-31.
Rissi, M., 'Die Hochzeit in Kana Joh 2,1-11', in ed. F. Christ, *Oikonomia*:
    Heilsgeschichte als Thema der Theologie, Hamburg, 1967, 76-92.
Salier, W. H., *The Rhetorical Impact of the Semeia in the Gospel of John*,
    WUNT 186, Tübingen, 2004.
Schnackenburg, R., *Das erste Wunder Jesu*, Freiburg, 1951.
Serra, A., *Contributi dell'Antica Letteratura Giudaica per l'esegesi di
    Giovanni 2.1-12 e 19.25-27*, Rome, 1977.
Smitmans, A., *Das Weinwunder von Kana. Die Auslegung von Jo 2.1-11 bei
    den Vätern und heute*, Tübingen, 1966.
Van Belle, G., *The Signs Source in the Fourth Gospel: Historical Survey and
    Critical Evaluation of the Semeia Hypothesis*, BETL 116, Leuven, 1994.
Vanhoye, A., 'Interrogation johannique et exégèse de Cana (Jn 2.4)', *Biblica*
    55 (1974), 157-67.
Williams, R. H., 'The Mother of Jesus at Cana: A Social-Science Interpre-
    tation of John 2:1-12', *CBQ* 59 (1997), 679-92.

(vi) The New Temple: 2.13-22

Hartmann, L., 'He Spoke of the Temple of His Body (Jn 2.13-22)', *SEÅ* 54
    (1989), 70-79.
Kerr, A. R., *The Temple of Jesus' Body: The Temple Theme in the Gospel of
    John*, JSNTSup 220, Sheffield, 2002.
Léon-Dufour, X., 'Autour du σημειον johannique', in R. Schnackenburg,
    in eds. J. Ernst and J. Wanke, *Die Kirche des Anfangs*, FS H. Schürmann
    (1977), 363-78.
Moloney, F. J., 'Reading John 2:13-22: The Purification of the Temple', *RB*
    97 (1990), 432-52.
Schnelle, U., 'Die Tempelreinigung und die Christologie des Johannes-
    evangelium', *NTS* 42 (1996), 359-73.

(vii) Nicodemus: 2.23–3.21

Auwers, J.-M., 'La Nuit de Nicodéme (Jean 3.2; 19.39) ou l'ombre du
    langage', *RB* 97 (1990), 481-503.
Bauckham, R. J., 'Nicodemus and the Gurion Family', *JTS* NS 47 (1996),
    1-37.

Becker, J., 'Joh. 3.1-21 als Reflex johanneischer Schuldiskussion', in eds. H. Balz and S. Schulz, *Das Wort und die Wörter*, FS G. Friedrich, Stuttgart, 1973, 85-95.

Bligh, J., 'Four Studies in St John. II. Nicodemus', *HJ* 8 (1967), 40-51.

Borgen, P., 'Some Jewish Exegetical Traditions as Background for the Son of Man Sayings in John's Gospel (Jn 3.13-14 and Context)', in ed. M. de Jonge, *L'Évangile de Jean: Sources, redaction, théologie*, BETL 44, Louvain, 1977, 243-58.

Burkitt, F. C., 'On "Lifting Up" and "Exalting", *JTS* (First Series) 20 (1918–19), 336-38.

De Jonge, M., 'Nicodemus and Jesus: Some Observations on Misunderstanding and Understanding in the Fourth Gospel', *BJRL* 53 (1970–71), 337-59.

De la Potterie, I., 'Jesus et Nicodemus. De Revelatione Jesu et vera fide in eum (Jo 3.11-21)', *VD* 47 (1969), 257-83.

—'Jesus et Nicodemus: De necessitatite generationis ex Spiritu (Jo 3.1-10)', *VD* 47 (1969), 193-214.

—'Naître de l'eau et naître de l'esprit. Le texte baptismal de Jn 3.5', *ScEs* 14 (1962), 417-43.

—'Structura primae partis Evangelii Iohannis (Cap. 3 et 4)', *VD* 47 (1969), 130-40.

Derrett, J. D. M., 'Correcting Nicodemus (Jn 3:2,21)', *ExpTimes* 112 (2001), 126.

Doignon, J., 'L'esprit souffle où il veut (Jean 3.8) dans la plus ancienne tradition latine', *RSPT* 62 (1978), 345-59.

Dschulnigg, P., 'Nikodemus im Johannesevangelium', *SNTU* 24 (1999), 103-18.

Frey, J., '"Wie Mose die Schlange in der Wüste erhöht hat…": Zur frühjüdischen Deutung der "ehernen Schlange" und ihrer christologischen Rezeption in Joh 3.14f.', in eds. M. Hengel et al., *Schriftauslegung im antiken Judentum und in Urchristentum*, WUNT 73, Tübingen, 1994, 153-205.

Goulder, M. D., 'Nicodemus', *SJT* 44 (1991), 153-68.

Julian, P., *Jesus and Nicodemus. A Literary and Narrative Exegesis of Jn. 2,23–3,36*, Frankfurt/New York, 2000.

Klaiber, W., 'Der irdische und der himmlische Zeuge: Eine Auslegung von Joh 3.22-36', *NTS* 36 (1990), 205-33.

Léon-Dufour, X., 'Et là Jésus baptisait" (Jn 3.22)', in *Mélanges E. Tisserant I Studi e Testi*, Vatican City, 1964, 295-309.

Létourneau, P., *Jesus Fils de l'homme et Fils de Dieu. Jn 2.23–3.36 et la double christologie johannique*. Montreal/Paris, 1993.

Longenecker, B., 'The Unbroken Messiah: A Johannine Feature and its Social Functions', *NTS* 41 (1995), 428-41.

Michel, O., 'Der Aufsteigende und Herabsteigende Gesandte', in ed. W. C. Weinrich, *The New Testament Age*, FS B. Reicke, Macon, GA, 1984, II 335-61.

Pryor, J. W., 'John 3.3, 5: A Study in the Relations of John's Gospel to the Synoptic Tradition', *JSNT* 41 (1991), 71-95.

Ruckstuhl, E., 'Abstieg und Erhöhung des johanneischen Menschensohns (Jn 2.23–3.36)', in eds. R. Pesch et al., *Jesus und der Menschensohn*, FS A. Vögtle, Freiburg, 1975, 314-41.
Sandnes, K. O., 'Whence and Whither: A Narrative Perspective on Birth ἄνωθεν (John 3, 3-8)', *Biblica* 86 (2005), 153-73.
Thüsing, W., *Die Erhöhung und Verherrlichung Jesus im Johannesevangelium*, Münster, 1960; 3rd ed., 1979.

(viii) John the Baptist: 3.22-36
Bammel, E., 'The Baptist in Early Christian Tradition', *NTS* 18 (1971–72), 95-128.
Boismard M.-E., 'Aenon, près de Salem (Jn 3.23)', *RB* 80 (1973), 218-29.
—'L'ami de l'époux (Jn 3.29)', in *A la rencontre de Dieu: Mémorial Gelin*, Paris, 1961, 289-95.
Lindars, B., 'The Parable of the Best Man (John 3.29)', *NTS* 16 (1969–70), 324-29.
Murphy-O'Connor, J., 'John the Baptist and Jesus: History and Hypotheses', *NTS* 36 (1990), 359-74.
Neyrey, J. H., and R. Rohrbaugh, '"He Must Increase, I must Decrease" (John 3.30): A Cultural and Social Interpretation', *CBQ* 63 (2001), 464-83.
Nicklaus, T., 'Notiz zu Joh 3,25', *ETL* 76 (2000), 133-35.
Pryor, John W., 'John the Baptist and Jesus: Tradition and Text in John 3.25', *JSNT* 66 (1997), 15-26.
Trocmé, E., 'Jean 3,29 et le thème de l'epoux dans la tradition préévangélique' *RSR* 69 (1995), 13-18.
—'Jean-Baptiste dans le quatrième Evangile', *RHPR* 60 (1980), 129-51.
Wink, W., *John the Baptist in the Gospel Tradition*, SNTSMS 7, Cambridge, 1968.
Zimmermann, M., and R. Zimmermann, 'Der Freund des Bräutigams (Joh 3,29): Deflorations- oder Christuszeuge', *ZNW* 90 (1999), 123-30.

(ix) The Samaritan Woman: 4.1-45
Argyle, A. W., 'A Note on John 4.35', *ExpTimes* 82 (1971), 247-48.
Baillet, M., 'Samaritains', *DBS* XI 773-1007.
Bienaimé, G., *Moïse et le don de l'eau dans la tradition juive ancienne: Targum et midrash*, Analecta Biblica 98, Rome, 1984.
Boers, H., *Neither on This Mountain nor in Jerusalem: A Study of John Four*, Atlanta, 1988.
Botha, E., *Jesus and the Samaritan Woman: A Speech-Act Reading of John 4.1-42*, Leiden, 1991.
Bowman, J., *The Samaritan Problem: Studies in the Relationships of Samaritanism, Judaism, and Early Christianity*, Pittsburgh, 1975.
Braun, F.-M., 'In Spiritu et veritate', *RThom* 52 (1952), 245-74, 486-507.
Briend, J., 'Puits de Jacob (Jn 4.5-6)', *DBS* IX 396-98.
—'Samarie', *DBS* XI 740-56.

Crown, A. D., *A Bibliography of the Samaritans*, American Theological Library Association bibliography Series 10, Metuchen, 1984.

Crown, A. D., ed., *The Samaritans*, Tübingen, 1989.

Crown, A. D., et al., eds., *Companion to Samaritan Studies*, Tübingen, 1993.

Cullmann, O., 'Samaria and the Origins of the Christian Mission', in *The Early Church*, ETr, London, 1956, 185-92.

Danna, E., 'A Note on John 4:29', *RB* 106 (1999), 219-23.

Daube, D., 'Samaritan Women', in *The New Testament and Rabbinic Judaism*, London, 1956, 373-82.

Day, J. N., *The Woman at the Well: Interpretation of John 4.1-42 in Retrospect and Prospect*, Biblical Interpretation 61, Leiden, 2002.

De la Potterie, I., 'Nous adorons, nous, ce que nous connaissons, car le salut vient des Juifs. Histoire de l'exégèse et interprétation de Jn 4, 22', *Biblica* 64 (1983), 74-115.

Díaz, J. R., 'Targum palestinense y Nuevo Testamento', *EstBib* 211 (1962), 337-42; ETr 'Palestinian Targum and New Testament', *NovT* 6 (1963), 775-80.

Ensor, P. W., 'The Authenticity of John 4.35', *EQ* 72 (2000), 13-21.

Freed, E. D., 'Did John Write his Gospel Partly to Win Over Samaritan Converts?', *NovT* 12 (1970), 241-56.

—'The Manner of Worship in John 4.23f.', in eds. J. M. Myers et al., *Search the Scriptures*, FS R. T. Stamm, Leiden, 1969, 33-48.

Harris, J. R., 'A Lost Verse of St John's Gospel?', *ExpTimes* 38 (1926–27), 342-43.

Herrojo, J., *Cana de Galilea y su Localizacion*, Cahiers de la Revue Biblique 45, Paris, 1999.

Hjelm, I., *The Samaritans and Early Judaism: A Literary Analysis*, JSOTSup 303, Sheffield, 2000.

Loewe, R., 'Salvation is Not of the Jews', *JTS* 32 (1981), 341-68.

Maccini, R. G., 'A Reassessment of the Woman at the Well in John 4 in Light of the Samaritan Context', *JSNT* 53 (1994), 35-46.

Margain, J., 'Samarit Pentateuque', *DBS* XI 762-73.

Muñoz-León, D., 'Adoración en espiritu y verdad. Aportación targúmica a la inteligencia de Jn 4.23-24', in eds. L. Alvarez Verdes et al., *Homenaje a Juan Prado: Miscelànea de estudios bìblicos y hebraïcos*, FS J. Prado, Madrid, 1975, 385-405.

Okure, T., *The Johannine Approach to Mission: A Contextual Study of John 4.1-42*, WUNT 2.31, Tübingen, 1988.

Park, S.-J., 'L'entretien avec la Samaritaine. Jn 4, 1-42', *Sémiotique et Bible* 96 (1999), 26-55; 97 (2000), 22-36.

Reim, G., 'Crux or Clue? The Rejection of Jesus at Nazareth in Johannine Composition', *NTS* 22 (1975–76), 476-80.

Robinson, J. A. T., 'The "Others" of John 4.38', in *Twelve New Testament Studies*, London, 1962, 61-66.

Schenke, H.-M., 'Jakobsbrunnen–Josephsgrab–Sychar. Topographische Untersuchungen und Erwägungen in der Perspektive von Joh 4.5,6', *ZDPV* 84 (1968), 159-84.

Schmid, Lothar, 'Die Komposition der Samaria-Szene Joh. 4.1-41. Ein Beitrag zur Characteristik des 4. Evangelisten als Schriftsteller', *ZNW* 28 (1929), 148-58.

Schnackenburg, R., 'Die "Anbetung in Geist und Wahrheit" (Jo 4,23) im Lichte von Qumrântexten', *BZ* NF 3 (1959), 88-94. ETr in *Christian Existence in the New Testament*, Notre Dame, 1969, II 77-115.

Schottroff, L., 'Johannes 4.5-15 und die Konsequenzen des johanneischen Dualismus', *ZNW* 60 (1969), 199-214.

Thyen, H., '"Das Heil kommt von den Juden"', in ed. D. Lührmann, *Kirche*, FS G. Bornkamm, Tübingen, 1980, 163-84.

Van Belle, G., 'The Faith of the Galileans: The Parenthesis in Jn 4:44', *ETL* 74 (1998), 27-44.

Van der Horst, P. W., 'A Wordplay in John 4.12?', *ZNW* 63 (1972), 280-82.

Van Unnik, W. C., 'A Greek Characteristic of Prophecy in the Fourth Gospel [Jn 4.4ff.]', in eds. E. Best et al., *Text and Interpretation*, FS M. Black, Cambridge, 1979, 211-29.

Vincent, L.-H., 'Puits de Jacob ou de la Samaritaine (Jn 4)', *RB* 65 (1958), 547-67.

Willemse, J., 'La patrie de Jésus selon Saint Jean 4.44', *NTS* 11 (1964–65), 349-64.

(x) The Roman Centurion: 4.46-54

Boismard, M.-E., 'Saint Luc et la rédaction du quatrième évangile (Jn 4.46-54)', *RB* 69 (1962), 185-211.

Feuillet, A., 'La signification théologique du second miracle de Cana (Jean 4.46-54)', *RSR* 48 (1960), 62-75.

Joüon P., 'Notes philologiques sur les évangiles: Jean 4.52', *BZ* 8 (1964), 58-88.

Kilpatrick, G. D., 'Jn IV.51: παῖς or υἱός?', *JTS* 14 (1963), 393.

Mead, A. H., 'The basilikos in Jn 4.46-54', *JSNT* 23 (1985), 69-72.

Park, S.-J., 'La guérison du fils d'un officier royal. Jean 4, 43-54', *Sémiotique et Bible.*

Schnackenburg, R., 'Zur Traditionsgeschichte von Jo 4.46-54', *BZ* 8 (1964), 55-85.

Schwarz, G., '"καὶ ἦν τις βασιλικὸς…" (Joh 4.46)', *ZNW* 75 (1984), 138.

Schweizer, E., 'Die Heilung des Könlichen, Joh 4, 46-54', *EvTh* 11 (1951), 64-71.

THE TITLE

ΕΥΑΓΓΕΛΙΟΝ ΚΑΤΑ ΙΩΑΝΝΗΝ

Since the publication, in 1869, of Tischendorf's *editio octava critica maior*, it has been customary to print the superscription as κατα ιωαννην, following ℵ (and B, κατα ιωανην). But ευαγγελιον κατα ιωαννην is found in the majority of manuscripts of the Byzantine tradition (including C L W^{supp} Ψ, and the 'Caesarean' witnesses Θ and *f*¹); in D, where it appears in the form ευαγγελιον κατα μαθθαιον ετελεσθη αρχεται ευαγγελιον κατα ιωαννην; and in two of the most ancient papyri, 𝔓⁶⁶ and 𝔓⁷⁵, written, at the latest, in the early years of the third century. Thus ευαγγελιον κατα ιωαννην is not only the most widely supported reading, but also the most ancient attested; and it is therefore to be preferred to the form κατα ιωαννην found in ℵ (and B), which can easily be explained as a handy abbreviation. In fact, if one is looking for the title of the work rather than the manuscript superscription, ℵ itself gives as the title ευαγγελιον κατα ιωαννην, at the end of the Gospel, as a *subscriptio*, following its pattern with Mark and Luke (that of Matthew having been omitted, probably by an oversight).

A few witnesses have αγιον ευ. κ. I., and some editions of the Peshitta read: 'the holy gospel of the preaching of John the Evangelist which he spoke and preached in Greek at Ephesus' (for the evidence see Tischendorf 739). But the absence of αγιον (or of any other addition) in the overwhelming majority of early codices makes it virtually certain that the formula ευαγγελιον κατα ιωαννην was the original title of the work.

The absence of the definite article before ευαγγελιον is in accordance with normal Greek practice when giving the title of a book, as in απολο-για σωκρατους or πλατωνος πολιτεια: there is nothing indefinite about the anarthrous nouns here (cf. MHT I 82). It is to be noted, however, that (as in the two examples just mentioned) ευαγγελιον is first and foremost a description of the content of the writing, probably inspired by Mk 1.1: it is the 'Gospel, the Good News' as preached in a tradition 'according to John' (compare Mk 14.9). Only later did the term acquire, by a quite natural extension, the secondary meaning of a written gospel-book.

This is evident from the fact that in the NT and in the Apostolic Fathers εὐαγγέλιον is found only in the singular, and in its primary sense of 'gospel-message'; and from the fact that the earliest Apologist, Aristides, uses the clumsy circumlocution εὐαγγελικὴ ἅγια γραφή to denote the book (or books) which he invites the Emperor Hadrian to examine.[1] Justin is the first witness of the plural form εὐαγγέλια,[2] and it is remarkable that in his extant writings neither the oral proclamation of the Christian gospel by the Church nor its content is ever termed εὐαγγέλιον; in Justin's writings, the word εὐαγγέλιον denotes, exclusively, a book.[3]

In the latter half of the second century the use of the plural with the meaning 'gospel-books' became widespread, partly as a result of the proliferation of what we call apocryphal gospels, partly as a reaction against Marcion's attempt to restrict the Gospel-message to one written gospel-book (Luke's), and partly because it was such a natural development of the language. True, apart from the text of Justin just mentioned (*I Apol.* 66.3), there is only one other known reference to gospels (in the plural) before Irenaeus, in the *Chronicon Paschale* of Apollinarius of Hierapolis, written under Marcus Aurelius. There we read στασιάζειν δοκεῖ κατ᾽ αὐτοὺς τὰ εὐαγγέλια (*PG* 5.1297 A). The very wording of this phrase implies that it was by then normal to speak of gospels in the plural, and as written books; and in Irenaeus, Clement of Alexandria and Origen, this usage is well established (see *PGL* 555ff.). Indeed, both Tatian's endeavour to harmonize our four canonical narratives into his *Diatessaron* (after A.D. 172) and Irenaeus' stress on the unity of the teaching in the 'fourfold gospel' (*Adv. haer.* III 11.7-8) may be seen as attempts to keep a balance when speaking of the gospels, by ensuring that the original and primary sense of 'Gospel' should not be lost: the Church possesses only one Gospel, albeit in four different versions.[4]

It is impossible to say whether the writers (or the final editors) of our four canonical gospels themselves attached the title 'gospel' to their books. Mark 1:1 is not conclusive proof, for it is not certain that it refers to Mark's *book*: it could refer to the content of the writing. But Hengel has argued well that, to distinguish the various codices in the library or

---

[1] *Apologia* 15: οὗ τὸ κλέος τῆς παρουσίας ἐκ τῆς παρ᾽ αὐτοῖς καλουμένης εὐαγγελικῆς ἁγίας γραφῆς ἔξεστί σοι γνῶναι, βασιλεῦ, ἐὰν ἐντύχῃς (J. Rendel Harris and J. Armitage Robinson in *Texts and Studies* I,1, Cambridge, 1893, 110[21-23]). That Aristides had in mind Luke's gospel is highly probable, in view of his strong emphasis at the beginning of ch. 15 on the virginal conception of Jesus; but since he there writes also of the son of God 'descending from heaven' and 'taking flesh', and invites the Emperor 'to look into the writings [plural] of the Christians' (ch. 16; 111[24-25]), one cannot exclude the possibility that he was also asking Hadrian to read the gospel according to John. For the text and translation of the beginning of ch.15, see the comment below on Jn 1.14a, p. 51 fn. 7.

[2] *I Apologia* 66.3 (ca. A.D. 150–155): οἱ γὰρ ἀπόστολοι ἐν τοῖς γενομένοις ὑπ᾽ αὐτων ἀπομνημονεύμασιν, ἃ καλεῖται εὐαγγέλια...

[3] He speaks of the preaching of the apostles in *I Apol.* 42.4; 45.5; 49.5; 50.12; 53.3; *Dial.* 114.4; 119.6, without ever calling it εὐαγγέλιον. But in the *Dial.* 10.2 we read of the 'wonderful divine commandments, ἐν τῷ λεγομένῳ εὐαγγελίῳ', and in 100.1, ἐν τῷ εὐαγγελίῳ γέγραπται.

[4] See G. N. Stanton, 'The Fourfold Gospel', *NTS* 43 (1997), 317-46, especially 329-35.

book-chests of a Christian community, the obvious step was to put a short title at the beginning of each manuscript, by which it could be precisely identified at a glance. In that case, the 'short title' (e.g. ευαγγελιον κατα ιωαννην) would in all probability be contemporaneous with the making of the first copies from the original manuscript.

One final point must be noted. In the Graeco-Roman world, the name of the author normally precedes the title of the book. Thus one finds πλατωνος πολιτεια, but απολογια σωκρατους (in the reverse order, since Socrates was not the writer of the book). Now no NT manuscript contains as a short title ιωαννου ευαγγελιον, though such usage would be perfectly legitimate in the case of an epistle (see Tischendorf on James, 1 Peter etc.) or of an apocalypse, and does in fact occur. *A fortiori*, no Greek manuscript reads ευαγγελιον ιωαννου[5] for it is always 'the Gospel of Jesus Christ' which is intended, and which is as a rule entitled quite simply '[the] Gospel', followed by the identification of the particular version, as in 'according to John'.[6]

[5] Though some Syriac texts (including the Curetonian) do. For the evidence see Tischendorf 739.

[6] For further detail, see M. Hengel, *Studies in the Gospel of Mark*, London and Philadelphia, 1985, cf. III: 'The Titles of the Gospels', 64-84, plus invaluable notes on 162-83. See also G.N. Stanton, *Jesus and Gospel*, Cambridge, 2004, 9-62.

I

THE PROLOGUE

1.1-18

The first 18 verses of the Gospel according to John are by custom known as 'The Prologue', a title which goes back at least to Jerome.[1] In this commentary, the Prologue is divided into four parts:

A. The Word of God in Creation and History (1.1-5).
B. John as Witness to the Light (1.6-8).
C. The Coming of the Light into the World (1.9-13).
D. The Word Become Flesh (1.14-18).

A. THE WORD OF GOD IN CREATION AND HISTORY (1.1-5)

1a	In the beginning there was the Word,
1b	and the Word was very close to God,
1c	and the Word too was God.
2a	This Word was, in the beginning, with God;
3a	Through it, all things came into being,
3b	and without it, not one thing came into being.
3c-4a	What has come into being† | in it was life,
4b	and this life was the light of mankind,
5a	and the light is shining in the darkness,
5b	and the darkness has never become master of it.

[† 3c: or What came into being]

---

[1] '…in illud prohemium caelo veniens eructavit In principio erat verbum' (*Prologus quattuor evangeliorum: Praefatio in Matthaeum*: printed in Aland, *Synopsis Quattuor Evangeliorum* 546).

Nowadays it is widely accepted that the core of this Prologue consists of a hymn, into which additional or explanatory matter has been inserted. Which verses belong to the hymn, and whether the verses assigned to the hymn were written by the evangelist or an editor or were taken over from another source, Christian or not, are questions much debated. They are discussed immediately after v. 18, in Excursus I.

1a. Ἐν ἀρχῇ. The absence of the article is normal, even classical, in such prepositional phrases, especially in designations of time (BDF 255 [3]). Thus Thucydides writes (I 35,5) ὥσπερ ἐν ἀρχῇ ὑπείπομεν, and Plato (*Timaeus* 28b), ἐν ἀρχῇ δεῖν σκοπεῖν. The phrase is therefore good Greek for 'at the beginning' and is not to be regarded as a Semitism.

It occurs only four times in the NT, here in Jn 1.1-2, in Acts 11.15 and in Phil 4.15, but the latter texts, which refer respectively to the first reception of the Spirit in Acts 2 and to the first preaching of the gospel in Macedonia, throw no light on the meaning of the phrase in Jn 1.1-2. In fact, the opening words of the Gospel are clearly intended to recall the first words of Genesis (1.1): Ἐν ἀρχῇ ἐποίησεν ὁ θεὸς τὸν οὐρανὸν καὶ τὴν γῆν (LXX). The first question, therefore, is to ask how the writer of Jn 1.1 understood these words of Genesis.

Gen 1.1 is a declaration that the first thing God created in our physical universe was just raw material, material which was to begin with in a state of chaos (v. 2);[2] this shapeless and chaotic mass God then proceeded to organize over a period of six days in order to produce a place suitable for human beings to live in. That Gen 1 is concerned with the creation only of the physical universe, and not of the world of spirits, is evident both from the list of the things that are made and from v. 26: 'Let us make man in our image, after our likeness'. The plural here is best taken (as in Isa 6.8, and very probably in Gen 3.22 and 11.7) as addressed to the attendant spirits in the heavenly court,[3] who are therefore considered as already in existence before the making of the material world.

ἦν is then an affirmation that ἐν ἀρχῇ, even before the raw material of the physical world was created, the Logos was already in existence.

Thus far, the assertion is identical with those in Prov 8.22-23 and Sir 24.9, which state that Wisdom existed before the world was made; but, in contrast to these two texts, John gives no hint that the Logos was created. Proverbs 8.22ff read: 'The Lord begot (?) me (קָנָנִי [qānāni] LXX, ἔκτισέν με) as the starting-point of his activity, the first of his acts of old. From eternity (מֵעוֹלָם [me'olām]: LXX, πρὸ τοῦ αἰῶνος) I was enthroned, from the beginning (מֵרֹאשׁ [mer'oš]: LXX, ἐν ἀρχῇ), before the origins of the earth...' Sirach 24.9 reads: 'From eternity, in the beginning [πρὸ τοῦ αἰῶνος, ἀπ' ἀρχῆς] he created me, and to eternity [ἕως αἰῶνος] I shall not cease to exist'. In Jn 1.1 there is no equivalent reference to the creation of the Logos, and this is significant, particularly when one compares it with the text of the Palestinian Targum on Gen 3.24. 'Two thousand years before the world was created, he created the

---

[2] This is true whether one construes the Hebrew absolutely as 'In the beginning God created...' (thus the majority of interpreters, and all the ancient versions), or as 'In the beginning, when God created...' (Rashi, Ibn Ezra, and some moderns). For detail, see F. Delitzsch, *A New Commentary on Genesis*, Edinburgh, 1888, I, 74-76.

[3] It is not a plural of majesty (which is never found in the Hebrew OT where God is speaking of himself) nor a plural of self-deliberation (the content of the whole chapter speaks against this). Cf. Delitzsch, *Genesis*, 98.

Law. He established the Garden of Eden for the just and Gehenna for the wicked.'[4] There is also a baraitah[5] in the Babylonian Talmud (*Pesahim* 54*a*) stating that 'Seven things were created before the world was created, and these are they: The Torah, repentance, the Garden of Eden, Gehenna, the Throne of Glory, the Temple, and the name of the Messiah'.[6] The Law (Torah) is here listed as having been created, and is even placed first in the list; therefore, since the Law is the medium by which the designs of divine Wisdom are outwardly expressed, it is reasonable to conclude, with Sir 24.1-29 (note especially v. 23), that Wisdom is logically and 'chronologically' antecedent to the Torah. This will be an important factor in assessing the relationship between the Logos, Wisdom and Torah.[7] For the moment, it is sufficient to note that in Jn 1.1 the verb ἦν asserts that the Logos was in existence ἐν ἀρχῇ, that is, before the creation of the material world, and that there is nothing to imply that this Logos was itself created.[8]

ὁ λόγος. Since the meaning of λόγος in this and the following verses cannot be finally determined except in the light of the Prologue as a whole, it must suffice to set down here various possible meanings and to indicate which is preferred. A full discussion is given in Excursus II.

Five basic and clearly differentiated meanings are theoretically possible. (1) In the Platonist sense, the term denotes a self-subsistent Form or Idea.[9] (2) In the Stoic sense, it denotes either the internal concept (λόγος ἐνδιαθέτος) or the external expression of the same (λόγος προφορικός). (3) For Plotinus and the Neoplatonists, the term denotes the first, ontologically necessary (i.e. non-contingent), emanation from the absolutely primary principle of all things, the One, and is more commonly spoken of not as Logos but as Mind (Νοῦς). (4) The Hebrew

---

[4] *Neophyti I: 1 Genesis*, ETr by M. McNamara, Edinburgh, 1992, 505. Though the text does not of itself imply that Eden and Gehenna were also created 2000 years before the world, this is its most natural meaning, with which one may compare Mt 25.34, 41.

[5] I.e. 'teaching not included in the Mishnah, but related to and contemporary with the teachings of the Mishnah, and recorded in the Gemara' (H. Danby, *The Mishnah*, Oxford, 1933, 141 fn.7).

[6] *The Soncino Talmud, Seder Mo'ed II: Pesahim* 54a, 265.

[7] See Excursus II.

[8] In 1 Jn 1.1, the phrase ὃ ἦν ἀπ' ἀρχῆς, referring to the incarnate Logos, presupposes its existence ἐν ἀρχῇ, as does the phrase τὸν ἀπ' ἀρχῆς in 1 Jn 2.13, 14.

[9] 'Platonist' is used (in preference to 'Platonic') because Plato himself did not use the term λόγος in presenting his theory of Ideas or Forms. See especially the *Theaetetus* 206d-10d, where Socrates argues that the three meanings of λόγος are the expression of thought, the correct enumeration of the constitutive elements of an object, and the determination of its distinctive characteristic ᾧ ἀπάντων διαφέρει τὸ ἐρωτηθέν (208c). Compare also the *Sophist* 259c-63e. In no text does Plato himself come anywhere near to equating λόγος with ἰδέα as denoting an ideal form or archetype (e.g. *Republic* VII 517b: ἡ τοῦ ἀγαθοῦ ἰδέα). The assimilation was made by the later Platonists, notably by Plotinus. See LSJ *s.v.* III 7 c, and IV 73 A 2 (Debrunner) and especially 79-86 B 2 (Kleinknecht).

OT presents the Word of God as creative of all things, revelatory of God's will and sovereignly effective of his decrees concerning human history, so much so that this Word may be considered as the external expression of divine Wisdom, with which it is closely identified. (5) In the Targums and in rabbinic thought, the Aramaic term Memra, meaning literally the *utterance* or the *Word* of God, is frequently found, but its precise meaning is much debated. (a) Perhaps the most widespread view is that which regards the Memra as nothing more than a reverential circumlocution to avoid pronouncing the Holy Tetragram, YHWH. (b) Others see the Memra as a kind of divine attribute akin to Wisdom, or to the Holy Spirit, or to the Name, which are virtually personalized in order to express God's activity in creation and in history while at the same time preserving untouched the immutability of the Godhead. It is thus a kind of literary form used to preserve the doctrine of divine transcendence. (c) Some Christian scholars have taken this rabbinical term to indicate a kind of intermediary hypostasis between God and his people. (d) But the most satisfactory meaning seems to be that which interprets Memra as 'neither an hypostasis, nor a simple replacement for the Name YHWH, but an exegetical term representing a theology of the name "*HYH*"'[10] (see below).

The first, strictly Platonist, sense is rarely, if ever used in interpreting John. The second, Stoic, sense was used in the early Trinitarian controversies (notably by Tertullian) in order to defend the unity of the Godhead; but few would maintain that this was the meaning intended here by the evangelist. The third, the Neoplatonist, sense exercised a profound influence on patristic interpretation, but, unless one regards the Fourth Gospel as a fore-runner of second-century Gnosticism, it is hard to see how anything resembling the philosophical Neoplatonist meaning could have been in the mind of the evangelist. His thought-world is far too Jewish.

The fourth, the OT, meaning is the meaning attached to the concept of the Logos in all the classical interpretations, and it may be taken as certain that the evangelist intended to include in his usage whatever the OT meant by the term Logos. This, however, need not restrain anyone from holding in addition that the primary sense of Logos in Jn 1 is the fifth one, namely, that the term Logos there stands for the Memra considered as the Holy, Ineffable, Name of God. That is, to speak of the Logos-Memra is to refer to the Deity revealed in the phrase 'I AM WHAT I AM' at Exod 3.14; and the meaning of this phrase is that the God of Moses does not merely exist in an ontological sense (*Sein*), but is also ever-present at the side of his creatures, ever ready to have mercy and to supply whatever help they may need in any situation (*Dasein*). The foundation of Israel's faith is that its God does actively intervene in this

---

[10] Thus Robert Hayward, *Divine Name and Presence: The Memra*, Publications of the Oxford Centre for Postgraduate Hebrew Studies, 1981, xii.

world, that is, the exact opposite of what is now termed deism. The Logos, the Memra, is 'He Who is There'. The sense of Jn 1.1a is therefore: 'In the beginning, before the material world was created, there existed the Word of God, the Compassionate, the All-merciful'.[11] This paraphrase accords perfectly with the Palestinian Targum of Gen 1.2: 'a spirit of love from before the Lord was blowing over the face of the waters'.[12]

1b. καὶ ὁ λόγος ἦν πρὸς τὸν θεόν. (1) It is often said that in the Koine, πρός with the accusative is, after a verb such as εἶναι, equivalent to παρά with the dative, as in Mt 13.56; 26.16[, 55 + πρòs υμαs *v.l.*], Mk 6.3; in that case, the meaning of the clause would be 'The Word was with God, was beside God' (*auprès de Dieu*), just as Wisdom is said to have been παρ' αὐτῷ (Prov 8.30), παρὰ κυρίου καὶ μετ' αυτοῦ εἰς τὸν αἰῶνα (Sir 1.1). Thus Bultmann, Barrett, Schnackenburg. (2) Others maintain that here the preposition has not lost its classical sense of relationship. Abbott (*JG* 2363-66) would render it as *devoted to, and in converse with* [God]; Westcott similarly. I. de la Potterie offers a more refined interpretation of this second view,[13] and argues against the first interpretation on four grounds: (a) No other text of John uses πρός with the accusative to denote proximity. (b) The Wisdom texts use παρά and μετά to express that sense, and John could easily have done the same. (c) John, to express the proximity of the Son to the Father, uses παρά σοι (17.5) and παρὰ τῷ πατρί (8.28), and employs the same construction to denote the nearness of one person to another (1.39; 4.40; 14.17, 23; cf. 19.25). He also uses μετά τινος (3.22, 25, 26 etc.) but never πρός with the accusative. (d) 1 John uses πρός with the accusative to denote orientation towards (παράκλητον ἔχομεν πρὸς τὸν πατέρα, 2.1; παρρησίαν ἔχομεν πρὸς τὸν θεόν, 3.21; cf. 5.14). De la Potterie concludes that πρὸς τὸν θεόν in 1.1 is the first member of a chiasmus with 1.18, and equivalent to εἰς τὸν κόλπον τοῦ πατρὸς, with the sense 'Le Logos était *tourné vers* Dieu'.[14]

Perhaps the difference between these interpretations should not be pressed too hard, for if the Logos was 'with God', it must have been in some relationship *to* God, and it is obvious that this cannot have been a local or spatial relationship in a material sense. De la Potterie's reasons do seem to tip the scale appreciably in favour of the second interpretation, in which πρός is taken to stress the close 'metaphysical' relationship between the Logos and God. Compare 1 Jn 1.2, ἀπαγγέλλομεν ὑμῖν

[11] The ambiguity of attribution for the adjectives is of course deliberate.

[12] *Neofiti I: 1 Genesis*, ETr by M. McNamara, 497. See further, Catrin Williams, *'I am He': The Interpretation of ʾANI HU in Jewish and Early Christian Literature*, Tübingen, 2000.

[13] *Biblica* 43 (1962), 379-81.

[14] Compare C. K. Williams, *The New Testament: A New Translation in Plain English*, London, 1952: 'The Word was face to face with God'.

τὴν ζωὴν τὴν αἰώνιον ἥτι ἦν πρὸς τὸν πατέρα, and 2.1, παράκλητον ἔχομεν πρὸς τὸν πατέρα; see also Jn 8.42 and 16.28. Thus v. 1b might be represented in English as 'The Word was very close to God', with all the ambiguity those words contain.[15]

1c. καὶ θεὸς ἦν ὁ λόγος. Ever since Chrysostom, commentators have remarked that the first clause (1a) asserts the pre-existence of the Logos, the second (1b) affirms that he was in a certain relationship with God, and the third (1c) states that he is some sense to be identified with God. The threefold ἦν thus leads up to a climax: the Word was God. The three statements taken together are the foundation upon which the teaching of this Gospel rests. Further, when the Logos is identified with the Memra in the sense defined above, the three statements become in addition a declaration that mercy, love and compassion beyond all telling belong from all eternity to the very nature and essence of the Godhead. This doctrine is perhaps the most distinctive characteristic of Johannine theology.

The absence of the article before θεός shows not merely that ὁ λόγος is the subject, and θεός the predicate (MHT III 183); it also 'indicates that the Word is God, but is not the only being of whom this is true' (Barrett), thus laying the foundation for the long and arduous discussions in early Christian history about the sense in which the Word could be said to be God (θεός), if there was only one God, and if the Word was not in every respect identical with ὁ θεός. English, like most languages, cannot reproduce the distinction between θεός and ὁ θεός, and the translation above endeavours to achieve a semi-satisfactory version by the insertion of the adverb *too*.

The chiasmus in 1bc (λόγος–θεόν, θεός–λόγος) has often been remarked; sometimes also, the symmetry between 1.1 and 1.18. Less often noticed is the fact that if the term Logos here stands for the Holy Name of God, the Memra, there is an all-embracing *inclusio* around the entire gospel, whose purpose is that 'believing, you may have life *in his name*' (20.31).

2. οὗτος as a resumptive pronoun is distinctly more emphatic than the natural choice, αὐτός, and the insertion of *Word* in the English translation is intended to reflect this. The position of the verb ἦν serves to place all the stress of the sentence on the complement: the Logos was, **ἐν ἀρχῇ, πρὸς τὸν θεόν.**

---

[15] Burney's suggestion (AOFG 29) that πρός is here a translation of the Aramaic לות (lwt), denoting either connexion with (= *apud*, παρά) or motion towards (= *ad*, πρός), has not been well received. Straight after the book's publication, G. R. Driver pointed out that this text, far from being in the strict sense an Aramaism, is simply 'an extension of many classical usages': see MHT II 467 for the reference and for examples. Nigel Turner, somewhat surprisingly, writes that it is 'is a Semitism and it may be due to the Aramaic lewĕthī (MHT IV 71)'.

Though the sentence may seem at first reading to be an otiose repetition of facts already stated in v. 1, it does in reality add a clarification, by reaffirming that from the very beginning the Logos was in close relationship to God (Barrett). It is more questionable whether this statement was inserted to prevent anyone from misunderstanding v. 1 as an assertion of the existence of two divine beings, a Logos–Theos and ὁ θεός, *the* God (so Bultmann), for it is difficult to imagine any first-century Christian thinking in terms of two deities. The most satisfactory explanation is that v. 2 by reaffirming, at this point, and in the strongest way possible, the nature of the Logos *in se* and *quoad Deum,* prepares the ground for the next statement, about the role of the Logos with respect to all that has been created.

3. πάντα δι' αὐτοῦ ἐγένετο, καὶ χωρὶς αὐτοῦ ἐγένετο οὐδὲ ἕν ὃ γέγονεν. This is the reading and punctuation of the Textus Receptus. A different punctuation will be discussed at the end of the commentary on this verse. Verse 3 punctuated as in the Textus Receptus may be interpreted in three ways.

1. *The verse is understood as referring to the creation.*
In Classical Greek and in the Koine, both πάντα and τὰ πάντα are used to denote 'the whole of creation, the entire universe' as distinct from God. Plato, for example, writes (*Epistula* 6.323d): τὸν τῶν πάντων θεὸν ἡγεμόνα τῶν τε ὄντων καὶ τῶν μελλόντων. Colossians 1.20 and Eph 1.10 use τὰ πάντα in the same way, to denote the whole of creation, the totality in each case being further emphasized by the addition of the words 'those that are in heaven and those that are on earth' (Ephesians; Colossians in the reverse order, and with one different preposition). So also Rev 4.11: σὺ ἔκτισας τὰ πάντα. The presence of the article in these texts and elsewhere is probably intended to stress the notion that *all* things, taken collectively (rather than 'every thing' taken distributively) were created (Revelation), reconciled (Colossians), given a new beginning (Ephesians)[16] etc. In that case, the *absence* of the article in the present verse (Jn 1.3) would indicate that *every single thing*, taken one by one, came into being through the Logos, a distributive sense which may also be intended in Rev 21.5, Ἰδοὺ καινὰ ποιῶ πάντα, individually. If this is the sense here, it would be more accurate to translate the Greek πάντα not as *all things*, but as *everything*, or even better, as *every thing.*[17] The translation above retains the plural *all things* to reflect the Greek plural.

[16] For this translation, see J. McHugh, 'A Reconsideration of Ephesians 1:10b in the Light of Irenaeus', *Paul and Paulinism: Essays in Honour of C.K. Barrett*, ed. M. D. Hooker and S. G. Wilson, London, 1982, 302-309.
[17] The only other texts in John where the same difficulty might arise are 3.31 and 10.29, but see the notes *in loco.*

δι᾽ αὐτοῦ: *through him*. Note that the text says 'through him', not 'by him' (ὑπ᾽ αὐτοῦ), a distinction which is well taken by the Latin versions' *per ipsum* (not *ab ipso*). This may be very significant, because in the Synoptics, διά with the genitive is rarely used to indicate a personal agent, and on two of the four occasions it is used in a bad sense.[18] In John the construction is more common, and is always used in a good sense: apart from the occurrences here and in v. 10.[19] διά with the genitive is always used of the contribution made by God's personal agents in the work of salvation. Thus the Baptist is his agent as witness (1.7), as is Moses as lawgiver (1.17). Both are superseded by one who remains for ever the supreme and only, definitive and irreplaceable, agent of salvation, Jesus Christ (1.17; 3.17; 10.1, 2, 9 and especially 14.6). Johannine usage tells rather against interpreting this half-verse as referring *solely* to the work of creation.

ἐγένετο: *came into being, was brought into existence*, the aorist denoting a fact completed in the past. The tense stands in (probably deliberate) contrast to that used of the Logos in 1.1, 2 (ἦν). At this point the author could have underlined the universality of the work of the Logos by inserting a phrase such as τὰ ἐν τοῖς οὐρανοῖς καὶ τὰ ἐπὶ τῆς γῆς; indeed, if he were writing a hymn, and that in proconsular Asia, such a line might have commended itself as almost a natural expansion of πάντα, as it is in the hymns of Eph 1.10 and Col 1.20. If he did first entertain and then reject this idea, it might have been because he was consciously thinking of Gen 1.1, in which 'heaven and earth' denote only the material creation (see above on 1.1), and do not include the spirits outside this world. This would seem to be the sense of the words in Rev 14.7; 20.11. The reason for mentioning this hypothesis is that the author may have wished to stress that everything without exception was brought into existence by the Logos. Hence, instead of writing 'the things that are in heaven and those that are on earth', which could have been be misinterpreted as denoting only the material world, terrestrial and celestial, he placed next a clause more emphatic still.

As in 1.29 etc., a positive statement is reinforced by the denial of its opposite. χωρίς means *apart from*, οὐδὲ ἕν (*si vera lectio*[20]) is even more emphatic than οὐδέν, and ὃ γέγονεν is in this context almost a technical term for *that which has come into existence*.[21] Thus the sense is that 'not a

---

[18] It is found seven times, but on only four occasions, namely, in Mt 11.2, of the Baptist's envoys; in Lk 18.31, of the prophets; in Mt 18.7 = Lk 17.1, of the one through whom scandals come; and in Mt 26.24 = Mk 14.21 = Lk 22.12, of him δι᾽ οὗ the Son of man is handed over.

[19] But see below, on 1.10.

[20] That οὐδὲ ἕν is the true original reading can scarcely be doubted, for among the papyri and uncials the only witnesses to οὐδέν are 𝔓⁶⁶, ℵ* and D, and among the minuscules, only *f* 1 and 1071.

[21] So also in a frequently cited text of Plato (*Timaeus* 28b), which is worth quoting in extenso. ὁ δὴ πᾶς οὐρανὸς - ἢ κόσμος ἢ καὶ ἄλλο ὅτι ποτὲ ὀνομαζόμενος μάλιστ᾽

single thing that has come into existence ever came into existence independently of the Logos'.

2. *The verse is understood as referring to the work of salvation.*
In John, and in the Johannine Epistles, the neuter plural τὰ πάντα is never found. By contrast, πάντα *without* the article is found on several occasions with reference to the work of Jesus on earth (notably in 3.35-36; 5.20; 13.3; 16.15; 17.7, 10; and especially 19.28). Secondly, there is the phrase δι' αὐτοῦ. Everywhere else in John διά with the genitive, when used of Christ, refers to his mediatory role in the work of salvation (see especially 3.17; 10.9; 14.6; 1 Jn 4.9; and above, on this verse, under 1). Thirdly, the verb γίνεσθαι occurs three times in this verse, each time with an indeterminate and neuter subject (πάντα, οὐδὲ ἕν, ὃ). Whenever this construction is found elsewhere in John, γίνεσθαι always applies to an historical *event*, which either *happened, took place* (1.28; 3.9; 13.19 [×2]; 14.22, 29 [×2]; 19.36) or which *will come to pass* (15.7). Verse 3, so interpreted, would then mean that *every single event* in the story of salvation which is about to unfold *takes place* only *through* the Logos,[22] and that *not one thing happens independently of* him. Some add, as a final and confirmatory argument, that on this interpretation, the Prologue would be framed in a double *inclusio*, with ἐγένετο twice at the beginning in 1.3, and twice at the end (1.14, 17), on each occasion referring to historical events.[23]

3. *The verse is taken as referring both to the role of the pre-existent Logos in the creation and also to the salvific work of the Word made flesh which is about to be revealed.*
The verbal similarity between 1.1 and Gen 1.1, and the repetition of 'And God said…' throughout Gen 1, make it hard to think that the role of the Logos in creation was absent from the writer's mind at Jn 1.3; but to affirm that is not to invalidate the arguments just given in favour of the second interpretation. There is no difficulty in accepting both, for such a double meaning would be entirely in keeping with the style and theology of the evangelist, and here in 1.3 it could well be fully intended (but contrast 1.9-10).

The foregoing interpretations of v. 3 assume the punctuation found in the Textus Receptus, but there is another, more ancient, manner of construing the final words of v. 3 and the initial clause of v. 4 which, though

---

ἂν δέχοιτο, τοῦθ' ἡμῖν ὠνομάσθω - σκεπτέον δ' οὖν περὶ αὐτοῦ πρῶτον, ὅπερ ὑπόκειται περὶ παντὸς ἐν ἀρχῇ δεῖν σκοπεῖν, πότερον ἦν ἀεί, γενέσεως ἀρχὴν ἔχων οὐδεμίαν, ἢ γέγονεν, ἀπ' ἀρχῆς τινος ἀρξάμενος. γέγονεν.

[22] The preposition is important: not *by* the Logos. See above on 1.2a. It will assume great importance in early patristic Trinitarian debate.

[23] I. de la Potterie, *La Vérité*, 162-64. The first to argue this point in print was apparently T. E. Pollard, 'Cosmology and the Prologue of the Fourth Gospel', *Vigiliae Christianae* 12 (1958), 147-53.

it does not affect the meaning of v. 3, makes a significant difference to the sense of v. 4.

3-4. Of the two ways of punctuating vv. 3-4, the first places a full point at the end of v. 3, after ὃ γέγονεν, whereas the second places a full point after οὐδὲ ἕν, and takes the words ὃ γέγονεν as the initial words of the sentence in v. 4. The text will thus read

> either 1. ἐγένετο οὐδὲ ἕν ὃ γέγονεν. ἐν αὐτῷ ζωὴ ἦν.
> or 2. ἐγένετο οὐδὲ ἕν. ὃ γέγονεν ἐν αὐτῷ ζωὴ ἦν.

The interpretation of v. 3 just given is in accordance with Reading 1.

Reading 2 is more difficult to explain, for the words ὃ γέγονεν in v. 3 and the first four words of v. 4 take on different meanings according to the manner in which they are construed; and they can of course be construed

> either as (a) ὃ γέγονεν / ἐν αὐτῷ ζωὴ ἦν.
> or as (b) ὃ γέγονεν ἐν αὐτῷ // ζωὴ ἦν.

One of these alternatives must be chosen in order to interpret and to translate Reading 2. The commentary will here indicate the sense which emerges according to the punctuation which the reader prefers to assign to it (and it is well to remember that the original text was not punctuated at all). A short history of the interpretation of the verse according to the punctuation adopted is given in Excursus IV, 'Longer Notes of Textual Criticism'.

Reading 2 (a) places a comma after γέγονεν, giving ὃ γέγονεν, ἐν αὐτῷ ζωὴ ἦν. On this reading, ὃ γέγονεν may be construed as an accusative of respect, giving the sense 'for that which has come into existence, there was life in him', but the evidence for such a grammatical construction is flimsy in the extreme,[24] and if that meaning had been intended, the text should have read rather, to make the antecedent clear, ἃ γέγονεν. A second possibility is to take ἐν αὐτῷ as referring not to the Logos, but to ὃ γέγονεν: 'As for that which has come into existence, there was life in it'. This would keep close to the text of Gen 1, especially if life is here understood as denoting purely 'natural' life.[25] It would make good sense here, but gives rise to problems when this life is identified with light in v. 4. The alternative is to take ὃ γέγονεν as the subject of the clause, and to translate it as 'that which has come into existence [or: come to pass]—in it was life', which makes little sense, if any. Unless the words are taken as an accusative of respect, the comma must come after ἐν αὐτῷ.

---

[24] The only possible examples in John are at 6.10, τὸν ἀριθμὸν ὡς πεντακισχίλιοι, where the grammar is self-evident, and at 8.25, τὴν ἀρχὴν κτλ., where the construction, whatever its meaning, must be idiomatic. See BDF 160.

[25] Thus A. van Hoonacker, 'Le Prologue du quatrième Evangile', *RHE* 2 (1901), 5ff.

Reading 2 (b) puts a comma after αὐτῷ, giving ὃ γέγονεν ἐν αὐτῷ, ζωὴ ἦν. The usual objection to this punctuation is that the second verb should be not ἦν but ἐστιν, a reading which is in fact found in ℵ D it syrᶜ cop, and several Gnostic writers (see UBS). Certainly, if one is thinking of the creation, it is more natural to expect 'What has come into existence in him *is* life'; but this objection has less force when one remembers that the perfect may be used in the sense of the aorist, a usage which Nigel Turner calls a 'resultative' rather than a 'present' perfect.[26] The verse could then mean 'What came into existence in him, was life'.

If, however, the words are taken to refer not to the creation but to Christ's work of salvation, they may be translated as 'What came [or: has come] to pass in him was life', which seems eminently reasonable.

Indeed, if this third interpretation of v. 3 is accepted, it suggests a most attractive double meaning affirming both that created life came into being through the pre-existent Word, and that it was through the Word made flesh that it was restored (cf. 3.5; 10.10; 11.25). One may then recall that in Gen 1, the creation proceeds from day to day, in a careful logical succession, establishing the conditions in which living things may grow until on the sixth day, when all is at last ready for the completion of the work, God creates the land-based beasts and finally the human race. In Genesis, all these things, from the first creation (light) to the last, were brought into existence through God's Word. So in the Fourth Gospel, all proceeds towards the restoration of life for the entire human race on the sixth day of the final week of Jesus' earthly life, with Paradise Restored.

4. ἐν αὐτῷ ζωὴ ἦν. The absence of the article before ζωή indicates that the writer is alluding not to an abstract concept of life apprehensible by the mind, but to an objectively subsistent reality ('a life'), and is asserting that there was in the Logos a principle of life, that is, a particular kind of life. Such a principle is, of course, found also in many kinds of creatures which in their different ways are 'living' beings which 'have' life, but all the living creatures which are observable on earth carry within themselves by nature the germ of death: they grow, mature, age, decline and die (cf. Zahn 54). In the Logos, by contrast, there is by nature, because of his relationship to God (ἐν ἀρχῇ ἦν πρὸς τὸν θεόν), uncreated life—ἡ κατὰ φύσιν ζωή (Cyril of Alexandria). Following the interpretations given above of v. 3, some will see this initial statement of v. 4 as an assertion that even before the creation there was in the pre-existent Logos a principle of life; others will see it as referring to the ministry of the Incarnate Word, and others as referring to both.

The meaning of the term ζωή, 'life', will therefore depend on the way in which the word Logos is understood. (1) If the meaning of Logos is here restricted to what has so far been stated about the Logos in vv. 1-3,

---

[26] MHT II 68-69 and 81-85. See also BDF 343 (3).

that is, if the term Logos is understood to denote, at this point in the Gospel, God's agent or instrument in creation (cf. Gen 1 etc.), and nothing more than that, then the term 'life' will in consequence be of wide and generic application (as in Gen 1.20-21, 24, 30); and though this would proclaim the greatness of God, so 'deistic' (if one may use the term) a view of the Logos hardly seems consonant even with the OT concept. (2) If, however, that same creative Logos is understood (as elsewhere in the OT) to have been in addition God's agent in the providential guiding of events in history (e.g. Isa 40.8; 55.10-11), then this implies that it has, at particular moments in time, ensured life and survival for God's people on this earth. (3) If the Logos is also a rule (*torah*) for the people as a whole, and a light for each individual (e.g. Ps 119.105), to guide them during their time on earth along the paths of righteousness, then this Logos is in an even more specific sense a source of what we may call the life of the spirit, 'enlightening the eyes' (Ps 19.9). (4) If 'Logos' is also here equivalent to the term Memra, and therefore connotes a whole theology of the name *YHWH* as defined above (p. 8), then it is capable of being a source of life for all humanity. The precise sense in which there is life in the Logos remains, however, to be disclosed, and its full implications will become clear only gradually, as the story of the Fourth Gospel unfolds. The evangelist begins by declaring that the first characteristic of 'the life which is in the Logos' is that it brings 'light' to humankind.

καὶ ἡ ζωὴ ἦν τὸ φῶς τῶν ἀνθρώπων. It would be absurd to say that this was so before the creation; the meaning of ἦν must therefore be that the life which came in the Logos *was destined to be* the light of the human race after the creation.

But what is the meaning of τὸ φῶς τῶν ἀνθρώπων? By qualifying τὸ φῶς with the words τῶν ἀνθρώπων, the writer makes it clear that he is not referring to natural light, as in Gen 1, for in that text the daylight is a precondition of life not only for humans, but for beasts and plants as well. Equally, he is not speaking of 'the light of the world' in the sense which that phrase has in Jn 8.12; see the note on ὁ κόσμος at Jn 1.10. The primary meaning must therefore be that the life which God has from the beginning given to human beings contains a special, and indeed unique, kind of enlightenment, namely, the faculty of reason. See Thomas Aquinas's collection of patristic authorities in his *Catena aurea* 8-9.

But there is more to the meaning of τὸ φῶς τῶν ἀνθρώπων than that. It is impossible to imagine any Christian steeped in Judaism thinking of the coming of Jesus as having been without preparation (cf. Gal 4.4; Heb 1.1 etc.), and here at the beginning of John's Gospel, the full sense of the words τὸ φῶς τῶν ἀνθρώπων must be interpreted not only in terms of the OT concept of that unique kind of 'life' which God has given to the human race (as the sentence demands) but also in terms of salvation history (which is implied). *Heilsgeschichte* is the key to this sentence.[27]

ἦν: 'The imperfect is the tense of incomplete action, duration and continuity' (MHT III 64). Therefore the life which was in the Logos has from the moment of creation been throughout history, πολυμερῶς καὶ πολυτρόπως (Heb 1.1), the source of light for humankind. It was through the life-giving Logos that our race was first endowed with the primal faculty of reason; and then, as the OT so often teaches (see Proverbs, Ecclesiastes, Sirach and Wisdom), God would enhance this gift in all who sincerely sought to do his will, by bestowing upon them the gifts of wisdom and prudence. The universalist horizon is particularly evident in Sir 24, where the enshrinement of Wisdom in the Torah marks the culmination of its descent to this earth, and in those four great chapters of the book of Wisdom (6–9), addressed to all the rulers of the earth, which discourse upon the folly of preferring any material prosperity to the possession of wisdom. Far beyond the frontiers of Israel, as well as inside its culture, the Word and Wisdom of God had from the beginning been engaged in a *praeparatio evangelica*. But a still deeper meaning is to come. Just as human reason is enhanced by the gifts of wisdom and prudence, so wisdom and prudence may in turn be further heightened by another gift of the one who first bestowed them.

τὸ φῶς: here the presence of the article is significant, for it would have been equally easy to write καὶ ἡ ζωὴ φῶς ἦν τῶν ἀνθρώπων. The article indicates that the author is now referring to the most outstanding, indeed the unique, source of light for humankind (MHT III 183). The second article, too, is significant, for it too could have been omitted (e.g. ἡ ζωὴ φῶς ἦν ἀνθρώπων); τῶν ἀνθρώπων, therefore, must refer to the whole human race (see v. 9).

The underlying reasoning of vv. 3c-4ab is that the life which was in the Logos, being uncreated, is of its nature imperishable.[28] Therefore, the life which comes to the human race through and in and from the Logos must contain within itself the possibility, the prospect, the expectation and even the sure hope, of one day sharing to the full in some deathless life. Hope of this nature will clearly be τὸ φῶς τῶν ἀνθρώπων κατ' ἐξοχήν—the light *par excellence* for all those who here on earth dwell in darkness and in the shadow of death (compare Lk 1.79; Ps 106.10, 14 in the LXX, and Isa 9.1; 42.7). This is one of the central ideas in Johannine theology.

5. καὶ τὸ φῶς ἐν τῇ σκοτίᾳ φαίνει. In early Greek, the usual term for darkness was ὁ σκότος, but the alternative τὸ σκότος became

---

[27] *Pace* Bultmann, 'The history-of-salvation perspective as a whole is lacking in John' (*Theology of the New Testament*, ETr, II 8).

[28] The next occurrence of 'life' is at 3.15-16, where it is characterized as ζωὴ αἰώνιος.

common in Hellenistic Greek, and the masculine form is nowhere found in the LXX or in the NT.[29] The feminine form σκοτία is Hellenistic and, by comparison with σκότος, rare; see LSJ and *TWNT* VII 425.

σκότος occurs six times in Matthew (4.16; 6.23; 8.12; 22.13; 25.30; 27.45), four times in Lk (1.79; 11.35; 22.53; 23.44), and once in John (3.19). With the *possible* exception of the three Synoptic references to darkness at the crucifixion (Mt 27.45; Mk 15.33; Lk 23.44), its reference is always metaphorical. σκοτία is found in only two Synoptic texts, Mt 10.27 and its parallel Lk 12.3, and as a variant reading at Mt 4.16;[30] it too is in all cases used metaphorically.

John, by contrast, has a distinct preference for the form σκοτία, which occurs eight times in his gospel (1.5 [×2]; 6.17; 8.12; 12.35 [×2], 46; 20.1) and six times in 1 Jn (1.5; 2.8, 9, 11 [×3]). There does not, however, seem to be any difference of meaning between the three terms, masculine, feminine and neuter, unless we hypothesize that the termination –ια, which so often represents an abstract noun, justifies one in translating σκότος as *the dark* and σκοτία as *the darkness*, with the latter being more pronouncedly metaphorical. Against this, σκοτία is in Jn 6.17 indubitably, and in Jn 20.1 almost certainly, literal. In any case, John's theology would have been no different had he written τὸ σκότος rather than ἡ σκοτία, in accordance with the general usage of the LXX and of the other NT writers.[31]

In religious literature the use of the term 'darkness' is almost certain to be metaphorical. It refers not to the absence of physical light, but rather to that 'encircling gloom' of doubt or depression, of uncertainty or despair, where it would be a grace to see but one step ahead (cf. Ps 119.105).[32] Similarly, LSJ records that in the *Iliad*, ὁ σκότος always refers to the darkness of death, mostly in the phrase τὸν δὲ σκότος ὄσσε κάλυψεν (*Il.* 4.461 etc.), but also in lines such as στυγερὸς δ' ἄρα μιν σκότος εἷλεν (*Il.* 5.47; 13.672). Again, the texts from Qumran about the struggle between the Prince of Light and the Angel of Darkness (1QS III 20-26), or between the children of light and the children of darkness (1QS I 9-10; II 16-17; III 24-25), serve to illustrate the currency of this metaphor in the religious literature of the age.

---

[29] It would be rather pedantic to object that the anarthrous nominatives in Mt 27.45, Mk 15.33e and Lk 23.44 could in theory be masculine.

[30] NA[26] cites for σκοτια א[1] B D W; Or[pt]; for σκοτει, א* C L Θ *f* 1 13 𝔐; Or[pt]. NA[27] prints σκοτει as the text, σκοτια as a variant.

[31] HR lists only three instances of σκοτία in the LXX (Job 28.3; Mic 3.6; Isa 16.3); there are more than 100 instances of σκότος. All the NT occurrences of σκοτία are listed above—two in the Synoptics and 14 in John and 1 John; there are 18 examples of σκότος in addition to the 12 instances in the gospels enumerated in the preceding paragraph.

[32] Cf. Conzelmann in *TWNT* VII 425.

In the OT, darkness is one of the constituent elements of the initial chaos (Gen 1.2) which is not annihilated, but brought under control by God and turned into a useful and subordinate part of his creation (Gen 1); indeed, the darkness serves to reveal God's glory (Gen 15; Pss 8; 19). Furthermore, even though it is regularly seen as a source of danger and a cause of disaster, these things too may serve God's purposes, as at the Exodus. The realm of darkness too is subject to God's will, because he is its creator (Ps 139.11-12), as the Community Rule of Qumran stresses: 'It is He [the God of Israel] who created the spirits of Light and darkness... And he loves the one everlastingly and delights in his works for ever; but the counsel of the other he loathes and for ever hates its ways' (1QS III 25–IV 1).[33]

σκότος and σκοτία can, of course, also be used with reference to blindness, and in particular of the mental incapacity to see what is in fact before one's eyes. This too qualifies as 'darkness', and the meaning of σκοτία in Jn 1.5 is that human existence is lived out in a world of deep darkness, a place without hope, until the uncreated light of eternal life in the Logos begins to shine into and through that darkness, just as the creation of physical light in the beginning initiated the ordering of the universe and the beginning of life on earth (Gen 1.3). σκοτία should therefore not be taken to refer directly either to those who are unbelievers, or to spiritual powers that rule in this present world (Eph 6.12), but to the cultural climate, the godless atmosphere, in which those who believe in God are so often called to live out their lives.

This is the first mention of the contrast between light and darkness in the Fourth Gospel, and two statements are made. φαίνει: the close parallel in 1 Jn 2.8 (ἡ σκοτία παράγεται καὶ τὸ φῶς τὸ ἀληθινὸν ἤδη φαίνει) is there certainly intended to refer to the age in which the writer is living (παράγεται, ἤδη), but neither there nor here in Jn 1.5 is there any reason to restrict the meaning of the verb to one particular era. The light is perpetually shining, just as the darkness always remains. ἐν τῇ σκοτίᾳ: the writer had available a wide choice of prepositions. He could, like Paul in 2 Cor 4.6, have written that light shone out of darkness, or have used ἐπί with the accusative, genitive or dative, implying that the light shone into or over or upon the darkness, thus clearly affirming that the darkness was overwhelmed and dispelled. By writing not ἐπί but ἐν, he stresses that the darkness remains, undispelled by the light. By the placing of φαίνει at the end of the clause, and the studied choice of the present tense, the superior power of the light is quietly affirmed.

καὶ ἡ σκοτία αὐτὸ οὐ κατέλαβεν. *Pace* Turner (MHT III 73), οὐ κατέλαβεν can only with difficulty be termed a gnomic aorist, since, though it expresses a repeated fact, the fact is not an axiom (compare BDF 333 [2]). The verb can mean either *has not overpowered, overwhelmed it* (so most Greek commentators since Origen, and many

---

[33] Translation by G. Vermes in *DSSE*, 3rd ed., 65.

modern writers[34]), or *has not understood, has not grasped, has not embraced it.* The Latin versions' *tenebrae eam non comprehenderunt* is ambiguous enough to be patient of both meanings, and perhaps indicates that both meanings were thought to have been intended by the writer, as several modern scholars (notably Barrett) affirm. *The darkness was not able to master it* (Knox) and *has never mastered it* (NEB = REB) seek to catch the double meaning that the darkness 'has neither extinguished the light nor understood it'. The translation given above is but a variation of this: *and the darkness has never become master of it*

So the opening paragraph of the Gospel ends. The conflict between the light-bearing life-giving Logos (cf. 8.12; 11) and the powers of darkness will be one of the principal themes of the Fourth Gospel.

---

[34] And also (if it is a quotation or a true parallel) the lines in the *Odes of Solomon* 18.6a: 'Let not light be conquered by darkness...' (translation by J. H. Charlesworth in *OTP* II 751).

B. JOHN AS WITNESS TO THE LIGHT (1.6-8)

Without warning, both the scene and the subject-matter change, and the reader is thrust into the world of time. With no connecting particle, the break in the train of thought is so abrupt that several modern scholars judge that v. 6 may have been the original opening of the Gospel, before the Prologue was added.[1] The only link with v. 5 is the theme of light: a man was sent from God to testify about the light that was shining in the darkness. Schnackenburg writes that the evangelist introduces the Baptist here precisely because of the key-word 'light', 'which is his favourite image for the work of the incarnate Son of God', and suggests, because of v. 8, 'that the disciples of the Baptist outside the Christian Church claimed this title for their master (cf. also 5.35)'.

> [6]There was a man sent from God—his name was John. [7]He came for testimony, to bear witness to the light, that through him, all might believe. [8]He was not himself the light, but came to bear witness to the light.[2]

6. The paratactical structure, common in Semitic languages, is also quite acceptable as Greek, and provides no positive ground for postulating that the sentence must be a translation from Aramaic or Hebrew.[3]

Ἐγένετο ἄνθρωπος. Mark too introduces the Baptist into the gospel story with the word ἐγένετο (1.5), which may be there translated, without any emphasis, as *There came, There appeared*, or even *There was once....* John's use of the same word at this point is more significant. His Gospel opens (Jn 1.1-2) with the imperfect tense ἦν, describing what was before creation, and then, in v. 3, changes over to the aorist ἐγένετο, when it begins to speak of the time-conditioned work of creation, and of history. Similarly, here in v. 6, the use of the aorist ἐγένετο in preference to ἦν signals that the story is moving into historical time,[4] and 'clearly refers not to this man's coming into existence, but to the mission itself' (Chrysostom). The choice of ἄνθρωπος over ἀνήρ is not significant, for with the possible exception of 1.30, John uses ἀνήρ only when he wishes to refer to a husband or a male.

Furthermore, the combination of the two words ἐγένετο ἄνθρωπος is almost certainly intended to suggest that the story now beginning marks a

---

[1] See Excursus I, 'The Structure of the Prologue'.

[2] The lines are here arranged to indicate that they are not part of the hymn.

[3] Contra Burney, Torrey et al.

[4] So, most emphatically, Cyril of Alexandria (I 7, 61bc); and also Aquinas fn. 109: *erat* was used when speaking *de aeternis*, *fuit* is now used *de temporalibus*.

momentous step forward in the salvation history of the human race. It is probably purely by accident that this exact verbal combination occurs nowhere in the LXX, but the two words clearly echo the LXX renderings of the Hebrew אִישׁ וַיְהִי [wayĕhi ʾiš] as καὶ ἐγένετο ἀνήρ (Judg 13.2 A, of Manoah; father of Samson, and 17.1 AB, of Micah), or καὶ ἦν ἀνήρ (Judg 13.2 B) or Ἄνθρωπος ἦν (1 Kgdms 1.1, of Elkanah, father of Samuel). Each of these texts introduces a new figure into the narrative, first by stating his tribe or homeland, and then by identifying him in the words καὶ ὄνομα αὐτῷ; similar constructions occur in 1 Kgdms 25.2-3; 2 Kgdms 9.2 and Esth 2.5. So also Lk 1.5 tells of the parentage, profession and tribe of the Baptist, in order to link his birth with the Temple and the ancient hopes of Israel (1.5-25, 68-79). Our lemma is essentially different. It says nothing about ancestry, profession or homeland; in this Gospel, it is enough that he is sent directly 'from God'.

ἀπεσταλμένος παρὰ θεοῦ. The periphrastic construction, in preference to ἀπεστάλη, has two advantages. First, the choice of the verb ἐγένετο is a reminder that both the existence of the Baptist and his mission are to be counted among 'all those things that came into being and into history' (1.3) only through the pre-existent Word (cf. 1.15, 30). Secondly, the perfect participle passive, ἀπεσταλμένος, places the stress on the abiding quality in the envoy rather than on the once-for-all fact of the mission. 'There was a man sent from God' rather than 'A man was sent from God'. In Classical Greek, the verb ἀποστέλλω is generally more emphatic than στέλλω or πέμπω, and is often used to denote the commissioning of a representative to discharge a particular task; this usage is even more widespread in Hellenistic Greek (*TWNT* I 397), where in legal contexts this verb underlines the fact that the person so commissioned is in truth duly authorized. Indeed, in religious contexts it was sometimes used almost as a technical expression to denote the pleni-potentiary delegate of a divine being. Thus Epictetus writes that 'the one who is in truth a Cynic...should know that he is sent as a messenger from God' (τὸν ταῖς ἀληθείαις Κυνικὸν...εἰδέναι δεῖ ὅτι ἄγγελος ἀπὸ τοῦ Διὸς ἀπέσταλται).[5] Irenaeus states that Menander, a disciple of Simon Magus, 'made himself out to be the saviour sent down from invisible (worlds?) for the salvation of humankind',[6] and Philo writes that Jacob's son Joseph, addressing his brothers, 'declared that he had not received his commission at the hands of men, but had been appointed by God (μὴ πρὸς ἀνθρώπων ἀπεστάλθαι ὑπὸ δὲ τοῦ θεοῦ κεχειρο-τονῆσθαι)'.[7]

---

[5] Dissertations III 22,23.

[6] I 23,5 = *SC* I 320, where the Latin reads 'se autem eum esse qui missus sit ab invisibilibus Salvatorem'. Compare Eusebius, *Hist. Eccl.* III 26, 1, where a rather different text uses ἀπεσταλμένος.

[7] *Migr. Abraham* 22, as translated in Loeb Philo IV 145. All the references in the paragraph above come from K. H. Rengstorf in I 397-99, where further detail may be found.

In the LXX, where it occurs over 700 times, ἀποστέλλω is for all practical purposes the equivalent of the Hebrew שׁלח [šlḥ], and, like that verb, in the overwhelming majority of cases it means to entrust, to charge, or to commission someone with a message or task. All the emphasis is on the authority of the sender, to whom the person of the envoy is wholly subordinate, and consequently on the respect due to his delegate. This stands out starkly in the sending of Isaiah (Isa 6.8) of Jeremiah (Jer 1.7) and of Ezekiel (Ezek 2.3). In each case there is also in the recipient the consciousness of a divine mission, and an obedient acceptance of the prophetic role, however arduous it may prove (*TWNT* I 399). ἀποστέλλω carries the same connotations over into the NT, stressing the commissioning, the task involved and the empowering authority behind the mission. Here, then, in Jn 1.6, the sense of ἀπεσταλμένος is that there was a man duly commissioned and charged with a particular task, by the authority of God. Note also that though this Gospel uses the noun 'apostle' only once (13.16), the use of the verb here may point to another all-embracing *inclusio* spanning the entire Gospel, with John being sent (ἀπεσταλμένος) at the beginning to present Jesus to Israel (cf. 1.31), and the Eleven being sent out at the end (καθὼς ἀπέσταλκέν με ὁ πατήρ, κἀγὼ πέμπω ὑμᾶς),[8] to present the message of salvation to the whole world (20.21).[9]

In παρὰ θεοῦ, the choice of παρά rather than ὑπό calls for the translation *from* as distinct from *by*, indicating the envoy's origin rather than his commissioner: in the LXX, παρά renders perfectly the preposition מֵאֵת (*de chez*, cf. Abel, *Grammaire* §50 *f*, and BDB 86 4). Further, the omission of the definite article before θεοῦ may well indicate that the commissioning of this envoy was not restricted to the one described in 1.1 as ὁ θεός, but can be predicated also of that Logos–Theos through whom all things came to pass (cf. 1.3). Thus we can say that the man was not merely sent ἀπὸ τοῦ θεοῦ or ὑπὸ τοῦ θεοῦ, but also διὰ τοῦ λόγου, and one may also suggest that παρὰ θεοῦ was intentionally chosen in order to embrace all three meanings.[10] The authority

---

[8] For the difference between ἀποστέλλω and πέμπω in the NT, see below on Jn 1.33 (and *TWNT* I 403-405).

[9] Origen II 29-31, nn. 180-88, prefers to explain the word 'sent' in Jn 1.31 by appealing to the doctrine of the pre-existence of souls. It would account for the Baptist's pre-natal holiness (Lk 1.44); indeed, he might have been more than human—an angel (Mal 3.1 = Lk 7.27), similar to the angel described in the Prayer of Joseph. (For the latter, see *OTP* II 713-14, with an Introduction by J. Z. Smith on 699-712.) Cyril of Alexandria, without naming Origen, denounces this 'widely circulated tale', and asserts that it was to counter this misinterpretation that the evangelist wrote ἄνθρωπος (I 7, 61cd).

[10] This interpretation may underlie the reading παρα κυριου in D*, which in a Christian MS probably refers to the Word before the Incarnation. It is not, however, a true variant reading, for it is nowhere else attested, and is corrected in D itself by the simple alteration of the initial kappa to theta (i.e. from K̄Ȳ to Θ̄Ȳ).

behind the message is not human, but divine.[11] See further the comment on 5.34a.

ὄνομα αὐτῷ 'Ιωάννης. The construction, with ellipsis of the verb, is typically Semitic,[12] and as it here introduces John, so in 3.1 it introduces Nicodemus (contrast 18.10, with a verb). But whereas in 3.1 Nicodemus is there described, 'John' is here considered sufficient for identification. This name occurs 18 times in the Fourth Gospel, and, by contrast with the Synoptics, always stands without patronymic or epithet; on every occasion it denotes the Baptist. Clearly, the readers know to whom the name John refers, and the next step must be to state what his task is.

7. The resumptive pronoun οὗτος, more emphatic than αὐτός, means *this one, the one just mentioned* (cf. BDF 290). It is difficult, probably impossible, to translate these nuances into English. ἦλθεν: he who had, by God's election and free initiative, been 'sent from God', *came* obviously 'from God', in the sense described in the comments on v. 6 under παρὰ θεοῦ. 'With this sentence, the place of the Baptist in salvation history is at once established'.[13] We are not yet told when, or from where he came, only why, and his task (i.e. God's purpose in sending this envoy) is described in three ever more precise expressions.

First, John came, in a general sense, εἰς μαρτυρίαν, that is, *in order to testify, to bear witness.* μαρτυρία here carries its primary, legal, meaning of testifying, of bearing witness to the true state of affairs because one has fuller knowledge than others. Ordinarily, testimony is given 'before a *tribunal* which has to give judgment on the matter, and this judgment *must* be based on the statement of the witness; on the other hand, the witness is *in duty bound* to make his statement, and in so doing commits himself to what he says'.[14] The Fourth Gospel frequently uses the vocabulary of litigation, reminding its reader especially of bearing witness (μαρτυρία, 14 times; μαρτυρεῖν 33 times) and of judgment (κρίνειν, 19 times; κρίσις, 11 times). John will be the first witness, both in the gospel-book (1.15) and in the story (1.32, 24; 3.26, 28); he is also the first witness invoked in what we may call the (unofficial) trial of

---

[11] 'Si quis obiiciat, nimis infirmum esse testimonium hominis, ut Christus probetur esse filius Dei: hic quoque in promptu est solutio, non citari Baptistam quasi privatum testem, sed qui divina auctoritate praeditus, angeli magis quam hominis personam substineat' (Calvin).

[12] It is not a solecism in Greek. ℵ* D* W^supp syr^c insert ην before ονομα, but it is deleted in ℵ and 'pointed out' in D; and syrc is notoriously pleonastic. Likewise, the *cui nomen erat* of the Latin versions is nothing more than an elegant rendering, not a witness to a different Greek text. So also, when Origen on one occasion writes ᾧ ὄνομα 'Ιωάννης (II 37 fn. 225, in *SC* I 362), the reconstruction is there recommended by the shape of his sentence; elsewhere he reads ο. α. I. (e.g. XXXII 17, in Brooke II 180 line 6; and Fragment 49 on 264).

[13] 'Mit diesem Satz ist zugleich der heilsgeschichtliche Ort festgestellt, den der Täufer einnimmt' (Johannes Schneider in *TWNT* II 669[10-11]).

[14] Bultmann ETr 50-51 fn. 5.

Jesus in Jerusalem, spanning chs. 5–10 (see 5.33-36a). Apart from one passing reference in the story of the woman of Samaria (4.39), he alone 'bears witness to Jesus' during the earthly ministry,[15] and in fact he does nothing else. In this Fourth Gospel, there is not a hint of the comminatory preaching attributed to him in the Synoptics, no reference to his attracting great crowds seeking baptism for the forgiveness of sins, much less to his baptizing Jesus (see on 1.32-34). John was indeed sent from God, but his sole task was to be a witness in the Great Trial in which Jesus was arraigned before an earthly tribunal, and humanity thereby arraigned before God.

Secondly, the Baptist's testimony was to be directed to one specific topic: ἵνα μαρτυρήσῃ περὶ τοῦ φωτός. The wording here repays close examination. μαρτυρεῖν περί is normal usage both in Classical and in Hellenistic Greek,[16] and is a particular favourite in this Gospel for *to testify concerning, with reference to*. The complete list is: Jn 1.7, 8, 15; 2.25; 5.31, 32ab, 36, 37, 39; 7.7; 8.13, 14, 18ab; 10.25; 15.26[; 18.23]; 21.24, cf. 1 Jn 5.9, 10, and the phrase is found nowhere else in the NT. John probably prefers this construction to μαρτυρεῖν with the dative (which occurs in 3.26; 5.33; 18.37) because it avoids any ambiguity: the Baptist did not come to bear witness *to* the light, but to others (including the readers). He was to bear witness περὶ τοῦ φωτός, that is, about the light which was shining in the darkness, and which the darkness had not understood (1.4-5). Origen asks why John did not bear witness about Life, or about the Logos, or about some other title of Christ, and answers that what the people that dwelt in darkness most urgently needed was Light.[17] It is worth mentioning also that whereas in 4b, 5a and 9a, the Latin versions translate τὸ φῶς as *lux*, in 7b and 8b, they read *ut testimonium perhiberet de lumine*. The Latin *lumen* is used primarily of the physical source from which light proceeds, and consequently comes to denote also the illumination; *lux* refers primarily to the ambient brightness which enables us to see, and only secondarily to the source. The Latin versions thus distinguish very precisely between Jesus as the bodily source from which light proceeds here on earth (*lumen*), to which the Baptist bears witness (7b, 8b), and the pre-existent Word as the source of that enlightenment (*lux*) which dispels spiritual darkness: compare the hymn *O nata lux de lumine*. Though the distinction cannot claim any foundation in Greek lexicography, it is an important indicator of the interpretation customary in the Latin Churches. For further detail on the witness borne by John, see below on 1.15.

---

[15] All other texts about bearing witness to Jesus concern the post-Resurrection age: 15.26 (the Holy Spirit), 27 (the disciples); 19.25 and 21.24 (the disciple whom Jesus loved).

[16] BDAG *s.v.* μαρτυρέω 1.a, citing Josephus, *Vita* 259 ('they bore testimony about my past conduct') and *Apion* I 217.

[17] II fn. 226 = *SC* II 362.

Thirdly, the ultimate purpose of the Baptist's divine mission and of his witnessing was ἵνα πάντες πιστεύσωσιν. To whom does πάντες refer? Obviously, to all those who physically heard the Baptist preaching; almost as certainly, to those who heard his message at second- or third-hand; and therefore, to all whom his message was to reach in future time, for to John there applied, even before the death of Jesus, the principle stated in Heb 11.4: 'he, being dead, still speaks' (cf. Zahn 64), as Jesus himself averred (Jn 5.35). πιστεύσωσιν: that all these 'might come to believe' (an inceptive aorist), though we are not yet told in what, or in whom (see below on 1.13). The evangelist 'sees all faith as a response to testimony… Nowhere do the concepts of μαρτυρεῖν and μαρτυρία stand out so strongly as in the fourth Gospel' (Schnackenburg ETr 251), and the divinely willed response to such witness (ἵνα) is faith.

δι᾽ αὐτοῦ: this apparently simple phrase is far from clear. The preposition itself can be used for anything from the bearer of a letter (e.g. Ignatius, *Rom.* 10.1; *Philad.* 11.2; *Smyrn.* 12.1) to a plenipotentiary agent, even in creation (Jn 1.3, 10; 1 Cor 8.6; Col 1.16): see BDAG. διά, therefore, does not specify the precise role of the Baptist in bringing everyone to believe; it merely intimates that this role was, in God's plan, that of a subordinate agent. And even so, the phrase remains ambiguous. Does δι᾽ αὐτοῦ mean that all might come to believe through John's witness, or through the Light, or through the Logos that is in 1.9 identified with the Light ? Grammatically, any one of these interpretations is possible. In favour of the first is the fact that there is no other instance in Johannine writings which speaks of believing *through* the Logos, or *through* the Light, and that διά can be used for a subordinate agent of God, as in 1.17, 'The law was given *through* Moses'. In favour of the second (or third) is the fact that in this Prologue, with the exception of the unemphatic and parenthetic phrase ὄνομα αὐτῷ/ Ἰωάννης, the pronoun αὐτός is everywhere used only for the Logos, the Light etc., and that it seems unlikely that the evangelist would say that 'all' were, in the divine Providence, intended to believe *through* the Baptist, when he stresses so firmly that the role of the latter was subordinate to that of Jesus. The first interpretation, taking δι᾽ αὐτοῦ to refer to the Baptist, is almost universally accepted, but Abbott, who discusses this text at length (*JG* 2301-304), defends the alternative vigorously, with several additional arguments. Haenchen also dissents.

8. οὐκ ἦν ἐκεῖνος, that is, 'the one previously mentioned' (BDF 291 [3]), was not *the* light, τὸ φῶς. Cyril remarks that the article indicates that John was not *the one* light, though he, like all the saints, can assuredly be called both a light (Mt 5.14), and a lamp (Jn 5.35).

ἀλλ᾽ ἵνα μαρτυρήσῃ περὶ τοῦ φωτός. Other occurrences of ἀλλ᾽ ἵνα used elliptically are to be found in 9.3; 13.18; 15.25 and 1 Jn 2.9 (BDF 448 [7]); the meaning is 'but on the contrary', with the main verb mentally supplied. Though many ask whether this verse is not redundant, its clear implication is that at the time the Gospel was published, some people did think that John was *the* light come into the world. The idea is far from absurd, for, as Chrysostom points out, 'as a general rule, the witness is greater than the one for whom he testifies, and more worthy of trust' (VI 69-70). The first clause (8a: οὐκ ἦν κτλ.) is therefore necessary to preclude this misapprehension among uninitiated readers, and the second (ἀλλ' ἵνα κτλ.) consequently advisable, in order to make a smooth transition from v. 7 to v. 9. Without 8a, 9 would read as an assertion that John was the one true light.

C. THE COMING OF THE LIGHT
INTO THE WORLD (1.9-13)

After vv. 6-8, marked off by the introductory ἐγένετο, the reappearance of ἦν returns the reader to the theme of 1.4-5, about the light that was in the Logos. Many would say that here the pre-Gospel Logos-Hymn resumes, though some prefer to attach v. 9 to the previous section and to place the recommencement of the Hymn at v. 10. The view taken here is that v. 9 is not part of a pre-Gospel Logos-Hymn but that it is more logical to place it in this section than in the preceding one, about the role of the Baptist.

9ab	The Word was the true light | that enlightens every one
9c	coming into the world.
10a	It was in the world,
10b	and it was through it that the world had come into being,
10c	yet the world did not recognize it.
11a	It came to what was its own,
11b	yet its own did not welcome it.
12a	But to all who did welcome it,
12b	it gave power to become children of God,
12c	to those who believe in its name.
13a	It was not through the union of blood-streams,
13b	nor through any carnal desire,
13c	nor through the desire of a husband,
13d	that they were begotten,
13e	but from God

9a. ῏Ην τὸ φῶς τὸ ἀληθινόν. The first point is that the Life which was, before creation, in the Word (1.4) was (ἦν, not ἐγένετο) even then τὸ φῶς τὸ ἀληθινόν. The use of the double, postpositive, article signifies a certain emphasis and, though the clause could be rendered as 'That was' (AV = KJV) or 'There was' (RV) the true light,[1] perhaps the best englishing is 'It was the true light', with a slight, and equal, vocal stress, when speaking aloud, both on the article and on the adjective. The usage is self-evidently metaphorical, but neither the nature of this light nor the manner of its operation are here described. The Greek states only that it is the light *par excellence.*

---

[1] Or even: 'The light was the true one', though it is pedantry to mention the fact, since no one proposes this version.

ἀληθινόν. The adjectives ἀληθής and ἀληθινός, though close, and sometimes even identical, in meaning, are not completely synonymous: see *JV* 1797, *TWNT* I 249-51 (Bultmann) and BDAG for details.

In Classical Greek, ἀλήθεια means *truth as opposed to lies* (its only meaning in Homer), and therefore comes to mean (later, after Homer) *truth as opposed to mere appearances*. Eventually, there is a confluence of the two connotations in the notion of *truthfulness, sincerity, honesty,* though LSJ gives no examples of this meaning before the fifth century B.C. The same development occurs with the cognate ἀληθής: in Homer it means *true as distinct from false*, and later, from the fifth century, *real as distinct from apparent*, that is, *genuine*. ἀληθινός is not attested until around 400 B.C., when it is found in Plato and Xenophon, but from its earliest usage it means, when applied to persons, *truthful* and *trustworthy* or, when used of things, *real* and *genuine* (see LSJ for the evidence).

Etymologically, ἀλήθεια originates from the prefixing of an α–privativum to the verb λανθάνω/λήθω, so that its root meaning is 'that which is not hidden, that which is not veiled'. It was therefore an ideal term waiting to be adopted in the Golden Age of Greek philosophy to denote that which is discovered by natural reasoning; and it was even more fittingly applied to those humanly undiscoverable secrets (in Greek, τὰ μυστήρια) which are disclosed only by the gracious gift of God. Hence it has always been a favourite term among the adherents of a revealed religion, not least in the Greek mystery-religions, and in Gnosticism.[2]

In Greek-speaking Judaism, however, ἀλήθεια and its word-group underwent a subtle but profound refinement. ἀλήθεια itself occurs about 190 times in the LXX.[3] On 107 occasions it translates a Hebrew or an Aramaic word; on 97 of them that word is a cognate of אמת ('mt), meaning *truth, fidelity*; on only ten occasions does it represent some other Semitic word (see HR). ἀληθής occurs about 25 times, 16 of them being translations of Hebrew or Aramaic; of these 16 instances, seven render the Hebrew noun אמת ('mt), and three the verb כון (kwn) in the Niphal, where it means *standing firm, steadfast*.[4] In the LXX, ἀληθής is applied to God only three times, once at Esth 1.20 (only in Codex A; a gloss perhaps?), and twice in the Wisdom of Solomon, at 12.27; 15.1. By contrast, its near-neighbour ἀληθινός is freely predicated of God (Exod

---

[2] BDAG *s.v.* ἀλήθεια gives many examples, biblical and extra-biblical, of the word's being used for 'the content of Christianity as the absolute truth'.

[3] In citing word-counts, especially from the LXX, 'around' or 'about' are regularly used because of the variations in the different editions of the text. All statistics about the LXX are based on HR.

[4] The remainder translate: (1) חכם (ḥkm) *wise*, in Job 17.10; (2) צדיק (ṣdyq) *true, correct*, in Isa 41.6; (3) קשט (qšṭ) *true*, in Prov 22.21 and *truly*, in Dan 2.47 LXX; (4) תושיה (tušiyyāh) from √ ישה yšh) in Job 5.12. meaning *abiding success*; (5) רב (rb) *extensive* (?) in Esth 1.20 (only in A); (6) טוב (ṭyb) *good*, in Isa 65.2 (only in Codex Sin., *lectio prima*, subsequently corrected).

34.6; Num 14.18; Pss 86[85].15; 103[102].8 etc.), of his words (2 Kgdms 7.28; cf. 3 Kgdms 17.24), of his works (Deut 32.4; Dan 3.27; 4.34) and of his judgments (Ps 19[18].9; Dan 3.27, 31; Tob 3.2, 5). Furthermore, ἀληθινός occurs twice as frequently as ἀληθής, about 50 times, of which 34 are translation, where it does duty for nine etymologically different words; but of these 34, twelve render the Hebrew אמת (ʾmt), or its root אמן (ʾmn), and a further six, all in Job, represent the root ישׁר (yšr) meaning *honest, virtuous, upright*. The other seven Semitic roots too are associated more with moral integrity than with the factual accuracy of affirmations or judgments.[5]

Thus both ἀληθής and ἀληθινός display in the LXX a strong measure of the Hebrew content of אמת (ʾmt), that is, of *faithfulness* and *reliability*, of *being true to one's promise, true to one's word*. Classical Greece would on the whole have expressed this concept by the word-group πίστις (see LSJ), not ἀλήθεια, but the introduction of this Hebrew element of faithfulness into the lexicon of Greek religion was profoundly to alter the balance of meaning in the word-group ἀλήθεια. In Judaism, to say that God was ἀληθής or (more usually) ἀληθινός was not so much an assertion that his sayings were free from error, as an affirmation that he is ever faithful, always true to his word. This harmonizes well with the proposal previously mentioned on Jn 1.1a, namely, that the primary sense of Logos is equivalent to the Memra, the very embodiment of God's everlastingly protective Presence (*sein ewiges Dasein*) as disclosed and affirmed in Exod 3.15 (see pp. 8-9).

It is astonishing, therefore, to discover, when we turn to the Gospels, that ' "Truth", in the Synoptics, occurs only in the phrase *"in truth"* (Mk 12.14, 32; Mt 22.16; Lk 4.25; 20.21; 22.59: ἐπ' ἀληθείας, except in Mt 22.16 [ἐν ἀ.]) and in Mk 5.33 "told him all the truth". As an attribute of God, or a subject of Christ's teaching, it is non-existent in the Three Gospels' (*JV* 1727*m*). Likewise, ἀληθής is found only in Mt 22.16 = Mk 12.14 ('We know that you are true'), never in Luke; and ἀληθινός, never in Matthew or Mark, and only once in Luke (16.11). In John, by contrast, ἀλήθεια occurs 25 times (plus 20 times in 1, 2 and 3 John), ἀληθής 14 times, ἀληθινός nine times (plus four in 1 Jn 2.8 and 3.20 [×3]), and ten times in Revelations). John is evidently writing out of a different world from that of the Synoptics, or for a different readership, or both. In the Gospels, the word-group ἀλήθεια is one of his most wide-ranging personal trade-marks.

[5] The roots are: (1) אמת (ʾěmɛt) or אמן (ʾmn) meaning *steadfast*; (2) ישׁר (yšr) *upright*, in Job 1.8; 2.3; 4.7; 6.25; 8.6; 17.8; (3) נקי (nqy) *guiltless, blameless*, once, in Job 27.17; (4) שׁלם (šlm) meaning *correct* or *perfect*, twice, in Deut 25.15, 25, of weights and measures; (5) תם (tm) meaning *of utter integrity*, twice, in Deut 32.4 and Job 1.1; (6) קשׁט (qšṭ: Aramaic) *true*, i.e. *in conformity with promises*, once, in Dan 4.34 Theod. (7) יצב (yṣb: Aramaic) *irrevocable, unalterable*, once, in Dan 6.12 [13] Theod. (8) שׂתם (štm) *clearsighted, discerning*, twice, in Balaam's prophecy, Num 24.3, 15; (9) טוב (ṭyb) *good*, once, in Isa 65.2.

The various connotations of the noun ἀλήθεια will be investigated at each of its occurrences in the gospel text (the next one is at Jn 1.14e). For the present, it is enough to explain the differences, in John, between ἀληθής and ἀληθινός. With the exception of the two occurrences in Jn 6.55 (see the notes *in loco*), ἀληθής always means *truthful, veracious, trustworthy in testimony*; in this sense it occurs six times with μαρτυρία (5.31, 32; 8.13, 14, 17; 21.24), three times with a verb of saying in a context of testimony (4.18; 10.41; 19.35), and three times with reference to God (3.33), or to Jesus (7.18), and in the phrase 'He who sent me' (8.26). It will be observed that eight of these twelve references occur in chs. 5– 10, in the course of 'the trial' in Jerusalem (see on 1.7, pp. 24-25).

ἀληθινός is different. It appears side by side with μαρτυρία only in 19.35, but Abbott argues that not even here does ἀληθινός mean merely *veracious*; it affirms also that the testimony is *founded on fact*. In 4.33 the word denotes *authentic*, as distinct from merely outwardly observant, worshippers; in 4.37 it refers to the *true* sense of a misunderstood proverb (see *JV* 1727i, and *in loco*). In 6.32 it points to that which is (though this is not at all apparent) the *true* bread; and in 8.16 it indicates the *right* judgment (though here too this fact is not evident to those there addressed). In 7.28 it refers to the one who in truth sent Jesus, and in 17.3 to the one true God. In all these texts, ἀληθινός points to something which is not at first glance, and not obviously or evidently, that which is sought after; but it is in the Fourth Gospel a literary marker, identifying that which will, in the end, prove the only *real* and *genuine* object of our knowledge or desiring. Where the definite article is repeated, and post-positive, as here in 1.9, the emphasis is strong, as in 6.32 and 15.1.

Bultmann has argued that in Hellenism, ἀληθινός, when used of divine things, means that which alone 'truly is', the Eternal (*das einzige wirklich Seiende, das Ewige*); and that, correspondingly, when the word is used to refer to human affairs, it ascribes to them a more than earthly character because they reveal, or are in contact with, the divine.[6] This accords well with the ending of the preceding paragraph.

In brief, τὸ φῶς τὸ ἀληθινόν denotes that qualitatively unique[7] light which is, though not evidently so to all, real, authentic and genuine. As

---

[6] *TWNT* I 250-51. He cites in support Philo, the Corpus Hermeticum, and (naturally) Heb 8.2 (ἀληθινὴ σκηνή) and 9.24 (ἀντίτυπα τῶν ἀληθινῶν). (1) Philo writes in *Leg. All.* I 32 [on Gen 2.7]: 'This earthlike mind is in reality also corruptible, were God not to breathe into it a power of real life (δύναμιν ἀληθινῆς ζωῆς)', by endowing it with 'divine breath', the nature of which Philo explains at length in 33-42 (Loeb I 166-75). Again, in *Vita Mos.* I 289 [on Num 24.2-5]: 'Thus saith the man who truly sees (ὁ ἀληθινῶς ὁρῶν), who in slumber saw the clear vision of God with the unsleeping eyes of the soul' (Loeb VI 427). (2) CH I 30 reads 'The closing of my eyes became a veritable vision (ἀληθινὴ ὄρασις)', and XIII 2 speaks of rebirth through silent contemplation as the ἀληθινόν ἀγαθόν.

[7] Schnackenburg I 254: ἀληθινόν 'can mean in Hellenism simply the divine being as qualitatively unique in its incomparable excellence'.

such, the phrase is the ideal expression to remind the readers that this
light has been from the first shining in the darkness, unrecognized (1.5),
and to prepare them for the next clause affirming its universal relevance,
and for the verses following, which will speak of its rejection and
recognition (1.10-13).

9b. ὃ φωτίζει. The verb, not attested before Aristotle, was, to begin
with, used only of physical light, at first intransitively (*to shine*), later
also transitively, usually of a heavenly light which *illuminates* an object.
The earliest examples cited for its metaphorical sense *to enlighten* come
from the LXX; and thereafter it becomes common in Greek religious
literature.[8] This the only time this verb is used in John; it marks the last
reference to light in the Prologue. The next mention of light is in 3.19-21,
a hymn about the acceptance or rejection of the light, just after the
discussion with Nicodemus.

πάντα ἄνθρωπον. (1) T. F. Glasson has suggested that the phrase
could perhaps be understood of a prenatal enlightenment, to which there
are parallels in rabbinic texts, and in 4 Esd 7.21; and even in the idea of
sin before birth (cf. Jn 9.2).[9] (2) Origen's commentary is unfortunately
lost, at this very point; he might have had some interesting comments
about the incarnation of souls.[10] (3) Many ask how it can be that, if the
Logos enlightens everyone, some remain unenlightened. Chrysostom
answers: 'If some wilfully close the eyes of their minds, and do not wish
to receive the rays of this light, it is not because of the nature of the light
that darkening comes over them, but because of the wickedness of those
who voluntarily deprive themselves of the gift'. He then applies this at
some length to the Jews, referring to Jn 9.22 (some were afraid to confess
Jesus in his lifetime) and citing 5.44. Calvin gives a similar answer to the
same question. Some, he writes, restrict the application of the phrase to
those who, reborn by the Spirit, share the life-giving light, but he himself
prefers to stand by the literal sense of 'all', and to say that the light which
is given to all humanity (as distinct from brute beasts) and restricted to
the, is the light of reason, albeit clouded by sin.[11] It is obvious that the
theological question raised by the affirmation of universal enlightenment
remains, however the Greek be construed.

---

[8] For the evidence, see LSJ, BDAG and *TWNT* IX 304 (Conzelmann). All the
examples cited are later than the LXX.

[9] 'John 1.9 and Rabbinic Tradition', in *ZNW* 46 (1958), 288-90.

[10] See above, p. 23 fn. 9.

[11] 'Caeterum bifariam hic locus exponi solet. Quidam enim notam universalem ad eos
restringunt, qui Spiritu Dei regeniti, lucis vivificae fiunt compotes…Sed quum omnes
generaliter ponat Evangelista qui in hunc mundum veniunt, mihi alter sensus magis
arridet…Scimus enim hoc homines prae aliis animantibus singulare habere, quod ratione
et intelligentia praediti sunt, quod discrimen recti et iniusti in sua conscientia insculptum
gerunt.'

9c. ἐρχόμενον εἰς τὸν κόσμον. There is no way of deciding on purely grammatical grounds whether ἐρχόμενον is a masculine accusative, qualifying ἄνθρωπον, or a neuter nominative, belonging with τὸ φῶς. Quite fortuitously, spoken English is able to reproduce this ambiguity, in the translation 'He was the true light that enlightens every one coming into the world'. Commas give the game away.

(1) If ἐρχόμενον is taken as qualifying ἄνθρωπον, the meaning is 'enlightening everyone who comes into the world'. This is the sense taken by all the early ancient versions (Latin *venientem*, Old Syriac, Bohairic), except the Sahidic (at least in part), by several Greek Fathers (Eusebius, Cyril of Alexandria and Chrysostom) and by some modern writers, notably Burney, Schlatter and Bultmann. In modern times, the main argument adduced in its favour is that the phrase כל באי העולם (kl b⁾y h⁽lm: every one coming into the world) is a common expression in rabbinic writings.[12] To this one may retort that the Aramaic phrase cited contains no equivalent for ἄνθρωπον;[13] that 'coming into the world' is, after ἄνθρωπον, a redundant synonym; and that the evangelist would have been more likely to have written πάντα τὸν ἐρχόμενον εἰς τὸν κόσμον.[14] Πᾶς (sing.) followed by the article and a participle is one of his favourite constructions: see 3.8, 15, 16, 20; 4.13; 6.40, 45; 8.34; 11.26; 12.46; 16.2; 17.3. 18.37; 19.12; cf. 6.37, 39; apart from 1.9, it is only in 2.10 that we find πᾶς ἄνθρωπος, without the article. Of those who prefer to construe the Greek in this way, most are content to see here a strong emphasis, and to ask why, if the Logos enlightens all who come into the world, so many remain unenlightened (see above on 9b).

(2) If ἐρχόμενον is taken as neuter nominative, in agreement with τὸ φῶς, the sentence means that the true light, which enlightens every man, was coming into the world. This also can be interpreted in two ways.

(a) The verb ἦν may be linked with the participle, to constitute a periphrastic imperfect: thus the NEB and REB read '...was even then coming into the world'. This could be understood as drawing attention to the durative nature of the verb. Abbott, for example, remarks that 'like the distinction between καταβαίνων and καταβάς [in 6.41, 48-51], there appears a distinction here between ἐρχόμενον and ἦλθεν [1.11], and the passage says, first, that the Light was "*continually coming*" to all mankind (more especially to the prophets and saints) and then that it definitely came in the Incarnation'.[15] On this view, the reference is to, and the

---

[12] See SB II 358-59.
[13] Bultmann (32 fn. 6 = ETr 52 fn. 3) suggests that ἄνθρωπον is inserted as an explanatory gloss by the translator of the underlying Aramaic hymn, and should be removed, but he does not explain why the word was ever put in.
[14] Interestingly, Origen, who says that both constructions have the same meaning (ἑκατέρως αὐτὸ ἑρμηνευτέον), clarifies the former by writing πάντα τὸν ἐρχόμενον εἰς τὸν κόσμον ἄνθρωπον. See Brooke II 216-17, Fragment 6.
[15] *JG* 2508, and cf. 2504-505.

emphasis on, the *praeparatio evangelica* both in the OT, and among the Gentiles.

(b) On the other hand, there are nine instances of the imperfect with a participle in John (1.9, 28; 2.6; 3.23; 10.40; 11.1; 13.23; 18.18, 25), and they seem on the whole to put a distance, rather than a close link, between the two words. Leaving aside 1.9, none of the other texts appears to stress duration, and here in 1.9 the imperfect is in addition separated from the participle by a clause. This makes it less probable that in 1.9 the intent is to say that the Light was 'continually coming', over a period.[16] The form is more often ascribed to Semitic influence, Aramaic in particular,[17] though Lagrange cautions that the occurrences in John are not exactly the same as Aramaic imperfects.[18]

Hence it is wiser to understand 1.9 as saying, first, that the Logos was the true light, and secondly that it was coming, or was about to come, into the world. This Gospel does not in any way deny that there was a relationship between the light of God's Word and humanity from the beginning (1.4: ἐν τῷ λόγῳ ζωὴ ἦν, καὶ ἡ ζωὴ ἦν τὸ φῶς τῶν ἀνθρώπων); but 1.9 affirms that at a particular moment in time, this light was, presumably in a entirely new sense, entering the world (cf. Gal 4.4; Heb 1.1, etc.). So in the RSV we read, 'The true light…was coming into the world', and in Barclay, '…was just about to come into the world' (where ἐρχόμενον is taken as a *futurum instans*). The decisive argument for linking ἐρχόμενον with τὸ φῶς is that in John, Jesus is called 'he who comes into the world' (6.14; 11.27), who came into the world (3.19, with φῶς; 9.39; 12.46 with φῶς; 16.28; 18.37), or who was sent into the world (3.17; 10.36; 17.18). 'The Light coming into the world' is, in John, little short of a technical term for Jesus, the Son of God (see on 1.15).

10. Κόσμος, the crucial word in this verse, is one of the most important in the entire Gospel, and deserves close attention.

THE MEANING OF Ὁ ΚΟΣΜΟΣ IN THE FOURTH GOSPEL

The original meaning of κόσμος is *order, good order, adornment* etc., from which it came to denote the *orderly pattern* of the moon and the seasons, of the planets and the stars, and hence, among the Ionian philosophers of the sixth century, what we call the Universe. There it first took on a spatial reference. This application was well established in Plato's day, though both he and Xenophon remark that it was a technical

[16] To say that this view about the construing of the participle ἐρχόμενον is, on grammatical grounds, less probable does not mean that one cannot simultaneously hold that the Word was active in the world under the Old Covenant.

[17] Thus MHT III 87-88 (with references to major grammars).

[18] 'Ces cas ne sont pas précisément des imparfaits périphrastiques à la manière de l'araméen, car le verbe substantif garde une valeur propre et un certain accent sur l'idée de l'être' (12). This is the interpretation favoured above.

usage among academics;[19] the more common terms were τὸ ὅλον or τὸ πᾶν. Later still, ὁ κόσμος came to be used of particular parts of space, such as the firmament or the heavenly spheres, or (especially in the plural) of the constellations within them. Finally, it was used, by hyperbole, for the inhabited world, the οἰκουμένη of the Greeks, the *orbis terrarum* of Rome. The earliest text cited in LSJ for this sense is an inscription, from Priene near Miletus, *ca.* 9 B.C., where the birthday of the divine Augustus is referred to as the beginning of good news to the world: ηρξεν δε τωι κοσμωι των δι αυτον εὐανγελι[ων ἡ γενεθλιος] του θεου, and the second (A.D. 67) hails ο του παντος κοσμου κυριος Νερων.[20] With the consolidation of Roman rule, it was only natural that the word κόσμος should have come to be virtually synonymous with the Roman Empire. This is the sense in Rom 1.8 ('your faith is spoken of throughout the entire world') and 1 Clem 5 (Paul 'taught righteousness to the whole world and reached the farthest bounds of the West').[21]

The outstanding merit of Greek philosophy is to have sought to describe the origin of our world by human reason rather than through mythology. The pre-Socratics all accepted that matter was there 'from the beginning', whether there was initially only one element (Thales: water) or four (Anaximander: earth, air, fire, water), or whether everything was always changing (Heraclitus). Plato, in the *Timaeus* 28ff., introduced into the discussion the idea of an intelligent maker or Demiurge; but his Demiurge was not a self-subsistent God, only a Divine Craftsman working to arrange, according to eternal patterns or 'Ideas', the unformed material before him. For Aristotle, 'the order of the universe is eternal (ἡ τοῦ κόσμου τάξις ἀΐδιος)',[22] '...without origin and incorruptible (ἀγένητον καὶ ἄφθαρτον ἔφη τόν κόσμον εἶναι)'.[23] The idea of a Creator-God is nowhere found in the Classical Greek philosophers.

It was otherwise in Alexandria, where the term κόσμος was taken up by philosophers who were also deeply religious Jews. The notion of creation by God's Word (Gen 1) was central to their faith: 'he spoke, and they were made; he gave the command, and they were created' (Pss 33.10; 148.6). Their cosmogony was expressed partly in myths and legends which had their origins in ancient Mesopotamia. For the rest, the

[19] *Gorgias* 507e-508a: 'Academics... call the whole of this Cosmos, not disorder or disarray' (οἱ σοφοὶ...τὸ ὅλον τοῦτο διὰ ταῦτα κόσμον καλοῦσιν, οὐκ ἀκοσμίαν οὐδὲ ἀκολασίαν). Xenophon, *Mem.* I.1.11 (Loeb IV 8-9): Socrates 'avoided speculation on the so-called "Cosmos" of the Professors' (ὅπως ὁ καλούμενος ὑπὸ τῶν σοφιστῶν κόσμος ἔφυ).

[20] For the detail see LSJ, MM and *TWNT* III 868-74. See also G.N. Stanton, *Jesus and Gospel*, Cambridge, 2004, 30-33.

[21] Translation by J. B. Lightfoot in *The Apostolic Fathers*, ed. and completed by J. R. Harmer, London, 1891, 59. The Greek reads: δικαιοσύνην διδάξας ὅλον τὸν κόσμον, καὶ ἐπὶ τὸ τέρμα τῆς δύσεως ἐλθὼν... ἀπηλλάγη τοῦ κόσμου, where κόσμος is, at its second occurrence, taken in a different sense.

[22] *De Caelo* II 14 296a33.

[23] Fragment 17, 1477a10. See also *De Caelo* I 10-12 279b4.

Israelites had been content to tell of God's creation in poetry and in story; they had admired its beauty without seeking to examine philosophically the principles underlying its harmonious order. Consequently, Hebrew had no proper word to designate 'the entire universe as an integrated unity'. It used instead 'heaven and earth' (Gen 1.1) or simply כֹּל (kol: 'all', as in Ps 8.7b; Isa 44.24; Eccl 3.1), but neither term expresses formally that 'all are but parts of one stupendous whole'.[24] Here the Jewish scholars of Alexandria saw a role for the word κόσμος.

One of them, Aristobulus,[25] was the first to substitute the term κόσμος for 'heaven and earth', when commenting on Genesis; he stressed, too, that, once created, it needed God's continual support for its conservation (διακρατεῖσθαι and συνέχειν).[26] Later Alexandrian scholars took up the Greek notion of ὁ κόσμος with enthusiasm, and none more than Philo. He 'distinguishes between the κόσμος νοητός on the one hand (= "the original principle behind all principles, after which God shaped or formed the universe", *Mig. Abr.* 103), the spiritual blueprint of the empirical world, and on the other hand, this world, which he calls κόσμος οὗτος (*Rer. Div. Her.* 75), κόσμος αἰσθητός (*Op. Mundi* 25), κόσμος ὁρατός (*Op. Mundi* 16)'.[27] The creative Word of God in the religion of Israel became, for Philo, an intermediary agent, like Plato's Demiurge, between God and the world. 'The image of God is the Word through whom the whole universe was framed' (λόγος δ' ἐστὶν εἰκὼν θεοῦ, δι' οὗ σύμπας ὁ κόσμος ἐδημιουργεῖτο, *Spec. Leg.* I 83 [Loeb IV 147]). The Greek concept of order (and beauty) in the material world was thus coupled with the Jewish idea of a personal, but entirely spiritual, God, and it was to this personal God that the order in the material world was ascribed.[28]

In the LXX (including 3 and 4 Maccabees), κόσμος occurs 71 times. In 19 texts it is a translation from the Hebrew, and on every occasion κόσμος means *ornaments, adornment*; it is never used to translate the Hebrew עוֹלָם (ʿolām). Seven instances are found in Sirach; they all mean *adornment*, except for 50.19, where the word means *liturgy*. In the

---

[24] Pope, *Essay on Man*, 266.

[25] He wrote around the middle of the second century B.C. Of his works, only two long fragments survive, cited in Eusebius, *Praep. Ev.* VIII 10 and XIII 12 (GCS Eus. VIII 1 451-54 and 190-97 or *PG* 21.635-39 and 1097-103). See Schürer III 579-87.

[26] See XIII 12: 'Orpheus is said to have written about the upholding of all things by divine power (περὶ τοῦ διακρατεῖσθαι θείᾳ δυνάμει τὰ πάντα)…that is, was brought into existence by God and is continually sustained by him (ὑπὸ θεοῦ γεγονυῖαν καὶ συνεχομένην ἀδιαλείπτῳ)' (*PG* 21.1097C). Compare Wis 1.7 (τὸ συνέχον τὰ πάντα) and 7.27b (μένουσα ἐν αὐτῇ τὰ πάντα καινίζει).

[27] *TWNT* III 8779-812.

[28] Indeed, so attractive was this Greek idea of κόσμος that by A.D. 100 its sense had passed over into Palestinian and Babylonian Judaism, so that both the Hebrew עוֹלָם (ʿolām) and the Aramaic עָלַם (ʿālam) acquired a spatial meaning. See *TWNT* III 881-82 for examples.

remaining 45 occurrences, which are not translation, the sense still remains, always, *adornment* or *array*, until one comes to the books of Wisdom and Maccabees. In Wisdom, ὁ κόσμος always means *the world*, in the sense of 'the entire universe' (18 times), a usage which is found also in 2 and 4 Maccabees.[29]

In the light of this LXX usage, it is at first surprising that in the NT the word κόσμος never means *order*, and only once (1 Pet 3.3) *adornment*. Further, in the Synoptic Gospels it is relatively rare. In Mark it is found only three times, or even twice (8.36; 14.9; 16.15[?]), in Luke three times (9.25; 11.50; 12.30). Matthew has nine (or eight) instances (4.8; 5.14; 13.35[?], 38; 16.26; 18.7; 24.21; 25.34; 26, 13). All mean, in a general sense, *the world*, denoting by this anything from the whole material universe (Mt 24.21; 25.34) to those parts of the earth where people live (Mt 13.38; Lk 12.30) or the people themselves who live on our planet (Mt 5.14; 18.7). Apart from Mt 4.8, all 15 examples are sayings placed on the lips of Jesus and the meaning would be equally well represented by the Aramaic עָלַם ('ālam).

In the rest of the NT, ὁ κόσμος only rarely denotes the Universe. The most prominent example is at Acts 17.24, in Paul's speech at Athens; the word is notably absent in the prayers of the believers at 4.24, and in Paul's speech at Lystra (14.15). Moreover, wherever κόσμος does mean *the Universe*, it is usually with reference to the act of creation: so ἀπὸ κτίσεως κόσμου (Rom 1.20), πρὸ καταβολῆς κόσμου (Eph 1.4; 1 Pet 1.20), ἀπὸ καταβολῆς κόσμου (Heb 4.3; 9.26. Rev 13.8). Two other texts of interest are Jn 21.25 ('the world itself could not contain the books that would be written') and 1 Cor 3.21-22 ('all things are yours, whether Paul or Apollos or Cephas or the world or life or death or the present or the future, all are yours'); but both are figurative, and do not necessarily refer to the Universe. It is therefore fair to say that in the NT, the word κόσμος refers to the Universe only where the context demands it, for example, when someone is referring to cosmology or astronomy, and that otherwise it refers to the planet earth, or the people on it, or to the countries around the Mediterranean, or even to the Roman Empire. It is much the same in every culture.[30]

In contrast to the Synoptic evangelists, John uses the word κόσμος persistently (75 times), and a further 22 examples occur in 1 John.[31] One may well ask why. The roots of the Fourth Gospel go deep, and grew to

---

[29] 2 Macc 7.9, 23; 8.18; 12.15; 13.14, four times as *king, sovereign,* or *creator of the world*; so also *4 Macc* 5.25. Did the usage start in the liturgy? In *4 Macc* 16.18, it means *the place where people live,* in 17.14 *the people who live there*; and in 8.23 we find the words, τί ἐξάγομεν ἑαυτοὺς τοῦ ἡδίστου βίου καὶ ἀποστεροῦμεν ἑαυτοὺς τοῦ γλυκέος κόσμου;

[30] Cf. Apuleius, *Metamorphoses* XI 17: 'quae sub imperio mundi nostratis reguntur'.

[31] There are 35 instances in Romans, Galatians, 1 and 2 Corinthians, and another eleven in the Corpus Paulinum.

maturity in Palestinian Judaism; but before or after A.D. 70 that tree had to be transplanted, to flourish afresh in a different climate, among the Greeks. Philo in Alexandria had been only too happy to accept the optimistic view of a world divinely ordered; but at the same time, other Jews elsewhere were reading and writing books about impending apocalyptic doom, and after A.D. 70 they seemed to have been proved right. The Fourth Gospel was written to present Jesus' teaching to the Greeks as well as the Jews (cf. Jn 12.20-23), and to interpret for all the significance of Jesus' life and death (12.24). For that purpose, the use of ὁ κόσμος to denote the inhabited earth, and in particular the Roman Empire, was a new linguistic tool ready to hand, for the word designated everyone who lived in that world (including the Emperor and his officials), and designated it as the spatial, the historical and the existential setting for their lives.

For Christians, this world was essentially impermanent: ὁ κόσμος παράγεται (1 Jn 2.17), παράγει τὸ σχῆμα τοῦ κόσμου τούτου (1 Cor 7.31). Yet nowhere in the NT is the word κόσμος used for a future world: we find ὁ αἰὼν ὁ μέλλων (Mt 12.32; Eph 1.21; Heb 6.5) and ὁ αἰὼν ὁ ἐρχομένος (Mk 10.30; Lk 18.30), but never ὁ κόσμος ὁ μέλλων or ὁ κόσμος ὁ ἐρχομένος. Christian writers, when speaking of the future, stayed with the OT usage of 'heaven and earth', a usage which still survives in the Christian creeds. Thus we read καινοὺς δὲ οὐρανοὺς καὶ γῆν καινὴν προσδοκῶμεν (2 Pet 3.13) and εἶδον οὐρανὸν καινὸν καὶ γῆν καινήν. ὁ γὰρ πρῶτος οὐρανὸς καὶ ἡ πρώτη γῆ ἀπῆλθαν (Rev 21.1). In the NT, the word κόσμος refers always to the material world that we know, and is never once used to denote the life of the world to come. Furthermore, with the exception of Jn 1.10b and Acts 17.24, nowhere in the NT is the κόσμος said to have been brought into being by God. The only conceivable explanation for these two facts is that in the NT, as in the early Christian writers, the term κόσμος is taken 'existentially' and refers to a world full of sinfulness and hostile to God. This is nowhere more true than in John.

Yet for Jewish or Christians believers, 'this world' is also the place of *Heilsgeschichte*, where God intervenes to save. The Christian hope of a 'new age', an age yet to come, has just been mentioned. The word αἰών occurs 13 times in John, once in the phrase ἐκ τοῦ αἰῶνος (9.32) and everywhere else in the conventional εἰς τὸν αἰῶνα (4.14; 6.51, 58; 8.35 [×2], 51, 52; 10.28; 11.26; 12.34; 13.8; 14.16). John, who never promises a new κόσμος, does not promise a 'new age' (αἰὼν καινός) either. His new heaven and new earth come into being when a new Jerusalem comes down out of heaven from God, to quote Rev 21.1-2.[32] These two facts are significant for the hypothesis of 'realized eschatology'.[33]

---

[32] Note the prefix and prepositions: καταβαίνουσαν ἐκ τοῦ οὐρανοῦ ἀπὸ τοῦ θεοῦ.
[33] The article αἰών in *TWNT* I 197-209 is also by H. Sasse.

'All the meanings that κόσμος can have blend with one another in the usage of the Fourth Gospel',[34] and therefore each occurrence must be closely examined to discern how many connotations are there implied. Among the Greeks, ὁ κόσμος denoted the theatre in which was played out, in full view of the gods, the drama of every human life. John had the script for the greatest drama of all time. In his church, intellectual belief in the godhead of Jesus was firmly established (Jn 20.28-29), a fact which placed Jesus in the relationship of creator to the entire universe (1.3 etc). When the central human figure in the story is a God crucified by those whom he created, the κόσμος (in the threefold sense of the Empire, the Earth and the Universe) is the only theatre large enough to accommodate the tragedy, and the audience must be men and women of all races, of every place and of every time. The κόσμος did not know him, and the κόσμος did not welcome him.

The Synoptic evangelists wrote of Jesus' earthly life in Palestine, and drew from it lessons for the present and the future. John takes the record of those historic years, and then, like a Palestrina or a Victoria, employs the plainsong of the Synoptics to inspire his own polyphony. He sees the events of Jesus' life as paradigmatic for all future time, and in manifold ways reinterprets the meaning of Jesus for the Graeco-Roman world of his own day. By so doing he seeks to offer to ages yet to come a deeper understanding of the reality, the ἀλήθεια, lying hidden beneath the external facts recorded in the annals. It is not too much to say that his starting-point is the concept κόσμος. With it, his gospel opens, here in 1.10, and with it, Part I of the Gospel closes: 'I came as light into the world...I came not to judge the world but to save it' (12.46-47). Part II opens with the words, 'Jesus knew that his hour had come that he should pass over from this world to the Father' (13.1). His parting words to the disciples before his arrest are 'Be of good heart! I have conquered the world' (16.33). His final words to Pilate are: 'For this have I been born, and for this am I come into the world, that I may bear witness to truth; everyone who is on the side of truth listens to my voice'. Pilate's answer is, 'What is truth?' (18.37-38). These are the last occurrences of the five thematical words κόσμος, ἀλήθεια, μαρτυρέω, ἀκούω and φωνή in the Fourth Gospel.[35]

This richly allusive pattern of meaning obtains wherever the word κόσμος occurs in John. The multiple allusions are clearly essential when we ask, for example, who is ὁ ἄρχων τοῦ κόσμου τούτου (12.31).

Before we proceed to comment further on the text of Jn 1.10, two remarks are necessary. (i) In all three clauses, the word κόσμος refers to the Universe only if the context clearly demands it, as was argued on p. 37. (ii) It is debated whether vv. 10-12 refers to the presence of the

---

[34] Sasse, in *TWNT* III 894.
[35] This is so if one agrees that 19.35 and 21.24-25 are editorial additions.

Logos in the world and in Israel before the coming of Jesus, or to the presence of Jesus on earth during his ministry. This is discussed after v. 11.

ἐν τῷ κόσμῳ ἦν. The unexpressed subject of the clause must be λόγος, not φῶς, because of the masculine accusative αὐτόν in the third clause. Because of the proximity of εἰς τὸν κόσμον at the end of v. 9, ἐν τῷ κόσμῳ must here mean 'in the world, where people live', referring equally to the place and the population. ἦν has so far been used to refer only to what was permanently, and even eternally, a fact; and the text here does not say that the Logos *came into* (εἰσῆλθεν εἰς) or *came down to* (κατέβη εἰς) the world. A comment above (p. 33) stated that it was less probable that 1.9c intended to affirm that the Light 'was *continually* coming into' the world over a period of time (interpretation [1]), and argued (mainly for grammatical reasons) that 9c meant that at a particular moment in time, this Light was, presumably in a entirely new sense, entering, or about to enter, the world (interpretation [2]). Here the statement in 9c is extended: the imperfect ἦν affirms that the Logos, as Life and as Light, was, after that first entry, always present in the world.

καὶ ὁ κόσμος. Though a reference to the whole Universe, as in 1.3a, is logically entailed, this is not the primary meaning here. The natural sense is that 'the world, where people live', had come into being only δι' αὐτοῦ. The sense of ἐγένετο differs slightly from that in 3a; here it is more correctly rendered into English by a pluperfect. Through the Logos 'the world *had come* into existence'.[36] It makes a poignant transition to 10c.

καὶ ὁ κόσμος αὐτὸν οὐκ ἔγνω. The same meaning of ὁ κόσμος must apply, with the stress here on the people living on this earth. They failed to recognize the Logos. The verb is almost certainly intended to be taken also in a Semitic sense, that is, as meaning 'to know and to respond with moral commitment', because of the parallel in 11b. For examples of this Semitic sense, see Isa 1.3; Jer 9.3; 22.15-16 and Hos 4.1-6.

After the first appearance of ὁ κόσμος in 1.9c, its triple occurrence in v. 10 is certainly a description, almost a definition, of the sense in which John is going to use the term. The three clauses make three statements about the world. (1) It came into existence only through the Logos, and presumably, therefore, was, in its original state, wholly good. In Gen 1 the refrain 'God saw that it was good' in vv. 4, 10, 12, 18, 21, leads up to God's judgment concerning the entire creation: 'God saw that it was very good' (v. 31). (2) The Logos was in the world from the moment of its creation. It is legitimate therefore to infer that the Logos beckoned the whole human race to enjoy perfect happiness in the beginning (Gen 2). (3) Even this first invitation was rejected (Gen 3). That the Logos was present in the Garden is an ancient interpretation, as can be seen from two texts in the Targum Neofiti. At Gen 3.8 we read 'they heard the voice of

---

[36] See the excellent remarks by *IBNTG* 16.

the Word of the Lord God', and at 3.10, 'the voice of your Word I heard in the garden'; and there are, in addition, several marginal glosses in these chapters which insert Memra, or the Memra of the Lord.[37] Thus in the Fourth Gospel ὁ κόσμος denotes the divinely created world which has, as Genesis teaches, rejected God, but which is at the same time not beyond salvation, rather the opposite: it is certain to be saved.[38] This is clear already in Gen 3.15, and it is most significant that the next occurrence of κόσμος in Jn is at 1.29, where the first words of the Baptist concerning Jesus are that 'he takes away the sin of the world'.

11. εἰς τὰ ἴδια. BDAG 4b gives as alternatives *home* or *property, possessions*, with examples for each, but mostly for the former; yet the two meanings are very often indistinguishable. Most of the occurrences in the LXX mean 'home' (Esth 5.10; 6.12; 1 Esd 5.46 [47]; 6.31 [32]; 3 Macc 6.27, 37; 7.8, 18, 20), though some refer to '[their] own affairs' (2 Macc 11.23, 26, 29). In the present context, a good interpretation would be *his homeland, his own country*, for ἦλθεν implies that this is a location more precise than the preceding one 'in the world', and Barrett observes that 'the aorist points to a unique coming'. (This would of course affect, even if it did not prejudge, the meaning assigned to οἱ ἴδιοι: see below.) It may also be noted that this coming is apparently subsequent both to the one mentioned in v. 9 (ἐρχόμενον εἰς τὸν κόσμον), and to the permanent presence (ἐν τῷ κόσμῳ ἦν) noted in v. 10.

καὶ οἱ ἴδιοι. These are people in some way personally connected with the Logos. The identification is discussed below. This term too, like τὰ ἴδια, is rare in the LXX (Sir 11.34; 2 Macc 10.14 *v.l.* in A†; 12.22).
αὐτὸν οὐ παρέλαβον. *Receive* has been the classic English rendering for centuries, no doubt because of the Latin *receperunt*; but JB, NRSV, NAB and REB choose *accept*, which conveys better the idea of an open-hearted welcome. The rendering preferred here, with Knox and Kleist, is *welcome*. παραλαμβάνω is in Classical Greek a regular term for *learning from a teacher*,[39] and is especially frequent for *the receiving of religious truth or heritage by living tradition* (e.g. 1 Cor 15.13; Gal 1.9; 1 Th 2.13; 2 Th 3.6).[40] In Aramaic, קבל represents the same idea of teaching accepted

---

[37] *Neofiti* I 500-505, or 56-64. Compare also the comment above on the Memra under Jn 1.1a, at ἦν (on pp. 8-9).

[38] A passage in Augustine, too long for full quotation, links this text with Eph 5.8 and 6.12, to speak of the Christian's high hope of salvation from the diabolically evil powers that preside over this present world in all its darkness. '...mundi dixit, tenebrarum harum; mundi dixit, amatorum mundi; mundi dixit, impiorum et iniquorum; mundi dixit, de quo dicit Evangelium: Et mundus eum non cognovit' (*Enarr. in Ps.* 54, 4).

[39] E.g. Plato, *Theaetetus* 198b: καλοῦμέν γε παραδιδόντα μὲν διδάσκειν, παραλαμβάνοντα δὲ μανθάνειν: see also *Laches* 197d and *Euthydemus* 304c.

[40] See G. Delling in *TWNT* IV 11-13, and, for extra-biblical references, BDAG.

by tradition (e.g. *Pirke Aboth* 1.1).[41] Thus the negatived οὐ παρέλαβον is somewhat stronger than οὐκ ἔγνω in 10c. In itself, the phrase signifies only a failure positively to accept, the absence of a true welcome; it does not necessarily imply a fully deliberate rejection.[42] Nevertheless, in the present context, if these words are taken to refer to Israel under the Old Covenant, there are many OT texts which stress that God's people has from time to time knowingly rejected him (e.g. Jer 3.25; 7.28; 9.12; 32.23; 40.3; 42.21; 44.23; Bar 1.18–2.10).

The juxtaposition of τὰ ἴδια and οἱ ἴδιοι makes it plain that the terms are connected. A minority (but including Maldonatus, Loisy, Bauer, Schlatter and Bultmann) takes τὰ ἴδια to denote 'the world that came into existence through him' and οἱ ἴδιοι to denote all humankind.[43] Others, however, understand the words as referring specifically to the land and to the people of Israel, where divine Wisdom had made itself a special dwelling. Proverbs 8.22-31 tell how Wisdom was with Yahweh before the creation, and how it shared in the work. Sirach 24 speaks the same language ('I came forth from the mouth of the Most High, and covered the earth like a mist', v. 3; cf. Gen 1; 2.6), adding that Wisdom finally found a dwelling-place in Israel:

> Among all these I sought a resting place;
> I sought in whose territory I might lodge.
> Then the Creator of all things gave me a commandment,
> and the one who created me assigned a place for my tent.
> And he said, 'Make your dwelling in Jacob,
> and take possession of your inheritance in Israel'.[44]
> …So I took root in an honoured people,
> in the portion of the Lord, who is their inheritance (Sir 24.8, 12).

Similar ideas are found in Sir 14.20–15.20 (note the wording in 15.1b, 'he who holds to the *law* will obtain wisdom') and 1.1-10, where the universality of God's gracious gift is unequivocally affirmed:

> The Lord himself created wisdom;
> he saw her and apportioned her,
> and poured her out over all his works,
> to be with all flesh according to his bounty,
> and he has lavished her upon those who love him (1.9-10).

The question therefore arises, whether Jn 1.10-13 refers to the presence of the Logos in the world and in Israel before the Incarnation, or to the presence of Jesus on earth during his ministry.

Schnackenburg draws attention to a commentary by Paul Schanz (1841–1905),[45] who states that Maldonatus (1534–1583) was the first to

---

[41] See Jastrow.

[42] 'Sometimes the emphasis lies…on the fact that the word implies agreement or approval' (BDAG *s.v.* 3).

[43] Aquinas, however (*pace* Lagrange, 13) prefers to take *sui* of the Jews (fn. 145).

[44] ἐν Ισραηλ κατακληρονομήθητι.

explain vv. 10-12 of the Incarnate Logos, with only Gaudentius to appeal to among the Fathers.[46] Maldonatus writes: 'I do not see how, before the Incarnation, the world either should or could have recognized the Word'.[47] Schnackenburg adds that the older view, which takes these verses to refer to the activity of the Word of God in the Old Covenant, prevailed until quite recent times.

Distinguished names can be cited on either side, but one fact, which is often overlooked, is antecedent to all supporting arguments. One group argues that since vv. 10-13 come after vv. 6-9, i.e. after the mention of the Baptist, they must refer to the public ministry of Jesus, whereas another group asserts that since vv. 1-13 come before v. 14, they must refer to what precedes the Incarnation.[48] R. E. Brown cites for the former interpretation Büchsel, Bauer, Harnack and Käsemann, and for the latter Westcott, Bernard and Boismard; both lists can be extended year by year. With so much honest scholarship on either side, common sense decrees that the two positions are perhaps not mutually exclusive alternatives, but complementary, for the arguments brought forward on one side may be justified in what they affirm, without thereby disproving the rival interpretation. In other words, the reception of the Word of God under the Old Covenant was repeated at the coming of the Word made Flesh. The Fourth Gospel would not be the first work of literature to carry two meanings, one evident at first reading, the other becoming clear only at the end of the story.

One further fact should not be overlooked. In all the Latin versions, the noun *verbum*, which was quite correctly assigned a neuter pronoun as far as v. 9b, abruptly receives a masculine one in 10c ('et mundus *eum* non cognovit'), a gender it retains at 11b and 12a ('sui *eum* non receperunt', 'quotquot autem receperunt *eum*'). This is the more

---

[45] *Commentar über das Evangelium des hl. Johannes*, Tübingen, 1885.

[46] CSEL 68 Tr. XII 8f. 112 = ML 22.827-1002.

[47] 'Ante… incarnationem non video quomodo aut debuerit aut potuerit Verbum mundus agnoscere…Nec enim de eo titulo Joannes agebat, quo populus Iudaeorum proprius et peculiaris dicebatur, quod ab eo electus esset…sed de eo potius quo universus omnino mundus erat, quia per ipsum erat factus'. Juan de Maldonado's two-volume *Commentaria in Quattuor Evangelia*, first published at Pont-à-Mousson in 1596–97, are still worth consulting. The two citations are from an edition by J. M. Raich, Mainz 1874, II 406 and 408.

[48] Obviously, it becomes more complex when commentators introduce their hypotheses about extraneous verses interpolated into a pre-Gospel hymn, but the principle at issue remains the same. Schnackenburg, for example, thinks that the original pre-Gospel hymn was thinking of the time before the Incarnation, and that the evangelist, after inserting v. 9, applied the text to the work of the Incarnate Logos. Brown argues that most of the phrases in vv. 10-12 are used in the Gospel to describe the ministry of Jesus: e.g. he came into the world as light (3.19; 9.5; 12.46) and was by his own rejected (4.44; 12.37). But this is exactly what the evangelist so clearly states in 12.38, 40, citing Isa 53.1 and 6.10, about the blindness of God's people. Wisely, Barrett comments 'It was the world which rejected Jesus'.

astonishing since the translator could have continued to use, in vv. 10-12, the ambivalent *ipsum*, which had done duty in vv. 3-4 ('omnia per ipsum...et sine ipso... nihil'). Could it be that the Latins were (subconsciously?) relating these verses to the Incarnate Word long before Maldonatus? The same question arises with the German versions from Luther onwards, which follow *das Wort* with *Er* in vv. 10-12. Such translations condition the reader to think of the Logos in 10-12 in terms of the Incarnation, and it is essential to remember that what is in question is whether 'the non-acceptance by his own' in this verse refers to the Logos before or after the Incarnation.

12a. ὅσοι δέ. A nominative absolute (*nominativus pendens*) such as this is common in the Koine, is also a common Semitic construction, and is more common in John (28 times) than in the Synoptics: this is its first occurrence (BDF 466 [2]). ὅσοι δέ denotes therefore everyone who received God's enlightening Word. Aquinas comments, 'to show that God's grace is distributed impartially to all who receive Christ', whether free or enslaved, male or female, Jew or Gentile, with quotations of Acts 10.45 and Gal 3.28.[49] **ἔλαβον αὐτόν.** There is no difference in meaning between ἔλαβον here and παρέλαβον in v. 11. J. H. Moulton calls attention to 'the survival in NT of a classical idiom by which the preposition in a compound is omitted, without weakening the sense, when the verb is repeated' (MHT I 115).[50] The simplex λαμβάνω can mean both *to receive what is offered*, not to refuse or reject it (Thayer) and *to accept or recognize someone's authority*, as in Jn 5.43; 13.20, where the verb is equated with 'to believe' (cf. 5.44 and 13.19). Where it is, as here, equated with the compound παραλαμβάνω, it includes also the idea of accepting the Word (either in the OT or in the person of Jesus) as presenting authoritative teaching handed down from God (see the comment on παραλαμβάνω, on pp. 41-42).

12b. ἔδωκεν αὐτοῖς ἐξουσίαν. The grammatical subject is still the Logos, as Bengel perspicaciously observes: 'ἔδωκεν. *dedit*: Gloria Christi, Unigeniti'. αὐτοῖς, resumptive of the first clause in 12a, embraces all who received the Word. In the NT, ἐξουσία is found far more often without than with the article; and with an abstract noun, there is sometimes no significance in its presence or omission.[51] ἐξουσία here denotes the possibility, the ability, a capability, and therefore the potential,

---

[49] 'Dicit Quotquot ut ostendat quod gratia Dei indifferenter datur omnibus recipientibus Christum'.

[50] He cites Euripides, *Bacchae* 1065, where κατῆγον, ἦγον, ἦγον answers to the English 'pulled down, down, down', and offers as further examples Rev 10.10 (κατέφαγον / ἔφαγον), Rom 15.4 (προεγράφη / ἐγράφη), 1 Pet 1.10-11 (ἐξηραύνησαν / ἐραυνῶντες), and Eph 6.13 (ἀντιστῆναι / στῆναι).

[51] MHT III 177 cites Plato, *Meno* 99a ἡ ἀρετή - 99e ἡ ἀρετή - 100b ἡ ἀρετή - ἀρετή; Rom 3.30 etc.

the power[52] 'to become children of God'. The clause affirms that this is a gift from the Logos.

τέκνα θεοῦ γενέσθαι. The phrase τέκνα θεοῦ is nowhere found in the Synoptics,[53] and only twice in John (here and at 11.52; plus 1 Jn 3.1, 2, 10; 5.2). Elsewhere in the NT it occurs only in Rom 8.16, 17, 21; 9.8; Eph 5.1 (? ὡς τέκνα ἀγαπητά) and Phil 2.15. Ephesians 5.1 is of Jewish inspiration,[54] and Phil 2.15 is in part a citation of Deut 32.5 in the LXX,[55] so that neither is of distinctively Christian origin.

The phrase υἱοὶ θεοῦ is equally rare. It occurs in Mt 5.9 (and 45, υ. τ. πατρός κτλ. = υἱοὶ ὑψίστου in Lk 6.35) in an OT sense, in Lk 20.36, in a similar sense ('they are equal to angels and are sons of God, being sons of the resurrection'), in Rom 9.26, citing Hos 2.1, and in 2 Cor 6.18, echoing 2 Sam 7.14; Isa 43.6, and Jer 31.9. The only NT examples of υἱοὶ θεοῦ used in a specifically Christian sense are Rom 8.14.19 and Gal 3.26.

For good measure, one may add that the only texts with υἱοθεσία in that sense are Rom 8.15, 23; Gal 4.5 and Eph 1.5 (but not Rom 9.4). It will not have escaped notice that, whether one is considering the words τέκνα θεοῦ, υἱοὶ θεοῦ or υἱοθεσία, all the non-Johannine texts which bear a distinctively Christian connotation are found either in Rom 8.14, 15, 16, 17, 19, 21, 23, or in Gal 3.26; 4.5, the two classic passages dealing with the topics of emancipation from slavery through faith, and of adoptive sonship.

υἱὸς θεοῦ in the singular always refers to Jesus Christ (Matthew 9 times; Mark 6 times; Luke 7 times; add Mk 14.61, υ. εὐλογητοῦ and Lk 1.32, υ. ὑψίστου). John uses υἱὸς θεοῦ, or its equivalent, 11 times; υἱὸς ἀνθρώπου 13 times; υἱός on its own 20 times; and υἱὸς μονογένης 4 times, almost 50 times in total. The sole NT author to use μονογένης of Jesus[56] (1.14, 18; 3.16, 18; 1 Jn 4.9), he declines to extend the title υἱός

---

[52] For detail on other senses see W. Foerster in *TWNT* II 559-71.

[53] Although the noun τέκνον is quite common there (Matthew 15 times; Mark 9 times; Luke 14 times).

[54] Compare SB III 605. One quotation reads: 'We are called "sons", as it is written, Sons are ye to the Lord your God [Deut 14.1]. He [R. Akiba] said to him: You are called both sons and servants. When you carry out the desires of the Omnipresent, you are called "sons", and when you do not carry out the desires of the Omnipresent, you are called "servants"' (*The Soncino Talmud, Seder Nezikin II: Baba Bathra* 10a, 45.) J. Gnilka comments: 'Bereits diese Analogie erhellt, das Eph 5.1 mentalitätsmässig jüdisch...konzipiert ist, obwohl die griechische imitatio-Idee vorgetragen wird. Die christliche Begründung folgt nach' (*Der Epheserbrief*, 1971, 244).

[55] This is not acknowledged by bold type in the UBS or by italics in NA[27]. The text reads (with the LXX allusions underlined): ἵνα γένησθε ἄμεμπτοι καὶ ἀκέραιοι, τέκνα θεοῦ ἄμωμα μέσον γενεᾶς σκολιᾶς καὶ διεστραμμένης, ἐν οἷς φαίνεσθε ὡς φωστῆρες ἐν κόσμῳ.

[56] Elsewhere in the NT, only of the three sick children in Lk 7.12; 8.42; 9.38 and in Heb 11.17 (of Isaac).

θεοῦ to any other person, while affirming that they have the power to become τέκνα θεοῦ.

Is there a difference, then, between being υἱοὶ θεοῦ and becoming τέκνα θεοῦ? It is notoriously difficult to define in English the difference between a couple's 'children', and their 'sons and daughters'. So also in Greek. τέκνον (√ τίκτω) describes the offspring from the viewpoint of the relationship to their progenitors, and is therefore on the whole used of small children, with an accompanying awareness of their weakness, their utter dependence on adults, their often total trust and guileless affection. υἱοί, and θυγατέρες, are more adaptable, and more comfortably used for maturing or adult offspring; they are also, for obvious reasons, more frequent in a legal context. Naturally, τέκνον will be the more intimate and affectionate term.

The Christian notion of divine filiation is clearly a development of the Israelite concept of God as Father, and, like its Israelite antecedent, it occurs in a context of emancipation from slavery. In particular, it spells emancipation from moral slavery (Rom 7), and also an interior liberation (as Paul so powerfully portrays in Rom 8.12-24) from any fear of God based on terror (*timor servilis*).[57] Paul there invokes the use in prayer of the word *Abba* as proof of entitlement to be τέκνον θεοῦ, as if this added something, somehow, to being υἱὸς θεοῦ, perhaps because of the degree of familiarity the word *Abba* presupposes (see Rom 8.15-16), perhaps because a child can plead lack of full adult discretion (Gal 4.3-7). John 1.12 asserts that the Logos has made it possible to become a child of God, with all its privileges such as total and trustful dependence, and with freedom from any vestige of *timor servilis*.

12c. τοῖς πιστεύουσιν εἰς τὸ ὄνομα αὐτοῦ. The phrase, in apposition to αὐτοῖς, is not a restrictive qualifier, but a defining one: to accept the Logos is *to believe and to trust in* its name. Though there was Life and Light *in* the Logos (1.3-4), the Logos itself has not as yet been given any other, additional, name, much less a specific or personal name (αὐτοῦ). The almost identical phrase, fractionally but adroitly altered, recurs, as all-embracing *inclusio* at 20.31, to form the solemn conclusion of the Gospel.

13. The text as it stands affirms that those who believe in the name of the Logos *were born* or *were begotten* of God. Note, '...*were born*' or '*were begotten*', not *are*. The aorist ἐγεννήθησαν implies a once-for-all event

---

[57] The term *timor servilis* is here used in the strict technical sense which it has in Thomas Aquinas. 'If someone is converted to God and clings to him through fear of punishment, this will be servile fear; but if it is through fear of offending God, it will be filial, since it is only natural that sons should be afraid of offending their father' (*Summa Theologiae* 2-2, q.19, a.2c).

in the past,[58] and stands in striking contrast with the perfect tenses in 1 Jn 2.29; 3.9 [×2]; 4.7; 5.1 [×2], 4, 18 (where contrast ὁ γεννηθείς). The spelling ἐγενήθησαν found in 𝔓⁷⁵ A B* Δ Θ 28 *pc* (as if from the root γίνομαι) is a natural mistake for a copyist, especially since both words are used for *to be born* (e.g. BAG *s.v.* γίνομαι I.1.a, citing Jn 8.58). For emphasis, a threefold denial precedes one affirmation.[59]

All are agreed that **οἳ οὐκ ἐξ αἱμάτων**[60] is intended to exclude birth as a result of (ἐκ) sexual congress, through the joining of two blood-lines, but no-one seems able to bring forward another example of the usage.[61] Augustine's remarks are still unbettered: the plural is not good Latin, but the writer preferred to retain it, because it expresses so clearly that human beings result from the union of two parents, one male and one female.[62] For 'Latin', read 'Greek'. **οὐδὲ ἐκ θελήματος σαρκός**. *Nor of urging of the flesh.* θελήμα, rare in Classical Greek, but frequent in Christian literature, means *will* or *desire*, and here specifically *the sexual desire or urge*, a sense found (according to many) in 1 Cor 7.37, and perhaps in Eph 2.3 as well. Note, however, that σάρξ here carries no hint of sinfulness, or of opposition to God, as it does in Rom 7 (see Rom 8.3). σάρξ is in itself neutral, and for John it will be the earthly dwelling-place of the Logos (1.14), the instrument of everlasting life (6.51-63).[63] **οὐδὲ ἐκ θελήματος ἀνδρός** is clear: *nor of the will of a husband* [or: *a male*], with the former sense much more likely. The three negative phrases thus affirm that the birth of believers comes not through sexual congress, nor from those natural urges which lead to sexual congress, nor from the desire of a husband, here considered as the one who initiates the move towards physical union. *They were begotten* (**ἐγεννήθησαν**) solely **ἐκ θεοῦ**, *from God.*

---

[58] Though it could, grammatically, be translated as a pluperfect, it would be absurd to write 'he gave to those who had been born of God the power to become children of God'.

[59] Lagrange, without suggesting any direct dependence, calls attention to *1 En* 15.4 ('même genre d'esprit sémitique'): ἐν τῷ αἵματι τῶν γυναικῶν ἐμιάνθητε, καὶ ἐν αἵματι σαρκὸς ἐγεννήσατε, καὶ ἐν αἵματι ἀνθρώπων ἐπεθυμήσατε;

[60] The plural is a *hapax legomenon* in the NT, unless one includes the variant readings in Rev 16.6 (accepted only by Tischendorf) and 18.24 (accepted, among modern editors, only by Tischendorf, Souter, Vogels and Bover).

[61] Euripides' *Ion* 693 is the closest parallel suggested (ἄλλων τραφεὶς ἐξ αἱμάτων), but is not quite exact, for it refers to the child born of the demi-god Apollo and the wholly human Creusa.

[62] 'Sanguina non est latinum: sed quia graece positum est pluraliter, maluit ille qui interpretabatur minus latine loqui secundum grammaticos et tamen explicare veritatem secundum auditum infirmorum.' In Hebrew, the plural form דָּמִים always denotes blood that stems from bleeding (e.g. blood shed by violence, but also blood-stains, the blood of menstruation, of birth etc.); see BDB 2 f and *HALOT* 5. There is no record that it was ever used in the sense ascribed to ἐξ αἱμάτων above.

[63] The only other references are in 8.15 and 17.2. The only depreciatory uses are at 8.15 and 1 Jn 2.16; but contrast with them 1 Jn 4.2 and 2 Jn 7.

But why should anyone think it was necessary to exclude such notions, and so unequivocally? Many authors suggest that the text should read not οἵ οὐκ...ἐγεννήθησαν but (in accordance with some ancient writers) ὅς οὐκ...ἐγεννήθη (see UBS). The sense of vv. 12-13 would then be: 'But to all who did welcome him, he gave power to become children of God, to those who believe *in the name of him who was born* not through the fusion of blood-streams, nor through any carnal desire, nor through the desire of a husband, but of God'. If this were the original text, the most probable interpretation would be that it is a reference to the virginal conception of Jesus Christ, though it could also be interpreted of the eternal generation of the Word. Against this opinion is the fact that not a single Greek MS has the singular reading ἐγεννήθη. Another argument advanced in favour of the singular is that it is rather odd to say that the Word gave to those who were born (or begotten) of God *power to become* children of God. On this, Barrett's is the most helpful suggestion, namely, that here there may be an allusion to the spiritual [re]birth of believers as adopted children, which is utterly unlike natural birth, and takes place through God's will alone. A detailed note on this matter is obviously desirable, and is printed in Excursus IV, 'Longer Notes on Textual Criticism'.

D. THE WORD BECOME FLESH (1.14-18)

14a	And the Word became flesh
14b	and came to dwell among us,
14c	and we beheld his glory,
14d	glory as of someone unique, from a father,
14e	full of grace and truth.
15a	John bears witness to him, and cries aloud,
15bc	This was he of whom I said, | There is one of my followers who has always taken precedence, by rank, before me, because he existed before me.'[1]
16a	For of his fullness have we all received,
16b	and grace for grace.
17a	For the law was given through Moses;
17b	grace and truth came through Jesus Christ.
18a	No one has ever seen God;
18b	it is that utterly unique One,† who is now returned into the bosom of the Father,
18c	that has been our guide, and shown and led the way.

[† 18b or: that one and only Son]

14a. So far, each new sentence of the Prologue except 12 (ὅσοι δέ) has begun with an asyndeton;[2] the **καί** here is therefore significant. Though fair play demands that the translation be left as *and*, to encompass all possible divergent meanings, this καί is certainly not merely copulative (BDF 442 lists 16 possible senses). (1) For those (e.g. Schnackenburg) who think that vv. 10-13 refer to the activity of the Word after the Incarnation, the best translation is *and indeed*, taking καί as a resumptive and confirmatory conjunction. (2) For those who interpret vv. 10-11 as referring to the activity of the Word before the Incarnation, the καί might be taken as a strong contrastive, meaning *and yet, and nevertheless*, i.e. in spite of the rejection referred to in vv. 10c and 11b, the Word became flesh. (The obvious objection to this is that v. 11 is far away, and that vv. 12-13 speak of those who accept the Word, so that the rendering *and nevertheless* is, as the text stands at present, quite inappropriate. The interpretation does, of course, make sense if vv. 12-13 are regarded as a later interpolation, and disregarded.[3]) (3) The conjunction, however, need not be solely adversative: καί is also used for 'emphasizing a fact as

---

[1] The lines are here arranged to indicate that they are not part of the hymn.

[2] I take v. 5 to be a continuation of the sentence in v. 4 (see above).

[3] Cf. Bernard cxliv and Haenchen, though both in fact take the καί in sense (3).

surprising or unexpected or noteworthy; *and yet, and in spite of that, nevertheless'* (BDAG 1 b eta, with references to Jn 1.5, 10; 3.11, 32; 5.40; 6.70; 7.28). Hence 'by an easy transition, the sense of addition sometimes recedes into the background, while the sense of climax predominates, a ladder of which only the top rung is clearly seen'.[4] On this interpretation, particularly when we recall the continuous asyndeton from v. 1 to v. 11, the most appropriate rendering is *and then, to crown all*—the Word became flesh. The καί is then a conjunction expressing astonishment, as the next words are intended to evoke adoration.

ὁ λόγος. The opening verse of the Gospel, pronouncing the name Logos three times, once in each of its three clauses, made each of those three statements programmatic for the entire Gospel: the Logos existed in the beginning, the Logos was very close to God, and the Logos was God.

Thereafter, the Prologue refrains from any mention of the term Logos until v. 14. In vv. 2-13, it is represented once by οὗτος (v. 2), and by the oblique cases αὐτόν, αὐτοῦ, αὐτῷ, but the term itself is never mentioned. Then in v. 14, ὁ λόγος reappears, just once, and for the last time in the Gospel, as a proper name. To be sure, a restatement of the subject was required after vv. 12-13, for the sake of clarity. Nevertheless, the fact that this is the last mention of the Logos makes it of supreme importance; and the final declaration about the Logos in the Fourth Gospel is that it 'became flesh'.

Before passing on, therefore, some notes on ὁ λόγος in v. 14 will not be out of place. It was suggested above, under Logos in 1.1a, that the author was thinking of the Word of God as revealed in the OT, and above all of the Memra.[5] This would explain why John in his Prologue writes only ὁ λόγος and not ὁ λόγος τοῦ θεοῦ, namely, because he wishes not so much to make a distinction or separation between the Logos and God, as to speak of the Logos for the moment in what is an indeterminate, but exceedingly close, relationship with God. θεὸς ἦν ὁ λόγος, as was the Memra, the Holy, Ineffable, Name of God—the 'I AM WHAT I AM' of Exod 3.15. To repeat what was stated on pp. 8-9, if ὁ λόγος, without addition, is taken as equivalent to the term Memra, then it denotes the Compassionate, the All-Merciful, God not just as existent in an onto-logical sense (*Sein*) but rather as One who is ever-present at the side of his creatures, ever ready to have mercy and to supply whatever help they may need in any situation (*Dasein*). This is surely the first and main reason that John chooses to write ὁ λόγος without adding 'of God'.[6]

---

[4] The words of J. D. Denniston, writing about καί in Attic Greek, in *The Greek Particles*, Oxford, 1934, 316-17.

[5] The comment on 1.1a (pp. 7-9) stated that of the five possible senses of Logos, three—the 'Platonist', the Stoic, and the Neo-Platonic (plus its cousin, the Gnostic)—were definitely not intended by the evangelist, and they are not considered here. See Excursus II.

[6] See also on v. 14b, ἐσκήνωσεν, and on v. 14c ἐθεασάμεθα τὴν δόξαν αὐτοῦ.

A second reason may have been that ὁ λόγος on its own is tanta-
lisingly vague. A person unfamiliar with Judaism, but well-versed in
contemporary ideologies, might perhaps have been intrigued enough to
inquire further, to see in what sense a pre-existent Logos could, as the
Christians taught, be said to have once been 'embodied' in a particular
historical human being. One thinks of Aristides' writing to Hadrian.[7]

Thirdly, the fact that ὁ λόγος as a proper name is, after v. 14, never
again found in the Gospel, must mean that it was there intended as a
technical term for the pre-existent Word up to the moment of its Incarnation (1.14). Christian theologians have interpreted it correctly by speaking
consistently thereafter of the *Incarnate* Word, in accordance with the
patristic adage: *verbum quod semel assumpsit nunquam dimisit.*[8]

Fourthly, since most readers approach the Gospel with a firm belief in
the Nicene dogma of the Holy Trinity, a plea for caution is here imperative. Those who listened to Jesus during his life-time did not come
already endowed with faith in a Trinitarian Godhead, nor did those who
heard the preaching of the Apostles: it was not a matter of teaching
people who already believed in a Holy Trinity that one of those divine
persons had become a human being. Neither in Judaism nor elsewhere is
there any trace of such a belief. Rather, as the following verses show, the
early Christians first saw the historical Jesus of Nazareth and then sought
to express in words what they beheld in him; and when the Fourth Gospel
was written, its author could find no other vocabulary to express his faith
than to say that Jesus was the very Logos who existed in the beginning,
face to face with God.[9]

The word **σάρξ** is not too frequent in John (six times in 1.13, 14; 3.6;
6.63; 8.15; 17.2; plus one occurrence in each verse of the six verses from
6.61 to 6.56, a section the provenance of which is much disputed), and
each text needs to be examined on its own. Here it stands, by synecdoche,
for ἄνθρωπος, that is, for the whole human being, not merely for the

---

[7] See above p. 2 fn. 1 on The Title, and note that one reference there suggested is
precisely Jn 1.14. 'Christians trace their origin from the Lord Jesus Christ, whom they
confess to be the son of the Most High God, by a holy Spirit come down from heaven,
for the salvation of humanity; and having been begotten of a holy virgin without seed or
any damage, he took up flesh and made himself visible to the human race, so that he
might call them back from their aberration into polytheism'. The text reads: οἱ δὲ
Χριστιανοὶ γενεαλογοῦνται ἀπὸ τοῦ κυρίου Ἰησοῦ Χριστοῦ· οὗτος δὲ ὁ υἱὸς τοῦ
θεοῦ τοῦ ὑψίστου ὁμολογεῖται ἐν πνεύματι ἁγίῳ ἀπ' οὐρανοῦ καταβὰς διὰ τὴν
σωτηρίαν τῶν ἀνθρώπων· καὶ ἐκ παρθένου ἁγίας γεννηθεὶς ἀσπόρως τε καὶ
ἀφθόρως σάρκα ἀνέλαβε, καὶ ἀνεφάνη ἀνθρώποις, ὅπως ἐκ τῆς πολύθεου πλάνης
αὐτοὺς ἀνακαλέσηται. Aristides, *Apology* 15.1.

[8] Chrysostom *in loco*: διαπαντὸς κατοικεῖ τὴν σκηνήν· τὴν γὰρ σάρκα τὴν
ἡμετέραν περιεβάλετο, οὐχ ὡς πάλιν αὐτὴν ἀφήσων. ἀλλ' ὡς διαπαντὸς ἔξων
μεθ' ἑαυτοῦ (Hom. 11.2 = Ben 65B). For the sense, see also John of Damascus *De fide* I.
III 27.

[9] The point is excellently made by G. Kittel in *TWNT* IV 134. For further detail on the
term Logos, see Excursus II.

flesh, but for the bones and blood and soul as well. It is worth adding, in view of the later Apollinarian controversy, that the evangelist would hardly have considered a body without any human intellect as matching his concept of the Word made flesh: he meant to affirm that the Logos became fully human, not that it did duty for the rational soul in a hominoid body that was devoid of a human mind or will.[10] If one asks why the evangelist did not use ἄνθρωπος, it might have been because the idea of a divine Heavenly Man, existing before creation, was at the time widely current in contemporary Judaism, as is fully evidenced by *1 En* 45–57. Briefly, this heavenly being, known as the Messiah, the Righteous One, and the Son of Man, reigned enthroned in glory, with dominion over all creatures, heavenly and earthly, and as judge of them all. It has been suggested that the evangelist, believing that the Logos was, even before the creation, not merely identified with, but identical with, this Heavenly Man, felt therefore unable to write 'he *became* man', and put instead 'he became *flesh*'.[11] Again, to say that ὁ λόγος ἄνθρωπος ἐγένετο could have been misinterpreted, by readers more familiar with Greek mythology than with Judaism, as meaning that the Logos was *changed into* a human being. It is perhaps worth mentioning also that in John, σάρξ does not stand for 'flesh' as corrupted by sin (frequent in Paul) but for flesh as mortal and physically weak.[12] The risk of these misunderstandings might have counselled the use of a circumlocution, as in Phil 2.7: ἑαυτὸν ἐκένωσεν μορφὴν δούλου λαβών, ἐν ὁμοιώματι ἀνθρώπων γενό- μενος, καὶ σχήματι εὑρεθεὶς ὡς ἄνθρωπος. But all these reasons taken together still do not explain why John expresses himself so differently, choosing σάρξ *simpliciter*, with no explanation, or why he writes ἐγένετο.

---

[10] An Easter sermon of Augustine, *Sermo 238, in fine*, ends with a comment on this text. 'Suscepit totum quasi plenum hominem, animam et corpus hominis. Et si aliquid scrupulosius vis audire; quia animam et carnem habet et pecus: cum dico animam humanam et carnem humanam, totam animam humanam accepit. Fuerunt enim qui hinc haeresim facerent, et dicerent quia anima Christi non habuit mentem, non habuit intellectum, non habuit rationem; sed Verbum Dei fuit illi pro mente, pro intellectu, pro ratione. Nolo sic credas. Totum redemit, qui totum creavit: totum suscepit, totum liberavit Verbum. Ibi mens hominis et intellectus, ibi anima vivificans carnem; ibi caro vera et integra: peccatum solum non ibi.' (Vol. V 1450 AB = Ben 994). The words are just as relevant nowadays, when a practical monophysitism is widespread among many Christians, because it is so often inadvertently preached. Compare also Bernard's comment *in loco*.

[11] A suggestion of J. Héring, 'Kyrios Anthropos', *RHPR* 16 (1936), 207-209: cf. *TWNT* VII 140 fn. 304. Cullmann, *Christology*, ETr 187, is not unsympathetic to the idea ('perhaps not incorrectly'…particularly if a pre-Christian hymn to the Original Man really lay behind the prologue). For further detail on this figure, see Excursus VI, 'The Son of Man in John'.

[12] 'Caro minime hic pro corrupta natura accipitur (ut saepe apud Paulum), sed pro homine mortali' (Calvin).

In the end, the only satisfactory answer is that σάρξ, more than anything else in the material creation, is diametrically opposed to the Logos. Flesh is the most vulnerable, the most corruptible, the most easily destructible, part of the human being—in a word the most impermanent. The Logos is the Eternal. Flesh is τὸ φθαρτὸν τὸ κατ᾽ ἐξοχήν. They are literally poles apart; but like a positive and a negative, they attract each other, and the attraction is creative. This is what John's Gospel is about.

ἐγένετο. To write ὁ λόγος σάρξ ἐγένετο is to exclude any possibility that the human flesh of Jesus was something similar to clothing which he had put on, something quite external to him, which he could discard at will. Had that been the evangelist's thought, he could easily have expressed it without ambiguity.[13] This does not mean that the Logos was *changed into* a human being. It has just been suggested that one reason why John used σάρξ, not ἄνθρωπος, might have been to preclude any such misinterpretation: no one would think that the Logos could be *changed into* material flesh, or even *changed into* a human being. Nor does the use of ἐγένετο imply that the Logos ceased to be God. The sense is that the Logos *became a human being without ceasing to be God.*[14] Thus the purpose of ἐγένετο is to emphasize that the Logos did not just 'dwell in' human flesh, did not just 'have' a human body in order to speak his part for one or more performances, like a Greek actor walking on stage with a particular mask.[15] He, the divine Logos, *was* in reality the principal character in the drama; the lines that he was to speak were lines written for him in eternity (cf. 3.34; 7.17; 8.28, 38; 12.48-50; 14.10); and the words he was to utter were the words of God.[16] Precisely because of this, a still deeper message is necessarily embodied in the ἐγένετο of v. 14. Eduard Schweizer comments: 'The underlying theological reason for the Incarnation lies therefore in this, that in the cosmic lawsuit between God and the world which accuses him, only an act of

---

[13] See the quotation from Chrysostom on p. 51 fn. 8.[13] But can one really imagine the author of the Fourth Gospel writing καὶ σῶμα ἐπίγειον ἐνεδύσατο ὁ λόγος (cf.1 Cor 15.40) or καὶ ὁ λόγος σῶμα ἑαυτῷ ἔλαβεν φθαρτόν (or rather, θνητόν: cf. 15.53-54)? Or καὶ ὁ λόγος σάρκα ἐπενεδύσατο (cf. 2 Cor 5.2)? Is it not significant that in speaking of Christ's advent upon earth, Paul, like John, consistently avoids the metaphor of dress?

[14] Two sentences of Athanasius deserve quotation for their perfect clarity. (a) ἀεὶ ὢν Θεὸς...ὕστερον καὶ δι ἡμᾶς γέγονεν ἄνθρωπος, καὶ σωματικῶς, ὥς φησιν ὁ ἀπόστολος, κατῴκησεν ἡ θειότης ἐν τῇ σαρκί. (b) οὐδὲ γὰρ ἐπειδὴ γέγονεν ἄνθρωπος, πέπαυται τοῦ εἶναι Θεός (*c. Arianos* III 31 and 38: *PG* 26.389A and 404C).

Barrett rejects the translation 'became', and writes 'perhaps ἐγένετο is used in the same sense as in v. 6: the Word came on the (human) scene as flesh, man', but this seems too feeble for John, and for this context.

[15] Augustine again: 'Aliud est enim Verbum in carne, aliud Verbum caro; id est, aliud est Verbum in homine, aliud Verbum homo' (*De Trin.* II 11, 6: VII 1 = Ben 777).

[16] See Augustine, *Sermo 187 In natali Domini*, fn. 3 (V/1 1286 CD = Ben 886).

witness—μαρτυρεῖν—which includes the commitment of the whole person—can evoke faith, not a mere communication of divine gnosis'.[17] See 18.37.

Schweizer's profoundly perceptive judgment can be taken one step further. If one asks why did John write the word σάρξ, it may be because σάρξ is also intimately bound up with the notion of sacrifice: see the comments on 6.51-56.

14b. On καί here and in the rest of the verse, see on 14a (pp. 49-50): its successive occurrences are not merely copulative, but represent steps always rising from one climax to another (κλῖμαξ meaning, literally, 'a ladder').

ἐσκήνωσεν. The verb σκηνοῦν occurs four times in the NT, here, and in Rev 7.15; 18.6; 21.3. Only Rev 21.3 is akin to our v. 14: Ἰδοὺ ἡ σκηνὴ τοῦ θεοῦ μετὰ τῶν ἀνθρώπων, καὶ σκηνώσει μετ' αὐτῶν.[18] Nor, on the face of it, is κατασκηνοῦν of much help. Three of its four NT occurrences (Mt 13.32 = Mk 4.32 = Lk 13.19) refer to birds nesting, as do both instances of the cognate κατασκήνωσις (Mt 8.20 = Lk 9.58). The one other text (Acts 2.26) is a quotation from Ps 16.9 LXX (ἡ σάρξ μου κατασκηνώσει ἐπ' ἐλπίδι).

The LXX contains only five instances of σκηνοῦν: Gen 13.12; Judg 5.17 (in B [×2]): 8.11; 3 Kgdms 8.12; all except the last refer to those who lived, physically, in material tents. This is certainly not the sense (even metaphorically) of ἐσκήνωσεν in 1.14. By contrast, κατασκηνόω (rare in Classical Greek: see LSJ) is found in the LXX (including variant readings) more than 60 times, in 55 of which it translates the Hebrew root שׁכן (shakan).[19] If one asks why, as a translation of this Hebrew verb, the Greek compound form is so much more frequent than the simplex, it is probably because the prefix κατα– brings out the idea of a long, and even permanent, residence: it is regularly used of Israel's dwelling in the Promised Land: e.g. Num 14.30; Deut 33.12, 28; Josh 22.29; 2 Kgdms 7.10 (cf. κατοικεῖν, καταπαύειν etc.).[20] κατασκηνοῦν is also used for God's first coming *down* to dwell in the Land (Num 35.34), or to dwell in

[17] 'Die theologische Begründung der Fleischwerdung liegt also darin, daß in dem kosmischen Rechtsstreit Gottes mit der ihn anklagenden Welt nur ein μαρτυρεῖν, daß den vollen Einsatz der ganzen Person in sich schließt, Glauben schaffen kann, nicht eine bloße Mitteilung göttlicher Gnosis' (*TWNT* VII 1406-10).

[18] The cognate nouns offer little help in settling on a precise definition, for their meanings in different contexts are too varied, as this list (complete for the NT) shows: σκῆνος in 2 Cor 5.1, 4, σκήνωμα in Acts 7.46; 2 Pet 1.13, 14, and σκηνή itself in Mt 17.4 = Mk 9.5 = Lk 9.33; Lk 16.9; Acts 7.43 [= Amos 5.6], 44; 15.16 [= Amos 9.11]; Heb 8.2, 5; 9.2, 3, 6, 8, 11, 21; 11.9; 13.10; Rev 13.6; 15.5; 21.3.

[19] In the MT, √ שׁכן (škn) occurs about 140 times, and is variously translated; but κατασκηνοῦν dominates among the verbs used.

[20] Further detail in *TWNT* VII 369-96 (Michaelis). Note 386-88 (σκηνόω) and 389-91 (κατασκηνοῦν; its sole OT cognate is κατασκήνωσις, at 1 Chr 28.2; Tob 1.4; Wis 9.8 [and possibly κατασκήνεσις, a variant there]).

the Temple (3 Kgdms 6.13; 1 Chr 23.25; 2 Chr 6.1); and after the destruction of the Temple, there is the promise that 'his name' would again dwell there (Ezek 43.7 and Neh 1.9; cf. Jer 7.12, of Shiloh). Thus κατεσκήνωσεν would have suited the theme admirably, but John does not use that form, and it is hard to think it was because he wished to stress that Jesus' life on earth was so transitory.

In fact, to understand the true thrust of John's ἐσκήνωσεν, we must turn from the LXX to the Hebrew, and some introductory remarks are required. A few altars were built here and there on special occasions by the patriarchs,[21] but they were not places of continuing worship; the Israelites had no permanent sanctuary until after the Covenant at Sinai (Exod 24). When Yahweh had revealed his proper name at Exod 3.15,[22] his first command, immediately after the sealing of the Covenant, was to gather materials to make a great tent, to be the visible sign of his presence in the camp (Exod 25–31). Two verses at the beginning of this passage are then of the utmost importance. (a) Exod 25.8. This is the first occasion in the Bible that Yahweh says, in a phrase that was to be central to his covenant-promises, וְשָׁכַנְתִּי בְּתוֹכָם (wĕšākanti bĕtokām), 'and I shall dwell among you'.[23] The same, or an almost identical, Hebrew phrase recurs, a second time, at Exod 29.45 (a promise, to be fulfilled after the consecration of the Tent); thirdly, at 1 Kgs 6.13, at the Dedication of the Temple; fourthly, at Ezek 43.7, and Zech 2.10, 11 RSV [Heb 2.14, 15], with reference to the divine presence returning to the Temple after the Babylonian Exile. These are the only six instances of the word וְשָׁכַנְתִּי (wĕšākanti = 'and I shall dwell') in the Hebrew Bible, and it is noteworthy that it is uttered only by Yahweh, the all-merciful, i.e. the speaker is always called 'Yahweh', never 'God'.[24] (b) In Exod 25.9 we encounter the noun הַמִּשְׁכָּן (hammiškan: LXX σκηνή), this too at its first time in the Hebrew Bible. It is commonly translated into English as the tabernacle or the Tent, but means literally the dwelling, the abode. A cognate of

---

[21] See R. de Vaux, *Ancient Israel*, 289-94. Only in Gen 35.1 is God said to have taken the initiative.

[22] In this context, it is worth mentioning 'the general Rabbinic rule that the name YHWH represents God's Attribute of Mercy, while ʾelohim stands for the Attribute of Justice' (Hayward, *Divine Name*, 39).

[23] The LXX translates this as καὶ ὀφθήσομαι ἐν ὑμῖν. See the comment on ἐν ὑμῖν at the end of v. 14b.

[24] שָׁכַנְתִּי (šākanti) is found without the initial waw consecutive in Ps 120.6 [RSV 5] and in Prov 8.12, neither of which is remotely relevant. Otherwise, not at all. Note that when Solomon asks, at the Dedication of the Temple, 'But will God indeed dwell upon the earth?' (1 Kgs 8.27 = 2 Chr 6.18), the Hebrew verb is not שׁכן (škn) but ישׁב (yšb). The nuance of difference seems to be that the former means *to settle down, to take up an abode* for a long while, or permanently, whereas the latter means primarily *to sit down*, and therefore simply *to take up residence*. See *LHVT* 334b, for ישׁב (yšb), and 843a, for שׁכן (škn). Yahweh has already promised that he will make his permanent home there, and Solomon wonders, 'Will he really take up residence here?'

shakan, it occurs 139 times in the MT, and with two or three exceptions,[25] wherever it is found in the singular, it denotes always (= 136 times) the 'physical abode' of Yahweh (BDB). This verb and this noun, each occurring, with reference to God's indwelling in the midst of Israel, for the first time in Exod 25, explain why John chose to write ἐσκήνωσεν; and they, by recalling Exod 25, and the dedication of Solomon's Temple, and the return after the Exile, disclose the full meaning of ἐσκήνωσεν. A medieval Latinist caught the OT allusions perfectly: *et tabernaculavit in nobis.*[26]

Further, at 25.8, Aquila, Symmachus and Theodotion all render the verb וְשָׁכַנְתִּי (wĕšākanti) normally, and quite correctly, as σκηνώσω. Aquila was much given to translating a Hebrew root by a similar Greek word, and the correspondence between *shakan* and σκηνοῦν must have seemed too good to miss. Perhaps it was noticed by Theodotion and Symmachus too; this would explain why three such disparate versions could, in Exod 25.8, arrive at the rarely used simplex σκηνοῦν instead of the commonly used compound κατασκηνοῦν. May not John have done the same?

Thus the καί before ἐσκήνωσεν marks yet another climax. When the Logos, the Memra, became flesh, there was the final dwelling-place of God among men, as Rev 21.3 declares: Ἰδοὺ ἡ σκηνὴ τοῦ θεοῦ μετὰ τῶν ἀνθρώπων, καὶ σκηνώσει μετ' αὐτῶν, where σκηνώσει must refer to God, especially as the verse continues with 'and God himself shall be with them'. Revelation 21.22 completes this picture of new Jerusalem with 'and I saw no temple in her, for the Lord God the Almighty is her temple, and the Lamb'. As in Rev 21–22, so throughout John's Gospel, there runs the theme of 'the Temple of his body': see 2.21; 19.34, 37; 20.25, 27.

ἐν ἡμῖν refers primarily to those who personally 'heard, saw and touched' Jesus (1 Jn 1.1), secondly to that particular generation, whether Jewish or Gentile; thirdly and by extension to all who hear the Gospel story to the end of time; and to all the human race.

Before moving to 14c, it is worth asking why the LXX did not always translate the verb וְשָׁכַנְתִּי (wĕšākanti) by καὶ κατασκηνώσω, but used instead, in Exod 25.8, καὶ ὀφθήσομαι ἐν ὑμῖν, and in Exod 29.45, καὶ ἐπικληθήσομαι ἐν τοῖς υἱοῖς Ισραηλ. (In the other four texts, it gives καὶ κατασκηνώσω, 3 Kgdms 6.13; Ezek 43.9; Zech 2.14, and κατασκηνοῦσιν, Zech 2.15). The reason for its choice of ὀφθήσομαι in

---

[25] Num 16.24, 27, where it is generally agreed that the original must have been not the dwelling 'of Korah etc.', but 'of Yahweh'; and Isa 22.16, poetically, of a tomb ('graving an habitation for himself in the rock' (RV).

[26] *Concilium Armenorum* (A.D. 1342) art. 2 in E. Martène, *Veterum scriptorum et monumentorum amplissima collectio* t. VII, Paris, 1733, col. 316 = *Sacrorum Conciliorum nova collectio* ed. J. D. Mansi, Florence, 1759–, 25, 1190 C; cited in C. F. Du Cange, *Glossarium ad scriptores mediae et infimae latinitatis*, new ed. by L. Favre, t. VIII, Paris, 1887, *sub voce*. See also RV[mg], 'tabernacled'.

Exod 25.8 is presumably to gloss the literal sense by hinting at the future visible presence of the Cloud over the Tent (Exod 33.7-11; 40.34-38; cf. Barrett), and the parallel gloss in 29.45 is intended to stress what the people's liturgical response to that visible divine presence will be.

All the Targums of these six texts mention the Shekinah: e.g. *Neofiti* at Exod 25.8 (McNamara), 'I will make the Glory of my Shekinah dwell among them', or 1 Kgs 6.13 'I will make dwell my Shekinah among the sons of Israel' (Harrington-Saldarini). The two (post-biblical) terms Shekinah (Hebrew) and Shekintah (Aramaic) both designate the 'Divine Presence' among the people of God. One translation including this idea would be, 'And the Word became flesh, and made his dwelling among us' (NAB: or, less literally, 'came to dwell among us', Knox, NEB).

14c. The third καί in v. 14 marks the final step on the ladder of climax. ἐθεασάμεθα has a strong and distinctive resonance: both the Latin *vidimus* and the English *see* are unduly feeble renderings. LSJ gives as the basic meaning *gaze at, behold*, 'mostly with a sense of wonder', followed by a fascinating list of examples. The same sense obtains in the LXX, where the word occurs only once in a translation from the Hebrew (at 2 Chr 22.6), but seven times in the 'Greek' books (Tob 2.2; 13.6, 14; Jdth 15.8; 2 Macc 2.4; 3.36; 3 Macc 5.47). In John, it often means to see one thing with the physical eyes, and to perceive therein, by the gift of God, something else, not self-evident, but profoundly true (cf. BDAG 2). Thus the Baptist sees a physical dove, and 'beholds' in it a sign of the Holy Spirit (Jn 1.32; cf. 1.38; 4.35; 6.5; 11.45). Note that ἐθεασάμεθα is aorist middle, and deponent. It may therefore be translated as 'we beheld, for a time, for ourselves (his glory, dwelling among us)'. Cf. 1 Jn 1.1-4.

τὴν δόξαν. The Hebrew word underlying δόξα, כָּבוֹד (kābod), is found three times in Genesis, where it is in no way connected with God.[27] As a religious term, it makes its first appearance in the very texts we have just encountered under ἐσκήνωσεν. 'The glory of Yahweh' is first mentioned by Moses and Aaron en route to Sinai, to calm the people's fears (Exod 16.7, 10); secondly, when Moses goes up the mountain to speak with God after the Covenant (24.16-17); and thirdly, when Moses asks to see Yahweh's glory (33.18), only to be told that he cannot see that face and live (33.20, 22). Naturally, the phrase recurs at 1 Kgs 8.11 and in Ezek 43.2, 5; 44.4. The ἐσκήνωσεν of 14b calls forth the ἐθεασάμεθα τὴν δόξαν of 14c.

αὐτοῦ. Of the Logos, clearly, but of the Word made flesh. Both the Shekinah and the Glory of Yahweh are regarded as being present in his humanity, in his flesh; but how that glory is there contained, and how it will be only slowly unveiled, and in what circumstances it will finally be completely revealed—these are among the major themes that are subtly developed throughout the Fourth Gospel. The first manifestation of Jesus'

[27] In Gen 31.1 it refers to the wealth accumulated by Jacob, and in 45.13, to that of Joseph. In 49.6 it is parallel to 'O my soul'.

glory at Cana (2.11) is matched by a reference, at the end of his public ministry, to the fact that Isaiah 'saw his glory' (12.41); and the discourse at the Supper begins (13.31-32) and concludes with references to his glory (17.1, 4, 5, 24).

14d. δόξαν ὡς. This is the first clue as to the nature of that glory of the Word made flesh, and Chrysostom rightly comments: 'The ὡς here is not one of comparison or illustration, but of confirmation and unambiguous definition'.[28] That is, it means not 'glory similar to that of...', or 'glory as though it were', but 'glory which truly is that of...': see BDAG 3 (a) α, and compare 1 Pet 1.19; 2.2. Michaelis observes that wherever ὡς introduces a fact, it is never followed by an article.[29]

μονογενοῦς παρὰ πατρός. J. H. Moulton comments, on this text: 'For exegesis, there are few of the finer points of Greek which need more constant attention than this omission of the article when the writer would lay stress on the quality or character of the object' (MHT I 83). There is no article either before μονογενοῦς or before παρὰ πατρός.

In the older English versions, μονογενής was translated as 'only begotten', but twentieth-century versions nearly all prefer 'only Son'. The danger with this new rendering is that it makes no distinction between the use of μονογενής without the accompanying υἱός (as here, and perhaps in v. 18), and its recurrence with υἱός in 3.16, 18. Bultmann, for example, writes that in v. 14, μονογενής, because it stands alone, must come from the evangelist's source, and must therefore be taken in a different sense from its other occurrences (47 fn. 2; ETr 72 fn. 2). It is not necessary to accept these two principles (which are far from being self-evident) in order to agree that μονογενής with and without υἱός may well carry two different meanings. In Excursus III, 'The Meaning of μονογενη in John 1.14, 18', it is argued at some length that in 1.14 the meaning to be preferred is 'of someone quite unique, coming [*or*: sent from] a father'. It is a commonplace to remark that in the Johannine writings, by contrast with the Synoptics and with Paul, Jesus alone is called υἱὸς θεοῦ, and all others are designated τέκνα (e.g. 1.13). This usage itself implies that in John the title 'Son of God' is considered to belong to Jesus alone, and to apply to him in a quite unique mode.[30] The view taken here is that at this point in the Prologue, the reader is told only that the Word become flesh

---

[28] τὸ δὲ, ὡς, ἐνταῦθα, οὐχ ὁμοιώσεώς ἐστιν, οὐδὲ παραβολῆς· ἀλλὰ βεβαιώσεως, καὶ ἀναμφισβητήτου διορισμοῦ.

[29] *TWNT* IV 749 fn. 15.

[30] Boismard writes succinctly: '...s'il est "l'Unique-Engendré", c'est en tant que Logos incarné' (*Moïse ou Jésus*, 116). The adjective 'incarné' is here of crucial importance, affirming as it does that μονογενής is not here (in v. 14, where it stands alone, without υἱός) to be taken as referring, in a Nicene sense, to the eternal generation of the Son *apud Patrem, ante omnia saecula*, but to the appearance on earth of that Word in the flesh. At a second reading, when one knows the whole content of the Gospel, the term μονογενής here can of course take on a deeper significance.

was at first seen as someone quite unique, coming from another most appropriately designated as a father (see the quotation from Moulton in the preceding paragraph).

παρὰ πατρός: 'The idea conveyed is not that of sonship only, but of a mission also' (Westcott), and of a mission for a special work (cf. 6.46; 7.29; 16.27; 17.8). For further detail see Excursus III, 'The Meaning of μονογενη in John 1.14, 18', and the comment on μονογενής at 1.18.

14e. πλήρης χάριτος καὶ ἀληθείας. The Latin *plenum gratiae et veritatis* attaches this phrase to *verbum* in 14a; so also (by bracketing the intervening words) the RV of 1881, and (by repositioning the phrase: 'dwelt among us, full of grace and truth'), the RSV (but not the NRSV). J. H. Moulton, writing in 1905, questioned whether an educated writer would have used the form πλήρης for an oblique case, and suggested that 'an original πλήρη was corrupted to the vulgar πλήρης in an early copy' ('a reading which D has either preserved or restored'), and that it would be more appropriate to take this πλήρη as qualifying δόξαν (MHT I 50). Since then, the evidence of the papyri has made it clear that, from the first century of our era onwards, πλήρης was regularly indeclinable when followed by a genitive (MHT II 162; III 315 [nb.]; MM 519; BDF 137 [1]). Thus the construction in the Latin, the RV and the RSV may safely be abandoned; and though Moulton's application to δόξαν can stand, it too is better relinquished.

If πλήρης is genitive, then it may qualify αὐτοῦ or μονογενοῦς or πατρός (or both the latter). Grammatically, there is no way to decide. Nor does this Greek phrase occur in the LXX. It is, however a perfect rendering of words in the Hebrew text of Exod 34.6, and if taken as an evocation of this text, it suits the context to perfection.

In 14b, ἐσκήνωσεν ἐν ἡμῖν contains an implicit allusion to the Shekinah in the desert (cf. Exod 25.8-9; 29.45). In 14c, ἐθεασάμεθα τὴν δόξαν αὐτοῦ alludes to Moses' request to see the Glory of Yahweh at Sinai (cf. Exod 33.18-22). 14d may then be taken as a refinement of the description of that glory (it is δόξαν ὡς μονογενοῦς παρὰ πατρός). 14e can then be taken to match Exod 34.5-6, where Yahweh fulfils his promise, made in 33.19, to 'proclaim before [Moses] his name, Yahweh'.[31] Exodus 34.5-6 is a solemn disclosure of the meaning of the Ineffable Name revealed at Exod 3.15, and may be translated thus: 'Yahweh descended in the cloud and stood with him [Moses] there, and he proclaimed the name "Yahweh"'.[32] Yahweh passed before him, and proclaimed, "Yahweh, Yahweh, is a God *merciful and gracious, slow to*

---

[31] The meaning of this phrase קרא בשם יהוה (qrʾ bšm yhwh), when used of creatures, is 'solemnly to call upon the name of Yahweh'; when used of God himself, it means 'solemnly to reveal himself by name' (as the context of Exodus makes clear).

[32] It is grammatically possible to construe this sentence either with Moses or with Yahweh as the subject of 'proclaimed'. Most prefer the latter interpretation.

anger, and abounding in merciful love and faithfulness (רַב־חֶסֶד וֶאֱמֶת: rab-ḥĕsĕd wĕ'ĕmɛt)...'" This is the first, and the most basic, OT reference underlying Jn 1.14e. It is by the Incarnation of the Logos that Yahweh, the most merciful God of Sinai, 'has made his dwelling among us'.

Chapters 33–34 of Exodus follow immediately after the painful apostasy of Israel in the episode of the golden calf (Exod 32), a fact which serves to underline the unmerited and uncovenanted mercy of God. Exodus 34.6 is aptly termed by Luther 'this sermon on the name of the Lord'.

It is therefore most significant that the almost identical formula recurs next in Num 14.18 (indeed, v. 17 makes an explicit reference back to the promise in Exod 34): 'Yahweh is *slow to anger, and abounding in merciful love...*'. This too is a prayer used immediately after a national apostasy, when the people tried to stone Moses and Aaron, Joshua and Caleb (Num 14.10). After this second apostasy, however, the MT omits from the prayer the final word (וֶאֱמֶת: wĕ'ĕmɛt), though the full version, with the two nouns, is found in a handful of MSS, in the Samaritan text of Exodus and in the LXX (*BHS*). It seems more likely, though, that the MT represents the better tradition, and that the formula of Exod 34.6-7 has in the later texts been deliberately truncated, because Moses, in pleading for mercy for the people, does not wish to remind Yahweh of the retribution he had threatened to inflict upon them. This interpretation would seem to be supported by the text of Deut 7.9-10, which places equal emphasis on Yahweh's loyalty to those who love him and on his sternness to those who hate him.

The other citations of the phrase from Exod 34.6 occur in the two great penitential services of the post-exilic period, at Joel 2.13 and at Neh 9.17 (here again, in both cases, in the truncated form, without the final וֶאֱמֶת [wĕ'ĕmɛt]: cf. also Jonah 4.2). Thus this 'definition' of the name of the Lord as all-merciful is attested at four major moments in the history of Israel, in the Law, in the Prophets and in the Writings. It is interesting that the phrase '*slow to anger, and abounding in merciful love [and faithfulness]*' does not occur in the story of the dedication of Solomon's Temple, either in 1 Kgs 8 or in 2 Chr 6. On the other hand, the faith of Israel during the period of the Second Temple is assuredly most accurately expressed in the psalms; and they repeat over and over again that the people of Israel trust in the Lord, and take refuge in him, because of his *merciful love and faithfulness* (Pss 25.10; 40.11-12; 57.11; 61.8; 85.11; 89.15; 115.1; 138.2 [nb]; cf. 26.3; 117.2).

The evangelist concludes this foundational statement about the Word become flesh, by declaring that everything that is true of the Memra (see above pp. 8-9) is now true of the Logos, and of the Logos made flesh. Though πλήρης in 14d can, grammatically, be taken as an attribute of the μονογενής (whether this be translated as 'only son' or 'someone utterly unique'), or of the one with the quality of a father, it is practically certain that in the mind of the evangelist it applied to the former (the μονογενής) as revealing that selfsame attribute of the latter (a father—see v. 18; and 14.9-11). The Word made flesh is, like Yahweh in Exod 34.6, רַב־חֶסֶד וֶאֶמֶת (rab-ḥěsěd wě°ěmɛt), 'abounding in merciful love and in faithfulness'. The phrase χάρις καὶ ἀλήθεία recurs in 1.17, after which it is never again found in the Gospel.

15. The climax past, asyndeton returns, and the apparent lack of a close logical connection with v. 14 led WH, RSV and NRSV to place the verse in parentheses; all others, wisely, do not (see UBS, and the remarks at the end of the comment on this verse).

Ἰωάννης μαρτυρεῖ περὶ αὐτοῦ καὶ κέκραγεν λέγων. The present tense μαρτυρεῖ and the perfect κέκραγεν affirm the perduring nature of John's witness up to the time of the writing of the Gospel. John is still witnessing; this interpretation seems preferable, in the present context, to treating μαρτυρεῖ as a 'vivid' historical present, *pace JG* 2479 and BDF 321. Likewise, the perfect κέκραγεν implies that his public proclamation is still echoing around the churches (compare MHT I 147[33], and, for examples of κέκραγα referring to the present, BAG 2 a). It is regrettable that so many English versions translate both verbs by a past tense (KJV RSV NRSV NEB [*ex parte*] REB NAB), even though the RV of 1881 had opted for the present in both cases ('beareth witness and crieth'): JB and NIV render by two present tenses, as does NJB ('John witnesses to him. He proclaims').

Οὗτος ἦν ὃν εἶπον. Thinking the accusative awkward, 'ℵ* rewrote the passage...and several other witnesses (ℵ[avid] B* C* Origen)...changed ὃν εἶπον to ὁ εἰπών' (*TCGNT*), but the lemma above is undoubtedly the original reading (see the evidence in UBS and the comment in *TCGNT*). When it is translated as 'This was the one I mentioned (*or*: meant)', the usage is both Classical[34] and Johannine (8.27: for further examples see BDAG *s.v.* λέγω 1b and εἶπον 1). ἦν: the imperfect is the correct tense to refer back to a chronologically anterior witness by the Baptist (namely, that yet to be related, in 1.27, 30). 'The insertion of ὑμῖν after εἶπον (D W[supp] X *al*) is a natural addition which copyists were prone to make' (*TCGNT*).

Ὁ ὀπίσω μου ἐρχόμενος. Almost all English versions render this phrase as 'He who comes after me', or the equivalent; indeed, the two most noteworthy exceptions, Moffatt ('my successor') and Barclay ('He

---

[33] Moulton there quotes Monro's *Homeric Grammar*, 31, 'Verbs expressing sustained sounds...are usually in the perfect' (in Homer), and adds 'This last remark explains κέκραγα, which has survived in Hellenistic, as the LXX seems to show decisively'. The conjunction of a present tense with the perfect of κέκραγα is found also in Attic Greek: κεκραγὼς καὶ βοῶν in Aristophanes, *Plutus* 722, βοῶν...καὶ κεκραγὼς in Demosthenes XVIII *De Corona*, 132.

[34] So common indeed, that LSJ, under εἶπον II 2 'name, mention', notes only one example (*Iliad* 1.90), followed by 'etc.' (The sole reference is to Achilles' oath, 'not even if you mean Agamemnon': οὐδ᾽ ἢν 'Α. εἴπῃ.)

follows me in time'), express even more forcefully that the words refer to one who comes, chronologically, later than John. So it was in the first edition (1953 = 1956) of the French *Bible de Jérusalem* ('lui qui vient après moi'); but in the second edition (1973 = 1992), we find 'Celui qui vient derrière moi', in which ὀπίσω is taken to denote not time, but place.[35] That this is the correct understanding can be argued on several grounds. (i) The use of ὀπίσω with the genitive to denote place (= *behind*) is quite foreign to Classical Greek, and even to Josephus (who in *Ant.* VIII 354 replaces the ἀκολουθήσω ὀπίσω σου of 3 Kgdms 19.20 with the normal Greek dative: ἠκολούθησεν 'Ηλία).[36] (ii) This employment of ὀπίσω with the genitive to indicate a relationship of place (not time) suggests that the phrase comes from a writer with a Hebrew rather than a Greek mind, and that the meaning is therefore *to be a follower of*. This is confirmed by the fact that the Hebrew הָלַךְ אַחֲרֵי (hālak ʾaḥăre) is in the LXX regularly translated by πορεύεσθαι ὀπίσω τινος, less often by ἀκολουθεῖν ὀπίσω τινος. See HR under ὀπιόω (1) a, and BDB under הלך (*hlk*) II 3 d (235) or (more conveniently) *DCH* I under אַחֲרֵי (ʾaḥĕre), 2 a (197). (iii) In these words here at Jn 1.15, one can perceive an echo of Jesus' call δεῦτε ὀπίσω μου (Mt 4.19 = Mk 1.17), and of the programmatic statement about discipleship, εἴ τις θέλει ὀπίσω μου ἐλθεῖν... (Mt 16.24 = Mk 8.34; cf. Lk 9.23, with ἔρχεσθαι), where the words ὀπίσω μου ἐλθεῖν | ἔρχεσθαι in the protasis are answered by ἀκολουθείτω μοι in the apodosis. Matthew 10.38 = Lk 14.27 (and cf. Lk 21.8) witness to the same usage. (iv) Thus 'as a general rule, wherever it is found in the NT together with the genitive of a person and a verb of motion, ὀπίσω has a theological meaning'.[37] Regrettably (for his is a fine article), the author of these words, Heinrich Seesemann, then writes that the three references in Jn 1.15, 27, 30, along with Mt 3.11 and Mk 1.7, are (judged on the basis of ὀπίσω) exceptions to this rule, and have no theological significance, but give only a time-reference. Seesemann is certainly correct in claiming that at Mt 3.11 and Mk 1.7, the words of the Baptist are intended to carry only a temporal meaning ('he who comes after, i.e. later than, me'); but it is hard to see no more than this in Jn 1.15, 27, 30, and to treat these Johannine texts also as exceptions to the OT usage mentioned above under (ii), and to the Synoptic texts mentioned under (iii). (v) Origen calls attention to the precision of this wording with ἐρχόμενος: insofar as Jesus went forward to be baptized by John, he may be said to have been a follower of John.[38] The preferable translation of ὁ ὀπίσω μου ἐρχόμενος is therefore not 'There is one who comes after me' but *There is one of my followers...*

[35] BDAG 2 b prefers to take this text (and also its parallels in Mt 3.11; Mk 1.7; Jn 1.27, 30) as meaning that the Baptist came after Jesus in time; but the OT passages there cited (3 Kgdms 1.6, 24; Eccl 10.14) are scarcely sufficient to determine the case.

[36] According to G. Kittel in *TWNT* I 2118-16.

[37] H. Seesemann in *TWNT* V 29020-22.

[38] Brooke II, Fragment 10, on 2211-10.

ἔμπροσθέν μου γέγονεν. Though Jesus came 'after John' in time
(compare the birth stories in Luke 1–2) and in his ministry, the sense of
ἔμπροσθέν μου γέγονεν is that he *has always been* (γέγονεν is
perfect) *one who takes precedence, by rank, before me.* For examples of
ἔμπροσθέν with this sense, see BDAG 1 b (ζ), which rightly comments
that if ἔμπροσθέν here referred to precedence in time, the following
words (ὅτι πρῶτός μου ἦν) would be a tautology.[39] Consequently, *There
is one of my followers who has always taken precedence, by rank, before
me.*

ὅτι πρῶτός μου ἦν. This is because Jesus existed before John, as
1.1-4 clearly affirm. For the superlative ousting the comparative, see
MHT I 79; II 32, 216 fn. 2 (noting that πρῶτός μου is not classical), and
BDF 62: 'Hellenistic has retained the superlative πρῶτος; πρότερος has
surrendered the meaning "the first of two" to πρῶτος, and now means
only "earlier"'.

Thus the meaning is 'John is still testifying and his cry still rings out
loud: This is the one I meant with "There is a follower of mine who takes
precedence before me, because he existed before me"'. This, the first
occurrence of ὀπίσω μου ἔρχεσθαι in John, has the Baptist designating
Jesus as one of his followers. The relevance of this fact will become clear
as the commentary begins to discuss this Gospel's presentation of the
Baptist and his disciples.

The phrase recurs in Jn 1.27, 30, and then, for the last time, at 12.19,
in ἴδε ὁ κόσμος ὀπίσω αὐτοῦ ἀπῆλθεν,[40] words which immediately
precede the great announcement, 'There were some Greeks among those
who had come up to worship at the feast' (12.20). In that final chapter of
Part I, when Jesus' public ministry has reached its close, the last words
uttered by the Pharisees are 'Behold, the world has gone after him'
(12.19). In that context, the words are surely intended to remind the
reader that the purpose of the Baptist's mission announced at the beginning ('so that all might come to believe', 1.6-7) has in fact been achieved,
and that the rhetorically phrased (but, ironically, so accurate) judgment of
the Pharisees unwittingly proclaims that it is no longer true, as was said
in 1.10, that 'the world did not know him'. (Compare the comment on
1.10.)

16. The majority of codices insert καί before ὅτι,[41] but the agreement of
𝔓⁶⁶·⁷⁵ ℵ B C* D L 33 it co tells against its inclusion, and no modern editor
places καί in the text. Yet its presence in so many MSS is testimony that

---

[39] Cullmann's view, that the clause refers to the absolute time of the Prologue
(*Coniect. Neot.* 11 [1947], 31), need not, however, be positively rejected, for ἔμπροσθέν
need not be so restricted to precedence in rank as to exclude the priority of the Word's
existence (cf. Jn 8.58, and BDF 214 [1]).

[40] The only other occurrences of ὀπίσω in John are at 6.66; 18.6 and 20.14, on each
occasion in the phrase εἰς τὰ ὀπίσω.

[41] NA²⁷ lists A C³ Ws Q Y f¹·¹³ 𝔐 lat sy bomss.

a large part of the tradition found the initial ὅτι awkward, and therefore
preferred the reading with καί, which made it easy to interpret this clause
as a continuation of the words of the Baptist (thus Origen, Theodore of
Mopsuestia and many of the Fathers). Chrysostom and Cyril of
Alexandria, however, do not read καί, and interpret the clause as words
of the evangelist, here adding his own testimony to that of the Baptist.
ὅτι may then be considered a very loose connective, which scarcely
subordinates its clause at all (cf. BDF 456 [1]; MHT III 318); it may be
translated as *For the fact is, that...*

'Of his fullness we have all received', referring to that fullness of
grace and truth mentioned in 1.14e. **ἐκ τοῦ.** After verbs meaning *to take
from, to eat of,* the partitive genitive (used for the divided whole) is in NT
Greek regularly replaced by ἐκ or ἀπό followed by the genitive (BDF
169 [2]). (ἐκ τοῦ) **πληρώματος** is therefore the direct object of
ἐλάβομεν. The word πλήρωμα is not here employed with the sense it has
in Col 1.19; 2.9; Eph 1.23; 3.19; 4.13, much less in a sense akin to that
which it has in Gnosticism; the OT allusions in 1.14e (pp. 59-61) are
more than sufficient to indicate a more convincingly authentic meaning.
We have received of the fullness of that grace and truth whose light first
dawned at Sinai.[42]

It is difficult, if not impossible, to conceive of the words **ἡμεῖς
πάντες ἐλάβομεν** (in the past tense) on the lips of the Baptist, even
before the preaching of Jesus has begun, particularly when the evangelist
elsewhere distinguishes both the Baptist and his followers from the
disciples of Jesus. The simplest and most meaningful interpretation is to
accept these words (ἡμεῖς πάντες ἐλάβομεν) as an affective expression
of profound gratitude on the part of the evangelist for the fullness of
grace and truth received by himself, his own generation, and all future
ages. 'All of us—the Twelve, the three hundred, the five hundred, the
three thousand, the five thousand, the many tens of thousands of Jews, the
whole totality of believers, of those that were then, and are now, and that
shall be—have received of his fullness' (Chrysostom).

Next, defining further the object of ἐλάβομεν, is an epexegetical **καί**
(= *that is to say,* BDF 442 [9]) followed by **χάριν ἀντὶ χάριτος,** in the
accusative (not the genitive) as denoting the undivided whole (cf. BDF
169 [2]), so that it too is the direct object of ἐλάβομεν.

ἀντί occurs 22 times in the NT, but in the Johannine writings, only
here.

(i) According to BDF 208 and MHT III 258, its basic meaning is
instead of, in return for, so that it is often akin to a genitive of price (e.g.
Mk 10.45, λύτρον ἀντὶ πολλῶν. Some authors, therefore, staying close

---

[42] Bultmann explains the words in terms of 'sharing in the fullness of the divine
Being', which he then illustrates at length from Gnostic, Neo-Platonic and similar texts
(ETr 77 fn. 1). Contrast Schnackenburg (in John, the word *pleroma* has nothing to do
with Gnostic or cosmological speculations).

to this meaning *instead of,* suggest that χάριν ἀντὶ χάριτος denotes the *substitution* of one grace for another. χάριν ἀντὶ χάριτος is then most often taken to refer to the *replacing* of the grace of the Old Covenant by the grace of the New.[43] Chrysostom expounds this interpretation with enthusiasm, pointing to Paul's references to the arrival of a new kind of righteousness (Phil 3.6), of faith (Rom 1.17: ἐκ πίστεως ἐις πίστιν), and of sonship (Rom 9.4; 2 Cor 3.11), all realized in a New Covenant 'not like the covenant I made with your fathers', and promised long ago in Jer 31.31. Not surprisingly, this elucidation of John by Paul has for centuries found favour in the Church, and has declined only as exegetes have become more aware of the crucial distinctions to be observed between the theological systems of different NT writers. The strongest arguments in favour of this interpretation are that Jn 1.17, especially with its initial ὅτι, seems to point directly to it, and that it is the explanation favoured by the Greek Fathers.[44]

Nigel Turner (MHT III 258) asks whether it may not refer to the Spirit who *comes in place of* Jesus, but this too seems quite alien to the immediate context, when Jesus himself has not yet begun his ministry.

(ii) A. T. Robertson, however, argued impressively that the original etymological meaning of ἀντί is *face to face* ('suppose two men at each end of a log, facing each other'), and that this root sense is never lost. Thus when a fish and a snake are placed opposite each other, what father would choose ἀντὶ ἰχθύος ὄφιν (Lk 11.11; cf. Mt 5.38, ὀφθαλμὸν ἀντὶ ὀφθαλμου). There is thus a fundamental idea of correspondence, and therefore of making a comparison between the value of two objects, from which the use of ἀντί meaning *instead of,* or for a genitive of price, is derived: see *GGNT* 572-74. On the basis of this understanding of ἀντί, J. M. Bover subsequently argued that the grace received (χάριν) must therefore *correspond to* (ἀντί) the grace mentioned earlier (in v. 14), and that it is consequently not a matter of one grace simply *replacing* another, but of a creature's receiving grace which *corresponds to,* and is analogous to, that fullness of grace and truth which is possessed by Jesus Christ.[45] Bernard too liked this idea, referring sympathetically ('a better suggestion') to an essay much earlier than Bover's, by J. A. Robinson.[46]

[43] M. Black, in *JTS* (First Series) 42 (1941), 69-70, asked whether an Aramaic play on words, which the translator missed, might not underlie the Greek. Its meaning, based upon two different Aramaic words, each written חסדא (ḥisdaʾ), would have been 'and grace instead of shame'. The idea did not find favour, and Black himself did not include it in his second or third edition of *An Aramaic Approach.* Even if one grants the hypothesis of an underlying Aramaic text, it is impossible to imagine any Jew ever referring to any aspect of the Old Covenant as 'shame'.

[44] De la Potterie (142 fn. 59) lists Origen, Chrysostom, Theodore of Mopsuestia, Cyril of Alexandria, Theophylactus and Euthymius.

[45] 'Χάριν ἀντὶ χάριτος (Ioh. 1,16)', *Biblica* 6 (1925), 454-60.

[46] 'On the meanings of χάρις and χαριτοῦν', in *St Paul's Epistle to the Ephesians,* 2nd ed., 1909, p. 223.

The weak point of this second interpretation is that ἀντί is nowhere found with the meaning *corresponding to* in the LXX, in Hellenistic Greek or in the NT.[47]

(iii) The majority of modern commentators, however, interpret χάριν ἀντὶ χάριτος as denoting not substitution, but *accumulation by succession*, "the ceaseless stream of graces which succeed one another" (Schnackenburg), i.e. *grace upon grace* or *grace after grace*.[48] The parallel always cited is in Philo, *De post. Cain* 145: ...ἑτέρας [sc. χάριτας] ἀντ' ἐκείνων [sc. τῶν πρώτων χαρίτων] καὶ τρίτας ἀντι τῶν δευτέρων καὶ ἀεὶ νέας ἀντὶ παλαιοτέρων... ἐπιδίδωσιν. One may point also to a line of Theognis (344), ἀντ' ἀνιῶν ἀνίαι ('grief upon grief'), to Aeschylus (*Agamemnon* 1560), ὄνειδος ἥκει τόδ' ἀντ' ὀνείδους, and to Chrysostom (*De Sacerdotio* VI 13: Ben. ed.535D): σὺ δέ με ἐκπέμπεις ἑτέραν ἀνθ' ἑτέρας φροντίδα ἐνθείς ('you are sending me away after giving me one head-ache on top of another'). On this view, χάριν ἀντὶ χάριτος records the continuity of the divine gift under the Old and the New Covenant.[49]

(iv) De la Potterie has strongly challenged the modern majority, beginning with a criticism of its appeal to the text from Philo. That text, he points out, does not refer to an *accumulation* of graces, but to a continuous series of graces, each *replacing* the preceding ones. Further, if the third interpretation were correct, one would have expected not ἀντί, but ἐπί. Again, John does not write of *graces* (in the plural), as does Philo, but of χάρις (in the singular) both in 1.16 and in 1.17, thus indicating that he is referring to the replacement of one specific and definite grace by another, equally specific and definite.

De la Potterie's major contribution is to have stressed that it is not sufficient to examine the meaning of ἀντί on its own, and that the formula τι ἀντί τινος must be investigated. Four cases are possible.

---

[47] A similar interpretation found favour at the Renaissance (among writers as diverse as Luther (WA 46, 654, with a polemical note against the doctrine of merit), Toletus and Cornelius a Lapide. It may be noted that the doctrine which this second interpretation expresses, even though it is not exegetically well-founded (being based on the supposed meaning of ἀντί), need not be rejected by those who prefer the next interpretation, the third.

[48] De la Potterie lists more than twenty authors up to 1975, including Schlatter, Lagrange, Bultmann, Barrett, Schnackenburg (143 fn. 64).

[49] Augustine's words on the text ought to be mentioned here, for though not exegesis in the modern sense, they have become a locus classicus in the history of interpretation (*In Ioannem* III 8-10: Ben 306C-308). '(8) Accepimus enim de plenitudine eius, primo gratiam; et rursus accepimus gratiam, gratiam pro gratia. Quam gratiam primo accepimus? Fidem... (9) Quid est ergo, gratiam pro gratia? ...Consecutus autem istam gratiam fidei, eris iustus ex fide...et promereberis Deum vivendo ex fide: cum promerueris Deum vivendo ex fide, accipies praemium immortalitatis, et vitam aeternam. Et illa gratia est. Nam pro quo merito accipies vitam aeternam? Pro gratia...(10) Quod ergo praemium immortalitatis postea tribuit, dona sua coronat, non merita tua.' This was the dominant view in the West during the Middle Ages (e.g. Aquinas, *In Ioannem* Lect. X 3, fn. 206).

(i) Where the two terms are different, and two parties are involved, the meaning of ἀντί is *in return for, in exchange for*: e.g. Prov 17.13, ὅς ἀποδίδωσιν κακὰ ἀντὶ ἀγαθῶν ('if someone returns evil for good...'). See also 1 Macc 16.17. (ii) Where the two terms are different, but only one party is involved, ἀντί is best translated *in preference to*: e.g. Wis 7.10, προειλόμην αὐτὴν ἀντὶ φωτὸς ἔχειν ('I chose to have her [Wisdom] in preference to light'). (iii) Where the two terms are the same, and two parties are involved, ἀντί means *in exchange for*. There is a clear parallel in Euripides' *Helen*, at line 1234: χάρις γὰρ ἀντὶ χάριτος ἐλθέτω. The colloquial English rendering 'one good turn deserves another' may serve to indicate that χάρις ἀντὶ χάριτος could itself be a cliché in Greek. (iv) Where the two terms are the same, and only one party is involved, as in Jn 1.16, the meaning of ἀντί must be, literally, *instead of*, as the Greek Fathers maintained, but it is not inappropriate to add that in this case the context often implies a preference for one rather than the other, as in Wis 7.10, because a comparison is inescapably entailed. Thus the first interpretation of ἀντί in v. 16b may, and should be, upheld, though with the firm proviso that the Old Law is seen not as a burden, but as a grace, which is superseded by a grace that is more attractive still.[50]

The principles to be stressed are that the grace of the Old Covenant was not inadequate, but that it was preparatory; and that the grace of the New Covenant is definitive (ἐξουσία τέκνα θεοῦ γενέσθαι), for this life and the next.

17. ὅτι may once again (cf. 16) be translated as *For the fact is, that...*; here it is explanatory of v. 16.

ὁ νόμος. This first occurrence of ὁ νόμος in the Gospel is particularly significant, since it stands in (contrasting) parallelism with 'the grace and truth that came through Jesus Christ'. Here the word νόμος does not denote the Pentateuch as distinct from the Prophetical Books or the Writings, or the Pentateuch insofar as it contains legislation; but rather the whole body of the teaching contained in the Law, the Prophets and the Writings, considered as deriving from, and remaining faithful to, the inspiration of Moses, and as such, constituting the divinely authoritative basis of the faith and the socio-religious life of Israel.[51] The literal meaning of the Hebrew word 'Torah' is *instruction, direction, guidance,* and like it, the LXX translation νόμος represents a concept which is deeply rooted in the will of the gods.[52] The words Torah and νόμος are

[50] On the whole section see de la Potterie, *La Vérité*, 142-50.

[51] The wording is my own, but compare Dodd, *Interpretation*, 77, and especially S. Pancaro, *The Law in the Fourth Gospel*, 515, 534-46.

[52] See Kleinknecht in *TWNT* IV 1016-29. The words of Antigone may stand for the universal belief of ancient Greece:

Nor did I dream that thou, a mortal man,
Could'st by a breath annul and override

therefore far removed from the modern idea of statute law, alterable at will by a human legislature.[53] Neither Torah nor νόμος designates the arbitrary or authoritarian commands of an all-powerful Deity who is answerable to no-one, as Marcion, and many to this day, would have it. Even Augustine, when commenting on this text, is not entirely free from a negative assessment of the Law, because he, like Paul (indeed, more than Paul), considers Law mainly in one aspect of its existential reality, as exposing sin, but without enabling fallen humanity to resist it.[54] John by contrast looks upon the Law (*Torah, Nomos*) as it was intended to be by God, neither arbitrary nor oppressive, but rather the source of light and life (Ps 119.105, 107) to all God's people (cf. Jn 1.4-5); for the most basic fact about the Law is that it is the Word of God (see the whole of Ps 119).

διὰ Μωϋσέως ἐδόθη. 'The Law is regularly regarded in Jewish sources as a gift of God to Israel' (Barrett). He cites Josephus, *Ant.* VII 338 (τὰς ἐντολὰς αὐτοῦ καὶ τοὺς νόμους οὓς διὰ Μωϋσέος ἔδωκεν ἡμῖν), *Pirke Aboth* 1.1 and *Siphre Deut* 31.4 § 305 ('Blessed be God who gave the Law to Israel through Moses our teacher'). It is a gift given *through* (not *by*) Moses (compare Acts 7.53). In this clause John writes ἐδόθη, because the Law was a gift received by a servant to pass on to those for whom it was intended; but in the parallel, 17b, he writes ἐγένετο, which implies the sovereign authority (βασιλέως μετὰ ἐξουσίας) of Jesus Christ (Chrysostom). 'Mosis non sua est lex: Christi sua est gratia et veritas' (Bengel).

ἡ χάρις καὶ ἡ ἀλήθεια. In 𝔓66 it syh** , δέ is inserted before, and in W after, χάρις. This reading implies a certain tension between Church and synagogue; more significant is the negligible attestation in favour of it. The lack of support for δέ only confirms the interpretation of v. 16 as indicating not the replacement of one grace by another, but the continuity in God's bestowal of grace; it also justifies the cautionary remarks about hostility to the Old Law which are set out in the comment on ὁ νόμος at

> The immutable unwritten laws of Heaven.
> They were not born today nor yesterday;
> They die not; and none knoweth whence they sprang.
> (Sophocles, *Antigone* 453-57. Translation by F. Storr in the Loeb edition.)

[53] It is unfortunate that so many European languages translate the term as *law, loi, Gesetz, legge, ley*, thus giving the impression that the Torah is akin to what Europeans call 'statute law'. English cannot avoid this, but other languages are more fortunate, and have less excuse. 'Torah' would be more adequately rendered into Latin etc. by *ius, droit, Recht, diritto, derecho*, words which denote a corpus of legislation that includes, and is based upon, carefully defined fundamental principles of jurisprudence. Statute law is variable to an extent that *ius, droit, Recht* etc. are not.

[54] 'Non erat ista [gratia] in Veteri Testamento, quia lex minabatur, non opitulabatur; iubebat, non sanabat; langorem ostendebat, non auferebat: sed ille [Dominus] praeparabat medico venturo cum gratia et veritate' (*In Ioannem* III 14). Contrast Chrysostom (on 16b): Καὶ γὰρ τὰ τοῦ νόμου καὶ αὐτὰ χάριτος ἦν.

1.16. For ἡ χάρις καὶ ἡ ἀλήθεια, see on v. 14e. This is the last occurrence of the word χάρις in the Fourth Gospel.

διὰ ’Ιησοῦ Χριστοῦ. The only other occurrence of the proper name 'Jesus Christ' is at 17.3, where the words are almost certainly a late addition to the text. If we discount this instance in 17.3, the formula in 20.31 ('that you may believe that Jesus is the Christ'), taken in conjunction with the wording here in 1.17b, may well represent an *inclusio* embracing the entire Gospel, in which the reader is at the end invited to profess faith in Jesus as the Christ, the Son of God, through whom (διά) the grace and truth promised in the Old Covenant *were brought into being* (ἐγένετο). See the comments above on ἐδόθη in this verse, on ἐγένετο in 1.3 (p. 12), and on the variant reading ὃ γέγονεν ἐν αὐτῷ ζωὴ ἦν (pp. 14-15).

18a. θεὸν οὐδεὶς ἑώρακεν πώποτε. Four words, which could stand in any sequence, are here skilfully ordered, closing the Prologue with supreme economy. As in 18b, any conjunction would have weakened, probably destroyed, the strength of this verse. The absence of the article before θεόν implies that no one had ever (previously) seen God *qua* God,[55] though they might have 'seen' him under shadows and figures at Mamre, at the burning bush, or in a vision (Gen 18; Exod 3; Isa 6). That is, no one had ever seen and known God in the way one knows oneself or another human being (cf. Exod 33.18-20). Contrast the past tense in 1 Jn 4.12 (θεὸν οὐδεὶς πώποτε τεθέαται) with the future tense in 1 Jn 3.2 (ὅμοιοι αὐτῷ ἐσόμεθα, ὅτι ὀψόμεθα αὐτὸν καθώς ἐστιν) and with 1 Cor 13.12. J. H. Moulton calls the perfect with πώποτε (1.18; 5.37; 8.33) 'an aoristic perfect of unbroken continuity' (MHT I 144; see also III 68f. 84). The sense is therefore that no one has ever, here on earth, seen God directly, face to face, in his divinity, though Christians see God's glory indirectly, in the humanity of the Word made flesh. See above on 14cd and compare 2 Cor 4.6 on the knowledge of the glory of God in the face of Christ.

18b. The evidence for the text of 18b is very finely balanced between **μονογενὴς θεός** (UBS[3] and NA[27]), and **ὁ μονογενὴς υἱός** (Tischendorf and von Soden). The former is preferred by the editors of the UBS[3] and NA[27] on the ground that it has earlier and better support among the Greek MSS of the Gospel, although ο μ. θ., with the article, is much better attested among the early Fathers. The latter, **ὁ μονογενὴς υἱός**, is the reading most widely attested among the totality of the MSS, the versions and the Fathers. Schnackenburg and Barrett rightly comment that the sense is substantially unaltered whether one reads ὁ μονογενὴς θεός or ὁ μονογενὴς υἱός (both prefer the former, not least because of 𝔓[66.75]). The shortest reading (**ὁ μονογενής**), though not accepted by any

[55] See the comment of J. H. Moulton at 14d.

of the major modern editions of the Greek NT, has much to commend it
(see UBS). For the detail, see Excursus IV, 'Longer Notes on Textual
Criticism 3', and the comment on μονογενοῦς παρὰ πατρός under
1.14d.

If μονογενὴς θεός (without the article) is accepted as the reading,
the most accurate translation would be *someone quite unique, and divine*
(so *The Translator's NT*, 1973, 452); if the article is included, one might
say *the one and only God* (*unicus deus*). If ὁ μονογενὴς υἱός is
preferred, the translation would be *the one and only Son* (cf. RSV, *the
only Son*). If ὁ μονογενής is accepted, then the entire clause may be
translated, with due respect for English idiom, by transposing ἐκεῖνος to
the beginning of the clause, and using an adverb, *utterly*, to ensure that
the force of the article be not lost. Accordingly, *that utterly unique One* is
the version used above on p. 49; the present writer's second choice would
be *that one and only Son.*

ὁ ὢν εἰς τὸν κόλπον τοῦ πατρός. Though it is often said that 'in
the Koine εἰς and ἐν are freely interchanged', this does not apply to all
NT books: in Matthew, in the Pauline and Johannine epistles, and in
Revelation, the old classical distinction between εἰς and ἐν is still very
much alive (MHT III 254-57; BDF 205-206). Also, we may add, in John,
and the distinction is particularly significant in this text.

In the major modern English versions the lemma is rendered: (i)
'which/who is in the bosom of the Father' (AV = KJV RV RSV); (ii)
'who is at the Father's side' (NIV NAB); (iii) 'who is nearest to the
Father's heart' (NEB REB JB); (iv) 'who is close to the Father's heart'
(NJB NRSV). Option (i) is clearly based on the assumption that in this
verse εἰς is equivalent to ἐν, which is how the Latin versions understood
it (*in sinu patris*). The other renderings, made after 1950, when NT
scholarship had become more sensitive to the distinction between the two
prepositions, avoid 'in'. Indeed, (iii) and (iv) gently hint that εἰς here
connotes more than close physical presence together, which is the sense
of ἐν τῷ κόλπῳ in 13.23.[56]

The metaphor is frequent in the OT to describe the most intimate of
human relationships: it is used of marriage (Deut 13.7 [6]; 28.54, 56 etc.),
of mother and child (1 Kgs 3.20; 17.19), and of God's care for Israel
(Num 11.12: for further detail see Schnackenburg). Here in Jn 1.18 the
phrase is probably intended to answer to the words ἐν ἀρχῇ ἦν ὁ λόγος
πρὸς τὸν θεόν: just as the pre-Incarnate Logos was, *in the beginning,
very close to God* (see on 1b), so the utterly unique human individual,
Jesus Christ, is at the end described as being permanently (ὁ ὢν) εἰς τὸν
κόλπον τοῦ πατρός. What exactly does this phrase mean?

---

[56] Compare the distinction between εἰς τὸν κόλπον 'Αβραάμ and ἐν τοῖς κόλποις
αὐτοῦ, Lk 16.22-23. One may note also that it would be a mistake to read into the
replacement of the word *bosom* by *side* or *heart* anything more than the updating of an
obsolescent metaphor.

The Greek Fathers (Chrysostom, Theophylactus, Theodore of Mopsuestia) and several Latin writers (Marius Victorinus, Thomas Aquinas,
Maldonatus) interpret the phrase as referring to the consubstantiality of
the Father and the Son. Augustine gives a psychologizing interpretation,
which was to become common in the Middle Ages: the Son knows the
secrets of the Father, and can therefore reveal them.[57] Both types of interpretation assume that the verse refers to intra-trinitarian relationships, and
that the preposition εἰς means *in*. De la Potterie, with a number of
(mostly French) writers, has argued for the translation, *qui est tourné vers
le sein du Père*, meaning that Jesus during his earthly life was ever
attentive to, and responsive to, the love of the Father.[58] In the second
edition of the French *Bible de Jérusalem* (1973) this translation replaces
dans le sein du Père of the 1956 edition.

The most satisfactory interpretation, however, is to take ὁ ὢν εἰς τὸν
κόλπον τοῦ πατρός as referring to the return of Jesus Christ into the
bosom of the Father. This interpretation, formerly upheld by B. Weiss, H.
J. Holtzmann, Zahn, Tillmann, Thüsing etc., has been newly presented by
René Robert.[59] Robert reasons that Greek provides many examples of a
verb followed by εἰς which express situation in a place and thereby
imply a preceding movement to that place. The construction is both
classical, and common.[60] There is a fine example in Xenophon (*Anabasis*
I ii 2), παρῆσαν εἰς Σάρδεις, which is neatly rendered *they presented
themselves at Sardis*.[61] Compare Jn 21.4 ('Jesus stood on [εἰς] the
shore').[62] No one denies that one of the central themes of John is that
Jesus, when his earthly mission is accomplished, will return to heaven,
whence he came (3.13; 6.62; 8.21), to the Father who sent him (7.33;
13.1, 3; 16.5; 17.11, 13), there to be glorified with the glory which he had
before the world was, with the Father (17.5). Indeed, in John, this is the
only message which the risen Jesus gives to Mary Magdalen (20.7). It
makes excellent sense therefore to translate ὁ ὢν εἰς τὸν κόλπον τοῦ
πατρός as *who is now returned into the bosom of the Father*, thus not

---

[57] Quid est, in sinu Patris? In secreto Patris...secretum Patris sinus Patris vocatur (*in loco*). This was the interpretation accepted by J. H. Bernard.

[58] This is the sense which de la Potterie gives also to πρὸς τὸν θεόν in 1.1b. See 'L'emploi de εἰς dans S. Jean et ses incidences théologiques', *Biblica* 43 (1962), 366-87, and also in *La Vérité*, 228-39.

[59] 'Celui qui est de retour dans le sein du Père (Jean 1,18)', *Revue Thomiste* 85 (1985), 457-63.

[60] W. W. Goodwin, *A Greek Grammar*, 1205.1, cites Thucydides I 96, αἱ ξύνοδοι ἐς τὸ ἱερὸν ἐγίγνοντο (i.e. involving the idea of going into the temple to hold the synods), and other examples. See also LSJ *s.v.* παρεῖναι I 5 = *to arrive at*. Abel, *Grammaire* §48 c Rem. II, instances Mk 13.3, καθημένου αὐτοῦ εἰς τὸ Ὄρος τῶν Ἐλαιῶν, Heb 11.9, πίστει παρῴκησεν εἰς γῆν τῆς ἐπαγγελίας, tc.

[61] The translation given by Carlton L. Brownson in the Loeb edition (1921).

[62] And what we may call a reverse example in Jn 20.7, χωρὶς ἐντετυλιγμένον εἰς ἕνα τόπον, 'rolled up [and put] into a separate place'. See *JG* 2305-309.

only giving an *inclusio* with πρὸς τὸν θεόν in 1.1b, but also, perhaps, recalling to the reader the prophetic word of Isa 55.10-11.

One serious objection to this interpretation is that it is nowhere found in the Greek Fathers. At this point Origen is not extant, but Chrysostom in his commentary and elsewhere, while citing the lemma as εἰς τὸν κόλπον, always interprets it as equivalent to ἐν τῷ κόλπῳ; and Cyril does likewise. Both Chrysostom and Cyril, and their contemporaries (Gregory of Nyssa, Epiphanius) appear to have understood the two Greek phrases as synonymous, as indeed they had by their time become. So did the Latin versions, which, without exception, render *qui est in sinu patris*.[63] But if the evangelist in his day used εἰς and ἐν with different meanings, then subsequent writers, by not adverting to this, would have misinterpreted this text; and there is much evidence to support the view that John did distinguish between εἰς and ἐν.[64]

Another important proposal concerning this lemma must be mentioned.[65] If in the Prologue the term Logos is equivalent to the Memra, may not the words ὁ ὤν in v. 18 be a conscious allusion to Exod 3.15, 'He Who Is'? The same participle occurs with this sense in the book of Revelation (1.4, 8; 4.8; 11.17; 16.5), though with reference to the Lord God, not to Jesus Christ. There are, however, in John's Gospel four verses where ἐγώ εἰμι is used absolutely, of Jesus Christ, and without any grammatical complement, namely Jn 8.24, 28, 58 and 13.19. In three of these (8.24, 28; 13.19) the words ὅτι ἐγώ εἰμι clamour to be interpreted against the background of Isa 43.10 (LXX) which in turn points back unmistakably to the revelation in Exod 3.15.[66] This is why, in each of these cases, the AV = KJV RV and RSV translate ὅτι ἐγώ εἰμι as 'that I am he', the NEB and REB, 'that I am what I am'. The awesome implication of these words becomes fully transparent only when the rendering of ὅτι ἐγώ εἰμι makes the cross-reference to Exodus abundantly clear, e.g. *that I am He Who Is*.[67] Consequently, if the term Logos in the Prologue does represent the concept of Memra, the possibility that the words ὁ ὤν at 1.18 are an allusion to 'He Who Is' should not be too

---

[63] The patristic references, both Greek and Latin, are most readily accessible in Tischendorf 8a.

[64] Compare *JG* 2305-308 and 2706-13 *passim*. On the equivalence of εἰς and ἐν, see MHT I 62-63 and 234-35, and Robertson, *Grammar*, 591-92.

[65] L. Devillers, 'Exégèse et théologie de Jean 1.18', *Revue Thomiste* 89 (1989), 181-217.

[66] Isa 43.10-11 reads in the LXX: γένεσθέ μοι μάρτυρες, κἀγὼ μάρτυς, λέγει κύριος ὁ θεός, καὶ ὁ παῖς, ὃν ἐξελεξάμην, ἵνα γνῶτε καὶ πιστεύσητε καὶ συνῆτε ὅτι ἐγώ εἰμι, ἔμπροσθέν μου οὐκ ἐγένετο ἄλλος θεὸς καὶ μετ' ἐμὲ οὐκ ἔσται· ἐγὼ ὁ θεός, καὶ οὐκ ἔστιν πάρεξ ἐμοῦ σῴζων. πιστεύειν ὅτι ἐγώ εἰμι occurs in Jn 8.24 and 13.19, γνῶναι ὅτι in 8.28.

[67] Jesus' statement is then so apparently blasphemous that on each occasion he immediately affirms that the Father is on his side ('I do nothing on my own authority, and he who sent me is with me', 8.28-29; 'he who receives me receives him who sent me', 13.20). Cf. Dodd, *Interpretation*, 95-96.

hastily discounted, for there is much patristic evidence which identifies the Word, the revealer on earth of the invisible Father, with the one who spoke from the burning bush.[68] Though, in the present writer's opinion, the primary sense of the phrase ὁ ὢν κτλ. refers to the return of the μονογενής into the glory of the Father, this does not exclude the possibility that the same words may hold a secondary meaning also, which, though not evident at first reading, will disclose itself to the reader who comes to understand the deepest truth of the Gospel (cf. Jn 20.28, 31). John 1.18b could then be turned into English as 'that utterly unique One [or: that one and only Son], He Who Is now returned into the bosom of the Father...'

ἐκεῖνος ἐξηγήσατο. The English versions cited above under 18b render these words as (i) 'hath declared him' (AV = KJV RV); (ii) 'has made him known' (RSV NRSV NEB REB NIV JB NJB); (iii) 'has revealed him' (NAB). The second version has a clear over-all majority, and the third is apparently a rank outsider.

The original, and etymologically self-evident, meaning of ἐξηγεῖσθαι is *to lead*, but this sense, though frequent in Classical Greek (LSJ), is, according to the lexicons, found nowhere in the LXX, the NT or cognate literature (BDAG). This last statement has recently been challenged.

In the NT, the verb occurs six times, five in the Lukan writings (at Lk 24.35; Acts 10.8; 15.11, 14; 21.19), and once here, in Jn 1.18. It is generally agreed that in the Greek of NT times, the verb ἐξηγεῖσθαι is used in three senses. It can mean *to recount, relate, report, describe, explain*, and this is the sense usually assigned to it in the five Lukan texts

---

[68] Justin may be a witness to a tradition of Palestinian, perhaps even of Samaritan, origin, when in terms reminiscent of Jn 1.14, 18, he links the invisible nature of the Father and the Incarnation of the Son with the episode in Exod 3.14-15. 'Neither Abraham nor Isaac nor Jacob, nor any other of humankind has seen the Father who is both the ineffable Lord of all things without exception (ἁπλῶς) and of Christ himself...whom the Father decreed should be begotten of the Virgin, and who once, long ago (πότε) became fire in order to speak to Moses out of the bush' (*Dial.* 127, 4; also in 128, 1). Similarly, in *1 Apol.* 62, 3 we read that 'our Christ conversed with Moses in the form of fire from a bush' (ἐν ἰδέᾳ πυρὸς ἐκ βατοῦ προσωμίλησεν αὐτῷ ὁ ἡμέτερος Χριστός), and in 63, 7, that 'an angel of the Lord spoke to Moses in flames of fire from the bush, and said, I am He Who Is, God of Abraham, God of Isaac, God of Jacob...', an idea repeated in 63.17. Irenaeus too makes the connection between the Word and the text of Exod 3.14, in his *Proof of the Apostolic Preaching*, chs. 2 and 46; this connection is all the more significant since elsewhere he ascribes and applies the phrase 'He Who Is' both to the Father and to the Son, and equally to each (*Adv. Haer.* III 6 2). Devillers refers (*Revue Thomiste* 89 [1989], 195-99) to two surveys of patristic usage, one by M. Harl, 'Citations et commentaires d'Exode 3.14 chez les Pères grecs des quatre premiers siècles', in *Dieu et l'Etre, Exégèse d'Exode 3.14 et de Coran 20.11-24*, Paris, 1978, 87-108, the other by G. Madec, '"Ego sum qui sum" de Tertullien à Jérôme"', in the same work, 121-39. One example, from Ambrose, must suffice: 'non Pater in rubo, non Pater in eremo, sed Filius Moysi locutus est'.

just mentioned. It is frequently used, as in Classical Greek, as a technical term meaning *to reveal, to impart to initiates* officially the secrets of the mystery-religions.[69] In Josephus, it is used with the sense *to interpret* the Law (*War* I 649; 2.162; *Ant.* XVIII 81). See LSJ and BDAG. All three usages would sit well with the preaching activity of the historical Jesus as described in our extant sources.

In 1977 de la Potterie challenged the accuracy of these common interpretations of the verb when they are applied to Jn 1.18.[70] The first sense, correct for Luke, he judges inadequate for John. The second and the third he finds oversimplified, alleging that they are uncritically reliant on a number of classical texts which have been regularly repeated since Wettstein (1751).[71] His criticism is that neither the noun ἐξηγητής, nor the verb ἐξηγεῖσθαι is ever found in Classical Greek with the meaning *to reveal*. In the classical texts quoted, wherever ἐξηγεῖσθαι is used of the gods, it means *to issue laws, to make edicts*; wherever it is used of 'exegetes' or diviners at sanctuaries like Delphi, it means that they *interpret* oracles or *explain* the meaning of laws.[72] There is no example of its ever being used to denote *revealing* new truths.[73] The translation *to reveal* cannot therefore be justified in terms of, or by references to, Greek or Hellenistic religion.

But, de la Potterie continued, that does not imply that ἐξηγεῖσθαι may not in fact, bear, at Jn 1.18, the sense *to reveal*, provided that this is interpreted against a Hebrew background. That would be a quite acceptable rendering of Job 28.27, at the end of the passage in which the writer asks, 'Where shall wisdom be found?' (vv. 12-28).[74] In τότε εἶδεν

---

[69] ἐξηγηταὶ δ᾽ ἐκαλοῦντο οἱ τὰ περὶ τῶν διοσημιῶν καὶ τὰ τῶν ἄλλων ἱερῶν διδάσκοντες ('Those who teach about celestial omens and other sacred matters were called "exegetes"'): Pollux 8, 124, cited in BDAG.

[70] *La Vérité*, 213-28.

[71] *Novum Testamentum Graece* I 841-42. The texts are easily accessible in F. Büchsel's article in *TWNT* II 910. De la Potterie lists a number of commentators, including Westcott, H. J. Holtzmann, Barrett and Brown, as upholding that the verb cannot be satisfactorily explained except by references to Greek or Hellenistic religion, while noting that others, e.g. Godet, Lagrange, Tillmann and Schnackenburg are 'either more circumspect or even reject the connection' (*La Vérité*, 215 fn. 291).

[72] There are two very clear examples of this meaning in Plato, in the *Republic* IV 427c, and in the *Laws* VI 759cd.

[73] On 218-19 fn. 308, he writes that the sense *reveal* is nowhere attested in the *TLG*, LSJ or any other standard Greek Lexicon, and caps this with a quotation from A.-J. Festugière: 'Je ne connais en vérité aucun texte où ἐξηγεῖσθαι = "donner une révélation"', in the latter's *Observations stylistiques sur l'Evangile de S. Jean*, Paris, 1974, 132.

[74] Lev 14.57 is clearly irrelevant. Four other texts bear the meaning *to recount, relate* (Judg 7.13; 4 Kgdms 8.5; 1 Macc 3.26; 2 Macc 2.13); 1 Chr 16.24 and Job 12.8 speak of *declaring* God's power or glory, which might include the secondary idea of revealing it by recounting it. So in Prov 28.13b the word *confess* could be construed as including revelation of one's sins to others. But all this is scarcely 'revelation' in the usual theological sense of the term.

αὐτὴν καὶ ἐξηγήσατο αὐτήν, ἐξηγήσατο could well be translated as *revealed* or—with a weaker sense—*made known*. One may compare also the cognate verb ἐκδιηγεῖσθαι in Sir 18.5 (τίς προσθήσει ἐκδιη-γήσασθαι τὰ ἐλέη αὐτοῦ); Barrett calls attention also, and particularly, to Sir 43.31, τίς ἑόρακεν αὐτὸν καὶ ἐκδιηγήσεται, 'Who has seen him and can describe him?', to which Jn 1.18 might seem a direct answer. ἐκεῖνος—'that one', the utterly unique One (ἐκεῖνος, particularly the resumptive ἐκεῖνος, being frequent in John).

One problem remains. The verb ἐξηγήσατο has no direct object. Nearly all translations supply one, usually 'him', that is, the Father, and it can rightly be argued that this must imply and include the Son (cf. Jn 14.5-11). Indeed, de la Potterie, in *La Vérité* (228) went so far as to translate 1.18b as 'Le Fils unique, tourné vers le sein du Père, il fut, lui, la révélation'. Later, however, in response to an article by R. Robert,[75] he abandoned this interpretation, pleading instead for the meaning *to walk in front*, and therefore for the translation *he is the one who has opened the way*.[76] Robert countered with a vigorous defence of what he had originally proposed: ἐξηγήσατο in 1.18 is intended to carry a double meaning, and to imply both *to guide* and *to explain*, just as both senses are implicit in Jn 14.6 ('I am the way...no one comes to the Father except through me'), particularly when this verse is taken in conjunction with 14.2 ('I am going, to prepare a place for you'). As a translation, Robert suggested *it is he who was the guide—it is he who was the way*, and even declared a preference (if a language cannot sustain the double meaning) for the latter.[77] The double meaning would, of course, dovetail with his version of 18b ('now returned into the bosom of the Father'). Indeed, his interpretation of the whole sentence from ὁ ὢν to ἐξηγήσατο has everything to commend it.[78] In an endeavour to capture all these nuances, the translation given above renders ἐξηγήσατο by three verbs: ... *has been our guide, and shown and led the way.*

If further evidence be needed to discern the evangelist's mind, there remain the Targums. In *Neofiti I*, at Exod 3.14, we read: 'And the Lord said to Moses: I am who I am. And he said: Thus shall you say to the

[75] Robert argued that it is not necessary to choose between the two meanings of ἐξηγεῖσθαι, *to guide* and *to recount*. 'La double intention du mot final du prologue johannique', *Revue Thomiste* 87 (1987), 435-41.

[76] '"C'est lui qui a ouvert la voie", La finale du prologue johannique', *Biblica* 69 (1988), 340-70.

[77] 'Le mot final du prologue johannique. A propos d'un article récent', *Revue Thomiste* 89 (1989), 279-88.

[78] One may mention also that Robert has also drawn attention to a very close parallel in Plato's *Republic* V, where, because of the presence of the verb *to follow*, the double meaning of *guiding* and *explaining* underlying ἐξηγεῖσθαι is but thinly veiled. Ἴθι δή, ἀκολούθησόν μοι τῇδε, ἐὰν αὐτὸ ἀμῇ γέ πη ἱκανῶς ἐξηγησώμεθα. 'Come, then, follow me on this line, to see if we can somehow or other explain it adequately' (474c). See also Book IV 427c. 'Un précedent platonicien à l'équivoque de Jean 1.18', *Revue Thomiste* 90 (1990), 634-39.

children of Israel: He who said and the world was from the beginning, and is to say again to it: Be!, and it will be, has sent me to you.'[79] The echoes of Jn 1.1-3 are unmistakable, and the thought certainly matches Boismard's vision of the return of humanity to be once more in the bosom of the Father (see Excursus I). These ideas are even more prominently marked in the same Targum at Exod 33.14: 'The Glory of my Shekinah will accompany amongst you and will prepare a resting place for you' (cf. Jn 14.2-3).[80] The idea of the Lord's going before Israel to *prepare a resting-place* for the people recurs in this Targum at Num 10.33 and Deut 1.33, where the Hebrew infinitive לָתוּר (lātur), eaning literally *to seek out by exploring, to scout out*, is rendered in the Aramaic by the verb לְמִתְקְנָה (lĕmitqānāh), the literal meaning of which is *to acquire, to take possession of*, and therefore *to prepare a place*. The phrasing is particularly poignant at Deut 1.32-33, which read: 'You did not believe *in the name of the Word* of the Lord your God, who led before you on the way to *prepare for you a place* for your encampment'.[81]

John 1.14, *we beheld his glory*, is replete with references to the memory of Israel's experiences at Sinai, which in turn remind the reader that even after the theophany on the high mountain, there was a lifetime's journey ('forty years') still to travel before the entry into the Promised Land. John 1.18 is then a declaration that, though no one has ever seen God, Jesus Christ during his earthly life has made known a God the like of whom the world had never seen, never imagined, never thought of. Like a new Moses, he leads God's people all the way to the Promised Land; and being a far greater leader than Moses, he has himself entered into it (Jn 14.2: compare Heb 3.3–4.16; 10.11-25; 12.2, ἀφορῶντες εἰς τὸν τῆς πίστεως ἀρχηγὸν καὶ τελειωτὴν Ἰησοῦν).

The evangelist, as he was writing these last lines of the Prologue, must have been fully aware that his Gospel was quite different from any other gospel book then circulating. Towards the end, in the discourse after the supper, he justifies the inclusion of the many novel teachings in his book by declaring that Jesus had promised to send, after his departure from the earth, another Paraclete, the Spirit of truth, to lead the disciples into all truth (Jn 14.16-20, 25-26; 15.26-27; 16.7, 12-15). If therefore ὁ ὢν εἰς τὸν κόλπον τοῦ πατρός be translated as *who is now returned to the bosom of the Father*, the word ἐξηγήσατο must imply that all the teaching given in the Fourth Gospel, long after Jesus' departure, by the Holy Spirit of truth, is also guaranteed by Jesus' authority (14.25-26; 15.26-27). Only then would the disciples begin to perceive that there was a divinely willed purpose even in the apparent failure of Jesus' life on earth.

---

[79] ETr by McNamara, 412.
[80] ETr by McNamara, 510.
[81] ETr by McNamara, 444. Compare the wording in Jn 1.12c and 14.2.

For the Synoptics, and for Paul, the crucifixion represents, in worldly terms, the execution of the wholly innocent Jesus, and justice therefore demands that God reverse this crime by the bodily resurrection (cf. Acts 2.22-36). But that leaves unanswered the question, 'If God is just, why does he not restore to life all who are unjustly executed, and why does he permit them to be executed in the first place?' The Fourth Gospel faces up to this question by boldly affirming that God so loved the world that he sent his only Son into the world, to display before the world the extent of his love (3.16). The message of John's Gospel is that Jesus, by voluntarily embracing the Cross,[82] has offered one perfect sacrifice (17.19a: καὶ ὑπὲρ αὐτῶν ἐγὼ ἁγιάζω ἐμαυτόν) which has achieved the salvation of the world (see on Jn 19.30, τετέλεσται). ἵνα ὦσιν καὶ αὐτοὶ ἡγιασμένοι ἐν ἀληθείᾳ (17.19b). Christians too are divinely called, generation after generation, to lead the world to advance out of barbarism by 'redeeming the time'[83] until human history reaches its close. Only someone utterly unique, He Who Is now returned into the bosom of the Father, could have shown and led the way.

---

[82] καὶ βαστάζων ἑαυτῷ τὸν σταυρόν at 19.17.
[83] ἐν σοφίᾳ περιπατεῖτε πρὸς τοὺς ἔξω τὸν καιρὸν ἐξαγοραζόμενοι (Col 4.5; cf. Eph 5.16).

EXCURSUS I

THE STRUCTURE OF THE PROLOGUE

The extent of agreement or disagreement about the plan or structure of the Prologue may be readily discerned from the way in which the major editions of the Greek NT divide it.

Tischendorf 8[a] (one paragraph, divided by capital letters)	1–5		6–8	9–18 [or: 9–14 and 15–18?][1]		
WH (one paragraph, divided by major and minor spaces, and capitals)	1	2–5 6–8	9–10	11–12 14(15)–18		
Von Soden (one paragraph, divided by spaces and capitals)	1–5		6–8	9–13	14	15	16–18
Nestle[1-22] (one paragraph, divided by spaces and capitals: Nestle[25], paragraph at 14)	1–5		6–8	9–13	25§	14–17	18
Vogels (one paragraph, divided by capitals)	1–5		6–8	9–13	14–18		
Merk (by paragraphs)	1–5		§ 6–8 § 9–13	§ 14–18			
Bover (divided by paragraphs, and by capital at 9)	1–5		§ 6–8 9–13	§ 14–18			
NA[27] (by paragraphs and capitals: by space and capital at 18)	1–5		§ 6–8 § 9–13	§ 14–17 18			
UBS[3] (by paragraphs and by capital at 9, but not at 18)	1–5		§ 6–8 9–13	§ 14–18			

[1] It is unclear whether in 1.15 the initial iota of Ἰωάννης has an upper case solely because it is a proper name, or because it also represents the beginning of a new section (probably, one feels, the latter).

It is helpful to compare also the variations between some of the major English language editions of modern times. The RV of 1881 has an undifferentiated paragraph, so that, setting aside versions by private individuals, editorial division into paragraphs began in practice with the RSV of 1946. All the divisions noted below are into paragraphs, and the versions are grouped not by date but by family.

RSV ([1]1946, [2]1952)	1–5	6–8	9–13	14–18 (= TNT)		
NRSV (1989)	1–5	6–9	10–13	14–18		
NIV (1978)	1–2	3–5	6–9	10–13	14	15–18
NEB ([1]1961, [2]1970)	1–5	6–9	10–14	15		16–18 (= REB)
REB (1989)	1–5	6–9	10–14	15		16–18 (= NEB)
JB (1966) and NJB (1985)	1–5	6–8	9–14 15	16–18		
NAB (1986)	1–5	6–9	10–11	12–13	14	15–18
TNT = BFBS (1973)	1–5	6–8	9–13	14–18 (= RSV)		
TEV = GNB (1966)	1–5	6–9	10–13	14	15	16–18

The disagreements here mostly concern the placing of vv. 9, 14 and 15, and are of little significance. Verse 9 is essentially a connective between vv. 8 and 10, necessary to avoid confusion about the subject of the verb in v. 10 (see the commentary), but whether it is attached to v. 8 or to v. 10 is, as far as its meaning goes, irrelevant; either placing is equally satisfactory. The NEB = REB and the JB = NJB are exceptional in attaching v. 14 to the foregoing verses, for no editor of the Greek text has this arrangement; it would be interesting to know how many non-English translations arrange it so (the German *Einheitsübersetzung* of 1980 does). Their reason for doing so is probably to keep v. 14 with other verses of a hymn (see below), which v. 15 is certainly not. Verse 15 is clearly an interpolation, to be separated and detached (e.g. by brackets, as in the RSV and NRSV) both from what precedes and what follows. It is clear from the pattern of paragraphing that editors are in general in agreement about the broad structure of the Prologue.

Given this very high measure of agreement about the structure of the Prologue as it now stands, it is somewhat surprising to discover what a wide variation exists when writers come to describe the contents of the different sections. By far the most popular description (and in the present writer's view, rightly so) is that which sees vv. 1-5 as speaking of the primordial existence of the Logos, and of its role in creation and history, of vv. 6-13 as outlining the historical advent of the Logos into the world, and of vv. 14-18 as celebrating the Incarnation of the Logos. Others who accept this same division have seen it not as an historical progression but as three concentric circles: that is, these writers understand the Prologue as spelling out first the revelation of the Logos in general (vv. 1-5), secondly, as telling of it in greater detail by reference to John the Baptist, and to the rejection of Jesus by his contemporaries (vv. 6-13), and finally, as celebrating the blessings of faith which through the Incarnation come to believers (vv. 14-18). This is practically the opinion of Godet, except that he, with clearer logic, ends the second section at v. 11 and attaches

vv. 12-13 to the third section, labelling the three sections 'The Word–Unbelief–Faith'.[2]

Westcott's quite personal analysis bespeaks a profoundly reflective theological mind, pastorally engaged. Part I consists simply of v. 1, 'The Word in his Absolute, Eternal Being'; Part II (vv. 2-18) is entitled 'The Word in Relation to Creation', subdivided into the essential facts (vv. 2-5), the historic manifestation of the Word generally (vv. 6-13), and the Incarnation as apprehended by personal experience (vv. 14-18). Though the angle is personal, and slightly unusual, the understanding of the text is much the same as in Godet and other scholars of the age. But with Westcott's death in 1901 (his commentary, edited posthumously by his son, did not appear until 1908), an era came to an end.

The first edition of Loisy's commentary (1903) set a new standard of acute critical observation for work on the Fourth Gospel. Its opening words affirm that the first five verses are in themselves a kind of general preface which summarizes in an abstract manner the theme of the Gospel, with the sole aim of linking it, from the start, and definitively, to the notion of the Logos, which will be mentioned only once more, later in the prologue, and never again in the body of the work. This general preface consists of ten propositions which fall into three groups, and each one of them is linked to the preceding proposition by repeating either the last word, or the most important word, of that earlier proposition (a process called, sometimes, *concatenatio*). In each group, the first proposition is presented as an assertion, the second as a development, and the third as a conclusion. The underlining corresponds to that of Loisy, 152.

> 1 Ἐν ἀρχῇ ἦν ὁ λόγος,
>   καὶ ὁ λόγος ἦν πρὸς τὸν θεόν,
>   καὶ θεὸς ἦν ὁ λόγος.
>
> 2 οὗτος ἦν ἐν ἀρχῇ πρὸς τὸν θεόν.
> 3 πάντα δι' αὐτοῦ ἐγένετο,
>   καὶ χωρὶς αὐτοῦ ἐγένετο οὐδὲ ἕν.
>
> 4 ὃ γέγονεν | ἐν αὐτῷ ζωὴ ἦν,
>   καὶ ἡ ζωὴ ἦν τὸ φῶς τῶν ἀνθρώπων·
> 5 καὶ τὸ φῶς ἐν τῇ σκοτίᾳ φαίνει,
>   καὶ ἡ σκοτία αὐτὸ οὐ κατέλαβεν.

(It will be observed that the connecting words of v. 2 sit rather awkwardly next to v. 1 and to v. 3: see the commentary, and see below in this excursus.) Loisy then proposes that, after this general abstract statement, vv. 6-18 represent an historical preface; the use of ἐγένετο in v. 6 marks the transition to history, as in Mk 1.4 and Lk 1.5. This second section starts by setting the Baptist's mission in the context of that of

---

[2] French 3rd ed., 1885; ETr I (1899), 326-28, and 381-86. He supplies names, but not references, for nineteenth-century scholars advocating the views referred to in this paragraph.

Jesus, first in a general way, dwelling on the unbelief of so many (vv. 6-13), then in a more precise way, pointing to the public manifestation of the Word made flesh (vv. 14-18). Lagrange (1925) summarizes the message of vv. 1-18 in practically the same terms, though in different words, and divides it into four parts (vv. 1-5, 6-8, 9-13, 14-18).

J. H. Bernard's work, published in 1928, one year after his death, is perhaps the first commentary (as distinct from an article) seriously to propose for examination a hypothetical reconstruction of a Logos hymn similar to those found in the Wisdom literature of the OT. Bernard suggested (pp. cxliv-cxlvii) that there was an original, pre-Gospel, hymn composed of vv. 1-5, 10-11, 14, 18. In vv. 3 and 5, the second line of a couplet repeats what has already been stated in the first line, and in vv. 4, 5, 11, and 14, an emphatic word is repeated in the following line, to give what is called in Hebrew poetry 'climactic parallelism' (cf. Pss 29.5; 93.3), so that the whole passage truly reads like an OT hymn in honour of the pre-existent Divine Logos. Bernard further suggested that this hymn ante-dated the Gospel, and it will be observed that the verses listed above as belonging to the original, pre-Gospel, hymn contain no mention of the historical names in the Prologue - John, Moses, Jesus Christ (in vv. 6, 15, 17), which must therefore be considered insertions by the evangelist; and that the verses omitted above contain only two parenthetical notes about the relationship between the Baptist and Jesus (vv. 6-9, 15), plus two exegetical comments, one in vv. 12-13 to correct a possible misunderstanding of v. 11, the other in vv. 16-17 to elucidate the meaning of 'grace and truth' in v. 14. Bernard notes that his suggested hymn does not embody argument (note the exclusion of vv. 12, 13, 16, 17) or contain the personal name of Jesus Christ. 'It is a Logos hymn of a triumphant philosophy, directly Hebrew in origin, but reflecting the phrases which had become familiar in Greek-speaking society' (p. cxlvi).[3] Bernard's cautious analysis yields a hymn of great beauty and lucidity, which in no way depends on opinions derived from presuppositions of the *religionsgeschichtliche* school about the origins of Christianity (and indeed, of religion).

In the ten years before Bernard's commentary was published, a new era had dawned. It had long been the custom for the books of the OT, and the Synoptics, to be dissected into their purported constituent parts, and the Johannine text was now to be subjected to the same process. For the Prologue, the first impulse came, in Britain, from J. Rendel Harris (1916), whose initiative was followed by C. Cryer (1921) and C. F. Burney (1922). Rendel Harris had published in 1909 the *editio princeps* of the *Odes of Solomon* from the Syriac, and followed it with a classic edition in 1915; at that time both he, and some other scholars, were inclined to regard this work as of Jewish-Christian origin, originating perhaps as early as the first century. By 1913, Bernard had rejected this dating as too early, and argued that the *Odes* were in fact Christian hymns from around

---

[3] Compare C. F. Burney's suggestion of an Aramaic hymn, and (for that age) J. Rendel Harris's *The Origin of the Prologue to St John's Gospel*, Cambridge 1917.

160–170. (It is now generally accepted that the *Odes* are certainly from the second century, probably from the earlier part, and of Syrian origin, with some slightly Gnostic overtones.) This background led Harris to suggest, in essays published between 1916 and 1922,[4] that the Johannine Prologue was based on a hymn to Sophia, akin to the compositions in the *Odes*. Though they contain 'no avowed verbal quotations either from the OT or the NT, ...the doctrine of the Logos is repeatedly dwelt on, in a way which recalls Johannine teaching' (Bernard, cxlvi).

Meantime, one group of German scholars was approaching the Bible with an understanding of the term 'revelation' that was very different from the meaning attached to it in traditional Christianity. The appellation of the group has never been properly anglicized, and it is still generally known either as the *religionsgeschichtliche* school, or as 'the history-of-religions school'. Its adherents hold that the entire Bible should be approached without any dogmatic principles, and should be interpreted simply by being scrutinized in its context, at that point in world history where it finds its place as an integrating part of humanity's cultural evolution. It is in this way that God gives 'revelation'. Rudolf Bultmann, in a *Festschrift* for one of the founding fathers of this school, Hermann Gunkel (1862–1932), set out to clarify the background to the Prologue of John in the light of these principles.[5] A second article (itself originally a lecture in October 1923) drew attention to a fresh source of information, the then recently published Mandaean texts.[6] Thereafter, Bultmann sought to interpret the Prologue of John not merely by examining it in the light of the books of Alexandrian Judaism, but by arguing that it was based upon a pre-Christian text (*Vorlage*) celebrating the mythological figure of a Logos-Redeemer. His theory is most conveniently outlined as it is presented in his commentary on John.

Bultmann classifies the Prologue as 'a piece of cultic-liturgical poetry, oscillating between the language of revelation and confession'. As a parallel to the revelation, he adduces a Naasene psalm quoted in Hippolytus, which starts with the beginning of all things, and then recounts how [Jesus] begs the Father to send him down to bring Gnosis to the suffering soul in the world.[7] As a parallel to the confession, he points to texts in the 7th and 12th *Odes of Solomon*, which call upon the community to extol

---

[4] *The Origin of the Prologue*, and 'Athena Sophia and the Logos' in the *BJRL* 1922.

[5] 'Der religionsgeschichtliche Hintergrund des Prologs zum Johannesevangelium', in *Eucharisterion. Festschrift für H. Gunkel*, II, Göttingen, 1923 (= FRLANT NF 19), 1-26. Reprinted in Bultmann, *Exegetica*, Tübingen, 1967, 9-35.

[6] 'Der Bedeutung der neuerschlossenen mandäischen und manichäischen Quellen für das Verständnis des Johannesevangeliums', originally published in *ZNW* 24 (1925), 100-46. Reprinted in Bultmann, *Exegetica*, Tübingen, 1967, 55-104.

[7] Hippolytus, *Elenchus* V 10 2, ed. by Wendland in the GCS $26:102^{23}$-104^3. An English version by R. McL. Wilson may be found in NTA II 807-808. W. Bauer's judgment is there cited, that 'The psalm is really entirely pagan. Only at one point has it been clearly Christianized by the insertion of the name *Jesus* instead of the deity originally there named' (807).

the praises of the Word.[8] The ideas behind the Prologue were thus circulating at the end of the first century, and it is not too difficult to discern which verses in the Prologue may have formed a pre-Christian hymn about the Logos. Bultmann's opinion is that vv. 6-8 and 15 cannot belong to the original cultic-liturgical hymn, because they are prose, because they interrupt the flow of the argument, because they are concerned with historical events, and because they have a polemical thrust, concerned with the Baptist. Further, vv. 12c-13 also disturb the rhythm of the hymn, and are to be explained as exegetical comments of the author. In addition, v. 17, the only verse in the Gospel to mention the proper name Jesus Christ, and also to use the Pauline antithesis between law and grace is certainly alien in spirit to the original pre-Gospel hymn. Verse 18 is probably to be regarded, on stylistic grounds, as an addition made to the original by the evangelist. The pre-Gospel hymn would therefore have consisted of vv. 1-5, 9-12b, 14 + 16, verses which he regards as stemming ultimately from a Gnostic hymn (akin to the Naasene psalm just mentioned). He conjectures (the term is his) that this hymn may have stemmed from a group of followers of the Baptist, among whom was the evangelist, who after his transition to the Christian community made various insertions in the hymn to urge his former co-religionists to turn, like him, to Christianity. The first edition of Bultmann's commentary appeared in 1941. It was not widely available for several years, and it is significant that the three influential works of Hoskyns (1940), Dodd (1953: Preface 1950) and R. H. Lightfoot (1956) have nothing to say about a pre-Gospel hymn in the Prologue.[9]

Since shortly after 1950, it has become almost routine for commentators to dissect the Prologue, though there are some notable exceptions (e.g. Barrett). Unfortunately there is no consensus on the literary criteria which should be employed to discern the different strata of authorship. Everyone agrees that the verses about the Baptist (6-8 and 15) are prose, and do not belong to a pre-Gospel hymn (if there was one), but there the agreement ceases. On the one hand, it is clear that certain verses tread to a regular rhythm of two or three stresses, often for two or three lines; on the other hand, some other lines which can also be read with that same rhythm hardly seem to qualify as poetry, and can with difficulty be classified as the kind of language one finds in a hymn (e.g. v. 12). Furthermore, even if it were possible to designate which lines are poetry and which are prose, it would not settle the dispute: Barrett has pointed out that 'antiquity in general found no difficulty in singing prose, and this is what early Christian hymns, from "O gladsome light" to the *Te Deum* for the

---

[8] Examples are given on page 2, fn. 2 of the German original, and on page 14, fn. 3 of the ETr of the commentary,.

[9] It may be mentioned that the commentaries of Hoskyns (d. 1937) and Lightfoot (d. 1953) are posthumous, and that Dodd did not see Bultmann's commentary as a whole until his book was completed (*Interpretation*, p. 121, fn. 2).

most part were'.[10] At the moment, too little is known about the hymnology of the epoch for anyone to make a firm judgment about what was the usual liturgical practice at the time.[11]

Except where there is a general consensus (as over vv. 6-8, 15), commentators who advance an opinion about the extent of the pre-Gospel hymn have stressed that their judgments is personal, and hedged by qualifications and hesitancy. Schnackenburg (1965) judged that the original hymn fell into four parts: vv. 1 + 3 - the work of the Logos in creation; 4 + 9 - its significance for the world of mankind; 10 + 11 the rejection of this work before the Incarnation; 14 +16, the Incarnation and salvation. This he regards as coming from a Christian community of converts from Hellenistic Judaism, probably in Asia Minor (cf. 1 Tim 3.16; 1 Pet 3.18). The present text, however, he would divide into three: vv. 1-5, 6-13, and 14-16 (or 14-18). R. E. Brown (1966) 'with great hesitancy' proposed as the pre-Gospel text: 1-2 - the Word with God; 3-5 - the Word and Creation; 10-12b the Word in the World; 14 + 16 the Community's Share in the Word. Verses 6-9 and 15 are excluded as dealing with the Baptist; 12c-13 are an explanation of how people become God's children, 17-18 an explanation of 'love in place of love'. Ernst Haenchen[12] chose for the original hymn vv. 1-5, 9-11, 14, 16-17, with the remainder as the additions of the evangelist; it represents the increasingly popular choice. Johannes Schneider (before 1970) takes vv. 1-5, 9-12b and 14-18 as the original hymn, stressing his conviction that it is the work of the evangelist himself.[13]

---

[10] In 'The Prologue of St John's Gospel', *NT Essays*, 37. He adds that 'the only way in which the poetic structure - in any serious sense of the adjective - of the Prologue can be saved is to maintain that it represents not Greek but Semitic verse, based not on quantity but on stress'. He then advances five reasons which make it difficult to believe this, notably that neither Josephus nor Philo nor the LXX translators seem to have recognized this factor of stress as a trait of Semitic poetry. Finally, he cites the hymn at the end of the *Poimandres* (CH I 31) which is certainly not Semitic, and certainly not verse. One may add also the *Gloria in excelsis,* the oldest Greek text of which is found in the Codex Alexandrinus among the *Odes* (in Swete, *The OT in Greek* III 810-12; in Rahlfs, *Septuaginta* II 181-83).

[11] In 1956, Serafin de Ausejo analyzed the form and content of the hymns in Phil 2.6-1; Col 1.15-20; 1 Tim 3.16 and Heb 1.2-4 in the light of the contemporary liturgical poetry in the synagogue, and also of the hymns used in Emperor-worship, or in the worship of Artemis, in Asia Minor. He concluded that (partly as a reaction against emperor-worship) the Christian hymns always had three parts, speaking of Christ's pre-existence, earthly life, and exaltation. Unfortunately, the author's attempt to discover the same tripartite structure in John 1 was less convincing: his three divisions were (i) vv. 1-5, 9-11, (ii) 13-14ab, and (iii) 14c-e.16.18. See '¿Es un Himno a Cristo el Prologo de San Juan?', *Estudios Biblicos* 15 (1956), 223-77, 381-427.

[12] In 'Probleme des johanneischen "Prologs"', *ZTK* 60 (1963), 305-34, and in the (posthumous) edition of his commentary (1980, ETr 1984).

[13] 'Die anonyme Größe "Gemeinde" besagt sehr weing, Eine "Gemeinde" bringt nich ein solches Lied hervor. Dahinter muß eine bestimmte, tief religiöse, theologisch schöpferische Persönichkeit stehen. Das kann nur der Verfasser des Evangeliums sein. Er

One other theory must be mentioned, that the Prologue has a detailed chiastic structure. The idea was first advanced, according to R. A. Culpepper, by N. W. Lund in 1931, but little noticed then, if at all.[14] Lund's attempt to discern chiastic structures in Jn 1.1-18 was over-ambitious: it is too elaborate to be convincing, and requires the omission of vv. 6-8 and 15 to succeed. An outline of it is given by Culpepper. Lund, however, rightly called attention to the modern usage whereby the terms 'chiasm' and 'chiastic' are extended from their original meaning in Greek rhetoric and applied to any regular repetition of words, phrases or even ideas when they recur in the inverse order in a sentence or paragraph. It is customary to mark the correspondent words or ideas A B C D E - E' D' C' B' A', or in some similar way.

In 1953, M.-E. Boismard, apparently without any knowledge of Lund's work, suggested that underlying the Prologue there was a very clear and definite pattern 'in the form of a parabola'. His analogy of a parabola is a more accurate description of the pattern, but the term chiasm has by now long since won the day. The fullest presentation of Bois-mard's theory is given in *L'Evangile de Jean* (1977). He proposes that there was a pre-Gospel hymn, in honour of the Logos, coming from a Jewish-Hellenistic background, but that it consisted of nothing more than vv. 1ab + 3-5, being also a short midrash on Gen 1.[15] The remainder of the Prologue was written by the one whom we may for convenience call the evangelist.[16] This means, of course, that this evangelist had sovereign liberty over all the material included in the Prologue, since practically all of it was his own creation. Boismard suggests, for example, that vv. 6-7a + c had in an earlier draft stood immediately before v. 19, introducing the appearance of the Baptist, as in Mark. In John, vv. 7b + 8 were added by the evangelist when he transferred those introductory verses to their present position (73: B 1). The reason that the evangelist made these changes, bringing in the Baptist at two specific points (6-8 and 15), was to create a great and solemn Prologue which would describe how the Word of God came down from heaven to bring life to the earth, and then,

wird den Hymnus zu irgendeiner Zeit geschaffen haben' (52). This commentary too is posthumous (1976).

[14] First in 'The Influence of Chiasmus upon the Structure of the Gospels' in the *Anglican Theological Review* [then from Evanston, Illinois] 13 (1931), 42-46; later in *Chiasmus in the New Testament*, Chapel Hill, N.C., University of North Carolina Press, 1942. The references are taken from R. A. Culpepper, 'The Pivot of John's Prologue', *NTS* 27 (1980), 1-31. The outline is on 2-3.

[15] His reason for omitting 1c and 2 is that these lines have a binary rhythm, while all the rest have a ternary one. It means, of course, that the original pre-Gospel hymn did not carry the statement that the Logos was God (1c), or stress by repetition that the Logos was, in the beginning, with God. These insertions would have been the work of the evangelist. Boismard does not mention any pre-Gospel hymn in his (semi-popular) book of 1953.

[16] So phrased to avoid introducing here the details of Boismard's general theory. In fact, he speaks of 'John II B'.

when its mission had been accomplished, returned to the God who sent it.

The guiding ideas in the evangelist's mind came from the hymns about Wisdom, as exemplified for instance in Prov 8.22–9.6; Sir 24.1-29, and Wis 9.9-12. Each of these speaks of the existence of Wisdom beside God before the creation, of Wisdom's part in creation, of its coming down to earth, eventually to God's Chosen People, and of the benefits it brings (see the commentary on 1.1a.11b and 18b). The evangelist was surely inspired also by the great lines of Isa 55.10-11: 'as the rain and the snow come down from heaven…so shall my word be, that proceeds from my mouth; it shall not return to me unproductive, - nay, it shall accomplish whatever I have desired' (LXX: ἕως ἂν συντελεσθῇ ὅσα ἠθέλησα). These words find their echo in the second part of the Gospel, particularly at those points where John wishes to emphasize the perfect accomplishment of all that Jesus had come to do. See Jn 13.3; 16.28; 17; and especially 19.28,30: εἰδὼς ὁ Ἰησοῦς ὅτι ἤδη πάντα τετέλεσται … εἶπεν, τετέλεσται.

To express this vision of *Verbum supernum prodiens, a Patre lumen exiens*,[17] the evangelist chose to deploy one of his favourite literary devices, and this time on the grand scale, to depict the descent and ascent of the life-giving Logos (p. 76). In the scheme below the verses concerning the descent are on the left, and are to be read downwards, while the matching verses on the right are to be read upwards. Catch-words are used to recall the contents of the verses on either side.

	THE DESCENT		THE ASCENT		
A	1-2 (beforehand)	The Logos with God	(afterwards)	18	A'
B	3 (in creation)	The Work of the Logos	(in recreating)	17	B'
C	4-5 Life & Light	The Gifts of the Logos	Grace for grace	16	C'
D	6-8 Then	The Role of the Baptist	Now	15	D'
E	9-11 Unrecognized	The Logos in the World	His Glory Seen	14	E'
	F 12-13	The Logos came so that those who received him F			
		might become children of God			

It is an impressive construction, which cannot be fairly appreciated except by checking the details in the Greek text of the Prologue.[18]

In an article published in 1980, R. A. Culpepper has done this, and also added a refinement to Boismard's plan: he divides section F into two (F + G), thus finding a 'pivot' for the structure at 12b (which he labels H).[19] His own configuration therefore ends:

---

[17] An Advent hymn, dating at the latest from the tenth century. 'Heaven's high Word proceeding forth, As light from our dear Father's side…'

[18] A. Feuillet, *Le Prologue* (1968), 160, offers but a slight variation on Boismard's plan. Verse 9 = 14 (E–E'), and vv. 10-11 = 12-13 (F–F').

[19] R. A. Culpepper, 'The Pivot of John's Prologue', *NTS* 27 (1980), 1-31. This article also supplies a bibliography of the topic from 1960 to 1980, listing several articles which contributed to the discussion at that time.

E 9-10	Unrecognized	The Logos in the World	His Glory Seen	14	E'
F 11	Israel	The Logos and His Own	Believers	13'	F
G 12a	ὅσοι δὲ	τοῖς πιστεύουσιν		12c	G
	ἔλαβον αὐτόν	εἰς τὸ ὄνομα αὐτοῦ			
H 12b	ἔδωκεν αὐτοῖς ἐξουσίαν τέκνα θεοῦ γενέσθαι			12b	H

In a second part of his article, Culpepper argues that this theme of becoming 'children of God' is central to John's Gospel. Even though the phrase τέκνα θεοῦ is not found in the LXX, the equivalent is. He examines the use of the word בֵּן (ben) = *son* in the Hebrew OT, and of παῖς in the book of Wisdom. He looks at parallels from Qumran ('sons of light', 1QS i.9; and 'sons of truth', 1QS iv.5), from Philo (especially *De Confessione Linguarum* 145-47), and from Rabbinic literature, and concludes with a survey of the Synoptics, Paul and 1 John. Through nine pages, Culpepper cites copiously to demonstrate that in the religion of Israel, it is not ethnic origin that is primary, but rather the moral and religious observance of the Covenants of Noah, of Abraham and of Moses. Affiliation with Israel either by descent or by conversion is usually presupposed, but it is only by obedience to the Word of God that one becomes a son, or child, of God. Finally, Culpepper observes that the phrase (τὰ) τέκνα (τοῦ) θεοῦ appears only twice in John's Gospel, here and at 11.52.[20] 11.52, coming as it does relatively near to the conclusion of Part I of the Gospel, may well mark, by matching 12b here, a Johannine *inclusio*. 'By claiming the designation τέκνα θεοῦ, the Johannine community was identifying itself (or perhaps more broadly all Christianity) as the heir to a role and standing which Israel had abdicated' (31).

Shortly afterwards, de la Potterie argued for a different mode of viewing the Prologue.[21] He prefers to compare it with three 'waves' rolling onshore one after the other, or with three successive movements interpreting afresh a musical theme. With the verses arranged as follows, he argues that the reader can discern the internal dynamism which carries the theme forward. The theme is 'revelation'.

The Language of Wisdom Literature	The Language of History	The Language of Faith
1-2 In the beginning...	6-8 There appeared ...sent from God	15 John witnesses: 'He was before me'
3-4.5a Light amid the darkness	9 The Word was the true light	
5b Light *versus* darkness	10-12 Mixed Response	16 'Of his fullness we have all received'
	13-14 The Word become flesh ...full of the grace of truth	17 the grace of truth 18 in the bosom of the Father = the Revelation

[20] In John, the word τέκνα occurs only once elsewhere, at 8.39.
[21] 'Structure du Prologue de saint Jean', *NTS* 30 (1984), 354-81.

His presentation is of course accompanied by detailed argument.
A little later (1987), Otfried Hofius proposed an impressively elegant
division into four strophes, each subdivided into A and B, the entire
hymn being dominated by parallelism of thought from line to line.[22] His
divisions are:

I   A   1a   Ἐν ἀρχῇ ἦν ὁ λόγος,   a
        b   καὶ ὁ λόγος ἦν πρὸς τὸν θεόν,   b
        c   καὶ θεὸς ἦν ὁ λόγος.   a
        2   οὗτος ἦν ἐν ἀρχῇ πρὸς τὸν θεόν.   b

    B   3a   πάντα δι' αὐτοῦ ἐγένετο,   a
        b   καὶ χωρὶς αὐτοῦ ἐγένετο   b₁
        c   οὐδὲ ἕν ὃ γέγονεν   b₂

II A   4a   Ἐν αὐτῷ ζωὴ ἦν,   a
        b   καὶ ἡ ζωὴ ἦν τὸ φῶς τῶν ἀνθρώπων·   b
        5a   καὶ τὸ φῶς ἐν τῇ σκοτίᾳ φαίνει,   a
        b   καὶ ἡ σκοτία αὐτὸ οὐ κατέλαβεν.   b

    B   9a   ἦν τὸ φῶς τὸ ἀληθινόν,   a
        b   ὃ φωτίζει πάντα ἄνθρωπον   b₁
        c   ἐρχόμενον εἰς τὸν κόσμον.   b₂

III A   10a Ἐν τῷ κόσμῳ ἦν,   a₁
        b   καὶ ὁ κόσμος δι' αὐτοῦ ἐγένετο,   a₂
        c   καὶ ὁ κόσμος αὐτὸν οὐκ ἔγνω.   b
        11a εἰς τὰ ἴδια ἦλθεν,   a
        b   καὶ οἱ ἴδιοι αὐτὸν οὐ παρέλαβον.   b

    B   12a ὅσοι δὲ ἔλαβον αὐτόν,   a
        b   ἔδωκεν αὐτοῖς ἐξουσίαν   b₁
        c   τέκνα θεοῦ γενέσθαι.   b₂

IV A   14a Καὶ ὁ λόγος σὰρξ ἐγένετο   a₁
        b   καὶ ἐσκήνωσεν ἐν ἡμῖν,   a₂
        c   καὶ ἐθεασάμεθα τὴν δόξαν αὐτοῦ,   b
        d   δόξαν ὡς μονογενοῦς παρὰ πατρός,   a
        e   πλήρης χάριτος καὶ ἀληθείας.   b

    B   16a ὅτι ἐκ τοῦ πληρώματος αὐτοῦ   a
        b   ἡμεῖς πάντες ἐλάβομεν   b₁
        c   καὶ χάριν ἀντὶ χάριτος.   b₂

---

[22] 'Struktur und Gedankengang des Logos-Hymnus in Joh 1.1-18', *ZNW* 78 (1987),
1-25. See also H. Gese, 'Der Johannesprolog', in *Zur biblischen Theologie. Alt-
testamentliche Vorträge*, Tübingen, 1983 (2 Aufl.), 152-201.

The literary structure may easily be grasped by referring to the letters on the right of the text. Strophes I and II each have four lines (two parallel distichs) in A, and three lines in B (of which the second and third are parallel). Strophes III and IV each have five lines in A (of which the first two are parallel), and three lines in B (of which the last two belong together, as in I and II). Hofius maintains that this Logos-Hymn is of Christian origin. It will be noted that he includes Jn 1.2 and 9 as essential parts of the hymn. The analysis is ingenious, and finely drawn, and merits close attention.

It is now almost universally accepted that there was a pre-Gospel hymn containing at least vv. 1, 3-5 and 10-11. There is an equally firm consensus that the verses about the Baptist (6-8 and 15) should be excluded, and also 12b-13. There is a growing tendency to exclude from the pre-Gospel hymn vv. 2 and 9, and a tendency in the opposite direction to include 12a. Verses 14 and 16 are nowadays generally seen as part of the hymn (but with notable exceptions), while v. 18 is usually excluded (again, with many exceptions). So Boismard summarized the situation in 1977, and it has not fundamentally changed.

Some principles may be laid down. If the evangelist made use of a pre-Christian hymn, even one of Jewish-Hellenistic origin, it is safe to say that this hymn would not have contained either the line 'and the Logos was God' (1c) or v. 2, and one can say with certainty that it would not have contained the phrase 'and the Logos became flesh' (14a). Equally we may exclude from a pre-Christian hymn the four verses about the Baptist (6-8 and 15). Verse 9 also must then be excluded, because it is only a (necessary) connective after v. 8. Verses 10 + 11 may quite properly remain, as being good examples of Jewish thinking about Wisdom, but the most reasonable conjecture to make is that, at this point, the evangelist broke off from the pre-Christian text and continued with his own words (so J. Gnilka). The pre-Christian hymn would in this case have been 1ab + 3 + 4 + 5, then 10 + 11, as follows.

1a   'Εν ἀρχῇ ἦν ὁ λόγος,
b   καὶ ὁ λόγος ἦν πρὸς τὸν θεόν,
3a   πάντα δι' αὐτοῦ ἐγένετο,
b   καὶ χωρὶς αὐτοῦ ἐγένετο οὐδὲ ἕν.
4a   ὃ γέγονεν | ἐν αὐτῷ ζωὴ ἦν,
b   καὶ ἡ ζωὴ ἦν τὸ φῶς τῶν ἀνθρώπων·
5a   καὶ τὸ φῶς ἐν τῇ σκοτίᾳ φαίνει,
b   καὶ ἡ σκοτία αὐτὸ οὐ κατέλαβεν.

10a ἐν τῷ κόσμῳ ἦν,
b   καὶ ὁ κόσμος δι' αὐτοῦ ἐγένετο,
c   καὶ ὁ κόσμος αὐτὸν οὐκ ἔγνω.
11a εἰς τὰ ἴδια ἦλθεν,
b   καὶ οἱ ἴδιοι αὐτὸν οὐ παρέλαβον.
[12a ὅσοι δὲ ἔλαβον αὐτόν,
σb   ἔδωκεν αὐτοῖς...]

It is easy to see that 11b does not mark the ending of a hymn, and that 12a, or 12ab, might be the continuation of it, but that the text of the Gospel has at this point begun to depart into strictly Christian realms.

If, however, the evangelist incorporated into his Prologue an already existent Christian hymn, then there are no grounds for excluding vv. 1c, 2 or 14a, or indeed any verses at all. Even if he did incorporate such a hymn, he might himself have been its author. Indeed, he himself might well have written the whole Prologue (Barrett, and, practically speaking, Boismard), for no clear literary criteria are available to prove for certain whether he did or did not. More about this hypothetical hymn it is impossible to say, except that if through the discovery of hitherto unknown texts, it became clear that either a Jewish or a pre-Gospel Christian hymn lies beneath the text of John's Prologue, this might lead to a deeper comprehension of the Gospel text. Likewise, some may find that one of the plans proposed above is of real help in understanding better the thrust of the argument. The fact that the plans differ from one another is not significant. It is always so with great literature, and the variety of interpretation which is legitimately possible with Virgil, Dante or Shakespeare only bears witness to the richness of the thought.

If, however, the gospel-writer put to use a hymn from a non-Jewish and non-Christian source, then the implications for the interpretation of the Gospel-text might be quite different, and even significant. One suggestion is that an originally Gnostic hymn was used (Bultmann 1923). That the Gospel itself is even tolerant of the basic tenets of second-century Gnosticism is, of course, disproved from the start by Jn 1.3, asserting that all things were made *through* the Logos; no Gnostic could have agreed that the entire material world was either good (Gen 1), or created by God through the Logos. Indeed, for a Gnostic, the one more objectionable affirmation conceivable is that 'the Word became flesh'; to a Gnostic, that declaration is the ultimate blasphemy. Nevertheless, there are those who still contend that there is a real affinity between the Johannine Prologue and Gnosticism, a relationship which does not rest merely on whether a Gnostic hymn was used by the evangelist. A deeper problem is involved, which is more conveniently addressed in a separate Excursus dealing with the Logos in the Prologue.

EXCURSUS II

THE LOGOS IN THE PROLOGUE

The sole purpose of this Excursus is to examine the background for the interpretation of the term Logos in the Prologue. More comprehensive articles on Logos may be found in the larger dictionaries.[1] Note too that Schnackenburg, in an Excursus entitled 'The Origin and Nature of the Johannine Concept of the Logos' (I 264-69 = ETr I 488-93) presents (in translation) a valuable collection of original texts about the Logos from the *Corpus Hermeticum*, the *Odes of Solomon* and from Nag Hammadi.

At the beginning of the twentieth century, Richard Reitzenstein sought to explain much of the Fourth Gospel in terms of Egyptian Gnosis, but subsequently, after the publication by Lidzbarski of the major books of the Mandaean religion (1915, 1920, 1925), he became convinced that the main influence on John was to be found not in Egyptian but in Iranian religion.[2] A synthesis of his theory may be found in the third edition of what is almost his final work, where he reaffirms that behind all the religions of the Near and Middle East there lies an old myth about a saviour sent from heaven to deliver all souls from darkness, and to lead them back to the kingdom of light. This saviour has many names—the Son of God, the Heavenly Man, the Logos, etc. For our present purpose, it is enough to cite the declaration that sometimes in the NT, 'mostly in non-Pauline passages, λόγος appears for the concept νοῦς, and it appears to contain within itself the two elements or essential attributes of deity, light and life',[3] a statement which Reitzenstein interprets in terms of Iranian mystery-religions (such as that of Mani). He had become convinced that within the Mandaean literature[4] it is possible to discern passages which

[1] E.g. *TWNT* IV (1942) *s.v.* λέγω, λόγος κτλ. 71-76, Philology (A. Debrunner); 76-89, Classical Greece and Hellenism, including Philo (H. Kleinknecht); 89-100, OT (O. Procksch); 100-140, NT (G. Kittel). *DBS* V (1957) *s.v.* Logos. 442-65, OT (A. Robert); 465-79 NT era (C. Mondésert, except 473-75, Alexandrian Judaism and Philo, by J. Starcky); 479-96, NT (J. Starcky).

[2] See R. Reitzenstein, *Poimandres*, Leipzig, 1904, and *Das iranische Erlösungsmysterium*, Bonn, 1921.

[3] Reitzenstein, *Die hellenistischen Mysterienreligionen*, Leipzig, 3rd ed., 1927, ETr by John E. Steely, *Hellenistic Mystery Religions: Their Basic Ideas and Significance*, Pittsburgh, 1978. The quotation above, and its interpretation, occur on 413-14 = ETr 526-27.

[4] None of the extant manuscripts is older than the sixteenth century, and the compilation is certainly post-Islamic, i.e. not much before A.D. 700.

can with confidence be dated back to the disciples of John the Baptist mentioned in Acts 18.14–19.7, of whom the Mandaeans of the eighth and following centuries are in his judgment the legitimate successors. Christianity too, in his opinion, arose out of this same Baptist sect. The Johannine Logos is therefore to be interpreted against the background of the Iranian redeemer-myth, by means of what we learn about it from the extant Mandaean writings. For further detail on Mandaism, see the excellent essay by C. H. Dodd in his *Interpretation*, 115-30. The texts published by Lady E. S. Drower (1953, 1959) have not materially altered the balance of the debate.

The theory as put forward by Reitzenstein won little favour, but as reworked by Bultmann, it had considerable influence in Germany and among the next generation of the 'history-of-religions school'.[5] Bultmann recognized that the points of comparison between the Mandaean and Johannine texts are not specifically Mandaean, but common to the many varieties of Gnosis current in the first two centuries of the Christian era. The contrasts between light and darkness, between life and death, between truth and lies, are frequent in all varieties of Gnosticism, and in other religions and philosophies too. What is distinctive in, and characteristic of, Gnosis 'hinges on the descent and return of a redeemer and revealer from on high', a figure who is often called Logos or Nous or Anthropos (Schnackenburg I 120 = ETr I 138). In Gnosticism, this redeemer comes to set free souls, which had once existed as purely spiritual beings in a heavenly world, from their bondage to matter, and to return them to their heavenly homeland; thus the coming of this redeemer presages 'a cosmic event which sets in motion an eschatological occurrence…as a process of nature by which the union of the essentially opposite natures, light and darkness, is dissolved'.[6] Clearly, John's idea of human life is far removed from this perception. In Bultmann's presentation, therefore, the Johannine redeemer is an entirely human person, Jesus of Nazareth, in whom the Logos (in the Gnostic sense of the first emanation from the one God) is (John does not tell us how) embodied. Jesus comes to set all humankind free by challenging them with the word of truth, so that each person must face up to, and make a moral judgment on, his or her own conduct. It is only by saying *Yes* to this word of God that each one discovers inner freedom, personal salvation and true life here on this earth. It is in this sense that Bultmann would speak of realized eschatology.[7] Bultmann is certainly not an ancient Gnostic. He is a modern existentialist.

The attempt to interpret the Fourth Gospel by means of the Mandaean literature is altogether too far-fetched to be convincing. A more obvious source of relevant background might be sought in the *Corpus Hermeticum*,

---

[5] In the two articles mentioned above on p. 82 nn. 5 and 6, and in his commentary on John. See also his *Theologie* (in the ETr II), especially §46.

[6] *Theologie*, 387 = ETr II 40.

[7] *Theologie* = ETr II §50 ('Faith as Eschatological Existence').

a collection of Egyptian origin, dating from the second or third centuries; parts of it may well be from the early second century. In its first treatise, the *Poimandres*, we read that 'out of light a holy Word came to hover over nature, and out of the humid nature pure fire leapt up on high…and the air, being light, followed the draught, rising up to the fire from the land and the water…' (I.5). If the opening of this quotation recalls Gen 1, the following words make it abundantly clear that the author is thinking in terms of the Stoic cosmogony, with its four elements of earth and air, fire and water.[8] Later we read that there is deposited within the soul an enlightening Logos by which the soul is united to itself, and to God (I.6-7), another distinctive characteristic of Gnosticism. A reading of the entire treatise makes it evident that the world of the *Poimandres* is not that of the evangelist, and is much closer to that of Egyptian non-Christian Gnosis.

By contrast, the *Odes of Solomon* are in fact very closely related to the Fourth Gospel, and it is even possible that their author was acquainted with it. References to the Word, however, are few, and can always be explained by reference to the OT alone. For example, the texts of Ode 16.19 ('the worlds are by his word'; cf. Jn 1.3) and of Odes 15.2; 18.6, where the Logos is light to the mind (cf. Jn 1.4-5) provide no further help for interpreting the term Logos than is already available in the OT.

Three texts from the library discovered in 1945 at Nag Hammadi, all dating from the middle of the second century, may be cited here, simply by way of example. The opening of the *Gospel of Truth* reads: 'The gospel of truth is joy for those who have received from the Father of truth the grace of knowing him, through the power of the Word that came forth from the pleroma, the one who is in the thought and the mind of the Father, that is, the one who is addressed as the Savior, (that) being the name of the work he is to perform for the redemption of those who were ignorant of the Father…' (16.31–17.4). Later we find: 'While [the Father's] wisdom contemplates the Word, and his teaching utters it, his knowledge has revealed it' (23.18-22), and 'In this way the Word of the Father goes forth in the totality' (23.33-35). Finally, we read that 'When the Word appeared, …it is not a sound alone, but it became a body' (26.4-8), bringing confusion among the 'jars' or 'vessels', that is, among human souls (26.10-29). In the first two texts quoted, the Word is entrusted by the Father with a function in revelation and salvation, but as the last text makes clear, this role is much closer to the role of the Saviour in Gnosticism than to early Christianity. The same can be said of two other treatises, the *Apocryphon of John* ('I am the Pronoia of the pure light': 31.11) and the *Trimorphic Protennoia* (with its frequent 'I am'

---

[8] The most convenient of texts on this point is in J. von Arnim, *Stoicorum Veterum Fragmenta*, Leipzig, 1905, 19-20 fn. 102, quoting Stobaeus, *Eclogae* I 17 3, and Diogenes Laertius VII 135-36 and 142.

sayings). All three works are Gnostic treatises which have been given, here and there, a thin varnish of Christian language.[9]

These Gnostic texts, like those of second-century Christian Gnostics such as the Valentinians, simply serve to show that in the Eastern Mediterranean there was a widely circulating myth which sought to explain the origin of the world and the problem of evil by a theory in which a being called the Logos played a significant but intermediary role. This provides a parallel with the work of the Logos in John's Prologue, but no justification for interpreting the Johannine Logos in terms of the Saviour envisaged by the Gnostics, whose task was to liberate pre-existent human souls from enslavement in matter.

Anyone searching for light on the Johannine Logos naturally turns to Philo, who sincerely and loyally strove to re-express the ancestral faith of Judaism in terms of Greek philosophy, and specifically as interpreted by the Middle Platonist school and the Stoics. Once again, Dodd provides an excellent survey in his *Interpretation* 54-74, of which 65-74 present Philo's understanding of the divine Logos. From the Platonists, Philo took the idea that this world (κόσμος αἰσθητός) is the copy of a higher world (κόσμος νοητός), and from the Stoics (who recognized no such supermundane existence) the idea that a rational principle within the material world (ὁ τοῦ κόσμου λόγος) held it all together. Then, taking from Judaism the doctrine that God created the world by his Word (Gen 1; Ps 32.6) and by his Wisdom (Wis 7.27), Philo suggested that just as a human word is the outward expression of a human thought, so God's Logos is the expression of divine Wisdom. According to Philo, therefore, there is a blueprint of creation (κόσμος νοητός), analogous to the world of Platonic Forms, in the mind or Wisdom of God; and when this is projected over formless matter by the Word (the λόγος προφορικός), the material world is brought into being. See *De Opificio Mundi* 16-20. This Logos is sometimes called the εἰκών of God and even his πρωτόγονος υἱός (though the personalization is not to be taken literally). It acts as God's intermediary in history (as in the OT), and relays the truth of God to individual souls. Here there is obviously an affinity of ideas with the world of the Fourth Gospel, but in Philo, the Logos is never fully personal, certainly never incarnate, and never the object of faith or love.[10]

Neither Philo nor the Gnostics is able to supply a convincing background which will account for all the attributes with which, according to John, the Logos of the Prologue is endowed: eternal, creator, sovereign Lord of all history, light of humanity, and Word made flesh. The OT, by contrast, can express all these attributes with the term 'the Word of our

---

[9] The texts cited are to be found in *The Nag Hammadi Library*, 3rd completely revised edition, Leiden, 1988, on 40, 43, 44, 122. The *Trimorphic Protennoia* is printed on 511-22.

[10] Thus Dodd, *Interpretation*, 73. For further details on the Logos in Philo, see the writers listed in Schnackenburg I 261-63 = ETr 485-87.

God'. To understand the term Logos in the Prologue, it is necessary only to study the meaning of the term in the OT, both Greek and Hebrew, and—we may now add—in the Aramaic translations too. Even if these Targums do not predate the Fourth Gospel, they are the best guide we possess to the Aramaic tradition in which John's Gospel was first formed. It is therefore on the basis of this background that the meaning of the term Logos has been expounded in the body of the commentary, particularly under vv. 1 and 14.

At the beginning of the Prologue, the central figure in the Fourth Gospel is introduced as the Logos. After the statement of the fact of the incarnation (Jn 1.14), the title is never used again. Instead, the evangelist writes only of Jesus, who 'embodies' the Logos in his flesh, to such an extent that death itself does not separate the Logos from his earthly body. John's narrative of the burial refers four times to 'the body of Jesus' (τὸ σῶμα τοῦ 'Ιησοῦ, 19.38 [×2], 40; 20.12), which in the end is identified with 'Jesus' (19.42, ἐκεῖ οὖν...ἔθηκαν τὸν 'Ιησοῦν). The climax of the Gospel then turns into a triumphant affirmation that the once torn and bleeding body which was crucified now lives again, its wounds not closed but glorified (Jn 20.20, and 24-29). *Ut in perpetuum victoriae suae circumferat triumphum.*[11] Nothing could be further from the Gnostic idea of a heaven-sent redeemer come to release human souls from imprisonment in the flesh and to lead them to a non-material, purely spiritual home.

And nothing could be closer to the traditions of Israel as embodied in the OT. There the Word of God is from the beginning creative (Gen 1 etc.) and the provident Saviour of God's people for the future good of all the human race (Isa 40–55). The sense of Jn 1.14 is that all that had previously been true of the Word and Wisdom of God in the OT is from a particular moment in time, the moment of the incarnation, embodied in Jesus of Nazareth, Jesus the Christ. Compare Heb 1.1.

The Fourth Gospel (like Matthew's) contains no narrative record of Christ's ascension. There are allusions to an ascension in the sense of an exaltation (e.g. Jn 3.13; 6.62; 20.17), but not in the sense of a departure and separation from his own (not even in 20.17). As in Mt 28.20, the narrative ends with Jesus still on stage, still facing and addressing all future ages. John 20.29 closes the book with Jesus proclaiming, 'Blessed are those who have not seen and yet have come to believe', Jn 21.23 with him declaring 'If I wish him to remain until I come, what is that to you?' Both endings express the same truth, that 'the Word of our God abides for ever' (Isa 40.8), publishing its message thereafter through the Church to the world in every age.

In calling Jesus the Word made flesh, the evangelist was equating him with the Memra, and thus with everything that term implies.[12] In so doing,

---

[11] Bede, *In Lucam* VI, on Lk 24.40.
[12] See pp. 8-9, and the comment under 1.14b, on pp. 54-57.

he had chosen from Israel's tradition the perfect formulation for presenting the distinctively Christian teaching to Judaism, in a context which Judaism could well understand. At the same time, by employing the Greek term Logos, he was presenting Jesus as the Saviour to all 'the Greeks' (cf. Jn 12.21) who sincerely sought the truth about God amid the perplexing world of Hellenistic religions.

THE MEANING OF ΜΟΝΟΓΕΝΗΣ IN JOHN 1.14, 18

English Versions of μονογενοῦς παρὰ πατρός

AV = KJV (1611)	as of the only begotten of the Father
Douay-Ch. (1749)	as it were of the only begotten of the Father
RV (1881)	as of the only begotten from the Father
RV[mg]	as of an only begotten from a father
RSV (1952)	as of the only Son from the Father
NRSV (1989)	as of a father's only son
NEB (1st ed., 1961; 2nd ed., 1970)	as befits the Father's only Son
REB (1989)	as befits the Father's only Son
NIV (1978)	of the one and only [Son] who came from the Father
NIV[mg]	of the Only Begotten who came from the Father
NAB (1986)	as of the Father's only Son
TEV = GNB (1966)	which he received as the Father's only Son
TNT = BFBS (1973)	such as belongs to the Father's only Son
JB (1966)	that is his as the only Son of the Father
NJB (1985)	that he has from the Father as only Son of the Father
Weymouth (1902)	as of the Father's only Son, sent from His presence
Moffatt (1913)	such as an only son enjoys from his father
Torrey (1933)	as of an only son, bestowed by a father
Knox (1945)	such as belongs to the Father's only-begotten Son
Williams (1952)	of the only Son from the Father
Kleist (1954)	such as befits to the Father's only-begotten Son
Phillips (1960)	as of a father's only son
Barclay (1968)	which an only son receives from his father

These versions have been widely used or influential.

The Problem

(1) The three pre-1901 versions (AV, RV and Douai-Challoner) have *only begotten*, which the twentieth-century ones (with the exception of Knox, Kleist, and NIV [and NIV[mg]]) have replaced with *only Son*.

(2) What a minority of the Revisers were striving for in 1881, namely, the reading in RV[mg],[1] has found approval only from Torrey, Philips, Barclay

---

[1] 'The marginal reading stood in the text in the First Revision. It is one among very many places where a conservative minority damaged the work by the operation of the two-thirds rule' (J. H. Moulton, in MHT I 83 fn. 1).

and NRSV: otherwise πατρός is always translated as if it had the article, and in addition referred, by capitalization, to [God] the Father.

(3) Apart from the agreements between NEB and REB, and between Phillips and NRSV, no two versions are identical. The translators, concerned to catch the nuances of ὡς and παρά, seem to have been less anxious about the anarthrous πατρός, and agreed on the interpretation of μονογενής.

(4) The purpose of this Excursus is to question whether it is certain that μονογενής means, in Jn 1.14, 'an only [or: only-begotten] son'. All the above versions (even NIV) consider that the idea of sonship is implied in the adjective. This was until around 1980 the common opinion of expositors, vigorously presented by F. Büchsel in *TWNT* IV (1942), 745-50, particularly on 745, fn. 6 and 749[7-11]; so also de la Potterie (*Vérité*, 181-91), Barrett, 2nd ed., 166, Dahms, 222-32, and Theobald. The meaning *unique*, however, preferred by Winter, D. Moody Smith, Fitzmyer and Pendrick, appears to be gaining more support.

The Lexical Data

(1) μονογενής occurs nine times in the NT.
(a) In Lk 7.12; 8.42; 9.38, it refers to an only child, and is always translated in the Latin versions as *unicus* (*–a*), not *unigenitus* (*–a*): that is, it could refer to an only *surviving* child.

(b) In Heb 11.17 the Vg gives 'et *unigenitum* offerebat qui susceperat repromissiones', the VL, 'et *unicum*'. Strictly speaking, both *unicum* and *unigenitum* are equally incorrect, since Isaac was not the only-begotten of Abraham: Ishmael was alive (note Gen 17.18; and the lovely midrash in *Sanhedrin* 89*b*). The usual (and surely correct) explanation is that Isaac was the *only-born* of *Sarah, through whom* the promise was to be fulfilled (Gen 17.19), and therefore the *only son as far as the promises went*. So Theophylactus, cited in Westcott, *Hebrews*, 366: πῶς δὲ μονογενὴς ἦν Ἰσαὰκ ὅπουγε καὶ τὸν Ἰσμαὴλ εἶχε; ἀλλ' ὅσον κατὰ τὸν ἐπαγγελίας λόγον μονογενής. The sense of μονογενής in Heb 11.17 is therefore 'this particular child, who was in a class by himself' (because of the divine promise; see Heb 11.18, citing Gen 21.12).

(c) In the other five NT references, Jn 1.14.18; 3.16.18, and 1 Jn 4.9, the Vg always renders *unigenitus*, but whether *only-begotten* or *only son* is a correct rendering of all five Johannine texts is the point under discussion. The VL reads *unicus* in more than one of these texts (see below), and it will not be forgotten that nowhere else in the NT is Jesus called μονογενής.

(2) The meaning of μονογενής in the OT.

(a) In the MT, the word יָחִיד (yahid) occurs eight times with the meaning *an only child* (Gen 22.2, 12, 16; Judg 11.34 [explicit]; Amos 8.11; Jer 6.26; Zech 12.10; Prov 4.3). In seven of these texts, the LXX translates it as ἀγαπητός. The only exception is Judg 11.34, where A has καὶ αὕτη μονογενὴς αὐτῷ ἀγαπητή, καὶ οὐκ ἔστιν αὐτῷ πλὴν αὐτῆς υἱὸς ἢ θυγάτηρ, and B, καὶ ἦν αὕτη μονογενής, οὐκ ἦν αὐτῷ ἕτερος υἱὸς ἢ θυγάτηρ. This is the only instance in the LXX where יָחִיד (yahid) is translated by μονογενής, and it is notoriously difficult to discern what was the original LXX of Judges.

The Targums render all the above eight texts with the same root יָחִיד (yahid), meaning *only, single, individual* (cf. Jastrow). The Vg too, translating from the Hebrew, renders all eight texts by *unigenitus* [-*a*]. The VL, however, following the LXX, gives *dilectum, dilectissimo, amantissimum* in Genesis, *dilectus* in Amos and Jeremiah; in Jdg 11.34 it has *unica*, in Zech 12.10 *charissimum*, and Prov 4.3 is lacking.[2]

(b) The word μονογενής appears in Tob 3.15; 6.10, [11,] 14 [15 S: not BA]; 8.17 [δύο μονογενεῖς]; Wis 7.22 and Bar 4.16 [Codd. A&V: BS read μονην]. In every case, both Vg and VL translate by *unicus* [-*a*].

(c) The texts just given under (a) and (b) list all the occurrences of μονογενής in the LXX. It is clear therefore (i) that the early Latin translators understood μονογενής, wherever it is found in the LXX, as meaning *unicus*; and (ii) that the real problem is to find out why the LXX translators did not render יָחִיד (yahid) by a word meaning *only-begotten* or *only-born*, but by a word meaning *dearly beloved*.[3]

(d) Delitzsch suggests[4] that in Gen 22.2 the LXX must have read יְדִידְךָ (yedidᵉka), but this suggestion, though it might account for a similar misreading at 22.12 and 16, can hardly extend to all the other texts as well. Hence, given that the fundamental meaning of the Hebrew root יחד is not so much *to be alone* as *to be united*, the LXX translators may well have understood יָחִיד (yahid) as meaning *uniquely cherished*. This would have been all the more likely if they did not know of an exact Greek word (other than μόνος) to denote an only child.

(3) The meaning of μονογενής in non-biblical Greek.

(a) LSJ gives '*the only member of a kin* or *kind*: hence, generally, *only, single,* παῖς Hes. Op. 376, Hdt. 7.221, cf. *Ev. Jo.* 1.14…' etc. The word

---

[2] According to B. Fischer (for Genesis) and P. Sabatier, *Bibliorum Sacrorum*, Cyprian once has *unicum* for Gen 22.2 (Test. III 15: CSEL III 127).

[3] The translations in the Targums and the Vg are of course much later, and may for our purposes be disregarded.

[4] *New Commentary on Genesis*, Edinburgh, 1889, II 86.

may be either a qualifying adjective with a noun (e.g. παῖς) as above, or may stand alone, signifying an only child: so Hesiod, *Theogony* 426, οὐδ', ὅτι μουνογενής, ἧσσον θεὰ ἔμμορε τιμῆς. But its first and fundamental meaning is *unique*, the clearest example of which occurs in Plato, *Timaeus* 31b: οὔτε δύο οὔτ' ἀπείρους ἐποιησεν ὁ ποιῶν κόσμους, ἀλλ' εἷς ὅδε μονογενὴς οὐρανὸς γεγονὼς ἔστιν καὶ ἔτ' ἔσται.

(b) Indeed, so certain is this primary sense that Dodd in 1952 felt constrained to argue that 'one who is μονογενής relatively to a πατήρ can be no other than the only *son*, although μονογενής (from μόνος and γένος) does not mean (at this period [i.e. NT times] at any rate) "only-begotten" (μονογέννητος), but "alone of his kind", "unique"' (*Interpretation*, 305 fn. 1).

However, the etymologically flawless formation μονογέννητος, and equally μονογένητος, figure nowhere in LSJ or the *PGL*, and (what Dodd could not have known) are nowhere to be found in the early Greek Christian writers of the first four centuries. A computer survey of *TLG* gave a nil return for Irenaeus, Clement of Alexandria, Origen, Didymus, Athanasius, Basil, Gregory of Nazianus, Gregory of Nyssa, Cyril of Jerusalem, Chrysostom, and also John of Damascus. It is safe to say that μονογέννητος and μονογένητος did not exist, and that μονογενής, the primary meaning of which is *unique, alone of its kind*, would therefore have been used to denote *an only child*.

(c) The word μονογενής does not, however, occur in Philo (cf. *TWNT* IV 747 fn. 9). In Josephus, it is found only in *Ant.* I 222 and V 264, the former being a retelling of Gen 22.2, where it qualifies 'Isaac', and the latter of Jdg 11.34, where it qualifies 'daughter'.

(d) The only instance in the Apostolic Fathers (cf. Kraft, CPA) is in 1 Clem 25.21, with reference to the phoenix: τοῦτο μονογενὲς ὑπάρχον ζῇ ἔτη πεντακόσια. J. B. Lightfoot comments (*Clement* II 87): ' "*alone of its kind*". This epithet is applied to the phoenix also in Origen, Cyril and Apost. Const. v.7', the last reference being 'evidently founded on this passage of Clement', so that it must have been understood in this same sense.

(e) Two texts in the Greek Apologists are relevant (cf. D. Ruiz Bueno, PAG, with its splendid index).
    (i) Aristides, *Apology* 15.3 (ca. 135?): γιγνώσκουσι γὰρ τὸν θεὸν κτίστην καὶ δημιουργὸν τῶν ἀπάντων ἐν υἱῷ μονογενεῖ καὶ πνεύματι ἁγίῳ καὶ ἄλλον θεὸν πλὴν τούτου οὐ σέβονται. Since Aristides is here addressing the Emperor Hadrian, the most appropriate rendering would be 'in a son who is quite unique, and in a holy spirit'.

(ii) Justin, *Dialogue* 98.5; 105.1, 2 (ca. 155–165). Three times in 98.5 and 105.1.2 we find Ps 21[22].21 quoted, where μονογενής means 'soul'. But another part of 105.1 reads: <u>Μονογενὴς γὰρ ὅτι ἦν τῷ πατρὶ τῶν ὅλων οὗτος</u>, ἰδίως ἐξ αὐτοῦ λόγος καὶ δύναμις γεγεν- νημένος, καὶ ὕστερον ἄνθρωπος διὰ τῆς παρθένου γενόμενος... It is certain that μονογενής is here used by Justin of the pre-Incarnate Word.

(f) To these one may add the Martyrdom of Polycarp 20.2 (ca. 156): διὰ τοῦ μονογενοῦς παιδὸς αὐτοῦ 'Ιησοῦ Χριστοῦ, and the Epistle to Diognetus 10 (at the latest, 150–200): ἀπέστειλε τὸν υἱὸν αὐτοῦ τὸν μονογενῆ) which is probably a quotation from 1 Jn 4.9 (cf. Lightfoot, AF 498).

(g) Around A.D. 150, the Valentinians were beginning to use the term Monogenes as a designation for their aeon Nous, and drawing a sharp distinction between the Monogenes and the historical Jesus. It was possibly for this reason that the term μονογενής was introduced, ca. 160–180, into the credal questions that lie at the origin of the Old Roman Creed, for its use in Christian writings before Irenaeus is (see above) rare (so J. N. D. Kelly, *Early Christian Creeds*, 142). It is certain that after Irenaeus the term is used both of the pre-Incarnate and of the Incarnate Word with the meaning 'only-begotten'. The problem is to discern how far back this meaning 'only-begotten' goes. The three texts cited above in (e)(ii) and in (f) seem to clamour for the meaning 'only-begotten', and for this meaning only; but all three appear to belong to the second half of the second century.

Towards a Resolution of the Problem

(a) The Western Creeds
It was probably ca. 200–250 that the Roman Creed came to be used in Latin. The words τὸν υἱὸν τὸν μονογενῆ were translated as *filium eius unicum* (i.e. not *unigenitum*), a rendering which has prevailed up to the present day. So too virtually all other Western Creeds (Milan, Ravenna, Aquileia, Carthage, Spain, Ireland) have *unicum* [-*o*]; only in southern Gaul and Alemannia, from ca. 500 to ca. 800, do we encounter *unigenitum* (see DS 10-36; 25-27 for the variant).
Almost all these Western Creeds read textually 'Et in Iesum Christum Filium eius unicum Dominum nostrum', and immediately afterwards (with slight textual variations) 'qui conceptus est de Spiritu Sancto et natus ex Maria virgine'. Thus *filium eius unicum*, meaning *his only son*, is used to refer not to the pre-Incarnate Word within the Holy Trinity, but to the historical figure, Jesus Christ, the one and only Son of God, who was conceived of the Holy Spirit and born of Mary the virgin. If this

represents the understanding of μονογενῆ in the baptismal liturgy of Rome ca. 220, may this not have been the interpretation accepted earlier? That is to say, μονογενής was *not* used to denote the Word *as co-eternal*, but to describe the Word *as made flesh* by stressing how unique he is among all members of the human race.

Some measure of support for this view may be found in the early Latin writers. (a) Tertullian, in *adv. Prax.* XV.6, has 'tanquam *unigeniti*' and (for 1.18) '*unigenitus filius*' (CCSG 2.1179[33.40-41]), but shortly afterwards, in XXI.3, writes: 'Huius gloria visa est tanquam unici a Patre, non tanquam Patris, praecedit enim: Deum nemo vidit unquam. Hic unicus sinum Patris disservit…' (CCSG 2.1194[16-19]). As these are the only three relevant references in his writings, it is legitimate to wonder whether some scribe has not harmonized the biblical text to make it match the Vg: there are only four MSS of the *adv. Praxean*, two of the eleventh century, one of the fifteenth, and one now lost (see CCSG introduction). (b) Cyprian also, in *Test.* I.7 and III.31, reads *unici*, not *unigeniti*, at Jn 3.18; and the *De rebaptismate* 13 similarly has *unicum* not *unigenitum* at Jn 3.16 (CSEL III 45[3]; 144[6]; Appendix 86[7]). (c) Lucifer of Cagliari, that treasure-trove of quotations from the VL, offers *unicum* for Jn 3.16,18 and for 1 Jn 4.9 (*De s. Athan.* II 23[25.30] and 16[46], in CCSL 8. 116; 105).

(b) The Eastern Creeds
The earliest Eastern Creed, that of Eusebius of Caesarea, reads: καὶ εἰς ἕνα κύριον Ἰησοῦν Χριστόν, τὸν τοῦ Θεοῦ λόγον, Θεὸν ἐκ Θεοῦ, φῶς ἐκ φωτός, ζωὴν ἐκ ζωῆς, υἱὸν μονογενῆ, πρωτότοκον πάσης κτίσεως, πρὸ πάντων τῶν αἰώνων ἐκ τοῦ πατρὸς γεγεννημένον, δι' οὗ καὶ ἐγένετο τὰ πάντα κτλ. (DS 40). So also the Nicene Creed: καὶ εἰς ἕνα κύριον Ἰησοῦν Χριστόν, τὸν υἱὸν τοῦ Θεοῦ, ἐκ τοῦ Πατρὸς μονογενη γεννηθέντᾶ, τουτέστιν ἐκ τῆς οὐσίας τοῦ Πατρος, Θεὸν ἐκ Θεοῦ, φῶς ἐκ φωτός, Θεὸν ἀληθινὸν ἐκ Θεοῦ ἀληθινοῦ, πρὸ πάντων τῶν αἰώνων ἐκ τοῦ πατρός, γεννηθέντα οὐ ποιηθέντα, ὁμοούσιον τῷ πατρί, δι' οὗ καὶ τὰ πάντα ἐγένετο, τά τε ἐν οὐρανῷ καὶ τὰ ἐν τῇ γῇ κτλ. (DS 125). Similarly, the traditional reformulation at Constantinople: καὶ εἰς ἕνα κύριον Ἰησοῦν Χριστόν, τὸν υἱὸν τοῦ Θεοῦ τὸν μονογενῆ, τὸν ἐκ τοῦ Πατρὸς γεννηθεντα πρὸ πάντων τῶν αἰώνων, φῶς ἐκ φωτός, Θεὸν ἀληθινὸν ἐκ Θεοῦ ἀληθινοῦ, γεννηθέντα οὐ ποιηθέντα, ἐκ τοῦ πατρός, ὁμοούσιον τῷ πατρί, δι' οὗ τὰ πάντα ἐγένετο (DS 150). All the Greek Creeds dwell upon the eternal generation of the Son before creation (DS 40-61), so that in them μονογενής is quite naturally and correctly interpreted as referring to this unique generation from eternity from the Father. Thus, for example, Cyril of Jerusalem· ἕνα δὲ λέγομεν Κύριον Ἰησοῦν Χριστὸν, ἵνα μονογενὴς ᾖ ἡ υἱότης (Cat. X 3), and Υἱὸν μονογενῆ, ἀδελφὸν ἕτερον οὐχ ἔχοντα, διὰ τοῦτο γαρ καλεῖται μονογενὴς ὅτι εἰς τὸ τῆς θεότητος ἀξίωμα καὶ τὴν ἐκ Πατρὸς γέννησιν ἀδελφὸν οὐχ ἔχει (XI 2).

Conclusion

It is thus not absurd to suggest that the meaning of μονογενής in Jn 1.14 is not *only-begotten*, or even *only son*, but rather *quite unique, in a class of his own*. This is the starting-point of the revelation in the Fourth Gospel, from which the nature of the Father and of Jesus' Sonship is gradually disclosed. The revelation begins with an assertion of the uniqueness of the historical Jesus, and then proceeds to affirm the truth of what he disclosed about the nature of God (vv. 16-18).[5] So too the earliest professions of faith, whether in Greek or Latin, require the candidate for baptism to affirm the unique excellence of Jesus as man. It was only when the need arose to formulate an unambiguous affirmation of his full divinity that the term μονογενής was applied to his eternal generation from the Father, long after the Fourth Gospel was written.

[5] See also G. Pendrick 'ΜΟΝΟΓΕΝΗΣ', *NTS* 41 (1995), 587-600. With a wealth of classical examples he reaches the same conclusion, in favour of the meaning *unique*, by a somewhat different route. The argument was also presented, with an application to German renderings, in *Von der Suche nach Gott (FS Helmut Riedlinger)*, Stuttgart-Bad Canstatt, 1998, 'Vom Sinn des μονογενής in Joh 1.14,18', 339-49.

LONGER NOTES OF TEXTUAL CRITICISM

The Punctuation of John 1.3-4[1]

Of the two ways of punctuating vv. 3-4, the first places a full point at the end of v. 3, after ὃ γέγονεν, whereas the second places a full point after οὐδὲ ἕν, and takes the words ὃ γέγονεν as the initial words of the sentence in v. 4.

ἐγένετο οὐδὲ ἕν ὃ γέγονεν. ἐν αὐτῷ ζωὴ ἦν.
Thus the Textus Receptus. This was the division presented in the first printed editions of the Greek NT, namely, Erasmus' NT (1516), and Ximenes' Complutensian Polyglot (printed 1514, published 1522). Stephanus, in his first three editions (1546, 1549, 1550) followed them, and when, in his fourth edition (1551), he introduced the division of chapters into verses, he naturally placed the verse ending, in accordance with the punctuation, after γέγονεν. So the division between 3 and 4 was consolidated, and this punctuation became generally accepted, especially through the editions of the brothers Elzevier (1624 [1st ed.], 1633 [2nd ed.]—the latter being the first to claim the sobriquet Textus Receptus). Even after the dethronement of the Textus Receptus in the mid-nineteenth century, this punctuation was retained by Tischendorf in his first seven editions (1841–1859), by B. Weiss (1894–1900), Souter (1910 [1st ed.], 1947 [2nd ed.]),[2] Vogels (1920 [1st ed.], 1922 [2nd ed.]), Merk (1933), and Bover (1943) plus Nestle, editions 1–25 (1898–1963). For centuries translators followed this reading, in the AV = KJV, RV, ASV, RSV (1946), NIV (1973), and—somewhat surprisingly—in the REB (1989).

ἐγένετο οὐδὲ ἕν (or: οὐδέν). ὃ γέγονεν ἐν αὐτῷ ζωὴ ἦν.
The second part here may of course be construed in two ways,

either as   (a) ὃ γέγονεν / ἐν αὐτῷ ζωὴ ἦν.
or as   (b) ὃ γέγονεν ἐν αὐτῷ // ζωὴ ἦν.

---

[1] The basic article assembling all the detail is by K. Aland, 'Eine Untersuchung zu Joh 1.3-4', *ZNW* 59 (1968), 174-209. See also the comprehensive study by Ed. L. Miller, *Salvation History in the Prologue of John: The Significance of John 1.3-4*, NovTSup 60, Leiden, 1989.

[2] But it should not be forgotten that Souter was supplying the Greek text underlying the RV of 1881.

One or other of these alternatives must be chosen in order to interpret and to translate reading 2 at all.

According to K. Aland, the first editor to propose this reading in modern times was E. Barton (Oxford, 1831). He was followed by Lachmann (1837), Tischendorf (ed. 8a, 1869), Tregelles (1870), Westcott-Hort (1881), von Soden (1913), Vogels (³1949), Kilpatrick in ²BFBS (1958), the Greek NT for Translators (1960), Tasker (1964), the UBS (1966) and NA²⁶ (1979) and NA²⁷ (1993). The growing preference for this reading during the second half of the twentieth century is reflected in the number of translations which adopt it: *Bible de Jérusalem* (1958), NEB (1961 [1st ed.], 1970 [2nd ed.]), NAB (1970), *Translator's NT* (1973). NRSV (1989).³ This is also the punctuation of the Sixtine Vulgate ('sine ipso factum est nihil: quod factum est in ipso vita erat') and of Wordsworth–White; the Clementine, however, reads, with studied ambiguity, 'factum est nihil, quod factum est, in ipso vita erat', an ambiguity which, unfortunately, later printers of the Latin Bible (the so-called Sixto-Clementine Vulgate) did not always preserve.⁴

(a) *The external witness of the Fathers, of the earlier uncials, and of $\mathfrak{P}^{75}$, is proof that though most later Greek MSS. of the Gospel favour reading 1, reading 2 is the more ancient interpretation of the text.* The fullest account of the Greek manuscript tradition is in Aland's article, on pp. 187-90. Of 148 minuscules examined by him, 121 have reading 1, though two of these (885 and 1814) are fifteenth-century commentaries which on this point diverge from the lemma of their text, which is 2. Of the remaining 27 minuscules, only five read 2, one from the twelfth century (850) and four from the fifteenth (149 880 1820 2129—2129 reading [ii] [a]). Of the 22 others, 17 place a punctuation mark both after οὐδέν, and after ὃ γέγονεν, so that it is possible to construe the text either as 1 or as 2. The remaining five are very confused, but all have a full point after γέγονεν. Thus the later Greek manuscript tradition is overwhelmingly in favour of reading 1.

The witness of the uncials, however, points in a different direction. Aland prints out a complete list, with the punctuation of the lemma in each of 33 manuscripts clearly indicated (pp. 189-90). The early uncials $\mathfrak{P}^{66}$ B ℵ* A have no division between the words at this point, only *scriptio continua*, and must therefore be left out of consideration. However,

---

³ It is also true to say that before 1950, nearly all commentators followed Reading 1 (exceptions are Westcott, Loisy, Bernard, Gächter, Bultmann, Hoskyns–Davey), and that since 1950 an ever-increasing number of commentators has argued in favour of 2 (notably Roman Catholic scholars, such as Boismard, Lacan, Lamarche, de la Potterie, R. E. Brown, van den Bussche, and Zimmermann).

⁴ The simplest and surest way of checking the various readings of the 'official' printed texts of the Vulgate is to consult *Biblia Sacra Vulgatae editionis Sixti V ...et Clementis VIII auctoritate edita... edidit Michael Hetzenauer*, 3a ed., Regensburg, 1929. On Jn 1.3-4, see Hetzenauer's long note on 1264.

the first uncials to contain punctuation, $\mathfrak{P}^{75c}$ (early third century), C (fifth century), and D (fifth to sixth centuries) testify unambiguously to reading 2 (with the corrector of C making it more precise as 2 [b]). Thereafter, however, from the turn of the sixth and seventh centuries, the uncials, now regularly punctuated, nearly all join with the minuscules to support reading 1. Thus E F G H S V W Ψ Θ etc., with reading 2 attested only in W^{supp} L 050* 0141. Taking this evidence in conjunction with that of the minuscules, it would appear that the construction 'That which was made in him was life' represents the early interpretation of the text, and that the alternative, reading 1 ('...was made nothing that was made') began to replace it in the Greek manuscripts at some time in the sixth century. The fact that 2 represents the more ancient understanding of the words is further supported by the evidence of Tatian's Diatessaron, of the Old Syriac (sy^c; sy^s is here missing), of the Coptic Sahidic, and of the Old Latin tradition; indeed, according to F. C. Burkitt,[5] this is also the correct reading of the Peshitta.

The strongest argument, however, in favour of reading 2 is that until around A.D. 300 all the Christian writers and all the heretics without exception understood the text in this way. Thus all the second-century Gnostics (who punctuate as in 2 [b], '*quod factum est in ipso, vita erat*'),[6] and Irenaeus in his polemic against them; thus Tertullian and Hippolytus, Clement of Alexandria and Origen.[7] Indeed, the two most powerful arguments in favour of reading 2 are that Irenaeus, who cites the text ten times (I 8:5; 9; 21:1; II 2:5; III 8:3; 11:8; 21:10; IV 32:1; V 18:2; Dem. 43) seems quite unaware of any other understanding of the words, for the first interpretation, had he known of it, would have been a crushing retort to his adversaries. Origen also, who customarily lists all conceivable interpretations, and who (*In Ioannem*. II 13-14: SC 120, pp. 214-17) castigates Heracleon for not observing the significance of the presence and absence of the definite article before θεός in Jn 1.1, is equally unaware of any construction other than 2. A full list of writers supporting 2 is given in UBS.[8] One may add that reading 2 was the usual interpretation accepted by all the Latin writers of the Middle Ages, following Augustine.[9]

---

[5] *JTS* 4 (1903), 436-38.

[6] On the Gnostic interpretation of this verse, see the masterly study by A. Orbe, *En los albores de la exegesis iohannea = Estudios Valentinianos II.*

[7] The references to Irenaeus, Tertullian, Clement and Origen may be found in K. Aland, *ZNW* 59 (1968), 190-94, and those to Hippolytus on 195-96.

[8] For a detailed defence of Reading 2, see Miller, *Salvation History*, 17-44.

[9] This can be very clearly seen in Thomas Aquinas's handbook of patristic quotations, completed in 1267, entitled *Catena Aurea in Quattuor Evangelia: In Ioannem* I, 7 (vol. 2: Turin, 1953, 332-33).

The internal evidence does not prove that reading 1 is certainly that intended by the evangelist. The fact that reading 2 is the more ancient interpretation of the text does not, of course, prove that this was the meaning intended by the original writer, or the evangelist. Barrett, while disclaiming any certainty, presents succinctly the internal arguments in favour of reading 1. He writes that this reading 'gives a better parallel structure to the clause because οὐδὲ ἕν is a frequent sentence ending when greater emphasis than a simple οὐδέν is required (e.g. Josephus, *Ant.* VI 266), and because after οὐδὲ ἕν, ὧν (rather than ὃ) γέγονεν would be expected. [Neither] of these reasons is convincing, and against them may be set (1) John's very frequent use of ἐν at the beginning of a sentence; (2) his frequent repetitiousness (nothing was made that has been made; cf. e.g. vv. 1ff.); (3) such passages as 5.26, 39; 6.53, which give a similar sense; (4) the fact that it makes much better, and more Johannine sense to say that in the Word was life, than to say that the created universe was life in him, and that this life was the light of men. The alternative ways of rendering (That which came into being—in it the Word was life; That which came into being—in the Word was its life) are almost impossibly clumsy. After a detailed discussion, Schnackenburg comes to the same conclusion.'[10]

If, however, ὃ γέγονεν refers to something other than the making of the material creation, these objections may not hold.

Was the Original Reading of the Verb in 1.12 Singular or Plural?

The controversy on whether the verb in Jn 1.12 should be read in the singular, ἐγεννήθη, dates back to Tertullian.[11] The UBS edition lists the manuscript evidence, and its editors rate the plural as virtually certain {A}. 'It appeared to the Committee that, on the basis of the overwhelming consensus of all Greek manuscripts, the plural must be adopted, a reading which, moreover, is in accord with the characteristic teaching of John. The singular number may have arisen either from a desire to make the Fourth Gospel allude explicitly to the virgin birth or from the influence of the singular number of the immediately preceding αὐτοῦ.' The majority of scholars agree, and the first translation bold enough to

---

[10] For a fuller discussion, see Miller, *Salvation History*, 18-27.

[11] The most comprehensive study of this reading is J. Galot, *Etre né de Dieu (Jean 1.13)*, Analecta Biblica 37, Rome, 1969, which has an excellent bibliography to that date. Also worth consulting are: F.-M. Braun, ' "Qui ex Deo natus est" (Jean 1.13)', in *Aux Sources de la Tradition chrétienne (Mélanges offerts à M. Maurice Goguel)*, Paris, 1950, 11-31, and A. Houssiau, 'Le milieu théologique de la leçon ἐγεννήθη', in *Sacra Pagina II*, BETL 13, Paris-Gembloux, 1959, 169-88. The main arguments are summarized in J. McHugh, *The Mother of Jesus in the New Testament*, London, 1975, 255-68.

emend was that by D. Mollat in the *Bible de Jérusalem* (1953).[12] Yet an imposing group of twentieth-century writers (including more Protestants than Roman Catholics) have pronounced themselves in favour of the singular as the original reading of the text.[13]

(a) All the Greek manuscripts without exception read the plural, as do all the ancient versions. The singular is found only in one Old Latin MS. (Codex Veronensis *b*, fifth century), in an eleventh-century Lectionary from Toledo whose authorship is attributed to Hildefonsus (657–667) (both of which have *natus est*), and in the Curetonian Syriac. (The last-named, however, has the antecedent relative pronoun in the plural, so that the literal translation would be 'those who...was born of God'. The confusion reappears in six MSS of the Peshitta, dating from the fifth to the tenth century)

(b) Direct patristic evidence for the singular, explicitly rejecting the plural, is limited to Tertullian,[14] who may have adopted this reading from Irenaeus.[15] Other evidence is indirect, and sparse. The *Epistle of the Apostles* 3 (ca. 140–180) appears to allude to this text.[16] Irenaeus on four or five occasions appears to presuppose the singular, or at least to show signs of acquaintance with it.[17] Ambrose and Augustine, who sometimes

---

[12] And in the one-volume edition of 1956. The plural replaced it in the (English) NJB (1985), but the French version still retains the singular.

[13] Among those who favour the singular are A. Resch, F. Blass, A. von Harnack (with qualifications), Th. Zahn, R. Seeberg, C. F. Burney, F. Büchsel, M.-E. Boismard, F. M. Braun, D. Mollat (references to these in Galot, 5-6).

[14] 'Quid est ergo non ex sanguine nec carnis voluntate nec ex viri, sed ex deo natus est ? Hoc quidem capitulo ego potius utar, cum adulteratores eius obduxero. Sic enim scriptum esse contendunt: "Non ex sanguine nec carnis voluntate nec ex viri, sed ex deo nati sunt", quasi supra dictos credentes in nomine eius designet.' These lines from *De carne Christi* 19.1, are Tertullian's only reference to Jn 1.13, apart from a passing mention in 24.2 of the same work ('Et non ex sanguine nec carnis voluntate nec ex viri, sed ex deo natus est Hebion respondit', i.e. he replies to Ebion that...). The two texts are in CCSG 2.907; 915-16 = PL 2.784B and 791A.

[15] *De carne Christi* was written around 212. In his *Adv. Valentinianos* 5,1, written between 208 and 211, Tertullian names Irenaeus as one of his sources 'quos optaverim sequi' (CCSG 2.756 = PL 2.548-49).

[16] The exact date and place of its composition are uncertain, but all are agreed that it was written at the outside between A.D. 140 and 210, probably between 140 and 180. Egypt, Palestine, Syria and Asia Minor have all been proposed as the place of origin. Chapter 3 is extant only in Ethiopic, and translates as: 'we believe that the word which became flesh through the holy virgin Mary...was born not by the lust of the flesh but by the will of God' (see Elliott *ANT* 559; James *ANT* 486; *NTA* I 193).

[17] The texts are: (1) 'non enim ex voluntate carnis, neque ex voluntate viri, sed ex voluntate Dei, Verbum caro factum est' (*Adv. Haer.* III 17 1 = Harvey II 83 = *PG* [16.2] 7.921-22 = SC 294); (2) 'cognoscit autem illum, is cui Pater qui est in caelis revelavit ut intelligat, quoniam is qui non ex voluntate carnis, neque ex voluntate viri natus est, filius hominis, hic est Christus Filius Dei vivi' (III 20 2 = Harvey II 103 = *PG* [19.2] 7.940A = SC 294); (3) perhaps also 'circumscripsit igitur genitalia viri in promissione Scriptura: imo vero nec commemoratur, quoniam non ex voluntate viri erat, qui nascebatur' (III 26 1 = Harvey II 117 = *PG* [21.5] 7.952A = SC 416); (4) 'et propter hoc in fine non ex

use the singular may well have been influenced, directly or indirectly, by Tertullian.[18]

(c) Yet the internal evidence in favour of the singular is strong. Galot has argued the case at length, and it will be sufficient to summarize only his most important arguments. (1) Why should such stress be placed on the negative aspects of spiritual regeneration? It throws no light on the nature of spiritual rebirth, and in no way prepares the reader for the statement immediately following, that 'The Word became flesh'. (2) How can those who have already been begotten of God (v.13) be given the power to *become* children of God? 'We are so accustomed to reading the plural that we no longer notice how bewildering it is, how difficult to accept' (Galot, 96). (3) On the other hand, if the singular be read, and taken to refer to the earthly birth of Jesus, it is easy to explain the three-fold negation as a triple affirmation of the virginal conception of Jesus against its first opponents, probably Ebionites. Irenaeus in particular never seems to have suspected that the text could bear any other meaning. (4) The Fourth Gospel sometimes asserts that the Word made flesh gives to those who believe in him the power to become or to share in what Jesus himself already is *par excellence* (e.g. 11:25; 12.36; 14.12). Would not this make excellent sense in 1.13?

There is thus a head-on collision between the arguments from external and internal evidence. Braun argues that the witness of Irenaeus (and perhaps Justin) should be preferred above all other external authorities, inasmuch as they were closely linked with Ephesus.[19] Galot suggests[20] (less convincingly) that an original singular was altered, some time between 160 and 190, to a plural, when the text was applied to the spiritual regeneration of believers; but are we to believe that not a single Greek text remained untouched by the correction? Barrett suggests that the reverse process may have been at work, namely, that John was 'declaring that the birth of Christians, being bloodless and rooted in God's will alone, followed the pattern of Christ himself'.

Burney and Torrey have argued that the Fourth Gospel was originally written in Aramaic, and even if their arguments are far from conclusive, a case can be made that some parts of it were. If Jn 1.13-14 had been written in Aramaic the copulative *waw* at the beginning of 14 could, by dittography, have been repeated at the end of v.13, thereby turning an

voluntate carnis, neque ex voluntate viri, sed ex placito Patris manus eius vivum perfecerunt hominem, uti fiat Adam secundum imaginem et similitudinem Dei' (V 1 3 = Harvey II 3173 = *PG* [16.2] 7.1123B = SC 28); (5) possibly also the short remark 'quod enim ex Deo natum est, Deus est' (I 8 5 = Harvey I 77 = *PG* 7.534B = SC 130).

[18] Augustine's best-known text with the singular (*Confessions* VII 9, 13 = PL 32.740-41) understands the verse as referring to the eternal generation of the Word apud Patrem. So also Loisy, 180-82. But in that case, would the threefold negation be necessary?

[19] See F.-M. Braun, '"Qui ex Deo natus est" (Jean 1.13)', in *Aux Sources de la Tradition chrétienne*, 26-30.

[20] Galot, 87-89.

Aramaic singular (אתיליד, ʾtyld) into a plural (אתילידו, ʾtyldw).[21] This would explain how the internal evidence can be all in favour of the singular, while all the Greek MSS without exception (but not the Curetonian Syriac!) have the plural. Furthermore, this might also explain why Irenaeus took the reading to be singular. He could have been in contact with a living tradition at Ephesus, or could have known an Aramaic or Syriac version differing from that in our Greek manuscripts.[22] This would seem to be a reasonable explanation of all the data, but it is unlikely to commend itself to many.

If the singular be read, then of course the relative οἱ at the beginning of the verse has to be corrected to ὅς, for which there is no evidence at all (though D* and itᵃ omit the relative altogether, leaving the sentence unconnected with the preceding one). This objection would not hold against the theory of an Aramaic original, where the singular and the plural of the relative pronoun are the same. If the singular be read, then the sense is that the Word gave the power to become children of God to those who believe in the name of 'the one who was born as a result not of the union of blood-streams, nor through any carnal desire, nor through the desire of a husband, but of God.'

A Note on the Text of 1.18b

The text of 18b is much debated. UBS gives the preference to μονογενὴς θεός, on the ground that it has earlier and better support among the Greek MSS of the Gospel (although ο μ. θ. is far better attested among the early Fathers); it places second μονογενὴς υἱός, which is the most widely attested among the MSS, versions and Fathers; and last, ὁ μονογενής. The UBS Committee gave their choice a {B} rating, with A. Wikgren emphatically dissenting, 'At least a D decision would be preferable'. The fullest information is still that in Tischendorf 8a (he strongly prefers ο μ. υ.), the longest dissertation that in F. J. A. Hort, *Two Dissertations*, 1876, 1-72. Zahn, 2nd ed., 703-708 = 5th ed., 714-19 and also Lagrange 26-28 discuss the matter at length. Schnackenburg and Barrett comment that the sense is substantially unaltered whether one reads ὁ μονογενὴς θεός or ὁ μονογενὴς υἱός (both prefer the former, not least because of 𝔓⁶⁶·⁷⁵). This may well account for the paucity of periodical literature on the topic.[23] The main arguments that come under consideration are as follows:

---

[21] I.e. reading אתילדוממרא and writing אתילדוממרא.

[22] 'A point of some interest [lies in]…the repeated instances that Scriptural quotations afford, of having been made by one who was as familiar with some Syriac version of the New Testament, as with the Greek originals. Strange *variae lectiones* occur, which can only be explained by referring to the Syriac version' (W. W. Harvey, the editor of *S. Irenaei…Libri Quinque adversus Haereses*, Cambridge, 1857, I, Preface, 5.)

[23] Malatesta (1920–65) lists none, Van Belle (1966–85) only one, D. A. Fennema ('John 1.18: "God, the Only Son"', *NTS* 31 [1985], 124-35).

(1) If one accepts o μ. θ. as the original text, it is easy to see why it was altered to o μ. υ., to distinguish the Son from the Father, to correspond with πατρός in the same verse, and by assimilation to Jn 3.16, 18; 1 Jn 4.9. It is more difficult to say why υἱός should have been changed to θεός (or rather Ῡ͞Σ to Θ͞Σ).

(2) 'The anarthrous use of θεός' (cf. 1.1) appears to be more primitive. There is no reason why the article should have been deleted, and when υἱός supplanted θεός it would certainly have been added' (*TCGNT*). But if the original reading was μονογενής θεός, without the article, why was one inserted in MSS with this reading? If μ. θ. is taken as two separate nouns (see *TCGNT* fn.), it translates well as 'three distinct designations of him who makes God known': 'an only-begotten [or: an only] Son, God, who is in the bosom of the Father'.

(3) The most serious weakness in the case for [o] μ. θ. is that its supporting witnesses are overwhelmingly Alexandrian, and that one cannot exclude the idea that doctrinal considerations may have led either to the insertion of θεός or to its substitution for υἱός.

(4) 'The shortest reading, ὁ μονογενής, while attractive because of internal considerations, is too poorly attested for acceptance as the text' (*TCGNT*). There are indeed formidable internal arguments for the opinion that ὁ μονογενής was the original text. (a) It would explain the intrusion either of θεός or of υἱός, as clarifying nouns, at a quite early date, and of their persistence afterwards. (b) It alone supplies a satisfactory explanation of the two divergent readings. (c) In Excursus III, it is suggested that around A.D. 150, the Valentinians were beginning to use the term Monogenes as a designation for their aeon Nous, and drawing a sharp distinction between this Monogenes and the historical Jesus. It is therefore possible that in 1.18 an original μονογενής was more closely defined as θεός or υἱός in the second half of that century. (d) If the meaning 'someone unique' is accepted for μονογενής in 1.14, it would have made excellent sense to repeat it here in 1.18, with the article. (e) Even so, ὁ μονογενής might have become an embarrassment in public or liturgical use by (say) the year 200, and have stood in need of clarification. On these grounds, the present writer prefers to regard ὁ μονογενής as the original reading, and to understand it as 'the unique One, that unique individual', referring to one visibly present on earth, Jesus Christ.

(5) Burney offers a different explanation of the origin of the two divergent readings (*AOFG* 40). He suggests that an original Aramaic יְחִיד/אֱלָהָא (yĕḥid ʾelahaʾ), in the construct, meaning 'the only-begotten of God' has been misread as יָחִיד אֱלָהָא (yaḥid ʾelahaʾ), as an absolute, and so rendered

'the only-begotten God'. It is odd that he should have expressed his idea
in this manner, for his argument would have been more cogent had he
suggested that יחיד אלהא (unvocalized) had been misread as an absolute,
when it was originally a construct.

(6) Perhaps the simplest explanation of all is to take Burney's idea one
step further. Suppose that at least this verse (with or without some others
in the Prologue) was originally written in Aramaic, and that the (unvocalized) word written down was יחידא (= yḥydʾ), with the final aleph
denoting the absolute state, that is, equivalent to ὁ μονογενής. Suppose
that someone then misread the word as though the final aleph was an
abbreviation for אלהא (ʾɛlahʾa), meaning *God*, and translated it as μονογενὴς θεός. This would account for the fact that μονογενὴς θεός
(without the article) is on balance the most anciently attested ($\mathfrak{P}^{66}$ ℵ* B
C* L) but that all the other Greek MSS (from $\mathfrak{P}^{75}$ onwards) and Fathers
use the article, whether they read θεός or υἱός.

Those who prefer to read μονογενὴς θεός may like the accuracy of
'the unique one, who is divine' (*The Translator's NT*, 1973, 452, attempt-
ing to represent as clearly as possible UBS); only the NAB is bold
enough to print a literal version, 'the only Son, God'. Other translations
are 'God's only Son' (NEB, REB), 'the only Son' (RSV) and 'God the
only Son' (NRSV), but the RSV alone makes clear what Greek text is
being translated. In the other three, the marginal notes are very confusing.

II

THE FIRST WEEK

1.19–2.12

That this section constitutes a literary unit is evident from the repetition of τῇ ἐπαύριον, *on the next day*, in Jn 1.29.35.43, indicating four consecutive days, to which the phrase in 2.1, τῇ ἡμέρᾳ τῇ τρίτῃ, *on the third day*, adds two more. The narrative is thereby set in the framework of a first 'week' in Jesus' ministry.[1] The six days are marked out as follows:

Day 1	1.19-28	John's witness about himself
Day 2	2.29-34	John's witness about Jesus
Day 3	1.35-42	Three of John's followers join Jesus
Day 4	1.43-51	Philip and Nathanael join Jesus
Day 6	2.1-12	The Wedding at Cana

A different arrangement is adopted here. The section is divided into three parts, by putting the first two days together, and the third day with the fourth. This results in two diptychs of approximately equal length, one about the witness of John (1.19-34), the other about the calling of Jesus' disciples (1.35-51), and a conclusion about the Wedding at Cana (2.1-12).

A. THE WITNESS OF JOHN THE BAPTIST (1.19-34)

The three Synoptics begin by describing the activity of John the Baptist: he is presented first as administering a baptism for the forgiveness of sins (Mt 3.1-10 ‖ Mk 1.1-6 ‖ Lk 3.1-14), and secondly, as introducing and baptizing Jesus (Mt 3.11-17 ‖ Mk 1.7-11 ‖ Lk 3.15-22). The Fourth Gospel nowhere states that John's baptism was 'for the forgiveness of sins', thus leaving open the possibility that, in the mind of this evangelist, John's baptism was to be regarded as a rite of merely external purification, to make its recipients fit for Jewish worship (compare Jn 2.6 and

---

[1] Some writers, reading πρωι instead of πρωτον in 1.41, have suggested that an extra day should be added for the events in vv. 41-42. They are perhaps attracted to this by the mention of the third day in 2.1, and hopeful of finding there an allusion to the Resurrection of Jesus (→ 2.1).

3.25), an interpretation which would seem to be confirmed by the absence in this Gospel of any reference to a call to repentance by the Baptist. Further, even though the fact of his baptizing is mentioned (1.25, 26, 33), the sole purpose of referring to it is, apparently, to elicit John's testimony to Jesus. From the first half of the Synoptic account there remains only the citation of Isa 40.3; from the second half, the descent of the spirit and the revelation of Jesus' sonship are retained, but the record of John's baptizing Jesus is suppressed, totally. For what purpose could a baptism by John serve, or what significance could it have, in the case of the Word made flesh?

1. *The Baptist's Witness about Himself (1.19-28)*

1.19 And this is the testimony of John, when the Jews from Jerusalem sent priests and Levites [to him,] to ask him, 'Who are you?' 20 He admitted and did not deny, but admitted, 'I am not the Christ'. 21 And they asked him, 'What then? Are you Elijah?' He said, 'I am not'. 'Are you the prophet?' And he answered, 'No'. 22 So they said to him, 'Who are you? We need to give an answer to those who sent us. What do you say about yourself?' 23 He said, 'I am the voice of one crying in the wilderness, "Make straight the way of the Lord", as the prophet Isaiah said'.

24 Some were also sent from among the Pharisees. 25 They questioned him and said to him, 'Then why are you baptizing, if you are neither the Christ, nor Elijah, nor the prophet?' 26 John answered them, 'I am baptizing in water; but standing among you is someone you do not recognize, 27 that follower of mine, the thong of whose sandal I am not worthy to untie'. 28 These things took place in Bethany beyond the Jordan, where John was baptizing.

19. καὶ αὕτη ἐστὶν ἡ μαρτυρία τοῦ 'Ιωάννου. In the Fourth Gospel, the name 'Ιωάννης everywhere denotes the Baptist except in four verses referring to 'Simon, son of John' (1.42; 21.15, 16, 17);[2] no other 'John' is mentioned by name. More significant is the fact that this 'Ιωάννης is never once referred to either as 'the Baptist' (twelve times in the Synoptics) or as 'the Baptizer' (Mk 1.4; 6.14, 24); the absence of the by-name almost certainly indicates that the evangelist does not regard John's function of baptizing as integral to the story which is about to be told.[3] In his mind, John came solely 'for witness' (Jn 1.7), and the narrative of the Fourth Gospel opens by recounting first of all the content of his witness.

ὅτε ἀπέστειλαν [πρὸς αὐτὸν][4] οἱ 'Ιουδαῖοι. In the Fourth Gospel, the meaning of οἱ 'Ιουδαῖοι oscillates, 'no doubt deliberately—

---

[2] There are many witnesses in each of these verses to the variant 'Ιωνα.

[3] It would in fact be more appropriate to refer to him in the Fourth Gospel as 'John the Witness' (some scholars do); but 'John the Baptist' is less puzzling for the average reader, and is the title in possession.

[4] Thus UBS[3] and NA[27], with square brackets. Of the early witnesses, some omit the phrase, some include it here, and some place it after Λευίτας (NA[27] gives the details).

with varying accent, and for various groups indifferently' (Schnacken-burg⁵). Here it refers to what would be termed in modern British English the 'Jewish establishment' in Jerusalem, that is, the political leaders and families of influence, though it should be stressed that, certainly in this first reference, the term οἱ 'Ιουδαῖοι is used in a quite neutral sense, without favour or animosity. **ἐξ 'Ιεροσολύμων.** The Hellenized form of the name, 'Ιεροσόλυμα, is always used by Matthew,⁶ Mark and John. The alternative form, 'Ιερουσαλήμ, is certainly closer to the Semitic original, and is sometimes said to be used when stressing the sacral character of the city.⁷ Though the distinction is attractive, it is of no help in inter-preting John's Gospel, since the Semitic form is never found there, in spite of the fact that so much of the Gospel centres on Jerusalem, the Holy City of pilgrimage and worship. In all likelihood, therefore, the evangelist uses 'Ιεροσόλυμα simply because that was the form in normal use throughout the Eastern Mediterranean.⁸ **ἱερεῖς καὶ Λευίτας.** This is the only place where either priests or Levites are mentioned in John; both belonged to the lower ranks of the clergy. The great majority of priests had no high social status, and the Levites were of a lower rank still: forbidden to take part in the offering of sacrifice, they provided the musicians, the doormen and the police force of the Temple. A profound social and educational gulf separated these two groups from the priestly aristocracy,⁹ and the implication of this solitary mention of 'priests and Levites' is that the authorities in Jerusalem were at first content to send a rather low-ranking delegation to report on John's pretensions and activi-ties. **ἵνα ἐρωτήσωσιν¹⁰ αὐτόν, σὺ τίς εἶ;** *...that they might ask him, Who are you?* The order of the words σὺ τίς εἶ; places the stress on the verb, that is, 'Who *are* you?' (contrast the order in v. 21, and the wording in v. 22).

20. καὶ ὡμολόγησεν καὶ οὐκ ἠρνήσατο, καὶ ὡμολόγησεν ὅτι...

The two verbs ὁμολογεῖν and ἀρνεῖσθαι are not infrequently both used in the same context, and by way of contrast; the lexicons quote

---

The most reasonable explanation for the variation is that the two words are a very early gloss inserted for greater clarity.

⁵ For the differing shades of meaning, see his long note in I 275-76 = ETr I 287.

⁶ With the solitary exception of the lament appearing in Mt 23.27: 'Ιερουσαλὴμ 'Ιερουσαλήμ...

⁷ E.g. J. B. Lightfoot, *Galatians*, 182, commenting on 4.26. He cites Bengel on Rev. 21.22: "Ιερουσαλὴμ est appellatio Hebraica, originaria et sanctior; 'Ιεροσόλυμα deinceps obvia, Graeca, magis politica'.

⁸ See the excellent note in MHT II 148-49.

⁹ For detail, see J. Jeremias, *Jerusalem*, 198-207 (on the priests), and 207-13 (on the Levites).

¹⁰ The variant ερωτησουσιν makes no difference to the meaning. The use of the future indicative instead of the subjunctive is not rare after classical times. See BDF 369 (2) and compare Goodwin §324.

Thucydides, Josephus and other writers, sometimes in a judicial context.[11] The emphasis here is trebly strong: *he confessed, and did not deny, but confessed that...* Ἐγὼ οὐκ εἰμὶ ὁ Χριστός. The ἐγώ is slightly emphatic, in answer to the stress (just mentioned) in the question at 1.19: *I am not the Christ* (ἐγώ is omitted in answer to the next three questions in v. 21). ὁ Χριστός is here used in an undefined sense, denoting assuredly *the Messiah*, but without determining precisely how that title was to be understood. If the expectation of a messianic king who would come to liberate the nation by force of arms had in post-exilic times often receded, it had by no means wholly disappeared.[12]

21. καὶ ἠρώτησαν αὐτόν, τί οὖν; σύ Ἠλίας εἶ;[13] Once the major question of any kind of Messianic claim is out of the way, curiosity is aroused. οὖν is an inferential particle, moving the narrative forward. τί οὖν; (a favourite phrase of Paul) means *In that case,* or *What then? Are you Elijah?* **καὶ λέγει, Οὐκ εἰμί.**

A NOTE ON ELIJAH

To understand this question and the answer, two texts from the book of Malachi must be considered. According to the first, Mal 3.1-4, Yahweh was to send 'a messenger'[14] (unnamed) to purify the Temple and its priesthood, in order to prepare the way for his own coming to the Temple. A second text, Mal 3.23-24 (= 4.5-6), reads, 'I will send you the prophet Elijah', to establish peace within Israel 'before the great and terrible day of Yahweh comes...lest I come and strike the land with a curse'. Here it is Elijah's task to preach repentance and reconciliation within families, in order to avert the wrath of God. These two verses about Elijah are often regarded as a later addition to the book of Malachi, because they have no logical connection with the preceding context. Thus it is by no means clear that the messenger alluded to in the first text, Mal 3.1-4 ('Malachi'), whose task would be to purify the priesthood and the Temple for the Day of the Lord, is necessarily to be identified with the figure of Elijah portrayed in the second text, Mal 3.23-24 (= 4.5-6), whose task was to establish peace within Israel and to avert the wrath of God.

[11] BDAG lists among others Thucydides VI 60,3, βεβαιοτέραν γὰρ αὐτῷ σωτηρίαν εἶναι ὁμολογήσαντι μετ' ἀδείας ἢ ἀρνηθέντι διὰ δίκης ἐλθεῖν; Josephus, *Ant.* VI 151, Σαοῦλος δὲ ἀδικεῖν ὡμολόγει καὶ τὴν ἁμαρτίαν οὐκ ἠρνεῖτο; and the *Martyrdom of Polycarp* 9.2, τοῦ δὲ ὁμολογοῦντος, ἔπειθεν ἀρνεῖσθαι κτλ.

[12] Schürer II §29 gives both an historical survey of Messianism over the period (488–513) and a systematic presentation of its ideology (513-54). See below 'A Note on Messianism in the Time of Jesus', at 1.41, p. 154.

[13] In the MSS, the last five words appear in many a different sequence, the diversity of which does not affect the meaning. See NA[27] and *TCGNT*.

[14] In Hebrew מַלְאָכִי (malʾĕki), meaning literally *my messenger*. From this text the anonymous author of the book acquired the name Malachi.

Sirach 48.10-12, in what is apparently a comment on this second text, affirms that Elijah will return 'to calm the wrath of God before it breaks out in fury'. It adds that he will also 'restore the tribes of Jacob', thus ascribing to Elijah a role assigned in Isa 49.6 to the Servant of Yahweh. Indeed, these words imply that Elijah at his return would have a political, as well as a religious role, if such a distinction would have any meaning in the ancient Jewish world.

Yet Billerbeck can write: 'In the Pseudepigrapha the figure of Elijah recedes far into the background. The redemption of God's people is there entrusted to other hands', such as the angels, the pious, or the Messiah, so that there was really nothing left for Elijah to do.[15] Confirmation of the diminishing interest in Elijah may be found by consulting a concordance of the Greek Pseudepigrapha: of more than 70,000 entries, only fifteen mention Elijah, of which twelve occur in the *Lives of the Prophets* (and four of them are variant readings).[16] Between 200 B.C. and A.D. 100, the figure of Elijah, the great deliverer and restorer of Israel promised in Mal 3.23-24 (= 4.5-6) and in Sirach, had faded into the background; but there still lingered the memory of 'the messenger' promised in Mal 3.1-4. This messenger began to be thought of as a forerunner not of the divine judge but of the Messiah, and was often identified with Elijah.[17]

It is against this background that the three Synoptics depict the Baptist. Matthew 3.4 and Mk 1.6 both remark that John wore a camel-hair tunic and leather belt, the apparel by which Elijah was identified (1 Kgs 1.8); but such dress was not unique to Elijah (compare Zech 13.4), and the two Gospel texts mean no more than that John the Baptist was, like Elijah, a prophet. Luke 1.17 is more pertinent: Zechariah's son will go before the Lord 'in the spirit and power of Elijah' to reconcile fathers and sons, 'to prepare his ways' (1.76), as was foretold in Mal 3.1, 23-24 (= 4.5-6). Here the role envisaged for Elijah is a purely spiritual one. Similarly, when the three Synoptics apply to the Baptist the words of Mal 3.1—'Behold, I send my messenger before me, to prepare the way ahead of me'—the purpose of the citation is to announce that John is no ordinary prophet, but the messenger sent on ahead to prepare the way for the Messiah (Mt 11.10 || Lk 7.27; Mk 1.2 adapts it very slightly). In these texts, the Baptist is clearly identified with the messenger of Mal 3.1, just as in Lk 1.17 he is presented as a new Elijah preaching reconciliation within Israel (Mal 3.24 [= 4.6]). Matthew can therefore write that the Baptist was, in one sense, 'if you are willing to accept it', the Elijah who was to come (Mt 11.14).

---

[15] SB IV-2 Exkurs 28, 'Elias', 780, with many references to justify the statements.

[16] *CGPAT*. There are twelve occurrences in the *Lives of the Prophets* (Obadiah, four times, Jonah, four times, Elijah, three times, Elisha, once; in *OTP* I 392-93 and 396-97), two in *4 Ezra* 26 (*ibid.*, 577-78) and one in the *Martyrdom of Isaiah* 2.14 (*ibid.*, II 159).

[17] For further detail on Elijah, see SB IV-2 Exkurs 28, J. Jeremias in *TWNT* II 930-47, and Schürer II 515-16.

The idea recurs in Mt 17.10-13 (|| Mk 9.11-13). When the disciples, immediately after the Transfiguration, ask Jesus about the opinion of the scribes, who said that Elijah was going to come and restore everything (καὶ ἀποκαταστήσει πάντα), Jesus replies that Elijah had already come, and had been not acknowledged, but mistreated (Mt 17.12). That is to say, Elijah had been prevented from accomplishing his work of restoring true religion in Israel. If Matthew and Mark think it legitimate to speak of the Baptist as sent by God to fulfil this role of reconciliation, why does the Baptist, according to John, so firmly disclaim the appellation?

One reason may be that the Fourth Gospel does not wish to resurrect the idea found in the second text of Malachi (3.23-24 [= 4.5-6]), that Elijah would avert the wrath of God 'before the great and terrible day of Yahweh'; contrast Jn 3.16-19. A second reason may be that the strange phrase attributed to the scribes by Matthew and Mark (καὶ ἀποκαταστήσει πάντα), which represents neither the Hebrew nor the LXX text of Malachi, was being misused and misinterpreted, and that the evangelist did not want anyone to think of the Baptist as destined by God to restore the earthly or political kingdom of Israel. In Johannine thinking, there was no function for the restoration of the political kingdom of Israel. Compare Acts 1.6 and 3.20-21; compare also Acts 3.22 with the next phrase in Jn 1.21.

ὁ προφήτης εἶ σύ; That is, the prophet like Moses, promised in Deut 18.15, 18-19, to whom reference is also made in Jn 6.14; 7.40, and Acts 3.22; 8.37.

καὶ ἀπεκρίθη, οὔ. In the Community Rule of Qumran, 1QS 9.11, it is laid down that the Rule is binding 'until there shall come the Prophet and the Messiahs of Aaron and Israel'.[18] Qumran has also supplied us with a 'Messianic' Anthology of *Testimonia* from Cave 4 (4Q175) which cites four texts together. First, Deut 5.28-29 is cited alongside 18.18-19, thus referring both texts to the Prophet like Moses; next comes the Oracle of Balaam in Num 24.15-17, on the warrior king from Jacob; and lastly, the blessing of Levi in Deut 33.8-11.[19] Both these texts from Qumran, the Rule and the *Testimonia*, envisage therefore a trio of the Prophet and two Messiahs, one priestly, one kingly, as heralding the end of the age. There is a parallel trio here in the Fourth Gospel. If John is, by his own avowal, neither the Messiah nor Elijah returned to earth nor the prophet like Moses, what is his role?

22. εἶπαν οὖν αὐτῷ, τίς εἶ; ἵνα ἀπόκρισιν δῶμεν τοῖς πέμψασιν ἡμᾶς· τί λέγεις περὶ σεαυτοῦ; ἵνα ἀπόκρισιν δῶμεν. John uses the verb ἀποκρίνεσθαι 78 times, far more than any other

---

[18] English Text in *DSSE*, 4th ed., 82.
[19] English Text in *DSSE*, 1st ed., 247f., 3rd ed., 295-96, 4th ed., 355-56.

evangelist:[20] the expression ἵνα ἀπόκρισιν δῶμεν may therefore be a deliberate variation, especially since the only other occurrence of this phrase in the NT is at Jn 19.9. Just as the priests and Levites, at the beginning of the Gospel, ask the Baptist to identify himself, 'that we may give an answer to those who sent us', so Pilate, at the end of the Gospel, asks Jesus to identify himself, by the words 'Where are you from?': ὁ δὲ Ἰησοῦς ἀπόκρισιν οὐκ ἔδωκεν αὐτῷ. Jesus gave Pilate no verbal answer; the answer is to be found in the dignity of Jesus' subsequent demeanour as portrayed in ch. 19. That answer, given equally to Pilate and to those who witnessed the consummation of Jesus' life according to Jn 19, is of course the ultimate answer to the questions first put to John the Baptist two and a half years earlier by the simple folk, priests and Levites, on behalf of 'the Jews in Jerusalem'.

At the start of the story, however, when the delegation insists that it must take back some answer to Jerusalem (Jn 1.22), the Baptist replies with a citation of Isa 40.3, a text used of him at the beginning of his ministry in all three Synoptics (Mt 3.3 ‖ Mk 1.3 ‖ Lk 1.4-6). Jn 1.23 reads ἔφη,

> ἐγὼ φωνὴ βοῶντος ἐν τῇ ἐρήμῳ,
> εὐθύνατε τὴν ὁδὸν κυρίου,
> καθὼς εἶπεν Ἠσαΐας ὁ προφήτης.[21]

Is the last clause, καθὼς εἶπεν Ἠσαΐας ὁ προφήτης, intended as part of the direct speech of the Baptist, or merely as a reference for the reader? Older translations left the matter undecided, but the introduction of quotation marks into editions of the Bible compels editors to make a choice. The RV, JB = NJB and NAB place the clause inside the quotation, the JB = NJB unambiguously so ('I am, as Isaiah prophesied...'); the NEB = REB, NIV, TNT, TEV = GN and NRSV put the words outside the quotation. It is impossible to decide for certain, and in any case, it is ultimately the evangelist who is alerting the reader to the fact that the Baptist is here claiming to fulfil the words of Isaiah. Barrett observes that the Baptist rests his claim to speak on 'the only authority that can be recognized within Judaism, the authority of Scripture. The words... identifiable Scripture—καθὼς εἶπεν Ἠσαΐας ὁ προφήτης.' On the only other occasion when the Fourth Gospel quotes from Isaiah, the author takes care to mention the prophet's name, three times (Jn 12.38-41), in verses which are the last direct quotations from Scripture before

---

[20] Matthew 55, Mark 30, Luke 46 (*NTVoc* 35). Elsewhere the verb occurs only at Col 4.6 and Rev 7.13.

[21] The words underlined represent the LXX. Matthew, Mark and Luke follow the LXX almost to the letter in reading ἑτοιμάσατε τὴν ὁδὸν κυρίου, εὐθείας ποιεῖτε τὰς τρίβους αὐτοῦ, but in John εὐθύνατε has been substituted for ἑτοιμάσατε. τὰς τρίβους αὐτοῦ: the LXX, reads not αὐτοῦ but τοῦ θεοῦ ἡμῶν. The agreement of the Synoptics over αὐτοῦ seems proof that the citation was taken from a set of Testimonia.

the close of Jesus' public ministry. Those verses in Jn 12 are quite openly presented as the reflections of the evangelist perceiving in the public ministry of Jesus the fulfilment of certain prophecies in the book of Isaiah. It is permissible therefore to see here an *inclusio*, calling the reader's attention at Jn 1.21 to the beginning of the public ministry of Jesus (where the writer quotes Isa 40.3), and to the end of that public ministry at Jn 12.38-41 (where he cites Isa 53.1 and 6.10).

ἐγὼ φωνὴ βοῶντος ἐν τῇ ἐρήμῳ κτλ.

The Hebrew of Isa 40.3 can be construed as meaning either 'a voice is crying' or (as in the LXX) 'someone's voice is crying'; the meaning remains unchanged. Here in John, ἐν τῇ ἐρήμῳ goes with the preceding words, to give the sense *the voice of one crying in the wilderness,* as in the Synoptics, LXX, Vulgate, Targum and Peshitta of Isaiah, and not with the following line. The MT (and 1 QIsᵃ, and 1 QS 8.14) construe the text as *in the wilderness prepare the way of Yahweh.* εὐθύνατε τὴν ὁδὸν κυρίου. Aquila and Theodotion have ἀποσκευάσατε, and Symmachus εὐτρεπίσατε; John may be citing from memory, or even condensing two lines into one and strengthening the verb, from 'make ready' to 'make straight'. Barrett suggests that John's choice of εὐθύνατε might have been inspired by the use of εὐθύνειν with ὁδός in Sir 2.6; 37.15; 49.9.

In the Synoptic tradition, the phrase from Isaiah is used to present the Baptist as the forerunner of Jesus (Mt 3.3 ‖ Mk 1.3 ‖ Lk 1.4-6). Our evangelist's insight into the Isaian text goes deeper (he is the only one who writes *as the prophet Isaiah said*). In Isa 40.8 the announcement of the restoration of Israel after the Babylonian Exile closes with the declaration *The word of our God endures forever*; the corresponding proclamation in Isa 55.10-11, *My word shall accomplish that which I purpose*, concludes the 'Book of the Return' (i.e. Isa 40–55). There can be little doubt that the author of the Fourth Gospel, by citing Isa 40.3, intends to call attention to the content of all the chapters from 40 to 55, which speak of the Creator's love for his creature (Isa 43.1, 15; 51.13; 54.5), of a Father's love for his child (43.1; 44.2, 21, 24; 45.11), and of his consequent redemption of his children from the bonds of slavery (cf. especially chs. 43–45); compare these themes with Jn 1.12-13; 3.16-18 etc. The reader of John's Gospel is therefore being invited to take to heart the lesson that "The word of our God endures for ever" (Isa 40.8), and to perceive the connection of the Isaian text with the incarnation of this Logos as described in the Prologue. The mention here in Jn 1.23 of *the voice of someone crying in the wilderness* is then a reminder from the evangelist that by the intervention of the all-powerful Word of God, a new Israel is again about to be brought into being, as formerly after the Exile. See also the comment above on Jn 1.3, πάντα δι' αὐτοῦ ἐγένετο κτλ., and below on 1.28 (on Bethany beyond the Jordan).

24. καὶ ἀπεσταλμένοι ἦσαν ἐκ τῶν Φαρισαίων.

Some English Versions translate this sentence as if it referred to the priests and Levites previously mentioned (e.g. "Now they had been sent by the Pharisees", RSV). That sense is accurate if the text is taken as καὶ οἱ ἀπεσταλμένοι, a reading which does in fact occur. However, the evidence cited in NA shows both that the earlier MSS omit the article ($\mathfrak{P}$66.75 ℵ* A* B C* L T Ψ 086 pc co; Or), and that the insertion is a later addition (ℵ² Aᶜ B C³ Wˢᵘᵖᵖ Θ 0234 f¹·¹³ 33 𝔐 boᵐˢ). If the article is omitted, the meaning is altered. The NEB, and the REB, are therefore more circumspect in translating 'Some Pharisees who were in the deputation' (asked him), and the NIV is cautiously neutral ('some Pharisees who had been sent'). But if one accepts that οἱ is not part of the original text, then the TNT and the NAB are surely to be preferred, when they translate 'Some Pharisees were also sent', thus making them a group entirely distinct from the priests and Levites named earlier. Priests and Levites would almost certainly have belonged to the party of the Sadducees (which is never mentioned in John). Verse 24 is therefore best rendered *and there were some sent from among the Pharisees*, thus contrasting the two groups.

25. καὶ ἠρώτησαν αὐτὸν καὶ εἶπαν αὐτῷ, Τί οὖν βαπτίζεις εἰ σὺ οὐκ εἶ ὁ Χριστὸς οὐδὲ Ἠλίας οὐδὲ ὁ προφήτης... The οὖν

serves both to connect 1.25 with the three questions some way back in vv. 20-21, and to move the discussion forward. It will be noted that the reader has not so far been told, in this Gospel, that John was baptizing, much less why; but the writer takes it for granted that his readers are familiar with the tradition. The question from the Pharisees, inquiring why John was baptizing if he was not one of the three eschatological figures, implies that they wanted to know whether his baptism had some other religious significance. Was he perhaps about to start an independent religious movement?

26. ἀπεκρίθη αὐτοῖς ὁ Ἰωάννης λέγων, Ἐγὼ βαπτίζω

ἐν ὕδατι.[22] In John's Gospel, ἀπεκρίθη or ἀπεκρίθησαν occurs, at the beginning of a sentence, 65 times with asyndeton, a construction which is found only once elsewhere in the NT (Mk 12.29): compare also Jn 1.23 (ἔφη), 39 (λέγει), 41 (εὑρίσκει) etc.[23] This asyndeton is certainly a literary characteristic distinctive of John. Not so ἀπεκρίθη λέγων or its equivalent; this is a Semitism frequently found in all four Gospels and elsewhere.[24] λέγων is here omitted by $\mathfrak{P}$75 f¹ pc e.

---

[22] The variant readings in NA²⁷ for 1.26 make little difference to the meaning. Some MSS. insert μεν and δε after εγω and μεσος respectively (f¹³ pc it boᵖᵗ), many more insert δε alone (see NA²⁷). The text above is supported by $\mathfrak{P}$59.66.75 ℵ B C* L 083 pc.

[23] Abel, *Grammaire* §80 e 4.

[24] In Hebrew, *answered* is followed by *and said* in (e.g.) Job 3.2; 6.1; 9.1; 12.1 etc. without adding anything to the meaning. As a result, phrases such as ἀπεκρίθη λέγων or

For comments on ἐγὼ βαπτίζω ἐν ὕδατι, see below under Jn 1.33.

In spite of the word ἀπεκρίθη, the Baptist does not in fact answer their question. Instead, he replies by changing the subject.

μέσος ὑμῶν ἔστηκεν[25] **ὃν ὑμεῖς οὐκ οἴδατε.** If the text is read thus, without δέ, the asyndeton gives a powerful contrast between the two clauses. *I am baptizing in water— standing among you is someone whom you do not recognize.* The clause ἐγὼ βαπτίζω is here (grammatically) answered by μέσος ὑμῶν ἔστηκεν in the co-ordinate clause; but the pronoun ἐγώ is balanced by ὑμεῖς in the subordinate clause, so that there is a double contrast in the sentence (compare *JG* 2399). John tells the Pharisees, in reply to their question, that something has happened which is far more important than what they seek to learn about his ministry of baptizing, and adds (with a slight emphasis, ὑμεῖς) that *they* do not know it. Already standing among them is a figure of first importance, whom they do not recognize.

27. ὁ ὀπίσω μου ἐρχόμενος, οὗ οὐκ εἰμὶ [ἐγὼ] ἄξιος ἵνα λύσω αὐτοῦ τὸν ἱμάντα τοῦ ὑποδήματος.

The textual variants take up four lines in NA[27], and several are easily explained by positing that some scribes read our v. 26 as a completed sentence; in that case v. 27 is not, and many of the variant readings are attempts to repair the text in order to make v. 27 into a sentence. The most popular correction was to insert αυτος εστιν before ο (A C[3] [Ψ] *f*[13] 𝔐 latt 𝔐), but it has little support among the early witnesses; indeed, ℵ* and B (+ *pc*) solve the problem in the opposite way, by omitting the first four words above, to join it with v. 26. The text above has over-whelming support, starting with 𝔓[66.75] and ℵ[2]: see NA[27]. The evidence for rejecting other variants is clear from NA[27].

... *that follower of mine the thong of whose sandal I am not worthy to untie.* For the justification of this translation of ὁ ὀπίσω μου ἐρχόμενος, see the comment above on 1.15. The balance of the evidence for and against the inclusion of ἐγω indicates that some scribes understood the text to imply that the Baptist wished to stress the contrast between the follower just mentioned, and himself.

The Rabbis, commenting on Lev 25.39-40, laid down that an Israelite slave should never be given tasks which were too exacting or too degrading, such as taking off his master's shoes or washing his feet (cf.

ἀπεκρίθη καὶ εἶπεν are common in Biblical Greek, LXX and NT alike: see MHT III 156 for examples.

[25] στηκει is found in B L 083 *f*[1] *pc*; Or[pt], and ειστηκει in 𝔓[75] (ℵ) *pc* f vg. But εστηκεν is supported by 𝔓[66] A C T[vid] W[suppl] Θ Ψ *f*[13] 33 Or[pt] and the great majority of MSS. There is no significant difference of meaning between the three readings, *pace* the valiant efforts of Abbott in *JV* 1725 *a g* and 1796. Context is the determinant factor. στηκει (pres. indic.) may be a revision intended to make clear to the reader that the verb refers to the present moment, and ειστηκει (perf. indic.) may be an example of itacism, especially if the text was being dictated. Compare MHT II 77.

1 Sam 25.41). The words are thus an assertion by the Baptist that compared with Jesus, he is not worthy even to be his slave (cf. also Jn 13.6-7).²⁶

In the Synoptic parallels (Mt 3.11 ‖ Mk 1.7 ‖ Lk 3.16) the adjective employed is ἱκανός (not ἄξιος), and *sandals* are mentioned (in the plural). In John's choice of words, ἄξιος can only mean 'as a person, worthy'. But why is τὸ ὑπόδημα, by contrast with the Synoptics, in the singular (as in Acts 13.25)? In 1978, attention was called to an all but forgotten patristic interpretation, namely, that Jn 1.27 contains also an implicit reference to the levirate law.²⁷ In Deut 25.9-10 (which lays down that law) and in Ruth 4.7-8 (the historical example), the rite of *halitzah* involves the unfastening and taking off of only one shoe or sandal; the LXX renders all four texts by ὑπολύειν τὸ ὑπόδημα (sing.).²⁸ It is significant, too, that, in spite of the scribal tendency to harmonize parallel texts of the Gospels, neither Tischendorf nor von Soden records here the existence of even one MS with the plural reading, ὑποδημάτων. The use of the singular in Jn 1.27 does not of course by itself prove that the wording is intended as a reference to this rite. But since the Baptist later refers to himself as 'the friend of the bridegroom' (Jn 3.28-30), it is most reasonable to interpret λύειν τὸν ἱμάντα τοῦ ὑποδήματος as denoting not merely unworthiness to perform a menial physical service, but also as a firm disclaimer of any title to be considered a rival to Jesus, or even as next in succession. See the notes on 3.28-30 and the comment on the word ἀνήρ at 1.30.

28. ταῦτα ἐν Βηθανίᾳ ἐγένετο πέραν τοῦ Ἰορδάνου, ὅπου ἦν ὁ Ἰωάννης βαπτίζων.

Since Origen, there has been endless debate about the location, and indeed about the very existence, of a Bethany beyond the Jordan. Its location is certainly a matter of legitimate interest, but it is more important to ask why the evangelist chose to interrupt his narrative at this point, in

²⁶ Rabbinical references in SB I 121. The most vivid is that of R. Joshua ben Levi (ca. A.D. 250): 'All manner of service that a slave must render to his master a student must render to his teacher, except that of taking off his shoe' (*Kethuboth* 96a, in the Soncino Talmud, *Nashim* II 610).

²⁷ P. Proulx and L. Alonso-Schökel, 'Las Sandalias del Mesías Esposo', *Biblica* 59 (1978), 1-37. Some Latin patristic texts are there cited and discussed, notably that of Jerome, who summarizes the interpretation with exemplary conciseness in his *Commentary on Matthew*: 'Hic [Mt 3.11] humilitas, ibi [Jn 1.27] mysterium demonstratur quod Christus sponsus sit, et Johannes non mereatur sponsi corrigiam solvere, ne vocetur domus eius iuxta legem Moysi et exemplum Ruth domus discalciati' (PL 26.30 = CC 77,18).

²⁸ The root חלץ (ḥlṣ) 'may signify both (a) *loosing* or *untying* sc. of the shoe strap, and (b) *releasing* sc. of the foot from the shoe' (The Soncino Talmud, *Nashim* II 702 fn. 10 on *Yebamoth* 102a). The rabbinical discussions of this law are extraordinarily detailed (see *Yebamoth* 12, and the Talmud), but it is never once suggested that both sandals need to be removed.

order to state that *these things happened in Bethany on the other side of the Jordan.* The topographical and textual questions are discussed separately, in Excursus V, 'Bethany beyond the Jordan'.

If one stands on the summit of the biblical Mount Pisgah and looks towards Jericho (cf. Deut 34.1), then the direct line from Pisgah to (ancient) Jericho crosses the Jordan at the ford of Al-Maghtas, about one mile north of Al-Hajlah, near Qasr al-Yehud.[29] Not surprisingly, Jewish tradition located in that area both Joshua's crossing into the Promised Land (Josh 3–4), and Elijah's departure eastwards across the Jordan (2 Kgs 2.8-14); later, by a quite natural extension of the typology used in 1 Cor 10.1-4, the baptism of Jesus was linked with the same place. The site was already a place of pilgrimage in A.D. 333, when the Pilgrim of Bordeaux wrote: 'From the Dead Sea to the Jordan, where the Lord was baptized by John, is five miles. There is a place there on the river, a hillock (*monticulus*) on the bank, where Elijah was taken up into heaven.'[30] Jerome too links the site of Jesus' baptism with the crossing of the Jordan and the departure of Elijah.[31] The same typology is commonplace among the Eastern Fathers too;[32] may it not have been a factor in the angle of vision of our evangelist also?

To introduce the ministry of the Baptist, all four evangelists quote Isa 40.3. Mark puts the Baptist's preaching 'in the desert' (1.4), to which Matthew adds 'of Judaea' (3.1), while Luke sets it 'in the region around the Jordan' (3.3). John alone locates that ministry, quite explicitly, πέραν τοῦ ᾽Ιορδάνου, *on the far side of the Jordan.* That is to suggest that for him, it is not the place-name 'Bethany' which is important here. The weight of his sentence rests rather in the affirmation that these events took place *on the far side of the Jordan.* In the light of the typological parallels just mentioned, it makes good sense to interpret v. 28 as a hint that what is about to happen is comparable with the entry of Israel into the Promised Land. In the course of the narrative, the reader will discover that the new Jeshua will not be a military saviour like his namesake,

---

[29] Pisgah is usually identified with Ras es-Siâgha, a peak some 700 m above sea level and 1100 m above the surface of the Dead Sea, 10 miles = 16 km east of the Jordan. Mount Nebo, about two miles east-south-east of Pisgah, 802 m, is the summit of the range. See Abel I 379-84. The intrepid Etheria (ca. A.D. 395) rightly rhapsodized about the view towards Jericho, 17 miles = 28 km away (*Itinerarium* 12, in *Journal de Voyage, SC*, 1971, 140-43).

[30] 'Inde [a mare mortuo] ad Jordane [*sic*], ubi dominus a Johanne baptizatus est milia quinque. Ibi est locus super flumen, monticulus in illa ripa, ubi raptus est Helias in caelo' (CSEL 39, 24), 166. A tiny hillock is still shown as Jebel Mar Elias. '*Vocable prétentieux*', writes Abel, adding that he cannot vouch for the antiquity of the appellation. See the photograph in *RB* 41 (1932), Plate V 1, opposite p. 240, and p. 248.

[31] *Epistula* 108 (PL 22.88 = CSEL 55, 321).

[32] Abel, in *RB* 41 (1932), 243-44, gives by way of example Athanasius, *In Ps. 41.7* (*PG* 27.202), Cyril of Alexandria, *In Psalmos* (*PG* 69.1005), and Theodoret, *In Iosue* (*PG* 80.464).

Joshua, and that it is not Elijah who is coming to set Israel free (compare Jn 1.20-21). Here in the Fourth Gospel (alone) attention is deliberately drawn to the circumstances specifically mentioned in the text of Isa 40. As then, so now, it is *from across the Jordan* that a voice is crying aloud in the wilderness, to inaugurate the new era. As then, so now, the message to be proclaimed (LXX: εὐαγγελίζεσθαι) to the people of Jerusalem (cf. Jn 1.19) and to the cities of Judah, is 'Behold your God!' (Isa 40.3-9).

2. The Baptist's Witness about Jesus (1.29-34)

[1.29] The next day he saw Jesus coming towards him, and said, 'Behold, the Lamb of God, who takes away the sin of the world! [30] This is the one concerning whom I said, "There is a man, a follower of mine, who takes precedence before me, because he existed before me". [31] Nor was I myself aware who he was, but the reason I came baptizing in water was in order that he might be revealed to Israel.' [32] And John bore witness, saying 'I beheld the Spirit descending like a dove from heaven, and it came to rest on him. [33] Nor was I myself aware who he was, but he who sent me to baptize with water said to me, "He upon whom you see the Spirit descending and resting, this is the one who is going to baptize with the Holy Spirit". [34] And I have seen and have testified that this is the Chosen One of God.'

Day 1 of this First Week (Jn 1.19-28) reported the Baptist's witness about himself, in which he emphasized his own subordinate role, and asserted that one of his followers would be greater than he. Day 2 (1.29-34) presents the Baptist as identifying this follower, for the benefit of his disciples. There is no indication of any change of location, and this is strange after the careful topographical statement in v. 28. The reader is, however, left free to imagine that the Baptist was continuing his ministry elsewhere, either on the west bank of the Jordan or perhaps further up-river. For the moment, the area is immaterial, but it will become of interest very soon (see the comment on 1.45).

29. τῇ ἐπαύριον βλέπει τὸν Ἰησοῦν ἐρχόμενον πρὸς αὐτόν. τῇ ἐπαύριον marks the dawn of a new day, when the Baptist *sees Jesus coming towards him*. The reader knows that though 'the true light was [continually?] coming into the world' (1.9c), 'the world' (in the Johannine sense) had not recognized it (1.10c). This true light 'comes' now to the Baptist. The Baptist *sees Jesus* not just physically, but with a mind enlightened by this true light, and declares publicly, who Jesus is, and what his function is to be (compare 3.31, ὁ ἄνωθεν ἐρχόμενος).

καὶ λέγει, ἴδε… ἴδε 'with a nominative as object is explained by the fact that, like ἰδού, ἴδε has become a stereotyped particle of exclamation' (MHT III 231), and consequently does not admit of a plural (see 1.36): *ecce agnus dei* is a perfect rendering. In John, this use of ἴδε can involve a challenge *to perceive with the mind* a truth not outwardly evident to human eyes, as when Pilate, presenting the thorn-crowned Jesus, says to the Jews, ἴδε ὁ βασιλεὺς ὑμῶν (19.14; see also 19.26-27). A parallel occurs in Rev 5.5-6, where the seer 'hears' the words 'Weep not; behold, the Lion of the tribe of Judah, the Root of David, has conquered…', and then 'sees' not a Lion rampant, but 'a Lamb standing, as though it had been slain'. So here in Jn 1.29. the Baptist *sees Jesus, and says, Behold the Lamb of God.* This first statement about Jesus by the Baptist is programmatic for the entire Gospel, and merits detailed consideration.[33]

BEHOLD THE LAMB OF GOD

ἴδε ὁ ἀμνὸς τοῦ θεοῦ ὁ αἴρων τὴν ἁμαρτίαν τοῦ κόσμου.

Why is Jesus here termed 'the Lamb of God'? In the context of that designation, does the participle ὁ αἴρων imply that Jesus was to be a sacrificial victim who made expiation for the sin of the world (compare ἱλασμός in 1 Jn 2.7; 4.10, and τὸ αἷμα 'Ιησοῦ in 1.7; 5.6), or does it mean only that he would in some way put an end to the reign of sin, without specifying that he would do so by making expiation? Does the 'sin of the world' refer to the sin of Adam, or to that sinfulness inherent in descent from him (as in Rom 5.12-19), or to the actual sins committed throughout history, or to all three?

The noun ἀμνός occurs four times in the NT, always with reference to Jesus Christ, in Jn 1.29, 36, in Acts 8.32 (citing Isa 53.7), and in 1 Pet 1.19.[34] It is more difficult to determine the meaning of the phrase ὁ ἀμνός τοῦ θεοῦ in Jn 1.29, 36, and four main interpretations have been proposed.[35]

---

[33] See especially SB II 363-70. Billerbeck's comments on Jn 1.29 are outstanding.

[34] In the LXX, the word occurs nearly 100 times, and denotes most often a lamb for sacrifice (47 times in Num 7; 28; 29 alone); on about 30 occasions it is qualified by the adjective ἐνιαύσιος, to indicate a male lamb not more than twelve months old. It is the usual translation of the Hebrew כֶּבֶשׂ (kebeś); this noun too normally denotes a lamb destined for sacrifice (BDB, KBR, *DCH*). In order to describe the same sacrificial offerings, Josephus uses ἀρνίον and ἀρήν or ἀρνός, sometimes with the adjective αὐτοετής as an alternative to ἐνιαύσιος (*Ant.* III 226 and 231-39 *passim*). In the LXX, ἀμνός is usually masculine, but can be feminine: see below, p. 128 fn. 43. ἀρήν is found only once in the NT, at Lk 10.3 (ὡς ἄρνας ἐν μέσῳ λύκων), perhaps because 'The contrast [between lambs and wolves] is as old as Homer (*Iliad* 22.263)' (BDAG).

[35] A parallel with the ram in the story of the binding of Isaac, Gen 22, was proposed by Melito of Sardis (*Frag. in Genesim, PG* 5.1216B-17A). It was still alive in the Middle Ages: 'vel dicitur agnus Dei, scilicet Patris, quia ipse providit homini oblationem ad offerendum pro peccatis sufficientem', with a reference to Gen 22.7 and Rom 8.32 (Aquinas, *In Ioannem*, XIV I fn. 257). The comparison was again put forward by G. Vermes in *Scripture and Tradition in Judaism*, 1961, 224-25, and G. Delling (see Barrett), but it has never won general acceptance.

(1) Christian piety has often understood the title 'Lamb of God' as pointing principally to the meekness and patience of Jesus in his sufferings, and hymns like the opening Chorus of Bach's St Matthew Passion have made this interpretation the most widely accepted in popular devotion: *O Lamm Gottes unschuldig*. The wording is thus taken as inspired either by Isa 53.7 (ὡς ἀμνὸς ἐναντίον τοῦ κείροντος αὐτὸν ἄφωνος, as in Acts 8.32), or alternatively, by Jer 11.19 (ἐγὼ δὲ ὡς ἀρνίον ἄκακον ἀγόμενον τοῦ θύεσθαι...). 'Lamb of God' is then interpreted as an allusion either to Jesus' silence before Pilate (Mt 27.12, 14 ‖ Mk 14.60-61; cf. Jn 19.9), or to his refusal to offer counter-violence at the time of his arrest (Mt 26.52-54 ‖ Mk 14.47-49 ‖ Lk 22.49-51 ‖ Jn 18.10-11), or to both. Yet any reader who accepts that there is an allusion to Isa 53 might well think that the term 'Lamb of God' connotes far more than the two instances of meekness, silence and non-resistance, just mentioned, and that an all-embracing reference to the sufferings of the Servant of the Lord described in that chapter is intended. This alternative interpretation is treated more extensively below.

(2) The words are intended as a reference to the Passover Lamb. The casual manner in which Paul in 1 Cor 5.8 introduces the phrase 'Christ our Passover has been sacrificed' implies that the notion was already familiar to the Corinthians (compare 1 Cor 10). So too in Jn 19.46, the phrase ὀστοῦν οὐ συντριβήσεται αὐτοῦ is most probably an allusion to Exod 12.10, 46 LXX (see the comment on Jn 19.46); and significant links with the Jewish Passover are intimated elsewhere in John's Passion narrative (see the comment on 13.1). Indeed, in the light of the OT allusions underlying Jn 1.14.17-18, further references to the Exodus are to be expected. Many authors consider that 1 Pet 1.18-19 views Christ as the Passover Lamb,[36] and the identification was commonplace long before the close of the second century.[37]

(3) The words are intended to recall the daily sacrifice of lambs, morning and evening, prescribed in Exod 29.38-46 and Num 28.3-8, often called the 'perpetual' sacrifice.[38] It is difficult to understand why some writers reject the parallel between this sacrifice and the idea of Lamb of God on the ground that the 'perpetual' sacrifice was not a sacrifice of expiation for sin.[39] The purpose of this particular rite as a whole was adoration and thanksgiving, and as a holocaust, it was regarded as

[36] Notably E. G. Selwyn, *The First Epistle of Peter*, London, 1946; F. L. Cross, *1 Peter, A Paschal Liturgy*, London, 1954; M. E. Boismard, 'Une liturgie baptismale dans la Prima Petri', *RB* 63 (1956), 181-208; 64 (1957), 161-83

[37] Justin, *Dial.* 40.1-2; 111.3, and especially C. Bonner (ed.), *The Homily on the Passion by Melito Bishop of Sardis*, London, 1940; or O. Perler (ed.), *Méliton de Sardes: Sur la Pâques*, SC 123, Paris, 1966.

[38] This rite was so central to Jewish worship that in A.D. 70 it was maintained until the Romans had captured the Antonia, and were assaulting the Temple itself. See Schürer, I 505-506; II 295-96, 299-301; and Josephus, *War* VI 93-94.

[39] SB II 368; Dodd, *Interpretation*, 233. See also Schnackenburg I 287 = ETr I 300.

the perfect type of sacrifice, because the burning of the entire carcass both symbolized and effected the complete and irreversible making over of the gift to God. However, within that rite, the presenting of the blood of the lamb had a particular purpose, 'to make atonement' for sin (ἐξιλασάσθαι, Lev 1.4), for 'it is blood that makes atonement' in that the sprinkling of the blood upon the altar presupposed, and symbolized, the irrevocable surrender of the living animal to God (Lev 17.11).[40] If in Jn 1.29 the phrase 'Lamb of God' is intended to affirm that Jesus is the antitype of this daily sacrifice in the Temple, then the sense is akin to the doctrine of Heb 9.11-14.

(4) Dodd argued vigorously that the expression 'Lamb of God', is probably, in its first intention, a messianic title, a symbol of the Messiah as leader of the flock of God. He adduces the frequency of this metaphor in apocalyptic literature[41] and in the Apocalypse of John, where ἀρνίον occurs regularly to denote a leader, the bell-wether of the flock (Rev 5.6; 7.17; 14.1-5; 17.14). This, moreover, is a meaning which would, historically, have been fully comprehensible on the lips of the Baptist even before Jesus' ministry had begun. The fact that the Book of Revelation uses ἀρνίον in preference to ἀμνός does not weaken his argument, for in Jewish Greek, either word denotes *a lamb*.[42] Dodd readily admits that there may also be hidden allusions to the Servant in Isa 53, and perhaps even to the idea of sacrifice; but with respect to the Passover Lamb, he is unenthusiastic.[43]

---

[40] R. de Vaux, *Studies in Old Testament Sacrifice*, Cardiff, 1964, 37; see also *Ancient Israel*, 451-54. On the daily sacrifice, see Schürer II 295-96, 299-301.

[41] Note in particular *1 En* 89.41-50, where the term *sheep* or *ram* is applied to Samuel, then to David and to Solomon; 90.6-12, where it is applied to Judas Maccabaeus; and compare *Test. Joseph* 19.8. See *OTP* I 67-71; 824.

[42] Thus J. Jeremias in *TWNT* I 344. ἀρνίον, originally a diminutive, and rare in Classical Greek, occurs four times in the LXX, and *lamb* is the exact meaning in all four of them: Jer 11.19 (ἐγὼ δὲ ὡς ἀρνίον ἄκακον ἀγόμενον τοῦ θύεσθαι); Jer 27.45 [= 50.45] (ἐὰν μὴ διαφθαρῇ τὰ ἀρνία τῶν προβάτων αὐτῶν); Ps 113[114].4, 6 (ὡς ἀρνία προβάτων). It occurs also in Aquila, at Isa 40.11, in *PsSol* 8.28, and in Josephus at *Ant.* II 221, 251, where כֶּבֶשׂ in Num 7.15; 23.12 is translated by ἀρνίον to distinguish it from κριός, *ram*. In the NT, ἀρνίον is found once in Jn 21.15, and 29 times in the book of Revelation.

[43] *Interpretation*, 230-37. Dodd's first argument (231) is that, in the LXX, save for a single variant in the Codex Alexandrinus at Exod 12.5, the term ἀμνός never denotes the paschal victim. To this, one can reply that the Jewish translators may have eschewed ἀμνός because the word could denote either a male or a female lamb, the second of which would not have been a valid paschal victim. For ἀμνός as feminine, LSJ refers to Theocritus 5.144 and 149 and AP 525; for the sensitivity of the LXX translators, one may point to Isa 53.7, where ὡς ἀμνὸς ἄφωνος is a clever rendering of the Hebrew כְּרָחֵל (kerĕhel), a *ewe-lamb*; the epicene adjective allows the Greek reader to interpret the comparison with the Servant as masculine. Dodd's second argument against accepting a true parallel between Jn 1.29 and Exod 12 is that it is not the function of the paschal victim 'to take away sin' (234). But, as Jeremias points out, even if the passover of later times was not an expiatory sacrifice, the original passover of the Exodus certainly had

Older books discuss what the Baptist understood by the term, and in the light of the Synoptic summary of his preaching,[44] it would appear most probable that the Baptist himself would have intended the term 'Lamb' to signify a Messianic leader. There is ample evidence that the Jewish people were eagerly awaiting a Messiah-King who would purge the world of all injustice and sin (compare Isa 11.1-9 with *PsSol* 17.26-37;[45] *2* [= *Syriac Apocalypse of*] *Baruch* 73.11-14;[46] 1QS [Rule] 4.20-21[47]), and that such a leader was regularly represented as a sheep or ram (see n. 41 above).

Today, however, exegetes ask what the evangelist (rather than the Baptist) understood by this title, and why the evangelist chose this term for his first public designation of Jesus. To answer these questions, it will be helpful to scrutinize the modifying phrase ὁ αἴρων τὴν ἁμαρτίαν τοῦ κόσμου in the light of the text of Isa 53.

First, the verb ὁ αἴρων. In Isa 53.11, 12 it is twice affirmed that the Servant of Yahweh *bore* the sins of many, for which the Hebrew text uses two different, but virtually synonymous, verbs, סבל (sbl) and נשׂא (nśʾ). Their root meaning is *physically to carry, to transport*, and in consequence, at Isa 53.11, 12, to *remove* iniquities and *take away* sins.[48] In these two verses the LXX translates both verbs by ἀναφέρειν,[49] among the primary meanings of which, in Classical Greek, is *to take upon oneself*, for example, danger, or false accusations (LSJ).[50] Consequently, τὰς ἁμαρτίας ἀναφέρειν in Isa 53.11, 12 is probably an interpretation of the Hebrew as meaning primarily *to carry the burden of* (and consequently *to take away*) *sins*.[51] The more usual LXX term for *removing*

redemptive power, for it brought into operation God's liberating covenant with Abraham, and it is with that first Passover in Egypt, not with its subsequent commemoration, that the Christian Passover is compared. See his *Eucharistic Words*, ETr, 2nd ed., 225-26, especially the footnotes. Further, Dodd's reasoning seems to presuppose that only a sacrifice specifically offered as expiation for sin can have expiatory value; but many would maintain that atonement can be achieved by other means, such as a sacrifice of adoration and thanksgiving (*satisfactio* as distinct from *satispassio*). Finally, αἴρων in Jn 1.29 does not necessarily imply that Christ did away with the sin of the world by making expiation for it: see the comment on this word in the text above.

[44] Notably Mt 3.7-12 and Lk 3.7-18: see below on 1.33.

[45] *OTP* II 667-68.

[46] *OTP* I 645.

[47] *DSSE*, 3rd ed., 66.

[48] Under נשׂא (nśʾ), the *DCH* V 513 comments that in its proper sense, the verb 'denotes the whole process of lifting up and transporting, *or any of its phases*' (italics mine). This is most relevant in elucidating the verb's figurative senses.

[49] Compare with these verses the use of ἁμαρτίας φέρειν at Isa 53.4.

[50] LSJ cites, under ἀναφέρω I.3, *take upon oneself*, κινδύνους (Thucydides 3.38), διαβολάς (Polybius I 36, 3), and even πολλῶν ἁμαρτίας in Isa 53.12; Heb 9.28 (of which BDAG writes 'more in the sense of *take away*').

[51] The Vulgate translates סבל (sbl) (in Isa 53.4, 11) by *portare* and נשׂא (nśʾ) (in 53.4, 12) by *tollere*, thus distinguishing between the meaning of the two verbs. This may well

sin is, of course, ἀφιέναι or ἄφεσις, the root meaning of which is (literally) *to release.*[52] The evangelist uses neither ἀναφέρειν nor ἀφιέναι. Instead, he chooses the most common Greek verb with the meaning *to take away, to remove,* αἴρειν,[53] even though it occurs only twice in the LXX with reference to the removal of sin (1 Kgdms 15.25; 25.28), or six times if one includes the compounds ἀφαίρειν (Exod 28, 34[38]; Mic 7.18) and ἐξαίρειν (Exod 34.7; Num 14.18). Hence if Jn 1.29 is in fact inspired by Isa 53,[54] then the evidence indicates that the evangelist, by choosing αἴρειν in preference to the LXX's ἀναφέρειν (or ἀφιέναι), had his eye on the Hebrew text, not on the Greek;[55] and therefore that he wanted to assert that Jesus *does away with* the sin of the world, rather than that he *carries the burden of it.*[56]

Some exegetes[57] want to go further, arguing that ὁ αἴρων means that Jesus Christ takes away sin by giving humanity the ability not to remain in sin, as is clearly taught in 1 Jn 3.5-9. This notion is certainly ultimately contained and foreshadowed in the words about the Lamb of God in Jn 1.29, but it is scarcely to be discerned at the first reading of the phrase. The full implications emerge only in the context of an understanding of the entire Gospel.

One may add that ὁ αἴρων is best understood as a futural present, *who is to take away* (BDF 323; *IBNTG* 7). 'As in our own language, we may define the futural present as differing from the future tense mainly in the tone of assurance which is imparted' (Moulton, in MHT I 120). So we find *auferet* in the translation of Irenaeus and in Cyprian,[58] and in the Old Latin versions listed in Tischendorf.

Secondly, the noun ἁμαρτία. In Isa 53 (LXX) this noun occurs in the singular only once, at v. 10, where it denotes a sacrifice for sin (אשם ʾāšām); otherwise, in this chapter it is always in the plural, at vv. 4, 5, 6 (our sins), 11 and 12 (their sins: the sins of many). The Sixto-Clementine

---

be deliberate, since Cyprian had earlier opted for the former understanding of the text, and Tertullian for the latter. Contrast Cyprian, 'ipse peccata multorum pertulit' (*Testimonia* II 15: CSEL 3, 1 80[16-17]), with Tertullian: 'Portare autem Graeci etiam pro eo solent ponere quod est tollere' (*Adversus Marcionem* IV 8, 4); 'delicta nostra ipse aufert' (*ibid.*, 10, 2).

[52] ἀφιέναι is used from Gen 4.13 onwards (HR; note especially Lev 4–5).

[53] See LSJ under αἴρω (see ἀείρω) III, *lift, take away and destroy,* where it cites τιμᾶν (Aeschylus, *Eumenides* 847), and κακά (Euripides, *Electra* 942).

[54] The only two occurrences of αἴρειν, in v. 8, do not refer to sin.

[55] Like Paul in Rom 5.12-19, see J. Jeremias in *TWNT* VI 543.

[56] αἴρειν with 'sin' as object occurs only twice in the NT, here at Jn 1.29, and in 1 Jn 3.5. It is certainly true that in Classical Greek, the verb can also mean (LSJ IV 5) *to take upon oneself, to undergo,* but only when used in the middle voice: e.g. πόνον (Sophocles, *Antigone* 907), πένθος (*Oedipus Tyrannus* 1225), βάρος (Euripides, *Cyclops* 473).

[57] Dodd, *Interpretation*, 237; Boismard, *Du Baptême à Cana*, 49; Schnackenburg, on this text and on 1 Jn.

[58] *Adv. haer.* III 10,3 line 86 in SC; *Testimonia* II 15, last line, in CSEL 3, 82.

Vulgate too reads the plural in these five verses, but the critical edition of
the Vulgate (1969) has in 53.12 'ipse peccatum multorum pertulit'. The
plural of the Sixto-Clementine in v. 12 is but feebly supported[59] and
presumably originated as a scribal correction: if *multorum*, then *peccata*.
One suspects that the same reasoning may have led the LXX translator of
53.12 to write the plural ἁμαρτίας, even though the Hebrew is
indubitably singular: חֵטְא־רַבִּים (ḥeṭaʾ-rabbim), *the sin of many*. This noun
חֵטְא (ḥeṭaʾ) often 'refers to an unforgiveable burden of sin transcending
individual acts, leading ineluctably to death through the connections
between acts and their consequences.'[60] The full meaning of 'the sin of
the world' in John's Gospel will not emerge until later, but the reader has
already been told that the Logos was in the world, though the world was
not conscious of his presence (Jn 1.10). So when the Baptist proclaims
that Jesus is to do away with 'the sin of the world', the reader may well
suspect that this is to be achieved through γνῶσις, enlightenment, and
through the recognition of the Logos by the world. For the moment,
however, it is sufficient to keep in the forefront of one's mind the fact
that the singular ἁμαρτία in Jn 1.29 looks back to Isa 53.12, and refers to
the Hebrew חֵטְא (ḥeṭaʾ) in the sense just described, as 'an unforgiveable
burden…leading ineluctably to death',[61] a burden which Jesus is going to
take away. The manner of release from this burden will be revealed as the
story unfolds.

Thirdly, the genitive τοῦ κόσμου. In Isa 53.11 the Servant is said to
justify 'the many' (MT: with the article), and in v. 12 to take away 'the
sin of many' (MT: without the article). The 'many' here mentioned must
certainly include those envisaged in 52.14-15, that is, those 'many nations
and kings' who are seized by astonishment and terror when they see
what the Servant of the Lord has suffered, and perceive that it was *their*
griefs, *their* sorrows, *their* iniquity that he took upon himself.[62] Joachim
Jeremias, however, has argued convincingly that in Isa 53.11-12 the word
'many' refers not just to the non-Israelite kings and nations mentioned in
52.14-15, but to 'everyone' in the world, Jew and Gentile alike (compare
Wis 5, which may have been inspired by Isa 53).[63] This universalist

[59] Only two MSS, both Spanish, are cited in support of the plural *peccata*, C =
Cavensis, ninth century, and Σ = Toletanus, tenth century.

[60] K. Koch in *TDOT* IV 315.

[61] In the Synoptics, ἁμαρτία appears in the singular only once, at Mt 12.31 (πᾶσα
ἁμαρτία), but in John, ten times; the plural is found six times in Matthew, six times in
Mark, eleven times in Luke, and five times in John.

[62] J. Jeremias, *Eucharistic Words*, ETr, 2nd ed., 229.

[63] Since neither Hebrew nor Aramaic had any word for 'all' in the sense of *every
single one of a group*, only a word for *the whole, the totality*, both languages supplied
this lack by speaking of *the many*, or even simply *many*. 'The form *with the article* has
throughout the inclusive meaning. *ḥarabbim* is in the entire Talmudic literature the
constant expression for "*the whole community*"' (*Eucharistic Words*, ETr, 2nd ed., 179)
and the same usage is found in Josephus. Moreover, even the form without the article
can, and often does, carry the same sense of *all*: compare, for example, Mk 1.34 (ἐθερά-

interpretation of Isa 53 is powerfully supported by the other NT passages concerning redemption which are based upon Isa 53,[64] and it fits perfectly with the definition of sin given in the preceding paragraph.

There are then, in the first place, many reasons for affirming that in Jn 1.29, the phrase ὁ ἀμνὸς τοῦ θεοῦ ὁ αἴρων τὴν ἁμαρτίαν τοῦ κόσμου is a deliberate allusion to the role of the Servant of the Yahweh as portrayed in Isa 53: Jesus will *put an end to the sin of the world*. The Johannine term κόσμος, in its existential sense, [65] is here substituted for the phrase οἱ πολλοί (in the sense of πάντες) used in Isa 53.

Secondly, in 1 Corinthians, Christ's death is already termed 'the sacrifice of our Passover Lamb' (5.7, τὸ πάσχα ἡμῶν ἐτύθη Χριστός); the proposed parallel between Jn 1.29 and Exod 12 may therefore be accepted without more ado (and compare Jn 19.36).

Thirdly, in the Epistle to the Hebrews, Jesus' death is presented as a sacrifice expiatory of sin (note Heb 2.17, πιστὸς ἀρχιερεὺς ... εἰς τὸ ἱλάσκεσθαι τὰς ἁμαρτίας τοῦ λαοῦ; 10.12, μίαν ὑπὲρ ἁμαρτιῶν προσενέγκας θυσίαν). So also in 1 John we find (2.2) αὐτὸς ἱλασμός ἐστιν περὶ τῶν ἁμαρτιῶν ἡμῶν, οὐ περὶ τῶν ἡμετέρων δὲ μόνον ἀλλὰ καὶ περὶ ὅλου τοῦ κόσμου (cf. 4.10). Could any Jewish writer (or editor) of the Fourth Gospel have written the words 'Lamb of God' without recalling the cessation of the perpetual sacrifice in A.D 70, and without envisaging both that event and the destruction of the Temple within a 'Christological' context (Jn 2.22; 11.48)? Against this background, to call Jesus 'the Lamb of God' is to point to him as the One who, himself alone, supersedes and replaces the perpetual sacrifice once offered in the Temple (compare Heb 8.13).

Fourthly and finally, why should the author or editor not have intended to include also the multi-faceted role of the Lamb as presented in the Apocalypse of John, particularly if he believed that the Baptist himself had, as a matter of historical fact, used the term 'Lamb' to point to Jesus as the great leader sent by God to set all Israel free?[66]

πευσεν πολλούς) with its parallels in Mt 8.16 (πάντας) and Lk 4.40 (ἑνὶ ἑκάστῳ) (*ibid.*, 180).

[64] Mk 10.45 ‖ Mt 20.28 has λύτρον ἀντὶ πολλῶν; Mk 14.24 ‖ Mt 26.28, τὸ ἐκχυννόμενον ὑπὲρ πολλῶν. Rom 5.15 contains two instances of the 'inclusive' sense, οἱ πολλοὶ ἀπέθανον and πολλῷ μᾶλλον ἡ χάρις τοῦ θεοῦ... εἰς τοὺς πολλοὺς ἐπερίσσευσεν. Heb 9.28 has εἰς τὸ πολλῶν ἀνενεγκεῖν ἁμαρτίας. In each case, πολλοί is a Semitism, and denotes *all*, just as the words in Isa 53.12, αὐτὸς ἁμαρτίας πολλῶν ἀνήνεγκεν, mean that the Servant took upon himself and took away the sins of all. For further detail see the article πολλοί, by J. Jeremias, in *TWNT* VI 536-45 and *Eucharistic Words*, ETr, 2nd ed., 179-82.

[65] See above on the Prologue, pp. 34-39.

[66] 'The deeper teachings of poetry are not disposed of by the superficial question: "Did the writer mean all that?" "No," we boldly answer, "and yet he said it, because he saw the truth which he did not, and perhaps at that time could not, consciously analyse" (B. F. Westcott, at the opening of a new girls' school in 1893). Quoted in *Life and Letters of Brooke Foss Westcott* by his son, Arthur Westcott. London, 1903, 26-27.

That the evangelist could have intended the Christian reader eventually to to perceive all these allusions is easily credible; by the same criteria, it is obvious that the Baptist, preaching in A.D. 28, could not himself have entertained such profoundly christological thoughts. Can one trace a line of development from the Baptist's preaching to the text of the Fourth Gospel which is credible, because it makes good sense?

Some authors have suggested that in Jn 1.29 ὁ ἀμνός τοῦ θεοῦ represents an Aramaic phrase טַלְיָא דֶּאֱלָהָא [ṭalyaʾ deʾlāhāʾ], in which the term טַלְיָא (ṭalyaʾ) is open to more than one interpretation. There are two such words, one meaning *lamb*, the other meaning *boy, son* or *servant* (like the Greek παῖς). One proposal is that an original Aramaic text containing this noun, and intended to mean 'the Servant of God', was misunderstood by a translator, and rendered as 'the Lamb of God'.[67] In that hypothetical, pre-gospel, Aramaic text, טַלְיָא (ṭalyaʾ) meaning *servant* would have dovetailed into the Isaian context just as smoothly as does the word παῖς in the LXX, and in its sense of *son* would have matched the early kerygma about Jesus (compare the only five instances of παῖς θεοῦ applied to Jesus: Mt 12.18, citing Isa 42.1; Acts 3.13, 26; 4.27, 30). A strong counter-argument, however, is that in the Targum of Isaiah the Hebrew עֶבֶד (ʿεbεd) is, naturally enough, always translated by the cognate Aramaic word עֲבֵד (ʿăbed), so that the word טַלְיָא (ṭalyaʾ) would hardly have evoked direct memories of the Aramaic version of Isaiah. Fortunately, a more convincing explanation is to hand.

The Targum of Pseudo-Jonathan at Exod 1.15 explains why the Pharaoh sought to exterminate the Hebrew children. It reads: 'And Pharaoh said that while he slept, he saw in his dream that all the land of Egypt was placed on one balance of a weighing-scale, and a lamb, the young (of a ewe) and in the other balance-scales; and the balance of the weighing-scales on which the lamb (was placed) weighed down'.[68] Clearly, the lamb represents Moses, and the word used is טַלְיָא (ṭalyaʾ). There is other evidence too that similar stories were current by the end of the first century A.D.[69]

If, then, the Baptist had said (in Aramaic): 'Behold the Lamb of God', it would have been an easily comprehensible term to denote a great liberator, and was perhaps already used of Moses, as in the Targum just cited. So even if טַלְיָא (ṭalyaʾ) did not evoke memories of the Servant in Second Isaiah, it may well have aroused memories of Moses in Exodus.

[67] The original suggestion was that the Aramaic had been mistranslated: so C. J. Ball, 'Had the Fourth Gospel an Aramaic Archetype?', *ExpTimes* 21 (1909–10), 91-93. Also Burney, AOFG 107f. The idea has been most clearly formulated by J. Jeremias, whose arguments are more subtle, in *TWNT* I 342-45 and V 700. A revised version of the second article, 'παῖς (θεοῦ) im NT', is printed in *Abba*, 191-216; see 194-95, 202-203.

[68] Targum Pseudo-Jonathan: Exodus, 162.

[69] See Josephus, *Ant.* II 205, and R. Bloch, 'Quelques aspects de la figure de Moïse dans la tradition rabbinique', in *Moïse, l'homme de l'Alliance*, Paris-Tournai, 1955, 93-167.

Indeed, when one recalls the strong under-currents of references to the Covenant of Sinai which alone explain Jn 1.14, 17-18, one might expect the narrative of the Gospel to open with further allusions to another Moses. Further, if the Baptist had in actual fact used the term 'Lamb of God', the memory of this designation would almost certainly have survived, and as the understanding of Jesus' person and mission developed after his Resurrection, this title would have been able to assimilate all the additional connotations listed above, of Suffering Servant (12.38), Passover Lamb (19.36), the supreme sacrifice (17.18), King of Israel (1.49; 12.13) and Saviour of the world (4.42). In short, the words of the Baptist are, in the Gospel, serve as a programmatic affirmation about Jesus at the very beginning of his public life.

It is significant that in Jn 1.29-31 the Baptist does not address these words about the Lamb of God to anyone in particular. The statement is directed to all future readers of the Gospel, and therefore the content of the saying need not be restricted to the Baptist's understanding of it at the beginning of the ministry of Jesus; it can embrace whatever the Christian Church understood by the words towards the end of the first century. Indeed, to elucidate the fullest meaning of the text in the light of 1 Jn 3.5-9, Augustine's comment can hardly be bettered. 'Tollit autem et dimittendo quae facta sunt, ubi et originale comprehenditur; et adiuvando ne fiant, et perducendo ad vitam ubi fieri omnino non possint.'[70]

30. οὗτός ἐστιν ὑπὲρ οὗ ἐγὼ εἶπον, 'Οπίσω μου ἔρχεται ἀνὴρ ὃς ἔμπροσθέν μου γέγονεν, ὅτι πρῶτός μου ἦν. Verse 30 reproduces Jn 1.15, with slight textual variations.[71] A more significant divergence is that where v. 15 has ὁ ὀπίσω μου ἐρχόμενος, v. 30 reads ὀπίσω μου ἔρχεται ἀνήρ. It is unlikely that the term ἀνήρ is here directed against a type of Docetism which denied that Jesus had a true physical body like our own;[72] ἀνήρ is more naturally taken as a declaration that the pre-existent One was already to be found among John's followers as a fully grown man. The sense is therefore: *This is the one concerning whom I said, 'There is a man, a follower of mine, who takes precedence before me, because he existed before me'.* For further notes, see the commentary above on 1.15.

31. κἀγώ: the contracted form suggests *I too* (Lagrange: *moi non plus*). **οὐκ ᾔδειν αὐτόν**: the pluperfect form of οἶδα here carries the meaning

---

[70] 'He takes away [sin] both by forgiving those things which have been done (in which the original sin is also included), and by helping us not to do certain things, and by leading us to a life where such things cannot possibly be done.' *Opus Imperfectum contra Iulianum* II 84 *in fine* (Ben. X 986).

[71] The first ἦν of v. 15 is naturally replaced by ἐστιν in v. 30, and ὃν εἶπον is replaced, at v. 30, either by ὑπερ ου or περι ου. The preferable reading is ὑπερ: see NA²⁷ for the evidence.

[72] Compare Schnackenburg on 1 Jn 4.2 and 2 Jn 7.

of an imperfect tense, as is clear in the Latin, 'et ego nesciebam eum'. Hence, *nor was I myself aware of him* (that is, at first).

ἀλλ' ἵνα is elliptic; literally, '*but* it was *in order that...*' **φανερωθῇ τῷ Ἰσραήλ**. The adjective φανερός is common in Classical Greek, but the verb φανεροῦν was a new coinage in Hellenistic times (LSJ; BDAG). It occurs only once in the LXX (and in Aquila) at Jer 40[33].6 (= *reveal*), but 49 times in the NT. In the Synoptics, the new verb is rare,[73] but it is regular enough in the Pauline and Johannine books. Indeed, 'for Paul the verb is a key term for the revelation of God's salvation (Rom 1.19) in the gospel of Jesus Christ (cf. 16.26)'.[74] It is used to refer to the coming of revelation in Col 1.26 (τὸ μυστήριον τὸ ἀποκεκρυμμένον ἀπὸ τῶν αἰώνων καὶ ἀπὸ τῶν γενεῶν - νῦν δὲ ἐφανερώθη τοῖς ἁγίοις αὐτοῦ), in 2 Tim 1.10 and in 1 Pet 1.20; and it is also used of the person of Christ in 1 Tim 3.16 (ἐφανερώθη ἐν σαρκί). The last-mentioned text is closest to the sense of the verb here in Jn 1.31, where it refers to the manifestation to Israel of God's Presence on earth by the physical and historical coming of Jesus of Nazareth. The Baptist here affirms that his mission was to make this fact known.

In John, **διὰ τοῦτο** is almost always placed at the beginning of the sentence (*JG* 2387); its position here therefore underlines the importance of the preceding ἵνα-clause. **ἦλθον ἐγώ**. Once ᾔδειν in 31a is understood as an imperfect, the aorist ἦλθον in 31b must have a pluperfect sense: *it was for this reason, that I had come*, or *was come*. **ἐν ὕδατι βαπτίζων**. In Hellenistic Greek, the present participle increasingly does duty for the future participle, often with a sense of purpose (BDF 339 [2c]): hence, *in order to baptize. Nor was I myself aware who he was, but the reason I had come to baptize in water was that he might be made manifest to Israel.*

With this statement, the evangelist sets aside the two Synoptic traditions that John's ministry of 'baptizing for the forgiveness of sins' was the divinely ordained prelude to Jesus' ministry (Mk 1.2-4 etc.), and that Jesus too had presented himself for this baptism. Matthew felt that some explanation was needed to justify Jesus' baptism by John, but the Fourth Evangelist distances himself still further from the Synoptic tradition. He avoids any hint that Jesus had received baptism (compare Mt 3.16-17 with Jn 1.32-34), because there could be no place for such a ritual in his account of the pre-existent Logos presenting himself in the flesh.

32. καὶ ἐμαρτύρησεν Ἰωάννης λέγων ὅτι. See the notes on μαρτυρία given above at Jn 1.7 and 15. The aorist ἐμαρτύρησεν denotes an

---

[73] It is found only at Mk 4.22, as a variant reading in D in the parallel at Lk 12.2, and in Mk 16.12, 14.

[74] P.-G. Müller, *EDNT* III 413. Rom 16.25-26: κατὰ ἀποκάλυψιν μυστηρίου χρόνοις αἰωνίοις σεσιγημένου, φανερωθέντος δὲ νῦν...

action completed in the past; contrast the perfect μεμαρτύρηκα in v. 34 (and see the note there).

τεθέαμαι. The perfect tense underlines the lasting result of the vision: *I have gazed upon, I have beheld* (RV). In Classical Greek, the verb θεᾶσθαι most often carries a sense of wonder, and is also used to denote intellectual perception (LSJ);[75] in Biblical Greek, it comes to mean *seeing, beholding,* 'with the physical eyes, but in such a way that a supernatural impression is gained' (BDAG 2). According to Matthew and Mark, Jesus 'saw' (εἶδεν) the descent of the Spirit (Mt 3.16 ‖ Mk 1.10 ‖ Lk 3.22); only in John does the Baptist 'behold' it. In the Johannine writings, θεᾶσθαι, when used of the contemporaries of Jesus, is always found in a context which speaks of faith in him (Jn 1.14, 32; 11.45; 1 Jn 1.1; 4.12, 14); and in the other three Johannine occurrences (Jn 1.38; 4.35; 6.5), Jesus himself is presented as seeing the need for, or the possibility of, faith.

THE BACKGROUND TO THE WORD ΠΝΕΥΜΑ AT JOHN 1.32-33

The usual translation of the biblical words πνεῦμα and רוּחַ (ruaḥ) is 'spirit'. The gravest shortcoming with this rendering is that western European philosophy has conditioned almost everyone under its influence to accept a dualist view of the universe, in which spirit is the opposite of matter, and the spiritual is defined as that which is not material. But 'spirit' is the classical rendering of the biblical terms, and we have nothing more suitable.

In the OT, the root meaning both of πνεῦμα and of רוּחַ (ruaḥ) is *air in movement*, and in many texts their meaning is *wind, breeze,* or *breath*; indeed, πνεῦμα has a cognate verb (πνεῖν) meaning *to blow* (either strongly or softly), or *to breathe*, and a cognate noun πνοή, found in Gen 2.7 (πνοὴν ζωῆς). Thus the first and basic reference of these two words is to something purely physical. From this, they acquired, in the OT, a second sense: they came to signify other forces which are, like the wind and the air, physically invisible, but which certainly produce observable effects, and are just as clearly felt (for example, anger, bitterness, or depression). Sometimes these 'spirits' appear to come from outside a person: clear examples are found in 1 Sam 16.14-23 (Saul); 1 Kgs 22.21-23 (Micaiah) and 2 Kgs 2.9, 15 (Elisha). Note, however, that these texts do not refer to a personal 'demon' or devil: neither the Hebrew nor the Greek noun has that sense in the Bible.[76] In the OT, רוּחַ (ruaḥ) and

---

[75] So Plato, describing the true goal of life in this world and in the next: τὸ ἀληθὲς καὶ τὸ θεῖον καὶ τὸ ἀδόξαστον θεωμένη (Phaedo 84A). For further examples see LSJ.

[76] In Hebrew, this sense first appears, almost certainly under Iranian influence, at Qumran and in rabbinical writings. See 1QS 3.13-26; 4, and Jastrow 1458b *s.v.* רוּחַ II 4). The Greek πνεῦμα does not indicate a personal devil until the first century B.C. (Dionysius of Halicarnassus, *Ant.* 1.31, and then the magical papyri: see LSJ V and

πνεῦμα in this second sense usually denote not an external power, but an interior disposition, that is, what we would call a mood, a disposition or a temperament. Examples of this usage are 'a broken spirit' (NEB, 'distressed': Isa 66.2), 'bitterness of spirit' (Gen 26.35: NEB, 'a bitter grief'), 'better the patient in spirit than the proud in spirit' (Qoh 7.8), 'a steadfast spirit' (Ps 51.9: NEB, NAB). Finally, in view of Jn 1.33, the reader should be alerted to the fact that the phrase 'holy spirit' occurs only three times in the Hebrew Scriptures, at Ps 51.12; Isa 63.10, 11, all three post-exilic.[77]

The same terms רוּחַ (ruah) and πνεῦμα, when used with reference to God, have quite a different meaning. There is a consensus among OT scholars that the Spirit of God is, like the Word of God, at work in creation, in the providential guidance of history, in teaching mankind through the prophets and the holy writings, and in guiding God's people both collectively and individually into the knowledge of truth. A few basic texts will suffice to illustrate this.

The Spirit of God is, like the Word of God, at work in creation (Ps 33.6; compare Gen 1.2-3); indeed, the same Spirit is required, and is all-sufficient, for the survival of the animal creation (Ps 104.29-30).

The Spirit of God is, like the Word of God (Isa 55.10-11), at work in history. Examples are to be found both in individuals (Gideon, Judg 6.34; Jephthah, 11.29; Samson, 13.25; 14.6, 19; 15.14) and in the principle of an all-ruling divine providence (Zech 4.6; 7.12; Isa 30.28 [NRSV, 'breath']; compare 4.4 and 40.7). All the texts just listed use the term 'the Spirit of Yahweh' (not 'of God'). Beside these we may set the classic affirmation of God's omnipresence in Ps 139.7: 'whither shall I go from thy Spirit?'

The Spirit of God is also portrayed in the OT as active in teaching. Notably clear examples are to be found in 2 Sam 23.2; Mic 3.8; Isa 11.2; 42.1-4; 48.16; Ezek 2.2; 11.5, and Neh 9.20, 30 (again, nearly all referring to the Spirit of Yahweh').

In short, the term רוּחַ (ruah) or πνεῦμα stands for the innermost Being of God as active and intervening in the world of his creation (Isa 40.13-14). It is present everywhere, and at all times (Ps 139.7; compare 143.10 and 51.10-12). Furthermore, a Day will come when the Spirit of Yahweh will intervene in history more directly than ever before (Joel 2.28-29, cited in Acts 2.17-18; compare also Ezek 36.26-27; Num 11.29; Hag 2.5 and Zech 4.6; 6.8). On that Day 'a shoot shall burgeon from the stump of

---

BDAG 4 c). Plato uses the cognate noun ἐπίπνοια in the Phaedrus 265 B, where he discusses the four temperaments.

[77] In the LXX the term 'holy spirit' is found also in Wis 1.5 (ἅγιον πνεῦμα); 7.22 (πνεῦμα νοερόν, ἅγιον); 9.17 (τὸ ἅγιον σου πνεῦμα). All the major Hebrew Lexicons set out the different senses of רוּחַ (ruah), but the most modern ones like the DCH are far superior in their treatment to older works such as BDB. The references are generously printed out in TWNT VI 357-63 (Hebrew) and 366-70 (LXX).

Jesse, and a branch shall grow from his roots', that is, a king of the line of David, upon whom shall rest the Spirit of Yahweh in all its fullness (Isa 11.1-2). This promise of a charismatic leader filled with the Spirit recurs in Isa 42.1 and 61.1-3.[78] Always and everywhere, the Spirit of God works in and through the material world.

The book of Daniel was the last book received into the Hebrew Bible, and from 150 B.C to A.D. 100, Judaism seems to have accepted as fact that the Lord was no longer sending his Spirit to chosen ones among the people of Israel: see 1 Macc 4.46; 9.27; 14.41 (written around 100 B.C.) and *2 [=Syriac Apocalypse of] Baruch* 85.1-3 (soon after A.D. 100; *OTP* I 651). The conviction that the voice of prophecy was silent led to the proliferation of pseudepigraphical works, which were by convention back-dated to an epoch in which the Spirit was still openly active. These books consistently stress that the Spirit will return, and soon. The *Testament of Levi* 18.7 and the *Testament of Judah* 24.2-3 promise respectively an eschatological priest and an eschatological king, each of whom will be filled with the Spirit (*OTP* I 795, 801): these books were composed between 135 and 63 B.C.[79] The *Psalms of Solomon*, from the first century B.C., speak of a Messianic King filled with the Spirit (17.37; 18.7: *OTP* II 668, 669),[80] and *1 Enoch* foresees a time when the Son of Man, the Elect One, will come, richly endowed with the Spirit (49.2-3; 62.3; *OTP* I 36, 43; perhaps first century A.D.).[81] In the days of the Herods, therefore, it appeared that God was speaking to Israel only through the Law, the Prophets and the Writings, and that the fulfilment of all the ancient promises still lay in the future. The present was a time of waiting.[82]

It is in this context that we must attempt to determine the force of the words 'Spirit' (Jn 1.32) or 'holy Spirit' (1.33), on the lips of John the Baptist, before Jesus' ministry had begun. On the lips of the Baptist, the term can only denote the creative and life-giving power of God operating in the material world to teach and to guide humanity in the paths of holiness and righteousness, as it had formerly done through the prophets; in short, the ideas expressed by Luke in the Benedictus (Lk 1.61-79). It is self-evident that the term 'holy spirit' should not at this point in the gospel narrative be interpreted in the context of the Christian Trinitarian dogma, as referring to the Third Person of the Trinity in contradistinction to the Father and the Son (see Jn 7.39).[83]

καταβαῖνον ὡς περιστεράν. ℵ reads ὡς π. κ., perhaps to make clear that the Spirit itself was coming down from heaven, not that the Spirit

---

[78] JB has an excellent short note on this topic at Ezek 36.27.

[79] See Schürer III-2, 774

[80] See Schürer III-1, 193-95.

[81] See Schürer III-1, 256-59.

[82] Further detail on the subject-matter of the last two paragraphs may be found in *TWNT* VI 813-28, *s.v.* προφήτης C, by Rudolf Meyer.

[83] Fuller treatment of the term is given on at 3.5; 7.39 etc.

was like a dove coming down from heaven. That the distinction is not pedantic can be seen from the number of MSS which read, instead of ὡς, ὡσεί: thus 𝔓⁶⁶ K P Δ 063. 0101 *f*¹·¹³ 28.700.892. 1241. 1424 *pm*. The distinction between ὡς and ὡσεί is well represented by that between *as* and *as if*; the former term asserts similarity, the latter draws attention to the fact that the comparison is imperfect.[84] Thus ὡσεί may well have been used to avoid implying that the main purpose was to emphasise the physical presence of a dove (contrast Luke's σωματικῷ εἴδει, 3.22).

ὡς περιστεράν (found in all four Gospels) certainly carries a symbolic meaning. The most obvious allusion is to Gen 8.8-12, where the restoration and recreation of life on earth is marked by the safe departure of Noah's dove, a scene that inevitably evokes the memory of God's Spirit hovering over the waters at the first creation (Gen 1.2).[85] Noah in his ark was also a figure of Christian baptism (1 Pet 3.20-21). But in the OT, the primary symbolism of the dove is as a figure of love (Cant 2.12, 14; 5.2, 14; 6.9), and in early Christianity the dove was 'the symbol of all kinds of virtues' (BDAG).[86] Thus the words, 'I have beheld the Spirit descending from heaven like a dove', are a declaration that Jesus was endowed with all manner of spiritual gifts from heaven,[87] as would naturally follow if the meaning of μονογενής is, as proposed in the comments on Jn 1.14 and 18, *utterly unique*.

ἐξ οὐρανοῦ is a doctrinal, not a cosmographical, term—'out of heaven', not 'out of the sky'. John, alone of the evangelists, makes no mention of the baptism of Jesus. He omits also the phrase about 'a voice from heaven' (Mt 3.17 ǁ Mk 1.11 ǁ Lk 3.22). The omission may be significant. Jewish rabbis of the time speak of the Bath Qol (literally, *a voice's daughter*, like an Echo), which was a technical term for a Voice from Heaven. It meant 'an echo audible on earth of a voice which usually came from heaven',[88] and several rabbinical texts affirm that although, after the last prophets Haggai, Zechariah and Malachi, the Holy Spirit had departed from Israel, God had in the meantime sometimes spoken instead by a Bath Qol, especially in the Temple.[89] To say that the Spirit came

---

[84] This distinction, though often valid, needs to be handled with care, for there is much variation between the readings in the MSS (see BDF 453 [3]).

[85] In the Targums Neofiti and Pseudo-Jonathan, at Gen 8.2, God sends 'a spirit of mercy' or 'a merciful wind', רוח דרחמי (rwḥ drḥmyn) to make the Flood waters recede. The same phrase occurs in Neofiti at Gen 1.2.

[86] For detail, see H. Greeven *s.v.* περιστερά in *TWNT* VII 63-72; on the symbolism, see G. J. Botterweck in *TDOT* VI 37.

[87] Billerbeck is sceptical that a dove can symbolize the Holy Spirit (SB I 123-25), but some texts which he cites do compare the Bath Qol in the Temple with the cooing of a dove. See H. Greeven in *TWNT* VI 66 with fn. 37, 38; and C 1 on 67-68.

[88] Otto Betz in *TWNT* IX 282.

[89] For the rabbinical texts, see Betz on φωνή in the *TWNT* IX 281-82 fn. 41-43; for other relevant texts, see also *TWNT* VI 383-84 on πνεῦμα (Erik Sjöberg); and V 530-32 on οὐρανός (Helmut Traub).

down from heaven like a dove is therefore to insinuate that there is henceforth no need for the Bath Qol as a replacement for the voice of God on earth.

καὶ ἔμεινεν ἐπ' αὐτόν. The aorist ἔμεινεν implies that something took place once and for all, and that the result is permanent. Translate: *and it came to rest upon him.* (Compare MHT III 72 on the perfective and constative aorists.) 'Only here is it affirmed that the Spirit remained upon Jesus (but see Lk 4.18). Full and permanent possession of the Spirit is the distinctive characteristic of the Messiah (cf. Isa 11.2; 61.1)' (Schnackenburg). Jerome makes a similar comment, on Isa 11.2, cited in Aland, *Synopsis*, 27[46-50]. The perfect τεθέαμαι implies that the revelation is etched on the Baptist's memory for ever.

33. κἀγὼ οὐκ ᾔδειν αὐτόν: see the note above at 1.31.

ἀλλ' ὁ πέμψας με…ἐκεῖνός μοι εἶπεν. Only the Fourth Gospel contains this statement about 'the one who sent him [the Baptist]', but the thought is the same as that in Lk 1.13-17. The resumptive ἐκεῖνος is typically Johannine, and more emphatic than the word οὗτος which occurs later in this verse.

βαπτίζειν ἐν ὕδατι. A comparison of the Synoptic parallels suggests that the original form of the Baptist's preaching was probably, 'I am baptizing you in water, but there is one coming, mightier than I, who will baptize you in fire' (i.e. the fire of judgment). This would sit well both with the preceding threat about worthless trees being thrown onto the fire (Mt 3.10 ‖ Lk 3.9), and with the words immediately following, about burning the chaff in unquenchable fire (Mt 3.12 ‖ Lk 3.17). This interpretation also harmonizes well with the Baptist's perplexity when he later hears that Jesus is preaching to all a message not of doom but of healing and forgiveness (Mt 11.2-6 ‖ Lk 7.18-23). It is easy to comprehend how the early Church reinterpreted the Baptist's words. Matthew and Luke glossed the original form by rewriting the second clause as 'he will baptise you *with a holy spirit and* with fire', thus giving a spiritual meaning to fire, as in Acts 2. Mark achieves the same effect by writing 'holy spirit' instead of 'fire' (Mk 1.8). It is of course possible (but less likely) that the Baptist originally spoke of a baptism 'with wind and fire'. What is certain is that his words as we have them in the Gospels represent a rephrasing for Christian catechetical purposes. Compare the conjunction of wind, fire and the Spirit in Acts 2.2-4.

ἐφ' ὃν ἂν ἴδῃς τὸ πνεῦμα καταβαῖνον καὶ μένον ἐπ' αὐτόν.

ἴδῃς. the use of the aorist subjunctive, rather than the indicative ὄψῃ, implies that the clause states a general principle, but is neutral on the likelihood of the condition's being fulfilled (BDF 380). The statement is then all the more convincing when the condition is fulfilled. For notes on the other words, see above under v. 32.

οὖτός ἐστιν ὁ βαπτίζων ἐν πνεύματι ἁγίῳ. The absence of the article with πνεύματι ἁγίῳ is significant, particularly since, in the corresponding texts of the Synoptic Gospels, almost all the manuscripts contain the article, with scarcely a variant reading (Mt 3.16 ‖ Mk 1.10 ‖ Lk 3.22).[90] At this point in the gospel narrative, before Jesus has started to preach, the anarthrous πνεῦμα ἅγιον can only carry the meaning which it had in contemporary Judaism: that is, it signifies the creative, life-giving, power of Yahweh, which has descended upon Jesus and in which he has therefore come to share. The Baptist had baptized symbolically, and externally, with cleansing water; Jesus, because he was endowed with 'the spirit', would be able to 'baptize' others, that is, to endow them inwardly with 'a holy spirit', God's life-transforming gift.

34. κἀγὼ ἑώρακα, καὶ μεμαρτύρηκα. If τεθέαμαι means *I have beheld* (see the comments above on Jn 1.32), then κἀγὼ ἑώρακα κτλ. point to what ensued. ἑώρακα, καὶ μεμαρτύρηκα: *I have seen and have attested.* 'Seeing' as 'clear perception' would naturally follow if the meaning of μονογενής is, as suggested in the comments on Jn 1.14 and 18, *utterly unique.*

ὅτι οὖτός ἐστιν ὁ ἐκλεκτὸς τοῦ θεοῦ. The generally accepted reading has υιος, not εκλεκτος, and the external textual evidence in favour of υιος is overwhelming. There is, however, some support, chiefly Western, for εκλεκτος. True, among Greek MSS, only א* has εκλεκτος, but the lacuna in 𝔓⁵ is of the right length for it; *electus* is found in b e ff* and Ambrose; the equivalent in syr^cur sin; and the conflate reading *electus filius* is attested by in ff^2c syr^pal mss sah. (The Codex Bezae is defective at this point.) *TCGNT* by a majority classed the reading as {B}.

No modern edition of the Greek NT has the reading εκλεκτος. It is therefore impressive to see the list of scholars who defend it. Schnacken-burg in 1965 listed Spitta, Zahn, Harnack, Lagrange, Loisy, Windisch, Cullmann, J. Jeremias, D. Mollat, van den Bussche, and Boismard;[91] to these may now be added R. E. Brown, I. de la Potterie (*La Vérité*, 83), W. Grundmann[92] and B. Schwank. Barrett and Lindars are also favourable. The *Bible de Jérusalem* adopts this reading, as does REB. It is hard to think of any reason why a Christian scribe should have wished to substi-tute εκλεκτος for υιος, and easy to see why one might have chosen to do the opposite. Nor need the alteration to υιος have been made under the pressure of Arianism; 'adoptionist' controversies were alive from A.D.

---

[90] The only exceptions occur at Mt 3.16, where the two articles in [το] πνευμα [του] θεου are absent from B and א.

[91] See Schnackenburg I 305 fn. 2 = ETr I 306 fn. 73.

[92] In 'Verkündigung und Geschichte in dem Bericht vom Eingang der Geschichte Jesu im Johannes-Evangelium', in *Der historische Jesus und der kerygmatiche Christus*, 1961, 2nd ed., 293 fn. 15.

190 onwards,[93] and what was more natural than to align the Fourth Gospel with the Synoptics by adjusting Jesus' title to that of 'Son' found in the other accounts of his baptism (Mt 3.17 ‖ Mk 1.11 ‖ Lk 3.22)?

Internal evidence argues strongly in favour of ἐκλεκτός. One powerful argument is that 'the Elect One' was among the leading titles used in contemporary Palestinian Judaism. In the Similitudes of *1 Enoch* (*1 En* 37–71),[94] this is the principal, and the most frequent, name for the coming eschatological Judge and Saviour,[95] a pre-existent being (48.3, 6 ‖ Isa 49.1, 2) also referred to as 'Son of Man' (46.2, 3, 4; 48.2) and 'Messiah' (48.10; 52.4), destined to be the light of the Gentiles (48.4 ‖ Isa 42.6; 49.6; Lk 2.32).[96] Reading ἐκλεκτός in Jn 1.34 thus puts a most meaningful, utterly Jewish and Palestinian, designation of Jesus on the lips of the Baptist. Secondly, ὁ ἐκλεκτός is not a customary title of Jesus in Christian writings.[97] Apart from 1 Pet 2.4, 6, it occurs only once in the received texts of the NT with reference to Jesus, at Lk 23.35, where the evangelist places it on the lips of the Jewish rulers: σωσάτω ἑαυτόν, εἰ οὗτός ἐστιν ὁ Χριστὸς τοῦ θεοῦ ὁ ἐκλεκτός (23.35). Note that this too is in a Palestinian context. Thirdly, if the reading ἐκλεκτός is accepted at Jn 1.34, the cross-reference to Isa 42.1 becomes unmistakable: the Hebrew there reads 'my Chosen One'.[98] The adoption of this reading for Jn 1.34 would thus accord with the Baptist's declaration of the abiding presence of the Spirit upon Jesus (1.32, 33), and of Jesus' mission to the world (1.9-13). The NRSV reads:

> Here is my servant, whom I uphold,
>   my chosen, in whom my soul delights;[99]
> I have put my spirit upon him,
>   he will bring forth justice to the nations.

One final reason for preferring ἐκλεκτός is that Jn 1.19-51 would then contain just seven titles for Jesus, with none of them repeated: (1) the Lamb of God, vv. 29, 36; (2) the Chosen One of God, v. 34; (3) Rabbi,

---

[93] Theodotus the leather-merchant of Byzantium: see Hippolytus, *Refutatio* VII 35; Eusebius, *HE* V 28.

[94] These chapters, once thought to be pre-Christian, are now generally dated in the first century A.D. It is certainly a Jewish, work, and from Judea. See E. Isaac in *OTP* I 6-8 and M. Black, *The Book of Enoch or 1 Enoch*, Leiden, 1985, 181-88.

[95] In *TWNT* V 686 fn. 247, J. Jeremias lists fifteen references: 39.6; 40.5; 45.3, 4; 49.2; 51.3, 5; 52.6, 9; 53.6; 55.4; 61.5, 8, 10; 62.1; cf. 46.3; 48.6; 49.4.

[96] *TWNT* V 686-87; J. Coppens, *La relève apocalyptique*, 128-38.

[97] It is never applied to Jesus in the NT, the Apostolic Fathers or the Apologists. Note that ὁ ἐκλελεγμένος (Lk 9.35) also is not used as a title.

[98] The LXX has: Ιακωβ ὁ παῖς μου... Ισραηλ ὁ ἐκλεκτός μου. Hellenistic Judaism applied Second Isaiah's Servant prophecies to the people as a collective unity, whereas Palestinian Judaism held fast to the view that the texts referred to an individual. See J. Jeremias *TWNT* V 682-83.

[99] In the Targum, this line reads: 'my Chosen One, in whom my Memra is well pleased'.

v. 38, 49; (4) Messiah, v. 41; (5) the Son of God, v. 49; (6) the King of Israel, v. 49; (7) the Son of Man, v. 51.[100]

Verse 34 also contains two instances of *inclusio*. This short section itself opens and closes with a reference to the 'witness' of the Baptist (1.20 is matched by 32-34). And just as this first narrative in the Gospel ends with ἑώρακα, καὶ μεμαρτύρηκα (1.34), so the last event that ends the earthly life of Jesus is followed by the words καὶ ὁ ἑωρακὼς μεμαρτύρηκεν (19.35).

---

[100] Those who prefer to accept in 1.34 the reading υἱος will find the sense elucidated at Jn 1.49.

EXCURSUS V

BETHANY BEYOND THE JORDAN

Three variants of Βηθανια are found: for the evidence see UBS.

(a) Βηθαβαρα (C² K T Ψᶜ 083 *f*¹·¹³ 33 pm sy. ᶜ·ˢᵃ·; Or);
(b) Βηθεβαρα (*f*¹³ sin);
(c) Βηθαραβα (x² 892ᵛˡ *pc* [syʰᵐᵍ]).

Minor variants such as Βηθαρα, Βιθαρα etc. (see Tischendorf or von Soden) are best taken as abbreviations, and disregarded.

Βηθεβαρα is certainly no more than a variant for Βηθαβαρα, and Βηθαραβα (by metathesis) probably so; the choice lies between Βηθανια and Βηθαβαρα (thus Barrett, expressing the general consensus).

Origen informs us that in his day Βηθανια stood 'in nearly all the copies' and was read by Heracleon, but that he himself had been unable to find any place of that name near the Jordan. He had heard, however, that a place on the river-bank called τὰ Βηθαβαρᾶ (note the plural, and the article) was pointed out as the spot where John used to baptize (δεικύσθαι δὲ λέγουσι παρὰ τῇ ὄχθῇ τοῦ Ἰορδάνου τὰ Βηθαβαρᾶ, ἔνθα ἱστοροῦσιν τὸν Ἰωάννην βεβαπτίκεναι). Origen therefore proposed that 'Bethabara' must be the true reading,[1] and it has in consequence been perpetuated not only in several manuscripts, but also by Eusebius and Jerome, in their identification of the site,[2] and by Epiphanius and Chrysostom.[3] Notwithstanding this ancient support, 'Bethany' has, since the end of the patristic era, been universally preferred.

All efforts to find material evidence for a Bethany located east of the Jordan have come to nothing, but historical geography can still help. Origen, first visited Palestine in A.D. 215, and his statement is clear: John was said to have baptized at a place called Bethabara. A hundred years later, Eusebius, in his *Onomasticon* (written before 331), relates that many pilgrims went to avail themselves of the cleansing water at this 'Bethabara beyond the Jordan'; and according to the Pilgrim of Bordeaux (A.D. 333), the site of the Lord's baptism was five (Roman) miles from

---

[1] VI 40 §§204-205 (*SC* 284-87, with valuable notes on the text of Origen, and on his different etymologies).
[2] Eusebius, *Onomasticon* in GCS 11.1:58-59, cited in ELS, 2nd ed., 165, though Jerome wisely let Bethany stand in the Vulgate.
[3] See Tischendorf for the references.

the Dead Sea.[4] This would place 'Bethabara' at the ford now named Al-Maghtas, near the Greek monastery of St John the Forerunner, historically known as Qasr el-Yehud. In the nineteenth century, this was the area favoured by Latin Christians, while a different place, about one mile further south, at the ford of Al-Hajla, was preferred by Orthodox Christians.[5] The separation was no doubt intended to prevent unseemly disorder, but it serves both to illustrate and to underline the more important fact that for 1800 years the location of Jesus' baptism was always set in the same area, about four or five miles from the point at which the Jordan reaches the Dead Sea.[6] Nowadays all pilgrims make their way to the more southerly ford of Al-Hajla, for the river-bank is there easier of access.

Through the scrub-land on the east bank there runs today a little brook, the Wadi el-Kharrar. It is formed from half a dozen springs of brackish water emerging from a cliff not quite two miles east of the Jordan, in a valley where shrubs, willows, tamarisks and Euphrates-poplars grow.[7] This inspired Dalman to propose that the Baptist and his disciples might have dwelt in one of those easily erected bowers, standing on piles, for safety against floods, made from reeds and the Euphrates-poplar 'similar to those which can be seen even today [i.e. 1900–1930] on the banks of the Jordan'.[8]

A small group of such dwellings in that area on the east bank well have been called, in Aramaic, בֵּית עַיְנָא (beyt ʿayînēʾ), 'Waterhouses', and turned into Greek as Bηθανια.[9] The same place, or an adjacent group of dwellings, might have been known (at the same time or later) as בֵּית עֲרֵבָא (beyt ʿărĕbĕh), 'Willow Houses', ʿărĕbĕh meaning, both in Hebrew and in Aramaic, a willow-tree.[10] Thus Bηθαραβα is not necessarily a mis-copying of Bηθαβαρα; it could, like Bηθανια = 'Waterhouses', denote a group of 'Willowhouses' on the east bank.

---

[4] Inde [a mare mortuo] ad Iordane [sic], ubi dominus a Iohanne baptizatus est milia quinque (*Itinera Hierosolymitana saec. III -VIII recensuit...* Paulus Geyer, CSEL 39, 24).

[5] W. M. Thomson gives a lively account of an Orthodox pilgrimage to the spot in April 1833. See *The Land and the Book*, London, 1878, 613-16.

[6] The only serious alternative proposal is that of L. Féderlin, *Béthanie au-delà du Jourdain (Tell el-Medesch)*, Paris [1908], who argues the claims of Tell el Medesh (better Khirbet et-Tamil) on the north bank of the Wadi Nimrin, about 2 miles (3.5 km) north-east of the Roraniyeh (Allenby, King Hussein) Bridge, and 300 yards from the Jordan. Lagrange calls this site, by reason of its position, 'très plausible' (*Jean*, 39). C. R. Conder's preference for the ford called ʿAbarah, north-east of Bethshean = Beisan, became widely known as a result of his entry under 'Bethabara' in the DBH I 276a (1898), but it never gained acceptance among scholars.

[7] Abel, *Géographie* I 176; Dalman, *Sacred Sites*, 89.

[8] *Sacred Sites*, 88. See also the vivid page of H. V. Morton, *In the Steps of the Master*, London, 1934, 104-105, describing precisely such a dwelling at that very spot.

[9] Jastrow 1072a, cites for this meaning of עַיִן 'Targum Gen 16.7 and frequently', with a number of other examples.

[10] Jastrow 1112a.

Quite evidently, no trace of such flimsy dwellings would ever survive, particularly when one calls to mind the frequent earth tremors in the region, in consequence of which the river bed must often have shifted since the time of Jesus.[11] Furthermore, if even in Origen's day there was no memory of a Bethania east of the Jordan, it is understandable that some later copyists too, finding no record of any such place, should have corrected the gospel text. Here the very paucity of witnesses to Betharaba (x^2 892[vl] *pc* syr[hmg]) is significant, for though Betharaba was not a widespread reading, it was considered important enough to merit insertion as a correction in ℵ around A.D. 600 (probably in Caesarea), as a variant reading in 892 (eighth–ninth century, Calabria?) and among the local traditions reverently recorded in A.D. 616, in the margins of the Harclean Syriac. 'Betharaba' has a solid claim to represent a Syro-Palestinian tradition of respected antiquity. 'Bethabara' is, of course, more widely attested, and most of the evidence appears to come from Palestine: C^2 is probably a sixth-century Palestinian correction,[12] K is the Codex Cyprius, f^1 can apparently trace its origins to third- or fourth-century Caesarea, and the Old Syriac is certainly from the churches of Syria or Palestine.[13] The substitution of Bethabara for Bethany is therefore most easily explained by positing that when Bethany (and Betharaba) had long disappeared from human memory, Bethabara was known to everyone in Palestine as a major ford. It stood on the Roman road linking Jericho with Esbus (Heshbon), and thus with the great trunk road from the Syrian frontier to the Gulf of Aqaba, built by Trajan and Hadrian to secure communications across the province of Arabia,[14] and 'everyone agreed' that that was the place where John baptized. This explanation of the textual tradition is essentially the same as that advocated by Dalman.

Many features of this proposed location of the Baptist's ministry are confirmed by the Madaba mosaic (sixth century A.D.), though it shows Bethabara, meaning literally 'Waterford House', on the west bank of the Jordan.[15] The name of the crossing, however, may quite easily have applied to both sides of the river, since τὰ Βηθαβαρᾶ is plural. On the

---

[11] Cf. Dalman, *Sacred Sites*, 92.

[12] Metzger, *The Text of the NT*, 49.

[13] Cf. Lagrange, *Critique Textuelle* II 60.

[14] See Abel, *Géographie* II 186, 230, and *Histoire de la Palestine* II 53-57. He gives further detail on Bethabara in *RB* 22 (1913), 240-43, with a fine photograph of the spot at that time, opposite p. 218, Plate II 2.

[15] The most accessible reproductions are in *DBS* V (1957), 631-32 and in *DACL* X-1 after 820. *AtBib* reproduces clearly the relevant part on p. 61, Plate 173. The classic edition, with coloured plates, is that of P. Palmer and H. Guthe, *Die Mosaikkarte von Medeba*, Leipzig, 1904. See also M. Avi-Yonah, *The Madaba Mosaic Map*, Jerusalem, 1954, for notes, and H. Donner, *The Mosaic Map of Madaba*, Palaestina Antiqua 7, Kampen, 1995.

east bank, the map has Αινων ενθα νυν ο Σαπσαφας (idiomatically,
'Springwell-le-Willows'[16]) no doubt to distinguish it from any other place
named Ainon (such as Ainon near Salim, Jn 3.23).[17]

---

[16] צַפְצָפָה (ṣapṣāpāh) denotes 'a species of willow that grows in waterless regions'
(Jastrow 1298).

[17] See also R. Riesner, 'Bethany beyond the Jordan', in *ABD* I 703-705.

B. THE CALLING AND TESTIMONY
OF THE FIRST DISCIPLES (1.35-51)

1. *The Calling of the First Disciples: 1.35-42*

[1.35] The next day John was again standing with two of his disciples, [36] and observing Jesus walking by, he said, 'Behold, the Lamb of God!' [37] The two disciples heard him saying this, and followed Jesus. [38] Jesus turned, and beheld them following, and said to them, 'What are you seeking?' They said to him, 'Rabbi' (which means Teacher), 'where are you staying?' [39] He said to them, 'Come and see'. They came and saw where he was staying; and they stayed with him that day, for it was about the tenth hour. [40] One of the two who heard John speaking, and followed him, was Andrew, Simon Peter's brother. [41] He first found his brother Simon, and said to him, 'We have found the Messiah' (which means Christ). [42] He brought him to Jesus. Jesus looked at him, and said, 'So you are Simon the son of John? You are to be called Cephas' (which means Peter).

35. τῇ ἐπαύριον πάλιν εἰστήκει ὁ Ἰωάννης καὶ ἐκ τῶν μαθητῶν αὐτοῦ δύο. That is, on the third consecutive day.[1] εἰστήκει, the pluperfect of ἵστημι, stands related as imperfect to the intransitive perfect ἕστηκα, which has a present meaning: translate therefore *was standing* (the Latin *stabat* is exact). John 1.40 tells us that one of the two disciples was Andrew, and it will be suggested that the other one is 'the disciple whom Jesus loved' (→ 1.39, at the end). The natural flow of the text implies that the location is the same as on the preceding day.

36. καὶ ἐμβλέψας τῷ Ἰησοῦ περιπατοῦντι. *And observing Jesus walking by.* In John, the verb ἐμβλέψας occurs only here and at 1.42; contrast the Vulgate's rendering in 1.36 [Iohannes] *respiciens*, with that in 1.42, [Iesus] *intuitus* (→ 1.42). An aorist participle with a present indicative verb (λέγει) is quite usual to denote coincident action (MHT III 79). ἴδε ὁ ἀμνὸς τοῦ θεοῦ → 1.29. The fact that the saying is here curtailed indicates that the intention is merely to remind the reader of the designation given in full in 1.29; the disciples' response is spelt out in the events next described.

---

[1] 𝔓[5vid.75], plus the early Latin witnesses b e r[1], the three Old Syriac texts [sin cur pal], and some bohairic manuscripts attest to the absence of πάλιν.

37. καὶ ἤκουσαν οἱ δύο μαθηταὶ αὐτοῦ λαλοῦντος. The textual variations in the order of the words οἱ δύο μαθηταὶ αὐτοῦ (see NA²⁷) are evidently due to a desire to make clear the reference of αὐτοῦ. αὐτοῦ certainly refers to the Baptist, but does it refer to 'his disciples' (οἱ δύο αὐτοῦ μαθηταί) or to 'him speaking' (ἤκουσαν αὐτοῦ οἱ δύο μαθηταὶ λαλοῦντος)? The two opposing attempts at clarification suggest that the ambiguous text above, given by NA²⁷, must be the original one.

ἤκουσαν followed by the genitive participle means that the two disciples *listened to him speaking* and acted accordingly (see BDAG ἀκούω 4). **καὶ ἠκολούθησαν τῷ 'Ιησοῦ.** Since ἠκολούθησαν is not imperfect, but aorist, the sense is not that they *began to follow* Jesus, like the crowds in Mk 2.15 (ἠκολούθουν), Mk 5.24 or Jn 6.2 (ἠκολούθει); it is rather that at that moment the two disciples left the Baptist to become thenceforward followers of Jesus, heeding the words of their first master (compare 3.27-30).

38. στραφεὶς δὲ ὁ 'Ιησοῦς. στραφείς must imply more than that Jesus turned around physically. It is almost the first recorded action of the Word upon earth,² and immediately precedes his first spoken words. This same participle στραφείς occurs twice in Matthew (9.22; 16.23), and seven times in Luke (7.9, 44; 9.35; 10.23; 14.25; 22.61; 23.28), always with Jesus as subject; and on each occasion it denotes a sudden and remarkable change of attitude on his part, nearly always followed by a wholly unexpected saying.

To the Jewish mind, the Hebrew verb underlying στραφείς would evoke instinctively the insistent prayers for the 'return of God' to his people. 'Return, O Lord! How long?' (Ps 90.13), or 'Restore us again, O Lord of hosts!' (80.4, 8, 20; compare v. 15), and 'Wilt thou not return and give us life?' (85.7; compare 71.20)—in all these prayers the Hebrew verb for 'return' and 'restore' is everywhere the same, שוב (šub).³ It is the normal word for the return of God to Israel, and for the return of Israel to God (compare Jer 12.15 with Isa 63.17). With this verb Zechariah opens his programme for rebuilding the community after the exile: 'Return to me, says the Lord of hosts, and I will return to you, says the Lord of hosts' (Zech 1.3), and Malachi, the last post-exilic prophet, speaks in virtually identical words (3.7).

---

² Only the oblique reference to the appearance of Jesus before the Baptist (vv. 32-34) precedes it.

³ The fact that שוב (šub) is most often translated in the LXX by ἐπιστρέφειν (only three times as στρέφειν: see HR) does not weaken the argument of this paragraph, but only suggests that the gospel writer was accustomed to using a Hebrew text rather than the LXX. The Hebrew versions of the NT by Franz Delitzsch and David Ginsburg both translate στραφείς (as does the Peshitta) by the root פנה (pnh). פנה (pnh) most commonly denotes the physical movement of turning, but it too can have a metaphorical usage (for example, in Pss 25.16; 69.17; 86.16; 119.132).

στραφεὶς δὲ ὁ ᾿Ιησοῦς. As soon as the two Israelites followed Jesus, *Jesus turned...* στραφεὶς implies that the Word of the Lord has turned once more towards his people, redeeming the promises made in Zechariah and Malachi at the end of the OT. In John, this verb στρεφείν is never again used of Jesus, for it never need be: the Word of the Lord will never turn back from his mission until his task is accomplished. Compare Isa 55.11, τὸ ῥῆμά μου, ὃ ἐὰν ἐξέλθῃ ἐκ τοῦ στόματός μου, οὐ μὴ ἀποστραφῇ, ἕως ἂν συντελεσθῇ ὅσα ἠθέλησα with Jn 19.30, τετέλεσται. The next occurrence of στρεφείν (in any form) is at Jn 12.40, in the citation of Isa 6.10, thus providing a sad *inclusio* at the end of the first part of the Gospel.[4] Though Jesus has *turned* to Israel, not all Israel has turned to him (Jn 12.37-43; cf. 1.11-12).

καὶ θεασάμενος αὐτοὺς ἀκολουθοῦντας λέγει αὐτοῖς, Τί ζητεῖτε... *Beholding them following, he said to them, What are you searching for?* On **θεασάμενος**, → τεθέαμαι at 1.32. **τί ζητεῖτε**; 'What are you searching for?' The first words uttered by Jesus in the Fourth Gospel address with matchless lucidity the primordial existential question of 'the world' (particularly in the Johannine sense: →1.10). Nowhere else in the NT does Jesus put this question, and John's Gospel is intended as the answer given by God's Eternal Wisdom, the light and the life of the world. In this question to the first would-be disciples, we encounter for the first time in this Gospel the verb ζητεῖν. Its last occurrence comes in the first words spoken by the risen Jesus, at 20.15: τίνα ζητεῖς; If we exclude from consideration ch. 21, this is the final question asked by Jesus in John's Gospel, and it is put to his last disciple (Mary Magdalen). The narratives it introduces in ch. 20 bring to an end the quest initiated at 1.38. The two questions thus make a perfect *inclusio*, embracing the entire Gospel. See 20.15; compare also 18.4, 7.

οἱ δὲ εἶπαν αὐτῷ, ῥαββί, ὃ λέγεται μεθερμηνευόμενον διδάσκαλε, ποῦ μένεις; The use of 'Rabbi', together with the gloss that it means in translation 'Teacher', reveals a desire on the part of the writer to retain authentic local colour and at the same time to explain its meaning to readers unfamiliar with such terms (one might compare 'pundit', originally a learned Hindu). In NT times, the guardianship and interpretation of the Law had long passed from the priests to the scholars or scribes, who were increasingly seen as the true spiritual leaders of the people, and the honorific appellation 'Rabbi' ('my lord', 'monseigneur'), from being at first a form of reverential address (as in the NT), eventually came to be an official title for a duly qualified scholar. According to the new Schürer, the use of 'Rabbi' as a title seems to have originated around the life-time of Jesus.[5] Thus to

---

[4] στρεφείν occurs thereafter only in 20.14, 16, of Magdalen.
[5] Schürer II 322-29. Neither Hillel nor Shammai is ever called Rabbi.

address Jesus as 'Rabbi' is to accord him the highest status as a teacher of Israel. In the light of Jesus' question, 'What are you searching for?', it would be most extraordinary if this courteous address, ῥαββί, ποῦ μένεις; was, in the mind of the evangelist, intended to be understood merely as an inquiry about the location of Jesus' residence beside the banks of the Jordan. In inquiring ποῦ μένεις, the two disciples were 'seeking' something more.

39. λέγει αὐτοῖς, ἔρχεσθε καὶ ὄψεσθε. ἦλθαν οὖν καὶ εἶδαν ποῦ μένει. *He said to them, Come and see. So they came and saw where he was staying.* Though ὄψεσθε is a future indicative, it would be pedantic to translate it as *you will see*; the Greek idiom is perfectly matched by the English idiom *Come and see*, where *see* hovers between a future (with *you will* not so much suppressed as understood) and an imperative (compare BDF 387; 362). The variant reading ἴδετε appears to be an attempt to escape from this ambiguity by choosing the imperative sense. Lagrange preferred ἴδετε on the ground that 'Come and see!' was a current rabbinical formula,[6] that ὄψεσθε 'doit être une élégance', and perhaps also because ἴδετε was attested by ℵ. Now, however, the weight of the early evidence (including 𝔓⁶⁶.⁷⁵) supports ὄψεσθε (see NA²⁷).

At first reading, these words appear to affirm nothing more than that the disciples accepted Jesus' invitation to visit the dwelling and spent the day there; but this can hardly be the full intent of the story. To make sense of vv. 35 to 40, the text must be read in the light of the Prologue. John 1.1 exhibits the close relationship, even identity, between the Logos in John and the concept of Wisdom in Prov 8, especially in the work of creation (8.22-31). Immediately after these verses, Wisdom appeals for disciples:

> Happy is the man who listens to me,
>   watching daily at my gates,
>   waiting beside my doors.
> For he who finds me finds life
>   and obtains favour from the Lord (Prov 8.34-35).

There follows the description of the house of Wisdom, a splendid palace with an inner courtyard adorned with seven pillars, the number symbolizing perfection.

> Wisdom has built a house for herself,
>   with seven columns of dressed stone.
> She has slaughtered a beast, she has spiced her wine,
>   she has also set her table.
> She has sent out her maids to call
>   from the highest places in the town,
> 'Let anyone who lacks maturity turn in here!' (Prov 9.1-4a).

---

[6] Compare Jn 1.46 and 11.34, and also SB II 371.

Similar language about feasting on Wisdom is found in Isa 55.1-3 and
in Sir 15.3; 24.1-22. If Jn 1.38-40 are read with these Wisdom texts in
mind, the verses disclose the spiritual message in the two reciprocal
and complementary questions, 'What are you searching for?', and
'Where do you dwell?'

In Sir 24.3-12 Wisdom declares that she has dwelt in the high
places, in the clouds and in the waves of the sea, in every people and in
every nation under heaven, but above all, in Israel. In particular, divine
Wisdom had been embodied in 'the book of the covenant of the Most
High God, the law which Moses commanded as an inheritance for the
congregations of Jacob' (24.23). For the writer of the Fourth Gospel, it
is Jesus in the flesh who is now the embodiment on earth of Eternal
Wisdom, saying

> 'Those who eat me will hunger for more,
> and those who drink me will thirst for more' (Sir 24.21),

for he himself is 'the bread of God coming down from heaven and
giving life to the world' (Jn 6.33; see also 6.35).

When Jesus asked the two disciples what they were searching for,
they replied ῥαββί, ποῦ μένεις. The Vulgate renders, *magister ubi
habitas?* Let the phrase be englished as 'Master, where is your dwelling?' The disciples, without being overtly conscious of the fact, are
implicitly asking 'Where does Wisdom dwell?' (and one thinks immediately of Job 28.12). *Jesus said to them, Come and see.* ἦλθαν οὖν
καὶ εἶδαν. They came and saw: both verbs are repeated, and the οὖν
is not otiose. οὖν will seem an insignificant particle to anyone who
reads these verses as no more than a narrative of Jesus' invitation to
view and visit his domicile, and this probably accounts for its omission
from many manuscripts.[7] But what if the gospel writer was convinced
that there was one greater than Solomon here?

ἦλθαν οὖν: they came because Jesus had initiated the conversation
by his first question, and because he had responded to their question by
inviting them to converse with him. καὶ εἶδαν ποῦ μένει. The
Vulgate is here subtly discriminating. The disciples' question reads,
magister ubi habitas? The translator replies: *venerunt et viderunt ubi
maneret.* At its second occurrence, μένειν is taken to mean not
habitare (= *to dwell permanently*), but *manere*, meaning *to stay for a
time, to be lodging* (the very first sense ascribed to μένειν in BDAG,
where further references are given, one of which recurs in this same
verse; compare also Jn 14.25). The Latin translator thus reminds us

---

[7] 'It [οὖν] does not always furnish a strictly causal connection, but may be used
more loosely as a temporal connective in the continuation or resumption of a narrative' (BDF 451 [1]). This second, less emphatic usage, might account for its absence
here in the majority of later Greek manuscripts, and—astonishingly—in all the Latin
manuscripts; but the early Greek tradition, beginning with 𝔓[66.75] ℵ A B C L N W[suppl],
is solid in its support (see NA[27] for the evidence).

that there are two answers to the question, 'Where does Wisdom dwell?' There is Wisdom's eternal dwelling-place πρὸς τὸν θεόν, and its temporary residence in which ἐσκήνωσεν ἐν ἡμῖν. Translate therefore: *They saw where he was staying.* **καὶ παρ' αὐτῷ ἔμειναν τὴν ἡμέραν ἐκείνην:** *and they stayed with him that day* (the meaning 'dwelt' is clearly here impossible).

The two disciples remained all that day (τὴν ἡμέραν, accusative of extent of time: Robertson 470). **ὥρα ἦν ὡς δεκάτη.** *It was around the tenth hour,* that is, the time at which people go home to take the main, perhaps the only, meal of the day, the evening meal (Lk 17.7). The evangelist does not mention any meal, or give any hint of what the little group discussed. He leaves the reader to surmise what came to pass.

> 'Come, eat of my bread
>   and drink of the wine I have mixed.
> Abandon thoughtlessness, and live,
>   and walk in the way of insight' (Prov 9.5-6).

Here the account of the first day of Jesus' activity on earth ends, with coming of the evening meal-time. So his last day on earth will end, with a meal, at which he will unveil to his disciples the fullness of God's love for them (Jn 13.1; 17.26).

We are not told the name of the other disciple mentioned in vv. 35, 37 and here in 39, but, given that the Galilean calling of Peter and Andrew is, in the Synoptics, always linked with that of James and John (Mt 4.18-22 || Mk 1.16-20 || Lk 5.1-11), it is not surprising that John the son of Zebedee has always been the prime candidate for the role, because James was martyred before Passover of A.D. 44 (Acts 12.2). It is also often said that the anonymity cloaks a discreet retirement into the background by the original witness to the story; or that it proceeds from a desire to avoid the embarrassment of giving precedence to the person in question over Simon Peter (compare Jn 20.5, 8).[8] Others suggest Philip rather than John, but → 1.43. However, when 1.35-39 are compared with 21.1-22, the prominence in both texts of the verbs στῆναι, ἀκολουθεῖν, and μένειν inclines one to conclude that the anonymous disciple of 1.35, 37, 39 was most probably 'the disciple whom Jesus loved', his identity here discreetly concealed. In that case, it would be hard to overestimate the significance for him of this, his first long evening in Jesus' company: παρ' αὐτῷ ἔμειναν τὴν ἡμέραν ἐκείνην. Or for the reader not to perceive the overarching *inclusio* between that Supper on the first day of Jesus' ministry and the Last.

---

[8] This is the 'classical' interpretation, in support of the view that the son of Zebedee is the author of the gospel.

40. ἦν 'Ανδρέας ὁ ἀδελφὸς Σίμωνος Πέτρου εἷς ἐκ τῶν δύο τῶν ἀκουσάντων παρὰ 'Ιωάννου καὶ ἀκολουθησάντων αὐτῷ. 'Ανδρέας ('a good Greek name', BDAG, with references) is identified by his relationship to Simon Peter. ὁ ἀδελφός: the article is usually present, and it does not imply that Andrew was the only brother.

41. εὑρίσκει οὗτος πρῶτον τὸν ἀδελφὸν τὸν ἴδιον Σίμωνα. For the textual evidence on the choice of readings between πρωτον, πρωτος and πρωι, see NA²⁷. In *TCGNT* we read that πρῶτον means 'that the first thing Andrew did after having been called was to find his brother', and 'that this reading was preferred by a majority of the Committee because of its early and diversified support (𝔓⁶⁶·⁷⁵ ℵᶜ B Θ *f*¹ *f*¹³ cop arm geo *al*)'; it is rated as {B}. 'The reading πρῶτος, attested by ℵ* and the later Greek tradition, means that Andrew was the first follower of Jesus who made a convert.' The acceptance of this reading by so many later MSS may have been influenced by a desire to emphasize the role of Andrew, the patron saint of Greece, in bringing Simon Peter to the Lord. πρωι, attested in no Greek MS, but implied in two or three Old Latin MSS, is almost certainly an attempt to spread the narrative more evenly over seven days and to have the marriage at Cana on the seventh.

Whichever reading be preferred, it is best to treat vv. 41-42 (or 40-42) as a footnote to the preceding scene, describing what Andrew did, perhaps 'in the morning'. Thus the narrative about Jesus closes at v. 39, and v. 43 marks the fourth day of the week with τῇ ἐπαύριον.

The presentation of Andrew's calling as prior to that of Simon Peter suggests that the narrative rests on very early tradition. **καὶ λέγει αὐτῷ, εὑρήκαμεν τὸν Μεσσίαν.** The term Μεσσίας occurs only twice in the NT, here and at Jn 4.25, and in each place a translation is supplied, to explain to the Greek-speaking reader what exactly the term means. **ὅ ἐστιν μεθερμηνευόμενον Χριστός.** *That is, in translation, Christ, or (the) Anointed.* In the words *We have found the Messiah, God's Anointed*, the content of the evening's conversation is disclosed. The sense is, 'We have found the true Messiah, one quite different from other claimants'.

A NOTE ON MESSIANISM IN THE TIME OF JESUS

Under the monarchy, the people of Judah developed as part of their religion a national ideology to express their hopes and dreams for the future. Much of it centred on the coming of an ideal king of the line of David who would ensure internal peace and justice throughout the land, and whose overlordship would be acknowledged by the Gentiles. The main texts are 2 Sam 7.12-19; Pss 2; 45; 72; 110; Isa 7.14 with 9.1-6; Mic 5.1, and Ezek 34.23. This theme is the central and unchanging factor in what is called Messianism.

With the end of the Davidic monarchy in 587 B.C., the people of Judah had to accept that they were henceforth destined to live in daily contact with the great empires of the world, Babylonia, Persia, Alexander and Rome. As their religious horizons widened, they began to think of God not primarily as King of Israel and then of the world, but vice versa. He was primarily King of the Universe, but the dream persisted, that he would one day send a Davidic king to restore the fortunes of his people. Only, the character of that earthly kingship changed. The earlier notion had envisaged a warrior like Joshua who would rule the Gentiles with a rod of iron (Ps 2.8-9), and fill the earth with their corpses (110.6). After the Exile, the prophets spoke in more spiritual tones. Isaiah's vision of swords beaten into ploughshares (2.4 || Mic 4.3) is more precisely focussed: a descendant of the house of David would come, rich in wisdom and understanding, to establish universal peace (Isa 11.1-10; 42.1-9). Both before and after the Exile, the dream was of earthly happiness, in this life and in this world.

The non-appearance of this promised son of David inevitably led, over the centuries, to a decline of interest in the figure. Even Daniel, writing at the height of the Maccabean age, does not look for a Davidic Messiah, only for a military victory (note Dan 2.44) of the 'people of the saints of the Most High' over all other empires in the world (7.9-27). Similarly, expectation of a messianic King, Davidic or not, does not figure anywhere in 1 Maccabees, in Sirach, Judith or Tobit. Assuredly, these books trust that God will re-establish righteousness on earth, but no Messianic King has any role in that work.

It is in the book 3 of the *Sibylline Oracles*, written probably in Alexandria around 163–140 B.C., that the notion of a heaven-sent king re-emerges. Though there is only one reference to this liberator, in lines 652-56, the entire section from line 692 to 795 describes how he by military action imposes peace, in the name of God, over all the earth.[9] The idea is clearer still in the *Psalms of Solomon*, composed probably in the time of Pompey (63–48 B.C.). Here we find full-blooded nationalism hoping for a king of the line of David to lead a revolt, crush the Gentiles, drive them from Jerusalem, and establish there his ideal kingdom (*PsSol* 17.21-44 [note v. 32]; 18.5-10 in *OTP* II 667-69). Other texts of interest are discussed in Schürer II 504-13, and a systematic presentation of the idea is given on pp. 514-49. The popular appeal of such a nationalist ideology in the time of Jesus is evidenced by the revolts of Theudas and 'the Egyptian' (Acts 5.36 and 21.38: see Schürer I 456, 464) and by the final uprising between A.D. 64 and 70.

Jesus had expressly refused to accept the title of Messiah as long as it was understood as denoting a warrior-king (Mt 16.20 || Mk 8.29 || Lk 9.20), and the Fourth Gospel reaffirms this uncompromisingly (Jn

---

[9] For the text see *OTP* I 376-79; for comment, see Schürer II 501-502.

18.11, 36). When, therefore, Andrew says 'We have found the
Messiah', the word 'Messiah' is to be understood not in the pre-exilic
sense, nor in the then contemporary sense, but in the spiritually refined
sense of the later prophets like the Second Isaiah. 'Messiah' in this
verse denotes not the populist leader of a national independence
movement, but rather that Lamb of God who is filled with the Spirit,
that Chosen One of God described by the Baptist (Jn 1.29, 32-34).
Compare Jesus' words to Pilate in Jn 18.36-37.[10]

42. ἤγαγεν αὐτὸν πρὸς τὸν Ἰησοῦν. *He brought him to Jesus.*
ἐμβλέψας αὐτῷ ὁ Ἰησοῦς εἶπεν. The Vulgate, which in v. 36 rendered ἐμβλέψας as *respiciens*, here translates *intuitus autem eum
Iesus*, implying that Jesus' gaze went deeper and saw further than that
of the Baptist. Where Jesus is the subject, the same preference for the
translation *intueri* is found in Mk 10.21, 27. Perhaps: *Jesus, regarding
him intently, said.*
**Σὺ εἶ Σίμων ὁ υἱὸς Ἰωάννου, σὺ κληθήσῃ Κηφᾶς, ὃ
ἑρμηνεύεται Πέτρος.** *So you are Simon the son of John? You are
to be called Cephas, which translates as Peter, or Rock.*[11] In contrast
with Mt 16.17, the reader is not told why Simon is going to be called
Cephas (Peter), or what it will signify. Its significance will be made
clear only in the penultimate episode of the gospel, at Jn 21.15-19,
where we read again, and for the first time since this initial encounter,
the phrase Σίμων Ἰωάννου, three times, in vv. 15, 16 and 17.[12] This
inclusio spans the entire gospel.

---

[10] For further detail see Schürer II §29, *'Messianism'*, 488-554, and *Redemption
and Resistance: The Messianic Hopes of Jews and Christians in Antiquity*, eds.
Markus Bockmuehl and James Carleton Paget, London, 2007.

[11] The Greek reads more smoothly as a question, but there is no way of deciding
whether it is a question or a statement. 'A majority of the Committee regarded Ἰωνᾶ
(read by A B³ Δ f¹ f¹³ and most of the later Greek witnesses) as a scribal assimilation
to Bar-Jona of Mt 16.17' (*TCGNT*). The name Jonah referring to a man (other than
the prophet) is so far unattested until the fourth century A.D. Hence others propose
that Ιωνα may be a contraction of the third variant, Ιωαννα (Θ 1241 *pc* vg), and that
both forms may be abbreviations of Johanan (compare 4 Kgdms 25.23 B; 1 Paral 26.3
A B). Ιωαννης would serve as a translation of any of these words. See J. Jeremias in
TWNT III 410 A²⁻²³, Dodd, *Historical Tradition*, 307; Schnackenburg I 311 Anm. 1 =
311 fn. 86.

[12] And with the same textual variation: see NA²⁷. The Fourth Gospel uses by
preference the designation 'Simon Peter' (17 times), and uses 'Peter' obviously for
brevity, where the two names have been given just before (1.45; 13.8, 37; 18.11,
16ff., 26-27; 20.3-4; 21.7, 11, 17, 20-21). Thus Schnackenburg I 311 Anm. 3 = 312
fn. 88. 'Simon' on its own occurs only where Jesus, in addressing the disciple very
solemnly, identifies him by his parentage (1.41, 42; 21.15ff.) The reason is that
neither 'Peter' nor 'Cephas' is, during the ministry of Jesus, a name; it is applied to
this disciple as a sobriquet.

2. The Testimony of the First Disciples: 1.43-50

[1.43] The next day he was minded to go to Galilee, and he found Philip and said to him, 'Follow me'. [44] Now Philip was from Bethsaida, the town of Andrew and Peter. [45] Philip found Nathanael, and said to him, 'We have found him of whom Moses wrote in the law, and the prophets too, Jesus, son of Joseph, from Nazareth.' [46] Nathanael said to him, 'Can anything good come out of Nazareth?'† Philip said to him, 'Come and see.' [47] Jesus saw Nathanael coming towards him, and said of him, 'Behold, one who is truly an Israelite, in whom there is no guile!' [48] Nathanael said to him, 'How comes it that you know me?' Jesus replied and said to him, 'Before Philip called you, when you were under the fig-tree, I saw you.' [49] Nathanael answered him, 'Rabbi, you are the son of God! You are Israel's king!' [50] Jesus answered and said to him, 'Is it because I told you that I had seen you under the fig-tree that you believe? You will see greater things than these.'

[†or: So something good can come out of Nazareth?]

43. τῇ ἐπαύριον ἠθέλησεν ἐξελθεῖν εἰς τὴν Γαλιλαίαν καὶ εὑρίσκει Φίλιππον. Jesus is usually taken to be the subject of ἠθέλησεν and of εὑρίσκει. Andrew is sometimes suggested, for the following reasons. 1.41 reads εὑρίσκει οὗτος πρῶτον τὸν ἀδελφὸν κτλ., and 1.43, καὶ εὑρίσκει Φίλιππον, so that if Andrew were in both cases the subject of εὑρίσκει, the πρῶτον of v. 41 would be easily explained. Again, if in v. 43 the words καὶ λέγει αὐτῷ ὁ Ἰησοῦς, ἀκολούθει μοι are eliminated as a later editorial insertion,[13] the story runs more smoothly, for Jesus is thus from vv. 43 to 46, so to speak, off stage. Verses 40-46 then become two parallel stories approximately equal in length about Andrew (vv. 40-43) and Philip (vv. 44-46), each bringing to Jesus a new disciple. On this interpretation, both Philip and Andrew begin their discipleship by (separately) introducing people to Jesus (1.40-46), as they will later appear together twice (6.6-9 and 12.20-22), on each occasion introducing people to Jesus. It is then a short step to suggesting that Philip was the unnamed companion of Andrew in 1.37-40.

This interpretation of v. 43 must be rejected, principally because Jesus was the subject of the preceding sentence (42b: ὁ Ἰησοῦς εἶπεν), but also because it is hard to imagine this evangelist ever referring to the travel plans of a disciple. It was Jesus who *had a mind to leave* 'for Galilee'; it is he (not Andrew) who finds Philip, and says to him **ἀκολούθει μοι**, that is, 'Follow me now to Galilee', because there that he is about to reveal his glory (2.12). This leads smoothly into the next verse.

---

[13] Thus Spitta, *Johannesevangelium*, 56-57; Wilckens, *Entstehungsgeschichte*, 35, and especially Boismard, 'Les traditions johanniques', *RB* 70 (1963), 39-42.

44. ἦν δὲ ὁ Φίλιππος ἀπὸ Βηθσαϊδά, ἐκ τῆς πόλεως Ἀνδρέου καὶ Πέτρου. Philip, like Andrew, is a thoroughly Greek name, but not rare among Jews at the time. He is mentioned in all the lists of the twelve apostles, always in the fifth place, after Simon and Andrew, James and John (Mt 10.3 ‖ Mk 3.18 ‖ Lk 6.14 ‖ Acts 1.13). ἀπό and ἐκ here have the same meaning. The significant word in the sentence is Bethsaida, meaning 'Fishers-Home'. Bethsaida was on the north-east shore of Lake Gennesareth in the territory of Herod Philip the tetrarch (*Ant.* XVIII ii 1 = 28; *War* II ix 1 = 168; III x 7 = 515; *Life* lxxii = 399), and therefore home to a mixed population of Jews and Gentiles.[14]

45. εὑρίσκει Φίλιππος τὸν Ναθαναὴλ καὶ λέγει αὐτῷ, ὃν ἔγραψεν Μωϋσῆς ἐν τῷ νόμῳ καὶ οἱ προφῆται εὑρήκαμεν. Nathanael is introduced solely by his impeccably Hebrew name; the reader will soon learn more about his character. *He of whom Moses wrote, in the Law*, is most obviously intended to evoke the blessing of Jacob in Gen 49.10 ('the sceptre shall not depart from Judah'), the oracle of Balaam in Num 24.16 ('a star shall come forth out of Jacob'), and the words in Deut 18.15, 18-19, where Moses assures the people that God will 'raise up a prophet like myself from among you'; → 'prophet' at 1.21c.

The prophets too wrote of him. Several texts were mentioned above in the note on Messianism at Jn 1.41, of which the most relevant for the present verse is Isa 11.1: 'there shall come forth a sprout from the stump of Jesse, and an offshoot (נֵצֶר = neṣer) shall grow out of its roots'. The same idea, though with a different Hebrew word (צֶמַח = ṣemaḥ) meaning 'branch', is found in Isa 4.1 ('the branch of the Lord shall be beautiful and glorious', RSV); in Jer 23.5-6 ('I will raise up for David a righteous Branch'); in 33.15 ('I will cause a righteous Branch to spring forth for David'); in Zech 3.8 ('I will bring my servant, the Branch'), and 6.12 ('the man whose name is the Branch... he shall build the temple of the Lord'). That both נֵצֶר = neṣer and צֶמַח = ṣemaḥ were equally applied to the Messiah is clear from the Targums. In the five texts just cited for צֶמַח = ṣemaḥ, the Targum of Jonathan always substitutes for this term the word 'Messiah, Anointed One': so we read in Jer 23.5, 'I shall raise up for David *the Messiah of* righteous*ness*', and find virtually identical renderings, with 'Messiah' or 'Anointed One', in the other texts. The same replacement occurs

---

[14] Its exact location is elusive, but it is usually identified with Khirbet el-'Araj, on the shore. Three kilometres to the east, a rocky hill now nameless and known simply as et-Tell was perhaps the site of the new town known as (Bethsaida) Julias built by Herod Philip and named after the daughter of Augustus, further evidence of a Gentile population in the area. For detail see Schürer II 171-72 (which leaves the identifications open); Abel, *Géographie* II 279-80; Dalman, *Sacred Sites and Ways*, 161-65; G. A. Smith, *Historical Geography*, 456-58.

with נֵצֶר = neṣer in Isa 11.1 ('*the Messiah* shall *be exalted* from *the sons of* his *sons*').[15] 'Offshoot' and 'Branch' were clearly equivalent technical terms for the Messiah who was to stem from the root of David, as this overtly messianic interpretation shows.[16]

That this was so in NT times is clear from three texts of Qumran. 4Q174, a collection of texts from 2 Samuel and the Psalter, contains at line 11 a comment on 2 Sam 7.11-14, 'He is the Branch of David (צמח דויד = ṣmḥ dwyd)'; 4QpGenᵃ = 4Q252 speaks at lines 3-4 of 'the Messiah of Righteousness, the Branch of David' (again, צמח דויד = ṣmḥ dwyd); and 4QpIsaᵃ = 4Q161 8-10 is a comment on Isa 11.1 (*DSSE*, 3rd ed., 294, 260, 268; *DSSE*, 4th ed., 354, 302, 321 respectively). The Testament of Judah 24, a mosaic of messianic allusions, also speaks of the Star rising out of Jacob as 'the Shoot of God' (24.4: οὗτος ὁ βλαστὸς θεοῦ ὑψίστου) and 'a rod of righteousness for the nations' (ῥάβδος δικαιοσυνῆς τοῖς ἔθνεσι).[17]

Ἰησοῦν υἱὸν τοῦ Ἰωσήφ. In Matthew, Jesus is called 'son of David' nine times; in Mark, three times; in Luke, three times; but never in John. The strikingly different phrase here in Jn 1.45, *Jesus son of Joseph*, since it is found nowhere else in the NT, gives pause for thought, and Boismard makes an attractive proposal. He suggests that the ministry of the Baptist here recorded took place at Aenon near Salim (compare Jn 3.23, and the comment there), and that this Aenon was on the edge of Samaria.[18] Since the Samaritans accepted as holy books only the five books of Moses, it was natural that they should revere as religious leaders only those who figured in those books, notably Moses (hence their interest in the 'prophet like Moses' of Deut 18.17-18) and of course Joseph, father of Ephraim and Manasseh, the two tribes whose territory embraced the central mountains of the

---

[15] The italics signify the divergence from the Hebrew text. The texts may be checked in *The Aramaic Bible: The Targums*.

[16] C. T. R. Hayward, in *The Targum of Jeremiah*, 111 fn. 3 refers to J. J. Brierre-Narbonne, *Exégèse Targumique des Prophéties Messianiques*, Paris, 1936, pp. 50-51; also to P. Humbert, 'Le Messie dans le Targum des Prophètes,' *RTP* 44 (1911), 6-7.

[17] *OTP* I 801; M. De Jonge, *The Testaments of the Twelve Patriarchs*, 77.

[18] This is part of Boismard's general theory concerning the composition of the Gospel, but it is not necessary to accept the whole theory in order to admit this proposal. That the Baptist answered the queries from Jerusalem at 'Bethany beyond the Jordan' (Jn 1.19-28) is eminently credible, and indeed v. 28 appears to imply that what followed took place somewhere else (or why put 28 at that point, and not later?). That the evangelist should have taken other stories which happened in other places and at other times, and linked them together as happening on successive days of one week, is also quite credible; and the intention of so grouping the episodes will, naturally, become clear only at the end of the week. One obvious advantage of Boismard's proposal is that the distance from the place of John's baptizing to Cana in Galilee is immediately reduced by more than a half, thus obviating the problem of reaching Cana 'on the third day' after leaving the lower Jordan.

ancient kingdom of Israel (Josh 16–17), the region known in NT times as 'Samaria'. Schürer writes that nothing precise can be known about the 'messianic expectations' of the Samaritans, because the extant sources are much too late,[19] but Boismard cites two texts which seem plausible enough, in which the patriarch Joseph is given the title 'Owner' of the land (= King) and placed next to Moses, 'the Prophet'.[20] Thus while the term 'son of Joseph' in Jn 1.45 certainly refers to Jesus' status as son of the carpenter of Nazareth, the phrase might have been chosen to evoke also the memory of Joseph the patriarch, from whom the Samaritans hoped for the restoration of the kingdom of Israel. If this scene is set not in Judaea, but in a largely Samaritan area, it would explain why Philip says 'son of Joseph' rather than 'son of David'.

τὸν ἀπὸ Ναζαρέτ. Nazareth is nowhere mentioned until it appears in the NT, and until the time of Constantine it remained a wholly Jewish town, or rather village, in which no Greek or Samaritan or Christian lived.[21] The name occurs only twice in John's Gospel, here and in v. 46,[22] and is quite clearly etymologically linked with the shoot or branch of a tree (נֵצֶר Nĕṣāret, from nĕṣɛr). No one who thought in Aramaic would have failed to recognize in this story the possibility of a link between the man from 'Branchtown' or 'Branchville' and 'the Branch of David'. 'Jesus son of Joseph, from Nazareth' hints at the one who will be both 'king of Israel' (for Samaria) and 'the Branch from the root of Jesse' (for the Jews). → Jn 1.49; 4.21-22, 25-26.

46. καὶ εἶπεν αὐτῷ Ναθαναήλ, ἐκ Ναζαρὲτ δύναταί τι ἀγαθὸν εἶναι; λέγει αὐτῷ [ὁ] Φίλιππος, ἔρχου καὶ ἴδε. *And Nathanael said to him, Can anything good come out of Nazareth? Philip said to him, Come and see.* The sentence, thus translated, is taken to mean that Nathanael is sceptical (some even say 'scornful') about the likelihood of anything good emerging from Nazareth. This interpretation, however, does not sit comfortably next to the high praise of Nathanael's character, by Jesus himself, in v. 47, and such a thought would have been more clearly expressed had the evangelist written δύναταί τι ἀγαθὸν γίνεσθαι. There is much to be said for translating Nathanael's words in a way which also does justice to his choice of the verb εἶναι: *So something good can come out of Nazareth?* Philip's answer, *Come and see,* suits either rendering equally well. Augustine suggests, and prefers, this alternative, while admitting

[19] Schürer II 513.
[20] Boismard. *Jean*, 93b.
[21] Epiphanius, *Adversus haereses* 30,11: *PG* 41.424, cited in ELS 2. For nomenclature and historical detail, see Abel, *Géographie* II 249; Dalman, *Sacred Sites and Ways*, 57-60.
[22] Not counting Ναζωραῖος in Jn 18.5, 7; 19.19.

that it was in his day not the usual interpretation.[23] Aquinas follows
him. On ἔρχου καὶ ἴδε → 1.39; the only difference is that here the
verbs are singular, and that ἴδε is indubitably imperative. These words
certainly include, as in v. 39a, more than an invitation to see Jesus
physically; they are an invitation to approach the house of Wisdom, as
in Prov 9.1-5 and Isa 55.1-3.

**47. εἶδεν ὁ ᾽Ιησοῦς τὸν Ναθαναὴλ ἐρχόμενον πρὸς αὐτὸν,
καὶ λέγει περὶ αὐτοῦ, ῎Ιδε ἀληθῶς ᾽Ισραηλίτης ἐν ᾧ δόλος
οὐκ ἔστιν.** *Jesus saw Nathanael coming towards him*: (that is,
physically and spiritually approaching him, for the two go together in
this story), *and said of him, Behold one who is truly an Israelite, in
whom there is no guile!*

᾽Ισραηλίτης occurs nine times in the NT: five times in Acts, as a
formal address to assembled Jews (2.22; 3.12; 5.35; 13.16; 21.28);
three times in Paul, when he is stressing his racial and religious creden-
tials (Rom 9.4; 11.1; 2 Cor 11.22); and here (only) in the gospels.[24]
ἀληθῶς ᾽Ισραηλίτης proclaims the genuineness of Nathanael's devotion to the God of Israel. The use of the adverb with a noun to mean
real, genuine, is both classical and common, and recurs in Jn 8.31.[25]
Here, as elsewhere in John, the Greek meaning of 'genuine' is com-
bined with the Hebraic meaning of 'being faithful to one's word' (see
JV 1727g).

ἐν ᾧ δόλος οὐκ ἔστιν. The absence of δόλος, that is, of any
deceitfulness, dishonesty or insincerity is a mark of one who is
righteous before God: see Pss 24.4; 32.2; 34.13; 139.4. Jacob had
signally lacked this quality: 'your brother came with guile and took
away your blessing' (ἐλθὼν ὁ ἀδελφός σου μετὰ δόλου ἔλαβεν τὴν
εὐλογίαν σου, Gen 27.35). Not so Nathanael.

**48. λέγει αὐτῷ Ναθαναήλ, πόθεν με γινώσκεις; ἀπεκρίθη
᾽Ιησοῦς καὶ εἶπεν αὐτῷ, πρὸ τοῦ σε Φίλιππον φωνῆσαι ὄντα
ὑπὸ τὴν συκῆν εἶδόν σε.** The point of v. 48 is that Jesus had some
knowledge which so astounds Nathanael that it elicits the great
confession of v. 49

Commentators are at a loss to decide what this knowledge was, or
to find a satisfactory explanation for the reference to the fig tree. It
may be that the evangelist intended to leave the matter equally
unknown to us; it may be that the early recipients of the gospel knew
what the saying referred to, and that this knowledge is long lost

[23] Augustine, *In Ioannem* VI 15.
[24] On the usage of the word, see also the comment on 'Israel' at Jn 1.49.
[25] Plato writes ἐκεῖνός ἐστιν ὁ ἀληθῶ οὐρανός (Phaedo 129e), and ἀληθῶς
ἀγαθοί (Laws 642cd). See also Ruth 3.12, ἀληθῶς ἀγχιστεὺς ἐγώ; Josephus, *Ant.*
IX 256, ὁ ἀληθῶ θεός; BDAG gives further instances.

(Dibelius).[26] The most common suggestion is that to study the Scriptures under a tree, and perhaps particularly a fig tree, was a common practice among the rabbis.[27] All these suggestions are merely surmises, which can be neither proved nor disproved.

49. ἀπεκρίθη αὐτῷ Ναθαναήλ, ῥαββί, σὺ εἶ ὁ υἱὸς τοῦ θεοῦ, σὺ βασιλεὺς εἶ τοῦ 'Ισραήλ. On ῥαββί, → 1.38. σὺ εἶ κτλ. is 'in the style of a confession of faith' (Schnackenburg).

ὁ υἱὸς τοῦ θεοῦ. This is not to be understood at this point in the narrative as a confession of metaphysical sonship in a Trinitarian sense.[28] Indeed, there is no clear evidence that in Palestinian Judaism the title 'Son of God' was ever applied to the Messiah even in a metaphorical sense during pre-Christian times, probably for fear of arousing misunderstanding in the non-Jewish world. The divine sonship of the Davidic Messiah had indeed been clearly declared in 2 Sam 7.14; Pss 2.7; 89.27-28; but these OT texts were intended only to affirm the legitimacy of the claim of the line of David to the throne, not to assert that there was some exceptional ontological relationship between God and the monarch. *1 Enoch* 105.2 has often been cited as an example of God's calling the Messiah 'my son', and for this reason often dismissed as a Christian interpolation; but since the discoveries of fragments of the work at Qumran, Matthew Black has argued convincingly that the reference is not to the Messiah but to Methuselah.[29] The only other texts which refer to the Messiah as 'son of God' are *4 Ezra* 7.28; 13.32, 37, 52; 14.9;[30] these do indeed have in the Latin 'filius meus', but the phrase is certainly a translation of the Greek παῖς, which is in turn a rendering of the Hebrew עַבְדִּי (ʿabdi), meaning *my servant,* not 'my son'.[31] Moreover, according to most scholars, *4 Ezra* was written around A.D. 100. Consequently, the title 'son of God' on the lips of Nathanael must bear a meaning not previously found in Judaism, namely, that Jesus enjoys an utterly unique relationship with God.[32]

---

[26] *Die Formgeschichte des Evangeliums*, Tübingen, 6th ed., 1971, 114 = *From Tradition to Gospel*, Cambridge and London, 1971, 117.

[27] Several references are given in SB II 371; note especially *Midrash R. Qoh.* 5.11 cited in SB I 858, or in the ETr (Soncino), 151.

[28] 'Si enim intellixisset eum esse Filium Dei per naturam, non dixisset *Tu es Rex Israel* solum, sed totius mundi', and then (on *maius his videbis*) 'ducam te ad maiorem cognitionem, ut scilicet credas me Filium Dei naturalem et Regem omnium saeculorum' (Aquinas).

[29] *The Book of Enoch or 1 Enoch*, 318-19.

[30] *OTP* I 537, 552, 553.

[31] See Eduard Lohse, υἱός, in *TWNT* VIII 361-63.

[32] Mowinckel too supports this view: see *He That Cometh*, 293-94. Further detail may be found in Dalman, *Worte Jesus*, 219-23 = ETr *The Words of Jesus*, 268-88; and in SB III 15-20.

σὺ βασιλεὺς εἶ τοῦ Ἰσραήλ. Apart from those texts which refer
to a monarch of the Northern Kingdom, the term 'King of Israel'
appears only twice in the OT, in Zeph 3.15 and in Isa 44.6, referring in
each case to Yahweh, king of Israel. Nowhere in the OT is the term
used of the expected Messiah. Among the Apocrypha and Pseudepigrapha of the OT, the title figures only once, in the Psalms of
Solomon (mid-first century B.C.), in [PsSol] 17.42, though the concept
is implicit from v. 21 onwards; it is safe to say that the author of this
psalm eagerly hoped for someone to lead a military revolt against the
Roman occupation army. This leader is called 'son of David' (21), 'the
Lord Messiah' (32) and 'king of Israel' (42).[33] The term 'King of
Israel' does not occur at Qumran, not even in the War Scroll, and is
certainly not a title in common use.

To discern the precise meaning of 'King of Israel', it is necessary to
compare it with 'King of the Jews'. All four Gospels stress that Jesus
was condemned as 'King of the Jews' (Jn 18.33, 39; 19.3, [14,] 19, 21;
Mt 27.11, 29, 33; Mk 15.2, 9, 12, 18, 26; Lk 23.3, 37, 38), and the
political implications of claiming that title are all too clear in the narratives. 'King of Israel', by contrast, is found in the NT only four times,
here in Jn 1.49, in 12.13, and in the mockery of the Jewish leaders on
Golgotha, at Mt 27.42 ‖ Mk 15.32. It is, however, an oversimpli-
fication to say that 'King of the Jews' carries political overtones, and
that 'King of Israel' does not; or that Jesus rejected the former title, but
accepted the latter. In NT times, in Palestinian Judaism, the terms used
by the indigenous population for self-designation were 'Israel' and
'children of Israel'.[34] Outside Palestine, those who shared the religion
of Israel would refer to themselves as 'Jews', and would use the terms
'Israel' and 'children of Israel' only in prayer, preaching and liturgy.[35]
King of Israel on Nathanael's lips is therefore wholly idiomatic from a
Palestinian. It has been suggested that perhaps the use of this title
implies that Nathanael had a nationalistic messianic expectation, and

---

[33] OTP II 667, 668. Note the editor's comment on 'the Lord Messiah'. The title
'Messiah' recurs in PsSol 18.5, 7 (OTP II 669).

[34] Thus the author of 1 Maccabees always uses 'Israel' for self-designation, when
writing in his own person, but always writes 'Jews' when quoting what Gentiles say
(e.g. 10.23; 11.50) or in recording diplomatic correspondence (e.g. 8.21-32; 12.1-23;
14.20-23; 15.1-9) and so forth. The rabbis were later to follow the same practice. In
the Palestinian literature of the age (Sirach, Judith, Tobit, Baruch, the Psalms of
Solomon, 4 Ezra, The Testament of the Twelve Patriarchs, 3 Enoch) the word 'Jews'
never once occurs, even though all others who did not belong to this group would
have designated its members simply as 'Jews'. See TWNT III 361-64 (K. G. Kuhn).

[35] TWNT III 364-66 (by K. G. Kuhn) and 372-74 (by Walter Gutbrod). Kuhn illustrates in detail how 2 Maccabees, representing Hellenistic Judaism, follows a usage
opposite to that of 1 Maccabees, and normally writes of 'Jews', reserving Israel for
liturgy and prayer.

that Jesus corrects him in v. 51.[36] Yet since there is only one known
example of the title's being used in that nationalist sense (*PsSol* 17.42:
see the preceding paragraph), it is legitimate to seek an alternative
explanation.

'Israel' occurs only four times in John (1.31, 50; 3.10; 12.13),[37]
denoting always the People of God as a religious, not a national, entity.
To be king 'of the Jews' would be to reign as an earthly monarch
merely over that part of God's people which happened to be alive on
earth at the moment. To be 'King of Israel' is to be God's viceroy on
earth, and to have a part assigned in the redemptive drama of God's
Chosen People, which stretches back in time and forward to the end
of time. So Nathanael, when he calls Jesus 'Israel's king', gives an
entirely new title to Jesus, the prima facie meaning of which is
messianic, the long-term, the divine (Jn 20.28, 31). The title, here at Jn
1.49, and at the entry into Jerusalem (12.13), has no political implications: both the first and the second part of the Gospel begin with a
statement that Jesus' kingdom is not of this world.

**50. ἀπεκρίθη ᾿Ιησοῦς καὶ εἶπεν αὐτῷ, ῞Οτι εἶπόν σοι ὅτι
εἶδόν σε ὑποκάτω τῆς συκῆς, πιστεύεις;** [38] Whether Jesus'
remark is translated as a question or a statement (*'You believe because
I told you...'*), its meaning is the same. **μείζω τούτων ὄψῃ.** *You will
see greater things than these.* ὄψῃ is singular, and the promise in this
verse is therefore to Nathanael alone, assuring him that he will witness
greater things than Jesus' knowledge of him when he was under the fig
tree: the phrase μείζω τούτων will recur at 5.20 and 14.12.

If the story had ended here, it would (with v. 51 omitted) have led
smoothly straight into the Wedding at Cana, the home town of
Nathanael,[39] where greater things began to take place. But the *greater
things* promised comprise more than the sign at Cana, as v. 51
explains.

---

[36] John Painter, 'Christ and the Church in John 1.51', in M. De Jonge, *L'Evangile
de Jean*, 1977, 359-62.

[37] 'Israelite' once (1.48), 'Jew[s]' 70 times.

[38] The variation from the text of 1.48 (ὑποκάτω with the genitive replacing ὑπο
with the accusative) is not significant: 'when repeating a phrase, John is apt to alter it
slightly, either by a change in the order of the words, or by using a different word'
(Bernard). Likewise with the variant readings for μείζω: μειζονα is the uncontracted
form, and μειζων an instance of the 'irrational ν' often found in certain manuscripts
(see MHT II 161, 113).

[39] According to Jn 21.2, the only other text where Nathanael is mentioned in this
Gospel.

3. 'You will see Heaven opened': 1.51

Verse 51 'has caused as much trouble for commentators as any other single verse in the Fourth Gospel' (R. E. Brown). Many think that this verse was inserted into an already completed narrative; but if it is such a subsequent addition to a previously finished text, it is impossible to decide whether the alteration was made by the evangelist himself, or by a later editor. In any case, all manuscripts contain it, so it is certainly part of the canonical Gospel.

Jesus said to him [λέγει αὐτῷ, in the singular], *Amen, Amen I say to you* ['Αμὴν ἀμὴν λέγω ὑμῖν, in the plural]; and the remainder of the sentence is in the plural. It is probably this unusual construction which first entices many to posit that v. 51 must have been written by someone other than the author of the verses in the immediate context; unusual though the construction may be, it serves to make a point quite clearly. Jesus solemnly assures Nathanael, who has just made the most remarkable profession of faith, that not only he, but his companions too, will see heaven opened and angels ascending and descending upon the Son of Man. This is the first occurrence of 'Αμὴν ἀμὴν λέγω ὑμῖν in the Gospel, where it appears 25 times, always on the lips of Jesus, where it denotes a more than usually solemn assurance that the statement which follows is both true and very important. The content of this particular saying, the first to be prefaced by 'Αμὴν ἀμὴν λέγω ὑμῖν, therefore demands close scrutiny.

ὄψεσθε τὸν οὐρανὸν ἀνεῳγότα καὶ τοὺς ἀγγέλους τοῦ θεοῦ ἀναβαίνοντας καὶ καταβαίνοντας ἐπὶ τὸν υἱὸν τοῦ ἀνθρώπου. These words raise three questions: What is the meaning of *the opened heaven*? What is the significance of *the angels ascending and descending*? And what is the meaning of *the Son of man*? On one point only is there a consensus, namely, that the phrase about the angels 'ascending and descending' is an allusion to Gen 28.12, because only there do these words occur, in this order, in the entire OT. In the LXX we read verbatim: καὶ τοὺς ἀγγέλους τοῦ θεοῦ ἀναβαίνοντας καὶ καταβαίνοντας. Why do the angels first go up and then come down?

Joachim Jeremias once proposed that this saying about the angels should be interpreted in the light of certain late Jewish ideas about Gen 28.17 and 22, according to which the stone of Bethel was the place of the presence of God, above which was the door leading into heaven.[40] The suggestion never found acceptance.

In 1922 Burney had called attention to a text in the *Midrash Rabbah* on Gen 28.12, which records a rabbinical dispute on whether

---

[40] 'Die Berufung des Nathanael (Joh. 1.45ff.)', *Angelos* 3 (1928), 2-5.

the angels were ascending and descending on the ladder (thus the LXX also), or on Jacob himself, for the Hebrew pronoun could bear either meaning.[41] The former opinion was favoured by the majority of rabbis, but the latter could not be excluded. Some rabbis who supported the second opinion held that the angels who ascended wished to compare the features of the earthly Jacob with his archetype in heaven before descending to be once more Jacob's guardians on earth.

Odeberg in 1929 proposed that the writer of Jn 1.51 accepted the second interpretation of Genesis, and substituted for 'Jacob' (understood as the personification of all Israel) 'the Son of Man' (intended to be understood as the embodiment of the new Israel). The sense of Jn 1.51 would therefore be that the Son of Man on earth was in constant touch with his archetype in heaven through thousands of ministering angels (Odeberg cites Dan 7.10).[42] Bultmann was sympathetic to Odeberg insofar as this interpretation unites Jesus the individual with his heavenly archetype, but critical of the proposal that *the Son of Man* embraced the whole community of believers, who would therefore themselves be destined to share here on earth Jesus' communion with the world above.[43] There is, however, nothing in John to corroborate the suggestion that Jesus had an archetype in heaven, or that angelic mediators could serve any useful function for him who was always one with the Father (Jn 10.30).

Wilhelm Michaelis suggested that Jn 1.51 was inspired by the Synoptic accounts of the Baptism and Temptation, and even rejected any reference to Gen 28.12.[44] Yet the differences are significant. The angels mentioned in John are not ministering angels, but mediators or messengers, and in John heaven is (apparently) not momentarily but permanently open.

More commonly, Jn 1.51 is explained by reference to the Resurrection, the Ascension or the Parousia of the Lord. The insertion of ἀπ' ἄρτι before ὄψεσθε is evidence that many copyists thought of this verse in terms of Mt 26.64,[45] and interpreted it, presumably, as referring to the coming of the Son of Man at the Parousia (compare Mt 16.27-28, 'with his angels'). Thus Bernard: 'The vision of this [final and glorious] Advent [cf. Dan 7.13] seems to be what is promised to Nathanael and his believing companions.'[46] It is a sensible and uncom-

[41] In the Soncino edition, the reference is LXVIII 12. Burney's somewhat different translation is printed out in Dodd, *Interpretation*, 245: they give the reference as 70.12.

[42] Odeberg, *The Fourth Gospel*, 33-45.

[43] Bultmann, *Johannesevangelium*, 74 fn. 4 = ETr 105 fn. 4.

[44] 'Joh. 1.51, Gen 28.12 und das Menschensohn Problem', *TLZ* 85 (1960), 561-78.

[45] For the textual evidence, see NA[27].

[46] I 68. Bernard also gives (70-72) a very useful selection of early patristic texts to support his affirmation that 'no commentator before Augustine suggests any connection between Gen 28.13 and Jn 1.51'. It is astonishing, but apparently true.

plicated explanation, and suits the context. Yet the words in John may
perhaps disclose a different meaning.

Surprisingly few commentaries on Jn 1.51 contain a cross-reference
to Isa 64.1, 'O that thou wouldst rend the heavens and come down!'
ἐὰν ἀνοίξῃς τὸν οὐρανόν... (= 63.19c in the LXX).[47] No one, as far
as I know, has in practice employed this verse of Isaiah for the interpretation of Jn 1.51, which is astonishing when one considers how
many hold that 1.51 was originally an isolated saying. Once again, the
Targum of Isaiah helps, for several sections represent the mainstream
of rabbinical exegesis between A.D. 80 and the revolt of Bar Kokhba
in 132–135.[48] In particular, many passages clearly presuppose 'the
national existence of God's people, whether as presently fallen into
decay or soon to be restored... Within this perspective, the Messiah,
repentance and Shekhinah[49] are all urgently desired; only their realization can bring about the restoration of the sanctuary and the return of
the house of Israel from exile.'[50]

'Who is this that comes from Edom, in crimsoned garments from
Bozrah, he that is glorious in his apparel, marching in the greatness of
his strength?' Thus Isa 63.1a-d, according to the RSV. The Targum
transforms this passage, in a rendering which comes alive if 'Edom'
and 'Bozrah' are taken as code-names for Rome. '*He is about to bring
a stroke upon* Edom, *a strong avenger upon* Bozrah, *to take the just
retribution of his people, just as he swore to them by his Memra*'. The
words in italics are interpretative, and have no corresponding words in
the Hebrew text. This militarist rewriting of the prophetical text is
exactly the message which would have appealed most in the years after
A.D. 70. Then comes the great prayer (63.15 to 64.12) centred on 64.1,
'O that thou wouldst rend the heavens and come down!' The prayer is
too long to cite in its entirety, but a glance at the Targum will show
how deeply its words must have been burnt into the minds and
memories of those Jews who lived in Palestine or elsewhere between
A.D. 70 and 135. In the Targum, the two verses 64.10-11 are rendered
very literally, as needing no interpretation, but the translation of other
verses illustrates how the devastation of Jerusalem and of the Temple
was interpreted at a theological and religious level. (Once again, the
words in italics are interpretative, and have no corresponding words in
the Hebrew text.) '[63.17]...*return your Shekhinah to your people* for
the sake of your servants, *the righteous, to whom you swore by your
Memra to make among them* the tribes of your heritage. [63.18] For a
little while your holy people possessed your sanctuary...[64.7] ...you

[47] Westcott, Barrett and Schnackenburg are among the rare exceptions.

[48] Chilton xxi-xxiii. See also Schürer I 104-105.

[49] Shekhinah, *sic*, and so throughout in B. D. Chilton's writing.

[50] In other passages, from a later age, 'the Messiah and the Shekhinah already
exist in God's sight, repentance has begun and even the sanctuary is already present,
albeit in heaven'. Chilton xx.

have *taken up the* face of your *Shekhinah* from us, and *handed* us *over*
into the hand of our *sins*.' These verses show how deeply Judaism
grieved over the departure of the Shekinah from the holy place, and
how earnestly the people longed for its return. In the light of this
longing, it may be significant that the prayer of 64.1 is omitted, and
that the following words are substituted: '*Not for them [the Gentiles]
did* you *incline* the heavens and *reveal yourself*. Is this version, one
wonders, a protest against the Christian teaching of the Incarnation?[51]

ὄψεσθε τὸν οὐρανὸν ἀνεῳγότα. In John, the verb ὄψεσθαι is
regularly used as a promise that the disciples will be given some
spiritual insight (Jn 1.39, 50, 51 [contrast 3.36]; 11.40; 16.16, 17, 19),
as distinct from merely bodily sight (θεωρεῖν): see *JV* 1598. ἀνεῳγότα is a second perfect participle, the only form in which ἀνοίγω is
intransitive (BDF 101 [p. 53]; BAG 2, citing also 1 Cor 16.9, θύρα μοι
ἀνέῳγεν μεγάλη). Translate therefore: *you will have sight of heaven
wide open*.

The word οὐρανός is relatively infrequent in John, except in chs. 3
and 6. Outside these chapters, it occurs only four times (Jn 1.32, 51;
12.28; 17.1); but it is found six times in ch. 3 (5, 13 [×3], 27, 31) and
nine times in ch. 6 (31, 32, 33, 38, 41, 42, 50, 51, 58). It is surely not
accidental that the term occurs mainly in contexts that speak of rebirth
through water and the Spirit, and of Jesus as the life-giving bread from
heaven. Perhaps here in 1.51 the writer (or editor) already has in mind
the manner in which the disciples *are going to see heaven wide open*,
through baptism and by sharing the life-giving Word at the eucharistic
table. Compare Rev 21.1-2, where the holy city, new Jerusalem,
'comes down' out of heaven, from God, and the dwelling of God
(σκηνή) is pitched on earth.

The angels ascending and descending furnish an unmistakable reference to the story of Jacob at Bethel (Gen 28.12), and the desire to
make a clear reference to the OT text is sufficient in itself to explain
the curious order of the two verbs. More to the point, the angelic trans-
migrations are not the central theme of that story.[52] Attention should
rather be directed first of all to Gen 28.13-15, where God promises
Jacob possession of the land, a numerous posterity, a destiny that will
prove to be a blessing for all peoples of the earth, and everlasting
divine protection. In the Targums, both Neofiti and Pseudo-Jonathan[53]
speak of '*the glory of the Shekinah of the Lord*' dwelling in that place
(Gen 28.16) and Pseudo-Jonathan adds that the place itself is '*founded
beneath the Throne of Glory*' (28.17). Such are their interpretations of

[51] Translation by Chilton 122-23.

[52] ἄγγελος (Matthew, 6 times; Mark 20 times; Lk 25 times) is hardly used in
John. It is found only here, at 1.51; at 12.19; and at 20.12. Jn 5.4 is inauthentic.

[53] But not that of Onqelos, which stays close to the Hebrew text, and does not
mention the Shekinah.

the Hebrew text, 'This is none other than the house of God, this is the gate of heaven' (28.17). In Jn 1.51 the allusion to Gen 28.17 is not hard to discern: the primary meaning is that the disciples will come to perceive that Jesus as Son of Man is the locus where the glory of the Shekinah is made manifest on earth. This is the only occasion in John where ἐπί followed by the accusative is used in a good sense with reference to Jesus. However, the reader should not forget the other promises made to Jacob in Gen 28.13-15, and in particular that the people descended from him, and from his father Abraham, was destined by God to be the source of blessings for all the nations of the earth.

The meaning of the term 'Son of Man' in this Gospel will be discussed in detail later, at Jn 3.14, and in Excursus VI, 'The Son of Man', but something must be said about its meaning here in 1.51. In the Synoptics, Jesus speaks of 'the coming of the Son of Man in the glory of his Father with his holy angels' and of 'the kingdom of God arrived in power' (Mt 16.27-28 || Mk 8.38–9.1 || Lk 9.26-27). The theme recurs in Mt 24.29-30 || Mk 13.26-27, which interpret the significance of the destruction of Jerusalem. That which to all Jews appeared to be the ultimate disaster, is presented in the Synoptics as ἀρχὴ ὠδίνων, *the onset of birth-pangs* (Mt 24.8 || Mk 13.8); that is, it is presented as having been, in God's plan, the occasion for Jesus' followers to make the final break from the ritual institutions of Judaism. When Christians *see these things happening*, they are to *know that summer is nigh* (Mt 24.32-33 || Mk 13.28-29 || Lk 21.29-30).

In Jn 1.41 and 49, the disciples are shown hailing Jesus as the Messiah, the one who was to restore the political kingdom by re-establishing the throne of David in Jerusalem. John 1.51 points away from this expectation, to the idea of an everlasting kingdom coming, as in Daniel's vision, not from earthly power, but down from heaven through One like a Son of Man (Dan 7.13-14). It is a promise to Nathanael (λέγει αὐτῷ) that he and all Jesus' disciples will see the fulfilment of the promise related in Mt 26.64 || Mk14.62 || Lk 22.69, that they *will see the Son of Man coming on the clouds of heaven*, will see heaven wide open (in the sense of Dan 7.13), and the glory of God, the divine presence or Shekinah, once again made manifest on earth. Though their bodily eyes will not see the restoration of the earthly Temple in Jerusalem, the disciples will be given the spiritual insight to perceive in the nascent Church the fulfilment of the promises to Abraham, Isaac and Jacob, of a new Israel with a multitudinous progeny through which all the nations of the world shall be blessed (Gen 28.13-14).

EXCURSUS VI

THE SON OF MAN

In the Synoptic Gospels, this phrase is on some occasions unquestionably intended to recall, and to identify Jesus with, the figure in Dan 7.13 (Mt 24.30; 26.64 || Mk 13.26; 14.62 || Lk 21.27; 22.69). There is no such indubitable allusion to Daniel in John, and consequently the precise import of 'Son of Man' in this Gospel is a more open question.

Until nearly 1900, most Christians understood the phrase, in the NT, as a reference either to the humanity of Jesus or to the figure in Dan 7.13. For the *status quaestionis* around 1900, see the admirable article by S. R. Driver in *HDB* IV (1902), 578-89; it is well to be reminded that Westcott in 1880 did not regard this term as derived from Daniel, but as expressing Jesus' relationship to all humanity, and that B. Weiss in 1884 held that it was not a first-century title of the Messiah. After 1900, the centrality of the term in the then intensive quest for the authentic words of Jesus initiated a century of debate which is still not concluded.

The Aramaic phrase in Dan 7.13 is a *hapax legomenon* in the Hebrew Scriptures. Daniel writes that he saw coming with the clouds of heaven כְּבַר אֱנָשׁ (kĕbar 'ĕnāš), *something like the offspring of a human being* (in contrast to the four animals mentioned immediately before). In Biblical Aramaic, the normal word for *a human being* is אֱנָשׁ ('ĕnāš) on its own, not בַּר אֱנָשׁ (bar 'ĕnāš, literally, *son of man*), the form found in Dan 7.13, which both the LXX and Theodotion translate quite literally, without the article, as ὡς υἱὸς ἀνθρώπου. In 1898 Gustav Dalman argued that in Dan 7.13, bar 'ĕnāš, *son of man*, was an uncommon and poetic expression for the eschatological figure there mentioned. He observed that, like the Hebrew בֶּן אָדָם (ben 'ādām, also *son of man*), the term is never found in the singular with the definite article (= בַּר אֱנָשָׁא, bar 'ĕnāšā), until it appears in Jewish-Galilean and Christian-Palestinian dialect; and con-luded that, when used with the definite article, it was ideally suited as a special title for Jesus, *the son of man*, the usual form in the NT.[1] Dalman's prestige ensured that this interpretation was widely accepted for nearly half a century.

---

[1] ETr *Words of Jesus*, Edinburgh, 1902, 235-67 = *Die Worte Jesu*, Leipzig, 2nd ed., 1930, I, 191-219.

In Germany, up to 1914, J. Weiss and A. Schweitzer were prominent advocates of the theory that Jesus shared with his contemporaries a firm conviction of the imminent arrival of a heaven-sent saviour, someone who would judge the world and establish on earth the kingdom of God.[2] Their view found little favour in the Anglo-Saxon world, which continued to see Jesus' use of the term 'Son of Man' as stressing his human nature, even when found in the context of Dan 7.13. Thus T. W. Manson took it as a portmanteau term embracing the idea of the Remnant, the Servant, the 'I' of the Psalmist, and the Danielic Son of Man; C. J. Cadoux similarly, and they are typical.[3] Among Catholics, the 'consistent eschatology' of pre-1914 Germany never found favour, except with Alfred Loisy,[4] and 'the Son of Man' in the Gospels retained its traditional meaning.

Nonetheless, ὁ υἱὸς τοῦ ἀνθρώπου is in Greek an odd phrase, and with the advent of the history-of-religion school, a non-Jewish origin was inevitably proposed, in Oriental mystery-religions. Bultmann and Odeberg looked to Mandaean or Manichaean (ultimately Iranian) Gnosis, and interpreted the phrase as equal to Primal Man;[5] even Dodd judged that the Johannine Son of Man had more affinity with the Anthropos of the Poimandres in the Hermetic literature, and with Philo, than with Jewish apocalyptic;[6] Siegfried Schulz thought that John had decisively modified the Jewish apocalyptic concept by interpreting it in terms of a Son of God, a redeemer from above (as in the Odes of Solomon).[7]

The majority of exegetes, however, continued to maintain that 'Son of Man' was a name or title essentially Jewish; that its origin was to be sought in Dan 7.13, and that its deeper meaning might be illustrated from *1 En* 37–71 and *4 Esd* 13;[8] and that in first-century Judaism, many awaited the imminent arrival of this 'Son of Man' from heaven. It is only fair to say that much of the evidence adduced in support of the last assertion is taken from the Gospels, notably by C. Colpe in the *TWNT*, and by J. Jeremias.[9] Of those who understood 'the Son of Man' in this

---

[2] See Kümmel, *The NT: The History of Investigation*, 226-44: 'Consistent Eschatology'.

[3] T. W. Manson, *The Teaching of Jesus*, 1931, 211-36 fn. 227; C. J. Cadoux, *The Historic Mission of Jesus*, London, 1941, 90-102.

[4] *L'Evangile et l'Eglise* (1902); *Autour d'un petit livre* (1902).

[5] Bultmann on Jn 3.9-21 *passim*, and *ZNW* 24 (1925), 138-39; H. Odeberg (1929).

[6] *Interpretation* (1953), 43-44, 71.

[7] S. Schulz, *Untersuchungen* (1957); *Das Evangelium nach Johannes* (1972), 62-64.

[8] The last two texts are the only Jewish texts dealing with the Son of Man in Dan 7, may date from the close of the first century A.D., and may have been influenced by Christian ideas. See NJBC 67:9, 15, 41 (R. E. Brown) or J. Coppens, *La Relève apocalyptique* II 119-55, 167-73. Even so, they could be expressing ideas that were abroad when the Gospels were taking shape.

[9] C. Colpe in *TWNT* VIII (1969), 403-81; J. Jeremias, *NT Theology*, Etr, London, 1971, 257-76.

apocalyptic sense, some maintained that during his earthly life Jesus
never identified himself with this figure, but that the term was assigned
to him after his death, as a title, by the Church. Thus J. Knox, H. E. Tödt,
F. Hahn, A. J. B. Higgins, N. Perrin, Teeple, and J. C. O'Neill.[10] Ph.
Vielhauer regarded all the Son of Man sayings in the Gospels as the
creation of the church.[11] Others judged that 'the Son of Man' was the only
designation which Jesus did accept during his lifetime, whether he used it
rarely or regularly, and however he may have understood it: for accepting
an identification with the figure in Dan 7.13 does not entail accepting an
apocalyptic interpretation, much less application, of that text. Daniel's
'Son of Man' could denote God's servants in Israel, both collectively and
symbolically, or a person representative of them and embodying their
destiny. So, with different emphases, E. Schweizer, R. H. Fuller, F. H.
Borsch, and M. D. Hooker.[12]

Meantime, another group was emerging which held that Jesus might
indeed have spoken of himself as son of man, but without thereby
intending to identify himself with the Danielic or any other apocalyptic
Son of Man. In a conference at Oxford in 1965, Geza Vermes argued that
the idiomatic use of bar něš or bar nĕšĕ was firmly attested in Palestinian
Aramaic, that is, in *Neofiti* I, the Palestinian Talmud and *Genesis Rabbah*.[13] Sometimes the phrase means simply *a human being*, or *humankind*
as a whole (as, e.g., in Mk 2.10, 28). At other times, it is equivalent to an
indefinite pronoun, such as *everyone, anyone, someone*, or (plural) *some
people, nobody*, and even (with the adjective 'one') *a certain person.* It
can also be (like the English 'one') a circumlocution for 'I', especially
when the speaker wishes to contrast himself with God or with others (Mt

---

[10] John Knox, *The Death of Christ*, 1959, 58; H. E. Tödt, *The Son of Man in the
Synoptic Tradition*, ETr, London, 1965; F. Hahn, *Christologische Hoheitstitel*, 1963 =
ETr (abridged) *The Titles of Jesus*, 1969; A. J. B. Higgins, *Jesus and the Son of Man*
(1964); N. Perrin, 'The Son of Man in Ancient Judaism and Primitive Christianity. A
Suggestion', *Biblical Research* 11 (1966), 17-28; 'The Son of Man in the Synoptic
Tradition', *Biblical Research* 13 (1968), 1-25; H. M. Teeple, 'The Origin of the Son of
Man Christology', *JBL* 84 (1965), 213-50; J. C. O'Neill, 'The Silence of Jesus', *NTS* 15
(1968–69), 153-57.

[11] Ph. Vielhauer, 'Gottesreich und Menschensohn in der Verkündigung Jesus', *FS
G. Dehn* (1957) = *Aufsätze zum NT* (1965); 'Jesus und der Menschensohn', *ZThK* 60
(1963), 133-77; H. Conzelmann, 'Gegenwart und Zukunft in der synoptischen Tradition',
ZThK 54 (1957), 277-96; *Grundriss der Theologie des NT* (1967).

[12] E. Schweizer, 'Der Menschensohn', *ZNW* 50 (1959), 185-209; 'The Son of Man',
JBL 79 (1960), 119-29; 'The Son of Man Again', *NTS* 9 (1956), 256-61; R. H. Fuller,
The Foundations of NT Christology, London, 1965, 34-43, 119-25, 151-55, 229-30, and
cf. 233-34; F. H. Borsch, *The Christian and Gnostic Son of Man*, London, 1970; M. D.
Hooker, *The Son of Man in Mark,* London, 1967, 182-98.

[13] Published as Appendix E in the third edition of M. Black, *An Aramaic Approach*,
1967, 310-28, especially 318, 320, 327. See also G. Vermes, *Jesus the Jew*, London,
1973, 160-91; *Studies in Judaism*, London, 1975, 147-65; 'The Present State of the "Son
of Man" Debate', *JJS* 29 (1978), 123-34.

9.11 ‖ Lk 7.34) or even with animals (e.g. Mt 8.20 ‖ Lk 9.58); but whenever 'the Son of Man' is used in this last sense, as a self-reference, it is always out of humility or modesty, or out of a genuine fear of humiliation, of danger or death. Vermes (pp. 327-28) concluded that bar nēšē (with the definite article) was never used as a 'messianic' designation, and was in fact, because of the circumstances in which it was customarily employed for the first person pronoun, quite unsuitable for use as a name or title. This would explain why it is never found in the Gospels as a title of address to Jesus, why it is normally placed on Jesus' own lips, and why in the Synoptics, no question was ever raised about its meaning, nor any objection to its use.[14] Dodd himself was an early convert to Vermes' view.[15] Lindars too came to see the term simply as a self-reference by Jesus, later applied to him as a title (sometimes Danielic) by the church.[16] P. M. Casey went one step further than Vermes, maintaining that the Aramaic idiom was used to make general statements (as in 'people like to be consulted'), and that Jesus used this idiom in order to say something about himself: only those Gospel sayings which fulfil this criterion are authentic, and the others, including all those connected with Dan 7, are creations of the church.[17]

Several writers sought to reconcile the old with the new. The Norwegian scholar Ragnar Leivestadt, while agreeing that Jesus used 'Son of Man' only as self-designation, added that Jesus employed the term 'in analogy with and by contrast with' ben David, but not as a title, since there was at the time no widespread belief in the coming of an apocalyptic Son of Man.[18] Moule argued that the Danielic term was not a name or a title, nor even a personal figure at all, but rather a symbol for God's martyred people, who would be ultimately vindicated; and suggested that Jesus adopted the term to express his vocation as one called to be the nucleus of all who stand in a right relationship to God.[19] J. Bowker and M. Black, accepting that 'Son of Man' was a self-designation, stressed that the term, by underlining the mortality of every human being, was

[14] Compare Vermes as in *Jesus the Jew*, 310. Fitzmyer, reviewing Vermes, agreed that there is no evidence in first-century Aramaic for Son of Man as a 'messianic' title, but contested Vermes's claim to have found positive proof of its use during the first century as a substitute for the first person pronoun: *CBQ* 30 (1968), 426. Their debate continued for years.

[15] *The Founder of Christianity*, London, 1973, 110-13, 178 fn. 25.

[16] Compare the essay from *Christ and Spirit in the New Testament*, FS C. F. D. Moule, Cambridge, 1973, with the chapter on John from his *Jesus Son of Man* (1983), both reprinted in *Essays on John*, 33-50 and 153-66.

[17] P. M. Casey, *Son of Man* (1979), 224-40; 'Method in our Madness', *JSNT* 42 (1991), 17-43; 'Idiom and Translation: Some Aspects of the Son of Man Problem', *NTS* 41 (1995), 164-82.

[18] R. Leivestadt, 'Der apokalyptische Menschensohn ein theologisches Phantom', *ASTI* 6 (1968), 49-105; 'Exit the Apocalyptic Son of Man', *NTS* 18 (1972), 243-67.

[19] C. F. D. Moule, *The Origin of Christology*, London, 1977, 14-17.

most appropriate to point to Jesus' role as the one who came to lay down his life for others.[20]

By 1980 the discussion of the meaning of the term was almost confined to the English-speaking world. In Germany the one large-scale work on the topic, *Jesus und der Menschensohn* (FS A. Vögtle, 1975) was for the most part a discussion of where to place the phrase in the literary stratigraphy of the Gospels. France seemed utterly uninterested,[21] but in Belgium Joseph Coppens completed, just two days before his death in 1981, what is the best survey of the problem down to 1980.[22] It must in all honesty be said that since then there has been little that is new, and much that is repetition. The reader desirous of additional detail is referred to Excursus VI, 'The Son of Man', in *Matthew* II, 43-52 of this series, by W. D. Davies and D. C. Allison (1991).

For the commentator faced with these divergent opinions, the only prudent course is to apply Occam's razor: to start by taking the term 'Son of Man' in a minimalist sense, as nothing more than a self-designation of Jesus, and then to inquire, on each occasion of its use, whether any further contextualization is necessary or appropriate. This method is particularly helpful for examining John wherever (as here) Synoptic parallels are lacking, and those writers whose interest has centred on John have in practice used it. Each in his or her own way has come to the conclusion that the evangelist, though assuredly adopting from elsewhere the concept of 'Son of Man', reinterpreted the term, and adapted it to his own purposes. For Schnackenburg, 'Son of Man' in John refers not to a future apocalyptic saviour, but expresses Jesus' understanding of himself as the bringer and giver of life, come down from heaven.[23] For Moloney (216), the phrase presents Jesus as the incarnate revealer of God among men. Coppens suggests that all thirteen Johannine references belong to a distinct stratum of the Gospel, and were introduced at the end of its writing, in order to reveal step by step to the reader the identity of the figure to whom it referred; the title was chosen to bid farewell to the classical but nationalist Davidic nomenclature of the Messiah, and because it was ideally suited to focus attention on Jesus' earthly ministry as his highroad to exaltation.[24] For Lindars, John at 5.27 uses the

---

[20] J. Bowker, 'The Son of Man', *JTS* 28 (1977), 19-48; M. Black, 'Jesus and the Son of Man', *JSNT* 1 (1978), 4-18. Black was still maintaining (against Vermes and Casey) that bar nĕšĕ functioned as a title in Classical Aramaic, *ExpTimes* 95 (1984), 200-206.

[21] See F. Neirynck et al., *The Gospel of Mark: A Cumulative Bibliography 1950–1990*, Leuven, 1992, compiled by F. Neirynck and others lists more than 200 entries on 'Son of Man' (pp. 667-68), of which only three are from France.

[22] J. Coppens, *La Relève apocalyptique du messianisme royale*. III. *Le Fils de l'homme néotestamentaire*, Leuven, 1981, 1-21: 'Position du Problème'.

[23] Though not in any Gnostic sense. Schnackenburg was concerned to contest any alleged influence from the then new finds at Nag Hammadi.

[24] Coppens, *La Relève*, 45-103: 'Les Logia du Fils de l'Homme dans l'Evangile johannique'.

originally self-referent phrase like a title reminiscent of Daniel, in order to refer to the one whose crucifixion reveals God's glory.[25] John Ashton follows the same method as the writers just mentioned, only to reach a conclusion at the opposite pole from that of Vermes: 'the remote origin of all the sayings is the Danielic Son of Man'.[26]

[25] Lindars, *Essays on John*, 164-65.
[26] Ashton, *Understanding*, 340.

C. THE WEDDING AT CANA IN GALILEE (2.1-12)

^{2.1} On the third day there was a wedding at Cana in Galilee, and the mother of Jesus was there. ² Jesus too was invited, and his disciples also. ³ The wine ran out, and the mother of Jesus spoke to him, saying 'They have no wine'. ⁴ Jesus said to her, 'What relationship is there, woman, between you and me, now that my hour is approaching?'† ⁵ His mother said to the servants, 'Do whatever he tells you'. ⁶ Now standing there were six stoneware jars, for the Jewish rituals of purification, each holding twenty or thirty gallons. ⁷ Jesus said to them, 'Fill the jars with water', and they filled them up to the brim. ⁸ Next he said to them, 'Now draw some out, and take it to the butler in charge', and they took it. ⁹ As soon as the butler tasted the water (which had become wine, and he did not know where it came from—the servants knew, those who had drawn the water), he (the butler in charge) called the bridegroom ¹⁰ and said to him, 'Everyone puts out first the good wine, and when they have drunk freely, the inferior; but you have been keeping the good wine until now'.

¹¹ It was at Cana in Galilee that Jesus did this, an inauguration of the signs, and disclosed his glory; and his disciples believed in him.

¹² After this he went down to Capernaum, with his mother and his brothers and his disciples; and there they stayed, but only for a few days.

[† or: …between you and me? My hour is not yet come.]

2.1. καὶ τῇ ἡμέρᾳ τῇ τρίτῃ. Dodd writes that 'the "third day" was in Christian tradition from earliest times the day when Christ manifested his glory in resurrection from the dead', and gently hints that an allusion to that event colours the narrative here (*Interpretation*, 300). Boismard is more forthright: 'the expression could not fail to evoke the resurrection of Christ' (*Jean*, 105), and many others accept this interpretation, seeing in the first manifestation of Jesus' glory (2.11) a foreshadowing of the glory of the Resurrection.[1] There are, however, serious reasons to question it.

Mark, in referring to the Resurrection of Christ, never uses the phrase 'on the third day', but always μετὰ τρεῖς ἡμέρας (8.31; 9.31; 10.34). Matthew writes, always, τῇ τρίτῃ ἡμέρᾳ (16.21; 17.23; 20.19, cf. 27.64), and so, as a rule, does Luke (9.22; 24.7, 46; cf. 13.32). Only once, in 18.33, does Luke employ the phrase employed in Jn 2.1, τῇ ἡμέρᾳ τῇ τρίτῃ, though this is the wording used in 1 Cor 15.4: ὅτι ἐγήγερται τῇ ἡμέρᾳ τῇ τρίτῃ. The variations are regular enough to be significant, and it is also noteworthy that, if we set aside the text under examination (Jn

---

[1] I myself formerly held this view (see *The Mother of Jesus*, 464, 396-99), but now observe that I made no use of the idea in commenting on the Cana pericope. Clearly, the parallel with the Resurrection had not contributed in any way to the elucidation of the text.

2.1), the Fourth Gospel nowhere employs the Synoptic concept of the Christ's Resurrection 'on the third day'. The closest, and only, approximation to it occurs in Jn 2.20, where Jesus affirms that he will replace the Jerusalem Temple ἐν τρισὶν ἡμέραις, 'within a period of three days'.

Some (like Bernard, or Mollat in the *Bible de Jérusalem*) find an extra day in ch. 1 either by positing nightfall after 'the tenth hour' in 1.39 or by reading πρωΐ at 1.41, so that the Cana story then supplies a climax on what is, by their counting, the seventh day of the week. Neither Bernard nor Mollat, however, sees in *the third day* at Jn 2.1 a reference to Jesus' Resurrection.[2]

There is, however, another possible interpretation of τῇ ἡμέρᾳ τῇ τρίτῃ in Jn 2.1, which involves no manipulation of the text of ch. 1. John 1.19-51 presents its story in four consecutive days (1.19, 29, 35, 43). The (emphatic) phrase τῇ ἡμέρᾳ τῇ τρίτῃ,[3] will therefore indicate the sixth day of the First Week of Jesus' ministry. Now, given the obvious reference to Gen 1.1 in Jn 1.1, may not this First Week of the Gospel story be intended to reflect that First Week of Gen 1 (creation by the Word), the climax of which is reached on the sixth day, in the world's first wedding (Gen 1.26-28)? And could not the First Week of the ministry also point towards the scene on the sixth day of the final week of Jesus' life, in which the mother of Jesus reappears, when all is accomplished? In Rev 19.6-7 the victory of the Crucified is termed 'the wedding-feast of the Lamb'; perhaps the evangelist too wishes to interpret that victory on Calvary in terms of a wedding from which there issues, instead of the children of Adam, a newly created race (→ Jn 19.25-28). Once again, this would be a carefully constructed *inclusio*.

γάμος ἐγένετο ἐν Κανὰ τῆς Γαλιλαίας. *There was a wedding in Cana of Galilee.* On Jewish wedding customs, see SB I 500-17; II 372-99.[4] Cana 'of Galilee' is so called to distinguish it from Kanah in Phoenicia, nearly 40 miles away, a town in Asher mentioned in Josh 19.28 [written Κανα in Codex A of the LXX], situated some 6 miles = 10 km south-east of Tyre. Cana in Galilee was from around A.D. 1650 to 1940 identified with Kefar Kenna, some 3 miles = 5 km north-east of Nazareth, where two churches, Orthodox and Latin, welcome pilgrims even today. This tradition, however, does not antedate the arrival of the Franciscans in 1620, and there is now a consensus that the Cana of NT times is rather to be sought some 9 miles = 15 km due north of Nazareth at Khirbet Qana (map reference 1787 2478). A handful of pitiful ruins today marks the site of this once fortified position on a hill overlooking,

[2] Others find in the phrase *on the third day* a reference to the revelation of God's glory at Sinai, particularly because of the Targum of Pseudo-Jonathan at Exod 19.16. So A. Serra and J. Potin.

[3] The reduplication of the article after the noun and before the adjective is mainly a Johannine usage, as a rule to stress the adjective (*JG* 1982–86).

[4] The earliest mention of a seven-day celebration is in Tob 11.19 (14 days according to Tob 8.19).

from a distance of about two miles, the main highway from Ptolemais via Sepphoris to Tiberias. Cana stood close to an important crossroads, and there, for a time, Josephus had his headquarters in A.D. 66–67 (*Life* XVI 86).[5]

καὶ ἦν ἡ μήτηρ τοῦ 'Ιησοῦ ἐκεῖ. Though the sense is beyond doubt (it does not matter whether ἐκεῖ means 'at Cana' or 'at the wedding'), the intriguing question is why the evangelist refers here (and in 2.12; 19.25-27) to 'the mother of Jesus' without mentioning her proper name. This will be discussed later (→ γύναι in v. 4a). When the story begins, his mother was already there, at the wedding.

2. ἐκλήθη δὲ καὶ ὁ 'Ιησοῦς καὶ οἱ μαθηταὶ αὐτοῦ εἰς τὸν γάμον. Note the double καί. It may be translated *both...and*, as in the AV = KJV ('and both Jesus was called, and his disciples...'), a usage which 'is almost peculiar to John in the NT' (*JG* 2162, cf. 2161-66). Subsequent English versions from the RV onwards prefer *also*, construing the first καί as in Jn 3.23; 18.2, 5, 18; 19.39; 20.6 (compare *JG* 2147, cf. 2152-56), and neglecting the force of the second. A handful of ancient MSS, including 𝔓⁶⁶*, also seem to have either overlooked or disregarded the double καί. Yet, especially after the verb ἐκλήθη in the singular, the double καί serves to underline the dual and complementary presence, both of Jesus and of his disciples: he is there to manifest his glory, they are to witness it.

οἱ μαθηταί must include the four (or five) already mentioned in ch. 1, though in view of the later occurrences of the phrase in 2.11, 12, 17, 22, there is no reason to think that in the Cana story the term is restricted to

⁵ For the evidence that Khirbet Qana (grid reference 1787–2478) is the authentic site, see especially Clemens Kopp, *Das Kana des Evangeliums*, Palästina-Hefte 28, Cologne 1940, or, more accessibly, in *Die heiligen Stätten der Evangelien*, 184-95 = ETr *Holy Places*, 143-54. Compare also Abel, *Géographie*, II 412-13; Dalman, *Sacred Sites and Ways*, 101-106 and 112; and for a useful collection of the historical texts, Baldi ELS, 2nd ed., 238-64. See also W. M. Thomson, *The Land and the Book*, 1878, 426-27 for a description of the site in those days. The standard work, setting out all the pertinent literary texts from Josephus to 1697, is by Julián Herrojo, *Cana de Galilea*. For the main road, see Abel, II 224 or D. Baly, *Geographical Companion to the Bible*, 122; it ran across the plain known as Sahl al Battuf or *campus Asochis*. Another, more northerly, route from Sepphoris to Ptolemais via Jotapata and Kabul (see Josephus, *Life* XLII, XLV = 213, 234) crossed the main road and passed close by Cana.

From Bethania = Bethabara (see Excursus V) to Cana is about 60 miles = 100 km in a straight line, more by road. Older writers comment that it is possible to make the journey on foot in three days: F. W. Farrar calls it 'easily possible, although it requires quick travelling' because he had done it himself. One might stop on the first night at Shiloh or Shechem, on the second at En-Gannim (= Jenin), and complete the journey on the third day (*The Life of Christ* I 1874, Chapter XI, p. 160). The reader is, however, free to hypothesize that (some of?) the events ascribed to the second, third and fourth days (Jn 1.29-51) took place upstream from Bethania = Bethabara, which would notably diminish the distance to be covered. → Jn 1.29, and 1.45 under υἱὸν τοῦ 'Ιωσήφ.

these. Wellhausen suggested that here in v. 2, the original text may have read, instead of 'disciples', 'brothers', on the basis of the *Epistula Apostolorum* 5: 'There was a marriage in Cana of Galilee. And he was invited with his mother and his brothers'.[6] Bultmann and Boismard are sympathetic, on the ground that it is easy to see why a scribe should have altered *brothers* to *disciples*, but not easy to understand the reverse.[7] One may reply that no manuscript or patristic reference supports the reading αδελφοι at v. 2; that the *Epistula Apostolorum* was written possibly after A.D. 150, and is far from being a direct citation; and that its wording may rest on a recollection not of v. 2 but of v. 12.

3. καὶ ὑστερήσαντος οἴνου. This reading is supported by virtually the whole tradition (see the *TCGNT*). Among modern editors, only Tischendorf adopts, instead of υστερησαντος οινου, the longer reading, οινον ουκ ειχον οτι συνετελεσθη ο οινος του γαμου. ειτα. Among commentators, Zahn, Loisy, Lagrange and Bultmann preferred this longer reading, partly, no doubt, because it is the original text of the then relatively recently discovered Sinaiticus, but sometimes at least on the basis of the argument that ὑστερήσαντος οἴνου 'is undoubtedly a smoothing over of the clumsy original text' (Bultmann). It is, however, surprising that Boismard, Fortna and the *Bible de Jérusalem* should hold to this opinion after the publication of 𝔓⁶⁶ and 𝔓⁷⁵. 'The shorter reading is attested by 𝔓⁶⁶.⁷⁵ ℵᵃ and all known uncial and minuscule manuscripts', as well as all versional witnesses except a.b.ff².j.r. syr harᵐᵍ eth (*TCGNT*).

ὑστερήσαντος οἴνου: *when wine had given out* (aorist). οἴνου has no article, indicating perhaps that there was no wine at all. οἶνον οὐκ ἔχουσιν: whether these words refer to the guests or to the hosts (or to both) is unclear, and is immaterial.

λέγει ἡ μήτηρ τοῦ Ἰησοῦ πρὸς αὐτόν. This is the first occurrence in the Gospel of the phrase λέγειν πρός, a more formal and respectful construction than λέγειν followed by the dative, which therefore underlines the importance of the words that follow.[8] **οἶνον οὐκ ἔχουσιν.** A passage in Irenaeus, the first commentator on these words, has generally been understood to mean that Jesus' mother was pleading for a miracle, which he was unwilling to perform at that time; the text of Irenaeus is difficult, but probably does include this idea.[9] Augustine too expressly states that Jesus here refuses to perform a miracle at his mother's request, and Chrysostom even sees, in the words which follow,

---

[6] Elliott, *ApocNT*, 559.

[7] Bultmann 79 Anm.6 = ETr 114 fn. 6; Boismard, *Jean*, 100b.

[8] See also 3.4; 4.15, 49.

[9] 'Properante Maria ad admirabile vini signum et ante tempus volente participare compendii poculo, Dominus repellens eius intempestivam festinationem dixit…' (*Adv. Haereses* III 16,7: *SC* 211, p. 314²²⁸⁻²³¹). For a discussion of the difficulties, see the note in *SC* 210, p. 324.

a reprimand to Mary for wanting to parade herself as the mother of a son who could work miracles. 'She wanted to place them under an obligation to her, and also to make herself more conspicuous because of her child. For she was doubtless subject to the same human failing as his brothers, who said, 'Show yourself to the world!', wishing to enjoy the reflected glory of his miracles. That is why he replied rather sharply...'[10]

Thomas Aquinas is more cautious. In explaining the role of Mary in this text, he writes that we need only place our needs before God, without inquiring how he may help; and that is why Mary simply mentioned to Jesus the shortage of wine.[11] Calvin too doubted whether Mary 'hoped for, or asked for, anything, since he had so far performed no miracle'. Rupert of Deutz (†1129/30) suggested that the arrival of Jesus and his disciples might have occasioned the shortage, if they had not originally been counted among the expected guests, a suggestion warmly commended by Maldonatus. The most gentle interpretation is that of Bengel: Mary wished politely to suggest that Jesus, and the rest too, should leave before the poverty of the newly weds was, to their embarrassment, exposed.[12]

Mary's words do not of themselves imply that she is hinting that Jesus should intervene, much less that he should perform a miracle, but the context, and the use of πρὸς αὐτόν, intimate that it was in the hope that Jesus would do something to help the newly wed couple.

4. λέγει αὐτῇ ὁ 'Ἰησοῦς. Jesus here uses the dative, not (contrast v. 3) πρός. **τί ἐμοὶ καὶ σοί, γύναι;** The various renderings of τί ἐμοὶ καὶ σοί in the main English-language versions illustrate both the broad measure of agreement about the sense of the phrase in Jn 2.4a, and the difficulty of catching the idiom in English.[13] Jesus' question, however translated, certainly implies that his mother had been hoping for some action on his part, and that he himself (at least initially) had not intended to intervene. Yet the Greek phrase contains more than Jesus' reaction to a plea that he should rescue a wedding-party from an embarrassing situation.

---

[10] *In Ioannem* Hom. 21,2: *PG* 59.130

[11] 'Ex reverentia quam ad Deum habemus, sufficit nobis ei tantum defectus nostros exponere... Qualiter autem nobis Deus subveniat, non est nostrum inquirere' [he cites Rom 8.26]. 'Et ideo mater eius defectum aliorum simpliciter exposuit, dicens *Vinum non habent*' (*In Ioannem* II 3, fn. 345).

[12] 'Hoc dicit: Velim discedas, ut ceteri item discedant, antequam penuria patefiat. In hunc Mariae sensum responsio Iesu non modo non dura videtur, sed amoris est plenissima.'

[13] AV = KJV = RV, 'Woman, what have I to do with thee?'; RSV, 'O woman, what have you to do with me?'; NRSV, 'Woman, what concern is that to you and to me?'; NEB, 'Your concern, mother, is not mine'; REB, 'That is no concern of mine' [*sic*]; JB, 'Woman, why turn to me?'; NJB, 'Woman, what do you want from me?'; NIV, 'Dear woman, why do you involve me?'; NAB, 'Woman, how does your concern affect me?'

τί ἐμοὶ καὶ σοί is an idiomatic Semitic expression found both in the OT and in the NT, and 'used to deprecate interference or, more strongly, to reject overtures of any kind. The shade of meaning can be deduced only from the context' (JB). In the OT it sometimes indicates a harsh protest, as when Jephthah protests against the invasion of his land (Judg 11.12), or when the widow of Zarephath complains to Elijah (1 Kgs 17.18). Elsewhere, it may betoken simply a refusal to become involved (2 Sam 16.10; 19.22; 2 Kgs 3.13). And there is certainly no hostility in 2 Chron = Paral 35.21, where the Pharaoh Necho says to Josiah, τί ἐμοὶ καὶ σοί, βασιλεῦ Ιουδα; οὐκ ἐπὶ σὲ ἥκω σήμερον πόλεμον ποιῆσαι, meaning 'Why should we fight? I am not marching against *you*'. The five occurrences in the Synoptic Gospels (Mk 11.24 || Lk 4.34; Mt 8.29 || Mk 5.7 || Lk 8.28) are all cries of the possessed, and may be accurately rendered as 'Why do you trouble us?' or 'What have you got against us?' or 'Leave us alone!' The same idiom, with the same meaning, is found both in Classical and in Hellenistic Greek.[14]

Many have taken the words τί ἐμοὶ καὶ σοί to be a merely rhetorical question, implying that Jesus cannot accept the request that he should do something about the shortage of wine. The evangelist, however, is a master of irony and an artist in double meanings. His ostensibly rhetorical questions are in fact real questions to which alternative answers are always possible, though not always self-evident. On the surface, the only possible reply will be that which common sense and worldly wisdom immediately seize, and recommend. But there will always be an alternative answer, accessible only by faith. Other examples of this technique are to be found in Jn 4.12 and 8.53, 57.[15]

From the OT and NT evidence listed above, it would appear that when Jesus says τί ἐμοὶ καὶ σοί he is declining to act as his mother wishes; yet she does not take this as a rebuff (2.5), and Jesus immediately provides a solution to the problem disturbing her. Vanhoye therefore suggests that the most satisfactory interpretation of these apparently inconsistent verses is to take τί ἐμοὶ καὶ σοί as a serious question. The phrase has been translated above as *What relationship is there between you and me?* That is to say, Jesus is here questioning the relationship that has up to this point bound him to his mother, and implying that he can no longer remain part of the Nazareth family. It is the Johannine equivalent of Lk 2.49 and 4.16-30.

The introduction of the term γύναι supports this interpretation. In the gospels, Jesus uses this form of address to several women, including those he has never met before (the Samaritan woman in Jn 4.21, and

[14] *JG* 2230; J. J. Wetstein, *Novum Testamentum Graece*, Amsterdam, 1751, I 355, on Mt 8.29. Those desirous of an extensive discussion of the idiom may consult Boismard, *Du Baptême à Cana*, 144-49, Olsson, 36-40, Lütgehetmann, 156-66, and the articles by Michl and Vanhoye; see the Bibliography on pp. xxxv-xxxvi.

[15] This is cogently argued by A. Vanhoye, 'Interrogation johannique et exégèse de Cana (Jn 2.4)', *Biblica* 55 (1974), 157-67.

Mary of Magdala in 20.13, 15; compare also 8.11; Mt 15.28; Lk 13.12).
'It is by no means a disrespectful form of address' (BDAG): this is how
Abraham's servant addressed Rebecca's mother (Josephus, *Ant.* I xvi 3 =
152), and Augustus, Cleopatra (Dio Cassius 51,12.5). Yet apart from the
two occurrences at Cana and Calvary in Jn 2.3 and 19.26, there is no text
in the Bible or in rabbinical writings where a son addresses his mother as
'Woman'. The choice of this unusual form of address therefore confirms
the view that in these two texts the evangelist wished to draw attention
away from Mary's blood-relationship with Jesus, in order to intimate that
she was to have, in the gospel story, a role very different from that of
simply being Jesus' biological mother. The words in Jn 2.4 are not Jesus'
last words to his mother (see 19.26). As so often, the reader will have to
wait for an *inclusio*, and it has already been suggested (see 2.1) that the
writer may have had in mind the sixth day in the first chapter of Genesis.

οὔπω ἥκει ἡ ὥρα μου. The Greek may be translated either as a
statement or as a question. If the words are a statement, they give the
reason why Jesus refuses to intervene, namely, because *My hour is not
yet come*. In that case, *is not* (AV = KJV; RV) seems preferable to *has not*
(RSV, and most modern versions), for ἥκειν underlines the aspect of
arrival. Its normal meaning is *to have come, to be arrived, to be present*.
In the NT, it often refers to an event of the eschatological age (compare
Ezek 7.7, 12, ἥξει ὁ καιρός), clearly so in Mt 24.14; Lk 19.43.[16]

If the clause is interpreted as a statement, a problem arises. 'The hour
of Jesus' should then, to be consistent, refer to a future moment when it
would be proper for him to intervene (by working wonders, some say) in
purely earthly affairs, and there is no evidence that in the Fourth Gospel,
'the hour of Jesus' ever has this meaning. Moreover, if οὔπω ἥκει κτλ.
indicates a refusal to intervene, either by a miracle or in some other way,
one has to explain why, after this refusal, Mary at once said, 'Do whatever he tells you,' and why Jesus apparently acceded to her request.

To counter these objections, many commentators point to the story of
the Syro-Phoenician woman in Mt 15.21-28 ‖ Mk 7. 24-30; to Jesus'
apparent reluctance to act in Jn 4.48; and to Martha's distress that Jesus
had not arrived in time to save Lazarus' life, 11.6, 14, 21-22. Similarly
here, they argue, his mother's quiet confidence allows Jesus, once he has
asserted his independence, to accede to her implicit request. Schnackenburg compares Jn 7.6-10, where 'the reader also has the impression that
Jesus acts differently from what his words in v.8 would lead one to
expect'. These comments are true, but they leave unexplained why Jesus
seems at first to have discountenanced his mother's approach.

The most common resolution of this problem is that advocated by
Augustine, namely, that Jesus' mother was asking for a miracle, and that
he, now that he was about to begin the work appointed by his heavenly
Father, could no longer hold himself at her bidding; but (Augustine adds)

---

[16] For other NT texts, see *EDNT* II 114-15, and *TWNT* II 929-30.

Jesus did promise that when the humanity he had received from his mother was hanging on the cross, he would once more acknowledge the claims of her from whom that humanity had been born.[17] Aquinas writes in almost identical words. But if this smoothes the passage from vv. 3 to 4, it leaves the logical connection between vv. 4 and 5 somewhat strained.

On the other hand, if the words οὔπω ἥκει ἡ ὥρα μου are not a state-ment but a question, their meaning is reversed, and the sense becomes 'Is not my hour already come?' Boismard is the most persistent advocate of this interpretation, which steadily gathered adherents over the twentieth century.[18] The underlying principle is that when a Greek sentence begins with a negative, it is often interrogative: for example, Lk 23.29 or Jn 18.11. Moreover, wherever in the NT the word οὔπω follows an interro-gative (as here in 2.4), it itself has an interrogative force. So we read in Mk 4.40, τί δειλοί ἐστε; οὔπω ἔχετε πίστιν; and in Mk 8.17 ‖ Mt 16.8-9, in a situation parallel to that at Cana, τί διαλογίζεσθε ὅτι ἄρτους οὐκ ἔχετε; οὔπω νοεῖτε οὐδὲ συνίετε; If the text be construed in this fashion, Jesus meets his mother's anxiety about the dearth of wine by asking 'Is not my hour now come?', indicating that he is about to intervene in some way or other.[19]

The most common objection to interpreting the words as a question is that οὔπω occurs twelve times in John, and that none of the other occurrences is interrogative. But none of the other Johannine texts comes immediately after a question, and the other eleven all have a connective particle, so that Jn 2.4 alone matches exactly the interrogative texts of Mk 4.40; 8.17 and Mt 16.8-9.[20]

A second objection is that Jn 7.30 and 8.20 clearly state that οὔπω ἐληλύθει ἡ ὥρα αὐτοῦ, *his hour had not yet come*, where the 'hour' indubitably denotes the hour of Jesus' departure and triumph. But could not his 'hour' embrace, in a broader sense, the divinely appointed time of Jesus' public ministry in its entirety? 'The Fourth Gospel is written from beginning to end *sub specie aeternitatis*; the predestined end is foreseen from the beginning' (Bernard), and the cross, though unmentioned by name until ch. 19, casts its long shadow forward over the years of the ministry.[21]

---

[17] *In Ioannem* 8,9 (on Jn 2.4) and 119,1 (on 19.25). See Jn 19.25-27.

[18] Boismard, *Jean*, 106, and in *Du Baptême à Cana*, 156. In modern times it has been proposed by Knabenbauer (1898) and Durand (1930), by Hugo Seemann, 'Aufgehellte Bibelstellen', *Benediktinische Monatschrift* 5-6 (1952), and sympathetically noted by A. Kurfess, 'Zu Joh. 2.4', *ZNW* (1952–53), 257. See also Michl, and especially Vanhoye.

[19] Thus Gregory of Nyssa, *In 1 Cor.* 15.28 (*PG* 44.1308 D) and Theodore of Mopsuestia, *In Ioannem* 2.4 (ed. Vosté 39; ed. Devréesse, 319). See also L. Leloir, Ephrem, *Commentaire de l'Evangile Concordant ou Diatessaron*, 5 (CSCO 145, 144f.; and the note in the *SC* edition [1966], 108).

[20] A. Vanhoye, 'Interrogation johannique et exégèse de Cana (Jn 2.4)'.

[21] Compare Jn 4.23; 5.25, 28 (ἔρχεται ὥρα); 7.6, 8 (ὁ καιρὸς ὁ ἐμός); 9.4; 11.9. See also Schnackenburg I 334-35 = ETr I 330.

The interpretation of v. 4 preferred here implies that both parts of the verse are declaring two (complementary) aspects of the same truth, and that the best way of putting them into English is to make the two sentences into one. *'What relationship is there, woman, between you and me, now that my hour is approaching?'* The story can continue, but in a direction different from what the reader might have expected. In fairness, it must be said that no modern English version for public use translates the second sentence as a question; but such versions are quite properly hesitant to adopt exegetical opinions before they are generally accepted.

5. ὅ τι ἂν λέγη ὑμῖν ποιήσατε are almost the very words used by the Pharaoh in Gen 41.55 LXX, except that Rahlfs' LXX reads (instead of λέγη) εἴπῃ. λέγη is in the present, not aorist, tense, so that in this context it must be either continuous or iterative. The meaning is therefore, *Whatever he may say to you* (from time to time), *do it* : MHT I 186; III 107.

It is not immediately obvious that the words are, at Jn 2.5, an intentional quotation of the LXX, for Joseph the patriarch does not appear to have any relevance to the Cana story; but in Gen 41.55 these words herald the climax of the Joseph story when all his brothers (that is, all Israel) go down to Egypt as suppliants before one whom they did not recognize, thus fulfilling the unconscious prophecy of his father Jacob, 'Shall I and your mother and your brothers come to bow ourselves to the ground before you?' (Gen 37.11). So when the wine had run out, the mother of Jesus used to the waiters virtually the same words as the Pharaoh had used of Joseph in Gen 41.55, and the quite unforeseen outcome was that Jesus' disciples came to believe in him.

Perhaps the evangelist does wish to present Jesus as the successor of Joseph the patriarch, 'the Owner of the Land'. The reader may compare the comment on Ἰησοῦν υἱὸν τοῦ Ἰωσήφ at 1.45.[22]

6. ἦσαν δὲ ἐκεῖ λίθιναι ὑδρίαι ἓξ κατὰ τὸν καθαρισμὸν τῶν Ἰουδαίων κείμεναι. That this is the most satisfactory text seems clear from the note in *TCGNT*; and the variant readings make no difference to the meaning. Spitta, Bultmann, Fortna and Boismard argue that some later scribes put κείμεναι immediately after ἓξ, or suppressed it altogether, because they judged that the words κατὰ τὸν καθαρισμὸν τῶν Ἰουδαίων make an unduly long separation between ἦσαν and κείμεναι. On the basis of this theory, these modern commentators propose that κατὰ τὸν καθαρισμὸν τῶν Ἰουδαίων represents an insertion into an earlier draft of the story.

λίθιναι ὑδρίαι. Water-jars were generally made of earthenware or stoneware, and were frequently, for safety, embedded in the ground; stoneware jars were more highly prized, because they were stronger, and

---

[22] Compare Boismard, *Jean*, 93b.

less liable to contract ritual uncleanness (compare Lev 11.33). On the laws of levitical cleanness, see Mk 7.3-4 and SB II 406-407.[23] To interpret κείμεναι as *lying on their sides* (and therefore empty) is to read too much into the verb, which can mean simply *placed* or *put there* (LSJ) (and therefore possibly standing upright, or embedded in the ground).

ἕξ, *six.* The number is almost certainly symbolic. For some, it is an imperfect number, being one short of the sacred Hebrew number, seven. So Boismard writes (*Jean,* 102a): 'c'est tout le principe des rites purificateurs du judaïsme qui est en cause, et qui doit être remplacé par un nouveau système symbolisé par le vin qui va remplacer l'eau'. Others (like the Pythagoreans) take six to be a perfect number (1+2+3): see Philo, *On the Creation* 89; Clement of Alexandria, *Stromata* VI 16. The first view is more appropriate here.

χωροῦσαι ἀνὰ μετρητὰς δύο ἢ τρεῖς. ἀνά followed by the accusative, though rare in Attic prose and found only 13 times in the NT (and a *hapax legomenon* here in John), is good Hellenistic Greek, especially with a distributive sense: see MHT III 265-66 and BDF 305. The Attic measure was almost exactly 40 litres, or about 9 gallons; 'two or three measures' is therefore rendered in nearly all modern English versions, in round numbers, as 'from twenty to thirty gallons',[24] that is, between 80 and 120 litres.

7-8. γεμίσατε...ἀντλήσατε...καὶ φέρετε. The change to the present imperative after two aorists looks strange, but φέρε and φέρετε are always found in the present (not the aorist) whatever the context, ἐνέγκατε in Jn 21.10 supplying the only exception in the NT (MHT III 75). Zerwick-Smith §244 suggests this is because 'the present expresses the notion of "setting about" an activity'.

In the NT, ἀντλεῖν occurs only in John, here in 2.8, 9, and in 4.7, 15. The LXX contains at the most nine instances, only six of them certain (HR), but given the rarity of the verb, these six texts are of interest. In Gen 24.13, 20, Abraham's servant Eliezer is seeking for a wife for Isaac, in order to arrange the first wedding from which God's Chosen Race will be born. In Exod 2.16.17 [B], 19, the context is of Moses drawing water for the daughters of his future father-in-law, an act leading to his own wedding. Jewish tradition interprets each of these texts in a similar fashion. In Gen 24.17, the *Midrash Rabbah* glosses the phrase 'a little water' with *but one mouthful;*[25] on Exod 2.19, it says of Moses that 'he only drew out one bucketful and with this watered all the flock there assembled, for the water was blessed at his hands'.[26] The sixth LXX text

---

[23] See especially, Roland Deines, *Jüdische Steingefässe und pharisäische Frömmigkeit : ein archäologisch-historischer Beitrag zum Verständnis von Joh 2,6 und der jüdischen Reinheitshalacha zur Zeit Jesu,* WUNT 2.52, Tübingen, 1993.

[24] Or (in round numbers) 15 to 25 US gallons (Brown I 100).

[25] LX 6 in the Soncino edition, p. 530.

[26] I 32 in the Soncino edition, p. 41.

is Isa 12.3, καὶ ἀντλήσετε ὕδωρ μετ' εὐφροσύνης ἐκ τῶν πηγῶν τοῦ σωτηρίου. In the Targum, this verse is rendered as: '*And* you will *accept a new teaching* with joy *from the chosen ones of righteousness*'.[27]

ἀρχιτρικλίνος is found nowhere in the Bible except in this passage. It denotes the one in charge of the arrangements for the meal. Chief steward, butler and head waiter are all appropriate, but none of them exact, equivalents.

9-10. ὡς δὲ ἐγεύσατο ὁ ἀρχιτρίκλινος τὸ ὕδωρ οἶνον γεγενημένον κτλ. The text does not state, or imply, that the entire contents of the six jars had been turned into wine. It is only what has been, on Jesus' orders, drawn out of the jars and tasted, that has been pronounced 'the best of wine'. For the use of a positive to express a superlative, see MHT III 31; compare the Vulgate's translation by *optimus* in Lk 8.15; 10.42; Heb 13.9, and the rendering given here by the NEB, REB and JB, *the best wine*. The Gospel states only that the steward tasted it. It does not say that the guests drank and were satisfied, or that bride and bridegroom rejoiced, or that Jesus pronounced some striking word. Is it not strange, too, that the *architriclinus* should call the bridegroom, to congratulate him, and not vice versa? Some commentators view the last clause as humorous or playful, but the real message of the text is that in the mind of the evangelist, the final remark conceals a second, deeper and truer meaning than the speaker could have foreseen or intended (Westcott).

Note the abrupt ending of the narrative. The story comes to a stop halfway through, with the reader left wondering what is the point of it. **σύ.** Here the pronoun carries some emphasis, being contrasted with **πᾶς ἄνθρωπος** (MHT III 37). **τετήρηκας** is a resultative perfect (MHT III 84). *You have been keeping the best wine until now.*

11. ταύτην ἐποίησεν ἀρχήν τῶν σημείων. The textual variants are evidence that many scribes sought to regularize the Greek by inserting την before αρχην, but since the reader of the Gospel has so far not heard about any 'signs' done by Jesus, '*a* start' is more accurate than '*the* start'. 'Signs' may be defined as notable events which reveal Jesus' glory to those who see them with the eyes of faith,[28] and the evangelist already has in mind other signs to which the wine-miracle at Cana, correctly interpreted, will provide the key. Origen calls it προηγούμενον τῶν σημείων, that is, 'a first, pre-eminent and primary sign', of greater

---

[27] Chilton's rendering in *The Aramaic Bible*.
[28] The matter will be discussed more fully at Jn 4.48. For the present, it is sufficient to note that people may physically observe an indubitably wonderful work, such as the Feeding of the Five Thousand (Jn 6.14) or the Healing of a Man Blind from Birth (Jn 9.20, 25) and yet fail to see the 'sign', i.e. fail to see what that event signifies, because they do not perceive the deeper truth enshrined in it (Jn 6.36-40, 44-45, 63-66; 9.39).

significance, he insists, than the healing miracles which will follow.[29]
ἀρχήν therefore does not indicate merely that that this sign is the first in
time (else, why not πρωτον to match Jn 4.54?), but rather that here is *an
inauguration of the signs* yet to come. Isocrates provides a perfect
parallel where the absence of the article is equally significant. ἀρχὴν μὲν
ταύτην ἐποιήσατο τῶν εὐεργεσίων, τροφὴν τοῖς δεομένοις εὑρεῖν
(*Panegyricus* 38).

καὶ ἐφανέρωσεν τὴν δόξαν αὐτοῦ. This is the first mention of
Jesus' 'glory' since Jn 1.14; what was there said about the fulness of
grace and truth is, with this ἀρχὴ τῶν σημείων, beginning to be
disclosed. 'According to the Johannine use of φανεροῦν, it is Jesus 1.31;
7.4; 21.1, 14, Jesus' δόξα, 2.11, God's ἔργα 9.3; 3.21, and God's Name,
17.6, which are revealed' (Olsson, 70). As the Prologue closes with the
reference to his glory, so does the First Week of his ministry.

One of the principal promises of the prophets was that the Glory of the
Lord would one day return to the Land, to Jerusalem and to the Temple
(Isa 35.2, 10; 40.5; 60.1-3; Ezek 43.1-5: compare *PssSol* 17.33-35).
Rabbinical Judaism too stressed the intense longing for the return of the
Shekinah to the Land and to Jerusalem: → Jn 1.51 on Jesus' promise,
'You will see heaven laid wide open'. It is surely significant that after the
first 'disclosure' of his glory at Cana, the precise meaning of which will
be discussed very shortly, Jesus goes almost at once to the Temple in
Jerusalem (→ 2.19-20, and compare Luke's use of δόξα in 2.32 to close
his Infancy narrative).

καὶ ἐπίστευσαν εἰς αὐτὸν οἱ μαθηταὶ αὐτοῦ. If the arrangement adopted in this commentary is correct, these calm words draw down
the curtain on the First Week, that is, the First Act of Jesus' public
ministry.

12. μετὰ τοῦτο κατέβη εἰς Καφαρναούμ. μετὰ τοῦτο occurs four
times in John (2.12; 11.7, 11; 19.28), μετὰ ταῦτα, eight times (3.22;
5.1, 14; 6.1; 7.1; 13.7; 19.38; 21.1). Abbott (*JG* 2394) prefers to interpret μετὰ τοῦτο as indicating a short interval, but acknowledges that it
might be intended to underline the completion of some significant period
or action of Jesus. Certainly it is always followed by some significant
word or deed of Jesus, and this is not the case after μετὰ ταῦτα (e.g.
19.38). Here in 2.12, μετὰ τοῦτο can hardly mean just 'next'. It serves
rather to call attention to 'this significant act at Cana, which completed
the first week of his ministry', after which Jesus moved down to Capernaum.

αὐτὸς καὶ ἡ μήτηρ αὐτοῦ καὶ οἱ ἀδελφοὶ αὐτοῦ. Exactly 3
miles = 5 km due west of Khirbet Qana (map reference 1787 2478) lies
Kaukab (map reference 1736 2484), where according to Julius

---

[29] *In Ioannem* X 12 66 (*SC* 157: 422-25).

Africanus[30] relatives of Jesus lived in the second half of the first century. Julius tells us they were known as δεσπόσυνοι ('the Master's people')[31] and that they took pride in preserving the memory of their connection with the Saviour's family; he asserts that some of them travelled far afield to preach the Christian message throughout Galilee and Syria.[32] It is likely that those 'grandsons of Jude' who were arraigned before Domitian and discharged should be counted among these δεσπόσυνοι.[33]

The nearness of Kaukab to Cana is sufficient to explain both the mention at this point, after the wedding, of οἱ ἀδελφοὶ αὐτοῦ, and their absence in v. 2, where they, as local people, are perhaps assumed to have been (like his mother) already at Cana. If they were (as Julius Africanus assures us) meticulous in preserving the genealogies of their family, it is more than probable that they would also have cherished any tradition about Jesus' presence at a wedding in Cana before his public ministry began.

καὶ οἱ μαθηταὶ αὐτοῦ καὶ ἐκεῖ ἔμειναν οὐ πολλὰς ἡμέρας.
Verse 12 records that the entire group, Jesus and his mother and his brothers and his disciples, moved to Capernaum and stayed there, but only for a few days. This verse is intended to harmonize the Fourth Gospel with the Synoptic tradition, according to which the public ministry really begins in Capernaum. Luke too mentions a (short?) pre-Capernaum, ministry at Nazareth (Lk 4.14-16).[34]

THE INTERPRETATION OF THE WINE MIRACLE AT CANA

There is nothing quite like this narrative anywhere else in the Gospels. Many Christians understand it as a record of the fact that Jesus did once change water into wine, at Cana in Galilee; others think the evangelist

[30] Officer in the army of Septimius Severus, friend of Origen, *floruit* A.D. 195–240. See Quasten, II 137-40; Altaner, 185-86.

[31] Note the ancient title for Jesus, ὁ δεσπότης, cf. Lk 2.29; Jude 4 ‖ 2 Pet 2.1; and perhaps Rev 6.10(?).

[32] The text occurs in Julius' *Letter to Aristides* (Eusebius *H.E.* I 7 14).

[33] Eusebius in *H.E.* III 19.1–20.7, on the authority of Hegesippus (*floruit* A.D. 150–190: Quasten, I 284-87; Altaner, 117-18). See Richard Bauckham's outstanding study of the group in *Jude and the Relatives of Jesus in the Early Church*, Edinburgh, 1990, 64-70, 94-101.

[34] The comment above on v. 2 reported that some commentators thought that μαθηταί had there been substituted for an original ἀδελφοί. This argument can be inverted, to say that the words καὶ οἱ μαθηταὶ αὐτοῦ were inserted in v. 12 only because they had already been mentioned in v. 2. In v. 12, the phrase is absent from 𝔓⁶⁶*.⁷⁵ B Ψ (ℵ and a few others omit the initial αὐτοῦ as well: see NA²⁷); might not these words have been inserted by a zealous scribe anxious to get everyone tidily off stage? It is impossible to be certain whether the words καὶ οἱ μαθηταὶ αὐτοῦ were or were not present in the original text; and it is not of great importance. ἐμειναν was probably corrected to the singular ἐμεινεν because otherwise the text speaks only of Jesus' movements (12, κατέβη; 13, ἀνέβη) (Schnackenburg).

intended it to be so understood; and others would regard that interpretation as a trivializing of divine omnipotence. The inherent improbability of this narrative's being the report of something which actually happened has naturally moved many writers to seek a more easily credible interpretation.[35]

From around 1900 to 1960, adherents of the school of the history of religions argued that the Cana story was inspired by Greek myths about Dionysus, the god of wine, whose feast on 5–6 January was later replaced by the Christian feast of the Epiphany. 'There can be no doubt that the story has been taken over from heathen legend and ascribed to Jesus' (Bultmann). One example frequently quoted relates how it was the custom at Elis to place three empty jugs in the shrine of Dionysus on the evening of 5 January, and to lock the doors; the next morning the jugs were found to be full of wine.[36] History, however, provides no example of any wonder-worker's actually changing water into wine (Lagrange).

A better example occurs in the novel *Leucippe and Clitophon* by the otherwise unknown Achilleus Tatius (A.D. 150–200), a Phoenician saga about Dionysus which tells how the god visited a herdsman noted for his hospitality, and gave him in return 'purple water, blood so sweet, harvest water, the blood of the grape'.[37] Hengel offers the most moderate presentation of the case for the influence of a Dionysus-motif, arguing that this text, albeit so late, supplies evidence that the idea might have taken root in rural Palestine long before the Christian era.[38]

It is, however, hardly necessary to go to Greece in order to find inspiration for a story about an abundance of wine at a Jewish wedding; now, in the twentieth-first century, it becomes very difficult to believe that our Jewish-Christian evangelist would have wanted to open his Gospel by introducing Jesus as a greater than Dionysos.[39] Another fundamental flaw in these history-of-religion interpretations is that they make the centre of the story the physical transformation of water into wine, and seem to regard the wedding as secondary, almost incidental to the narrative.

By the middle of the twentieth century, the positivist ideal of history as the disinterested observing and recording of actual happenings was

[35] E. Little, in *Echoes* 9-16 ('The Scandal of Cana'), lists some representative twentieth-century views.

[36] The story is told in Pausanias VI 26,2 (around A.D. 173) and in Athenaeus I 61 (A.D. 230). A similar story about a temple on the island of Andros tells how, on the feast of Bacchus, 5 January, wine flowed from the temple for seven days until, once out of sight of the temple, it lost its taste and became like water (Pliny, *Historia Naturalis* II 231 and XXXI 16; also in Pausanias VI 26,2). Other tales about wine in the cult of Dionysos are listed in Lagrange, *Jean*, 61. Barrett too collects all the useful parallels, on 2nd ed., 188-89. Bultmann, 83 Anm. 3 = ETr 119 fn. 1 and Schnackenburg I 343-44 = ETr I 340 give several similar references to modern writers on the subject.

[37] In the Loeb edition, II.2.1-6.

[38] Hengel, 108-12.

[39] *Pace* Linnemann (1974), Fortna (1989), 52, and especially Walter Lütgehetmann (1990), 339-40.

already receding, and with it the confident conviction that the Fourth Gospel cannot be termed 'historical'. Exegetes began to ask instead what was meant by calling this gospel 'historical', and to seek new ways of understanding it. One or two[40] saw the Cana episode as a sign contrasting Jesus' baptism in the Spirit (Jn 1.33) with the ritual cleansings of Judaism (2.6) or of John the Baptist (3.22-25; 4.2); but their suggestions did not find wide favour.

Others, who proposed to see in the text a reference to the Holy Eucharist, met with a more kindly reception.[41] For these, the wine of Cana forms a diptych with the bread that fed the Five Thousand, as the two scenes sometimes do in early Christian art. Both scenes occur near the time of Passover, and at the third Passover, Jesus' hour is come. The earthly food and drink are thus seen as symbols of the body and blood of Christ that would be offered to the disciples at the Supper, by which the forgiveness won upon the Cross is communicated to all humankind, replacing the Jewish rites of purification. Indeed, some consider that Irenaeus interpreted Mary's words in Jn 2.3-4 as a (premature) plea for the gift of the Eucharist,[42] and one (André Feuillet) has suggested that Jesus' action at Cana was a sign intended both to indicate the transformation of the Old Covenant into the New, and at the same time to hint at the gift of the eucharistic wine.[43] That a secondary application to the eucharist may underlie the gospel story is possible; but that it is the primary symbolic meaning seems impossible since John (alone of the evangelists) does not mention the institution of the eucharist at the Supper.

Schnackenburg, whose doctoral thesis (1951) was entitled *Das erste Wunder Jesu*, sums up all the evidence clearly and judiciously in his commentary (1965).[44] He concludes that the 'sign' reveals Jesus himself as the gift of the Father, superseding the gifts of the Old Covenant (Jn 1.17), the order of grace with its sacraments and its doctrine being as superior to the Law of Judaism as the choicest wine is to water, life-giving though the latter most certainly is. More precise than that, Schnackenburg is not prepared to be, and R. E. Brown, in 1966, delivers an equally cautious concurrent judgment (I 103-11).

Yet it is legitimate to attempt to be more precise. In 1963, Dodd suggested[45] that the original nucleus of the pericope might have been a parable about a wedding feast. As the gospel tradition developed, this parable came to be interpreted as an event in the ministry of Jesus. So, for

[40] E.g. K. L. Schmidt, 40-41, and F. M. Braun, 'Le baptême', 353, 384-85.

[41] So Cullmann, *Urchristentum und Gottesdienst*, 4th ed., Zürich, 1962, 65-71 = *Early Christian Worship*, 68-71, and Strathmann, NTD 2, 6th ed., 1963, 59. Dodd is not unsympathetic: *Interpretation*, 298; *Historical Tradition*, 224.

[42] So W. Wigan Harvey in his edition of 1857 (*S. Irenaei* II 88), and the French editors of Irenaeus in the *SC* (see their note on III xvi 7 at p. 315 fn. 3, in *SC* 210: 324).

[43] 'L'heure de Jésus et le signe de Cana', *ETL* 36 (1960), 5-22.

[44] 'The deeper meaning': I 341-44 = ETr I 337-40

[45] *Historical Tradition*, 226-28.

example, many critics think that Mark's story of the cursing of the fig-tree (Mk 11.12-14, 20-25) 'has passed over from the status of a parable to that of an actual happening' (compare Luke's parable of the barren fig-tree in 13.6-9). Dodd put forward his suggestion as no more than a conjecture, but one may suggest a transition in the opposite direction that would illustrate its possibility. Everyone speaks of the Parable of the Good Samaritan (Lk 10.29-37); but Luke does not say it is a parable. When Jesus replied, 'A certain man went down from Jerusalem to Jericho', his ἄνθρωπός τις could well have been autobiographical, like οἶδα ἄνθρωπον in 2 Cor 12.2, 3. In that case, an actual event in the life of Jesus has, in the common understanding of Christians, for almost two thousand years been turned into a parable. Might not the reverse have happened, too? There is, however, a still simpler explanation.

The main point about this pericope is that it concerns a (Jewish) wedding, and that the mother of Jesus was there (Jn 2.1). It is the wedding, rather than the wine-into-water motif, which was the centre of interest for the evangelist.[46] The exegete should therefore start by inquiring why the evangelist gave so prominent a place, at the beginning of Jesus' ministry, to a wedding.

Once Hosea had introduced into Israel's religion the language of marital love (chs. 1–2, especially 2.19-20 [ETr] = 21-22 [MT]; 11.1-4), later writers began to speak of the Covenant of Sinai as the moment when God had first wedded himself to Israel (Jer 2.2), and to look forward to an era when Yahweh and Israel would once again be united as bridegroom and bride, in faithfulness and everlasting love (Isa 54.1-8; 61.10; 62.4-5). The New Covenant promised in Jer 31.31-34 and Ezek 37.26-28 would take effect when the exiles of Judah 'returned' to Yahweh with their whole heart (Jer 24.5-7), saying 'Let us join ourselves to Yahweh in an everlasting covenant which will never be forgotten' (50.5). The image reached its high point in the allegorical interpretation of the Song of Songs, which made possible the acceptance of this poem into the Canon of Hebrew Scripture. In the OT, the bridegroom and bride were always Yahweh and his Chosen People, Israel.

In post-biblical Judaism the OT conception of the Covenant of Sinai as a wedding was not forgotten, but from the first century of the Christian era onwards, the rabbis also (and more usually) likened this present age to the period of betrothal: 'This world is like the betrothal... The actual marriage ceremony will take place in the Messianic days.'[47] Even then, the bridegroom is always Yahweh, never once the Messiah. In the words

---

[46] Note that the evangelist does not say that the water was *changed* into wine: no verb meaning *changed* occurs in the Gospel. Jn 2.9 refers simply to the 'water *become* wine', and 4.46 'where he *made* the water wine'.

[47] *Midrash R. Exod* XV 30 on 12.2 (in the Soncino ed. XV 31, 204). Other texts are cited in SB I 517. See also J. Jeremias, *TWNT* I 652, on γαμέω, and on νύμφη in *TWNT* IV 1094-96.

of Isa 54.5, cited in that same rabbinic text, 'Your Maker is your
husband: Yahweh Sabaoth is his name'.

A wedding feast would normally take seven days (Judg 14.12; Tob
11.19),[48] and as always in the Mediterranean, wine would be in plentiful
supply. Abundance of wine was also a blessing promised for, and
characteristic of, the Day of Yahweh, the end of time, as we read at the
conclusion of Hosea (14.7) and of Amos (9.13-14); compare Jer 31.12
and Zech 10.7. Genesis 49.10-12 proclaims that the coming of the king
from the tribe of Judah will be celebrated amid wonderful harvests from
the vines (cf. 27.28),[49] and the same promise recurs (with reference to the
Day of the Lord) in Joel 2.21-24 and 4.18. Other texts which mention an
abundance of wine, normally along with rich harvests of corn and oil, are
Isa 62.8-9; Hos 2.8, 15, 22 = [MT] 2.10, 17, 24; Amos 9.14; Joel 2.24;
Zech 9.17. Conversely, lack of wine is a sign of abandonment by God as
a result of the people's unfaithfulness (Isa 16.10; 24.7-11; Hos 2.9, 12 =
[MT] 11, 13; Amos 5.11; Joel 1.5, 10).

R. E. Brown (I 105) calls attention also to *1 En* 10.19 and *2 Bar* 29.5
(*OTP* I 18 and 630), which promise a thousandfold fruitfulness of the
vines. Irenaeus even claims, on the authority of the Elders who had seen
John the disciple of the Lord, that this image (indeed, ten thousandfold)
had, according to that same John, been used by Jesus himself.[50]

Now it is ridiculous to think that the abundance of wine promised in
the OT is meant to signify a liberal supply of alcoholic drink, particularly
when it symbolizes the table fellowship of God's eschatological kingdom. That would be to accuse the prophets of Israel of crass materialism.
In the OT, wine is also a symbol of God's holy wisdom, of divine
revelation. So in Isa 55.1 we read, 'Come, buy wine and milk without
money', and in Prov 9.4-6, 'Eat of the bread and drink of the wine that I
have mixed for you'. Sirach 15.3 and 24.19, 21 refer to the water of
wisdom (not to wine); but 31.27 reads 'Wine is like life to men, if you
drink it in moderation' (see also vv. 25-31, and 40.20). The metaphor of
wine to connote wisdom is used also by Philo, who spells out the spiritual
sense that he intends to convey. 'Let Melchizedek instead of water offer
wine, and give to souls strong drink, that they may be seized by a divine
intoxication, more sober than sobriety itself'.[51] 'And when the happy soul
holds out the sacred goblet of its own reason, who is it that pours into it
the holy cupfuls of true gladness, but the Word, the Cup-bearer of God

---

[48] Further detail in SB I 504-18 (on Mt 9.15).

[49] Hengel (p. 100) asserts that this was one of the most important prophecies in
Judaism, and adds: 'It is equally instructive that the wine-cup, pitcher, grape-leaf, and
grape appear frequently on the coins of the uprisings of 66–73 and 132–135, which were
motivated by eschatological-Messianic considerations'.

[50]*Adv. Haereses* V 33:3 = *SC* 153: 414-16. For a commentary, see A. Orbe, *Teología
de san Ireneo* III, Madrid-Toledo, 1988, 418-25.

[51] *Legum Allegoriae* III xxvi 82 (Loeb I 354-55).

the Master of the feast (ὁ οἰνοχόος τοῦ θεοῦ καὶ συμποσίαρχος λογός) who is also none other than the draught which he pours…'[52]

Three OT motifs, then, provide a starting-point for the interpretation of the Cana story: the marriage-bond between Yahweh and Israel, the comparison of the re-establishment of the new Covenant with a wedding (Jer 31.2-14, 23-28; Isa 54.1-8; 61.10–62.5), and the blessing of this union with 'an abundance of corn, wine, and oil' (Jer 50.5; cf. 31.12-14) on the day of that 'everlasting covenant which will never be forgotten' (Jer 50.5).

In the NT too, the wedding-feast is a symbol of the coming of salvation, the fulfilment of time. It features three times in the parables: in that of the King's Son (Mt 22.1-14), of the Ten Virgins (Mt 25.1-13), and of the Waiting Servants (Lk 12.35-36). Further, with only two possible exceptions (here at Jn 2.9 and at Rev 18.23), in the NT the word for *bridegroom*, νυμφίος, always refers to Jesus Christ. Thus νυμφίος is found in Mt 9.15 (twice) ‖ Mk 2.19-20 (twice) ‖ Lk 5.35 (twice) ('the children of the bridal chamber cannot fast as long as the bridegroom is with them'); these are also the only verses in which the word νυμφών (*bridal chamber*) occurs in the NT, once in each gospel.[53] Elsewhere, νυμφίος is found four times in Mt 25.1, 5, 6, 10 (the delayed Parousia?), and three times in Jn 3.29. In addition, references to the Church as the bride of Christ clearly imply that Christ was regarded as the heavenly bridegroom (2 Cor 11.2; Eph 5.25; Rev 19.7; 21.9), and Rev 19.9 speaks of the wedding feast of the Lamb. By the time John's Gospel came to be written, around A.D. 90, Jesus of Nazareth was known to all his followers, and accepted by them, as the bridegroom, the King's Son.

When we recall that the bridegroom of Israel expected at the end of time is always Yahweh, never the Messiah, it becomes evident that in the Cana story, on the sixth day of the First Week, the evangelist is subtly (not yet overtly) presenting the Word made flesh as the bridegroom standing at the threshold, come to claim his bride, the people of Israel. Compare Jn 1.11: 'He came to what was his own'. Instinctively, one thinks also of Rev 3.20—'Behold, I am standing at the door, and knocking!' (and compare Jn 3.29)—not that Jesus is the bridegroom-in-the-Cana-story, whom he saves from embarrassment; but in another sense, it *is* Jesus who is envisaged as the true bridegroom, for it was he who had been keeping the best wine until that day.[54]

---

[52] *De Somniis* II xxxvii 249 (Loeb V 554-55).

[53] Unless one reads νυμφών (א B* L 00138. 892. 1010. *pc*) rather than γάμος in Mt 22.10: but see NA[27] for the textual evidence on that text.

[54] The motif of Jesus as the bridegroom and that of new wine as a metaphor for his new doctrine are juxtaposed in all three Synoptics (Mt 9.14-17 ‖ Mk 2.22 ‖ Lk 5.33-39). There the mention of 'new wine' 'occurs in a context which refers to the shattering effect of His impact upon existing institutions' (Dodd, *Interpretation*, 298; pp. 297-300 are very important, especially for the cross-references to Philo).

Seen against this background, the account of the wedding at Cana is a symbolic narrative about realized eschatology. It was only natural that as the Church developed, the metaphor of drinking the water of wisdom should be applied to the teaching of Jesus, as it had formerly been applied to the teaching of the Old Covenant (Sir 15.3). That the metaphor was early established in Christian catechesis is clear from 1 Cor 10.4, and it is a major motif in the Fourth Gospel (→ Jn 4.13-14; 7.37-38). The same theme recurs in Rev 7.17; 21.6; 22.1, 17 where we read of drinking from 'the springs of the water of life'.

Since wine too was in the OT a symbol of divine wisdom (see above), when the evangelist wished to make a comparison between the teaching of the Old and of the New Covenant, both God-given, both life-giving, yet essentially different, it was perhaps natural for him to think in terms of the contrast between water and wine. Even the water used for purification among the Jews was (apparently) in short supply, and the wine had run out, yet Jesus did not replace them with something created *ex nihilo*. He ordered the servants to fill those (old?) water-jars from the usual well-spring (ἀντλήσατε). It was via Jewish sources that Jesus' heart-warming wine would be provided. The wine stands for Jesus' teaching, and in particular his interpretation of the Holy Writings of Israel and Judaism (→ 2.7-8, the Targum of Isa 12.3).[55]

This is in fact the interpretation of Origen and of Augustine. Augustine's first homily on this text begins by observing that every year rain-water is turned into wine, and on a far grander scale than at Cana, yet nobody marvels, simply because it happens all the time. Augustine then writes: 'excepto miraculo, aliquid in ipso facto mysterii et sacramenti latet' (*Tract.* 8.3), a sentence which may be translated as 'setting aside the miracle, some hidden, some secret and symbolic meaning lies concealed in what was actually done'. He expounds this meaning in the following homily, beginning with the principle 'bonum vinum Christus servavit usque adhuc, id est, evangelium suum' (*Tract.* 9.2). The writings of the OT, read without Christian understanding, were like water (2 Cor 3.14-16), but when interpreted by the risen Lord (Lk 24.13-47) became like wine. 'Mutavit ergo aquam in vinum Dominus noster Iesus Christus, et sapit quod non sapiebat, inebriat quod non inebriabat.' 'Our Lord Jesus Christ changed the water into wine, and what previously had no taste began to have a taste, what before did not intoxicate became intoxicating' (*Tract.* 9.5). Origen's commentary on Jn 2.1-11 is, unfortunately, not extant, but other texts show that this was his interpretation too.[56]

---

[55] Braun, *Jean le théologien*, II 198-99 (and compare the entire volume); III 80-81; Boismard, from *Du baptême à Cana* (1956) onwards.

[56] At his first visit to Cana, Jesus 'brings us joy…and gives us to drink of the wine that proceeds from His power, which was water when it was drawn, but became wine when Jesus transformed it. And truly before Jesus the Scripture was water, but from the time of Jesus it has become wine to us' (Origen, *In Ioannem* XIII.62 cited in Dodd, *Interpretation*, 299 fn. 2 = GCS 10:294[30]-295[1] = fn. 438 in the *SC* edition). There is a

The canonical text itself contains some suasive evidence that it was intended to be read as a symbolic narrative. The first indication is to be found in the way the central fact of the narrative, the discovery that water has become wine, is presented. The chief steward alone tastes the water, and one sip leads him to utter his remark.[57] Further, it is only when the drink is tasted that it is found to have been turned into wine; was there no visible change in colour, no fragrance of a bouquet? Lastly, there is no hint that anyone other than the chief steward touched the drink; and the text clearly reads: 'when he had tasted *the water* (become wine)'.

οἶνον γεγενημένον. Unless these crucial words are taken as declaring a physical change of water into wine, the commentator has to explain what they are meant to signify, and why they were inserted. One may suggest that this very phrase οἶνον γεγενημένον contains a second clue indicating that this story was intended to bear a symbolic meaning. In Jn 6.52, we read that the Jews began to debate among themselves, saying 'How can this man give us his flesh to eat?' The Gospel does not tell us that Jesus then explained that his words were not meant to be taken literally; on the contrary, it boldly asserts that Jesus at once added 'and drink my blood' (6.53). Is it not possible that when the Cana story was included in the Gospel, the words 'which had become wine' were inserted for the benefit of those who would otherwise have been mystified by the remark of the chief steward, wondering why he had spoken in so enigmatic a manner about the water he had just tasted? By inserting οἶνον γεγενημένον (2.9), the evangelist (or the final redactor) sought to anticipate any misunderstanding, judging that the presence of these two words would lead people to ask quite seriously what was meant by speaking of water that had become wine. After all, Luke wrote that Jesus had promised his disciples that they would eat and drink at his table in his kingdom (Lk 22.30), but no one interprets these words as an assurance that they would one day share together gourmet meals with vintage wines in a royal palace. The writer of the Fourth Gospel might reasonably have judged that, given the clue of οἶνον γεγενημένον, any reader would recognize that the words of the steward contained a hidden meaning, and embodied a truth more profound than the speaker realized or intended (compare Jn 11.51).

Was this story of the wedding at Cana simply made up for kerygmatic or for catechetical purposes? Several authors have claimed to have detected in it an earlier, pre-Johannine, source which was subsequently

similar text in Frag. 74 *In Ioannem* = GCS 10:541[26-28], where Origen points to the link between this gift at Cana and the restoration of good order in the Father's house; see also *In Cant.* 1 = GCS 33:94-95. Other patristic texts in a similar vein are presented by Smitmans, 217-24.

[57] γεύεσθαι is often used of a small quantity. Compare the comment above on Jn 2.7-8: Abraham's servant Eliezer requested only 'one mouthful' of water from Rebecca's newly filled pitcher (Midrash Rabbah).

edited by the evangelist when it was incorporated in the gospel.[58] Even if such a source existed, one must still ask whether the Gospel narrative can plausibly claim any historical credibility.

The comment above on Jn 2.12 suggested that perhaps some members of 'the Master's' family in Kaukab (the δεσπόσυνοι) could recall that Jesus had once attended a wedding at Cana at which the wine had run out; that at his suggestion, water had been served in place of the wine; and that the steward in charge of the feast, when he tasted this water, said, perhaps as a witticism, perhaps as a sagacious comment, 'You have kept the best wine until now'. Could not the family recollection of an event like this lie at the origin of the gospel story?

The wedding was placed on the sixth day of the First Week of Jesus' ministry (→ 2.1). Now, though the Gospel does not say that Jesus gave any teaching on this occasion, presumably he was not entirely silent, and it is not far-fetched to suggest that, if he spoke, he said something about the wedding. In that case, might he not have spoken about the institution of marriage (Gen 1–2), about Hosea's profound meditation on marriage as a symbol of God's love, and about God's promise to restore the broken bonds of love even with Samaria and her daughters (Hos 14.4-7; Ezek 16.53-55)? 'As the bridegroom rejoices over the bride, so shall your God rejoice over you' (Isa 62.5). The δεσπόσυνοι of Kaukab would have been unlikely to forget the occasion.

The evangelist is therefore declaring that Jesus on this occasion at Cana spoke in a manner which was, in comparison with the most wholesome water of wisdom found in Jewish teaching, even more attractive, the choicest wine. That is to say, Jesus at Cana began to instruct his disciples in the understanding of Holy Scripture (→ Jn 1.39), an action which points to the correct understanding of the later σημεῖα (→ 2.11, Origen). It is no accident that the final 'I am' saying in this Gospel is 'I am the true vine' (15.1; compare Sir 24.17, 19, 21).[59] It serves as a reminder of the first sign at Cana, the 'inauguration of the signs', and represents yet another *inclusio*. Jesus alone is the source of life-giving wisdom.

It only remains to ask why the evangelist put this narrative here, and his use of the word γύναι provides the clue. Genesis 1.27-28 places the world's first wedding on the sixth day of the First Week of creation. The Cana episode, on the sixth day of the First Week of Jesus' ministry, spells Jesus' departure from his family to undertake his life-work: hence γύναι, not 'mother' (→ 2.4). She who was his biological mother has fulfilled her role of bearing him and rearing him. So has Judaism. It is she who now says to him 'They have no wine', words which may connote for the thoughtful reader, and especially for the Jewish Christian after the Fall of

---

[58] And the various efforts to reconstruct that source do, to an unusual degree, converge. See Excursus VII, 'A Literary Source of John 2.1-11?'

[59] Hengel, 100.

Jerusalem in A.D. 70, that the people of Israel are no longer able to celebrate worthily and joyfully their marriage to their God ($\rightarrow$ 2.20).

But on the sixth day of the Final Week of Jesus' life, when all is accomplished, 'the mother of Jesus', this same Daughter[60] of Zion, will be honoured with a new role, as will Jesus' Jewish disciples (see 19.25-27). On that day there will be another wedding, a wedding of truly cosmic importance, its bride a new Jerusalem with citizens from all the nations of the world (Isa 60–62), the wedding of the Lamb (Rev 19.6-9; 21.1-4).

---

[60] Note the upper case initial.

A LITERARY SOURCE FOR JOHN 2.1-11?

Of the many attempts to distinguish in the Fourth Gospel different strata, most have dealt with the whole Gospel or with a large section of it. This Excursus is concerned only with Jn 2.1-11, and is offered simply as an example of what might be done in detecting a literary source, without any great confidence in its verisimilitude. It is a revised version of what was printed in *The Mother of Jesus* in 1975, pp. 462-66.

Before Bultmann, M. Dibelius suggested that Jn 2.4b, at least part of v. 5 and v. 11 were added by the Evangelist[1]; similarly K. L. Schmidt, who contended that vv. 3, 4 and 11 betray the touch of the evangelist.[2] It was Bultmann's commentary (1941) which made the quest fashionable. He maintained that the evangelist added (1) the phrase 'on the third day' in v. 3; (2) the words in 9b, 'and he did not know where it came from, but the waiters knew, they who had drawn the water'; (3) the main part of v. 11, 'and he manifested his glory and [they] believed in him', 'his disciples' being perhaps an addition by a later editor. It is strange that Bultmann does not see any Johannine addition in vv. 4-5.

Schnackenburg thinks that the mention of Jesus' hour in v. 4 and the second half of v. 11 betray the hand of the evangelist, but otherwise makes no firm statements about editorial insertions, on the ground that evidence is lacking. C. K. Barrett and R. E. Brown too do not commit themselves at all in their commentaries. But the seed sown by Bultmann spread.

Since 1970 R. T. Fortna has been perhaps the most diligent seeker in the quest for sources, and in *The Fourth Gospel and its Predecessor*, Cambridge, 1989, p. 53, he offers an analysis of the Cana story. He considers the following phrases to be editorial insertions:

v. 1:   'and on the third day'—'in Galilee';
v. 3:   from (v. 3) 'to him, They have no wine' as far as v. 5, 'His mother said', so that the text reads 'Jesus' mother said...to the servants';
v. 6:   'in accordance with the Jewish rite of purification';
v. 9:   'and did not know where it came from, but the servants who had drawn the water knew';
v. 11: 'at Cana of Galilee (and he manifested his glory)'.

---

[1] *Die Formgeschichte des Evangeliums*, Tübingen, 1st ed., 1919; 2nd ed., 1933 = 4th ed., 1961, p. 98 = ETr *From Tradition to Gospel*, Cambridge and London, 1971.
[2] 'Die johanneische Character', in *Harnack-Ehrung* (1921), 37-38.

Several others before and after him have also considered vv. 4-5 to be wholly or partly an insertion into an earlier text by the Evangelist. The proposals of Boismard and Lamouille (*Jean*, 101-104) are not dissimilar, but are too complex for summary here.

If one takes as guide the fifty positive literary characteristics proposed by E. Schweizer and E. Ruckstuhl, and the references to this passage in Abbott's *JV* and *JG*, and eliminates whatever these writers judge to be a positive indication of the evangelist's style, the result is the following passage:

1 γάμος ἐγένετο ἐν Κανὰ τῆς Γαλιλαίας, καὶ ἦν ἡ μήτηρ τοῦ Ἰησοῦ ἐκεῖ· 2 ἐκλήθη δὲ καὶ ὁ Ἰησοῦς καὶ οἱ μαθηταὶ αὐτοῦ εἰς τὸν γάμον. 3 καὶ ὑστερήσαντος οἴνου λέγει ἡ μήτηρ τοῦ Ἰησοῦ πρὸς αὐτόν, οἶνον οὐκ ἔχουσιν. [...]

6 ἦσαν δὲ ἐκεῖ λίθιναι ὑδρίαι ἓξ κατὰ τὸν καθαρισμὸν τῶν Ἰουδαίων κείμεναι, χωροῦσαι ἀνὰ μετρητὰς δύο ἢ τρεῖς. 7 λέγει [τοῖς διακόνοις] ὁ Ἰησοῦς, γεμίσατε τὰς ὑδρίας ὕδατος. καὶ ἐγέμισαν αὐτὰς ἕως ἄνω. 8 καὶ λέγει αὐτοῖς, ἀντλήσατε νῦν καὶ φέρετε τῷ ἀρχιτρικλίνῳ· οἱ δὲ ἤνεγκαν.

9 ὡς δὲ ἐγεύσατο ὁ ἀρχιτρίκλινος τὸ ὕδωρ [...] φωνεῖ τὸν νυμφίον [...] 10 καὶ λέγει αὐτῷ, πᾶς ἄνθρωπος πρῶτον τὸν καλὸν οἶνον τίθησιν καὶ ὅταν μεθυσθῶσιν τὸν ἐλάσσω·

σὺ τετήρηκας τὸν καλὸν οἶνον ἕως ἄρτι.

11 ταύτην ἐποίησεν ἀρχὴν τῶν σημείων ὁ Ἰησοῦς ἐν Κανὰ τῆς Γαλιλαίας.

In this text, the following words of the Gospel text have been left out.

(1) τῇ ἡμέρᾳ τῇ τρίτῃ. The reduplication of the article after the noun and before the adjective is mainly a Johannine usage (*JG* 1982-86).

(2) γύναι. Only in Jn 2.4 and 19.26 does Jesus address Mary as 'Woman'.

(3) Verses 4-5. οὔπω occurs twice in Matthew, five times in Mark, once in Luke, and thirteen times in John. It is used of Jesus' 'hour' in 7.30 and 8.20, of his 'time' in 7.6 and of his Ascension in 20.17. Contrast 13.1 and 17.1. See *JV* 1719, 1728.

(4) ὅ τι ἂν λέγῃ. (ἐ)άν τις occurs 19 times in the Synoptics, 24 times in John, four times in 1 John, and only twice in the rest of the NT.

(5) οἶνον γεγενημένον. The use of a perfect participle for a very recent happening is typical of John: cf. 5.10; 6.13 etc (*JG* 2506*a*). It is also typical of him to let the reader into the secret about the sense of a story: cf. Jn 2.21 (also *JG* 2016-18).

(6) οὐκ ᾔδει πόθεν ἐστίν, οἱ δὲ διάκονοι ᾔδεισαν. Chiasmus: (see *JG* 2554-57). οἱ ἠντληκότες τὸ ὕδωρ in apposition, but probably corrective, meaning 'Well, not exactly *all* the waiters, only those who had drawn the water'. For a similar construction see Jn 11.45, and for a forceful corrective, 4.2. Compare *JG* 1939. ὁ ἀρχιτρίκλινος is inserted at the end of v. 9 for clarity.

(7) καὶ ἐφανέρωσεν τὴν δόξαν αὐτοῦ, καὶ ἐπίστευσαν εἰς αὐτὸν οἱ μαθηταὶ αὐτοῦ. Except for οἱ μαθηταὶ αὐτοῦ, all these expressions are characteristic of John.

III

A NEW JERUSALEM

2.13–4.54

The hope of a New Jerusalem was central to the faith of Judaism, especially in the years between A.D. 70 and 100,[1] when the Fourth Gospel was taking its final form. The next part of the Gospel is interpreted in the light of this Jewish conviction about the certainty of God's restoring Jerusalem, and it has been divided into two sections, unequal in length. The first (Jn 2.13-25) speaks about the New Temple, while the second (Jn 3–4) contains the evangelist's vision of the new order in the New Jerusalem. For the sub-division of this second section, see the introduction to chs. 3–4.

A. THE NEW TEMPLE (2.13-22)

The Synoptics contain a similar story, which they place in the final week of Jesus' earthly life—Matthew and Luke on the day of his entry into Jerusalem (Mt 21.12-17 ‖ Lk 19.41-46), Mark on the day after it (Mk 11.15-17; note, in v. 12, τῇ ἐπαύριον). Their narratives, interpreted by reference to Mal 3.1-4 and Zech 14.21, are customarily entitled 'The Cleansing of the Temple'. From patristic times until around 1900, scholars discussed whether the accounts in the four Gospels referred to one and the same or to two different events, mainly because John places the incident close to a Passover two years before Jesus' death (Jn 2.13), but also because of differences in the descriptions of the expulsion, and in the sayings ascribed to Jesus.[2]

---

[1] See Schürer I 521-28, particularly p. 527: 'The Apocalypse of Baruch [= 2 Baruch] and *4 Ezra*, which originated at this time, provide a vivid and authentic explanation of the religious mood prevailing in the first decades after the destruction of the Holy City.' Such hope lived on until Hadrian's definitive victory over Bar Kokhba in A.D. 135.

[2] Chrysostom preferred to see two separate events ('probably': εἰκός, *In Matthaeum* Hom. 67.1), and Augustine had no doubts ('manifestum est non semel sed iterum', *De consensu evangelistarum* II 67 129). This view was accepted by Aquinas, Calvin, Maldonatus ('probably'), and many others down to Godet (1864), Westcott (1884),

Few exegetes now maintain that the variations in the Gospel accounts are evidence of two different incidents, because there is general agreement that in all four Gospels the order of the narratives is often determined not by the chronological sequence of events in Jesus' life, but by other, literary, considerations. In the Synoptic tradition Jesus is presented as making but one visit to Jerusalem during his public ministry; the story about the Temple therefore has to be placed there, at the end. Yet according to Mark, when two witnesses at his trial swore they had heard Jesus saying that he would destroy the Temple, 'their evidence did not agree' (14.57-59). A clue to the interpretation of this text may be found in the Mishnah, which states that 'They used to prove witnesses with seven inquiries: In what week of years? In what year? In what month? On what date in the month? On what day? In what hour? In what place?' (*Sanhedrin* 5.1). Mark 14.59 therefore seems to carry the implication that the episode happened some considerable time before the trial of Jesus, for there would hardly have been a problem in finding two witnesses had the offending statement been made only three or four days previously. It is impossible to determine even an approximate date.

It will facilitate the exegesis to examine first the nomenclature used for 'the Temple'. In Jn 2.13-22, nearly all the classical English versions (AV = KJV RV RSV NRSV NEB) translate both ἱερόν (vv. 14, 15) and ναός (vv. 19, 20, 21) as *temple*.[3] Only a few differentiate. For ἱερόν, here and elsewhere in the NT, NIV gives *Temple courts*, and NAB, *Temple area*; at Jn 2.14, REB gives *Temple precincts*. For ναός, RV[mg] and JB give *sanctuary*, but NJB reverts to *Temple*. Why this convention of using one English term for the two distinct Greek nouns?

ἱερόν designates 'the temple at Jerusalem, including the whole temple precinct, with its buildings, courts etc.' (BDAG). In this sense it occurs 70 times in the NT (the only instance of any other reference is at Acts 19.27). ναός, in its proper sense, denotes a building which is considered as the dwelling place (√ ναίω) of a god. It is used in this sense of the Temple building in Jerusalem (as distinct from the surrounding area) in Lk 1.9, 21, 22; in Mt 23.35; in Mt 27:51 ‖ Mk 15.38 ‖ Lk 23.45 (τὸ καταπέτασμα τοῦ ναοῦ); and also by Josephus, in the *War* V v 4 = 207, 209, 211 and in *Ant*. XV xi 3 = 391. In Josephus, however, the word ναός can also designate the whole Temple area (*War* VI v 3 = 293; *Apion* II ix 119), and in Mt 27.5, it must refer to the precincts, not the building. Only the context can determine its precise reference. Thus it is uncertain whether in Mt 23.16, 17 and 21 ναός denotes the building alone (it probably does), or the area. Similarly, it is not possible to determine whether the saying about destroying the Temple refers to the central

---

Knabenbauer (1898) and Zahn (1908). From 1900 onwards, it has been increasingly accepted that there was only one such incident; thus Holtzmann (1901) and Loisy (1903). V. Taylor, *Mark*, 461-62, gives a good survey of the discussion from 1900 to 1950.

[3] The Vulgate also, and the Nova Vulgata, render both Greek terms by *templum*. Luther too renders both as *Tempel*.

building alone or to the entire complex (Mt 26.61; 27.40 ‖ Mk 14.58; 15.29); and the question is clearly irrelevant.[4]

In the Pauline literature, Christians themselves are said to be a ναὸς θεοῦ, a dwelling-place of God (1 Cor 3.16, 17; 2 Cor 6.16), their bodies a temple of the Holy Spirit, ναὸς τοῦ ἁγίου πνεύματος (1 Cor 6.19). The metaphor is part and parcel of the doctrine of the divine indwelling, expressed also by the verbs οἰκεῖν (Rom 8.9, 11; 1 Cor 3.16), ἐνοικεῖν (Rom 8.11; 2 Tim 1.14, of the Spirit; Col 3.16, of the Word of Christ), and κατοικεῖν (Eph 3.17, of Christ dwelling by faith in hearts). If all the fullness of the Godhead dwells in Christ Jesus (Col 1.19; 2.9), and if he and the Holy Spirit dwell in human hearts, then the community of believers can truly be called a temple of God (see Eph 2.21-22). It is because of this doctrine that the classical English versions mentioned above translate ναός in these Pauline passages as *temple*, to affirm the presence of God dwelling (√ ναίω) in the heart; and for this same reason the rendering *temple* has been retained for ναός in Jn 2.19, 20, 21, to stress that these texts refer to God's dwelling-place rather than to a humanly created sanctuary.[5]

2.13 The Jewish Passover was near, and Jesus went up to Jerusalem. [14] In the Temple he found dealers in cattle and sheep and pigeons, and money-changers sitting there. [15] Making a little whip out of cords, he drove them all out of the Temple (the sheep and the cattle as well), and as for the money-dealers, he spilled their small change and overturned their counters. [16] Then he said to those who were selling pigeons, 'Take these things away from here, and stop making my Father's house into a house of trade.' [17] His disciples recalled that it was written, 'Zeal for your house will consume me.'

[18] The Jews therefore said to him by way of rejoinder, 'What sign have you to show us for doing these things?' [19] Jesus in reply said to them, 'Destroy this temple, and within three days I shall raise it up.' [20] The Jews then said, 'This

[4] For further detail on ἱερόν see *TWNT* III 230-47 (G. Schrenk). The LXX translators preferred to designate the Temple at Jerusalem as οἶκος ἅγιος, τοῦ θεοῦ, τοῦ κυρίου, ναὸς ἅγιος, rather than ἱερόν, possibly because the latter term was regularly employed to denote pagan temples (232[21-30]). In the LXX translations, the only instances of ἱερόν with reference to Jerusalem occur in Ezek 45.19 (a mistranslation); 1 Paral 9.27; 29.4; and 2 Paral 6.13 (Hebrew missing). Yet ἱερόν is, by contrast, common in those historical books of the LXX which were written in Greek, 1 Esdras and 1–4 Maccabees (232[33]-233[3]; see HR). For the usage in Josephus and Philo, see *TWNT* III 233-34. On ναός, see *TWNT* IV 884-95 (O. Michel). - τὸ τέμενος, regular in Classical Greek to denote a piece of land dedicated to a god, is rare in the LXX (10-12 times), and refers most often to a pagan temple: e.g. 1 Macc 1.47; 5.43, 44; 2 Macc 1.15; 10.2; 11.3 (HR). It is not found in the NT.

[5] Most recent translators concur. - ναός in Jn 2 is rendered *sanctuary* by John Lingard (1836), Richard Weymouth (1903), James Moffatt (1913) and James Kleist (1954); and as *holy place* by Charles K. Williams (1952). But C. C. Torrey (1933), R. A. Knox (1946), J. B. Phillips (1960), the Good News Bible = TEV (1966), the Translators' NT (1973) and William Barclay (1968), all retain *temple* (like the classical versions listed above).

temple has been under construction for forty-six years, and you are going to raise it up in three days?' [21] He, however, had been speaking about the temple of his body. [22] So it was that, after he was raised from the dead, his disciples recalled that he had said this, and came to believe the Scripture and the word that Jesus had spoken.

13. ἐγγὺς ἦν (of time) recurs, always with reference to a Jewish feast, in Jn 6.4; 7.2; 11.55. **τὸ πάσχα τῶν Ἰουδαίων.** The evangelist evidently thinks of the Jews as a religious group distinct from Christians. It was a long time since the followers of Jesus had shared in the Jewish Passover (compare 1 Cor 5.7, '*our* Passover'), and some prospective readers might even have needed to be informed that πάσχα was the name of a Jewish feast (Jn 6.4; 11.55). **καὶ ἀνέβη εἰς Ἱεροσόλυμα ὁ Ἰησοῦς.** From almost anywhere in Palestine (and certainly from Capernaum, 2.12) one *goes up* to Jerusalem, so that ἀναβαίνειν is virtually a technical term for a pilgrimage to the Holy City (5.1; 7.8, 10; 11.55; 12.20).

14. καὶ εὗρεν[6] ἐν τῷ ἱερῷ τοὺς πωλοῦντας. John alone mentions the sale of cattle and sheep, a fact which in the past contributed to the conviction that Jesus intervened on two occasions in the Temple.

βόας. *Cattle* (NEB REB JB NJB NIV NRSV) is better than *oxen* (AV= KJV RV RSV), since *oxen* might suggest bulls for sacrifice. In fact, a bull for sacrifice was rarely required—only for a sin of the high priest bringing guilt on the entire people (Lev 4.3-12; compare 16.6, 11) or for a sin of the whole people (4.13-21), but not for a sin even by the (civil) ruler (4.23). On feast days, and only on feast days, two bulls were offered in the Temple (e.g. on each of the seven days of Passover, Num 28.16-25): see Schürer II 308. These rules hardly suggest that large numbers of oxen customarily stood corralled waiting to be purchased for sacrifice. The picture is rather of a general cattle-market with beasts for sale, for such cattle-marts were held in the Temple court from time to time. See SB I 851-52 and J. Jeremias, *Jerusalem*, 48-49, for the primary references. **πρόβατα** originally denoted any small four-footed animals, as distinct from fowl, but in Attic Greek and thereafter, it refers predominantly to *sheep*. Here in 2.14 it could include goats as well, particularly since they too were permissible for the Passover sacrifice (Exod 12.5). For detail, see LSJ; BDAG; *TWNT* VI 688-92. **περιστεράς.** *Doves* or *pigeons* were stipulated as sin-offerings for those unable to afford a lamb (Lev 5.7, and compare 5.11).

καὶ τοὺς κερματιστὰς καθημένους. κερματιστής (= *money-changer*), a *hapax legomenon* in the NT, is found only here and in literature dependent upon it (MM). Yet as Greek its formation is impeccable, and its presence here so close to κολλυβιστής (v. 15) may indicate the hand of an editor seeking an elegant variation. All money used in the Temple had to be of Tyrian currency, that normally used in commerce. At

---

[6] The form without the augment is normal in the Koine: see BDF 67 (1).

this epoch it was somewhat lighter than the official Roman currency, which stood at par with the Attic standard coinage. Therefore, given the high prices always obtaining in Jerusalem, supervised money changers were needed to ensure that pilgrims should receive a proper exchange rate for their foreign currency. See Schürer II 272 fn. 54; 66-67 fn. 210; J. Jeremias, *Jerusalem*, 33, 121.

15. καὶ ποιήσας φραγέλλιον ἐκ σχοινίων. Just as John alone mentions cattle and sheep, so he alone mentions the little whip made out of cords to drive out the animals. φραγέλλιον, a *hapax legomenon* in the NT, is a loanword from the Latin *flagellum*, with dissimilation from λ to ρ, as in the vulgar Latin *fragellum*: see MHT II 103, 396; BDF 5 (1b); 41 (2). **πάντας** (masculine), that is, all the traders (*JG* 1929). **τά τε πρόβατα καὶ τοὺς βόας:** τε, with their sheep and cattle *as well*. τε, rare outside Acts, occurs only three times in John, at 2.15; 4.32 and 6.18: see BDF 443 (1). **καὶ τῶν κολλυβιστῶν ἐξέχεεν τὸ κέρμα καὶ τὰς τραπέζας ἀνέτρεψεν.** κολλυβίστης is a *small money-changer* (LSJ; MM) as distinct from a big banker (τραπεζίτης, see LSJ). Translate: *and as for the money-dealers, he spilled their small change and overturned their counters.*[7]

16. καὶ τοῖς τὰς περιστερὰς πωλοῦσιν εἶπεν, ἄρατε ταῦτα ἐντεῦθεν. The pigeon-sellers are simply bidden to take their trade outside, away from the Temple, and to *stop making* (**μή** with the present imperative **ποιεῖτε**) *the house of my Father a house of trade*. (μὴ ποιεῖτε) **τὸν οἶκον τοῦ πατρός μου οἶκον ἐμπορίου.** In the Synoptic tradition, Jesus justifies his actions by citing Isa 56.7 ('My house shall be called a house of prayer') and Jer 7.11 (not 'a den of thieves'). In John, the thought is sharpened to *my Father's house*, the first occasion in this Gospel that Jesus speaks of '*my* Father'. The introduction of this term into this narrative presents it as a subtle hint to the onlookers[8] (and a very clear reminder to John's readers) of the source of the authority that Jesus has for his action. In John, we have too, instead of the text from Jeremiah, *a house of trade*, an implicit reference to the final verse of Zechariah (14.21), where the word translated *Canaanite* in older versions (AV = KJV RV) is now normally given its alternative meaning, *trader* (RSV NEB: see KBR II 485-86). The last chapter of Zechariah foresees the ingathering of all the righteous Gentiles to worship with Israel in Jerusalem, and its final verse proclaims that everything in the Temple shall be sacred and yet freely available to any person of any race who seeks to do service to the Lord.

17. The verb **ἐμνήσθησαν** occurs only three times in John (2.17, 22; 12.16), and always in this form, the first aorist of μιμνήσκεσθαι. This is

---

[7] The variant readings for this verse in NA²⁷ do not affect the meaning.

[8] 'Subtle to the onlookers' in the story because, at least in theory, the term might have been used by any faithful Jew.

a deponent and reflexive verb meaning *to recall to mind* (BDAG),[9] and its
subject is always **οἱ μαθηταὶ αὐτοῦ**, *his disciples.*[10] The first two texts
occur at the start of Jesus' public ministry, the third at its close. If the
interpretation given of the Cana episode in 2.1-12 is correct, the use of
ἐμνήσθησαν here may be an early hint to the reader to be on the watch
for further OT testimonies. **ὅτι γεγραμμένον ἐστίν.** Matthew, when
he wishes to cite Scripture, always uses γέγραπται (9 times), as does
Mark (7 times); Luke uses both γέγραπται (9 times) and γεγραμμένον
(5 times). John uses γέγραπται of Holy Scripture only once (8.17);
more often (7t.) he uses the periphrastic perfect participle γεγραμμένον
with εἶναι (as here) and in 6.31, 45; 10.34; 12.14, 16; 15.25. There is no
difference in meaning between the two formulas, but the periphrastic
construction may indicate an author accustomed to thinking in Aramaic:
compare 19.19, 20; 20.30, and see MHT III 87-89; BDF 352.

ὁ ζῆλος τοῦ οἴκου σου καταφάγεταί με. A small number of
witnesses (Tatian, φ, lat syr boh geo Eusebius) read κατεφάγεν, the
reading in the LXX.[11] The Gospel has altered the aorist of the LXX Ps
68.10 to a future, *will eat me up, will devour me.* Westcott was convinced
that the text as cited refers to Jesus' burning zeal for the holiness of
God's house, and not to his future Passion; Loisy too rejects any suggestion that the first and direct reference is to Jesus' future sufferings.
Bultmann, by contrast, interprets the verb as meaning that Jesus' zeal for
the house of God will cost him his life;[12] similarly Schnackenburg, who
refers to 'the mortal hatred of the "Jews" which is soon to be aroused (cf.
5.16, 18)'. Brown stresses that the evangelist must have had in mind the
immediate context of the Psalm-verse cited, where the psalmist in the
preceding verse speaks of alienation from his blood-brothers and his
family (Ps 69 [LXX 68] 8-9); and he suggests that the alteration of the
LXX κατεφάγεν to the future tense (in Jn 2.17) may be a pointer
towards the Passion. Given that Ps 69 is quoted in Acts 1.20; Rom 11.9-
10; 15.3, and is very probably envisaged in Jn 15.25; 19.28, the evangelist may well have intended to incorporate here a covert reference to
Jesus' suffering (→ 2.22). Indeed, when one recalls the Synoptic insis-
tence that Jesus taught his disciples about his inevitable destiny (δεῖ in
Mk 10.45 ‖s), may he not have conversed with them before his Passion
about the perennial relevance of Ps 69?

**18. ἀπεκρίθησαν οὖν οἱ 'Ιουδαῖοι καὶ εἶπαν αὐτῷ, τί σημεῖον
δεικνύεις ἡμῖν ὅτι ταῦτα ποιεῖς;** In the Synoptic Gospels, it is 'the
high priests, the scribes and the elders' who ask 'by what authority' Jesus

---

[9] As distinct from μνημονεύειν, *to keep in mind, to retain in the memory,* Jn 15.20;
16.4, 21.

[10] The fact that the disciples have not been mentioned earlier in this pericope is not
proof that v. 17 is a later insertion into an earlier source.

[11] Rahlfs is surely right in judging (LXX II, apparatus) that καταφαγεται at Ps 68.10
in B and א stems from Jn 2.17.

[12] Compare the NEB '…will destroy me'; the REB reverts to 'will consume me'.

has acted (Mt 21.23 ‖ Mk 11.27-28 ‖ Lk 20.1-2), and to whom Jesus retorts, inquiring by what authority the Baptist had exercised his ministry. The Fourth Gospel presents the same challenge to Jesus, but reworded as a request for a *sign*, and ascribed not to the leaders of the people, but to the Jews in general. It is not unreasonable to infer that the sign requested will be given to the Jews as a whole.

19. λύσατε. John, alone of the Gospels, employs the simplex λύειν, which here does not differ in meaning from καταλύειν. As in Classical Greek, the imperative may simply be the equivalent of a concessive clause (BDF 387 [2]; Robertson 948-49):[13] in this context, *even though you destroy...* Note the contrast with the allegation at Jesus' trial before the Sanhedrin, according to Mt 26.61 ‖ Mk 14.58. There, and also at Mt 27.40 ‖ Mk 15.29, it is Jesus who, it is alleged, threatens to destroy the Temple; here in John, the text reads λύσατε, that is, *suppose you* (the Jews) *destroy...*[14] In comparison with the Synoptic phrasing, the Johannine wording makes it easier to construe **τὸν ναὸν τοῦτον** as referring in some way to Jesus' physical body, the interpretation which v. 21 seems to call for.[15] In support of this view, it is sometimes suggested that Jesus might have pointed to his body; but of such a gesture, there is no hint in the text. Yet whether the words τὸν ναὸν τοῦτον refer to Jesus' body or to the Jewish Temple, the Gospels agree that Jesus alone will rebuild it (οἰκοδομεῖν, Matthew, Mark) or raise it up (ἐγείρειν, John). And indeed, Mark opens the door to a deeper understanding of these words by distinguishing between τὸν ναὸν τοῦτον τὸν χειρο-ποίητον and ἄλλον ἀχειροποίητον (14.58).

καὶ ἐν τρισὶν ἡμέραις. ἐν with the dative may express either the point or the duration of time; here, it clearly denotes duration, *within three days* (BDF 200 [2]).[16] Yet the phrase ἐν τρισὶν ἡμέραις must not be understood as meaning 'within 72 hours'; rather, it is a regular Semitic idiom signifying 'within a very short, but undefined, time' (compare Hos 6.2; Lk 13.32).[17]

ἐγερῶ. The primary sense of ἐγείρειν is *to awake someone from sleep* (Mt 8.25; Acts 12.7), from which it comes to mean *to raise someone from the sleep of death*, that is, *actively to raise someone from the dead* (Jn 12.1, 9, 17): in this last sense it is mostly used of Jesus' Resurrection (texts are listed in BDAG). But ἐγείρειν can also mean *to raise up, erect or restore a building*. It is so used of the post-exilic

[13] Compare Sophocles, *Antigone* 1037, 1168.

[14] Greek, unlike English, does not employ the second person plural as an indefinite pronoun. Such a usage is not even mentioned in BDF 130, 280-81, or Robertson 678, 683. λύσατε must refer to the Jews.

[15] Lindars 144 (surprisingly) rejects the suggestion that v. 19 may include a reference to anything more than the fact of Jesus' bodily Resurrection.

[16] Abbott (*JG* 2331) contrasts Mt 26.61 ‖ Mk 14.58, διὰ τριῶν ἡμερῶν (omitted by Luke), which he takes to mean *after an interval of three days* (see also *JG* 2715).

[17] 'The idiom is a common Semitic one, and examples in Aramaic are frequent' (M. Black, *Aramaic Approach*, 2nd ed., 151-52 = 3rd ed., 205-206).

Temple in 1 Esd 5.43, of the walls of Jerusalem in Sir 49.13, and of the Temple (ναός) in Josephus (*Ant.* XV xi 3 = 391; XX x 1 = 228); further extra-biblical examples from Hellenistic Greek are listed in BDAG 9. **αὐτόν.** Here, because of the antecedent τοῦτον, the primary reference must be (not to Jesus' physical body but) to the Temple.

20. τεσσεράκοντα καὶ ἓξ ἔτεσιν. According to Josephus, the reconstruction of the Temple began in the eighteenth year of King Herod, 20–19 B.C.;[18] the work on the outer courts took eight years, that on the Temple building itself, eighteen months (*Ant.* XV xi 5-6 = 410–423), and further work continued until A.D. 62–64 (*Ant.* XX ix 7 = 219). Forty-six years from the commencement of the work would bring one to A.D. 27–28, thus dating this first Johannine Passover in A.D. 28, a year which fits exactly with the common opinion that Jesus was crucified in A.D. 30. ἔτεσιν. Where Classical Greek uses the accusative to express duration of time, the Koine uses either the accusative or the dative (BDF 161 [2]; 201; compare the variant readings at Jn 14.9). *Pace* BDF 200 (2), it would seem wiser to classify this dative in 2.20 as denoting the extent of time already involved rather than the period within which something had been accomplished. 'It has taken forty-six years to build this temple' (RSV NEB) could be taken to mean that the work had been completed, though this is not necessarily implied by the aorist **οἰκοδομήθη**:[19] compare Ezra [LXX, 2 Esdras] 5.16, ἀπὸ τότε ἕως τοῦ νῦν ᾠκοδομήθη καὶ οὐκ ἐτελέσθη. The NRSV corresponds better with the historical context, and with the testimony of Josephus: 'This temple has been under construction for forty-six years'. **ὁ ναὸς οὗτος** should therefore here be taken as denoting the whole complex of Temple buildings whose reconstruction had begun under Herod the Great.[20]

---

[18] In the *War* I xxi 1 = 401, Josephus writes that work began in the fifteenth year of Herod's reign. 'Both statements point to the same year 20–19 B.C., for Herod the Great was appointed King of Judaea in 40 B.C. but only succeeded in gaining possession of his kingdom in 37 B.C. with the conquest of Jerusalem. There were therefore two methods of reckoning the chronology of Herod's reign (*War* I xxxiii 8 = 665; *Ant.* XVII viii 9 = 191) which differed by three years' (J. Jeremias, *Jerusalem*, 22[39]). With this correction in mind, see for further detail Schürer I 292 fn. 12 and 308-309 fn. 71.

[19] The form without the augment is normal in the Koine: see BDF 67 (1).

[20] Origen points out that the 46 years cannot apply to Solomon's Temple unless one starts counting from the fifth year of David's reign in Hebron (two years before he entered Jerusalem!) to the eleventh year of Solomon (1 Kgs 6.38), and adds that there is no clear evidence about the rebuilding under Zerubbabel or the Maccabees (X xxxviii 22 = 254-60). Clement of Alexandria (*Stromata* I xxi = 128,1) and Eusebius also (*Demonstratio evangelica* VIII ii 64 = GCS 23:379; *Eclog. prophetarum* III xlvi = *PG* 22.1179 CD) sought to refer the 46 years to the Second Temple.

Augustine interpreted the number 46 symbolically. In Greek, the letters of ADAM, which represent 1 + 4 + 1 + 40, total 46; and can also represent the four points of the compass, Ἀνατολή, Δύσις, Ἄρκτος, Μεσημβρία. His interpretations, based on Pseudo-Cyprian, *De montibus Sina et Sion* 4 (CSEL 3, 3, pp. 107-109), though long since deplored (Maldonatus), were still taken seriously by H. Vogels, 'Die Tempelreinigung

21. ἐκεῖνος is frequently used by all the evangelists as an adjective, but its use in the singular as a personal pronoun is almost confined to John,[21] and when, outside dialogue, he uses it to express his own words, it carries considerable emphasis (*JG* 2381-82). In this context, the evangelist (or a final editor) may be using ἐκεῖνος as the Pythagoreans did, to refer (after his death) to 'the Master'; ἐκεῖνος would be equivalent to 'He' with an upper case initial (BDAG α [γ], and *JG* 2731). **ἔλεγεν**: here, the imperfect may be rendered *was* or *had been* (speaking); but → v. 22. On *the temple of his body*, see the essay below, pp. 213-16.

22. ὅτε οὖν ἠγέρθη ἐκ νεκρῶν. The passive ἐγείρεσθαι is normal in the NT to speak of Jesus' Resurrection (e.g. Rom 4.25; 6.4, 9, 1 Cor 15 *passim*; BDAG [7], but in John, this passive occurs only here at 2.22 and at 21.14 (contrast ἐγερῶ in v. 17, and 10.18), and may therefore betoken the hand of a final editor. **ἐμνήσθησαν οἱ μαθηταὶ αὐτοῦ,** *his disciples recalled,* → 2.17. **ὅτι τοῦτο ἔλεγεν**: here, the Greek imperfect needs to be rendered by an English pluperfect, *had said* (MHT III 67).

καὶ ἐπίστευσαν τῇ γραφῇ: *came to believe the Scripture,* that is, (πιστεύειν with the dative) *to believe in the truth of the Scripture.* ἡ γραφή occurs 11 times in John, at 2.22; 7.38, 42; 10.35; 13.18; 17.12; 19.24, 28, 36, 37; 20.9 (and its plural at 5.39, ἐραυνᾶτε τὰς γραφάς). In every case except 2.22; 17.12 and 20.9, ἡ γραφή (in the singular) refers to an OT text cited in the context. It is quite plausible that 17.12 refers back to the text already quoted at 13.18; that 20.9 refers to Ps 16.10, cited in Acts 2.27 and 13.35; and consequently that Jn 2.22 also may refer to a specific OT text. In that case, the quotation from Ps 69 in Jn 2.17 should prompt the interpreter to examine first, for v. 22, before any other text, this Ps 69. We find that vv. 15-16 may be applied to Jesus' Resurrection, and that v. 22 is the Scripture envisaged in Jn 19.28-29. Hence 'the Scripture they came to believe in' (2.22) is most probably the promise of Ps 69.36-37, that 'God will save Zion and rebuild the cities of Judah', with which one may compare the prayer of the *Shemoneh 'Esreh* 14 (see below). **καὶ τῷ λόγῳ ὃν εἶπεν ὁ Ἰησοῦς,** that is, the word uttered in Jn 2.19.[2223] λόγος reminds the reader that this is the term regularly used for revelation by God, especially through Jesus (BAG 1 b).

---

und Golgotha', in *BZ* 6 (1962), 102-107 and by J. Daniélou, in *Etudes d'exégèse judéo-chrétienne,* Paris 1966, p. 115.

[21] The two exceptions are at Lk 18.14 and Mk 16.10.

[22] The variant reading ᾧ in the majority of manuscripts (because of the attraction of the relative, BDF 294) makes no difference to the sense, and the text above (ον ειπεν) is found in 𝔓66.76 vid ℵ A B L 050 083 *pc* (see NA27).

THE SIGN PROMISED: JESUS WILL RAISE UP A NEW TEMPLE

The Meaning of σημεῖον in the Fourth Gospel

In the Synoptic Gospels, δύναμις is the usual term for an *act of power*, a *miracle*, done by Jesus, or in the name of Jesus. In this sense, it occurs 10 times: Mt 7.22; 11.20, 21, 24 ‖ Lk 10.13; Mt 13.54, 58 ‖ Mk 6.2, 5; and compare Mk 9.39. In John's Gospel, δύναμις does not occur even once, in any sense.

In the NT as a whole, the second most common term for a miracle is τέρας, meaning *something prodigious, astounding, a preternatural marvel*. The word occurs 16 times, always in the plural, and always in conjunction with σημεῖον, in the phrase σημεῖα καὶ τέρατα (or vice versa). The texts are Mt 24.24 ‖ Mk 13.22; Jn 4.48; Acts 2.19, 22, 43; 4.30; 5.12; 6.8; 7.36; 14.3; 15.12; Rom 15.19; 2 Cor 12.12; 2 Thess 2.9; Heb 2.4. It is striking that in the Acts and in the Epistles, 'signs and wonders' always originate from God, and are evident tokens of his beneficence, whereas the Gospels appear to disapprove of them. In Mt 24.24 ‖ Mk 13.22 they are denounced as the fraudulent tricks of pseudo-Messiahs and false prophets, plausible enough to beguile even God's elect. The solitary reference in John (4.48) reproves those who, unless they *first see signs and wonders*, will not begin to believe.[24]

Other NT words for miracles are παράδοξα (Lk 5.26; frequent in ecclesiastical Greek, but a *hapax legomenon* in the NT); ἔνδοξα (Lk 13.17: *hapax legomenon* in the NT with reference to miracles); and perhaps τὰ θαυμάσια in Mt 21.15 (again, a *hapax legomenon* in the NT). τὸ θαῦμα, so common in ecclesiastical Greek to denote a miracle (*PGL*; see also BDAG 1 b), occurs nowhere in the NT, the Apostolic Fathers (unless one counts the *Martyrdom of Polycarp* XV 1) or the Apologists.

With the sole exception of τέρατα in Jn 4.48, none of the above terms is found in the Fourth Gospel. It is as if the writer was anxious that people should not look upon Jesus as someone renowned for astounding preternatural deeds (4.48; 20.29), but should instead ask themselves what message lies concealed in the often, humanly speaking, incredible events of his life. To refer to these events, John uses two words only, ἔργον (often equated with, or identified with, the works of the Father) and σημεῖον.

ἔργον occurs 17 times in John's Gospel with reference to Jesus' activity, and is the term preferred by Jesus himself: 16 of the references are on his lips, and 7.3 is attributed to his brothers. σημεῖον too occurs 17 times in the Gospel, but unlike ἔργον, it is—perhaps significantly—mostly used by others about Jesus. Only twice is it found on Jesus' lips, at 4.48 and 6.26, in each case in conjunction with a negative, qualifying the verb ἰδεῖν. Of the other 15 occurrences, seven are ascribed to Jews (2.18; 3.2; 6.30; 7.31; 9.16; 10.41; 11.47) and eight belong to the narrator

---

[24] For further detail on the phrase 'signs and wonders', → 4.48.

(2.11, 23; 4.54; 6.2, 14; 12.18, 37, and the final verse, 20.30). In these texts, except for 2.18 (δεικνύεις); 4.48 and 6.26 (ἰδεῖν), σημεῖον is always linked with the verb ποιεῖν, and is usually found in a context relating to faith. The usage both of ἔργον and of σημεῖον is of course due in the end to the decision of the evangelist.

The full significance of σημεῖον in John's Gospel is most easily elucidated by a comparison with its usage in Classical Greek and in the LXX. In ancient Greece, σημεῖον was a general term for any sign, mark or signal (LSJ, *TWNT* VII 202-206), but three usages of the word, from outside the field of religion, are of particular interest as background to the Fourth Gospel. σημεῖον can denote facts or words that supply evidential proof; it can denote, in the Logic of Aristotle, a probable but not completely conclusive argument (= τεκμήριον); and in Stoic and Epicurean philosophy, it can denote the starting-point of a process of reasoning from observable facts to certainty about something which is non-observable. Examples are given in LSJ II 1-3.

In a religious context, the Greeks used σημεῖον to denote atmospheric or meteorological phenomena envisaged as heaven-sent signals or warnings of future events, signals which were themselves usually in need of interpretation (e.g. Plato, *Phaedrus* 244c). Against this background the words σημεῖα and τέρατα were often juxtaposed, and regarded as virtually synonymous. Thus Polybius uses the phrase σημεῖα καὶ τέρατα when castigating the Romans for their superstitious panic at the approach of Hannibal after the battle of Cannae (III 112 [18] 8f.; Diodorus Siculus, when describing an eagle's swooping down upon a pigeon being offered in the temple of Apollo (XVI 27); and Plutarch, to report the superstition of Alexander the Great as he lay dying (*Alexander* 75,1). For further examples, see *TWNT* V II 205[25]-206[12].

The phenomena referred to all represent natural events regarded as symbolic, prefigurative, presages of future happenings; and the general public agreed that skilful interpretation was necessary to discern the exact significance of each portent. The same usage occurs in Jewish writers. Philo regards σημεῖα as virtually equivalent to τέρατα, ὀνείρατα and χρησμοί (*De Aeternitate Mundi* 2); he even writes that God created the sun, moon and stars 'not only to send light upon the earth, but also to give timely signs of coming events (ὅπω σημεῖα μελλόντων προφαίνωσιν)', of which he gives ample illustration (*De Opificio Mundi* XIX 58). Josephus too assures the reader from the outset that he will not fail to record 'the signs and portents' that preceded the taking of Jerusalem (*War* I Preface 11 = 28), a promise that he richly redeems by later relating many alleged portents, such as that a star resembling a sword stood over the city, and a comet continued for a year (VI v 3 = 288-300). Such stories were a conventional feature of the historiography of the age.

At the same time, none of these meteorological or other phenomena are in any technical sense 'miracles', if that term is understood to mean 'beyond the ordinary powers of nature'. Further, in contrast with OT usage, none of the Greek σημεῖα are 'demonstrative signs' by which the divine authority of words spoken by God's messengers is authenticated, for the Greeks had neither a religious doctrine nor a philosophical concept of the Word of God. Consequently, wherever Philo (e.g. *Vita Moysis* I xiv 76, 77; xv = 90-91; xvi 95) or Josephus (e.g. *Ant.* II xii 3, 4 = 274, 276; xiii 1 = 280) use σημεῖον or τέρας to tell of God's authentication of a human messenger, the story is always taken from the LXX. Compare also *Ant.* VIII xiii 6 = 343 (Elijah at Carmel). It is to the LXX, therefore, that one must turn first for the background to the Johannine use of σημεῖον.

The Hebrew noun אוֹת (ʾot) occurs 79 times in the MT, 75 of which are in the LXX translated by σημεῖον, so that the two words, Greek and Hebrew, are, in the OT, as good as synonymous. 39 of these texts occur in the Pentateuch, 19 in Isaiah, Jeremiah and Ezekiel, totals that together represent nearly four-fifths (58) of the 75 occurrences. All these texts about 'signs' refer, without exception, to things or events which are visible to all, but which also disclose, to those who know how to interpret them, some truth about God. The signs vary greatly one from another, and only the context enables one to discern in what sense some material event is 'a sign'. For example, the sun, moon and stars (Gen 1.14) or the rainbow (9.12-13) speak in a quite different manner from the blood of the lamb on the doorposts and lintel (Exod 12.7, 13), or the great deeds at the Exodus (4.1-19; Num 14.11, 22). Utterly different again are the sign of Immanuel (Isa 7.14) and Ezekiel's abstention from mourning (Ezek 24.15-24). Thus signs may be prodigious events indicative of divine action (see *DCH*), but are not necessarily so. Nor are signs of such a nature as to compel human beings to obey God: they can be, and not infrequently are, neglected, even by those who claim to be his servants (Num 14.11, 22; Deut 1.22-46). What these signs of the OT have in common is that they all witness to the fact that God is, in a particular context, addressing a message to those who perceive the sign. Hence to interpret the outwardly observable 'material' signs there is usually some explanatory discourse, some 'word of the Lord'. For further detail on the OT texts see G. von Rad, *Theologie des AT* (1960), II 107-11, 371; *TDOT* I 167-88, especially 176-79 on 'Faith Signs'; *TWNT* VII 209-11 and 217-19; and for the differing contexts in which אוֹת (ʾot) occurs, the *DCH* I 166-68.

Similarly, in the LXX, anything by which God authenticates the word of a prophet is called a σημεῖον (e.g. the birth of a male child, Isa 7.14). So also in the Fourth Gospel, σημεῖον, wherever it occurs, is the marker for an event which concerns the status or nature of Jesus, and which discloses the presence or action of God (Jn 3.2). This event may be something so astounding as to be humanly speaking incredible; but it need not be so (→ 4.48, 54).[25] An event may be witnessed, and regarded as astounding, by (literally) thousands of people, who may nonetheless fail utterly to 'see the sign' (→ 6.26, 30, 36), that is, to perceive the truth which the event as sign discloses (9.16; 11.47; 12.37). For 'signs' exert

---

[25] Compare Origen, *In Ioannem* XIII 64 = 450 (*PG* 14.521 B; GCS 10.296; SC 222: 278).

no incontrovertible power; rather, they provoke conflicting reactions (7.40-44; 9.16; 10.19-21; 11.45-46). To discern that a sign is authentic, or to perceive its true meaning, requires a gift from the Father (see 6.37, 44-46). Thus, though the fundamental meaning of σημεῖον is to be sought in OT usage, the word itself is admirably adapted for explaining the message of the Gospel to a Greek audience. For it can denote facts or words used as evidential proof, a probable if not utterly conclusive argument, and the starting-point of a process of reasoning from observable facts to certainty about something which is not naturally observable.[26]

The Temple of His Body

A comparison of the question raised in the Synoptic Gospels ('By what authority?') with that in John ('What *sign* do you show?') causes the reader to pause, and to ponder in what manner Jesus' saying about 'raising up this temple' can be construed as a 'sign'. The usual interpretation is that the words refer to Jesus' raising his body to life after the Crucifixion, because of the statement in v. 21: 'he was speaking of the temple of his body'. This, though true, is as an interpretation not wholly adequate.

For certain problems arise if Jesus' words about 'the raising of this temple within three days' are restricted to the Resurrection of his physical body. First, 'the Jews' (not just their leaders → 2.18) have asked for a sign, and there is no evidence that after the Resurrection Jesus ever presented himself in the flesh to 'the Jews', or to any significant group of them (except for those who were already his disciples), in order to convince them that he was truly alive. Secondly, nowhere else in the NT is the phrase ἐν τρισὶν ἡμέραις, *within three days*, used with reference to Jesus' Resurrection (→ 2.1); the phrase occurs only here, in Jn 2.19-20, and in Mt 27.40 ‖ Mk 15.29, on both occasions with reference to Jesus' rebuilding of a temple. Thirdly, as was stated above (→ 2.19), ἐν τρισὶν ἡμέραις must not be taken to mean 'within 72 hours', but as a regular Semitic idiom signifying 'within a very short, but undefined, time' (compare Hos 6.2; Lk 13.32).

The key to resolving these problems is found in the Synoptic Gospels. In one group of texts,[27] we read that some Jews came to Jesus 'seeking from him a sign from heaven' (Mk 8.11-13 ‖ Mt 16.1-4 and 12.38-39 ‖ Lk 11.16, 29-32). Mark bluntly states that 'no sign at all will be given to this generation'. Matthew and Luke affirm that no sign will be given except the sign of Jonah, but Matthew's comparison of Jesus' time in the tomb with Jonah's three days and three nights in the belly of the whale (in 12.40) has unfortunately obscured the fact that Luke, and even Matthew in his other text at 16.1-4, do not propose this interpretation of

---

[26] See above, p. 211.

[27] So phrased because I take Mt 16.1-4 to be a doublet of 12.38-39. The other instances of σημεῖον in the Synoptics (those which do not refer to Jesus' Resurrection) are found at Mt 26.48; Mk 16.17, 20; Lk 2.12, 34; 23.8.

the parallel. Mt 12.41-42 and Lk 11.31-32 both find the analogy not in Jonah's survival, but in the repentance of Nineveh: while the people of Israel thought Jonah was dead, he was proving himself very much alive by the success of his preaching in—of all places—Nineveh.

The second group of Synoptic texts concerning a 'sign' from heaven is found in Mt 24.3, 24, 30 ‖ Mk 13.4, 22 ‖ Lk 21.7, 11, 25. There the disciples ask Jesus when the Temple of Jerusalem will be destroyed, and what will be the sign of the approaching ending of their world. All three Synoptics describe the wars, the famines and the persecutions of the disciples which were to take place between A.D. 30 and the Fall of Jerusalem in A.D. 70, when the whole world would collapse. Then 'the sign of the Son of Man' would appear in heaven (Mt 24.30), coming on the clouds to assemble his chosen ones. After winter, spring. When the disciples see all these terrible sufferings of Jerusalem, they are to know that summer is near (Mt 24.29-36 ‖ Mk 13.24-32 ‖ Lk 21.25-33). Note in Mt 24.8 ‖ Mk 18.8, ἀρχὴ ὠδίνων, *the onset of birth-pangs*, and compare Jn 16.21.[28]

Those texts in the Pauline literature where the local community of Christians is called the temple of God, and of the Holy Spirit, were listed at the beginning of this section. Christians as a community are also called the body of Christ (Rom 12.4-5; 1 Cor 12.12-30; Eph 1.23, cf. 4.12-13, 15-16; 5.23; Col 1.18, 24). Not surprisingly, therefore, Jesus' saying about 'raising up within three days the temple of his body' has from early times been interpreted as referring not merely to the Resurrection of his physical body, but also to the raising up of that body which is the Church. See the *Epistle of Barnabas* 16; Irenaeus, *Adv. haer.* V vi 2 (*SC* 153: 80-82; Harvey II 335-36); Clement of Alexandria, *Frag.* 36 in GCS 3:218[20ff.] = MG 9:768-69;[29] Origen, *In Ioannem* X xxxv 20 = 228; xxxix 23 = 263 (GCS 10:209, 263; *PG* 14.369D-372A, 380CD; SC 150: 520, 542); and Augustine, *Enarrationes in Psalmos* 111.1, where, commenting on Jn 2.19, he writes: 'est enim corpus Domini ipsa sancta Ecclesia, cuius caput ascendit in caelum, qui est maxime lapis vivus, lapis angularis...' (he cites 1 Pet 2.4-6).

The evangelist, by depicting the Jews as asking for a 'sign', gives Jesus the opportunity to offer them a sign. The sign Jesus promises is that if, as a consequence of their actions, the Temple in Jerusalem should be destroyed (→ λύσατε in 2.19), a new Temple will quickly replace it, a Temple raised up by him which will be evidence of the authority he had possessed during his life on earth, and a visible sign of the power he exercises after his death. The burgeoning of the Christian Church after A.D. 70 is thus presented by the evangelist as a heavenly sign to 'the

---

[28] A. Feuillet, 'Le discours de Jésus sur la ruine du Temple d'après Marc 13 et Luc 21.5-36', *RB* 55 (1948), 481-502; 56 (1949), 61-92; and 'La synthèse eschatologique de s. Matthieu (24–25)', in *RB* 56 (1949), 340-64; 57 (1950), 62-91, 180-211.

[29] Note Claude Mondésert, 'A propos du signe du Temple: un texte de Clément d'Alexandrie', *RSR* 36 (1949), 580-84.

Jews' which they are invited, summoned and challenged to interpret. The evangelist is entreating the Jews to understand this event in the light of Israel's history.

From the early years of the Israelite monarchy some had questioned the propriety of constructing a great permanent building for the worship of Yahweh (see 2 Sam 7.5-7; 1 Kgs 8.27), and the questioning did not wholly cease, as may be seen from the story of the Rechabites in Jer 35.1-11, and the post-exilic protest in Isa 66.1.[30] It is significant that this last text makes the climax of Stephen's speech in Acts 7.48-49. In NT times, too, not all Jews participated in Temple services. The Essenes had withdrawn from worship in Jerusalem, as had the Qumran community, though the latter were confident that they would one day return to it, after the reconquest of the sanctuary (1QM 2.1-6). The Essenes and the 'monks' of Qumran were, however, unrepresentative minorities, and for the majority of Jews, Temple worship was central to their faith.[31] Even after the catastrophe of A.D. 70, Judaism did not cease to believe that God would rebuild Jerusalem, and that right early: see 2 Bar 31.4-5; 32.2-4 and *4 Ezra* 10.21-23, 44-59 (*OTP* I 631, 546-47), two works of Jewish-Palestinian provenance, written after A.D. 70 (perhaps around A.D. 100). For in mainstream Judaism, the Temple in Jerusalem 'was the meeting point between heaven and earth, its Service being an earthly representation of heavenly reality' and therefore having significance for the whole created world.[32] From this belief it followed naturally that Temple worship would not cease even in the messianic kingdom; and the cessation of worship after A.D. 70 was inevitably regarded as purely temporary, a conviction reflected in the *Shemoneh 'Esreh* (A.D. 70–100?) 14 and 17.[33]

The evangelist was composing his Gospel during the years when the Temple and the Holy City lay in ruins, when the nation had been mercilessly killed, or deported, or enslaved. As a Jew, he had to ask himself, What is God's plan for his Chosen People? As a disciple of Jesus, whom he revered as the most perfect example of Israelite virtue (→ 3.2), and indeed as the unique embodiment on earth of grace and truth (→ 1.14, 18), he saw (from Ephesus?) that the Christian ἐκκλησία, the new scion from the stock of Israel, was already bringing the faith of Abraham and the teachings of the God of Israel to a wider world. Was not this extension of the faith of Israel to the Gentiles (compare Isa 45) a σημεῖον in the OT sense, a datum in history clamouring for interpretation? And a σημεῖον in the Greek sense also, supplying evidence to be considered,

[30] R. de Vaux, *Ancient Israel*, 329-30.

[31] On the Essenes, see Schürer II 570[56]; on Qumran, II 582[27], 588-89.

[32] C. T. R. Hayward, *The Jewish Temple*, London and New York, 1996, Foreword, and Introduction, 8-15.

[33] For the *Shemoneh 'Esreh*, see Schürer II 455-63; for further references, 529-30. For other examples of expectations concerning the future 'new Jerusalem', see P. Volz, *Die Eschatologie der jüdischen Gemeinde im neutestamentlichen Zeitalter*, Tübingen, 2nd ed., 1934 = Hildesheim, 1966, 371-76.

evidence affecting the balance of an argument, and the starting-point of a process of reasoning from observable facts to a conclusion about something not naturally observable.

Westcott's words, 'the old Church is transfigured and not destroyed', express succinctly and precisely the teaching of John's Gospel about the Temple of Christ's body as a sign. The book of Revelation carries the same message in analogous symbols. The Temple of God that is in heaven will be opened wide (Rev 11.19), and a 'Great Sign' will be disclosed (12.1): a new Jerusalem coming down out of heaven from God, like a bride adorned for her husband (21.2). But this new Jerusalem is no earthly city constructed around a physical Temple-building, for the Lord God almighty is its Temple, and the Lamb (21.22).

B. THE NEW PEOPLE (2.23–4.54)

Chapters 3 and 4 fall naturally into four sections, dealing respectively with Judaism, the followers of the Baptist, the Samaritans, and the God-fearers (if we take 4.46-54 as a rewriting of the story of the centurion's servant). In the first three sections, the evangelist calls into question the sufficiency of Judaism, of the 'Baptist movement', and of the religion of the Samaritan people; in the fourth section, he tells the God-fearing Gentiles who frequent the synagogue not to wait for signs and wonders before beginning to believe (4.48). In three of the four sections, the person representing the group responds positively (in 3.30, the Baptist; in 4.29, the Samaritan woman; in 4.50, the official). Nicodemus, personifying the sympathetic stream of Pharisaic Judaism (3.2), remains at this stage puzzled (3.7, 9-10), because, for the development of the argument and the unfolding of the drama, it is essential that the response of Judaism should remain at this stage non-committal.

1. Nicodemus: The Presentation of the New Order to Judaism (2.23–3.21)

[2.23] While he was in Jerusalem at Passover at the festival, many began to believe in his name, perceiving the signs which he was doing; [24] but Jesus for his part would not trust himself to them, [25] since he knew them all, and had no need of evidence from others about anyone, because he knew by intuition what people were like.
[3.1] There was however one person, from the party of the Pharisees, Nicodemus by name, a member of the Jewish Council, [2] who came to him by night and said to him, 'Rabbi, we know that you are a teacher come from God, for no one can perform these signs which you are performing unless God be with him.' [3] In reply, Jesus said to him, 'Amen, amen, I say to you, Anyone who is not born afresh cannot see the kingdom of God.' [4] Nicodemus said to him, 'How can a person who is old be born? Surely it is not possible to enter into one's mother's womb a second time and to be born?' [5] Jesus answered, 'Amen, amen, I say to you, anyone who is not born of water and spirit cannot enter the kingdom of God.' [6] Whatever is born of the flesh is flesh, and whatever is born of the spirit is spirit. [7] Do not be astonished that I said to you, You must be born afresh. [8] The wind blows wherever it wills, and you hear the sound of it, but you do not know where it comes from or where it is going. So it is with everyone who is born of the spirit. [9] In reply, Nicodemus said to him, 'How can this be? [10] In reply, Jesus said to him, 'Are you, the teacher of Israel, failing to recognize these things? [11] Amen, amen, I say to you, we are speaking of what we know, and bearing witness to what we have seen; and you are not accepting our testimony. [12] If I told you earthly things and you do not believe, how will you believe if I should mention to you heavenly things?

[13] What is more, though no one has ascended into heaven, there is someone who has come down from heaven, the Son of Man. [14] And just as Moses raised up on high the serpent in the wilderness, so the Son of Man must be raised up on high, [15] in order that everyone who believes may, because of him, never lose that life which is eternal. [16] For God loved the world so dearly that he gave the Son, the unique one, so that everyone who believes in him may not perish nor ever lose that life which is eternal. [17] For God did not send the Son into the world in order to condemn the world, but so that through him the world might be saved. [18] Whoever believes in him does not have sentence pronounced; but whoever does not believe is already sentenced, by the very fact of not having believed in the name of the unique Son of God.

[19] And the discriminating factor is this, that light is come into the world, and people loved the dark rather than the light, because their actions were evil. [20] For every one whose behaviour falls below acceptable standards comes to hate the light and does not advance towards the light, lest his actions be exposed. [21] But whoever practises the truth is advancing towards the light, so that it becomes manifest that <u>his</u> actions are performed in accordance with God's will.

Verses 23-25 are evidently intended to link the two narratives before and after, and may be the work either of the evangelist or of an editor.[1] **23. ἐν τῷ πάσχα ἐν τῇ ἑορτῇ.** These words are, if translated *at the Passover, at the feast*, clumsy, and contrary to John's style elsewhere when referring to a Jewish feast (compare 6.4; 7.2; 11.55; 12.1; 13.1). It is preferable to translate ἐν τῇ ἑορτῇ as *at the festival*, in the sense of *among the festal throng* (so also in 7.11).[2] **ἐπίστευσαν** is an inceptive or ingressive aorist, *began to believe* (BDF 331; 318 [1]; MHT III 71-72). **εἰς τὸ ὄνομα αὐτοῦ** is the first occurrence of this phrase since 1.12c, at which point the Logos had not received any name other than Logos. In 1.14, 18 he was called μονογενής, and in 1.17, identified with Jesus Christ. Here, in 2.23, no particular name is specified, but there is doubtless a cryptic allusion to 2.16, Jesus' first reference to 'my Father'. In order to retain, without disclosing, this latent meaning, the clause may therefore be glossed as 'many were beginning to believe that he was what he claimed to be'. **θεωροῦντες αὐτοῦ τὰ σημεῖα ἃ ἐποίει,** *perceiving the signs which he was doing.* The proleptic αὐτοῦ is perhaps due to Aramaic influence (MHT III 41). So far, this Gospel has not recorded any signs accomplished in Jerusalem, but the assertion returns in 3.2. The difficulty diminishes if 'sign' is understood as any act or word which makes people ask profound and existential questions about God.

[1] Lindars suggests (50, 134-36, 145) that in an original edition of the Gospel, the Temple episode stood after Jesus' triumphal entry into Jerusalem (after 12.19), and that Jn 2.23-25 had therefore once followed immediately after 2.13, connecting the Cana episode with that of Nicodemus. See also Excursus VIII, pp. 257-58.

[2] J. Jeremias, *Eucharistic Words*, 71-73 supplies several instances of this sense; see also LSJ 4, and BDAG, εἶναι ἐν τ. ἑ. = *to take part in the festival.* Other references are cited by C. Burchard, 'Fussnoten zum neutestamentlichen Griechisch,' in *ZNW* 61 (1970), 157-71 (157).

24. αὐτὸς δὲ 'Ιησοῦς. αὐτός may again be proleptic, and evidence of Aramaic influence, as in v. 23 (MHT III 41), or (more likely here) simply a Greek attributive, meaning *for his part* (NEB) *on his part* (NRSV; compare MHT III 194), stressing the contrast between the two instances of πιστεύειν, in 23 and 24. **οὐκ ἐπίστευεν αὐτὸν αὐτοῖς,** *would not trust himself to them*; here, the sense of πιστεύειν is just the opposite of that in v. 23. It is a 'descriptive imperfect' (Robertson 883), because *he knew them all* **(25)** *and had no need of evidence from others about anyone* (REB). **αὐτὸς γὰρ ἐγίνωσκεν τί ἦν ἐν τῷ ἀνθρώπῳ** ('for he himself knew what was in man') may for greater clarity be interpretatively rendered *because he knew by intuition what people were like.* No grounds are given for this statement that Jesus was a superlative judge of character, but it fits well with the assertion that he was an utterly unique person (→ 1.14). It may also be intended to point the reader to Jer 17.9-10 ('I search the mind and test the heart'), and to the comment nearby in Jer 17.12-13, about the Lord as 'the shrine of our sanctuary, the hope of Israel, and the fountain of living water' (Jer 17.12-13, NRSV), phrases which could stand as titles for the three pericopes in John chs. 2, 3 and 4. See also Jn 7.37-38; 19.34.

3.1. It is not unusual for John to use **ἦν δέ** towards the beginning of a passage, in order to introduce a subject that will headline the theme. Compare in this section 3.23 (the Baptist); 4.6 (the well of Jacob), 46 (the king's official); elsewhere, 5.5 and 8; 7.2; 11.1; 19.41. ἄνθρωπος **ἐκ τῶν Φαρισαίων,** *belonging to the party of...*, 'upholding the doctrines and practices of' the Pharisees; for this sense of ἐκ, see MHT III 260 (as in οἱ ἐκ τοῦ Πλατῶνος = [*the*] *Platonists*). The words define succinctly the man's religious character. For an outline of the teachings and practices of the Pharisees, with an excellent bibliography, and citation of the main relevant passages from the original sources, see Schürer II §26, pp. 381-403. **Νικόδημος ὄνομα αὐτῷ.** The name was common among Jews and Gentiles alike (BDAG refers to Wettstein, Dittenberger and Preisigke for examples), but there are no grounds for identifying John's Nicodemus with any other person named elsewhere.[3] He is mentioned by name in Jn 3.1, 4, 9; 7.50; 19.39.

ἄρχων τῶν 'Ιουδαίων. From ancient times, throughout the Greek world, ἄρχων denoted a man in a position of authority in a city or state or civic body, including even the Roman Senate (LSJ; BDAG; MM).[4] The

---

[3] The Jewish references are presented in SB II 412-19. The individual most frequently suggested, also known as Buni ben Gorion, was, according to the Talmud, one of three rich men in Jerusalem who during the siege by Titus sought to relieve the distress from their own stores (*Gittin* 56a; in the Soncino ed., *Nashim* 4, 256). Billerbeck argues convincingly that this Nicodemus (Hebrew form, נקדִּמוֹן = Naqdemon) was not even a disciple of Jesus, let alone the figure envisaged in the Fourth Gospel. Note the comprehensive article by R. Bauckham noted on p. xxxvi.

[4] Josephus cites three letters, one from Julius Caesar to Sidon; one from Julius, son of Mark Antony, to Ephesus; and one from Claudius to Jerusalem, in which the writers

word is common in the LXX, with the same meaning (HR), and was an ideal term to designate to Greeks a member of the supreme council of the Jews, the Sanhedrin (*TWNT* I 486³⁷-87³⁴). ἄρχων indicates that Nicodemus was a member of this body, and shared in its political, juridical and judicial authority (7.50).⁵ Hence the customary English translation *a ruler of the Jews* (AV = KJV RV RSV NAB), or, more recently, *a leader of the Jews* (TEV NJB NRSV). A less literal but more exact version is *a member of the Jewish Council* (NEB REB; compare NIV, *of the Jewish ruling council*). The phrase is certainly the emphatic, perhaps even the predicative, part of the sentence (*JG* 2290a). ᾿Ιουδαῖοι is here devoid of any unfriendly overtones; it is simply the term in common use around the Empire to denote the race whose religion centred on the Temple at Jerusalem, as it is also in 7.11; 8.31; 10.19; 11.19, 31, 33, 36; 12.9, 11 (W. Gutbrod in *TWNT* III 379²⁹-80¹⁹). → ᾿Ισραήλ in 3.9.

2a. οὗτος ἦλθεν πρὸς αὐτόν. ἔρχεσθαι πρὸς [τὸν ᾿Ιησοῦν], found so far only at 1.47 (where it is used of Nathanael), recurs in each of the next four sections. It occurs here, and in 3.20, 21 (an *inclusio* for this Nicodemus episode?); in 3.26 of the followers of the Baptist; in 4.30, 40 of the Samaritans; and in 4.47 of the king's official. The use of αὐτόν here, rather than ᾿Ιησοῦν, indicates that in the author's mind, the literary unit commences not at 3.1, but earlier, probably at 2.23.

νυκτός. The statement in 19.38 about Joseph of Arimathaea's timidity has led many to interpret the remark in 19.39 about Nicodemus ('who first came by night') as indicative of similar pusillanimity, but this does not follow from the text either of 19.39 or of 3.2. The Book of Psalms begins by proclaiming the blessedness of those who ponder the law of the Lord day and night (Ps 1.2), and an abundance of rabbinic texts proclaims the virtue of studying the law deep into the night (SB II 419-20). Nicodemus seeks not the cover of darkness but the blessings of the night, and the evangelist here intends to present him as coming to the true light who enlightens everyone coming into the world (→ 1.9; 3.21).

καὶ εἶπεν αὐτῷ, ῥαββί. Nicodemus courteously accords to Jesus the status of a professional teacher of Jewish Law (→ 1.38). In John, **οἴδαμεν** is often used, especially by the Jews, with the sense *we know*

---

address themselves to the ἄρχουσι βουλῇ δήμῳ of the city (*Ant.* XIV x 2 = 190; XVI vi 7 = 172; XX i 2 = 11). In the LXX and the NT the word βουλή is never found with the meaning *council,* only *counsel* (MM); but local councils certainly existed in Palestine in NT times (Schürer II 184-88).

⁵ His role was probably more important than that of a βουλευτής (= councillor, used of Joseph of Arimathaea in Mk 15.43; Lk 23.50). Some hold that the βουλή was distinct from the Sanhedrin, and concerned only with the administrative institutions of the city of Jerusalem (Schürer II 207). Josephus too distinguishes between ἄρχοντες and βουλευταί (*War* II xv ii 1 = 405). Questions concerning the Sanhedrin are complex: see Schürer II §23 III 199-226 and E. Lohse in *TWNT* VII 858-69.

for certain (even though it may quickly transpire that their assurance is mistaken). So here, 3.11; 7.27, 28; 9.24, 29, 31. Since in 3.10-11 εἰδέναι occurs close to γινώσκειν, this is an appropriate place for a short note about their respective connotations.

εἰδέναι *AND* γινώσκειν *IN THE FOURTH GOSPEL*

From around 1900 it has been accepted that classical usage (particularly of Attic literary Greek) is not always a good guide for the interpretation of Hellenistic Greek, and by 1950 many exegetes agreed there was no significant difference in meaning between εἰδέναι and γινώσκειν.[6] In 1959 this view was challenged by I. de la Potterie who argued that in the Fourth Gospel a clear distinction in meaning could still be discerned.[7] His opinion has since been accepted and supported by a number of writers.[8]

LSJ gives as the basic sense of γινώσκειν, *to come to know, perceive,* and in past tenses, *know.* Hence, to *recognize, discern, realize* something not recognized etc., before. LSJ writes 'as distinct from οἶδα, *know by reflection,* γινώσκω = *know by observation*'; it cites Thucydides I 69,3, γνόντες δὲ εἰδότας, *once they realize that you are aware,* and Demosthenes XVIII 276, ἐγὼ δ᾽ οἶδ᾽ ὅτι γιγνώσκετε τοῦτον ἅπαντες, *I am aware that you all perceive this.* For οἶδα, LSJ gives *I see with the mind's eye, I know, I am acquainted with the fact.*[9] Thus, γινώσκειν denotes knowledge as something acquired, by discovery, experience or thought, whereas εἰδέναι denotes knowledge as something possessed, something known as a fact.[10] Not that the confident self-assurance implied by the use of οἶδα is always justified; John's employment of οἴδαμεν for irony makes the contrary quite clear (6.42; 7.27, 28; 9.24).

---

[6] Dodd, *Interpretation* 152; Barrett, 2nd ed., 162-63; BDF 126 (1aβ). Bultmann in *TWNT* I 688-715 (on γινώσκω) and Seesemann in V 120-22 (on οἶδα) do not even ask whether there is any lexical difference.

[7] 'οἶδα et γινώσκω. Les deux modes de la connaissance dans le quatrième Évangile', *Biblica* 40 (1959), 709-25. He stresses that this was the view of J. B. Lightfoot, *Notes on Epistles of St Paul*, London, 1895; of Westcott, on Jn 2.24 and elsewhere; and of Abbott in *JV* 1621-29.

[8] See B. Snell, *Journal of Hellenic Studies* 93 (1973), 172-84 = *Der Weg zum Denken und zur Wahrheit* (Hypomnemata 57, 1978), esp. 21-43; D. W. Burdick, 'οἶδα et γινώσκω in the Pauline Epistles', *New Dimensions in NT Studies*, eds. R. N. Longenecker and M. C. Tenney, 1974, 344-56; A. Horstmann in *EDNT* II 493-94 *s.v.* οἶδα (contrast I 250-51, where W. Schmithals *s.v.* γινώσκω does not discuss the lexical distinction).

[9] *S.v.* εἴδω on p. 483. The reasoning behind the translations is that οἶδα, grammatically a perfect form used as a present with the meaning *I know,* stems from the same root as the second aorist εἶδον, *I saw.*

[10] De la Potterie (710-11) cites two texts of Plato: τὸ γὰρ γνῶναι ἐπιστήμην που λαβεῖν ἐστιν (*Theaetetus* 209e), and τὸ γὰρ εἰδέναι τουτ᾽ ἔστιν· λαβόντα του ἐπιστήμην ἔχειν καὶ μὴ ἀπολωλεκέναι (*Phaedo* 75d).

The verb γινώσκειν occurs 57 times in John's Gospel, thirteen times with Jesus as subject. Eleven of the thirteen refer to contingent historical matters in Jesus' earthly life. For example, Nathanael's πόθεν με γινώσκεις; (1.49) is clearly an inquiry for the source of Jesus' human knowledge, *How do you come to know me?* The same type of natural human knowledge is envisaged in 2.24-25; 4.1; 5.6, 42; 6.15; 10.14-15, 27; 16.19; 21.27. The remaining two occurrences (10.15; 17.25) refer to Jesus' knowing the Father, but here there are special reasons for the choice of γινώσκειν, and it makes good sense to interpret these texts also as speaking of Jesus' human knowledge of the Father.

εἰδέναι, *to know*, occurs 84 times in John's Gospel, of which perhaps 24 have Jesus as subject. Two of these occurrences (with the plural οἴδαμεν) may safely be discounted (→ 3.11; 4.22). Of the remainder, three, though of no doctrinal significance, confirm the sense ascribed above to εἰδέναι (6.6, 61; and especially 7.15, πῶς οὗτος γράμματα οἶδεν μὴ μεμαθηκώς;). Two other texts illustrate the certainty implied by οἶδα (5.32; 8.32), two more the total confidence of Jesus in God (11.42; 12.50). Of the remaining fifteen, five declare that Jesus knows whence he came and who sent him (7.29; 8.14, 55 thrice), seven proclaim his knowledge and foreknowledge concerning his sufferings (6.64; 13.1, 3, 11, 18; 18.4; 19.28), and in the last three, Peter affirms that Jesus knows he loves him (21.15, 16, 17). Thus the 19 truly significant texts all employ εἰδέναι to represent the uniqueness and the certainty of Jesus' knowledge and of his relationship with God.

Where εἰδέναι has as its grammatical subject people other than Jesus, the negative οὐκ εἰδέναι or its equivalent regularly recurs. Thus the Baptist says to his disciples οὐκ οἴδατε (1.26), and twice of himself οὐκ ἤδειν αὐτόν. Jesus says the same to Nicodemus (3.8), to the Samaritans and to his own disciples (4.22, 32), that is, to all the Israelite groups mentioned in chs. 3–4. The same charge recurs in Jesus' words to the Jews during the debates in the Temple (7.28; 8.14, 19), and in ch. 9, where these Jerusalem debates reach their climax, εἰδέναι = *to know* (etymologically indistinguishable from εἰδέναι = *to see*) is found eleven times, but six times with a negative. One may also note the occurrences of εἰδέναι used ironically (7.28 twice) or in an unfulfilled condition (4.10; 8.19). The Passion Narrative too repeatedly affirms that while 'Jesus knew' (see above), the disciples 'did not know' (13.7; 14.5 [cf. 7]; 15.15, 21; 16.18); and the account of the finding of the empty tomb contains four instances of 'do not, did not know' (20.2, 9, 13, 14), with εἰδέναι. All the more striking therefore is the use of εἰδέναι without a negative, in 10.4; 11.22, 24; 19.35; 21.12, 24, denoting interior certitude; but these texts come, so to speak, only at the very end of the story.

γινώσκειν, by contrast, is regularly used to depict the progressive development in the disciples' knowledge of Jesus from ch. 6 onwards. This meaning appears first at 6.69, and thereafter at 7.17; 8.28, 32; 10.38 (nb); 12.16; it is prominent in the account of the Supper, 13.7, 12, 28;

14.7, 9, 20; 17.3, 7, 8, 25. γινώσκειν in this sense is closely related to πιστεύειν, and does not merely denote deeper knowledge; it connotes also, because of the biblical sense of *know*, a closer union with, and greater love of, Jesus and of God (Schnackenburg I, Excursus VII 514-15 = ETr I 565-66). All the more significant is its total absence from the story of the man born blind; γινώσκειν does not occur in ch. 9, only εἰδέναι (11 times, in vv. 12, 20, 21 [×2], 24, 25 [×2], 29 [×2], 30, 31).

In addition, γινώσκειν, *to recognize, come to know,* is used of the world in 1.10; 14.31 [contrast 14.17]; 17.23, 25 (an *inclusio,* here at the end, with 1.10?). It is used also of Jews in Jerusalem in 7.26; 8.52, 55 and 10.38, which makes the careful distinction, ἵνα γνῶτε καὶ γινώσκητε (compare *JV* 1627).

It remains only to state that, where γινώσκειν and εἰδέναι occur together, or in close proximity, it is always worth comparing them very carefully. See 3.8 and 10; 7.15 and 17; 7.27-29; 8.55; 10.4-5 and 14-15; 13.7, 11-12; 14.5-7; 16.18-19; 21.17. A survey of the above texts fully justifies de la Potterie's claim that, in the Fourth Gospel, the classical distinction between the two verbs was by no means dead, and is still relevant for interpretation.[11]

2b. [οἴδαμεν ὅτι] **ἀπὸ θεοῦ ἐλήλυθας** is not a normal OT expression for a divine emissary ('send' is the more usual verb: 1 Sam 15.1; 16.1; Isa 6.8; Jer 1.7 etc.), but ἐλθεῖν occurs frequently in the NT for the appearance of Jesus (Bultmann[12]). In John, ἀπό regularly denotes someone's place of origin (1.44, 45; 7.42; 11.1; 12.21; 19.38; 21.2); hence ἀπὸ θεοῦ is used both by the gospel-writer (13.3) and by the disciples (16.30) when referring to Jesus' heavenly origin, as seen from their point of view.[13] The perfect ἐλήλυθας, *you are come,* implies an abiding presence, and is regularly found on the lips of Jesus himself (5.43; 7.28; 8.42; 12.46; 16.28; 18.37). In this first occurrence, in 3.2b, ἐλήλυθας ('come as a teacher') makes a fine *inclusio* with its last occurrence, ἐλήλυθα in 18.37 ('I am come to bear witness to the truth'); in both, the context is 'the kingdom'.

διδάσκαλος is, by position, emphatic; its precise connotations are debated. By NT times, many in Israel, believing that the age of prophecy was over (cf. Deut 34.10), had accepted that the will of God could be known only by scrutinizing the holy writings. Thus the professional exponents of the Law, the 'scribes', emerged as the spiritual guides of the people, and in matters of religion, their only teachers. See Rengstorf *TWNT* II 155-60; Schürer II 322-36. So if in Jn 3.2 διδάσκαλος is taken

---

[11] The noun γνῶσις is nowhere found in the Johannine writings of the NT. 'Perhaps intentionally' (Bultmann, *TWNT* I 711[6]).

[12] He ascribes the usage to Gnostic roots. See his commentary on Jn 1.6, p. 30 fn. 3 = ETr p. 50 fn. 3.

[13] Jesus himself uses παρὰ θεοῦ (16.27; 17.8), emphasizing the enduring relationship rather than the (humanly envisaged) temporary 'distancing'.

in this, its primary sense, Nicodemus is hailing Jesus as a new and heaven-sent interpreter of the Law and the prophets. However, the Torah had never asserted that the age of prophecy had terminated. On the contrary, Deut 18.15-19 had clearly stated that God would one day send a prophet like Moses, to teach with authority in the name of Yahweh: 'I will put my words in his mouth' (v. 18). It is unlikely that Nicodemus is here presented as consciously acknowledging Jesus to be this prophet on a par with Moses; but one cannot exclude the possibility that a reference to this motif (reserved for future disclosure) was already in the mind of the evangelist. Compare J. L. Martyn, *History and Theology*, 106 and fn. 166. Nor should one forget that the Davidic Messiah, too, possessed, in addition to his role as governor, a teaching function: 'the Spirit of the Lord speaks by me, his word is upon my tongue' (2 Sam 23.2), an idea prominent in Isa 11.2. (See W. Bittner, *Jesu Zeichen* 1003-108; O. Betz, *Jesus Der Messias Israels*, 413; W. A. Meeks, *The Prophet-King*; W. Nicol, *The Semeia*, 83-90.) Thus the evangelist, when he wrote ἀπὸ θεοῦ ἐλήλυθας διδάσκαλος, might well have had in mind all three references (doctor of the Law, prophet and king) → 3.10. Compare also the text in Papyrus Egerton 2.45-47: διδασκαλε Ιη(σου) οιδαμεν οτι [ἀπο θῦ] εληλυθας α γαρ ποιεις μα[ρτυρει] υπερ το[υ]ς προφας παντας. The Papyrus may be an allusion to John 3.2, or to a common source.

ταῦτα τὰ σημεῖα refers to 'the signs just mentioned' (in 2.23: see *JV* 2553c), and therefore identifies Nicodemus as one of those who had 'come to believe in Jesus' name' (2.23). **σύ** is moderately emphatic, and **ἐὰν μὴ ᾖ ὁ θεὸς μετ' αὐτοῦ** is a standard biblical formula (e.g. Gen 21.20, 22; 39.2, 3, 21, 23). After this respectful and sympathetic opening on the part of Nicodemus, Jesus' teaching begins.

3. The connection with v. 2 is not immediately transparent, but **ἀπεκρίθη** implies a logical link. So does **ἀμὴν ἀμὴν λέγω σοί** (5 times in John: 3.3, 5, 11; 13.38; 21.18), or ἀμὴν ἀμὴν λέγω ὑμῖν (20 times in John), for this phrase, while stressing the importance of the words which follow, also carries in every instance a reference to what has gone before. When used after the verb ἀποκρίνεσθαι, ἀμὴν ἀμὴν λέγω is a *reply* to an observation (1.51 [cp.50]; 3.3, 5; 5.19; 6.26; 8.34, 51 [cp.49]; 12.24 [cp.23]; 13.38).[14] When used without a closely preceding ἀποκρίνεσθαι, it is an *explanation* or expansion of something that has already been said (5.24, 25; 6.32, 47, 53; 8.58; 10.1, 7; 13.16, 20, 21; 14.12; 16.20, 23; 21.18). It may of course be both a reply to, and an explanation of, something said before, but it is never unrelated to what precedes.[15] Note also the further remarks about ἀμὴν ἀμὴν λέγω at 3.11.

---

[14] The references in square brackets indicate the verse in which the preceding ἀποκρίνεσθαι occurs.

[15] These three sentences are to a large extent quotation from Bernard 68, 348, but amplified, and emended for greater precision.

ἀπεκρίθη therefore invites the reader to interpret Jesus' words in 3.3 as a *reply* to Nicodemus' gracious greeting. The opening sentence of this section (2.23) contained the phrase πιστεύειν εἰς τὸ ὄνομα αὐτοῦ, its first occurrence since 1.12, which stated that 'those who believed in his name' would be enabled 'to become children of God'.[16] Nicodemus believed in Jesus' name (→ 3.2; 2.23); Jesus' reply is about to disclose that Nicodemus (whatever his age) will be enabled to begin a new life as one of the children of God, and ἀμὴν ἀμὴν λέγω σοι stresses the importance of the words that follow.

In Mt 18.3, underlying the Greek στραφῆτε there may be an Aramaic verb (tûb, hᵃzar, or hᵃdar) which would give the interpretation 'Unless you turn back again and become like children...'[17] It is suggested that this dominical saying has been transposed in Jn 3.3. **ἐὰν μή τις γεννηθῇ.** Like the Hebrew ילד (yld), γεννᾶσθαι can mean either *to be begotten* (from a father) or *to be born* (of a mother). Here it will be translated *born*, since this English word too can refer to either parent. **ἄνωθεν** can bear three meanings: (1) *from above* (= *desuper*), preferred by most Greek Fathers, Aquinas, Loisy, Bernard, Schnackenburg and de la Potterie (p. 200), which assigns to ἄνωθεν here the sense it has in 3.31, and in Jas 1.17; 3.15, 17;[18] (2) *from the very beginning* (Lk 1.2), *from very early on* (Acts 26.5), which is not relevant here; and (3) *again, anew* (= *denuo*) as in Gal 4.9, favoured by most Latin writers, Syriac and Copts, and preferred, among modern exegetes, by Westcott,[19] Bultmann and Boismard 118 (2a). Older English versions favour (3),[20] but there has recently been a shift towards (1).[21] ἄνωθεν could of course carry a double meaning, encompassing both (1) and (3), the interpretation preferred by Loisy, 1st ed., 307, Lagrange (cautiously), Barrett, Brown and many others, and possibly intended by those who translate *anew*.[22] On this interpretation, ἄνωθεν here means, on the lips of Jesus, *from above* (1), but is misunderstood by Nicodemus as meaning merely *again* (3). Boismard's view is very similar: ἄνωθεν means *again, a second time* (3), but this is taken by

[16] They would in fact be 'begotten of God', if in 1.13 the plural ἐγεννήθησαν is read. In this commentary the singular was preferred in 1.13, not least because those who have already been begotten of God cannot acquire the ability to become children of God (→ 1.13, on pp. 46-48).

[17] See J. Jeremias, *NT Theology* I 155-56, citing linguistic parallels in support of his contention that 'these verbs are often used alongside another verb to express our 'again'', and giving references to other writers up to 1969. So also Origen, *Fragment* 35 (Brooke II 249). Dodd, *Interpretation*, 304, dissents, as does Schnackenburg.

[18] This sense of ἄνωθεν also suits best the (explanatory?) ἐκ πνεύματός in 3.5. Compare also 'begotten of God' in 1.13; 1 Jn 2.29; 3.9; 5.1, 4, 18.

[19] '...not mere repetition (*again*, AV), but an analogous process (*anew*, RV)', in I 136-37.

[20] *again* in AV = KJV REB NIV [JBᵐᵍ?], *over again* in NEB, *anew* in Tyndale RV RSV NRSVᵐᵍ.

[21] *from above*, in RVᵐᵍ RSVᵐᵍ NIVᵐᵍ NAB JB NRSV.

[22] For further detail see especially Schnackenburg.

Nicodemus to mean a second physical birth, whereas Jesus' intention was to point to the need for a second, but this time spiritual, birth. The double meaning can be expressed in English by *reborn from above*, but only by sacrificing the ambiguity.

Anyone who is not born afresh cannot see the kingdom of God. **οὐ δύναται.** The verb δύνασθαι occurs 36 times in John, and is always, in sense, negatived, either by οὐ or μή, by οὐδεὶς or τίς (in 6.60), by πῶς (in 3.4; 5.44; 6.52; 9.16), or by τί in a question (1.46). In the present passage, this 'negative' usage occurs six times (3.2, 3, 4 [×2], 5, 9), stressing that no human being can start a new life here on earth except by the gift of God (→ 3.27; 6.44, 65; 14.17: note Bultmann on 3.3-5). These first occurrences of δύνασθαι since 1.46 highlight the depth of the irony in that earlier verse.

ἰδεῖν τὴν βασιλείαν τοῦ θεοῦ. The words *kingdom of God* occur only twice in John, at 3.3, 5. In the OT, the NT and in Judaism, this term never refers to a territory or to a nation settled in a territory, but always to the *sovereign rule of God*, based on the radical and unlimited love of God calling each person to a life in love, here and now (Luz 202a). It is therefore chiefly an eschatological concept denoting a new order in society within which God reigns, and which may consequently be regarded as imminent or arriving, as already present or still to come, perhaps soon, perhaps in a distant future. Though this kingdom is of its nature invisible to human eyes, it was widely believed that its presence or approach might be detected, by those who had God-given insight, from certain signs.

The Pharisees' belief in a future life led to a keen interest in the signs of its approaching. Thus Mk 8.11-13 presents them as seeking from Jesus a sign from heaven (compare Mt 16.1-4), and Lk 17.20-21 portrays Jesus as telling them that the coming of the kingdom of God was not to be discerned μετὰ παρατηρήσεως, *by the close observation of external signs*,[23] because that kingdom was already *among them* or *within them, in their hearts* (ἐντὸς ὑμῶν, see BDAG *s.v.* βασιλεία). Matthew 12.28 ‖ Lk 11.20 stress that the kingdom had in some sense already arrived during the lifetime of Jesus (ἔφθασεν), as was evident from his power over evil spirits. Matthew 12.24 makes it clear that this saying is a reply to the Pharisees; and Lk 11.37-54 implies the presence of Pharisees among the critics in the crowd (11.15-16). But a still clearer manifestation of the kingdom was promised for the future: Mk 9.1 affirms that some of the bystanders would not die before they 'saw' the kingdom of God arrived in power, ἕως ἂν ἴδωσιν τὴν βασιλείαν τοῦ θεοῦ ἐληλυθυῖαν ἐν δυνάμει. Mark 9.1 ‖ Lk 9.27 and Jn 3.3 are the only NT texts which speak of 'seeing the kingdom of God', and in each case the writers use the aorist (ἴδωσιν, ἰδεῖν), which can be idiomatically

---

[23] The signs may be atmospheric, meteorological or historical, regarded as signals from heaven about future events.

rendered as *see for oneself.* The parallel in Mt 16.28, which also uses ἴδωσιν, confirms this.

So Nicodemus comes as the representative voice of the Pharisees: *we know* (plural)...*because of the signs.* He speaks for those who have already progressed from mental consideration of the signs (θεωρεῖν, 2.23) to 'knowing for certain' that Jesus is a teacher from God (3.2); and Jesus invites him (that is, all sympathetic Pharisees) to take the one further step needed to complete the journey and *to see the kingdom of God* (3.3).

οἴδαμεν and ἰδεῖν are from the same stem (ἰδ–), possibly even (given the prevalence of itacism) similar in pronunciation. Nicodemus' statement and Jesus' answer then throw light on each other, by chiasmus.

Nicodemus   <u>οἴδαμεν</u> ὅτι ἀπὸ θεοῦ ἐλήλυθας διδάσκαλος,
                <u>οὐδεὶς</u> γὰρ <u>δύναται</u> ταῦτα τὰ σημεῖα ποιεῖν
                <u>ἐὰν μὴ</u> ᾖ ὁ θεὸς μετ' αὐτοῦ.
Jesus   <u>ἐὰν μή</u> τις γεννηθῇ ἄνωθεν,
                οὐ δύναται
                <u>ἰδεῖν</u> τὴν βασιλείαν τοῦ θεοῦ.

Many commentators (including Bernard, Bultmann, Barrett and Schnackenburg) take this ἰδεῖν in 3.3 to be in practice synonymous with εἰσελθεῖν in 3.5, with both verbs meaning *to experience*, but it is preferable to distinguish between the two. Westcott does so, citing Hermas, *Sim.* IX 15, which clearly distinguishes between ἰδεῖν τ.β.τ.θ. and εἰς αὐτὴν εἰσελθεῖν. On this interpretation, Jesus, in 3.3, is, at one level, inviting the Pharisees *to open their eyes* (ἰδεῖν is a punctiliar aorist) to the fact that the kingdom of God has arrived, in his lifetime; and the evangelist, in a deeper sense, is inviting his own contemporaries around A.D. 80–90 *to make their entry* (εἰσελθεῖν) into the kingdom, the New Jerusalem, already present in their day (→ 3.5).

4. πῶς δύναται ἄνθρωπος... indicates the perplexity of Nicodemus, **μὴ δύναται,** his unbelief (though not positive disbelief: it is a question). Both questions reveal the crassness of his misunderstanding in taking the words to refer to a second physical birth. The verse is a reminder that one may rightly speak of starting a new life, even in old age.

5. Jesus' words are both an answer and an explanation (→ 3.3). In order *to enter the kingdom of God,* a person must *be reborn,* that is, start a new life (→ 3.4). This entails more than merely perceiving that the kingdom has arrived (→ 3.3). Rebirth, and the commencement of this new life, are said to come about ἐξ ὕδατος καὶ πνεύματος, *of water and spirit.* This phrase (without the article), refers to a rebirth which the early Church regarded as taking place through baptism (1 Pet 1.3, 23; Tit 3.5). In the NT, γεννᾶσθαι ἐκ occurs only in John and 1 John: → ἐκ at Jn 3.6.

Some writers (Wellhausen, Merx, Bultmann) have judged the words ὕδατος καί to be an interpolation, during the redaction of the Gospel, in order to ensure a reference, church-inspired, to baptism. Others (Wendt, Bernard, and many since) agree, but consider them an entirely justified gloss, added to bring the saying of Jesus into harmony with the belief and practice of a later generation (Bernard). Their reasons are that ἐκ πνεύματος on its own, without ὕδατος καί, accords better with ἄνωθεν understood as *from above*; that there is no mention of water in the explanatory verses which follow, 6-8; and that since the need for Christian baptism was never preached before the death of Jesus, it is incongruous even to hint at the idea in discussion with Nicodemus. If the evangelist were purporting to set down solely the record of a conversation held during Jesus' earthly life, these reasons would be suasive; but if John was interpreting Jesus for a different generation, then the case is altered. καὶ πνεύματος is then well interpreted as epexegetical, as Calvin perceived.[24] The four words ἐκ ὕδατος καὶ πνεύματος were probably always in the text, from the beginning. Their sense is that baptism in water alone would not of itself effect rebirth: there must be a new beginning by the creative advent of the Spirit. For further detail, see the comment at 4.1-2, where Johannine baptism is compared with baptism conferred in the name of Jesus.

Jeremiah, Ezekiel and Daniel had all seen in the destruction of Jerusalem and of its Temple a manifestation of the sovereignty and power of the God of Israel, and had spoken with confidence of the restoration of the city and its Temple. Ezekiel 36.1-7 was supremely applicable to the desolation in Judaea after A.D. 70, but so was 36.24-28. These latter verses speak of bringing the people home from the nations into their own land; of cleansing them with clean water from all uncleanness; of giving them a new heart and a new spirit; and of Yahweh's putting his own spirit within them. There follows the description of the resurrection of a new people (ch. 37) and of the building of a new Temple (chs. 40–48). These texts, along with Ezek 11.16-20 and Jer 31.31-34, are fully adequate to account for the phrase *reborn of water and spirit*, especially since Ezekiel's influence will be seen again in Jn 4 (compare Ezek 16.44-55). John, like Ezekiel, dwells not on past punishment, but on the positive gifts of the Spirit and of the New Temple (→ 2.23). (That is why the Baptist speaks of Jesus' baptising with a holy spirit, but not with fire; → 1.33). The book of *Jubilees* also associates the ideas of purification, the gift of the spirit and divine filiation (I 23-25: *OTP* II 54), as does 1QS 4.19-21 (*DSSE*, 4th ed., 74-75).

In the light of these prophetical and contemporary texts, and of the practice of the early Church, it is difficult to deny that the evangelist here has in mind Christian baptism as the gateway into the kingdom. This is

---

[24] *In Ioannem* 3.5: 'non est insolens copulam exegetice sumi, quum scilicet posterius membrum explicatio est prioris', where *exegetice* carries the meaning 'epexegetically'.

the last mention of the *kingdom of God* in the Fourth Gospel, probably because John does not wish to engage in needlessly distracting discourses confirming that Jesus was not a political or military Messiah, and that neither are his followers militant nationalists (see 18.36-37). Instead, he proceeds to explain the nature of the new life into which people need to be reborn.

Verses **6-8** comment on 3.5. Verse 6 explains why rebirth is necessary. *Whatever is born of the flesh is flesh, and whatever is born of the spirit is spirit.* **τὸ γεγεννήμενον** (neuter) *notat ipsa stamina vitae novae*, as in Lk 1.35 (Bengel: → 3.8). **ἐκ.** 'In Johannine thinking, the nature is determined by its origin, as appears from the frequent εἶναι ἐκ, which affirms both origin and type of being.'[25] This is the first occurrence of **σάρξ** since 1.13-14. In John, σάρξ is never found with the Pauline sense, to denote human nature as sinful and averse from God (as in Rom 8.4-6; Gal 5.16-17, 19); in John, σάρξ denotes human nature as transitory, and when left to itself, capable of dealing only with matters concerning this world, its only destiny to die.[26] Consequently, 6a does not mean that whatever is born by human intercourse is of its nature sinful, only that, left to itself, it is incapable of entering into another, 'eternal', world, and into a super-human relationship with God.[27] The statement thus reminds the reader of 1.13-14, of being *born not of flesh but of God*. 3.3-8 contain the first instances of γεννᾶσθαι (seven in all) since 1.14; they are the only references in John's Gospel to being *born of the Spirit* or of God. 3.5-8 contain also four instances of **πνεῦμα**, hitherto found only at 1.32-33, which affirmed that the Spirit was permanently abiding upon Jesus, μένον ἐπ' αὐτόν, from the beginning of his ministry (1.33). Three strands of thought thus converge here: of the inadequacy of the flesh, of the possibility of rebirth, and of the abiding presence of the Spirit in Jesus.

The meaning of σάρξ is often defined by antithesis, as in 'flesh and blood', 'flesh and bones', or (in Greek) 'flesh and soul', σάρξ καὶ ψυχή.[28] In John, however, the defining antithesis is not 'blood', but πνεῦμα, the *Creator Spiritus* of God. Thus the words in 3.6 are a firm assertion that there are two distinct forms of life, one wholly enclosed in 'this world', one open to an other-worldly dimension. γεγεννημένον (in the perfect, not the aorist tense) implies that a permanent effect results from being born of the flesh or of the spirit: compare 1 Jn 3.9; 4.7.

---

[25] Schnackenburg, who adds in the footnote, '3.31; 8.23, 44, 47; 15.19; 17.14, 16; 18.36f.; 1 Jn 2.16, 21; 3.8, 10, 12, 19; 4.1-3, 4-6; 5.19', and a cross-reference to his *Johannine Epistles*, Excursus viii; xii.

[26] σάρξ occurs only 12 times in John (1.13, 14; 3.6; 6.51-56 [6 times], 63; 8.15; 17.2). For its meaning, see E. Schweizer in *TWNT* VIII 139[16-17].

[27] It represents what classical Western theology terms 'natural man'.

[28] See *TWNT* VIII 99-104, especially no. 6 on 102-103. For the distinction σάρξ - ψυχή, see *Od.* XI 219-22; Euripides, *Medea* 1200, 1217, 1219.

7. μὴ θαυμάσῃς (aorist): *Do not be astonished.* θαυμάσῃς and **σοι** are singular, addressed to Nicodemus, whereas ὑμᾶς in the third clause is plural. **ὑμᾶς** refers first to those whom Nicodemus represents (→ οἴδαμεν, 3.2), secondly to all humankind (→ ἐάν μή τις, 3.3.5). On **δεῖ γεννηθῆναι ἄνωθεν**, → 3.3. The reason that Nicodemus must not be astonished is given in the next verse.

8. τὸ πνεῦμα. In Greek, as in Hebrew, the word translated *spirit* can denote the wind, the air we breathe, and the breath by which animals have life, thus encompassing a range of meanings impossible to reproduce by one word in English. The first part of this verse is directed to Nicodemus alone (**ἀκούεις** and **οἶδας** are singular). (1) Some commentators take the verse to be a parable about the wind, the sound of which is audible to all, though its origin and ultimate destination remain incomprehensible. In that case, οὕτως affirms that this parable is applicable to everyone reborn of the Spirit. Thus Chrysostom, Cyril of Alexandria, Lagrange, Bultmann and Schnackenburg. (2) Most ancient writers take τὸ πνεῦμα to refer directly to the Spirit. Thus Ignatius, *Philad.* 7.1; Origen, *Frag.* 37 (Brooke II 252); Augustine, Aquinas (detailed survey) and Bernard. See also Doignon. (3) Recent interpreters tend to favour the double meaning, embracing both (1) and (2). Thus Loisy, Barrett ('it means both'), Brown, de la Potterie, and especially Cullmann.[29] The last sentence (**οὕτως ἐστὶν κτλ.**) is the important one, explaining why Nicodemus should not be astonished or even surprised. As always, Bengel writes perceptively: the masculine participle **ὁ γεγεννημένος** *maturam nativitatem significat*, contrasts with the neuter form in 3.6 (→). Later, the Gospel will state that this Spirit is essentially the gift of the exalted Lord, bestowed only after his exaltation (7.39c; 19.34; 20.22-23). 3.8 is a qualification of that general principle, affirming that the Spirit is already at work, invisibly, during the public ministry of Jesus (see 3.34).

9-12. Nicodemus' answer reiterates his continuing perplexity (→ 3.4). As in 3.4, **πῶς δύναται κτλ.** indicate his total incomprehension: *how can what Jesus suggests be possible?* **10. ὁ διδάσκαλος**, with the article, *the* (outstanding) *teacher.* Compare the *Martyrdom of Polycarp* 122: ὁ τῆς Ἀσίας διδάσκαλος. Jesus returns the compliment given by Nicodemus in 3.2. **τοῦ Ἰσραήλ** (genitive, not ἐν Ἰσραήλ): Nicodemus is *the* (outstanding) *teacher of Israel*, not just one among several *in* Israel. On the connotations of *Israel* (as distinct from τῶν Ἰουδαίων), → 1.50. **οὐ γινώσκεις** (not οὐκ οἶδας: → 3.2) is a 'progressive present', best understood as a question: *are you failing to recognize these things?* The question may imply that Nicodemus thinks of entry into God's kingdom

---

[29] 'Der johanneische Gebrauch doppeldeutiger Ausdrücke als Schlüssel zum Verständnis des vierten Evangeliums,' *ThZ* 4 (1948), 360-72 (on 364) = *Vorträge und Aufsätze 1925–1962* (1966), 176-86.

as a gift that comes only by physical descent from Abraham. If so, the words of Jesus in 3.6-8 are a reminder to him (and to Jewish readers of the Gospel) that the concept of 'new creation' is not novel, but widely attested both in the OT (→ 3.5) and in rabbinical teaching (SB II 421-23). The relevance of descent from Abraham is discussed later, in Jn 8.30-40, as if on cue after Nicodemus' next appearance (7.50). There (7.51) Nicodemus pleads that Jesus should be given a fair hearing, intimating perhaps that he has meantime been reflecting on Jesus' words in 3.3-12, and has begun to ask himself whether Jesus is not something more than an outstanding exponent of the Law (→ 3.2).

11-12. ἀμὴν ἀμήν κτλ. → 3.3. Dodd observes that this phrase 'is often used by this writer to make the transition from dialogue to monologue, and 3.11 is best taken as a kind of heading to the reflections which follow' (*Interpretation*, 328 fn. 3). σοί in v. 11, εἶπον and εἴπω in v. 12, all singular, show that Jesus is still addressing his remarks to Nicodemus. ἡμῶν indicates that Jesus is speaking not merely on his own behalf, and ὑμῖν, that the remarks are also directed to a wider group, which Nicodemus represents, namely, Pharisaic Judaism: → 3.1.

The significance of the seven plural verbs which follow in vv. 11-12 is debated. οἴδαμεν (like διδάσκαλος in v. 10) answers to the οἴδαμεν of Nicodemus in 3.2, but why all the other plurals? Nowhere else does Jesus use the 'majestic plural', but A. von Harnack accepted this as akin to one, as did Lagrange; and J. Jeremias recalls that a similar idiom was common in Galilean Aramaic.[30] Some ancient writers interpreted the plurals as indicating that Jesus was here speaking on behalf of himself and the Father (as in 8.28, 38; 12.49-50), and even of the Spirit: thus Chrysostom, Cyril and Aquinas. Tillmann and F.-M. Braun suggested that the evangelist is here associating himself with the witness of Jesus. Bultmann thought the intention was to retain an air of mystery by not disclosing so early in the Gospel that Jesus alone is the revealer come from heaven, noting that in 3.13-21 and 31-36 Jesus speaks of himself, but only in the third person. The most satisfactory proposal is that the evangelist intends Jesus' statement to be understood as an affirmation on behalf of all his followers, not only at the time of his earthly ministry, but also at the time of the writing of the Gospel (Barrett, Schnackenburg[31]).

This last interpretation may be strongly confirmed by a proposal of Klaus Berger, who argues that the expression ἀμὴν ἀμὴν λέγω ὑμῖν/ σοί is of Christian, Jewish-Hellenistic, origin, and that, like analogous phrases in apocalyptic literature, it was used to affirm that the words following it contain revelation (18-28). The expression, he suggests, was

[30] *NT Theology* I 304-305, fn. 9, referring also to Dalman, *Grammatik*, 2nd ed., 265-66.

[31] For the origin of this approach see Holtzmann (1893) and Loisy (1903). Compare also Dodd, *Interpretation* 328 fn. For further detail see especially Schnackenburg.

originally an assertion (similar to an oath) by which the visionary solemnly attested that he was communicating faithfully what he had seen; later, it was an affirmation by the community that it too was in turn passing on exactly the message once proclaimed (32). Berger proposes, finally, that the double ἀμὴν ἀμὴν κτλ. in John represents a double authentication of what follows. The expression is a guarantee, first, that the words which follow faithfully represent what Jesus, the source of the tradition, taught as something he had seen or heard from the Father; and secondly, that the community has with equal fidelity preserved that teaching for subsequent generations (116). This understanding of ἀμὴν ἀμὴν λέγω ὑμῖν/σοί certainly fits the present context to perfection, as the following paragraphs will confirm.

ὃ οἴδαμεν λαλοῦμεν. On οἴδαμεν, → 3.2. λαλεῖν occurs 59 times in John, of which 50 refer to Jesus. Only three times is the verb used of normal human speech: in 1.37 (the only occurrence before 3.11) two disciples heard the Baptist *speaking*; in 7.13, where it is is negative (οὐδεὶς παρρησίᾳ ἐλάλει περὶ αὐτοῦ); and in 9.21, of the man born blind. In six other texts, λαλεῖν is used of those who speak the word of God: see 3.11 (the only plural); 9.29, of God to Moses; 12.29, of an angel to Jesus; 12.41, of Isaiah; and 16.13 (twice) of the Spirit of truth. → λαλία in 4.42; 8.43. The use of λαλεῖν in John is thus virtually restricted to Jesus' *speaking the word of God* (50 times). καὶ ὃ ἑωράκαμεν μαρτυροῦμεν. The verbs ἑωρακέναι and μαρτυρεῖν occur together four times in John, at 1.34 (of the Baptist), 3.11, 32 and 19.35, all fundamental texts about witness (and compare 1 Jn 1.2). 3.12ab might be rendered and glossed as *I solemnly assure you that we are speaking* (on behalf of God) *about something that we know for certain, and are bearing witness to what we have seen*. καὶ τὴν μαρτυρίαν ἡμῶν οὐ λαμβάνετε: *and yet you are not accepting our testimony*. The words τὰ ἐπίγεια and τὰ ἐπουράνια, *hapax legomena* here in the Johannine writings, are commonly antithetical (compare 1 Cor 15.40; Phil 2.10; BDAG gives further examples), and underline the antithesis in the thought. If they cannot accept τὰ ἐπίγεια, that is, even the need (surely self-evident on this earth) to start life afresh, how will they ever come to believe (πιστευσετε)[32] τὰ ἐπουράνια,[33] if Jesus should mention to them[34] matters, which are, like heaven itself, outside our κόσμος

---

[32] The variant -ευετε on the second occasion (𝔓⁷⁵ etc. → NA²⁷) should, if accepted, be interpreted as a future (compare BDF 323). If -ευετε was the original reading, πιστευσετε would be a (correct) interpretative gloss.

[33] Bultmann, adducing several supporting texts, claims that this distinction between earthly and heavenly indicates a Gnostic source, and then interprets the Gospel verse accordingly. Schnackenburg, while admitting that there are no perfect verbal parallels, finds sufficient explanation for the antithesis in the thought-world of Judaism and of John. Thüsing, *Erhöhung*, 257, interprets τὰ ἐπουράνια as things revealed through the Paraclete after Jesus' final departure; but unconvincingly.

[34] 'Mention', in order to represent εἰπεῖν, not λαλῆσαι.

into which the Logos came?[35] Compare Wis 9.16-17, and → Jn 3.33, 36. Up to this point in the Gospel, no one has been said positively 'not to believe';[36] indeed, several have *come to believe* (2.11, 22, 23), but **οὐ πιστεύετε** takes up the οὐ λαμβάνετε of v. 11, and puts it more strongly. The charge now is that Nicodemus' and his group, though not positively rejecting the testimony of Jesus and his followers (disbelief), are as yet not positively accepting it (unbelief). On **πῶς**, → 3.4, 9.

We are speaking of what we know, and bearing witness to what we have seen; and you are not accepting our testimony. This translation implies that all the present indicatives in 3.11-12 are to be taken as 'continuing' presents. This in turn implies that the words are not only those of Jesus speaking to the synagogue of A.D. 28–30 (λέγω, σοί in v. 11; εἶπον and εἴπω in v. 12), but also of the early Church (οἴδαμεν, λαλοῦμεν κτλ.), which is here addressing Judaism around A.D. 80–90, and indirectly, 'the world' (see 1.10-11; 12.37-43; 15.17-20). Here (if we except the gloss on the Psalm at 12.13) the word *Israel* occurs for the last time in this Gospel at 3.10 (1.31, 50; 3.10; 12.13). The term *Israel*, denoting as it does the People of God as a religious, not a national, entity (→ 1.50), harmonizes admirably with the close of Jesus' address to Nicodemus, by suggesting the question, around A.D. 80–90, 'Who is truly the teacher of Israel?'

No clear criterion enables one to decide for certain where Jesus' words to Nicodemus are (in the mind of the author) supposed to end. It could be after 3.12 (the last occurrences of εἶπον and εἴπω), or after 13, or after 15.[37] The most attractive point seems to be after 3.12. If 3.13-15 are then understood as comment on the preceding verses, by the evangelist or an editor, the last clause of 3.15 brings the passage to an appropriate and graceful conclusion.[38]

---

[35] See H. Traub in *TWNT* V 526-27, 542.

[36] 2.24 (of Jesus) clearly does not count.

[37] Schnackenburg writes: 'The discourses of Christ are always clearly recognizable as such, mostly because they are in the first person, …[and] the evangelist never interweaves them with reflections of his own. The only two passages in John about which there may be any doubt are 3.31-36 and 3.13-21' (ETr I 360).

[38] Schnackenburg suggests that 3.13-21 (and 3.31-36) may have been originally reflections of the evangelist circulating without a definite context, inserted later in a 'revised edition' of the Gospel, to answer the question left hanging in the air at 3.12. He suggests (tentatively) that 3.31-36 formed the first part of a 'kerygmatic discourse' in which the evangelist presented his reflections on Jesus as someone come down from heaven, and that 3.13-21 represents the second part of the same discourse, which speaks of Jesus as one who has now ascended. The disciples who first edited the Gospel, thinking (rightly) that the texts had been occasioned by the Nicodemus passage, placed 3.13-21 after 3.12 because of the echo of ἐπουράνια (12) in ἀναβέβηκεν εἰς τὸν οὐρανόν (13); and 3.31-36 after 30 because ὁ ὢν ἐκ τῆς γῆς in 3.31 was interpreted as referring to the Baptist (30) (ETr I 360-63). Compare J. Painter in *The Four Gospels 1992*, eds. F. Van Segbroeck et al., FS Neirynck, Leuven, 1992, III 1877.

13. καί = *What is more*, introducing a new argument in addition to that mentioned in v. 12. **εἰ μή** may be equivalent to ἀλλά, since both translate the Aramaic אלא (ʾllāʾ) (BDF 448 [8]; cf. MHT II 468); alternatively, εἰ μή may be rendered simply as *except for* (the sense is unaffected). **οὐδεὶς ἀναβέβηκεν εἰς τὸν οὐρανόν**, though not a direct quotation, is a clear echo of Deut 30.12.[39] There the Deuteronomist, contemplating the devastation of the Land (29.23-28), calls upon Israel to return to the Lord (30.2), affirming that there is no need for a second Moses to bring down the word of God, because that word is very near to them (30.12-14), if they will only listen to it, and so have life in the Promised Land (30.15-20). For Jews living in the immediate aftermath of A.D. 66–70, the relevance of this text from Deuteronomy would be self-evident, and the renderings in the Palestinian Targums show how earnestly they took its message to heart. *Neofiti* I reads: 'The law is not in the heavens, that one should say: Would that we had one like Moses the prophet who would go up to heaven and fetch it for us…',[40] and another, 'If only we had someone like the prophet Moses, who would go up to the heaven and bring it to us'.[41] John 3.13 is a Christian answer to this yearning, and to the question posed in Deut 30.12; cf. also Rom 10.6-8. The evangelist, as convinced as the Deuteronomist of the perennial nearness of God's word, reassures the Jewish reader that there is no need for a second Moses to go up into heaven to meet God, because there already is *Someone who came down from heaven*, **ὁ ἐκ τοῦ οὐρανοῦ καταβάς, ὁ υἱὸς τοῦ ἀνθρώπου.**[42] The verse, chiastic in structure, is similar to 1.18 (→ εἰς τὸν κόλπον); 3.31; 6.62; 20.17, and to Eph 4.9-10.[43] This is the first occurrence of ὁ υἱὸς τοῦ ἀνθρώπου since Jn 1.52 → 3.14.[44]

14-15 flow smoothly as a second statement addressed specifically to Judaism. **καθὼς Μωϋσῆς ὕψωσεν τὸν ὄφιν** recalls Num 21.8-9, interpreted as in Wis 16.5-7: when Moses set up his image of the death-bringing serpent, only those who gazed upon it with faith in God were

[39] And of Prov 30.4; of Bar 3.29; and of 2 [4] Esd 4.8, which speak of bringing wisdom from heaven; compare also Wis 9.16-17.

[40] McNamara 141. In the Soncino edition of the *Midrash R. on Deuteronomy* VIII 6, J. Rabinowitz observes that the text of the midrash on verse 12 is probably intended to have an anti-Christological bearing.

[41] M. Klein, *The Fragment Targums of the Pentateuch according to their Extant Sources*, II, Translation, Rome, 1980, 84, cf. 181.

[42] P. Borgen argues, on the basis of Jewish texts, that the sense is rather that the Son of Man in heaven first ascended to the throne of God (Dan 7.13), there to be installed in office before descending to earth, and later re-ascending to heaven.

[43] The variant which adds at the end of the verse ο ων εν τω ουρανω appears to deem it necessary to stress that the Son of Man is now in heaven.

[44] All modern editors except Tischendorf and Vogels exclude from their text at the end of 3.13 ο ων εν τω ουρανω (so NA²⁷). J. Delobel argues that the case for excluding these words is not irrevocably concluded, and probably never will be settled to everyone's contentment: see J. Coppens, *Le Fils de l'homme néotestamentaire*, 49-50 fn. 11.

healed. Some Targums give a similar interpretation: 'anyone who was bitten by the serpent would raise his face in prayer towards his Father in Heaven, and would look at the serpent, and live' (Klein, Fragment-Targums II 157, cf. 71). Compare Pseudo-Jonathan: '...and [if] his heart was paying attention to the Name of the Memra of the Lord, then he lived' (E.G. Clarke in AramB 4, 247). The evangelist points Judaism to this episode as a key to understanding the Crucifixion. ὄφις, *hapax legomenon* in this Gospel, recalls both Gen 3.1-15, and Rev 12.9-15; 20.2, all texts concerning a fight to the death against Satan. Chrysostom has a fine exposition of the parallel in his *Hom.* 27.2: θάνατος ἀπώλεσε, καὶ θάνατος ἔσωσεν. Compare the ensigns mentioned in Isa 11.10, 12; 49.22; 62.10, and → Jn 19.38-42.

οὕτως ὑψωθῆναι. In Classical Greek, ὑψοῦν means both *to lift high, to raise up* (physically), and *to elevate, to exalt* (metaphorically), but it is late and infrequent. In the LXX, by contrast, ὑψοῦν occurs around 260 times, mostly in religious contexts, meaning *to exalt, to glorify, to save* and even *to redeem*. See *TWNT* VIII 604-605 for examples, noting the parallel in Isa 52.13, ὁ παῖς μου καὶ ὑψωθήσεται καὶ δοξασθήσεται σφόδρα. In the LXX, humiliation (ταπείνωσις) is not seldom the precondition of exaltation. The LXX usage passed over into the NT (Lk 1.52; 14.11; 18.14; Mt 23.12), and ὑψωθῆναι can mean *to be raised to the highest honour* (Mt 11.23 ‖ Lk 10.15), in which sense it is applied even to the death and exaltation of Jesus (Acts 2.33; 5.31; Phil 2.8-9, ἐταπείνωσεν, ὑπερύψωσεν). In John's Gospel, the usage is special (3.14 [×2]; 8.28; 12.32, 34). There ὑψωθῆναι refers first to physical *elevation on high*, and as such is employed as a cypher for crucifixion; secondly, in stark contrast with Phil 2.8-9, this crucifixion (*mors turpissima crucis*) is itself presented as the final *exaltation* and *glorification* of Jesus here on earth (Jn 13.31; 17.1: see Isa 53.13 above); and thirdly, this 'exaltation on the cross' represents, at one and the same time, the first stage in Christ's *exaltation into heavenly glory* (compare ἀναβέβηκεν κτλ. in 3.13; 6.62; 20.17 with ὑψωθῆναι in 12.34).[45] The Syriac equivalent of ὑψωθῆναι means *to be crucified*; and in Palestinian Aramaic, the same root זקף (zqp), meaning *to be raised on high* (physically), can also mean *to be crucified*. It occurs in this sense in Ezra 6.11 and in the Targums of 1 Chron 10.10; Esth I 9.13, II 7.10 [or 9];[46] but the Syriac and Aramaic terms could not bear the second meaning of *being exalted, raised to a higher estate or position*.[47] Greek, however, could bear the double

---

[45] It is astonishing that Zahn (199-201, and even when commenting on 8.28, at 409) should have maintained that ὑψωθῆναι, when used of Jesus, always referred to his Ascension into heaven.

[46] Black, *Aramaic Approach*, 3rd ed., 141, citing G. Kittel, 'Zur angeblichen antiochenischen Herkunft des vierten Evangelisten', *ZNW* 35 (1936), 282-85. See also G. Bertram in *TWNT* VIII 608.

[47] See F. C. Burkitt, 'On "Lifting Up" and "Exalting"', *JTS* (First Series), 20 (1918–19), 336-38.

meaning, *to be crucified* and *to be exalted into glory*, as later writings
show (*PGL*). One classic work on the subject is by Thüsing (see especially 3-35); note also Létourneau, 176-78.

δεῖ. ὑψωθῆναι δεῖ τὸν υἱὸν τοῦ ἀνθρώπου recurs, with the variation δεῖ ὑψωθῆναι, in 12.34, the only two instances in John where δεῖ is
used with Son of Man.[48] Many trace the origin of this clause to the first
prediction of the Passion in the Synoptic tradition (Mt 16.21 || Mk 8.31 ||
Lk 9.22), where Mark and Luke both read δεῖ τὸν υἱὸν τοῦ ἀνθρώπου
πολλὰ παθεῖν...καὶ ἀποκτανθῆναι as does Matthew, except that he
writes [δεῖ] αὐτόν, which has as antecedent (in 16.13) Son of Man.[49] The
Synoptic logion is generally interpreted to mean *it is necessary* (in the
sense that 'it is divinely ordained') *that the Son of Man must suffer many
things...and be killed.* John has rephrased the thought to express his own
theology of the Cross. Eight times in John we read that the Jews *sought to
kill* Jesus (5.18; 7.1, 19, 20, 25; 8.37, 40; 11.53), but never once that he
'was killed'. With reference to Jesus, John uses θάνατος twice (12.33 =
18.32) and ἀποθνήσκειν five times (11.50, 51; 12.33 = 18.14, 32), but
always in the context of the words of Caiaphas, referring to Jesus' death
as seen by his contemporaries. (Cf. 10.18.) In 3.14, the words δεῖ
ὑψωθῆναι may be glossed as *it is* in God's design, historically *necessary*:
hence, *the Son of Man must be raised up on high.*

τὸν υἱὸν τοῦ ἀνθρώπου. The term υἱὸς τοῦ ἀνθρώπου occurs 13
times in John, 1.51; 3.13-14; 5.27 (without article); 6.27, 53, 62; 8.28;
9.35; 12.23, 34 [×2]; 13.31. Zahn observes that in John, it occurs on the
lips of Jesus only where there is a contrast between heaven and earth, or
between humiliation and exaltation, except in 9.35, if the phrase is there
the true reading (195 fn. 55). As for the meaning of the term, one can
hardly imagine that the evangelist, writing for Christians around A.D 80-
90, did not have in mind the Danielic Son of Man, but for a broad outline
of the discussion, see Excursus VIII, 'The Interpretation of John 3 in the
Twentieth Century', pp. 257-58.

15. The TR, the Sixto-Clementine Vulgate, and the AV = KJV all follow
the reading ο πιστευων εις αυτον μη αποληται αλλ εχη, the text
found in most Greek and Latin codices known at that time. The words μη
αποληται αλλ are, however, interpolated from 3.16; they occur only in
MSS which also read here in 3.15 εις αυτον (𝔓63vid ℵ A Θ Ψ 086 *f*13
𝔐), and should be deleted. The variants επ αυτον and επ αυτω may also
be set aside. Among modern editors, only von Soden retains εις αυτον;
all others read εν αυτω. See NA27.

---

[48] Elsewhere, δεῖ is used of Jesus at 3.30; 4.4; 9.4; 10.16; 20.9.

[49] In the Synoptics, 'the Son of Man' recurs in the second and third predictions of the
Passion, but δεῖ is replaced by a future tense or equivalent: Mt 17.22-23 || Mk 9.31 || Lk
9.43; Mt 20.18-19 || Mk 10.33-34 || Lk 18.31-33.

This is the only occasion in the Gospel where πιστεύειν, a favourite word of John (96 times; in 1 John, six times), is followed by ἐν with the dative. In John, πιστεύειν can be sometimes be used absolutely (1.7, 51 etc.), or (when it means *to trust someone's word as true*) with a simple dative (4.21, 50; 5.24, 38, 46, 47 etc.); but when it denotes an act of religious faith, it normally takes εἰς with the accusative (34 times), and that is presumably why so many scribes wrote εἰς αυτον here.[50] If therefore the true reading in Jn 3.15 is not εἰς αὐτόν but ἐν αὐτῷ, customary Johannine usage counsels that ἐν αὐτῷ should be construed not with ὁ πιστεύων but with the following word, ἔχῃ. ἐν αὐτῷ is then emphatic.[51] In that case, the renderings in the RV NIV JB ('that everyone who believes may have eternal life in him': similarly REB) are to be preferred to that given in the RSV NRSV NAB ('that everyone who believes in him may have eternal life').

ἵνα here implies, as well as intention, the sense *before it will be possible.* πᾶς ὁ πιστεύων, the first instance of this phrase with πᾶς in the Gospel, implies both belief in a fact and a trust resultant from that belief (→ 1.12c). Here it is an alternative way of phrasing the message to Nicodemus, about restarting life anew by rebirth of the Spirit: it recurs in 3.16, in 6.40, and at the close of the public ministry in 12.46. The use of πᾶς indicates that the principle does not apply to Nicodemus alone, but to all who believe, without distinction of time or place. In John, ἔχειν, wherever it has as object ζωὴν αἰώνιον (eight times: 3.15, 16, 36; 5.24, 39; 6.40, 47, 54), stands always in the present tense, meaning therefore *to hold on to that which one already has* (confirmed at 12.25, by the future φυλάξει): this is certainly the force of ἔχῃ as a present subjunctive.

ζωὴν αἰώνιον. The Gospel has affirmed the need for rebirth to see or to enter the kingdom of God (3.3, 5), but from that point onwards, it never mentions the kingdom of God. Instead, the teaching of Jesus centres on 'life eternal', which is presented as God's great gift to those who believe in that teaching. This first example of the word ζωή since the Prologue (1.4) is also the first of 17 occurrences of ζωὴ αἰώνιος in this Gospel (3.15, 16, 36; 4.14, 36; 5.24, 39; 6.27, 40, 47, 54, 68; 10.28; 12.25, 50; 17.2, 3). In John, the adjective αἰώνιος occurs only with ζωή, always after the noun, and always without the article, until its very last occurrence in 17.3 (ἡ αἰώνιος ζωή), where its identity is, as it were, finally disclosed. αἰώνιος does not mean simply *unending* (= ἀΐδιος), though that notion is clearly included, but 'belonging to that Other World,

---

[50] πιστεύειν + ἐν with the dative occurs in the LXX (Jer 12.6; Ps 105 = 106.12; Sir 32.21), with the meaning *to put one's trust in*, but in the NT this construction occurs once only, at Mk 1.15, the sense of which is consequently debated (see BDAG 1 a ε, and 2 a ε; and note MHT I 67-68).

[51] John places an adverbial phrase with ἐν *before* the verb when the phrase is emphatic or metaphorical (1.1; 5.39: 13.35; 16.30: *JG* 2636c [3]). Here ἐν αὐτῷ is also quasi-instrumental (compare *JG* 2332; BDF 219).

where God will grant us to share fully in his own life, in another Age': in this commentary the translation *life eternal* will normally be used as an appropriate abbreviation for *life which is eternal*. For this sense of αἰώνιος see BDAG 3; Turner, *Christian Words*, 455-57; J. T. Forestell, *The Word of the Cross*, 113-14; F. Mussner, ΖΩΗ, 186. **ἐν αὐτῷ** means, in this context, that every believer who contemplates here on earth the Son of Man crucified, risen and exalted (ὑψωθείς) will, by perceiving him as victorious over the death-bringing serpent, be enabled to hold fast to that eternal life into which the disciples of Jesus are here on earth reborn (3.3-8). ἐν αὐτῷ is translated *because of him* in an attempt to embrace, simply and briefly, the multifarious possible meanings of **ἐν** with the dative: see Robertson 584-91 and Abel, *Grammaire* §47a-j, 211-14. Hence (14b-15): *The Son of Man must be raised up on high, in order that everyone who believes may, because of him, never lose that life which is eternal,* and which is, for the believer, already begun. See 7.38.

Nicodemus, representative of 'mainstream' Judaism, had come seeking light amid the darkness of night (→ 3.2), but remained, at the end, puzzled (3.7, 9-10). The plan of the Gospel requires that the response of Judaism should be at this stage non-committal, for the great debate with Judaism does not begin in earnest until ch. 5.

3.16-21: A CHRISTIAN HYMN?[52]

The section addressed to Judaism (3.1-21) concludes with a passage similar to a Greek chorus, commenting on the scene with Nicodemus. Part of it is perhaps a Christian hymn about God's love for the world, and about the need for each individual to choose between darkness and light (3.16-18). The rest is a message of warning to those who deliberately disobey the dictates of their conscience, but of encouragement to all who, eschewing improper behaviour, live in accordance with their innermost conscience. The latter may be sure that they are advancing towards the light (3.19-21).

In these verses, 3.16-21, the great themes of the Gospel recur to an extent not seen since the Prologue. ὁ κόσμος, used four times in the Prologue, and then once by the Baptist at 1.29, reappears, five times in four verses, in 3.16-19 (and it will occur 45 times in chs. 13–18). φῶς, used six times in the Prologue, first reappears here, five times, in 3.19-21, again contrasted with darkness (here σκότος, *hapax legomenon* in John). 3.16 and 18 refer to ὁ υἱὸς ὁ μονογενής, the only instances of this term in the Gospel outside the Prologue. Most significantly, 3.16 introduces for

---

[52] For the reasons justifying a major break here, see the last paragraph of the commentary on 3.12, and the two footnotes there from Schnackenburg. At this point, several commentators postulate a different order of the text. Bernard and Bultmann rearrange the verses as 3.16-21, 31-36, 22-30, and Schnackenburg as 3.31-36, 13-21, 22-30. Further detail in Excursus VIII.

the first time the verb ἀγαπᾶν (see also 3.19, 35), a word which occurs only seven times in the first twelve chapters, but 30 times in chs. 13–21. The leading themes of the Gospel are here vigorously reaffirmed.

3.16. οὕτως γὰρ ἠγάπησεν ὁ θεὸς τὸν κόσμον. οὕτως stresses the quality and the depth of God's love (see BDF 2, 3), and the word-order of the clause underlines it, for this first occurrence of the verb ἀγαπᾶν precedes its grammatical subject, emphasizing that love. ὁ θεός. Only here in John's Gospel is the word 'God' the subject of the verb *to love*. True, elsewhere 'the Father' is often said to love Jesus, and, in three verses, the disciples (14.21b, 23; 17.23); but at 3.16, Jesus has scarcely begun to teach about his Father. Indeed, he has only once mentioned his name (→ 2.16). Hence ὁ θεός is used here, and the very first statement about God since the Prologue is that he *loved the world*, that is, the world seen 'existentially', as it really is, full of sinfulness and estranged from its Maker (see Prologue, pp. 39-40). τὸν κόσμον is also, by its position, emphasized. Compare Rom 5.8; 8.3 and 1 Jn 4.9, 14. Aquinas has a fine paragraph on this love (fn. 477).

ὥστε τὸν υἱὸν τὸν μονογενῆ ἔδωκεν. οὕτως...ὥστε is a regular combination in Greek (BDAG 2). On τὸν υἱὸν τὸν μονογενῆ, → 1.14d and Excursus III.[53] The clause probably alludes to Gen 22.12, 16, as does Rom 8.32, but there are subtle differences between John and Paul. While Paul stays closer to the LXX, with οὐκ ἐφείσατο, John stays closer to the Hebrew, but in place of the Hebrew, *did not withhold* (חשׂך ḥśk), he writes, more positively, *gave*. Again, Paul in Rom 8.32 uses παρέδωκεν of God *handing* his Son *over* to his redeeming passion; in John, παραδίδοναι is (with one exception, 19. 30) used only (pejoratively) of men *handing over* Jesus to his fate (Judas, 6.64 etc., nine times; the High Priests, 18.30, 35). John's choice of ἔδωκεν in preference to παρέδωκεν is therefore significant, intimating that God was not *handing over* his Son to suffering, but rather *giving him* as a gift to the world,[54] and that the reason for this giving was (ἵνα πᾶς ὁ πιστεύων κτλ.) so that *everyone who believes in him may not perish nor ever lose that life which is eternal*. → 3.15. Note also, in this context of rebirth to a new life (3.3-8), the parallel with ἔδωκεν in 1.12b.

---

[53] After τον υιον, the TR, and consequently many writers, read αυτου. So do von Soden, Vogels, Merk and Bover, on the authority largely of those witnesses which in 3.15 read εις αυτον and μη αποληται αλλα. NA²⁷ rightly prefers to follow 𝔓⁶⁶.⁷⁵ ℵ* B Wˢᵘᵖᵖ, and to omit αυτου, an omission which heightens the importance of the qualifying adjective, τον μονογενη.

[54] With due respect to the long list of those who equate ἔδωκεν with παρέδωκεν (*tradidit*): Chrysostom, Theophylactus, Maldonatus, Westcott, Loisy, Lagrange, Bultmann, Brown et al. The view adopted in the text above is that of Vanhoye, Schnackenburg, and de la Potterie.

17. οὐ γὰρ ἀπέστειλεν ὁ θεὸς τὸν υἱὸν εἰς τὸν κόσμον ἵνα κρίνη τὸν κόσμον, ἀλλ' ἵνα σωθῇ ὁ κόσμος δι' αὐτοῦ. *For God did not send the Son into the world in order to pass sentence on the world, but so that through him the world might be saved.* This is the first occurrence of ὁ υἱός absolutely (i.e. without any qualification at all); it occurs seven times, usually in connection with oJ pathvr (3.17, 36; 5.19; 6.40; 8.36; 14.13; 17.1). Once again, the word-order is illuminating: οὐ γὰρ ἀπέσ-τειλεν and σωθῇ are by position emphatic. ἀπέστειλεν is the second example (after the Baptist, 1.6) of a divine mission; on the connotations of the verb, → 1.6; 20.21. κρίνη is translated by the AV = KJV RSV NRSV JB NIV NAB as *condemn*, but by the RV NEB REB NJB as *judge.*[55] Note that God, and not the Son, must be the grammatical subject of κρίνη, because God is the subject in the main clause, and because the next clause substitutes the passive σωθῇ, when referring to what is done through the Son. σωθῆναι means *to be healed, to be put right.* The verb occurs only six times in John (3.17; 5.34; 10.9; 11.12; 12.27, 47), and 12.47 makes a strong *inclusio* with 3.17, with the double reference to saving, not judging, the world; note also, in 4.42 and 1 Jn 4.14, ὁ σωτὴρ τοῦ κόσμου. The verb σώζειν never occurs in the Johannine Epistles, and neither the verb nor the noun σωτήρ in the book of Revelation.[56] One possible reason for the relative rarity of these words is that the terms 'salvation' and 'saviour' might have been seen as religiously ambiguous (mystery religions, gnosticism) and/or politically compromising (ruler cult). See the references in BDAG. ἵνα σωθῇ ὁ κόσμος, not a relatively small company of the elect, as believed by the Gnostics (see Schnackenburg, referring to CH I 22-27).

18. ὁ πιστεύων εἰς αὐτὸν οὐ κρίνεται κτλ. Whoever believes-and-trusts in him does not have sentence pronounced; but whoever does not believe-and-trust is already sentenced, by the very fact of not having believed-and-trusted in the name of the unique Son of God. Note the parallel between this verse and 1.12d. Only the dual rendering believe-and-trust can faithfully reproduce the sense of the Greek πιστεύειν εἰς followed by the accusative. The phrase has hitherto occurred only in 1.12d and 2.23, but will henceforward be frequent, where it will be rendered (as is customary) simply as believed. μὴ πεπίστευκεν. The tense (perfect) makes clear that the unbelief is not just one act but a persevering state of mind, which rejects the idea of the fatherhood of God as preached—uniquely—by Jesus (εἰς τὸ ὄνομα τοῦ μονογενοῦς υἱοῦ τοῦ θεοῦ).

19 explains in other words the ground for the differentiation made in v. 18. αὕτη δέ ἐστιν ἡ κρίσις. A literal rendering might be, '*The*

[55] The verb κατακρίνειν is not found in John except in 8.10, 11.
[56] σωτηρία, however, is found in the hymns at Rev 7.10; 12.10; 19.1.

differentiation proceeds from this'. Barclay translates, *The fact which really judges men*... ὅτι τὸ φῶς ἐλήλυθεν εἰς τὸν κόσμον. τὸ φῶς was last mentioned in the Prologue, as *the true light, which enlightens every individual*, and as ἐρχόμενον εἰς τὸν κόσμον (→1.9). ἐλήλυθεν affirms that this light is now arrived, and come into the world. That is, the Son who stands in an utterly unique relationship to the Father is now, on earth, 'light' to the world. καί, introducing a contrast, is probably a Semitism, = *but.* ἠγάπησαν οἱ ἄνθρωποι μᾶλλον τὸ σκότος ἢ τὸ φῶς. Note the contrast with what God loves (3.16); οἱ ἄνθρωποι is a well-chosen variant for 'the world' in the preceding clause. On τὸ φῶς and τὸ σκότος → 1.4-5; on ὁ κόσμος → 1.10. ἦν γὰρ αὐτῶν πονηρὰ τὰ ἔργα. If γάρ is taken in a causal sense, the words mean that morally evil actions lead people to prefer darkness to light; alternatively, γάρ can be evidential, and then the sense is 'as may be seen from their evil actions'. The former view is more Pauline, the latter more in keeping with John, and to be preferred, because otherwise the first clause of 3.20 is a superfluous repetition. One may render, leaving open the alternative interpretations of 3.19d: *And the discriminating factor is this: that light* (τὸ φῶς) *is come into the world, and people loved the dark rather than the light, because their actions were evil.*

20 and **21** rephrase the thought of vv. 18 and 19, first negatively, then positively. 3.20 points to the practical misbehaviour which prevents a person from advancing into the light, and 3.21 describes the converse. Note the close syntactical parallels between verses 20 and 21 (ὁ πράσσων–ὁ ποιῶν, the double ἵνα), the structuring of both sentences around ἔρχεται πρὸς τὸ φῶς, and the contrast between **πᾶς ὁ** [φαῦλα πράσσων] and (21) **ὁ δὲ** [ποιῶν τὴν ἀλήθειαν]. Compare this last with 4.13.14 (πᾶς ὁ πίνων...ὃς δ᾽ ἂν πίῃ), both contrasting the many who go wrong with the individual who does what is right (*JG* 2574a).

φαῦλα πράσσων. φαῦλος occurs in Jn 3.20; 5.29; Rom 9.11; 2 Cor 5.10 (with πράσσειν), in Tit 2.8 (with λέγειν) and in Jas 3.16 with πρᾶγμα. It denotes, as in Classical Greek, *that which is below the gener-ally accepted standard,* and hence *unacceptable, improper behaviour.* In the present context, πράσσειν means *to do habitually*; it is frequently (though not always, cf. 2 Cor 5.10) used of doing evil, by contrast with ποιεῖν, the verb used for creativity, see Jn 5.29 (*JG* 2584). φαῦλα are by no means as bad as πονηρά (Jn 3.19), but habitual improper behaviour (φαῦλα πράσσειν), of which one is (correctly) ashamed, does not lead anyone in the right direction. On the contrary, such a person **μισεῖ τὸ φῶς καὶ οὐκ ἔρχεται πρὸς τὸ φῶς.** μισεῖ, a gnomic present stating a general rule, may also be inchoative (compare *SMTNTG* 12; Robertson 880; MHT III 63), and may legitimately be glossed, if not translated, as *begins to hate, comes to hate* the light (which has come into the world of darkness, → 1.5, 9), *and does not advance towards it,* even though it is shining in his direction. ἵνα μὴ ἐλεγχθῇ, *for fear that his actions may* *be exposed* (BDAG 1 gives for ἐλεγχθῇ, *exposed*). Hence, *Every one whose behaviour falls below acceptable standards comes to hate the light and does not advance in the direction of the light, lest his actions be exposed.*

21. ὁ δὲ ποιῶν τὴν ἀλήθειαν is a Semitism (אמת עשה = ʿśh ʾmt) meaning *to act with integrity, to behave in a trustworthy fashion* (Gen 24.49; 47.29; Josh 2.14: *DCH* I 329a), and therefore 'to act in accordance with one's interior beliefs and one's pledged word'. Barrett's interpretation of the words as meaning, in John, to practise the true (Christian) faith and life seems to infer too much at this stage in the narrative. It seems preferable to take the phrase as referring to those (particularly of the Jewish faith) who are still seeking after the truth about God. **ἔρχεται πρὸς τὸ φῶς**, *is advancing towards the light.* **ἵνα φανερωθῇ** stands in contrast with ἵνα μὴ ἐλεγχθῇ in v. 20. ἵνα is here used in two senses, the first instance in v. 20 clearly denoting purpose, whereas ἵνα φανερωθῇ here in 21 points merely to the result which follows (an 'ecbatic' clause, cf. MHT III 102-103). Contrast with τὰ ἔργα αὐτοῦ in v. 20, **αὐτοῦ** τὰ ἔργα, where αὐτοῦ is emphatic by position. ὅτι **ἐν θεῷ** ἐστιν εἰργασμένα. The prepositional usage is sometimes termed an ἐν of accompaniment: it 'is classical enough and belongs to the Koine, but its use in the LXX to render ב seems to have suggested an increase of use in the NT' (MHT III 252). It may be interpreted as *with the help of God*, or better (with Euthymius, who equates the phrase with κατὰ θεόν) *in accordance with God's will*, a rendering which naturally embraces the first interpretation as well. **ἐστιν εἰργασμένα.** The periphrastic construction, common in the NT, gives a rather elegant emphasis, with no change in the meaning.[57] *But whoever practises the truth is advancing towards the light, so that it becomes manifest that <u>his</u> actions are performed in accordance with God's will.*[58]

If these verses in Jn 3.16-21 are read with the destruction of the City and of the Temple in mind, and understood in that context, the reader will observe how they echo the thought of the Psalmist (Ps 43.3):

> Send forth your <u>light</u> and your <u>truth</u>, and let them <u>lead</u> me;
> let them <u>guide</u> me to your holy mountain, and to your dwelling-place.

In the mind of the evangelist, the dwelling-place of God is to be found not in the earthly, but in the New Jerusalem. The theme will recur in Jn 4.20-21. Compare also the comment at the end of 3.36, and note the close parallels between Jn 2.23–3.2; 3.11-21 on the one hand, and Jn 12.37-50 (especially vv. 37, 42, 43, 46-48) on the other.

---

[57] See BDF 4 and 352. The aorist passive εἰργασθῆναι does not appear anywhere in the NT, OT Pseudepigrapha, Apostolic or Apologetic Fathers.

[58] See also Excursus VIII, 'The Interpretation of John 3 in the Twentieth Century'.

2. John the Baptist:
The Presentation of the New Order to His Followers
(3.22-36)

Between 150 B.C. and A.D. 100 there existed in Syria (including therein Palestine and Transjordan) a number of religious groups in which baptism, regular bathing and sprinkling with water played a preponderant role. The Essenes, with whom one may include the Qumran communities, are the best-known, thanks to Josephus.[1] Hegesippus mentions along with them another Jewish sect, hostile to Christianity, called the Hemero-baptists.[2] This group, according to Epiphanius, was distinguished by the practice of bathing daily, both summer and winter, in order to cleanse themselves of every fault of body and soul; they left Jerusalem before A.D. 70, and thereafter disappear from history.[3] Book 3 of the *Sibylline Oracles*, a Jewish work written around A.D. 80, probably in Syria or the Jordan Valley, or perhaps Asia Minor, contains lines appealing for a baptism of repentance by total immersion (ll. 162-70); the thoughts are not unlike the preaching ascribed to John the Baptist.[4] Finally, Acts asserts that some twenty years after the Crucifixion, Apollos from Alexandria (18.24-26), and some disciples in Ephesus (19.1-7), were familiar only with John's baptism, never having heard about baptism in the name of Jesus. Common to all these 'baptist movements' was the conviction that a religious rite of symbolically cleansing the body in water would be more effective for removing spiritual defilement than the offering of an animal in sacrifice. In this culture, the followers of John the Baptist would have found a natural home.[5]

> [3.22] After this Jesus and his disciples went into the Judaean territory, where he spent some time with them, baptizing. [23] John also was baptizing, at Aenon near Salim, because there were many springs there, and people were presenting themselves and being baptized, [24] for John had not as yet been put in prison. [25] Now a discussion arose on the part of John's disciples and a Jew on the subject of purification. [26] And they came to John, and said to him,

---

[1] *War* II viii 2-13 = 119-61 [129 for bathing]. For rites of purification at Qumran, see the Damascus Rule (CD 10.10-13), the War Rule (1QM 14.2-3) and the Community Rule (1QS 3.4-5; 5.13). On the Essenes in general see Schürer II §30: 555-90.

[2] In Eusebius, H.E. IV xxii 7.

[3] See *Panarion* 17 (in Williams' translation, I 41-42). The Hemerobaptists are briefly mentioned in the *Pseudo-Clementine Homilies* ii 23 and in the *Apostolic Constitutions* VI vi 5. They may be identical with those whom Justin, writing around A.D. 135, calls simply 'Baptists' (*Dial.* 80).

[4] *OTP* I 388.

[5] This commentary accepts that the NT accounts of the role and teaching of the Baptist as the Forerunner of Jesus are based on trustworthy tradition. For a brief outline of some other views on this question, see Excursus IX.

'Rabbi, he who was with you on the other side of the Jordan, the one to whom
you have been bearing witness, here he is, himself baptizing, and everyone is
going to him.' [27] John answered by saying, 'No one can take any thing as his
own possession unless it be given him from heaven. [28] You yourselves are my
witnesses that I said, "I am not the Christ, but am an envoy sent on ahead of
him". [29] It is he who holds the bride in his arms that is the bridegroom, and the
bridegroom's friend, the one who stands and listens for him, is overjoyed to
hear the bridegroom's voice. That is why the joy that I am now experiencing
fulfils all my desires. [30] He is destined to grow ever greater, I to grow less and
less.'

[31] The One who comes from above is superior to all. Whoever issues from
the earth belongs to the earth, and whatever that person says is of earthly
origin. The One who comes from heaven is superior to all. [32] He bears witness
to what he has seen and heard, yet no one is accepting his testimony; [33] though
one who did accept his testimony put the seal of his own authority on this—
that God is true to his word. [34] For the One whom God sent speaks the words
of God, since he does not bestow the Spirit by measuring it out. [35] The Father
loves the Son, and has put everything in his hands. [36] He who believes in the
Son has eternal life; he who does not obey the Son shall not see life, but the
wrath of God rests upon him.

3.22. μετὰ ταῦτα. This is the first of the eight occurrences of the
phrase in John (3.22; 5.1, 14; 6.1; 7.1; 13.7; 19.38; 21.1). On each
occasion it means simply *next, after this*, and in contrast to μετὰ τοῦτο
(four times in John: 2.12; 11.7, 11; 19.28), signifies nothing more than
temporal sequence (→ 2.12). **ἦλθεν ὁ 'Ιησοῦς καὶ οἱ μαθηταὶ
αὐτοῦ εἰς τὴν 'Ιουδαίαν γῆν** marks a change of scene. Bultmann
renders γῆν as *Landschaft* = *countryside*, citing Aeschylus, *Eumenides*,
993, καὶ γῆν καὶ πόλιν, but a more likely word to denote *the open
country* would have been χώρα, as in Jn 11.54-55 (→ also BDAG);
compare the distinction drawn between πᾶσα ἡ 'Ιουδαία χώρα καὶ οἱ
῾Ιεροσολυμῖται πάντες, at Mk 1.5. Though Jesus may well have spent
time in the countryside, it is preferable to take εἰς τὴν 'Ιουδαίαν γῆν as
indicating here that administrative region whose northern boundary ran
within ten miles of Gerizim, that is, *the Judaean territory*, with all the
socio-religious conditions implied (compare Schürer II 184-98, 'The
Jewish Region').[6] **καὶ ἐκεῖ διέτριβεν μετ' αὐτῶν.** διατρίβειν, *to
spend time*, a thoroughly classical word, is rare in the LXX (six times); in
the NT, it occurs only twice in John (3.22; 11.54), and eight times in
Acts. Some therefore ascribe its presence to an editorial insertion, but the
choice of διατρίβειν can be equally well explained by a desire to
sidestep the theologically loaded μένειν. Not all English versions
succeed in expressing clearly the distinction between these two Greek
verbs. *Remained there* (RSV REB) is an invitation to assume that the

---

[6] The boundary is given by Josephus in the *War* III iii 4 and 5 = 48 and 51. The
capital of the northernmost toparchy, Acrabatta (= 'Aqraba) lies 9 m sout-east of
Neapolis, and Annath Borcaeus is identified with the modern Berkit, 9 m due south of it
(Schürer II 6-7, and especially 192 fn. 32).

Greek must be μένειν, and *stayed there* (NEB JB NJB) tempts one to think it is probably so. The translation *spent some time there* (NIV NRSV) evades that danger, and also expresses well the (surely significant) transition from the aorist ἦλθεν to the imperfect **καὶ ἐβάπτιζεν**, here implying duration. Compare NAB: ...*where he spent some time with them baptising*. This is the only text in the NT or elsewhere which affirms that Jesus, during his public ministry, baptized: for further discussion of this question, see the comment on 4.1-2.

23. ἦν δὲ καὶ introduces the second section of this part (→ 3.1). ὁ **Ἰωάννης**. The Baptist was last mentioned in 1.19-41. It is preferable therefore to read, here and in v. 24, with NA²⁷, the definite article, and to construe it as 'anaphoric', indicating *the one previously mentioned* (*JG* 1968-69; BDF 260; MHT III 167). **βαπτίζων ἐν Αἰνὼν ἐγγὺς τοῦ Σαλείμ, ὅτι ὕδατα πολλὰ ἦν ἐκεῖ.**

THE LOCATION OF AENON NEAR SALIM

From the fourth century onwards, Aenon near Salim has been identified with the area around Tell ar-Radgha, 8 miles = 12 km south of Scythopolis (= Beisan), at the grid reference 1998–2008. Half a dozen springs lie within a mile or so (clearly shown in Abel, *Géographie*, I 143; see also 447). The earliest mention of this site is in Eusebius' *Onomasticon* (GCS 11.1:141): *Aenon iuxta Salim... ostenditur nunc usque locus in octavo lapide Scythopoleos iuxta Salim et Iordanem*, a localization confirmed by Jerome (*ibid.*, 153) and by the pilgrim Aetheria-Egeria (fn. 15) in A.D. 385. The texts are printed in EBS, 2nd ed., 265-68; compare also the Madaba map. The Byzantine texts are collected in Kopp, *Die heiligen Stätten*, 166-72. The attraction of this identification is that it keeps the Baptist's activity close to the River Jordan, and near to a group of springs. The location is still favoured (though sometimes with a question-mark) in some late twentieth-century Bible maps. The weakness of the identification is that nowhere in the vicinity is there any place-name evocative either of Aenon or of Salim (according to Abel, *Géographie*, I 447; II 442).

Edward Robinson first (1852), then Conder (1882) and later Albright (1924) argued that the two place-names are found in proximity only in the region around Nablus. They suggested that the Johannine Salim was to be identified with the Arab village of Sâlim, 2.5 miles = 4.5 km east of Tell Balata (= the biblical Shechem), and Aenon with 'Ain Farah, 7.5 miles = 12 km north-east of this village. Abel, who in his *Géographie* (1938) had upheld the identification with Tell ar-Radgha (above), later opted decisively for 'Ain Farah on the ground that 'les sources médiocres qui se font jour dans le jungle au sud de Beisân...ne supportent pas décidément l'identification des sources de Jean 3.22s.' (*Histoire* [1952], I 441). 'Ain Farah (grid 1825–1884) certainly has abundant springs, but in spite of this, there is no trace of any settlement nearby, except for Tell el-Farah (the ancient Tirzah?), abandoned around 600 B.C., presumably because of malaria, which was endemic there until after 1950. Thus 'Ain Farah cannot be the Johannine Aenon, not only because of its distance from Salim (7.5 miles = 12 km), but even more because the Baptist would hardly have chosen an uninhabited and mosquito-ridden marshland as a centre for his ministry. There is, however, a different site, Khirbet 'Einun, some 5 miles = 8 km further up the valley (grid 1875–1898), near the top of a hill, at 439 m. De Vaux has suggested that when the population left 'Ain Farah for a healthier location, they kept the old name (Aenon) for their new village, even though it had no springs at all. This site is rightly rejected by Bernard, both because of its lack of water and of its distance from Salim. Bernard gives the distance as 7 miles, but that is only by direct flight; otherwise Khirbet 'Einun is 12.5 miles = 20 km distant from Salim, on a most difficult road which has to climb over two mountain ranges.[7]

Boismard, followed by Murphy-O'Connor, starts by identifying the Johannine Salim with the Arab village of Sâlim, citing both ancient and medieval texts to illustrate the continuity of the name ('Aenon', 219-21). Today's Sâlim stands at the grid reference 1815–1795, though Albrecht Alt placed the ancient Salim half a kilometre further west, at Khirbet es-Sheikh Nasrallah (*Salem*, Palästinajahrbuch 25 [1929], 52ff.). From either spot, five springs are clearly visible on the eastern slopes of Mount Gerizim, and there are several others in the vicinity (Dalman, *SSW*, 212-14). In 128 B.C. John Hyrcanus attacked Shechem and destroyed the temple on Gerizim (Ant. XIII ix 1 = 255; War I ii 6 = 63); in 107 B.C. he sacked Samaria, and presumably Shechem as well (Ant. XIII x 2-3 = 275-83; War I ii 7 = 64); and at Tell Balata = Shechem, there are no archaeological signs of subsequent occupation (Schürer I 207, 520-21; II 18-19; G. E. Wright, *Shechem. The Biography of a Biblical City* [New York–Toronto, 1965], Appendix 4 by R. J. Bull, 214-28). Thus when the Fourth Gospel identifies the Springs in the area ('Aenon') as being *near Salim*, it is because Salim was in A.D. 28–30 the village closest to those springs. In those years, and later, when the Gospel was being written, Shechem did not exist. And once Flavia Neapolis (the future Nablus) had been founded, in A.D. 72–73, its rapid expansion and importance would easily account for the fact that a little area only a mile or so outside the city, formerly known as 'The Springs', simply disappeared from the topographical nomenclature of the district. Compare, in Excursus V, 'Bethany

---

[7] Bernard adds a third reason, namely, 'it is not likely that John the Baptist was labouring among the Samaritans (cf. 4.9)'. The references supporting the statements in the paragraph above are in Murphy-O'Connor, *NTS* 36 (1990), 364 (note that his grid references give northings before eastings, whereas this commentary follows the British usage, citing first eastings and then northings, as above).

Beyond the Jordan', the suggestion about the disappearance of the names Bethania and Ainon.

The location of the site is important, because the writer wished to assert that while Jesus was baptizing in Judaean territory (3.22), John also (καί) was baptizing not that far away, though in Samaritan territory, *because there were many springs there* (mark the plural, ὅτι ὕδατα πολλὰ ἦν ἐκεῖ); and John's ministry was meeting with success. **καὶ παρεγίνοντο καὶ ἐβαπτίζοντο.** *People were presenting themselves* (to John) *and being baptized.*

3.24. οὔπω γὰρ ἦν βεβλημένος εἰς τὴν φυλακὴν ὁ Ἰωάννης. The periphrastic ἦν βεβλημένος may be due to Aramaic influence, but the perfect participle may perhaps have been chosen to stress the duration of John's incarceration (*IBNTG* 17-18). The verse certainly implies that the reader knows the fact of the Baptist's imprisonment (even though it is never again referred to in the Fourth Gospel), but why is it mentioned here?

One suggestion is that the writer wishes to make a subtle emendation to the Synoptic tradition about the Baptist. According to Mt 11.2-15 ‖ Lk 7.18-28, the Baptist in prison sent some of his disciples to ask Jesus whether he was 'the one who was to come'. The question may be intended to imply either that the Baptist was on his part still unsure about Jesus' role, or that he wished his disciples to hear the answer directly from Jesus; it is impossible to determine which of the two suggestions is correct. The important fact is that in the Synoptic tradition, the question provides the occasion for Jesus to proclaim that in the days before the coming of the kingdom of God the Baptist is the greatest person ever born. The Fourth Gospel is about to reciprocate the eulogy, by making the Baptist, in his last words on earth, a wholehearted witness to the superior status of Jesus (3.25-30).

A second reason for mentioning John's imprisonment is to prepare the ground for 4.35-38, where Jesus states that the fields of Samaria are ripe for harvesting. 3.23-24 are then a clear hint that the seed had already been planted there, by the Baptist, and inform the readers of something unrecorded in the Synoptic tradition, namely, that John, before his imprisonment, had ministered in Samaritan territory, with real success.[8]

25. ἐγένετο οὖν. John, after a parenthesis, is fond of a resumptive οὖν; compare 2.18; 4.42 (*JG* 2633; Robertson, 433 fn. 3). **ζήτησις**, a *hapax legomenon* in the Johannine writings, is translated *argument* (NIV), *dispute* (NEB NAB), *debate* (REB), *discussion* (RSV NRSV JB NJB). Nothing in the word itself enables one to decide between the various renderings. **ἐκ τῶν μαθητῶν Ἰωάννου.** Some take this as equivalent to the partitive genitive, with something like ἐν τισίν or ἐν τοῖς

---

[8] J. A. T. Robinson and Boismard.

understood (so MHT III 208), to give the meaning *a discussion [among some] of John's disciples.* That is possible, but it is more attractive to take ἐκ τῶν μαθητῶν as indicating the source of the dispute, *on the part of John's disciples*, as in Herodotus V 21 (ζήτησις ἐκ τῶν Περσέων) or Dionysius Halic. VIII 89 4 (ζήτησις ἐκ παύτων). **μετὰ 'Ιουδαίου.** Both 'Ιουδαίου and 'Ιουδαίων are ancient readings, with support rather evenly divided (see NA²⁷). 'Ιουδαίου is preferred, on the ground that the text is less likely to have been altered from the plural to the singular (thus *TCGNT*). On μετά with the genitive of the person, Abbott writes that 'except in Revelation, it is not used in the NT with verbs of contention *e.g.* "fight *with* (i.e. *against*)", a use apparently confined to Hebraic Greek. In John, when it is used of people "talking" or "murmuring" or "questioning with one another (μετ' ἀλλήλων)", the speakers *are all on one side*, either the Jews against Jesus, or the disciples wishing to question Jesus...': thus Jn 6.43; 11.56; 16.19 (*JG* 2349; see also 2350). Hence: *Now a discussion arose on the part of John's disciples and a Jew on the subject of purification.*

περὶ καθαρισμοῦ. In John, καθαρισμός is found only here and at 2.6 (where it refers to ritual purification by water). Most English versions translate *purification* (or a cognate form), but NAB has *ceremonial washing*, and NIV, *ceremonial washings*. It is impossible to be precise about the questions discussed; one can only exclude anachronistic ideas. There would have been no question of purification from sin *ex opere operato*, in the sense (for example) in which the early Church understood the effect of infant baptism; or of suggesting that those who were repentant had, in the name of God, been cleansed from sin by the act of physical washing. Reception of John's baptism would have been the outward expression of repentance, a plea for divine mercy both here and now, and at the future judgment; but more than that we cannot say. Indeed, when judged against the Jewish background, the whole question of 'purification' is so bound up with the concept of what is termed 'defilement' (e.g. by contact with a dead body, or with blood) that it is almost impossible for Christians of today to discusss the issues profitably. See H. Thyen in *EDNT* II 218-19 (with bibliography).

26. καὶ ἦλθον πρὸς τὸν 'Ιωάννην κτλ. John's disciples are clearly the subject of ἦλθον, and probably so is the Jew as well. The use of the honorific **ῥαββί** (8 times in John + in 20.16, ῥαββουνι), is significant, for this is the only text in the NT where this title is addressed to someone other than Jesus. The writer thus represents the Baptist not as a solitary preacher living rough in the desert (as always in the Synoptics), but as the respected teacher of a well-defined religious group. **ὃς ἦν μετὰ σοῦ πέραν τοῦ 'Ιορδάνου** is a reference back to 1.26-36,[9] where the Baptist

---

[9] πέραν τοῦ 'Ιορδάνου occurs in Jn 1.28; 3.26; 10.40*. Elsewhere, only in Mt 4.15, 25 ‖ Mk 3.8, Mt 19.1 ‖ Mk 10.1.

spoke so reverently of Jesus (note 1.34, ἑώρακα καὶ μεμαρτύρηκα). ᾧ. In John, περί is the more common construction after μαρτυρεῖν (see 5.31), but the dative is found in 3.26.28, and (with τῇ ἀληθείᾳ) in 5.33; 18.37 (cf. 3 Jn 3). The distinction (if there is one) lies perhaps in this, that the dative is used when mentioning just the fact of witnessing, περί when the content needs to be stressed or clarified. Here in 3.26 the dative, far from being the sign of an editor (*pace* Brown), is a cross-reference to 1.26-36. **σὺ μεμαρτύρηκας.** It is sad that all the major English-language versions except the RV (*thou hast borne witness*) overlook the tense. In John especially, the perfect tense frequently calls attention to the abiding significance of an act (compare 19.22): thus ᾧ σὺ μεμαρτύρη-κας, *to whom you have been bearing witness*, implies that this witness continues, and has not been withdrawn. See *JG* 2473 and MHT III 83-84. **ἴδε οὗτος βαπτίζει καὶ πάντες ἔρχονται πρὸς αὐτόν.** '*Here he is*' (ἴδε), *himself baptizing, and everyone is going to him*. Many writers take this sentence to imply that John's disciples were disturbed by Jesus' actions, and even jealous of his success, but the text itself is utterly neutral, and does not warrant that interpretation.[10] The words '*to whom you have been bearing witness*', with the perfect tense indicating an abiding witness, and with their reference back to 1.26-36, represent both the Baptist and his disciples as being fully aware of Jesus' high destiny. 3.26 is certainly a literary construct by the evangelist to introduce the verses which follow, but it is a simple statement of fact: nothing in its wording supports the claim that it imputes jealousy to the followers of the Baptist. For some further detail on this matter, see Excursus IX, 'John the Baptist and His Followers'.

27. ἀπεκρίθη Ἰωάννης καὶ εἶπεν. The Baptist responds by declaring that Jesus is superior to him, and that he himself is happy to acknowledge this visible reversal of their respective roles. These are the last words of the Baptist to his disciples. **οὐ δύναται ἄνθρωπος λαμβάνειν οὐδὲ ἕν ἐὰν μὴ ᾖ δεδομένον αὐτῷ ἐκ τοῦ οὐρανοῦ.** In John, the present infinitive is used after δύνασθαι in order to enunciate a general law, to express what one can habitually do, whereas the aorist refers to a particular act (*JG* 2496). *No one can take a single thing as his own possession, unless it be given him from heaven.* That is to say, the Baptist has no ground to feel aggrieved if others—even his own disciples—should choose to go to Jesus (3.26); they are not the Baptist's personal property. And if ἄνθρωπος is understood as referring to Jesus, the conclusion is the same: Jesus has a right to them. The statement is true whether the clause is taken as referring to the following of Jesus during his earthly ministry

---

[10] Compare Chrysostom, Hom. 29.2 *initio* (on Jn 3.25): 'Look carefully, please, at the gentle phrasing of the evangelist. He does not launch into a tirade, but tries to soften, as far as he can, the charge' (of jealousy on the part of John's disciples).

(compare 6.44, 65), or as the evangelist's reflection, sixty years later, about those who have been 'given' to Christ by his Father (6.37, 39, 40 etc.).

28. αὐτοὶ ὑμεῖς μοι μαρτυρεῖτε. μοι is omitted in many manuscripts, perhaps by scribes who were conscious that περί was the normal usage after μαρτυρεῖν in John; so it is, but the Baptist's disciples are not here testifying to others about their teacher's character (that would be unthinkable on his lips). Some modern writers see this dative as a sure sign of a later editorial hand (→ 3.26), but it is best taken as a dative of advantage, *my witnesses*. **ὅτι εἶπον [ὅτι] οὐκ εἰμὶ ἐγὼ ὁ Χριστός.** The clumsiness of ὅτι εἶπον ὅτι explains the confusion among the manuscripts attested in NA[27]. The second (bracketed) ὅτι is a prime example of the ὅτι recitativum, 'the equivalent of inverted commas' (Turner), whereby direct speech is preferred in narrative, and sometimes even mingled with indirect speech (MHT III 325-26). On the content, → 1.20. **ἀλλ' ὅτι ἀπεσταλμένος εἰμὶ ἔμπροσθεν ἐκείνου.** The words refer back to 1.27, 30 (and 1.15), where ὀπίσω (local, not temporal) gives the sense *a follower of mine* (*pace* BDAG 2b). ἔμπροσθεν here corresponds to ὀπίσω there, and is (as normally) local. *You yourselves are my witnesses that I said, I am not the Christ, but am an envoy sent on ahead of him* (compare NIV NRSV). **ἐκείνου** indicates 'the one just mentioned' (BDF 293 [1]), i.e. that *follower of mine* (who is indeed the Christ).

29. Dodd considered that this verse probably reflected an authentic saying of the Baptist.[11] Lindars suggested, on the basis of Mk 2.18-20, that it may have been originally a saying of Jesus subsequently transferred to the Baptist, but his idea has not found acceptance.[12] On the meaning of the text as it stands in the Gospel, a general consensus obtains.

According to the OT, and in Judaism, the bridegroom awaited at the end of time is always understood to be Yahweh, never the Messiah, but by A.D. 80–90, the followers of Jesus had accepted that his coming in the flesh was the fulfilment of time, the inauguration of the eschatological age. Jesus was for them the King's Son, come to claim his bride, the new Israel of the New Covenant. For further detail, see 'The Interpretation of the Wine Miracle at Cana', pp. 188-97. This is the context in which v. 29 must be interpreted.

ὁ ἔχων τὴν νύμφην νυμφίος ἐστίν. To translate verbatim, *He who has the bride is the bridegroom*, is implicitly to arraign the evangelist on a charge of serious tautology. A more accurate version,

---

[11] *Historical Tradition*, 279-87, especially 282-85.
[12] *NTS* 16 (1969–70), 324-29 = *Essays on John*, 15-20; and in his commentary.

with epexegesis, would be, *It is he who holds the bride in his arms that is the bridegroom*,[13] a rendering intended to suggest how the words would have been understood, by Christians and followers of the Baptist alike, around A.D. 80–90. The Baptist is then asserting that the very fact that large crowds are converging on Jesus is itself evidence that Jesus has won the heart of the bride (Israel), and must be the bridegroom. The evangelist, moreover, by placing these words on the lips of the Baptist, is also reasserting, in a manner only thinly veiled, the message proclaimed 'on the other side of the Jordan', 'Behold your God!' (→ 1.19-51, especially 1.29). ὁ δὲ φίλος τοῦ νυμφίου represents the Hebrew 'Shoshᵉbin', denoting a friend who acted as the bridegroom's agent in the arranging of a marriage, and who also had a prominent place in the wedding festivities (BDAG). His role was more extensive than that of best man or groomsman (*garçon d'honneur, Brautführer*), for it was the duty of the Shoshᵉbin to arrange the ceremonies, to ensure that the bride was bathed, appropriately dressed and adorned, and was then publicly escorted from her father's house to her new home.[14] ὁ ἑστηκὼς καὶ ἀκούων αὐτοῦ χαρᾷ χαίρει διὰ τὴν φωνὴν τοῦ νυμφί. According to some Jewish texts, the Shoshᵉbin was to stand guard outside the bridal chamber until the bridegroom called out to assure him that the union had been consummated with a virgin bride.[15] The Baptist by his ministry had striven to ensure that the bride was cleansed, duly clothed in righteousness, and brought to her intended spouse (compare Eph 5.27); it only remained for him to hear that the bridegroom had taken her as his own. Hence χαρᾷ χαίρει, a cognate dative, common in Biblical Greek, and parallel to the Hebrew infinitive absolute: see MHT II 444; III 241-42.

John's last words to his disciples are αὕτη οὖν ἡ χαρὰ ἡ ἐμὴ πεπλήρωται, the first occurrence of πληροῦσθαι in this Gospel. Jesus later mentions χαρὰ πεπληρωμένη (three times) at the end of his own ministry, to presage the joy of his disciples (cf. 15.11, ἡ ἐμὴ ἐν ὑμῖν; 16.24, ὑμῶν; 17.13, τὴν ἐμὴν ἐν ἑαυτοῖς). χαρὰ πεπληρωμένη is 'the joy that leaves nothing to be desired'. *That is why the joy that I am now experiencing fulfils all my desires.* **30.** ἐκεῖνον δεῖ αὐξάνειν, ἐμὲ δὲ ἐλαττοῦσθαι. *He is destined to grow ever greater, I to grow less and less.* δεῖ, in the sense of *divinely destined*; αὐξάνειν is contrasted with ἐλαττοῦσθαι possibly in the sense of *wax and wane*. Thus many

---

[13] To explain this translation, one may point out (a) that under ἔχω, BAG gives as the very first sense (I 1 a; cf. BDAG 3a), 'lit. *hold in the hands…* Of holding in the hand without ἐν τῇ χειρι (Josh 6.8) ἑ. κιθάραν Rev 5.8', plus 8.3.6 etc.; (b) that LSJ, under ἔχω (A) A I, reads, '4. *have to wife* or *as husband* (usually without γυναῖκα, ἄνδρα)', citing Od IV.569; VII 313; Il. III 53 etc. But to translate *He who takes to wife the bride is the bridegroom* would be an even worse tautology than the verbatim version rejected at the beginning of the paragraph in the text above.

[14] See I. Abrahams, *Studies in Pharisaism* II 213; J. Jeremias in *TWNT* IV 1094⁴⁻¹¹.

[15] SB I 45-46. The main text is bKetuboth I 5, 12a (pp. 63-64 in the ETr).

Greek and Latin Fathers (see BAG *s.v.* αὐξάνειν 3.): Origen points to the Daystar, which when it first appears, seems brighter than the sun (Frag. 45).

In *An Aramaic Approach*, 3rd ed., 146-49, Matthew Black suggested that underlying the words of the Baptist in 3.27-36 is an Aramaic poem or prophecy rich in parallelisms and clever wordplay detectable by translation into Aramaic, the wordplay being particularly evident in vv. 29-30 and 31-32. Black's arguments are fully and fairly presented by Barrett (2nd ed., 222-27), whose verdict is 'not proven'. Subsequent commentators have been equally reluctant to accept Black's case, but it deserves a kinder fate than premature oblivion, for it is ingenious and interesting, and not impossible. If true, it would, of course, increase the likelihood that the Gospel text represents accurately words spoken by the Baptist.

3.31-36: WORDS OF THE BAPTIST OR THE EVANGELIST?

Whether 3.31-36 are intended to be read as a continuation of the words of the Baptist is debated, and the introduction of quotation marks into editions of the Bible has made studied neutrality no longer practicable. The AV and RV, like the TR, had no such problem, but the NIV JB NJB print 31-36 as words of the Baptist, a view acknowledged in RSV[mg] and NRSV[mg]; Black, Barrett and Boismard also interpret the words as ascribed to the Baptist. Most modern versions, however, close the inverted commas after 3.30, thereby excluding vv. 31-36 from the Baptist's speech: thus RSV NRSV NEB REB [NIV[mg]] NovaVulgata. This is the opinion of Bengel, Westcott and Lagrange, who take the words as a comment by the evangelist. Whichever view one takes will inevitably influence one's assessment of the content of the text; and *vice versa*, one's interpretation of the content will inevitably affect one's judgment about the intended speaker.

Many, perceiving no strong connection between 3.31-36 and the preceding verses ascribed to the Baptist, have judged vv. 31-36 to be a comment by the evangelist, but misplaced. F. W. Lewis[16] in 1910 and Moffatt[17] simply removed the problem by suggesting that 3.22-30 should be transferred, to follow after 2.12, a proposal that found no welcome because it contributed nothing to the better understanding either of the relocated verses or of the sequence of events in ch. 2 (see Bernard, xxiii-xxiv). The suggestion may, however, have alerted others to the appositeness of reading 3.31-36 immediately after 3.21. This was suggested

---

[16] *Disarrangements in the Fourth Gospel*, Cambridge, 1910, 25-31.

[17] *Introduction*, 553 fn.

(first?) by Cadoux in 1919,[18] broadcast by Bernard (xxiv), and accepted by Bultmann: their preferred reordering was 3.16-21, 31-36, 22-30, with v. 30 leading smoothly into 4.1. Schnackenburg has a slight variation on it: he places 3.31-36 after 3.12, to give 3.1-12, 31-36, 13-30. Bernard, Bultmann and Schnackenburg all agree that in vv. 31-36 the evangelist is speaking for Jesus. Brown[19] (with Boismard) regards vv. 31-36 as a variation on 3.11-21 and also on 12.44-50; and with Dodd (*Interpretation*, 309), he prefers to think of 3.31-36 as the evangelist's recapitulation of the whole chapter.

The last-mentioned opinion has much to commend it, and it will have a strong appeal for those who are firmly convinced that the task of the exegete is to explain the text as it stands unless insuperable difficulties prevent one from making good sense of it. 3.31-36 will therefore be interpreted in terms of their present context, and the view taken in this commentary is that 3.31-36 are, like 3.16-21, a comment by the evangelist, serving the same role as a Greek chorus (→ 3.16).

31a. ὁ ἐρχόμενος is used of Jesus in Jn 1.15, 27; 11.27; 12.13, and here in 3.31, twice. Since 'the present participle…is timeless and durative' (Robertson, 891), it can signify the One who is/was to come in the future; the One who is always coming in the ever-present 'Today' (compare Ps 95.7d, and → Jn 1.9); the One who came at a precise moment in time now past (Gal 4.4; Heb 1.1); and all three. It will be translated as *The One who comes,* intended as a title, without limiting its reference either to the past, or the present or the future. **ἄνωθεν**, in the present context, can only mean *from above* (contrast Jn 3.3). The word recalls 3.2 (ἀπὸ θεοῦ ἐλήλυθας), and 11-13 (especially ὁ ἐκ τοῦ οὐρανοῦ καταβάς, v. 13). **ἐπάνω πάντων ἐστίν**, *is superior to all* (compare BDAG ἐπάνω 3, which cites Cebes 26.3, ἐπάνω πάντων ἐστί). *The One who comes from above is superior to all.*

31b. ὁ ὢν ἐκ τῆς γῆς. The words are a direct pointer to Gen 2.7, where humanity was fashioned out of dust ἀπὸ τῆς γῆς, and the same thought is found in 1 Cor 15.47. ὁ ὢν ἐκ τῆς γῆς denotes the human being as creature (but not as sinner). **ἐκ τῆς γῆς ἐστιν καὶ ἐκ τῆς γῆς λαλεῖ.** *Whoever issues from the earth belongs to the earth, and whatever that person says is of earthly origin.* One consequence of this 'earthly' origin is that the creature's knowledge of God is limited to what can be known by natural means (the 'natural theology' envisaged in Rom 1.18-21). The wording is strikingly different from that in 1 Jn 4.5: αὐτοὶ ἐκ τοῦ <u>κόσμου</u> εἰσίν, διὰ τοῦτο ἐκ τοῦ <u>κόσμου</u> λαλοῦσιν καὶ ὁ

---

[18] 'The Johannine Account of the Early Ministry of Jesus', *JTS* 20 (1919), 311-20, on 317.

[19] See his pp. 160, 147

κόσμος αὐτῶν ἀκούει. The κοσμός of Imperial Rome is not to be equated with the γῆ of the Garden of Eden before the primordial sin (see the essay at 1.10, 'The Meaning of ΚΟΣΜΟΣ in the Fourth Gospel').

31c. ὁ ἐκ τοῦ οὐρανοῦ ἐρχόμενος is clearly parallel to ὁ ἄνωθεν ἐρχόμενος in 31a, its meaning even more explicit. NA²⁷ puts square brackets around ἐπάνω πάντων ἐστίν. Their inclusion or exclusion makes no material difference to the content of the passage (and this probably accounts for the confusion). For an assessment of the textual evidence, see *TCGNT*.

32. The verse recapitulates what Jesus said (in the plural, ἑωράκαμεν, μαρτυροῦμεν), both on his own account, and on behalf of his followers, in 3.11-12 (→). Here, however, since the verbs are in the singular, and their subject is 'the One who comes from heaven', they merit a second scrutiny. The perfect in ὃ **ἑώρακεν** indicates the abiding memory of the vision (the 'durative' sense = *and still sees*): compare BDF 318 (4); Robertson, 895-96; contrast MHT III 85. καὶ **ἤκουσεν**: John always uses the (non-durative, punctiliar) aorist when describing Jesus as having heard something from the Father (3.32; 8.26, 40; 15.15: → *JG* 2451). **τοῦτο μαρτυρεῖ**: though the testimony of the One who comes from heaven (= **τὴν μαρτυρίαν αὐτοῦ**) is being submitted in evidence at the present moment, it is not being accepted by anyone (**οὐδεὶς λαμβάνει**). These words cannot be intended as a saying of the Baptist, for they would be in open contradiction to the report of the alleged success of Jesus' preaching in 3.26. No such difficulty arises if the verse is attributed to the evangelist, affirming that *The One who comes from heaven bears witness to what he has seen and heard, yet no one is accepting his testimony*.

33. ὁ λαβὼν αὐτοῦ τὴν μαρτυρίαν. ὁ λαβών (aorist) must, because of its tense, designate the Baptist, and must mean that he, during his lifetime, had accepted the testimony of Jesus (αὐτοῦ). ²⁰ **ἐσφράγισεν** (3.33; 6.27) here means *to authenticate, to certify something as genuine*, as a seal does when affixed to a document (BDAG 4). **ἀληθής** here = *true to his word*. Therefore: *One who did accept his witness put the seal of his own authority to this—that God is true to his word.* The meaning of this statement is explained in 34 (γάρ).

34. ὃν γὰρ ἀπέστειλεν ὁ θεὸς τὰ ῥήματα τοῦ θεοῦ λαλεῖ. The last five words indicate clearly that 'the one whom God sent' refers primarily to Jesus (→ 3.11 on λαλεῖν), but without excluding the Baptist; he too was 'sent from God' (1.6; 3.28), and therefore he too 'speaks the word of God' (again, → 3.11 on λαλεῖν). *He whom God sent speaks the words of God.* **οὐ γὰρ ἐκ μέτρου δίδωσιν τὸ πνεῦμα.** 'ἐκ μέτρου is

---

²⁰ The insertion of οὗτος (after μαρτυρίαν) in 𝔓⁶⁶ᶜ emphasizes this.

found nowhere else in the Greek language' but must be the opposite of ἐν μέτρῳ, and must therefore mean *without using a measure* (BDAG). The subject of the clause is unexpressed. For some, it is God who *does not bestow the Spirit by measuring it out*, for others, the One whom God has sent, but the resultant possession of the Spirit will be immeasurable, whoever bestows it. Thus 3.33-34 affirm (1) that the Baptist during his lifetime accepted the testimony of Jesus; and (2) acknowledged that Jesus' preaching was (like his own) the word of God. The evangelist is entreating the disciples of the Baptist to recognize that they will not lose anything by accepting the teaching of Jesus, because God's Spirit is not quantitatively divisible.

35-36. Apart from the two references in the Prologue (1.14, 18), and the one cryptic allusion in the Temple (→ 2.16), the word 'Father' has not appeared in the Gospel until now. This makes it most improbable that 3.35-36 were intended to be read as uttered by the Baptist, for nowhere in the NT is he ever presented as speaking of the Fatherhood of God. Nor are the verses intended to be read as words of Jesus, for the last (and only) speaker mentioned in this passage (3.27) was the Baptist, and in the Fourth Gospel the reader is always told whenever Jesus begins to speak. 3.35-36 are therefore the comment of the evangelist (or of an editor) as he ends this section. Here he addresses to the disciples of the Baptist the same gentle but clear admonition with which he concluded the previous section, addressed to Nicodemus and the Jews: compare 3.35-36 with 3.15-18.

35. ὁ πατὴρ ἀγαπᾷ τὸν υἱόν. On ἀγαπᾶν, → 3.16, noting the context there and in 3.17. Here the simple fact is stated, as the ground for the second clause, **καὶ πάντα δέδωκεν ἐν τῇ χειρὶ αὐτοῦ.** There is no significant difference in meaning between the wording here and that in 13.3 (*JG* 2334c), unless 13.3 refers to the act of conferring power (ἔδωκεν[21]...εἰς τὰς χεῖρας), and 3.35 to its resultant possession (δέδωκεν ἐν). On the Father's love for the Son, see 10.17; 15.9; 17.24, 26.

36. ὁ πιστεύων εἰς τὸν υἱὸν ἔχει ζωὴν αἰώνιον. → 3.15-16. **ὁ δὲ ἀπειθῶν τῷ υἱῷ.** ἀπειθῶν, a *hapax legomenon* in the Gospels, is here best interpreted as 'refusing to accept the testimony of the Son' (who speaks the words of God, 3.34). Thus BDAG; *EDNT* I 118 ('a technical term for non-acceptance of the Christian faith', P. Bläser); and Bultmann, *TWNT* I 118-19, citing Rom 11.30, 32; Gal 3.22; Heb 4.6, 11; Eph 2.2; 5.6. Anyone who does not accept that testimony **οὐκ ὄψεται ζωήν**, *shall never see life*. The phrase recalls Jn 3.3, that only those who are 'reborn from above' can 'see' the kingdom of God. To enable this to happen, there is One who stands in no need of rebirth, ὁ ἄνωθεν ἐρχόμενος (3.31), the υἱὸς μονογενής, the utterly unique One who came into this

---

[21] If this is the true reading: → 13.3.

world (1.10; 3.16) παρὰ πατρός (1.14), in order to show all humankind what the Fatherhood of God entails. ἐν αὐτῷ ζωὴ ἦν (1.4), and ἐκεῖνος ἐξηγήσατο: → 1.18; 3.11, 32. If anyone refuses to accept his testimony, **ἡ ὀργὴ τοῦ θεοῦ μένει ἐπ' αὐτόν.** To refuse to accept the teaching of Jesus, Son of God, revealing the Father's all-merciful love, as epitomized for example in the passage 'God loved the world so dearly' (→ 3.16-18), is to place oneself in a relationship with God in which strict justice, as between creature and Creator, and that alone, must hold sway. Then one thinks instinctively of Ps 130.3, and is relieved to recall the verses which follow after it. ἡ ὀργή (here) is a *hapax legomenon* in John.

According to the Synoptic tradition, the Baptist began his ministry by calling upon sinners to save themselves from 'the wrath that is about to come' (Mt 3.7 ‖ Lk 3.7), and he was possibly perplexed (his disciples certainly were) to learn later that Jesus was preaching not of the wrath but of the mercy of God.[22] But among the great prophets of Israel, the wrath of God is never the final word, and neither could 'the wrath about to come' be God's final word to his people. The Fourth Evangelist, in these last verses addressed to the followers of the Baptist, is appealing to them to reconsider their position, to remember that their master had always insisted that 'God is true to his word' (3.33), and to reflect that, even after the destruction of Jerusalem by the Romans, manifold mercies as yet undisclosed must still be awaiting God's people, to give them a future and a hope (Jer 29.11).

---

[22] See Mt 3.7-12 ‖ Lk 3.7-9, 15-17, and Mt 11.2-11, 16-19 ‖ Lk 7.18-35. T. W. Manson, *The Sayings of Jesus*, London, 1949, 40-41 and 66-71, is outstanding on these verses.

THE INTERPRETATION OF JOHN 3
IN THE TWENTIETH CENTURY

The shifts in twentieth-century exegesis of this chapter are instructive. In the early years, much of the discussion about the Fourth Gospel turned on how far any of the discourses record the actual words, or represent at least the substance, of Jesus' teaching, during his life on earth. Some, like Westcott, Zahn and B. Weiss, continued to uphold very conservative positions, while others such as Loisy (cautiously, 1903), H. J. Holtzmann and Wellhausen, Schmiedel and Jülicher, contended that the discourses in John represent not the teaching of Jesus during his earthly life, but the evangelist's exposition of the faith of his own generation, presented as having been uttered on earth by the Logos.[1] The Nicodemus pericope is an ideal test case.

Some British writers sought to circumvent many of the problems simply by rearranging the text of the Gospel. Thus Moffatt, in his translation of the NT (1913), placed 3.31 after 3.21, and 3.22-30 between 2.12 and 2.13. Bernard (1928) suggested (pp. xvi-xxx) that 3.22-30 should be transposed to follow (instead of preceding) 3.31-36, a simple adjustment (adopted also by Bultmann) whereby the verses about the Baptist (22-30) lead smoothly into 4.1;[2] in exchange, vv. 31-36 become a comment confirming the statements in 3.19-21, about bringing light into the world.

More radical relocations were also proposed. G. H. C. MacGregor, in the Moffatt NT Commentary (1928), proposed to read: (1) 3.1-13, 31-33, 22-30; 4.1-2, and (2) 12.30-32; 3.14-15; 12.34; 3.16-21; 12.35-36 (with 12.33 as a gloss, or possibly a doublet of 3.14-15).[3] Shortly afterwards, Greville P. Lewis sought (like others) to resolve two problems at the same time, the awkwardness of some texts in ch. 3, and the dating of the Cleansing of the Temple. In his view, the original order in the Gospel was: 12.1-19; 2.13–3.11; 12.20-32; 3.14-15; 12.34; 3.12-13, 16-21;

---

[1] For references, see Sanday, *Criticism*, 1-41; W. F. Howard, *Fourth Gospel*, 33-83.

[2] C. J. Cadoux had suggested this in 'The Johannine Account of the Early Ministry of Jesus', *JTS* 20 (1919), 311-20, on 317.

[3] MacGregor had previously set out his ideas in 'A Suggested Rearrangement of the Johannine text (Jn 3.14-36 and 12.30-36)', *ExpTimes* 35 (1923–24), 476-77. In his commentary, see both 77-85 and 268-69.

12.35-41, but many of these verses were relocated by the evangelist, who added 12.33 as a comment.[4]

But mere rearrangement of verses was not enough to answer the fundamental question raised by Liberal Christianity. If the Gospels do not represent (at least substantially) the teaching of Jesus, then whose teaching do they represent? Bultmann judged much of ch. 3 to have been composed by the evangelist on the basis of a 'Revelatory Discourse' of (pre-Christian) Gnostic origin, the closest parallels to which are found in Mandaean texts (see his footnotes on 3.9-21). His commentary on ch. 3 rests on the hypothesis that John applied to Jesus a Gnostic view of the Redeemer. Schnackenburg, while open to the possible influence of Hellenistic religions, finds parallels rather in Jewish texts: see his commentary, and his Excurses V and VI. Like Bernard and Bultmann (and for the same reason), he too places 3.22-30 immediately before 4.1; but he prefers to close the Nicodemus narrative after 3.12, and to insert at that point first 3.31-36, and then 3.13-21. He takes both passages to be the evangelist's reflections on the dialogue with Nicodemus set out in 3.1-12, to answer the question left hanging in the air at 3.12.

Since 1970, none of the major commentaries on the Greek text (Barrett, 2nd ed., 1978, B-L 1978, and the posthumous commentary from Haenchen ([†1975] 1980; ETr 1984), has significantly altered (or sought to alter) the classical methods of searching for the doctrinal content of the Nicodemus passage. Nor have the various articles of narrative or rhetorical criticism. And the repositioning of allegedly dislocated texts is no longer so fashionable. The most profound change in the understanding of John 3 has been the gradual, slow but sure, acceptance in the major Christian Churches that the truth of the Gospel's teaching does not depend upon, and therefore does not stand or fall with, subjective certainty that the believer is there reading (at least substantially) the very words of the historical Jesus. By contrast with the position prevailing in 1900, it is now widely agreed that the doctrinal message of the New Testament (for those who accept it as revelation) is to be found in the canonical text of the written Gospel, whether the words are those of the historical Jesus or of the evangelist or of an editor.

---

[4] 'Dislocations in the Fourth Gospel. The Temple Cleansing and the Visit of Nicodemus', *ExpTimes* 44 (1932–33), 228-30. Similar ideas were advocated by F. Warburton Lewis, 'The Arrangement of the Texts in the Third Chapter of St John', *ExpTimes* 37 (1925–26), 179-81; J. H. Michael, 'The Arrangement of the Texts in the Third Chapter of St John', *ExpTimes* 37 (1925–26), 428-29; and J. G. Gourbillon, 'La parabole du serpent d'airain et la "lacune" du chapître III de l'Evangile selon s. Jean', *Vivre et penser* 2 = *RB* 51 (1942), 213-26, who advocated 12.20-31; 3.14-21; 12.32-36a; 12.44-50; 12.36b-44.

JOHN THE BAPTIST AND HIS FOLLOWERS

There is nowadays general agreement that the Baptist summoned his generation to seek pardon for their sins before God's judgment descended on the land in the not far distant future. The NT gives no details about the manner in which the baptizands confessed their sins, but it may well have been in words similar to those used on the Day of Atonement (*Yoma* 3.8; 4.2; 6.1),[1] or in the ceremony at Qumran for the renewal of the Covenant (1QS 1.22–2.1). The rite of baptism in water would then have set a public seal on the declaration of willingness to repent, and to turn to a life of obedience to God as revealed in the Law. In all likelihood an individual confessed and was baptized only once, given that the day of judgment was held to be imminent. There is still debate about the nature of the 'baptism by fire' and ἐν πνεύματι (storm-wind? or a later Christian interpretation?), and about who was to initiate this baptism of judgment. Would it be God himself, or the Son of Man, or some other figure, or possibly God working with and through the Son of Man (compare *1 En* 48–50: *OTP* I 35-36)?

Unlike the Synoptics, the Fourth Gospel nowhere presents the Baptist as preaching of an imminent judgment, and does not explicitly mention his 'baptism of repentance for the forgiveness of sins' (Mk 1.4). This silence about the possibility of securing pardon for sins by receiving John's baptism, and the various negative statements about him ('he was not the light, not the Messiah, not the prophet' etc.) led Wilhelm Baldensperger to assert (in 1898) that the writer of the Fourth Gospel was distinctly hostile to those disciples of the Baptist who did not eventually follow the way of Jesus.[2] His thesis was so widely accepted that Kümmel could write in his *Introduction to the NT* that 'Baldensperger first proved that there was in John a recognizable polemic against the disciples of John the Baptist'.[3] At the close of the twentieth century, judgments are

---

[1] Cited in H. Danby, *The Mishnah*, 165, 166, 169.

[2] *Der Prolog des vierten Evangeliums, sein polemisch-apologetischer Zweck*, Freiburg-im-Br., 1898.

[3] ETr revised ed. 1975, 199. Goguel, too, *Jean-Baptiste*, 1928, 76 represents the thesis as virtually proven, citing among other supporters M. Dibelius, *Die urchristliche Ueberlieferung von Johannes dem Täufer*, FRLANT, Göttingen, 1911, 119, and W. Bauer, *Das Johannesevangelium*, Tübingen, 2nd ed., 1925, 15-16 (contrast the 1st ed., 1913, 12).

more qualified, and though many exegetes would agree that there was at
least tension, and perhaps even a measure of antagonism, between the
Johannine community and the 'Baptists', many of them add that it should
not be exaggerated. For a survey of the arguments on this issue, see
Schnackenburg, I 148-50 = ETr I 167-69, and (for detail), his article 'Das
vierte Evangelium und die Johannesjünger', *Historisches Jahrbuch* 77
(1958), 21-38; R. E. Brown *John* I LXVII-LXX and 69-71; *Birth of the
Messiah*, 282-85; *Community*, 68-71.

John has three references to 'the disciples of the Baptist'.[4] John 1.35
and 37 contain not a trace of hostility, but begin the story of the calling of
Jesus' first disciples. Neither is there is any proof that 3.25-26 betray
antagonism on the part of the writer towards the Baptist's disciples,
unless the words attributed to them are construed as an expression of
envy, an interpretation which is not self-evident (see the commentary).

Given the paucity of NT evidence, it is not surprising that some have
interpreted the figure of John the Baptist by appealing more to the wider
historical background. One example is Robert Eisler, according to whom
the Baptist was, like the Zealots, a champion of Jewish national independence, a man who spent over forty years (5 B.C.–A.D. 35) calling
upon the people to revolt against any ruler (such as the Herods, or the
Romans) not of pure Israelite stock as prescribed in Deut 17.14-15.
Inevitably, he came in the end to believe that the Baptist was himself the
Messiah.[5] The fragility of the foundations was exposed by Maurice
Goguel even before the final version of Eisler's work was published, a
judgement which subsequent scholarship has, with few exceptions,
confirmed.[6] Goguel himself accepted that Jesus and John did for a time
exercise parallel ministries, but thinks they separated before John's
imprisonment because of differences over the role of John's baptism
(→ 3.24-25).[7]

It is, however, an assured fact that a number of religious groups
claiming to trace their origin to John the Baptist survived after NT times,
though their profile is obscure because the documentation, mainly from
the Pseudo-Clementine literature, is scanty, and of uncertain interpre-

---

[4] The term figures also in the Synoptics: Mt 9.14 || Mk 2.18 || Lk 5.33; Mt 11.2 || Lk
7.18; Mt 14.12 || Mk 6.29; Lk 11.1.

[5] *ΙΗΣΟΥΣ ΒΑΣΙΛΕΥΣ ΟΥ ΒΑΣΙΛΕΥΣΑΣ*, Heidelberg, I 1929; II 1930: ETr
(abridged) *The Messiah Jesus and John the Baptist*, 1931, 221-311. Eisler's prodigiously
erudite work (and his theory) is now virtually forgotten, because (as he himself admitted)
it rests upon the postulate that the interpolations in the Old Slavonic translation of
Josephus (made in Lithuania around A.D. 1250–1260) are based upon historically
trustworthy fragments written in Aramaic. These additions in the Old Slavonic version
are most easily accessible (in English translation) in H. St. J. Thackeray's edition in the
Loeb Library, *Josephus* III 635-61 (prepared with the assistance of Dr Eisler).

[6] *Jean-Baptiste* (1928), 20-33 and 297-302 (the latter written on the basis of proof-
sheets obligingly supplied by Dr Eisler, but not published until 1930). For the judgment
of subsequent scholarship on Eisler's work, see Hengel, *The Zealots*, Excursus I, 16-18.

[7] *Jean-Baptiste*, 86-95, 257-71; *Jésus*, 2nd ed., 210-13.

tation. One group, separated from, and even hostile to, the Christian Church, existed in Syria and in Asia Minor around A.D. 230, and may have survived until around A.D. 300. The most one can say for certain is that some of these groups believed that John the Baptist was the Messiah, and others that he was at least superior to Jesus.[8]

For a summary of the historical questions concerning the Baptist, see J. Gnilka, *Jesus of Nazareth*, 71-79; and for an exhaustive treatment, J. P. Meier, *A Marginal Jew* II (with extensive notes), 'John without Jesus', 19-99; 'Jesus with and without John', 100-233.

---

[8] The most complete study is still that by Joseph Thomas, *Le mouvement baptiste en Palestine et Syrie 150 av. J.C.–300 ap. J.-C.*, Gembloux, 1935: on this topic see pages 114-39, 'Les Johannites aux premiers siècles chrétiens'. For the evidence that these disciples, around A.D. 230, regarded the Baptist as the Messiah, see *Clem. Recogn.* I 53-54 and 60 (*PG* 1.1237-38 and 1240); for their view of him as superior to Jesus (around A.D. 300?), see *Hom.* II 17 = *Recogn.* 61 (*PG* 1.1308) and *Hom* II 23-24 = *Recogn.* II 8. See also, G. N. Stanton, 'Jewish Christian Elements in the Pseudo Clementine Writings', in eds. O. Skarsaune and R. Hvalvik, *Jewish Believers in Jesus*, Peabody, 2007, 305-24.

3. *The Samaritan Woman:*
The New Order Presented to the People of Samaria (4.1-45)

^{4.1}As soon as the Lord became aware that the Pharisees had heard that he, Jesus, was making, and baptizing, more disciples than was John ² (and yet Jesus himself was not baptizing personally—only his disciples), ³ he left Judea and went back again to Galilee.

It is generally agreed that 4.1-3 are an editorial insertion to explain how Jesus came to be in Samaria. For that, however, vv. 1 and 3 would have been sufficient, and the awkward parenthesis of v. 2 is therefore commonly attributed to a second editorial hand. This hypothesis would account for the clumsiness of the final shape of the sentence, and for the textual variants in it, which are discussed separately.[1]

4.1. ὡς οὖν ἔγνω ὁ Κύριος ὅτι ἤκουσαν οἱ φαρισαῖοι ὅτι Ἰησοῦς πλείονας μαθητὰς ποιεῖ καὶ βαπτίζει ἢ Ἰωάννης... According to Josephus (*Ant.* XVIII v 2 = 116-19), Herod had arrested the Baptist because he feared that John's preaching might lead to political unrest (Schürer I 345-48); perhaps Jn 4.1 is intimating that the Pharisees in Judea had similar fears about civil disorder being aroused by Jesus' preaching (cf. 11.47-48). Or they might have been apprehensive about the religious implications of his activity in Jerusalem (2.14-25, noting 24): established authority is by nature suspicious of novel teaching by a popular but unauthorized preacher. If 4.1-3 are indeed redactional, then whoever inserted these verses may have had both political and religious factors in mind. This understanding of the verses accords well with the translation of ἔγνω as *became aware* (→ 3.2a).

2. ...καίτοιγε Ἰησοῦς αὐτὸς οὐκ ἐβάπτιζεν ἀλλ᾽ οἱ μαθηταὶ αὐτου... καίτοιγε, *hapax legomenon* in the NT, is an emphatic adversative,[2] and the imperfect tense (οὐκ ἐβάπτιζεν) is striking, an affirmation that 'throughout this period' Jesus did not personally take part in the baptisms. The verse is intended to clarify the statement in 3.22 that 'Jesus was baptizing in Judea'. Some say that 4.2 was inserted in order to correct 3.22 on a matter of historical fact, others that it is 4.2 which needs deleting, but both suggestions reflect modern preoccupations ('What really happened?'), rather than those of first-century Ephesus. The purpose of 4.2 is to ensure that 3.22 is not understood as implying that Jesus had during his earthly life admitted people to what was later called

---

[1] See Excursus X, 'ΚΥΡΙΟΣ OR ΙΗΣΟΥΣ IN 4.1a?' The omission of η Ιωαννης in 4.1 by some major uncials (A B* L Wˢ Γ Ψ) may be similarly explained, as a move to lighten an overloaded sentence.

[2] Compare J. D. Denniston, *The Greek Particles*, Oxford, 1954, 555-64.

Christian baptism (7.39), for the first-century disciples knew instinctively
that there was a genuine difference between baptisms before, and
Christian baptism after, Jesus' death: compare Acts 1.5; 2.38, 41; 11.16;
19.3-5. It would have been important to underline this distinction if Jesus
and his followers had in fact practised some form of baptism (Jn 3.24)
akin to the rites used by the Baptist and other religious groups in the
region,[3] including a general confession of sins, similar to those made in
the Temple on the Day of Atonement or at Qumran during the ceremony
for the renewal of the Covenant.[4]

**3. ...ἀφῆκεν τὴν 'Ιουδαίαν καὶ ἀπῆλθεν πάλιν εἰς τὴν
Γαλιλαίαν.** *...he left Judea and went back again to Galilee,* where the
Pharisees were less numerous, and probably not overly sympathetic to the
rigorism of some leaders of the party in Jerusalem (Schürer II 402 fn.73;
Freyne, *Galilee,* 319-23). For ἀφῆκεν (Chrysostom, ἀνεχώρησεν ἀπό)
with an impersonal object, compare Josephus, *Ant.* II xvi 1 = 335,
στρατῷ τῷ ἀφέντι τὴν Αἴγυπτον. On τὴν 'Ιουδαίαν, meaning *the
administrative territory of Judea,* → 3.22. πάλιν, with verbs of *going,*
usually means *back* (BDAG 1 a): some major uncials (A B* Ψ) and
Chrysostom (see Tischendorf) omit it, perhaps to polish the text by
eliminating a superfluous adverb. See also *TCGNT.*

4.4-12: THE ENCOUNTER AT JACOB'S WELL

[4] Now he had to go through Samaria. [5] Consequently he came to a village in
Samaria called Sychar, near the parcel of land which Jacob had given to his
son Joseph. [6] Jacob's well was there, and so Jesus, exhausted as he was by the
journey, without more ado sat down beside the well. It was about the sixth
hour.

---

[3] For further detail see p. 243, or consult Joseph Thomas, *Le mouvement baptiste en
Palestine et Syrie* (1935).

Tertullian (*De baptismo* 11,4: CChr 1.286) and Chrysostom (*In Ioannem* 29,1,
commenting on Jn 3.22: *PG* 59.167) both affirm that baptism with the Holy Spirit was
not given until after the Resurrection (Jn 7.39; 16.7). So also Leo (*Epist.* 16,3: PL
54.699), Theophylactus, Euthymius and Rupert of Deutz.

Augustine was perhaps the first to propose that the baptism mentioned in Jn 3.22; 4.2
imparted both forgiveness and the gift of the Holy Spirit, though without the latter being
openly perceived. 'Baptizabat, quia ipse mundabat; non baptizabat, quia non ipse
tingebat' (*In Ioannem* 15,3); 'sic etiam Spiritus sanctus latenter dabatur ante Domini
clarificationem' (*De Div. Quaest. LXXXIII,* fn. 62). See also *Epist.* 44,10 and 265,5, which
assert that Jesus had most probably already baptized his own disciples. Thomas Aquinas
(on Jn 4.2, Lect. I, ii, fn. 554) preferred Augustine's view over that of Chrysostom, and
Maldonatus (on Jn 3.22) unwisely refused to countenance any other (see Lagrange, *Jean*
91, on 3.22). For some twentieth-century discussions see the Bibliography on p. xxxvi.

[4] For an example of the former, see H. Danby, *Mishnah, Yoma* 3.8 = 4.2 = 6.2
(pp. 165, 166, 169); of the latter, 1 QS 1.22–2.1.

⁷ There came a woman of Samaria to draw water. Jesus said to her, 'Give me a drink!' ⁸ (for his disciples had gone away into the city to buy food). ⁹ The Samaritan woman said to him, 'How is it that you, being a Jew, ask for a drink from me, being as I am a Samaritan woman?', for Jews do not associate with Samaritans. ¹⁰ In answer, Jesus said to her, 'If you had been aware of the bountiful gifts of God, and who it is that is saying to you, "Give me a drink", it would have been you that would have made the request, and he would have given you living water'. ¹¹ The woman said to him, 'Sir, you have nothing to draw with, and the well is deep; where do you get that living water? ¹² Surely you are not greater than our father Jacob, who gave us the well, and drank from it himself, and his sons, and his livestock?' ¹³ Jesus said to her, 'Every one who drinks of this water will thirst again, ¹⁴ but whoever takes one sip of the water that I shall give him will never thirst; on the contrary, the water that I shall give him will become in him a spring of water welling up into eternal life'. ¹⁵ The woman said to him, 'Sir, give me this water, that I may never again know thirst, nor always be coming through here to go on continually drawing water'.

4. ἔδει δὲ αὐτὸν διέρχεσθαι διὰ τῆς Σαμαρείας. *Now he had to go through Samaria.* This was the normal route from Jerusalem to Galilee, shorter than that along the coastal road or by way of the Jordan Valley (Josephus, *Life* 52 = 266-70; *Ant.* XX vi 1 = 118; *War* II xii 3 = 232-33, all succinctly summarized in Barrett), and Jesus was at the time perhaps only 7 miles = 11 km from the boundary with Samaria (→ 3.22). **ἔδει.** Josephus writes that 'for rapid travel, it was essential (πάντως ἔδει) to take this road' (*Life* 269); in John the further implication of a divinely ordained plan cannot be excluded.⁵ → οὖν at 4.5.

John 4.4-42 has no parallel in the Synoptic Gospels, though according to Lk 9.52 and 17.11, Jesus did on at least one occasion travel through Samaritan territory, and both Acts 8.1-25 and Jn 4.35 imply that, by the time the Fourth Gospel was written, many Samaritans were already followers of 'the Way' (Acts 9.2). One motive for the narrative in Jn 4.4-42 is no doubt to make clear that the Samaritans are not second-class citizens in the household of God (compare Eph 2.11-22), but to understand fully the importance of their inclusion among the new people of the New Jerusalem, one must bear in mind the centrality of Samaria in the ancient history of Israel.

When Abram was called to leave his home, 'he went out, not knowing where he was to go' (Heb 11.8); only when the family came to the (Canaanite) sanctuary at Shechem, the oak of Moreh, was he assured that this was the land God had chosen for him and his descendants. Here he built an altar, so that in OT tradition Shechem is the place where true worship in the promised land began (Gen 12.1-7). The location is significant, for Shechem stands at the geographical centre of the 'Holy

---

⁵ Thus Cullmann, *Heil als Geschichte*, 255 = *Salvation in History*, 278.

Land'.[6] Abraham never returned there, but went on southward to Bethel, Mamre and Beersheba (12.8; 13.18; 21.22-31), peacefully grazing his livestock as he went, and so staking out a claim to be accepted as a friendly alien by those already resident there. Two generations later, Jacob returned to Shechem, and there bought a parcel of land, the first demesne acquired by and for the heirs of Abraham (33.18-20). Here Joseph's bones were, at his own request, buried (Gen 50.24-25; Exod 13.19; Josh 24.32; Acts 7.16). Here Joshua summoned the tribes for the foundational ceremony of the inter-tribal federation (Josh 24). And though in the course of history the Northern Kingdom became a traditional adversary of Judah, the restoration of Samaria remained a constant element in the hope of God's people, certainly until the Exile (Ezek 16.51, 53; with ch. 23 compare 37.21-28; note also Hos 1–3; 11, and Jer 31.1-9). → Jn 4.20-24. After the Return from Babylon, Samaria was increasingly regarded by the majority of Jews as a region corrupted by the transportation into it of 'people from Babylon, Cuthah, Avva, Hamath and Sepharvaim' (2 Kgs 17:24), five cities with five patronal gods (→ Jn 4.18). All these facts are relevant for understanding the present story.

5. ἔρχεται οὖν. 'Setting aside instances where οὖν introduces words of the Lord, we find that it either introduces an act of special solemnity, or else— as is most frequently the case— it is applied to His various journeys' (*JG* 2198). It is *as a result of* the decision to travel through Samaria, itself *a result of* the decision to leave Judea for Galilee, that Jesus comes to Sychar: the triple οὖν (4.1, 5, 6) calls attention to those contingent circumstances without which the drama would not have taken place.

εἰς πόλιν τῆς Σαμαρείας. For εἰς with the sense of πρός = *to,* but not *into,* see BDAG 1 b; BDF 207 (1). πόλις here means (like the Italian *paese*) simply *an inhabited locality,* not necessarily a large one, and in this context, *a village.* **λεγομένην Συχάρ,** *called Sychar.* Sychar, a *hapax legomenon* in the Bible and up to this point quite unknown to history, was presumably, during Jesus' lifetime, an identifiable locality not far from the Well, and is commonly identified with the ancient Shechem. Shechem had been destroyed in 128 B.C., and Flavia Neapolis was not founded until A.D. 72, so Sychar, a *hapax legomenon* in the Bible and up to this point quite unknown to history, was presumably, during Jesus' lifetime, an identifiable locality very near to the Well. Around A.D. 30, it would have been a small but significant place (→

---

[6] Halfway between the foothills of Mount Hermon (= Dan) and Beersheba, at the mouth of the only east–west pass through the mountains, surrounded by springs, nature made Shechem 'the uncrowned queen of Palestine' (J. Murphy-O'Connor, *The Holy Land*, Oxford, 3rd ed., 1992, 377-79). See also G. A. Smith, *Historical Geography*, 115-21: 'The View from Mount Ebal'.

3.22, Excursus XI, 'Shechem and Samaria in New Testament Times', and
Excursus XII, 'The Identification of the Site of Sychar').

πλησίον τοῦ χωρίου ὃ ἔδωκεν 'Ιακὼβ [τῷ] 'Ιωσὴφ τῷ υἱῷ
αὐτοῦ. The gift is not recorded in the OT, and the statement is probably
a deduction from the reference in Josh 24.32 to the purchase reported in
Gen 33.18-20; perhaps the writer also mentally identified that piece of
land with the mountain slope (Hebrew, *shechem*) which, according to
Gen 48.22, was Jacob's legacy to Joseph (though this was not acquired
by purchase but by force, Gen 34). In any case, the statement is of little
help in fixing the location of Sychar. Two villages are nowadays proposed as alternative candidates, 'Askar, and Balâta, and the debate is still
open (see Excursus XII, pp. 304-305). One awkward fact is that both are
blest with a fine supply of water. 'Askar, about 1100 yards north-
northeast. of Bir Yakub (Jacob's Well), 'possède une source abondante...
dont l'eau entretient de beaux vergers' (Abel, *Géographie*, II 473).
Balâta, about 500 yards west of the Well, has 'a strongly flowing spring'
(Dalman, *Sacred Sites and Ways*, 214), 'Ain Balâta. Why should anyone
want to walk from either place to Jacob's Well in order to carry back a
bucketful of water?

A traveller from the south comes upon Jacob's Well before reaching
either Balâta or 'Askar, and might be ready to stop at the first source of
water. This would explain Jesus' presence there (→ Jn 4.6). But why did
the woman from the village go there? One suggestion is that she was a
woman of ill repute (see 4.17-18), perhaps anxious to avoid the general
company gathered at 'Ain Balâta; another is that she preferred the softer
rain-water in the Well to the hard, limestone-filtered water elsewhere in
the neighbourhood.[7] All such speculations are pointless. The evangelist
depicts Jesus talking alone with the woman, as he had already done with
Nicodemus (3.1-9), and would later do with Pilate (18.29-40), because
she was in God's plan the divinely designated representative of her
ancient and elect people. Compare the comments on ἔδει in 4.4 and on
ἔρχεται οὖν in 4.5.

6. ἦν δὲ ἐκεῖ πηγὴ τοῦ 'Ιακώβ. πηγή is technically *a spring*, not *a
well*, but since this one was at the bottom of a deep shaft, there is little
advantage in deserting the customary translation: → 4.11 and 'Spring of
Living Water', on pp. 273-79. The absence of the article before πηγή is
normal in Biblical Greek, influenced by the Hebrew construct (MHT III
179-80): the phrase denotes a definite well (Jacob's), not just *a* well of
Jacob. The gospel narrative presupposes that this well, though nowhere
mentioned in the OT, was revered by the Samaritans as having been used
by Jacob (4.12).[8] **ὁ οὖν 'Ιησοῦς.** Once again, οὖν (→ 4.5): it is *because*

---

[7] On the latter suggestion see G. A. Smith, *Historical Geography*, 375-76.

[8] The authenticity of the traditional site is not disputed. Dalman, *Orte und Wege*, 249-
56 = *Sacred Sites and Ways*, 209-15, and Kopp, *Die heiligen Stätten*, 196-211 = *The*

he was exhausted by the journey that *Jesus without more ado sat down at the well.* **κεκοπιακὼς ἐκ τῆς ὁδοιπορίας ἐκαθέζετο.** Even the weariness and the sitting down—contingent circumstances—are essential to the story, and what was apparently casual was divinely foreordained (see *JG* 2272). ἐκαθέζετο, an imperfect with an aorist meaning, (*had*?) *sat down* (BDAG; BDF 101, *s.v.*). For **οὕτως** = *just, simply, at once, without more ado,* see LSJ IV or BDAG 4: ἁπλῶς καὶ ὡς ἔτυχεν (Chrysostom). **ἐπὶ τῇ πηγῇ** may mean either on the stone surround or on the ground beside the well: Chrysostom's ἐπ᾽ ἐδάφους can denote either, more probably *the ground*, but sitting down on either might have put Jesus at risk of being ritually unclean.[9]

ὥρα ἦν ὡς ἕκτη. *It was about the sixth hour* (cf. 19.14). Only one OT text links Jacob with a well, Gen 29.1-12, when he is going to seek a wife in Haran. Jacob reached this well while it was still broad daylight (29.7), and was waiting there when Rachel arrived. Rachel was to be the mother of Joseph, father of Ephraim and Manasseh, the tribes who were to occupy the territory known throughout history as Samaria. So John presents Jesus waiting, like Jacob for his bride, at a well, about midday, and in Samaria.

7-8. ἔρχεται γυνὴ ἐκ τῆς Σαμαρείας ἀντλῆσαι ὕδωρ. Compare the comment at 4.5 on ἔρχεται οὖν: the woman's arrival is divinely ordained for this moment, when the Saviour is waiting for her at this particular spot, in Samaria, when she comes, like Rachel, to draw water.

In this region Hosea had been the first of all the prophets to declare that God loved his people tenderly, even when they had deserted him (Hos 1–3), and to formulate the unsurpassable and immutable quality of that divine love in the simple metaphor 'I will betroth you to me for ever' (2.19). John, in describing Jesus as arriving exhausted at Jacob's Well, is presenting the bridegroom coming in person to Samaria, to take home his long-lost bride (compare Hos 2.14-23; 14.4-7). The scene depicts the fulfilment of the final words uttered by the Baptist, that the bridegroom of Israel is come (Jn 3.28-30).[10] κεκοπιακὼς ἐκ τῆς ὁδοιπορίας (4.6): the Son of God is prepared to travel any distance to bring the errant home. *Recordare Iesu pie quod sum causa tuae viae: quaerens me sedisti lassus.*[11] → 3.16.

Holy Places, 155-66, relate its post-biblical history, the main primary sources for which, from Eusebius to A.D. 1626, are printed in ELS, 2nd ed., 218-28, nos. 269-96.

[9] Though this cannot be positively demonstrated from contemporaneous Jewish laws, the possibility should be borne in mind. → 4.9.

[10] For much of what follows see F.-M. Braun, *Jean III*, 90-95, and G. Bienaimé, 154-99 *passim* and 278-81.

[11] From the *Dies Irae*, a thirteenth-century Sequence for the Faithful Departed, to be found in editions of the *Missale Romanum* from 1570 until 1970, and from 1971–72 onwards, in the *Liturgia Horarum* vol. IV.

Jesus and the woman were alone at the time, because (**8**) the disciples had gone to seek (earthly) food (by purchase) in the nearby locality (→ 6.5). There is no hint of the number of disciples envisaged, and the fact that they all went shopping is doubtless intended to clear the stage so that Jesus and the woman may be alone. The statement about 'buying food' may be intended (like 6.5) to remind the reader of Isa 55.1-2.

7. The woman came ἀντλῆσαι ὕδωρ, literally, *to draw water with a bucket.* λέγει αὐτῇ ὁ 'Ἰησοῦς, δός μοι πεῖν. Jesus, like Eliezer in Gen 24.14, 17, asks for a drink of water. The aorist πεῖν implies 'just a little drink', perhaps 'just a sip',[12] but the Samaritan woman, in contrast to the generous Rebecca, at first demurs.[13]

9. She does not directly refuse, but reminds Jesus that Jews would not drink, even from Jacob's Well, if the water had been in some way in contact with a Samaritan.[14] οὐ γὰρ συγχρῶνται 'Ἰουδαῖοι Σαμαρί-ταις. The object of συγχρῶνται is Σαμαρίταις, and two meanings are possible: (1) *to associate closely, on friendly terms, with* someone, and even *to trade with* (BDAG), or (2) *to use the same vessels for eating and drinking.* The second sense is proposed by D. Daube (*JBL* 69 [1950], 137-47), followed by Barrett. On either interpretation, the sentence is intended to explain why the woman was astonished. The words are omitted in ℵ* D a b e j and by Tischendorf ('loyal to his codex Sinaiticus', Schnackenburg), probably because they sound odd on the lips of the Samaritan.[15] They certainly read more like an explanatory gloss to help the reader than as an utterance of the woman of Samaria. The absence of the article before both 'Ἰουδαῖοι and Σαμαρίταις, even when both are definite, is unique in John and points with fair certainty to an editorial insertion (B-L).

---

[12] Compare the Midrash Rabbah on Gen 24.17, '"Give me to drink, I pray thee, a little water of thy pitcher"—but one mouthful' (LX 6, Soncino, 529-30).

[13] B-L sets out several parallels with the marriage of Rebecca, noting also that in Gen 24.7 Abraham says to his servant, 'Yahweh will send his *angel* before you...': compare Mal 3.1 and the role of the Baptist. See p. 136, §81 III A 1 a) *in fine.*

[14] On the Samaritans, see Schürer II 16-20. 'Inasmuch as their observance of the Torah in regard to tithes and the laws of purity falls short of Pharisaic requirements, they are judged by the rabbis to be in many respects on a par with Gentiles' (19-20). Note the references to *Niddah* 4.1-2; 7.5, and to 'Purity Laws' in II 475-79. On factors which render an earthenware vessel unclean, see *Kelim* 2,3,4 (Danby 606-10) *passim,* and especially Roland Deines, *Jüdische Steingefässe und pharisäische Frömmigkeit* (1993). See also R. T. Anderson, 'Samaritans' in *ABD* V 940-47, and R. J. Coggins, *Samaritans and Jews,* London, 1975.

[15] Modern editions can signify the ending of direct speech by quotation marks or (as here in UBS) by the insertion of brackets; ancient scribes not blest with such conventions would sometimes be perplexed about the point at which direct speech ended.

10. There are four points to note here. (1) εἰ ᾔδεις τὴν δωρεὰν τοῦ
θεοῦ. The identical phrase τὴν δωρεὰν τοῦ θεοῦ occurs elsewhere in
the NT only in the story of Simon Magus (Acts 8.20), also set in Samaria,
where it refers explicitly to the giving of a holy spirit by the laying on of
hands (8.17). The word δωρεά (11 times in the NT), always denotes a
'graciously offered' gift of God, four times with reference to the Spirit
(Acts 2.38; 10.45; 11.15; Heb 6:4). It differs from its cognates δῶρον and
δώρημα, in that it is more regularly found in legal contexts which stress
both the greatness of the gift and the freedom of the giver: *municificentia*
renders it well. Thus it is used for *a legacy* and especially for *bounty*
distributed to soldiers or faithful retainers, of which Aristotle remarks:
ἀναπόδοτος δόσις ἡ δωρεά (*Topica* 125a, 18, cited in LSJ), 'δωρεά is
an unreturnable, irrevocable gift'. BDAG lists examples from Plato to
Philo and Josephus referring to the *bountiful gifts of God*, and it is strange
that the word is relatively rare in the LXX.[16] In the papyri it is used also
for *a wedding present*, and served as evidence of a contract fulfilled.[17]
The Gospel does not at this point make clear in what this bountiful gift of
God consists, but leaves the reader, like the Samaritan woman, wondering
what it is.[18] The explanation is soon forthcoming: → 4.15, under 'Spring
of Living Water'. (2) καὶ τίς ἐστιν ὁ λέγων σοι, δός μοι πεῖν.
λέγειν on the lips of Jesus underlines the importance of the words
uttered, and alerts one to a possible hidden meaning: had she known the
identity of the man who was asking for 'just a sip' of water (this must be
the meaning of the aorist πεῖν), she would have realized that he was in
fact seeking not to receive, but to confer, a favour. ὁ λέγων σοι thus
initiates a dialogue terminating with a perfectly matching *inclusio* in v.
26, ἐγώ εἰμι, ὁ λαλῶν σοι (→). (3) σὺ ἂν ᾔτησας αὐτόν. In the
protasis, the personal pronoun was not expressed (εἰ ᾔδεις); σύ in the
apodosis is therefore emphatic (*JG* 2400). Moreover, in σὺ ἂν ᾔτησας,

---

[16] Disregarding the accusative δωρεάν used as an adverb, δωρεά used to denote *a gift*
is found only in 1 Esd 3.5; Wis 7.14; 16.25; Dan^LXX 2.48; 11.45; Dan^TH 2.6; 5.17; 2 Macc
4.30; 3 Macc 1.7.

[17] Fr. Büchsel in TWNT II 169; and G. Schneider in *EDNT* I 363-64.

[18] Odeberg, *The Fourth Gospel*, 150, is, I think, alone in suggesting that δωρεά τοῦ
θεοῦ is here the equivalent of the תורה מתן (mtn twrh), a technical term among the rabbis
for 'the gift of the Torah', as the supreme gift of God (which Odeberg thinks is to be
superseded by Jesus). But the Samaritans already possessed 'the gift of the Torah', and it
is hard to construe the meaning as 'if only you understood it'. Moreover, in the OT
prophets, the supreme gift of God comes in the outpouring of the Spirit making possible
the perfect observance of the Law at the End-time (Jer 31.31-33; Ezek 36.26-27; Joel
3.1-4). See Eichrodt, *Theologie* II 32-34 = ETr II 57-60. See also Jn 7.37-39.

Augustine, and almost all later Latin writers, opt for the Holy Spirit; Chrysostom,
and most of the Greeks, for the grace of the Holy Spirit. Others suggest Christ himself, or
the gospel teaching (Ammonius, Euthymius, Theodoretus), or encountering Jesus, and so
on. Maldonatus lists the various suggestions (with references). Some of these are
permissible applications for a preacher, some unjustifiable refinements of the writer's
thought, which is to be discerned from the significance of water as God's gift.

'the unusual position of ἄν calls strong attention to the hypothesis' (*JG* 2553*a*), stressing that 'you would most certainly have asked', by contrast with the more normal order in the following clause (καὶ ἔδωκεν ἄν σοι). (4) **ὕδωρ ζῶν** provides the first climax, naming the object of God's munificence. → 'Spring of Living Water' on pp. 273-79.

11. The woman[19] temporizes, but not disrespectfully. After all, she could reasonably have asked why Jesus, if he had access to living water, had asked her for a drink in the first place (Chrysostom), and the fact that she does not put this question is a strong signal not to interpret this dialogue as if it were meant to be taken as a stenographer's account of a conversation.[20] This woman is the first person in John's Gospel to address Jesus as **κύριε**, *Sir*, and does so three times, with increasing respect (4.11, 15, 19). The same courteous mode of address to Jesus by those who were not yet his disciples recurs in 4.49; 5.7; 9.36, 38, and also (with a double meaning, of course) in 20.15. It is not expressly stated that the paralytic in 5.7 came to believe in Jesus, but all the others who begin by addressing Jesus as *Sir* soon become his disciples (4.29, 39, 42, 53; 9.36, 38). **οὔτε... καί**, in Classical Greek very rare (MHT III 340), indicates that the two facts mentioned are correlative (BDF 445 [3]; *pace JG* 2258). **καὶ τὸ φρέαρ ἐστὶν βαθύ.** The water is usually about 100 feet or 30 metres below the surface,[21] lighter and more pleasant to the taste than the hard water from the neighbouring springs (Abel, *Géographie*, I 448). *Where do you get the living water from?* is a logical conclusion leading into v. 12.

12. μή indicates a question expecting a negative answer, = *numquid* (MHT III 282-83 and *JG* 2235). **σύ** is emphatic. *Is it really possible that you*... **ἔδωκεν.** No OT text attests that Jacob actually dug the well (compare Gen 33.18-20), but the woman calls attention to its age and importance, affirming that it was bequeathed by Jacob to supply water for his family and livestock. (Hence the variant δεδωκεν (𝔓⁶⁶·⁷⁵ C *f*¹³) would

---

[19] UBS³ and NA²⁷ place η γυνη in square brackets, judging its presence or absence equiprobable: UBS gives the evidence, *TCGNT* its evaluation.

[20] Contrast D. Fr. Strauss, *Life of Jesus* (ETr), 305-308.

[21] The variations in depth cited in different books result from measurements taken at different times of the year, or from the amount of rainfall that year, or (all too often in the past) from the custom of dropping a stone to illustrate the depth to visitors. G. A. Smith, in his *Historical Geography* (1st ed., 1894) wrote 'It is impossible to say whether the well is now dry, for many feet of it are choked with stones' (p. 374), and a Scottish minister, Andrew Thomson, describes how in the spring of 1869, 'there was a hole without fence around it of any kind, and less than a yard in diameter; - and this was the mouth of Jacob's Well. We looked down, and apparently about fifteen feet from the mouth, it was clogged up with great stones' (*In the Holy Land*, London, 1882, 213-14). J. Murphy-O'Connor quotes both 35 m (in *The Holy Land*, 1st ed., 1980, 210) and (in 4th ed., 1998, 287) 22.5 m.

have seemed more natural on the lips of the Samaritan.) In the LXX the normal term for cattle is κτήνη, and **τὰ θρέμματα** (*hapax legomenon* in the NT and absent from the LXX), a common word for a domesticated animal, especially a sheep or goat (LSJ: BDAG; MM), is here the *mot juste* to refer to Jacob's livestock, for he was not a breeder or keeper of oxen and cows (LXX, κτήνη), but a semi-nomad.[22] The customary rendering *cattle* (so AV to RSV, NEB and REB) is therefore misleading: *flocks* is preferred by Kleist, NAB and NRSV (but that excludes goats and donkeys), *flocks and herds* by NIV. *Small livestock* would be ideal, but seems pedantic. We shall use simply *livestock*.

'*Surely you are not greater than our father Jacob?*' Only one person in the five books of the Torah answers to this description, the one who having 'nothing to draw with' gave Israel 'living water' at Rephidim (Exod 17.1-7) and Kadesh (Num 20.2-18), where 'water came forth abundantly, and the congregation drank, and their cattle' (20.11), passages which we should nowadays regard as two versions of the same story about water produced from a rock-face. The Samaritan woman is then implicitly asking Jesus whether he is the prophet like Moses, the one spoken of in Deut 18.15, 18-19. This 'prophet like Moses' was sometimes called the *Ta'eb*, that is, 'the One who will return', or possibly as 'the One who will restore [everything]', who was expected to be, like Moses, not just a political ruler, but also a teacher.[23] → Jn 4.25. But (see above, on μή), she expects the answer 'No'. Her mindset is locked in the past (see also 4.20), so Jesus from this point onwards begins to speak only about the future. Note the parallel in 8.53.

13. Jesus refuses to accept the woman's challenge to reveal another source of drinking-water because drinking-water like that supplied at Rephidim and Kadesh does not satisfy for very long. Instead, he rewords his earlier conditional (4.10) offer to the woman, implicitly admitting that it was rather strange that he had asked her for water when it should have been the other way round, and explaining why he had first made a request for a drink. It was to open a dialogue, so that she, from recognizing the greatness of his gift, might come to perceive the greatness of the giver (→ 4.10 on τίς ἐστιν ὁ λέγων σοι). **πᾶς ὁ πίνων** (present participle)

[22] R. de Vaux, *Ancient Israel*, 3.

[23] *ta'eb*, תָּאֵב is the participle of the Aramaic verb תוב, meaning both *to return* and *to restore*: see Jastrow 1649. The former is the more common understanding of the term in the Samaritan context, but J. Jeremias, in *TWNT* VII 89[31ff], prefers *wiederherstellen*. There is no primary material earlier than, or contemporaneous with, the NT to supply further detail: see *TWNT* I 387[17]-88[2] (A. Oepke); IV 863-64 and VII 90[2-8] (J. Jeremias) and Schnackenburg on Jn 4.25. The importance of this expectation for the Samaritans is evident from the fact that Deut 18.18-22 is added to the Tenth Commandment in their version of Exod 20 after v. 17, an addition now attested also in 4Q158 (= 4QRP[a])and 4QTest (= 4Q175). See E. Tov, *Textual Criticism of the Hebrew Bible*, Minneapolis, 2nd ed., 1992, 88.

implies that everyone (not just the woman he is addressing) *who habitually drinks* or *continues to drink* of the water from Jacob's Well will be
thirsty again.

14. ὃς δ' ἂν πίῃ κτλ. (aorist) *but whoever takes one sip*[24] *of the water
that I shall give him will never again know thirst; on the contrary, the
water that I shall give him will become, in him, a spring of water welling
up into eternal life.* Note the futures, ἐγὼ δώσω, οὐ μὴ διψήσει, δώσω,
γενήσεται. **οὐ μὴ διψήσει.** Compare Isa 49.10 (cited in Rev 7.16) on
the time of salvation, and Sir 24.21 on the wise person's ever-increasing
thirst for more wisdom during this earthly life. So the living water
promised by Jesus will never fail because it comes direct from the
ultimate divine source, giving both life and light, as promised in Ps 36.9-
10 (Aquinas). On **εἰς τὸν αἰῶνα**, see below at v. 15. πηγὴ ὕδατος
ἁλλομένου was preferred perhaps because of its alliterative assonance
with the Hebrew עלה (ʿlh), used in Num 21.17; but compare also Prov
18.4 in the LXX:

> ὕδωρ βαθὺ λόγος ἐν καρδίᾳ ἀνδρός,
> ποταμὸς δὲ ἀναπηδύει καὶ πηγὴ ζωῆς.[25]

15. λέγει πρὸς αὐτὸν ἡ γυνή. Up to this point in the conversation,
λέγειν, whether used of Jesus or of the woman (Jn 4.7, 9, 10, 11, 13) has
always been followed by the dative. λέγειν πρός (as distinct from
λέγειν τινί) is in John more formal and more respectful: hitherto it has
appeared only at 2.3 and 3.4 (and will return at 4.49). Here, especially
when reinforced by **κύριε**, it serves to underline the seriousness and the
sincerity of the woman's request. She asks Jesus to give her once for all
(**δός**, not δίδου) *this water* (**τοῦτο** τὸ ὕδωρ),[26] that she *may not thirst
ever again* (**ἵνα μὴ διψῶ**) nor *keep coming through here* (**διέρχωμαι**[27]
ἐνθάδε)—to Jacob's Well!—*to go on continually drawing water*
(**ἀντλεῖν**, not, as in 4:7, ἀντλῆσαι). This ἵνα μή followed by the
present subjunctive is *hapax legomenon* in John (Westcott), and therefore
among the most emphatic negatives in the Gospel, particularly when
followed by εἰς τὸν αἰῶνα. The tenses of the four verbs used by the
woman constitute a fourfold affirmation of her complete acceptance of
Jesus' offer.

[ἵνα μὴ διψῶ] **εἰς τὸν αἰῶνα** provides the first instance in John of
the phrase εἰς τὸν αἰῶνα, which, apart from one exception in 9.32 (ἐκ

---

[24] The variant ο δε πινων (in א* and D) seems to be a correction, but it loses the
force of the distinction between the present and the aorist.

[25] B-L 139-40 quotes three parallel texts from the Samaritan *Memar Marqah* 2,1 and
6,3.

[26] In John, this word, when used as a pronominal adjective, seems to carry a certain
emphasis if it precedes the noun: cf. οὗτος in Jn 9.24; 11.47; 12.34; 21.23.

[27] Thus 𝔓⁶⁶ and א*, and justifiably preferred by NA²⁷.

τοῦ αἰῶνος), is the only form in which αἰών occurs in this Gospel. Elsewhere in the NT εἰς τὸν αἰῶνα is not common (15 times),[28] but in John's Gospel, it occurs 12 times (4.14; 6.51, 58; 8.35 [×2], 51, 52; 10.28; 11.26; 12.34; 13.8; 14.16), mostly on the lips of Jesus. In this first occurrence, it refers to a woman's artless desire to have an unfailing supply of the most fundamental necessity of life, water, εἰς τὸν αἰῶνα. Jesus, starting from this point, promises to lead her into a richer and more profound understanding of what life itself is, by pointing towards an αἰών which, far from terminating at bodily death, will then, and then only, blossom into full perfection. The full connotation of the concept emerges only in the subsequent occurrences of the term until, in its last occurrence at 14.6, Jesus promises to his disciples the gift of another Paraclete, the Spirit of truth, who will remain with them εἰς τὸν αἰῶνα, *for all future time*. Already in 4.14 we have just re-encountered the term ζωὴ αἰώνιος, here for the first time on Jesus' lips, a term which occurs 17 times in the Gospel (3.15, 16, 36; 4.14, 36; 5.24, 39; 6.27, 40, 47, 54, 68; 10.28; 12.25, 50; 17.2, 3—always anarthrous except at 17.3); and the adjective αἰώνιος occurs nowhere in this Gospel except in this phrase, *eternal life*. See the conclusion of the following essay.

With the δώσω of living water in 4.14, compare the δώσει in 6.27 and δίδωσιν in 6.35 of life-giving bread; and the identical responses—δός μοι (4.15) and δὸς ἡμῖν (6.34).

SPRING OF LIVING WATER

The word מַיִם (mayim) is found over 500 times in the Hebrew OT, more than 200x in the Torah and about another 100 times in Joshua–Judges, 1–2 Samuel and 1–2 Kings. Almost everywhere, it denotes just the natural element *water*, and in the books mentioned, its use even in the simple simile 'like water', is extremely rare.[29] Similarly, in the Torah, the only books accepted by the Samaritans as the Word of God, there are about 40 references to wells, none metaphorical. Further, the Hebrew phrase translated *living water* (מַיִם חַיִּים [mayim ḥayyim]), which occurs eight (or seven) times in the Torah, refers on every occasion to the physical element alone, and is never a metaphor: thus Gen 26.19, *a well of spring water* (NRSV); Lev 14.5, 6, 50, 51, 52; [15.13?],[30] and Num 19.17,

---

[28] Elsewhere it sometimes denotes the inclusion or exclusion of something *for all future time in this world* (thus Mt 21.19; Mk 3.29; 11.14; Lk 1.55; 1 Cor 8.13), and sometimes occurs in connection with a citation from the LXX (2 Cor 9.9; Heb [all six relating to Melchizedek] 5.6; 6.20; 7.17, 21, 24, 28; 1 Pet 1.25); the other instances are both Johannine, 1 Jn 2.17; 2 Jn 2.

[29] Gen 49.4 (Reuben's instability); Deut 12.16, 24; 15.23 (blood poured out like water); Josh 7.5 (hearts turned to water) and 2 Sam 14.14—only six instances out of more than 300 occurrences.

[30] *Living* is here omitted in some MSS of the LXX (B A).

denoting *fresh* or *running water* (NRSV) for cleansing. The phrase *a well of living water* occurs once only[31] in these five books, with reference to the well found by Isaac's servants (Gen 26.19: LXX, φρέαρ ὕδατος ζῶντος).

With this background, it is not surprising that the Samaritan woman should understand Jesus' phrase about 'living water' in Jn 4.10 as a reference to drinking-water. She naturally thinks in terms of her local well, τὸ φρέαρ (Jn 4.11, 12), and raises two objections to his offer of 'living water' in v. 10: (1) Jesus has no bucket and the well is deep; (2) surely he cannot be claiming to have found a new well in the vicinity?

Jesus counters her first point by discreetly substituting for τὸ φρέαρ the word πηγή (v.14, without the article) thereby moving the dialogue on to a new plane: he speaks not of *the well*, but of *a spring*. φρέαρ denotes a well purposely dug by human labour, πηγή, a natural spring created by God (BDAG). A well once dug may run dry, as the Well of Jacob often does after a low winter rainfall;[32] a natural spring is fed by 'the waters that are under the earth', and flows eternally at God's behest (Gen 1.9). In the LXX πηγή appears nearly 100 times. It is the translation always given, on more than 50 occasions, for two Hebrew words denoting a natural spring which are rarely metaphorical;[33] but on 14 occasions πηγή stands for מָקוֹר (mĕqor), which occurs several times as a metaphor (KBR II 627). In eight texts (all in the Wisdom Books) we find πηγὴ ζωῆς. In Proverbs, this *fountain of life* is said to flow from the mouth of the righteous (10.11), the teaching of the wise (13.14), the fear of the Lord (14.27), from wisdom (16.22) and from wise counsel of the heart (18.4); similarly in Sir 21.13b, from the counsel of the wise.[34] Psalms 36(35).9 attributes the origin of this source of life unequivocally to the Godhead: 'With you is the fountain-head of life, and it is in your light that we see light'.[35] In short, once Wisdom has built her house and set her table (Prov 9.1, 2), it is not from any earthly well (φρέαρ) that she summons people to drink at her banquet, but from the rivers of delight that flow from the 'fountain-head of life' in the house of the God of Israel (Ps 36[35].9). This 'fountain-head of life' embraces all that external enlightenment of the mind on matters of truth and goodness which flows ultimately from God alone, the supreme embodiment of which is to be found, according

[31] Twice, if the LXX reading is accepted at Gen 21.19.

[32] G. A. Smith, *Historical Geography*, 372; Abel, *Géographie*, I 144.

[33] עַיִן ('ayin) = *spring* (around 30 times in the Pentateuch and historical books), and מַעְיָן (maʿyān) (around 20 times). They stand in contrast to any *well* (בְּאֵר [beʾer]), *cistern* (בּוֹר [bôr]) or *water-tank* (גֵּב [geb]) dug out by human labour.

[34] The RSV here renders (inexplicably) 'and his counsel like a flowing stream'. Contrast NRSV: 'and their counsel like a life-giving spring'

[35] The eighth text, Cant 4.15, though metaphorical, contributes nothing to the understanding of John.

to Sir 24.21, 23, 30-33, in the Law of Moses.[36] This is the 'living water' of which Jesus invites the Samaritan woman to drink.

Outside the Pentateuch, in strong contrast with the usage there, the phrase living water appears only as a metaphor. The LXX twice renders the Hebrew phrase as ὕδωρ ζῶν (Cant 4.15; Zech 14.8), but in Jer 2.13 it gives πηγὴ ὕδατος ζωῆς (A ℵᶜ have ζῶντος), and in 17.13, πηγὴ ζωῆς.[37] In these two texts Jeremiah writes that the people have 'forsaken [Yahweh] the fountain of living water', and they are the only OT texts apart from Ps 35(36).9 which identify this 'fountain-head of life' with God. In each context Jeremiah is reproaching God's people for their neglect of true religion (Jer 2.8; 17.15-18), while assuring them that there are solid grounds for hope (cf. 3.12-14; 17.13a). For the days are coming when they will return (30.3) and reconstruct their country (31.2-14), when God will establish a new commonwealth, with Israel and Judah reunited, on a foundation more solid than the Mosaic Covenant, a covenant written in their hearts (31.31-34). In OT terms, this declaration is truly breath-taking: the people that had abandoned the very fountain of living water are promised a future superior to everything that Moses gave. Ezekiel echoes the same message: God will cleanse the people with clean water, give them a new heart and a new spirit, enabling them to keep the Law (Ezek 36.25-27). His text about water flowing out of the sanctuary in the New Jerusalem to bring life to the dried-up land even beyond Judah's borders (47.1-12) is similarly optimistic: 'future salvation is here promised for the territory outside the sanctuary' (Zimmerli, *Ezekiel*, ETr II 509b). Ezekiel's message is recalled in Zech 13.1; 14.8: living waters shall flow out from Jerusalem. Joel too foretells an age when God will pour out his Spirit on all flesh and a fountain shall come forth from the house of the Lord (3.1-2; 4.18 = EV 2.28-29; 3.18). This living water is, quite simply, the knowledge of the word and wisdom of God as contained in the tradition of Israel.[38]

These texts from the Wisdom Books and the Prophets, so clearly remembered in Rev 21.6 and 22.1, must have been in the mind of the evangelist too (cf. 7.38), for the metaphor was common enough in NT times. *Baruch* 3.12 refers to 'the fountain of wisdom'. Philo speaks of God himself as ἡ πηγή τῆς σοφίας, imparting every form of knowledge to the mortal race (*De Sacrificiis* XVII 64: Loeb II 142), and of the supreme Divine Word, τὸν ἀνωτάτον λόγον θεῖον, as 'that supreme and most excellent Spring, which the All-Father declared by the mouth of

---

[36] A Thanksgiving Hymn from Qumran uses the same metaphors, speaking about God-given wisdom as *a well, a fountain of life, a spring of living waters* etc. (1 QH VIII, listed as fn. 14 in Vermes, *DSSE*, 4th ed., 213-14).

[37] Jer 2.13 and 17.13 are the only OT texts which mention together *a spring* and *living water*. Gen 26.19 and Cant 4.15 speak of a *well* of flowing water, but not a *spring* (of a בְּאֵר (beʾer) = φρέαρ, but not a מָקוֹר (māqor) = πηγή).

[38] Pancaro, *The Law*, 473-85, provides a good survey of twentieth-century exegesis up to 1975, with ample references to the texts from Qumran.

prophets' (*De Fuga* XVIII 97 and XXXVI 197: Loeb V 62,116). The same expressions are found in Qumran (see below), in the *Odes of Solomon* (11.6-8; 30) and regularly among the Rabbis (SB II 443-43, 483, 485, 492).[39] The suggestion that Jesus was inviting the Samaritan woman (and by implication her people) to examine more closely how the prophets and the teachers of wisdom had interpreted the Books of Moses is attractive; but can one argue that the evangelist intended to imply this by a simple reference to 'a spring of living water'? Everyone knows that the Samaritans accepted as the Word of God only the Torah.

Here the second question put to Jesus, 'Are you greater than our father Jacob?', becomes relevant, for it allows him to continue his discourse by speaking about the Torah. As explained above (→ Jn 4.12), the woman's question alludes to the prophet like Moses mentioned in Deut 18.15-18: can Jesus, like Moses, provide water for the people on their earthly journey? Jesus' reply in Jn 4.13-14 is 'Yes—and it will slake all thirst for ever!' The woman's reference to *livestock* in Jn 4.12 is proof that she has in mind only the water shared by humans and beasts alike, but the phrase she uses in John ('his children and his livestock') does not occur anywhere in the OT with reference to Jacob. Its equivalent, however, occurs both in Exod 17.1-7 and in Num 20.2-13, in the two stories about Moses miraculously producing water by striking a rock-face. Indeed, these are the only texts anywhere in the OT where such a phrase, equivalent to 'ourselves and our livestock', does occur (Exod 17.3; Num 20.4, 8, 11). Thus the wording of the question in John confirms that the challenge from Samaria means: 'Are you greater than Jacob, are you the prophet like Moses?' → 4.12 and fn.17.

At Exod 17.1-7 and Num 20.2-13 none of the Palestinian Targums gives any midrashic interpretation of the Hebrew text: the water from the rock at Rephidim and at Meribah is understood to be simply drinking-water. But after the strife at Meribah, when Moses leads the people along the edge of the desert east of Edom and Moab, there is a third revolt, again because of the poor food and lack of water (Num 21.5-6). On this third occasion, the Lord answers not with abundant water from a rock-face, but with a scourge of poisonous serpents, until the people repent (21.4-9), and it is only after their repentance, when they resume their journey (21.10-17), that they come upon a source of water, where they dig a well (21.16-18). John, in 3.14-15, has just made use of the story about the revolt recounted in Num 21.4-9, and about the bronze serpent which brought healing in the desert; he turns now to the well mentioned immediately after that episode, in Num 21.10-17. The drinking-water supplied earlier at Massah and Meribah was a miraculous gift which God did not repeat: the story in Num 21.10-17 is about the last well encountered in the desert, which had to supply water throughout the

---

[39] For the detail see *TWNT* VI 135-60 (L. Goppelt).

whole journey until Israel reached the edge of the Promised Land, and the Targums, alert to the difference, are anxious to explain its significance.

In the MT, the key words in Num 21.16-18 are that the water was given to the people by God (v. 16), and sprang up for them (v. 17). The Palestinian Targums, in sharp contrast to their sober renderings of the episodes at Massah and at Meribah, paraphrase this present passage to an extent which alters its meaning. 'It is the well which the princes *of the world, Abraham, Isaac and Jacob, dug from the beginning; the intelligent ones of the people perfected it, the seventy sages who were distinguished; the scribes of Israel, Moses, and Aaron, measured it… It was given to them* (as) a gift' (*Neofiti*).[40] Here the well dug in the desert is interpreted as denoting the Divine Revelation to the Patriarchs, and its expression in the Torah; the place-name Mattanah (MT, v. 18) is translated as *a gift*; and this is the well whose waters, in Jewish tradition, followed the people and enabled them to reach the Promised Land. These Targums then relate that '*swelling torrents*' of this water, '[going] *up with them to the tops of the high mountains*', then '*down with them to the deep valleys*', accompanied the Israelites 'as a gift of God' until they reached the steppes of Moab (*Neofiti*, Num 21.19-20).[41] Such a gravity-defying stream needs explaining, and so the *Damascus Document* (written around 100 B.C.?) affirms not merely that the Well symbolizes the Torah ('they dug a well rich in water', CD III 17) but boldly states in a comment on Num 21.18, that 'The Well is the Law' (CD VI 5). Philo too interprets the Well of Num 21 in a figurative sense: it symbolizes wisdom which lies deep below the surface, to drink of which is needful and delicious above all things (*De Ebrietate* XXIX 112-13: Loeb III 378); and also understanding (ἐπιστήμη) which has long been hidden but is finally found (*De Somniis* II, XLI 271: Loeb V 564).[42] The evidence of Qumran and Philo is proof that the symbolic interpretation represented in the Palestinian Targums was broadly known when the Fourth Gospel was written: and this is the key to understanding Jn 4.14-15. Jesus is telling the Samaritan woman that this is how the stories in the Torah concerning water should be understood. Far better than to drink of Jacob's Well is to drink deep of the living water of the Word of God.

The narrative in John opened with Jesus asking the woman to let him have a drink of water from Jacob's Well (δός μοι πεῖν, 4.7) and this first part ends with her begging him to give her that special, living water of which he had just spoken (κύριε, δός μοι τοῦτο τὸ ὕδωρ, 4.15). The reversal of roles began when Jesus said (4.10) 'If only you were aware of

---

[40] Trans. McNamara, pp. 119-20. The words in italic are those which diverge from the Hebrew. McNamara observes (119 fn. 20) that this paraphrase is for the greater part found also in Onqelos, in Pseudo-Philo (*LAB* 10.7; 11.15; 20.8) and the Tosefta.

[41] Similarly the Fragment-Targums and Pseudo-Jonathan. Compare 1 Cor 10.4 on the rock (Num 20.7-11) which supplied water thereafter.

[42] The *Vita Mosis* I 255-56 (Loeb VI 408) gives no similar interpretation.

the bountiful gift of God'. The verb διδόναι occurs 75 times in John,[43] and it refers mostly to a gift from God, or from Jesus, in the order of grace. διδόναι figured twice in the Prologue (1.12, 17) and four times in 3.16, 27, 34, 35, with reference to God's gracious gifts to 'the world'. Now, in 4.7-14, in order to stress its importance, διδόναι recurs seven times,[44] water being the gift at each step forward in the dialogue. By the end of this section (in v.15), petitioner and donor have exchanged roles, the nature of the longed-for water has altered, and what began as an urgent plea by Jesus for a sip of water proves to be the divinely ordained occasion for God's offering to the people of Samaria the waters of salvation (compare Isa 12.3). 'Ille autem qui bibere quaerebat, fidem ipsius mulieris sitiebat' (Augustine, *In Ioannem* XV 11).

The question, 'Are you greater than our father Jacob, who gave us the well?' (Jn 4.12), also opens the path to a further level of interpretation. There is no allusion in the OT to Jacob's finding or digging any well: indeed, only one OT text links Jacob with a well, Gen 29.1-12, when he is seeking a wife in Haran. The Palestinian Targums interpret this episode as follows *'When our father Jacob raised the stone from above the mouth of the well, the well overflowed and came up to its mouth, and was over-flowing for twenty years—all the days that he dwelt in Haran'* (*Neofiti*).[45] If this midrashic interpretation was commonly known when the Gospel was being written, then the woman is possibly asking (perhaps ironically) whether Jesus can (like Jacob) provide a supply of natural spring-water that will surge up to the surface. The idea has its attraction partly by reason of the word ἁλλομένου in Jesus' reply (→ 4.14), but there is another, stronger, argument in its favour.

The evangelist is here portraying Jesus as the bridegroom of Israel (→3.29) come to offer to the long estranged people of Samaria access to *a spring of living water* (Jer 2.13; and → Jn 4.6). Jeremiah, in 2.13, is reiterating the theme of Hosea, of God's enduring love even for his faithless bride (2.2; 31.32), summoning both the Northern and Southern Kingdoms to return together to Yahweh (3.11-25); then Samaria and the fertile hills of Ephraim (31.5-6) will joyfully worship together with Judah in Zion (see also 31.7-34).[46] Ezekiel too had spoken of Samaria's returning to life (16.51, 53; with ch. 23 compare 37.21-28), as well as Jerusalem (40–48). See also Zech 10.6-7. The Prophets, like the Wisdom writers, are convinced that the source of new life will be the knowledge of the one true God as known and handed down in Israel.

---

[43] Seldom with a purely secular meaning, and even then only in conventional phrases: e.g. Jn 1.22; 19.9 with ἀπόκρισιν, and in 18.22; 19.3 with ῥάπισμα.

[44] Not counting ὃ ἔδωκεν Ἰακώβ in 4.5, because it is outside the dialogue.

[45] Trans. McNamara, 139-40. Note that this text occurs at 28.10. Similarly in the Fragment-Targums, and Pseudo-Jonathan (at 28.10), but not in Onqelos.

[46] On the texts mentioned, see W. McKane, *Jeremiah* (ICC), and particularly his comments (II clvii-clx) on chs. 30–31.

The Fourth Gospel, in presenting the New Jerusalem, had to include Samaria, and the evangelist, by glossing *spring of living water* as *a spring of water welling up into eternal life*, has superimposed on Jeremiah's words a new dimension. ζωὴ αἰώνιος, a concept practically unknown in the LXX (only Dan 12.2; 2 Mac 7.9, 36), is central to John, where its full meaning is only gradually disclosed as the Gospel proceeds (cf. 17.3). So far, the term has occurred three times (3.15, 16, 36), always to affirm that everyone who believes will have life eternal. The *spring of water surging up into life eternal* is thus a metaphor for the knowledge of God continuous with, but even more profound than, that revealed in the Torah (see 1.17). ὁ δέ θεός πλέον τι ἢ ζωή, πηγή τοῦ ζῆν, ὡς αὐτός εἶπεν, ἀέννaos. 'God is something more than Life, an ever-flowing Spring of living, as He Himself says' (Philo, *De Fuga* XXXVI 198: Loeb V 116). This leads into the second part of the narrative.

In the prophets, the promise of living water is sometimes accompanied by the promise of the gift of a new spirit (Ezek 36.25-27; Joel 3.1-2 = EV 2.28-29; also Isa 44.3 and Zech 12.10 [pour out a spirit] with 13.1; 14.6), for the Spirit of God was regarded as the power which would bring into being and sustain the new Age of the End-time.[47] So far, in John's Gospel, the Spirit has been only briefly mentioned, in 1.32-33 by the Baptist; by Jesus in 3.5, 6, 8; and in 3.34, 'God is not parsimonious in bestowing the Spirit'. In 4.16-26, Jesus, as he describes the future age which is coming into being, introduces into the dialogue the motif of the Spirit. → 4.23.

POSTSCRIPT: ON A SUGGESTION BY BULTMANN

'That the water of Jn 4.10-15 is not the water of the Messianic age of salvation…, but is based on the Gnostic usage, specifically as in Od. Sol., is shown by the parallels and by the fact that the meaning of ὕδωρ ζῶν is governed by the contrast with natural spring-water' (Bultmann, ETr 185 fn. 3 = German 136 fn. 3). The footnotes on pp. 184-85 (= German 135-36) supply copious references to the Odes and to other writings. Today, few (if any) consider the Odes as inspired by non-Christian Gnosticism.[48] F.-M. Braun, *Jean le théologien*, I 242-45, argued in 1959 that the author of the Odes was fully familiar with the Gospel of John, and in 1977 J. A. Emerton considered the debate closed: 'The Odes are plainly Christian in their present form'.[49] J. H. Charlesworth expressed the general consensus: while there are 'striking and significant parallels' with the Gospel of John, one should not readily assume that the Odes are dependent on John,

[47] See W. Eichrodt, *Theologie des AT* II §13 III. 32-34 = ETr II 57-60.

[48] It is a matter of regret that in his first volume, published in 1965, Schnackenburg wrote of 'the Gnostic Odes of Solomon' (I 463,466 = ETr 427, 430).

[49] 'Notes on Some Passages in the Odes of Solomon', *JTS* 28 (1977), 507-19.

but should inquire whether they do not come from the same type of Christian community, during the late first or early second century.[50]

Of the other texts cited by Bultmann, the majority come from Mandean literature, of which the dates and places of origin are quite uncertain. Kurt Rudolph writes that 'the most ancient go back to the 4th century' and 'are connected in many ways with the ancient gnostic tradition as we encounter it especially in Syria (Gospel of John, Odes of Solomon)' (*Gnosis*, p. 346), but this assessment is hardly sufficient to sustain the weight of the thesis of Bultmann stated above.

4.16-30: SEEKING THE HAND OF THE BRIDE

[16] He said to her, 'Go, call your husband and come back here'. [17] In reply the woman said to him, 'I have no husband'. Jesus said to her, 'You have done well in saying, I have no husband, [18] for you have had five men and the one you have at present is not your husband. What you have just said is true.' [19] The woman said to him, 'Sir, I perceive that you are a prophet. [20] Our fathers have worshipped on this mountain, but you say the place where one must worship is in Jerusalem.' [21] Jesus said to her, 'Woman, believe me, an hour is coming when you will worship the Father neither on this mountain nor in Jerusalem. You are at present worshipping something of which you are unaware, for salvation is from the Jews.

[23] 'But the hour is coming' [and now is] 'when those who are genuine worshippers will worship the Father in spirit and truth, for indeed those are the people the Father seeks to have as his worshippers. [24] God is spirit, and those who worship him must worship in spirit and truth.' [25] The woman said to him, 'I am aware that a Messiah is going to come' [the one we call Christ]; 'when he comes, he will disclose everything to us'. [26] Jesus said to her, 'I who am speaking to you am he'.

[27] At this point his disciples arrived and were amazed that he was talking with a woman. (No one, however, said, 'What are you trying to find out?' or 'What are you talking about with her?') [28] In consequence, the woman left her water jar, and went off to the village, and said to the people, [29] 'Come and see a man who told me everything I have ever done! Is it really possible that this is the Messiah?' [30] They came out of the village and began to make their way towards him.

16. ὕπαγε, *Go*, is the popular word for '*go, depart*', used only in the present, and in the NT, most frequently in John (BDF 101 under ἄγειν). It is regularly used with the meaning *to go home* (see BDAG; *JV* 1652a, 1655, 1658; and note Jn 7.33; 8.14 etc.). **φώνησον τὸν ἄνδρα σου.** Chrysostom suggests this was in order to share the gift; Augustine interprets it symbolically, as meaning 'bring your intelligence into play' (and see that the promise concerns spiritual water). Bengel submits, more prosaically, that the woman seems to have thought it was to help her to

---

[50] In his Introduction to the Odes of Solomon, *OTP* II 725-34, noting particularly pp. 728, 730, 732.

carry home more of the new water! These three interpretations are evidence enough that the clause is meant solely to carry the narrative forward. καὶ ἐλθὲ ἐνθάδε. English usage demands *come back here*.

17-18. καλῶς εἶπας ὅτι ἄνδρα οὐκ ἔχω. 'Sad irony', writes Westcott, citing Rupert: 'clementiae manum porrigens pepercit pudori'. English idiom suggests that ἔσχες be translated *you have had*, but it would be just as acceptable to use *you had*, thus making a sharp contrast with ἔχεις. τοῦτο ἀληθές is a 'predicate adjective' (BDF 272; MHT III 225 *JG* 1894), which, taken with εἴρηκας, gives the sense, 'This statement you have just made is true'.[51]

The interpretation of vv. 17-18 turns on how one understands the words πέντε γὰρ ἄνδρας ἔσχες, which may for the moment be translated as *You have had five husbands*. Some deny *a priori* that these words represent an actual historical saying of Jesus, for how could he possibly have known that this woman had had five husbands? Others try to maintain their authenticity by introducing unattested and unprovable hypotheses;[52] and yet others (including many fundamentalists) regard the statement as clear evidence of Jesus' preternatural knowledge. All three groups take it for granted that the Gospel represents Jesus as saying that the woman had herself, as a matter of historical fact, had five husbands (or men) during her lifetime. Against this, the fact that the woman is not portrayed as overcome by guilt, shame or even embarrassment at Jesus' words suggests that one should not too readily impute to her personally a life-time of unchastity, or assume that the evangelist is implying this.

Since D. Fr. Strauss published *Das Leben Jesu* in 1832, many have interpreted the five husbands symbolically, arguing that, just as the woman is a symbol of the Samaritan people, so the five husbands represent the five foreign cults introduced into Samaria after its inclusion into the empire of Assyria (2 Kgs 17.24-34). This interpretation has sometimes been rejected on the ground that 'not 5 but 7 divinities are mentioned, some of which are female' (Bultmann); to which one may reply that in many such cults, a god was worshipped along with his consort (as at *Sepharvaim* 17.31), and that Josephus certainly saw them as five cults, not seven (*Ant.* IX xiv 3 = 288). Another argument adduced against the allusion to 2 Kgs 17 is that those foreign gods were worshipped simultaneously, whereas the Samaritan woman had her husbands successively;

---

[51] The variant αληθως could be interpreted as meaning *You have truly said this* - but that is a fact which is not in dispute; the variant may therefore be set aside as an attempt to clarify the sense by using simpler wording.

[52] Of which quite the most charming is that of H. E. G. Paulus, cited by Strauss. 'While Jesus sat at the well, and the woman was advancing from the city, some passer-by hinted to him that he had better not engage in conversation with her, as she was on the watch to obtain a sixth husband' (*Life of Jesus*, ETr 306, referring to Paulus' *Das Leben Jesu* I a 187 and his Commentary *in loco*.) Detail on Paulus in W. G. Kümmel, *The NT: The History of the investigation of its Problems*, London, 1975, ETr 90-93.

but this is to interpret the parallelism as an allegory, and 'the Evangelist does not use allegorization, but rather symbolic representation as his main literary device' (again, Bultmann).[53]

The word ἀνήρ occurs only eight times in John's Gospel, five of them in this text, 4.16-18 (elsewhere only at 1.13, 30; 6.10): compare the five loaves and the two fish in ch. 6, where *loaves* occurs five times (6.5, 7, 9, 11, 13) and *fish* twice (6.9, 11).[54] The fivefold repetition of ἀνήρ is very probably an intimation that one should be on the watch for symbolism. Further, in Aramaic (or Hebrew, or Samaritan) one term for *husband* is *ba'al*, the name of the god of the Canaanites, the plural of which (*be'alim*) was used by the Israelites as a designation for all false gods. Hence πέντε ἄνδρας ἔσχες can signify either *You have had five husbands* or *You have had five be'alim* (that is, five *false gods*), or both.[55] The woman in the story is naturally presented as understanding Jesus' words in the first sense as *five husbands* or (more probably?) *five men*, whereas the evangelist intended to intimate also that Samaria had not always given its worship exclusively to the God of Israel.

19. The woman, astounded at Jesus' knowledge of such intimate details of her life (compare 4.29), replies: *Sir,*[56] *I perceive that you are a prophet* (compare Lk 7.39). Now if he was in truth a prophet, he would be able to speak on behalf of God. By asking for a drink (Jn 4.7), Jesus had already shown that he did not consider the drinking vessel she had touched to be unclean; the woman, by asking for a drink from him (4.15), had reciprocated the courtesy. Clearly, he did not consider himself bound by every Jewish custom; how far was he prepared to go in overriding convention and tradition? Would he be prepared to abandon even the principle of worship solely in the temple at Jerusalem?

In **20-24** προσκυνεῖν is the dominant verb.[57] It appears to have entered the Greek language around 600 B.C., when the Greeks came into contact with the Persians, to denote *prostrating oneself* before a superior being such as a king or a deity or their images. Greeks found this custom of prostration repugnant (Herodotus VII 136 in contrast with VIII 118; Demosthenes, *Or.* XXI c. Median 549, 106), but in classical times

---

[53] Bultmann also cautiously wonders whether the number five was chosen at random, or because of its importance in Gnosticism, but remains studiously non-committal.

[54] Compare also the seven instances of διδόναι in 4.7-14 (see the essay 'Spring of Living Water' on pp. 273-79).

[55] The same problem may be observed in the modern translations of texts like Jer 3.14 (RV, *husband*; RSV NRSV JB NAB, *master*); 31.32 (RV RSV NRSV, *husband*; JB NAB, *master*). One may wonder whether the ancient Israelites (or the Samaritans) would have known the difference (*DCH* II 237; KBR I 143).

[56] κύριε is omitted by ℵ* *pc*: → on ἐν Ἱεροσολύμοις at 4.20.

[57] For detail consult LSJ; BDAG; *JV* 1640-51; JG 2019; *TWNT* VI 759-67 (HGreeven); *EDNT* III 173-75 and KBR I 296a.

accepted the verb into their language while moderating its significance: οὐδένα γὰρ ἄνθρωπον δεσπότην ἀλλὰ τοὺς θεοὺς προσκυνεῖτε (Xenophon, *Anabasis* III ii 13). In Attic Greek its meaning ranges from *adoration* to *receiving respectfully*, but it is followed by the accusative, thus effectively eliminating any hint of prostration. After Alexander, as Greece came into closer contact with Oriental cultures, the original meaning of the verb as *to show reverence by prostration*, and kissing the feet, the hem of a garment or even the ground, re-emerged on many occasions (especially in descriptions of foreign etiquette) and with it the custom of employing the dative for the person so honoured. The Koine admits both constructions, with the accusative and the dative. For examples see LSJ; BDAG.

In the LXX προσκυνεῖν is almost everywhere the translation[58] of the Hebrew form הִשְׁתַּחֲוָה (hištaḥăwāh), a verb which itself originally stressed the physical gesture of *bowing down in reverence* (KBR I 296a), and which in the Hebrew Bible was regularly used for worshipping Yahweh (or some other deity): note Ps 95.6. In the LXX, therefore, προσκυνεῖν may be used absolutely as a technical term for a pilgrimage to Jerusalem (e.g. Ps 5.7); it is usually followed by the dative of the deity adored, or of the person to whom deference is shown (e.g. 1 Kgdms 2.36; 25.23; 2 Kgdms 14.33). On those few occasions where προσκυνεῖν is followed by the accusative, the Jewish writer may be indicating disapproval of the acts of obeisance there described, and is certainly distinguishing between them and the worship of God.[59]

Outside Revelation (24 times) and Matthew (13×), the NT is sparing and cautious in its use of προσκυνεῖν,[60] and of the 11 instances in John, nine occur here in 4.20-24.

In **20** προσκυνεῖν occurs twice, referring once to *this mountain* and once to *Jerusalem*. **ἐν τῷ ὄρει τούτῳ** that is, on Mount Gerizim, overlooking Shechem. According to the Samaritans, *this mountain*, not Jerusalem, was 'the place which Yahweh had chosen' for the liturgical worship enjoined by Moses in Deut 12.5, 11, 14; 16.2; 26.2 (note the proximity of 11.29 to ch. 12). This, they held, was the site of the altar demanded by Moses in 27.4 (the Samaritan text here reads *Gerizim* instead of MT's *Ebal*),[61]

---

[58] On more than 150 occasions, *TWNT* VI 761, fn 23. See HR.

[59] Gen 37.7, 9; Exod 11.8; 2 Chr 24.17; Isa 44.15; *EpJer* 5 has both accusative and dative; Esther 4.17 (×2). *JV* 1642a gives brief comments on them.

[60] It occurs only twice in Mark, at 5.6 (the Gadarene demoniac) and 15.19 (the soldiers' mockery). In Lk 4.7, 8 (‖ Mt 4.9, 10) Satan uses it in the Temptation story, only to be rebutted by Jesus' citation of Deut 6.13 ‖ 10.20 (according to the reading in A); elsewhere in Luke it is found only in a doubtful reading at 24.52. In Acts it occurs only at 7.43; 8.27; 10.25; 24.11.

[61] In Deut 27.4, where the command to set up an altar reads in the MT 'on Mount Ebal', the Samaritan text reads 'on Mount Gerizim'; and in the text of the Decalogue, the Samaritans count the first precept as introductory, and then add as the Tenth Command-

which Joshua had built and where he had first offered sacrifices in
Canaan (Josh 8.30-33). Everyone knew that the sanctuary at Jerusalem
had come into existence many centuries later: compare Ps 78.54 with vv.
67-68. And at some to us uncertain date, probably after 425 B.C., the
Samaritans had built their own temple on Gerizim.[62] It was destroyed in
129–128 B.C. and there is no record that it was ever rebuilt. **προσ-
εκυνήσαν.** The woman speaks of Samaritan worship as something in the
past (aorist), but of the Jerusalem Temple as still functioning.[63] **ἐν
Ἱεροσολύμοις** (as distinct from Ἱερουσαλήμ) is the form always found
in John: there is no significance in the fact (see BDAG). The omission of
κύριε in Jn 4.19, and of **ὁ τόπος** in 4.20, by א* *pc*, is probably not a
scribal error but a deliberate correction by scribes who judged it inappropriate that the Samaritan woman should (in spite of her polite κύριε in
v.11) at this stage address Jesus as κύριε or refer to the Jerusalem
Temple as ὁ τόπος, that is 'The [Holy] Place' (5.13; 11.48; 14.2-3)
'where one must (**δεῖ**) worship'. *Our fathers have worshipped on this
mountain, but you say the place where one must worship is in Jerusalem.*
'To a Samaritan no question could appear more worthy of a prophet's
decision than the settlement of the religious centre of the world' (Westcott). Later, undatable, Samaritan tradition places both the call to sacrifice
Isaac on Mount Moriah, and the dream of Jacob at Bethel (Gen 22.2;
28.1-22) on Mount Gerizim.

21. The woman had addressed Jesus, very courteously, as a prophet
(4.19). Jesus replies with equal courtesy that her question about the
proper place for worship is no longer relevant. **πίστευέ μοι, γύναι.**
With πιστεύειν, the present (not the aorist) is the form normally used for
the imperative (MHT III 75), and always in John. Jesus' use of γύναι
commends the retention of κύριε (*contra* א*) in v.19. These words form a
fine *inclusio* with Jesus' words in v.26. **ὅτι ἔρχεται ὥρα.** *An hour is
coming.* This phrase, without the article, is always best interpreted as
denoting the time after Jesus' departure; it occurs seven times in Jn (4.21,
23; 5.25, 28; 16.2, 25, 32). **ὅτε οὔτε ἐν τῷ ὄρει τούτῳ οὔτε ἐν
Ἱεροσολύμοις.** After the destruction of their Temple by Hyrcanus, the
Samaritans did not cease to worship on Gerizim,[64] and they have in fact
continued to do so (perhaps with interruptions) until the present day. It
has also been suggested (without much success) that some form of
sacrificial worship may have continued for a while in Jerusalem after

---

ment the order to worship on Mount Gerizim, by inserting as Exod 20.17b and as Deut
5.18b the following verses, in this order: Deut 11.29a; 27.2b-3a, 4a, 5-7; 11.30. See E.
Tov, *Textual Criticism of the Hebrew Bible*, Minneapolis, 2nd ed., 1992, 94.

  [62] See Schürer II 17-19.

  [63] See Excursus XI, 'Shechem and Samaria in NT Times', pp. 302-303.

  [64] For NT times compare Josephus, *Ant.* XVIII iv 1 = 85-87, observing particularly
note *c* in the Loeb edition, p. 61.

A.D. 70.[65] The gospel, however, is not concerned to determine the correct locality for earthly liturgy, but to transcend that question by declaring that the very principle of worship is about to be altered, irrevocably. *Neither on this mountain nor in Jerusalem will you worship the Father.* προσ-κυνήσετε τῷ πατρί. In v. 20 the woman had used the verb προσκυ-νεῖν absolutely, and in the past tense, of her own community; here in v. 21 Jesus speaks of the future, uses the dative (the common LXX form for offering liturgical praise to Yahweh), and introduces the term τῷ πατρί. Since the Prologue (1.14, 18), God has been referred to as Father once in the presence of the Jews (2.16), once in the context of the followers of the Baptist (3.35), and now three times in a conversation with a Samaritan (4.21, 23 [×2]). The term will become frequent from ch. 5 onwards, but 4.21 is the first occasion on which *the Father* is used on its own,[66] 'a usage characteristic of John and almost peculiar to him' (Westcott). προσκυνήσετε, *you will worship*: this, the first declaration in John that God is in future to be adored as *Father*, is here addressed only to the Samaritans. It is uttered at the most ancient holy place in the Land (→ 4.4), and is presented as the solution to the ancient inter-tribal schism, in an elegant and subtle counter-balance to 'our fathers' in 4.20. The principle will be extended to everyone in 4.23-24.

22. In v. 20 the woman had spoken of the past, and in v. 21, Jesus had spoken of the future. In v. 22 Jesus, by-passing entirely the nature or legitimacy of Samaritan worship in the past, proceeds to speak about the present. The Samaritans are not to be required positively to renounce worship on their holy mountain, any more than Jews are to be required positively to renounce worship in the temple at Jerusalem. ὑμεῖς προσκυνεῖτε ὃ οὐκ οἴδατε. *You are worshipping something of which you are unaware*, or alternatively, paraphrased, *you are unaware of what you are at present worshipping.* On this sense of οἴδατε, → 3.2a, εἰδέναι, pp. 221-23. The Samaritans are certainly worshipping the God of Abraham and the God of Moses; it is simply that they are unaware of his solicitude for them as their Father. They treasure the five books of Moses, but undervalue their own prophet, Hosea, who before, and more than, any other prophet, spoke of Yahweh's fatherly love for his people: 'When Israel was a child, I loved him, …it was I who taught Ephraim to walk, picking them up in my arms, even though they did not realize [LXX: οὐκ ἔγνωσαν] that it was I who was caring[67] for them' (Hos 11.1, 2-4). ἡμεῖς προσκυνοῦμεν ὃ οἴδαμεν. Jesus, and those for whom he speaks (that is, those who were later to follow him) are *fully aware* of what they are worshipping (again, note οἴδαμεν, not γινώσκομεν, → 3.2a).

---

[65] The texts adduced are discussed in Schürer I 521-23.

[66] In 3.35 it is used in conjunction with τὸν υἱόν.

[67] For this figurative sense of רפא (rpʾ) see, among others, Macintosh (ICC), 443-44.

ὅτι ἡ σωτηρία ἐκ τῶν 'Ιουδαίων ἐστίν. σωτηρία, a *hapax legomenon* in John, is never found in 1, 2 and 3 John, and only three times (in hymns) in Revelation (7.10; 12.10; 19.1); σωτήρ is equally rare in the Johannine writings (→ Jn 4.42; 1 Jn 4.14; never in Revelation). The clause is probably redactional, not intended to be regarded as an utterance of Jesus to the woman at the well. On σωτηρία, BAG wrote: '... 2. quite predominantly, *salvation*, which the true religion bestows', a definition which would be acceptable not only throughout Judaism (LXX) and the Christian Church, but also among the many Mystery Religions of the ancient world. (BDAG deletes that definition, but supplies numerous examples where that sense would apply: see also *TWNT* VII 1003-1004; *EDNT* II 327, 329.) Whoever wrote this clause in John felt the need to assert strongly, perhaps to Christian converts among the Samaritans, perhaps also to any non-Jewish readers, that salvation originated among (ἐκ) the Jews. This accords with the evangelist's iterated reminders that many Jews were favourable to Jesus during his earthly life (2.23; 8.31; 10.21; 11.45; 12.9-11).[68] → 4.42, ο σωτηρ του κοσμου.

23-24. ἀλλὰ ἔρχεται ὥρα → 4.21. The words **καὶ νῦν ἐστιν** should not be understood as Jesus' words, but as a clarification inserted by the evangelist or an editor. **οἱ ἀληθινοί** means *genuine, authentic*. On **προσκυνήσουσιν τῷ πατρί** → 4.21, 22, and Excursus XIII, 'In Spirit and Truth'. The OT prophets had promised that the Spirit of God would bring into being and sustain a New Age in the End-time,[69] and so Jesus, as he begins to describe that new age which is beginning to take shape (ἔρχεται ὥρα), calls attention to the role of the Spirit. The worship of the community will be essentially different from the liturgy previously practised on Gerizim and in Jerusalem, because it will be conducted **ἐν πνεύματι καὶ ἀληθείᾳ.**[70]

25. οἶδα ὅτι Μεσσίας ἔρχεται ὁ λεγόμενος Χριστός. οἶδα and its ancient variant οιδαμεν (𝔓66c א2) attest that the woman is stating an article of her belief, and of that of her people. Many commentators have interpreted Μεσσίας here as a reference to the *Ta'eb*, the Restorer predicted in Deut 18.18 (→ 4.13, fn. 17); Odeberg and Bultmann, for example, suggest that the woman is explaining that this *Ta'eb* is the

---

[68] H. Thyen, 'Das Heil kommt von den Juden', in FS Bornkamm, 163-84.

[69] See W. Eichrodt, *Theologie des AT* II §13 III. 32-34 = ETr II 57-60. See also above pp. 273-79, 'Spring of Living Water'.

[70] The original text of Sinaiticus (א*), εν πνευματι αληθειας, is attested nowhere else; it may have been influenced by a recollection of 14.17; 15.26 and/or 16.13, but it was rejected even by Tischendorf in favour of the corrector's emendation to ἐν πνεύματι καὶ ἀληθείᾳ. This may be significant for judging the value of א* and of אc in other places.

Samaritan equivalent of 'the one whom you (Jews) call Messiah', but it is uncertain whether the Samaritans ever called their *Ta'eb* 'Messiah'.[71] The woman is using the terminology of Judaism, and it is reasonable to perceive in her use of 'Messiah' a pointer by the evangelist to the text of Gen 49.10, which all the Targums interpret as 'until the King Messiah comes', that is, the Anointed King of the tribe of Judah, and of the house of David.[72] The same interpretation has been accepted by virtually all Jewish scholars in later times.[73] The translation, ὁ λεγόμενος Χριστός, is best taken as an editorial gloss interpreting Μεσσίας for those (Greeks?) unfamiliar with that word.[74] It is also a typically Johannine clue to notice (→ 4.29).

ὅταν ἔλθῃ ἐκεῖνος. The resumptive ἐκεῖνος underlines her use of the Jewish term *Messiah*. Contained in this usage is the idea that she would be quite prepared to accept from Judaism a Messiah, that is, a new David, who would be—like her interlocutor—open and full of kindliness towards her people. For David was the only king who had ruled over the two kingdoms of Judah and Israel in an age when each was fully independent of the other, and when there was certainly no Temple in Jerusalem, and probably none on Gerizim either. Unlikely though it is that the woman herself thought so profoundly, the evangelist may well have had this vision in mind when he placed on her lips the word 'Messiah'.

ἀναγγελεῖ, a word meaning generally *report, announce, proclaim*, is prominent in the LXX with the meaning *disclose, proclaim what is unknown* (HR, 4 columns, with 184 examples rendering the Hiphil of נגד (ngd); see BDAG 2). ἡμῖν ἅπαντα. Nothing in the OT or in Judaism suggests that the Messiah was to be omniscient, much less that he was going to disclose or proclaim all things, but even so, ἅπαντα [or παντα] is emphatic (because it stands at the end of the sentence) and deserves attention. Classical Greece said of prophets that 'they knew all things'. Thus in the *Iliad* I 70, Chalcas knew all things present, past and future, ἤδη τά τ' ἐόντα τά τ' ἐσσόμενα πρό τ' ἐόντα; *Oedipus Rex* 300 reads, ὦ πάντα νωμῶν Τειρεσία; in Euripides' *Helen* 922, the prophetess Theonoe is upbraided with αἰσχρον τὰ μέν σε θεῖα πάντ' ἐξειδέναι. πάντα εἰδώς was used derogatively to mean 'a know-all' (Dio Chrysostom, *Or.* xxxiv, 4; xxxv, 2), but also as the distinctive

---

[71] The wide acceptance of the identification was probably due to the work by the distinguished Orientalist Adalbert Merx, *Der Messias oder Ta'eb der Samaritaner*, Giessen, 1909. The earliest text to mention a Messiah of the Samaritans is Justin, *Apologia* 53,6, but maybe Justin's evidence was sound: he was born in Shechem-Neapolis.

[72] The Hebrew text of Gen 49.10 is awkward, but probably means 'until Shiloh comes' (as in AV = KJV, RV): see the footnotes in RSV NRSV NEB REB (which interpret it otherwise).

[73] *Bereishit-Genesis*, translation and commentary by Rabbi Meir Zlotowitz, Brooklyn, 1986, II 2152-53.

[74] It is therefore, in my English version, placed in brackets.

characteristic of a true prophet. It is thus attributed to Apollonius of Tyana (*Life* vii 8) and in the Pseudo-Clementine Homilies, we read 'The true prophet is the one who always knows everything (ὁ πάντοτε πάντα εἰδώς), things past as they used to be, things present as they are, and things future as they will be' (Hom. II 6,5; see also III 11,2-15).[75] The Samaritan woman is simply stating, in her own way, an obvious truth, universally accepted, that a prophet knows everything. See Jn 14.26; 16.13-15 (14, 15, ἀναγγελεῖ), 30; 18.4; 21.17.

26. λέγει αὐτῇ ὁ Ἰησοῦς, **Ἐγώ εἰμι, ὁ λαλῶν σοι.** This is the first of the 'I am' Sayings in John's Gospel, in which Jesus reveals himself, here as the Messiah awaited by, and sent to, Israel (understanding by Israel all the Twelve Tribes). The sudden appearance of this claim, and in this context, is astonishing, since nowhere in the NT are the traditional Jewish beliefs about a royal Davidic Messiah more firmly laid aside than in the Fourth Gospel (Dodd, *Interpretation*, 228-40). But a re-examination of the conversation shows that it starts with the woman addressing Jesus as a Jew (v. 9) and with Jesus entering into dialogue on that presupposition (v.10: τίς ἐστιν ὁ λέγων σοι), after which she inquires whether he is greater than Jacob (v. 12), then concedes that he is a prophet (v. 19), and finally learns that he is the Messiah (vv. 25-26). Note (an *inclusio*) that ὁ λέγων σοι at the start of the dialogue (v. 10) is replaced at the end by ὁ λαλῶν σοι (v. 26), the verb signifying revelation. [76]

ὁ λαλῶν σοι defines the true function of his messianic role. It is insufficient to translate this phrase as *who am conversing with you*: see the comment at 3.11 on λαλεῖν, illustrating that in John this verb is virtually restricted to those, principally Jesus (45 times), who *speak the word of God* (cf. 18.36-37). Compare the five very clear examples at 8.25, 26, 28, 30, and contrast Jesus' refusal to reveal himself to the Pharisees in 10.24. Thus this first occurrence of Ἐγώ εἰμι on Jesus' lips carries a powerful doctrinal statement, partly concealing and partly revealing for those with eyes to see, who and what he is, the Word of God incarnate.

After the mention of Jesus as the bridegroom in 3.29, the scene in ch. 4 is therefore a pictorial representation of the fulfilment of Hosea's words of hope. All that Hosea had hoped for, all that the down-trodden Samaritans had longed for during more than a century, are here presented as fulfilled in the coming of Jesus to bring to the poor the water of life eternal:

---

[75] Many other examples in van Unnik, 219-28.

[76] See Judith M. Lieu, 'Messiah and Resistance in the Gospel and Epistles of John', in eds. M. Bockmuehl and J. N. Carleton Paget, *Redemption and Resistance: The Messianic Hopes of Jews and Christians in Antiquity*, FS W. Horbury, London, 2007, 97-108.

'I will speak tenderly to her,
and make the Valley of Misfortune a Gateway of Hope,[77]
and there she shall answer as in the days of her youth...
I will betroth you to me in faithfulness;
and you shall know the Lord' (Hos 2.14c-15bc, 19-20).

27. ἦλθαν, widely used in the Koine as an alternative to ἦλθον (BDF 81 [3]), is found in John only here and at 1.39. Even here the great majority of witnesses read ἦλθον (אᶜ AB³CDL and all other uncials), as did Lachmann, Tischendorf and Souter; but א* B* have ἦλθαν, followed by WH and most modern editors. ἦλθαν here may be a signal to a reader in the liturgy that the verb is third person plural, not a first person singular continuing Jesus' words in v.26 so as to read (with the variant in E K U 69.124) και επι τουτο ηλθον.

ὅτι μετὰ γυναικὸς ἐλάλει. γυναικός, *with a woman*, i.e. any woman at all. This was held to be inappropriate for any man, but especially for a rabbi: see *Pirke Aboth* 1,5 (Danby 446), and *Aboth Rabbi Nathan* 2,1d: 'No one should hold a conversation with a woman on the street, not even with his own wife, and certainly not with any other woman, because people talk' (full texts in SB II 438, and I 299-301). **τί ζητεῖς.** 'ζητεῖν in John hardly ever means a vague "wish", but "to seek", "to strive for"' (Schnackenburg): therefore, 'What are you trying to find out?' or 'What is the purpose of your conversation?'. **τί λαλεῖς μετ' αὐτῆς;** All the leading English-language versions from Tyndale and AV up to NRSV and REB inclusive render this as 'Why are you talking with her?' (REB) or the equivalent. In contrast, all the German-language versions I have consulted, from Luther to the present day, give 'Was redest du mit ihr?' or the equivalent. The first rendering probably arose from an over-emphasis on the astonishment of the disciples, but it makes the two verbs ζητεῖν and λαλεῖν almost tautologous. The alternative, 'What are you talking with her about?' (NJB, in line with the revised [French] *Bible de Jérusalem*), makes the second question a happy complement to the first. It appears also in the 'Wycliffian' NT of 1384: *What spekest thou with her?*

Translating τί λαλεῖς as 'What are you talking about with her?' also preserves the typically Johannine double meaning both of ζητεῖν and of λαλεῖν. At the mundane ('earthly') level, the disciples 'never asked' about the purpose or the topic of their conversation. As a result they forfeited the opportunity to learn there and then that Jesus was seeking to fulfil the will of the Father by taking the first step towards the reconciliation and restoration of Samaria, in revealing himself as the Messiah. The fact that the disciples did not ask even τί λαλεῖς directs attention to 4.26, ἐγώ ειμι, ὁ λαλῶν σοι (→): in John, λαλεῖν is virtually restricted to Jesus speaking the word of God. Compare and 3.11; 4.26; 5.30; 8.25, 26, 28, 30.

[77] For this rendering compare Macintosh, *Hosea*, 74-75.

28. ἀφῆκεν οὖν τὴν ὑδρίαν αὐτῆς ἡ γυνή is a neat phrase to take her off-stage while Jesus holds a private discussion with his disciples (= vv. 31-38), and at the same time to make clear that she will certainly soon be back. On οὖν compare the note at 4.5.

29. ἄνθρωπον (anarthrous).[78] This is the first occurrence of ἄνθρωπος referring to Jesus, the Word made flesh. In John, Jesus applies the term to himself only once (8.40), preferring to describe himself as 'Son of Man' (Excursus VI). The Samaritan woman here in 4.29, and the blind man before he comes to faith, who courteously speaks of ὁ ἄνθρωπος ὁ λεγόμενος Ἰησοῦς (9.11), are the only future disciples who, in John, refer to Jesus as an ἄνθρωπος. Otherwise (οὗτος) ὁ ἄνθρωπος is used of Jesus only by the Jews (5.12; 7.46; 9.16, 24; 10.33; 11.47, 50; 18.14, 17) and by Pilate (18.29; 19.5). Here in 4.29, δεῦτε ἴδετε ἄνθρωπον ὃς εἶπέν μοι πάντα ὅσα ἐποίησα marks the start of the woman's journey into faith. **πάντα ὅσα** is slightly stronger than the variant παντα α: hence *have ever done* (NRSV). She does not summarize the conversation, but merely states the central fact, a fact which is sufficient to prove that the stranger just arrived must certainly be a prophet (→ 4.25). **μήτι** usually indicates that a negative reply is expected, but it can also be used, where the questioner is in doubt, to mean *perhaps* (as here): see BDAG; MHT III 283; BDF 427 (2) and (3). 'Is this man perhaps the Messiah?' The double occurrence of Messiah in 4.25 and 29 may represent an intentional *inclusio* with its only previous appearance at 1.41 (the next instances are at 7.26-27, 41-42). Compare the final paragraph on ο σωτηρ του κοσμου at 4.42.

30. Many scribes sought to rectify the initial asyndeton (see the apparatus in NA[27]), but it is not uncharacteristic of John (MHT III 340). ἐξῆλθον ... **καὶ ἤρχοντο.** On the aorist followed by an imperfect see *JG* 2465. Note the parallel to 4.30 in 6.5.

4.31-37: AN INTERLUDE

> [66] In the meantime the disciples were imploring him, saying, 'Rabbi, have something to eat!' [32] but he said to them, 'I have food to eat which you are unaware of'. [33] So the disciples said to one another, 'Could anyone have brought him something to eat?' [34] Jesus said to them, 'My food is to do the will of him who sent me, and to accomplish his work. [35] Don't you say, "Another four months and the harvest will be here?" Look, I tell you! Raise your eyes, and behold the fields, how they are already white for harvesting. [36] The reaper is already taking in what he deserves, and gathering fruit for life

---

[78] The choice of ἄνθρωπος over ἀνήρ is not significant, for with the solitary exception of 1.36, ἀνήρ in John always refers to a husband (5 times in 4.16-18) or a male (1.13; 6.10). ἀνήρ is found nowhere in 1, 2 and 3 John, and in Revelation once only, at 21.2.

eternal, so that sower and reaper rejoice together. [37] For in this case the saying is true, "One sows and another reaps". [38] I sent you to reap that for which you did not labour; others have laboured, and you have entered into their labour.'

31-38. Several words in this 'Interlude' are found nowhere else in John's Gospel. They are μεταξύ (31), ὁ θερισμός (35 [×2]*) and ὁ θερίζων (36 [×2], 37, 38), μισθός (36), ὁ σπείρων (36, 37, and compare κόκκος 12.24), to which one may add κοπιᾶν (4.6, 38 [×2]) and κόπος (4.38). Even βρῶσις (4.32; 6.27, 55), βρῶμα (4.34) and φαγεῖν (only in 4.31-33 [3 times]; 6 (11 times); 18.28) attract attention by their presence here. As a result, several writers judge that these verses originate from someone other than the author of the main part of the Gospel; unfortunately, these unusual features of vocabulary do not enable one to determine whether the verses were inserted into the text after this part of the Gospel was completed, or whether the Evangelist took over a passage written earlier by someone else, and put it into his Gospel at the time he was composing this narrative about the Samaritans.

31. μεταξύ is scarcely found in the LXX (see HR), and then (as in the NT) it is nearly always as a preposition. Most modern English versions translate ἐν τῷ μεταξύ as *meanwhile*, but this rendering hardly brings out the emphasis (compare BDAG 1 b α): better, *in the meantime*. The three words then make a tight connection with v. 30: the reader knows that the townspeople of Sychar are already on their way and *In the meantime*, Jesus is informing the disciples that the fields of Samaria are ripe for harvesting, as they will presently see (4.39-42; *JG* 2668). The deferential form ῥαββί, hitherto used only by those who were not yet Jesus' followers (1.38, 49; 3.2), indicates the disciples' respect for, and distance from, him: compare 6.25; 9.2; 11.8. ἠρώτων. In the Koine (as distinct from Classical Greek), ἐρωτᾶν means, not merely *to ask a question*, but also *to invite, beseech*, or *implore*.

32-34. On οἴδατε (32) → 3.11. On οὖν (33) → 4.3; on μή τις → μήτι at 4.29. '*Is it possible that someone…*' ἐμὸν βρῶμα, without the article may be, grammatically, the predicate (*JG* 1994; MHT III 183-84; BDF 252; 393 [6]; 394) but here it makes no difference to the sense.

βρῶσιν ἔχω φαγεῖν (32)…ἐμὸν βρῶμα (34). The distinction between βρῶσις and βρῶμα is a very fine one, if one exists at all: perhaps βρῶσις denotes food as that which nourishes, βρῶμα, as that which is eaten. In 32 Jesus uses the less concrete word, βρῶσις, to express himself in a figurative sense, but when the disciples fail to comprehend (33), he switches to the more concrete term βρῶμα, and defines it in words that exclude any possible misunderstanding of it as physical food (ἵνα ποιήσω κτλ.). In both Greek and Oriental religious texts, words for food and drink are commonly used metaphorically (τροφή, ἄρτος, γάλα), but βρῶσις and βρῶμα are hardly ever so employed, either in Classical

Greek or in the Koine, and never once in the LXX (TWNT I 642-43). In
the NT, the two nouns are used figuratively only here in Jn 4.32, 34 and
in 6.27, 55, unless one counts also 1 Cor 3.2; 10.3. B-L suggests as a
possibility that Jesus' declining to eat at this juncture is meant to recall
that Abraham's servant, when seeking the hand of Rebecca, would not eat
until he had delivered his (divinely ordained) message.

On 4.34 (ποιεῖν) τὸ θέλημα τοῦ πέμψαντός με, see 5.30 and 6.38,
39; on καὶ τελειώσω αὐτοῦ τὸ ἔργον, see 5.36.

35-36. ἤδη. The textual evidence (see NA²⁷) does not warrant a firm
decision whether this word should be attached to the preceding or to the
following sentence, and in this context it does not make too much
difference. It seems, however, to give a better sense if it is taken with
v. 36, especially since John elsewhere places ἤδη at the beginning of a
clause (4.51; 7.14; 9.22; 15.3). **36.** μισθόν, without article, is a regular
Greek usage (Mt 10.41; LSJ and BDAG): it can mean either *pay* or
reward.

35. There is no evidence that the words **ἔτι τετράμηνός κτλ.** are a
proverb, or that they are not. They may simply be a statement that four
months still remain to harvest-time, τετράμηνος being an adjective, with
χρόνος understood (BDAG): this clause, so understood, has often been
used to date the incident at some time in the winter.[79] The sense in this
context would then be 'There is time enough yet'. Jesus counters that
expectation of the disciples by an emphatic **ἰδοὺ λέγω ὑμῖν**, with the
ancient Hebrew phrase **ἐπάρατε τοὺς ὀφθαλμοὺς ὑμῶν**,[80] and with
the aorist imperative **θεάσασθε** (not the future indicative!): they constitute a threefold command, 'Look! Raise your eyes, and behold!'
Though *JG* 2246 suggests translating ἰδού (4.35; 12.15; 16.32; 19.5) here
in 4.35 as *but*, it is better to take it (compare BDAG) as serving to arouse
interest at a new turn in the story.[81] It is not fanciful, only logical, to infer
that Jesus already sees several Samaritans coming down the road with the
woman. There has been no interval of waiting for the gradual ripening of
the crop: 'the harvest is ripe on the same day on which the seed has been
sown, for already the Samaritans are pouring out of the village and
coming to Jesus' (R. E. Brown).

---

[79] There is always at least a four-month period of waiting between the last sowing and
the first harvesting, dependent on the land, the crop, the weather and the time of year (SB
II 439-40; Dalman, *Arbeit*, III 1-12, 'Die Zeit der Ernte').

[80] [In the OT] 'the expression nĕśēʾ ʿenayim, "to lift the eyes" is extremely
widespread and refers to eager looking, particularly since it is normally followed by רָאָה
rāʾā "to see" (35 times)' (*TDOT* X 38).

[81] This is the only instance of ἰδοὺ λέγω ὑμῖν in the NT (unless one counts 1 Cor
15.31, ἰδοὺ μυστήριον λέγω ὑμῖν). Is it here preferred to ἀμὴν ἀμὴν λέγω ὑμῖν (25≈
in John), in order to introduce the word ἰδού, *Look!*, albeit in the singular?

36-37. The interpretation of these verses turns upon the identification of ὁ θερίζων. The term is certainly not used generically, to mean 'any harvester' (BDF 252 [2]). Schnackenburg suggests that Jesus is the harvester, his Father the sower. Those, however, who take ἤδη as making a close connection with v. 35 generally interpret 'the harvester' as Jesus, and 'the sower' as the Baptist. This dovetails with the interpretation of 3.23 given above, arguing that the Baptist exercised his ministry in the vicinity. μισθὸν λαμβάνει means that the harvester is collecting his due reward, that is, the approaching Samaritans, whom he will shepherd towards and into life eternal. ἵνα in the last clause of v.36 is not final but consecutive,[82] ὁ σπείρων is the subject, and ὁμοῦ can mean either *at the same place* or *at the same time* (BDAG), or, obviously, both. The sense is therefore that the Baptist can share in the rejoicing over the success of Jesus' ministry in Samaria. Thus [ὁμοῦ] χαίρῃ matches 3.29 (ὁ δὲ φίλος τοῦ νυμφίου... χαρᾷ χαίρει), just as the thought of 3.28-30 harmonizes with the interpretation preferred here, and leads smoothly into v. 37. ἐν γὰρ τούτῳ ὁ λόγος ἐστὶν ἀληθινός κτλ. *For on this occasion the saying holds true, that while one sows, another reaps.* In the context, this saying is most appropriately referred to the ministry of Jesus' disciples mentioned in 3.26 and 4.1-2, reminding them that their success has been built on the labours of others—especially of the Baptist and his followers.

38. The aorist ἀπέστειλα is the most awkward word in the sentence[83] because John, in contrast to the Synoptic writers (e.g. Mt 9.27–10.8 ‖ Mk 3.13-19; 6.6-13 ‖ Lk 9.1-6; 10.1-12), does not record that Jesus ever sent his disciples on a missionary journey until after his Resurrection (Jn 20.21). Most commentators would probably agree that ἀπέστειλα is here a word 'spoken in anticipation with prophetic assurance' (*GANT*); compare the same verb in Jn 17.18[84] and cf. 6.62-65, 70-71.

If that is so, and if an editor inserted v.38 after the Gospel was completed, then this editor may have intended by these words to indicate that others besides Jesus and his disciples, or even others besides the Baptist and his disciples, had taken part in preaching the Word of God in Samaria. Lagrange thinks of Moses and all the prophets as the sowers, citing for this interpretation 'Origen and all the Fathers'; so also Aquinas, who interprets the past tense *misi* of the pre-resurrection preaching of the Apostles to Israel according to Mt 10.5 (n. 654). John often views the present as a completed result of the past (*JG* 2477) and out of chronological order (2480).

---

[82] Compare *IBNTG* 142. Abel, *Grammaire* §79f, observes that the usage is frequent in the LXX, influenced by the Hebrew, which used the same construction for purpose and for consequence.

[83] ἀπεσταλκα in ℵ and D is perhaps an attempt to smooth over the difficulty.

[84] The future perfect had dropped out of use (BDF 65 [1b]; 352).

Cullmann suggested that perhaps the writer had in mind that the success of Peter and John in their mission to Samaria (the reapers) rested in part on the labours of Philip and the Hellenists (the sowers) (Acts 8.4-40). Brown surmised that the story in John might have been preserved as an argument against Christians in the Jerusalem Church who might have wanted even Samaritan converts to change their allegiance to Jerusalem as part of the Christian life (compare Acts 2.46). Perhaps Jn 4.38 might be interpreted as an (otherwise unattested) Saying attributed to the Lord in the early Church and inserted here to affirm a universal principle.

4.39-45: JESUS ACCEPTED IN SAMARIA AS THE SAVIOUR OF THE WORLD

[39] Many Samaritans from that village came to believe in him because of the woman's word testifying that 'He told me everything I had ever done'. [40] So when the Samaritans reached him, they implored him to stay awhile with them; and he stayed there a couple of days. [41] Many more came to believe because of his word [42] and said to the woman, 'It is no longer by reason of what you said that we are believing, because we have heard for ourselves, and are now aware that this is in truth the Saviour of the world.'

[43] After the two days he departed from there into Galilee. [44] For Jesus himself had testified that a prophet has no honour in his own country. [45] When therefore he came to Galilee, the Galileans welcomed him, having seen all that he had done in Jerusalem at the feast, for they too had gone to the festival.

39. ἐκ δὲ τῆς πόλεως ἐκείνης. John, in contrast with the Synoptics, uses πόλις sparingly: seven times only before the Passion Narrative, at 1.44 (Bethsaida) and 11.54 (Ephraim), with both places identified, five times here (for Sychar), and then once at 19.20.

Compare the comment at 4.18 on the woman's five partners. One may surmise that in this section entitled 'The New Jerusalem', John is implying that this New Jerusalem is beginning to take shape in Samaria, as ὁ υἱός ὁ μονογενής (→ 3.16) comes to claim his bride. This interpretation calls attention to the full significance of **πολλοὶ ἐπίστευσαν εἰς αὐτόν**: it is the first instance of this phrase in John, and the first of seven occurrences (4.39; 7.31; 8.30; 10.42; 11.45; 12.11, in the imperfect; 12.42). The omission of εἰς αὐτόν in ℵ*pc a e may have originated from a scribal reluctance to attribute to the Samaritans faith 'in Jesus' before the Resurrection; but at this point, the faith alluded to is simply faith in Jesus as Messiah (4.29). Mark the wording διὰ **τὸν λόγον** τῆς γυναικὸς **μαρτυρούσης**, for it affects the understanding of v. 42.

40. ὡς οὖν ἦλθον πρὸς αὐτὸν οἱ Σαμαρῖται, that is, the Samaritans who had been accompanying the woman down the road (→ 4.35), **ἠρώτων**[85] **αὐτόν μεῖναι** (aorist), *to make his abode, to take up*

---

[85] The imperfect tense is normal with this verb whenever it awaits a fulfilment in a further action by another agent (MHT III 65; BDF 328).

residence there, the aorist indicating a new act (as distinct from μένειν, denoting the continuation of an action already begun).[86] **παρ᾽ αὐτοῖς.** μένειν παρά τινι is John's normal usage for *to stay (physically) with someone*, as in 1.39, here at 4.40 and in 14.25. **καὶ ἔμεινεν ἐκεῖ.** Origen observes that John does not write that Jesus stayed 'in their village', or 'in Samaria', but simply *there*, with those who had come to believe. There, where Abraham had offered the first sacrifice in Canaan, where Jacob had bought the first parcel of land, below the mountain where Joshua had proclaimed the first Constitution of Israel (Josh 24) and where a temple lay in ruins, near the site of Shechem where no walled town remained, there he stayed. Rupert of Deutz observes that Jesus never 'stayed' in Jerusalem (contrast 2.12; 7.9; 10.40; 11.6, 54).

δύο ἡμέρας. The English idiom, *a couple of days*, like the German *ein paar Tagen*, indicates just a short stay, without chronometric exactitude (as the translation *two days* would in modern speech imply). Instinctively one thinks of Hos 6.2 ('after two days he will revive us': LXX, ὑγιάσει ἡμᾶς μετὰ δύο ἡμέρας), for given the prominence of Hosea in the interpretation preferred above, this verse would then make an ideal conclusion to the narrative.[87] Two days was all he needed to bring his long-lost bride back home (→ Jn 4.6).

41. Many more came to believe because of Jesus' word (διὰ τὸν λόγον αὐτοῦ) than had come to believe because of the woman's testimony in v.39. **42. διὰ τὴν σὴν λαλιάν.** In Classical Greek λαλιά meant *chatter*, but by NT times it meant simply *speech*, denoting *spoken language* in any form: in Mt 26.73 = Mk 14.70 Peter is identified by his Galilean accent. In the light of Jn 4.39 and 41, we should have expected rather διὰ τὸν λόγον σου, for John restricts the verb λαλεῖν almost exclusively to those who 'speak the word of God'. The choice of λαλιά over λόγος here in 4.42 depicts the Samaritans—the many believing Samaritans (v. 39)—as recognizing that the woman had indeed been speaking to them the word of God.[88] **αὐτοὶ γὰρ ἀκηκόαμεν,** *because we have heard for ourselves*, the perfect signifying completeness (thus *JG* 2450), or perhaps *because we have just heard for ourselves* (→ 4.18 on εἴρηκας). **καὶ οἴδαμεν,** *and are (now) aware*: see the note at 3.2a on εἰδέναι. **ὅτι οὗτός ἐστιν ἀληθῶς ὁ σωτὴρ τοῦ κόσμου.**

---

[86] Chrysostom's commentary reads (XXXV 1) ἐβούλοντο διηνεκῶς αὐτὸν κατέχειν, but Boismard contends that this phrase is added by the Compiler of the Homilies (*Un évangile pré-johannique* II, 2, 181).

[87] On this text see Macintosh, *Hosea* (ICC), 220-24

[88] The variant σην μαρτυριαν in א* D may have arisen from a desire to avoid using λαλια since it was considered a less precise and rather plebeian term, or from a desire to render explicit the interpretation proposed above. The only other occurrence of λαλιά in the NT is at Jn 8.43.

Ο ΣΩΤΗΡ ΤΟΥ ΚΟΣΜΟΥ

This title, so common in later Christian worship, occurs only twice in the NT, here and at 1 Jn 4.14.

In the LXX the noun σωτήρ is applied almost everywhere (over 30 times) to Yahweh alone (e.g. Isa 45.15, 21; Wis 16.7; Bar 4.22). Three exceptions refer to ancient 'judges of Israel' as saviours (Jdg 3.9.15; 2 Esd 19.27 [= Neh 9.27]), but otherwise σωτήρ is never applied to any human figure (not even to the Davidic Messiah). In fact, the LXX seems deliberately to avoid using it of the Davidic Messiah, as at Zech 9.9: ἰδοὺ ὁ βασιλεύς σου ἔρχεταί σοι, δίκαιος καὶ σῴζων αὐτός, and at Isa 49.6: ἰδοὺ τέθεικά σε ... εἰς σωτηρίαν (G. Fohrer in *TWNT* VII 1013).

At the other extreme, Josephus never uses σωτήρ with reference to God, but does use it of Vespasian (War III ix 8 = 459; VII iv 1 = 71) and even of himself (Life 47 = 244, and in 50 = 259, κοιναὶ παρὰ πάντων ἐγίνοντο φωναὶ καλούντων εὐεργέτην με καὶ σωτῆρα). In Greek literature σωτήρ was an honorific appellation, applied to benefactors and philanthropists, to philosophers and statesmen, to kings and emperors (e.g. Antiochus Epiphanes): see the extensive documentation in *TWNT* VII 1006-1014 (W. Foerster). Thus Hadrian is regularly called ὁ σωτὴρ τῆς οἰκουμένης or τοῦ κόσμου (1011[15-26]), not for any single achievement, but for his many individual acts of beneficence, and the title σωτήρ was in no way reserved to him alone (1011[28-44]). In the *Corpus Hermeticum* the title never occurs, and it is rarely found in any Gnostic Writings except under Christian influence (1019-1020).

In the NT σωτήρ occurs with reference to God at Lk 1.47; 1 Tim 1.1; 2.3; 4.10; Titus 1.3; 2.10; 3.4; Jude 25, and also, 16 times (see the next paragraph), to Jesus Christ, predominantly in the later books, from which one may reasonably infer that the title was neither claimed by Jesus nor attributed to him during his earthly life. The carefully restricted LXX usage might have made the first Jewish Christians wary of calling Jesus σωτήρ; it might have seemed too much. Among non-Jewish Christians, however, the same word might have seemed on its own too little (see the preceding paragraph), endangering the unique role of Jesus by attributing to him a term normally used to designate a political saviour.[89] Its exact connotation must always be discerned from the context.

Thus in Lk 2.11 the meaning of σωτήρ is clear from the fact that Luke 1–2 presents Jesus as the long-expected, freedom-bringing Messiah (see 1.68-75), born in 'the city of David'; 'Saviour' would have been an indispensable title in the protocol for the proclamation of this royal birth. Likewise in Acts 5.31 (see Barrett *in loco*) and 13.23 Jesus is called Saviour for bringing his people forgiveness from their sins. In Phil 3.20 Jesus is the Saviour awaited from heaven at the end of time (compare

---

[89] That is, reversing the argument of W. Bousset in *Kyrios Christos*, 1913, 293-99, that Christians adopted the title σωτήρ because it was used in pagan cults, particularly of rulers. See Barrett, *Acts*, 290, on 5.31.

1 Thess 1.10, though this parallel lacks the term σωτήρ). Ephesians 5.23 refers to the exalted Christ, as do 2 Tim 1.10 (note v. 10cd); Tit 2.13; 3.6 (and therefore 1.4 as well). 2 Peter 1.11; 2.20; 3.2, 18 show that around A.D. 100 κύριος καὶ σωτήρ was an accepted title of Jesus Christ (for σωτήρ see also 1.1).

The lexical data from the LXX and Greek literature clarify the import of ὁ σωτὴρ τοῦ κόσμου in Jn 4.42 (and compare 1 Jn 4.4). The adjunction of τοῦ κόσμου makes clear that in Jn 4.42 σωτήρ is not just the equivalent of a local civic honour (as in Josephus), and the LXX usage compels one to ask what ὁ σωτήρ might connote when applied by a Jewish writer to a man. Placed on the lips of the Samaritans, and being neither Judaic nor specifically Samaritan, it raises profound questions about Jesus.[90]

The reader of this Gospel is fully aware of the great significance of the term κόσμος in the mind of the evangelist (→ 1.9), and of the writer's predilection for *inclusio*. It is worth noting that after the Prologue, in the section running from 1.19 to 4.54, κόσμος first occurs at the point where Jesus enters into the narrative, at 1.29 (ὁ ἀμνὸς τοῦ θεοῦ ὁ αἴρων τὴν ἁμαρτίαν τοῦ κόσμου), and that its seventh and last occurrence is at 4.42 (ὁ σωτὴρ τοῦ κόσμου). The other five occurrences, in 3.16, 17 [3 times], 19, are all concerned with God's love for this world, contain the only mention outside the Prologue of μονογενής (τὸν υἱὸν τὸν μονογενῆ ἔδωκεν. The μονογενής, the utterly Unique One, is truly the Saviour of the World, the One who discloses how God so loved the world. Aquinas observes that the Samaritans here 'confitentur Christum Salvatorem singularem, verum et universalem', citing Isa 45.15 (vere tu es Deus absconditus, Deus Israel, Salvator) and Acts 4.12 (n. 663).[91]

43. μετὰ δὲ τὰς δύο ἡμέρας. When the evangelist uses a cardinal number with ἡμέρα, he does not use the article (2.19, 20; 11.6, 17; 12.1; 20.26) except here in 4.43. Therefore, *the two days*, probably because the writer saw them as fulfilling the promise in Hos 6.1-3, by initiating the conversion of Samaria.[92] → 4.40.

---

[90] Where σωτὴρ τοῦ κόσμου is found in *The Testaments of the Twelve Patriarchs* (Levi 10.2; 14.2; Dan 6.7 [and 9, τῶν ἐθνῶν]; Benjamin 3.8, ὁ ἀμνὸς τοῦ θεοῦ καὶ σωτὴρ τοῦ κόσμου), it is safe to say that this comes from Christian authors or editors, and so contributes nothing to a better understanding of the phrase in the NT. See H. W. Hollander and M. De Jonge, *The Testaments of the Twelve Patriarchs: A Commentary*, 1985, 82-85.

[91] The addition of ὁ χριστός at the end of the verse, though supported by a quantitatively large number of witnesses and consequently accepted for centuries in the Textus Receptus, is unjustified by the manuscript tradition (see NA[27]) and has been rejected in every modern critical edition beginning with Tischendorf's *8a* in 1869. See NA[26] Appendix II Textuum Differentiae = NA[27] Appendix III Editionum Differentiae on Jn 4.42, where this variant is not once recorded.

[92] Though no OT text looks more appropriately matched to the NT than Hos 6.2, neither the NT nor the early Fathers cite this text as evidence for the Resurrection. The

44. The saying about a prophet's being unwelcome 'in his own country' is found in Mt 13.57 ‖ Mk 6.4 ‖ Lk 4.24, but its presence here at Jn 4.44 is puzzling. Why should Jesus go 'into Galilee', knowing that he will not be welcome there? 'The text appears to be utterly illogical' (Origen XIII 53; GCS 10:283 = SC §364).

Origen therefore suggested that 'his own country' must refer to Judea, where Jesus had already experienced antagonism (compare Jn 2.18-20, 23-25; 4.1-3), commenting that πατρὶς δὴ τῶν προφητῶν ἐν τῇ Ἰουδαίᾳ ἦν (XIII 54; GCS 10:284 = SC § 372). Some modern exegetes adopt a similar view, arguing that Jerusalem, the home of every Jew, must be pre-eminently the home of the Messiah (Schlatter), and so for Jesus too his 'proper home' (Hoskyns), but this seems to read too much into ἰδίᾳ, which is here simply the equivalent of the possessive pronoun: see MHT I 87-90; III 2, 4, 191-92, and note that all three Synoptic parallels read not ἰδίᾳ, but αὐτοῦ. Bultmann and Brown suggest that Jesus knew that the welcome he would receive in Galilee (Jn 4.45) would be as shallow as that which, according to 2.23-25, he had received in Jerusalem, just the popular enthusiasm given to a wonderworker. Schnackenburg suggests that Jesus might have been seeking to retire for the moment from the stress of conflict in Jerusalem (compare 7.3-8), while knowing that he would encounter non-acceptance in Galilee too, simply because he was a Galilean (6.41-42, 52, 60-66). None of these views seems entirely satisfactory.

πατρίς can denote either a large geographical territory, a *native country*, or a very small locality, such as someone's *home town*. As parallels to the saying that a teacher is unwelcome in his own πατρίς, BDAG mentions Dio Chrysostom 30 (47), 6, πᾶσιν τοῖς φιλοσόφοις χαλεπὸς ἐν τῇ πατρίδι ὁ βίος; Apollonius of Tyana, Letter 44, to his brother, μόνη μέχρι νῦν ἡ πατρὶς ἀγνοεῖ, in Philostratus I 354,12 = Loeb II 436; and Epictetus 3,16,11, asserting that the philosopher avoids his πατρίς. All three parallels refer to the teacher's native ground, the home town or neighbourhood where his family background is only too well known, exactly as in Mk 6.2-4 ‖s and Jn 6.42. In Jn 4.44, therefore, πατρίς is best taken as referring not to Galilee in general, but, specifically, to Nazareth, in accordance with Jn 1.45-46; 18.5, 7; 19.19.[93]

The traveller from Samaria would cross the boundary and enter the district of Galilee at a point not two miles distant from Nazareth.[94] At no

---

first to do so was Tertullian in *Adv. Marcionem* IV 43 (CCL I,161) and *Adv. Iudaeos* 23 (CCL 2.1389): Wolff, *Hosea*, ETr 1974, prints the two texts both in Latin and in translation, together with many useful references. See also J. Dupont, 'Ressuscité "le troisième jour"', *Biblica* 40 (1959), 742-61, particularly 745-46.

[93] This represents a slight variation from the interpretation given by Chrysostom (XXXV 2) who says that Jesus went to Cana because his πατρίς was Capernaum, which rejected him (Lk 10.15).

[94] Josephus states that the most southerly point of the frontier of Galilee was 'a village in the Great Plain called Xaloth' (*War* III iii 1 = 39: Loeb II 587), to be identified

other time in John's narrative is Jesus so close to his native town. Perhaps that is why the writer feels it imperative to explain why Jesus did not go there, but instead, travelled on further into Galilee. ἐμαρτύρησεν in v. 45 has a pluperfect sense,[95] and provides the explanation: *because he had openly affirmed that a prophet finds no honour on his home ground*.

45. ὅτε οὖν ἦλθεν, → 4.5. *So it was* that when he reached Galilee, the Galileans *welcomed* him. ἐδέξαντο, *hapax legomenon* in John, was chosen perhaps (Schnackenburg) under the influence of the proverb in the form found at Lk 4.24, δεκτός. They *welcomed* him, as others had done in Jerusalem, because of what they had seen him do there ἐν τῆ ἑορτῆ, *at the festival*:→ Jn 2.23. Significantly, John does not here use λαβεῖν, which would imply that they *accepted* him, the verb he prefers to designate genuine faith (1.12; 5.43; cf. 3.11, 32-33; 12.48; 13.20 [4 times]; 17.8). → 4.48.

---

with the modern Iqsâl = Iksal (map reference 1807 2320), only 3 km south-east of Nazareth. See also his *Life* 44 = 227: Loeb I 85; Dalman, *Sacred Sites and Ways*, 62, 190.
    [95] See *SMTNTG* 48, 52; *IBNTG* 11.

ΚΥΡΙΟΣ OR ΙΗΣΟΥΣ IN 4.1a?

In 1869 Tischendorf, induced presumably by the reading in his newly found treasure, the Codex Sinaiticus, was the first editor to print Ιησους in the Gospel text at Jn 4.1a, but for ninety years thereafter, until 1960, nearly all others (H S V M N²⁵) continued to retain κυριος, as in the TR. The only exceptions were Friedrich Blass (1902)[1] and J. Bover (1943).

In 1960 G. D. Kilpatrick, in his *Greek–English Diglot* (1960), produced privately for translators of the British and Foreign Bible Society, replaced κυριος by Ιησους; so did R. V. G. Tasker in *The Greek New Testament* (1964), but he was merely supplying the Greek text underlying the NEB. Since that time Ιησους has usually been preferred in editions of the Greek text, as in all those from the United Bible Societies or from the Institute in Münster (including NA²⁷), plus the *Synopses* of J. B. Orchard (1983) and B-L (1986); the solitary exception is the (revised) *Synopsis* of A. Huck and H. Greeven (1981). Most modern English-language Versions since 1960 have also followed the Bible Societies, adopting the reading Ιησους, though the commentators have been rather more reluctant to abandon κυριος. See Van Belle 173-74.

There is good external evidence for either alternative (see NA²⁷), and in the *TCGNT*, the reading accepted, Ιησους, is classed only {C}, indicating 'a considerable degree of doubt' as to which is the superior reading (xxviii). The editorial committee judged that if κυριος had stood (as subject of εγνω) in the original text, it is unlikely that it would ever have been displaced by Ιησους, because the triple occurrence of Ιησους makes the text irksome to read; whereas if Ιησους had originally been the subject of εγνω, 'more than one copyist may have smoothed the passage by changing the first instance of Ιησους to κυριος' precisely to avoid this clumsiness. Perhaps in the original text the subject of the verb was not expressed, so that some scribes later supplied Ιησους, others κυριος (often written as ΙΣ̄ and ΚΣ̄). Thus *TCGNT* 205-206.

In 2002 Gilbert Van Belle entered a powerful plea for the reinstatement of κυριος.[2] In assessing the external evidence (set out fully in *UBS*³), he draws attention to Aland's 'five Categories' of witnesses, of

---

[1] *Evangelium secundum Ioannem*, Leipzig, 1902. See Lagrange, *Critique textuelle* II (1935), 8-9, on the idiosyncratic character of this work.

[2] G. Van Belle, '*ΚΥΡΙΟΣ* or *ΙΗΣΟΥΣ* in John 4.1?', in ed. J. Denaux, *New Testament Criticism and Exegesis*, FS J. Delobel, BETL 161, Leuven, 2002, 159-74.

which the first three ('very special', 'special' and 'distinctive') are of primary significance.[3] In Category I, Ιησους is found in ℵ alone; in II, in Θ alone; in III, only in 086 and f^1. κυριος, by contrast, occurs in Category I, in 𝔓[75] B; in II, in C and 083; in III, in A Δ Ψ and f^{13}. (Van Belle concedes that the original reading of 𝔓[66] is uncertain, though the 'corrected' one is K̄Σ̄.)

But Van Belle insists also on the 'intrinsic probability' of κυριος in this context. After an encyclopaedic survey of editions, versions and (from 1826) commentaries, he concludes that here in 4.1 (and in 6.23; 11.2) κυριος represents the original text. Many would agree, but would ascribe the term to a redactor or a glossator (so, e.g., Bernard I 132, also XXXIII). Van Belle, however, contends that it was the evangelist himself who wrote κυριος, to recall attention to the content of the passage immediately preceding, in which the heavenly status of him whom the Father has sent is explicitly declared (3.31, 34-35). Thus F. Godet 1902, 292; ETr 1886 (repr. 1978), 417. C. F. Keil (1881) likewise suggests that κυριος is there to remind the reader that Jesus was throughout his life fully aware of the mission assigned to him by God, and left Judea, to withdraw to Galilee, because that was at this point an integral part of God's plan (4.3; → ἔδει in 4.4); compare also the more than human knowledge ascribed to him in 4.16-18, 29. κυριος as a designation of Jesus is indeed, in John, a resurrection-title, but the evangelist knew this, and therefore employed it, sparingly and significantly, at critical points in the narrative. Here its presence would signal a powerful *inclusio* with 4.42.

To sum up, the simplest way of accounting for the origination of the two readings is to posit that originally the subject of εγνω was not expressed (thus Barrett, R. E. Brown, *TCGNT*); but no surviving manuscript attests its absence—all contain either Ιησους or κυριος. It seems virtually certain therefore that neither word was written in *scriptio plena*, but only as Ῑ̄Σ or K̄Σ̄. There is no clear and objective criterion to determine which of the two nouns was the earlier or the original, or whether the noun was first inserted in the text by an editor, a glossator, or by the evangelist himself. κυριος is preferred in this commentary, partly because of its earlier attestation, but mainly because it is so unusual, and is therefore the more difficult reading.

---

[3] See Van Belle 161-62, and K. Aland, *Text of the New Testament*, ETr, Grand Rapids, 1987, 106, 159-63.

SHECHEM AND SAMARIA
IN NEW TESTAMENT TIMES

It is impossible to say when the Samaritan temple on Gerizim was first built, perhaps around 330 B.C. (see Josephus, *Ant.* XI viii 1 = 322-24, and Appendix B p. 509, in the Loeb edition, vol. VI; Schürer II 17-19), but it was totally destroyed in 129–128 B.C. by John Hyrcanus I (*Ant.* XIII ix 1 = 255-56; Schürer I 207). That it was never rebuilt is clear from the fact that the Jews observed the anniversary of its destruction as a day of rejoicing (*Megillat Taanith* §8). In the same campaign Hyrcanus captured Shechem and no doubt left it ravaged, with any fortifications in ruins; but it is too much to state (with Schürer II 161) that Josephus asserts that the town was, like the temple, destroyed at the same time. In *Ant.* XIII ix 1 = 255; *War* I ii 6 = 63, the verb Josephus uses is αἱρεῖν, and αἱρεῖν implies rather that the localities mentioned as 'captured' continued to exist thereafter. Twenty years later, however, between 111 and 107 B.C., when Hyrcanus conquered the 'massive stronghold of Samaria' (Σαμά-ρειαν πόλιν ὀχυρωτάτην), he 'utterly effaced' that ancient historic capital (πᾶσαν αὐτὴν ἠφάνισεν) of the Northern Kingdom (1 Kgs 16.24), destroying its very foundations, 'until no sign remained that a city had ever been there' (*Ant.* XIII x 2-3 = 275-81; *War* I ii 7 = 65: Schürer I 209-10). For the next two centuries the region was under the control either of the Hasmoneans or of the Herodians or of the Romans.

After Pompey's conquest of Jerusalem in 63 B.C., the city of Samaria was refounded by the proconsul Gabinius (57–55 B.C.: Schürer I 245-46), repopulated by the Romans and later considerably enlarged by Herod the Great, but as a Roman colony and a Hellenized city, renamed in honour of the Emperor Augustus, Sebaste, the modern Sebastiyeh (*Ant.* XIV v 3 = 88; XV vii 3 = 217; viii 5 = 292; *War* I viii 4 = 166; xxi 2 = 403; Schürer II 160-64). Non-Jewish and firmly loyal to Rome, it supplied a substantial part of the troops stationed in Judaea under successive military governors (Schürer I 363-64).

While Sebaste flourished, the ancient Shechem became, to judge by the size of Tell Balâta, a mere village which had never recovered from the destruction wreaked by John Hyrcanus and his sons, all bitterly hostile to the Samaritan nation. The episode in John 4 is therefore located about 8 miles (12 km) away from Sebaste, in an economically depressed area, where the native population had been under the dominion of alien rulers for over one hundred years.[1]

In A.D. 67, the fighting men of Samaria gathered on Mount Gerizim, planning to join in the revolt against Rome, only to be virtually annihilated (*War* III vii 32 = 307-15). After the War, new *coloniae* were of course established by the Romans, one of them in A.D. 72 across the strategic defile of Mabartha[2] between Ebal and Gerizim; it was entitled *Colonia Prima Flavia* (thus Pliny), and also *Neapolis.* This new foundation soon became the principal city of the region, eclipsing even Sebaste, and, because of its location, about one Roman mile from the site of Tell Balâta,[3] came in time to be identified with the ancient Shechem (Schürer I 520-21; II 163-64). Nevertheless, between A.D. 72 and 90, 'the creation of this cosmopolitan city at the foot of their holy mountain must have seemed to the natives of Samaria an outrage' (M. Baillet, *DBS* XI 1001). It was in these years after the foundation of Neapolis that the story of Jesus' encounter with the woman of Samaria was being publicly presented as part of the Christian Gospel to the world. [4]

[1] On Josephus' animosity against the Samaritans, see *Ant*. IX xiv 3 = 290-91, plus, in the Loeb edition, the other references listed in vol. VI, fn. *a.* on p.155: *Ant*. XI 19ff., 84ff., 114ff., 174ff., 340ff.; XII 257ff.

[2] An indigenous local name, *War* IV viii 1 = 481, erroneously given as *Mamortha* in Pliny, *Natural History* V xiii = 69 *in fine.*

[3] Eusebius, *Onomasticon,* the Pilgrim of Bordeaux, and Jerome, *Epistula* 108, cited in ELS, 2nd ed., 269-71.

[4] See also at Jn 3.23, the comments on 'The Location of Aenon', pp. 245-47.

THE IDENTIFICATION OF THE SITE OF SYCHAR

The first to localize the site was the Pilgrim of Bordeaux (A.D. 333) who records that it was one [Roman] mile from Joseph's funeral monument 'at Sechim' 'to Sechar' (ELS, 2nd ed., fn. 270 = CSEL 39, 20). ELS, 2nd ed., 218-28 prints 28 texts, ranging from Eusebius of Caesarea to 1626.

Sychar is a *hapax legomenon* in the Bible, and until recently it was commonly identified with the village of 'Askar, 1100 yards north-northeast. of Bir Yakub (Jacob's Well), at grid 1776–1806. Many still favour that location, but others now prefer the little village of Balâta, about 500 yards west-northwest of the Well (grid 1769–1798). Joseph's memorial is today shown some 300 yards north of the Well, but perhaps the site of his tomb has altered since A.D. 333 (for the convenience of pilgrims?).

The main arguments are stated concisely both by Brown I 169 (in favour of Balâta) and by Schnackenburg I = ETr 422-23 (in favour of 'Askar). The fullest presentations are by Kopp and Delcor, both favouring 'Askar. See also J. Briend, who has a slight preference for 'Askar. Everything turns on whether there was during the lifetime of Jesus an inhabited locality at the site of the modern 'Askar. Some think there was, partly because of the similarity (though not identity) of name. They identify it as Sychar, and then interpret the evidence of Eusebius, Jerome and others accordingly. Those convinced that there was no village at all at modern 'Askar until Arab times (the Arabic word means simply 'military camp') locate the ancient Sychar at the site of the modern Balâta. The Sinaitic and Curetonian Syriac both read *Suchem,* not *Sychar*, perhaps to replace an obscure name by a well-known one (*Pons Aelii* is more familiar as Newcastle-upon-Tyne), an indication that the scribes had in mind ancient Shechem, close by modern Balâta. Some suggest that the name Sychar may in the course of time have moved from there 1 km north-east, and later have been assimilated with 'Askar.

There can be no conclusion to the debate until new and decisive archaeological evidence is forthcoming (thus Kopp, very firmly), and since the exact identification of the site does not affect in the slightest the interpretation of the Gospel's teaching, the wisest counsel is to await reports of future excavations. There have been no excavations since 1967.

For further discussion, see the following:

C. Kopp, *Die heiligen Stätten* (1958), 196-211 (= ETr *The Holy Places*, 155-66) (both with fine photographs). The evidence from Eusebius, Jerome and other witnesses presented on pp. 205-10 of the German edition is omitted from the ETr (p. 154, see fn. 48).

M. Delcor, 'Vom Sichem der hellenistischen Epoche zu Sychar des Neuen Testaments', *ZDPV* 78 (1962), 34-48 = *Religion d'Israël et Proche Orient Ancien*, 1976, 389-403.

J. Briend, 'Puits de Jacob', in *DBVS* IX (1975), 386-98.

Z. Stefanovic, 'Jacob's Well', in *ABD* III 608-609.

EXCURSUS XIII

'IN SPIRIT AND TRUTH'

The interpretation of this phrase in Jn 4.23-24, has long been a paradigm of the changing patterns of NT scholarship. The two nouns will be examined first separately[1] and then as a pair.

ἐν πνεύματι

Several Greek writers, under the influence of Platonic philosophy, interpreted πνεῦμα here as that which is distinguished from, opposed to, and contrasted with, the material body, because it is neither σῶμα nor σάρξ nor ὕλη in any way. Thus Chrysostom writes: 'When he says, *God is Spirit*, this means simply that he does not have a body. Therefore the worship of the one who is not corporeal must also be of the same kind, and performed by that which in us is incorporeal, that is, by the soul and by purity of mind.'[2] The same interpretation recurs in Theodore of Mopsuestia, Ammonius, Theophylactus and Euthymius, the last of whom writes οὐ σωματικῶς - ἀλλὰ πνευματικῶς, because πνεῦμα [ὁ θεὸς] τουτέστιν ἀσώματος (*PG* 129.1196). Many Latin writers thought much the same, but, following Augustine, judged the principal teaching of the verse to lie in the implication that the new worship would not be restricted to any particular localities on earth: thus the *Glossa ordinaria* ('non in templo, non in hoc monte, sed interius in intimo templo cordis').

Unsurprisingly, at the time of the Reformation, some began to ask questions about the relevance of this text to the forms of Christian worship. For the Lutherans, Philip Melanchthon declared in 1531 that it excluded all theories which argued that some sacrifices had value *ex opere operato*.[3] John Calvin in his *Commentary* (1553) wrote that it certainly excluded 'an excessive multitude of ceremonies' (*immodica caerimoniarum turba*), and called for 'inner faith of the heart,...purity of

---

[1] As in de la Potterie, *La Vérité*, 673-79: note also 680-706.

[2] ὅταν δὲ εἴπη, Πνεῦμα ὁ Θεὸς, οὐδὲν ἄλλο δηλοῖ, ἢ τὸ ἀσώματον. δεῖ τοίνυν τοῦ ἀσωμάτου καὶ τὴν λατρείαν τοιαύτην εἶναι, καὶ διὰ τοῦ ἐν ἡμῖν ἀσωμάτου προσφέρεσθαι· τουτέστιν, διὰ τῆς ψυχῆς καὶ τῆς τοῦ νοῦ καθαρότητος. *In Ioann*. 33, 2 = 191 DE.

[3] 'Haec sententia clare damnat opiniones de sacrificiis, quae fingunt ex opere operato valere, et docet, quod oporteat spiritu, id est motibus cordis, et fide adorare.' *Apologia Confessionis*, Art. XXIV *De Missa* 27, in *Die Bekenntnisschriften der evangelisch-lutherischen Kirche*, Göttingen, 2nd ed., 1952, 357[7-11].

conscience and self-denial' (*interior cordis fides, quae invocationem parit, deinde conscientiae puritas, abnegatio nostri*). In his *Institutes* he pleaded that any external ceremonies should be few, easy of observance, dignified, and clear in meaning (IV 10, 14; ETr II 1191-93), but neither there nor in his *Commentary* is he specific about the implications of these principles.[4] Some Spanish Jesuits alleged indeed that 'Protestants' were invoking Jn 4.23 to justify the abolition of all liturgical ceremonies,[5] but such was never the teaching of the Churches of the Reformation, and it is significant that Robert Bellarmine, at the very point where he is arguing against the chapter of Calvin's *Institutes* just mentioned, does not make this accusation (see his *De Controversiis* III, II, c. 32, arg. 7[um] 15-17). The first introduction of a regular pattern of 'purely interior and spiritual worship' without any external ceremonies at all is generally ascribed to George Fox (1624–1691) and the Society of Friends (from around 1650 onwards).

The eighteenth-century Enlightenment led inevitably to a radical re-examination of the practical implications of Jn 4.23, 'in spirit and in truth'. It was soon widely accepted that *spirit* here referred to the human intellect and will, that is, to those elements by which a human being is identified and distinguished from all other animals. Then the year 1859 saw the publication of Charles Darwin's *Origin of Species* and of John Stuart Mill's *On Liberty*, and many previously hallowed presuppositions were called into question. In 1863 Ernest Renan (1823–1892) published a *Vie de Jésus* which immediately became a best-seller (60,000 copies in the first four months), partly because of its exquisite French prose, and partly because it expressed what many people of that era wanted to believe: that a gentle, tolerant Jesus had preached a religion in which difficult dogma and uncomfortable law would have no place. Chapter XIV opens with the statement that 'Jesus despised all religion which was not of the heart' and ends with a paragraph pronouncing that 'the day on which Jesus uttered this saying ["shall worship the Father in spirit and in truth"] he was truly Son of God. He pronounced for the first time the sentence upon which will repose the edifice of eternal religion...until the end of time.'[6] Though Renan's book is not a work of scholarship and was never highly esteemed in the academic world,[7] its influence was none the

---

[4] He comments on 4.23: 'Quid sit Deum colere *in Spiritu et veritate*, ex superioribus dilucide patet, nempe, ablatis veterum rituum involucris, simpliciter retinere quod spirituale est in Dei cultu.'

[5] De la Potterie (675 fn. 91) cites 'especially Salmeron, Maldonatus, Ribera, Bellarmine and Toledo', the last of whom writes: 'omnes ceremonias, et ritus Ecclesiasticos tollunt, et sola conscientiae mundicia, adorandum Deum existimant'.

[6] *Vie de Jésus*, 13th ed., Paris, n.d. (1916?), 235 and 244 = ETr (Everyman's Library) 1927, 136 and 140.

[7] Charles Gore concludes his Introduction to the edition in Everyman's Library by describing it as 'an exquisitely conceived and executed romance rather loosely or remotely based upon history'.

less immense, and its publication may serve as a marker of the start of the popularization of 'liberal theology'. Even unquestionably conservative exegetes interpreted the phrase in Jn 4.23 in language which would have been quite acceptable to Renan and other liberal theologians.

Thus Godet commented in 1864: '*Spirit* here denotes that deepest element of the human soul by which it can hold communion with the divine world…' and truth is its corollary: 'the worship rendered in the inner sanctuary of the spirit is the only true one, because it alone corresponds to the nature of God—its object: "God is a spirit"' (ETr II 116). Similarly Westcott in 1880 (and 1908): 'In biblical language [*spirit* denotes] that part of man's nature which holds, or is capable of holding, intercourse with the eternal order, in the spirit (1 Thess 5.23). The spirit of man responds to the Spirit of God. Compare [John] 6.63.' Zahn (1908) draws out at some length the implications of this interpretation: the genuine worshipper will never be obliged to frequent particular places or buildings, or to conform in the observation of days, times or forms.[8] Lagrange too could write in 1925 (*Jean*, 113) : 'Il faut entendre…$\dot{\epsilon}\nu$ $\pi\nu\epsilon\dot{\upsilon}\mu\alpha\tau\iota$ d'une disposition humaine; l'esprit de l'homme est ce qu'il y a en lui de plus pur, de plus semblable à Dieu… L'action de l'Esprit Saint peut être aisément déduite, mais n'est pas indiquée expressément.'

The most obvious weakness of this interpretation is its banality. Neither Jews nor Greeks needed to be reminded that the inward devotion of an upright heart was superior to merely formal acts of external worship, even liturgical ones: compare 1 Kgs 8.27-30; Isa 66.1; Mal 1.11; 1 Sam 15.22 and Hos 6.6. Moreover, 'the cultic worship of God is [in Jn 4.23] contrasted, not with a spiritual, inward form of worship, but with the eschatological worship' (thus Bultmann 140 and fn. 3 = ETr 190 and fn. 4).

A second defect in the interpretation of $\dot{\epsilon}\nu$ $\pi\nu\epsilon\dot{\upsilon}\mu\alpha\tau\iota$ proposed above lies in its understanding of $\pi\nu\epsilon\hat{\upsilon}\mu\alpha$ $\dot{o}$ $\theta\epsilon\acute{o}\varsigma$ in Jn 4.24a. BDAG (here reproducing BAG) gives as the fourth sense of $\pi\nu\epsilon\hat{\upsilon}\mu\alpha$ *an independent noncorporeal being, in contrast to a being that can be perceived by the physical senses, spirit*, and then cites Jn 4.24a as the solitary NT text where $\pi\nu\epsilon\hat{\upsilon}\mu\alpha$ bears this meaning when applied to God (833b). The definition is indubitably applicable to God; but it is difficult to concur that it furnishes a complete and fully satisfactory statement of what the evangelist, when referring to God as *Spirit*, intended (in the light of his Hebrew background) to intimate and to imply.[9]

---

[8] 'Geist bildet auch hier den Gegensatz zum Fleisch und zu allem, was des Fleisches Art hat, zu bestimmten Örtlichkeiten, wohin man wallfahren, zu Gebäude, in denen man sich einfinden, zu sinnlich wahrnehmbaren Handlungen, die man vollziehen muss.' See also the rest of the page (244).

[9] Every other NT reference to God as Spirit is classified under the fifth, sixth or eighth sense, and Jn 4.24a should have been listed under the fifth or eighth.

ἐν ἀληθείᾳ

Similar problems arise when ἐν ἀληθείᾳ in Jn 4.23-24 is interpreted solely in terms of a Greek background.

All Greek writers were familiar with Plato's allegory of the cave (*Republic* VII 514-17A), in which a group of prisoners believed that some shapes they were watching on a wall in front of them were the only reality in the world, until they were released from their chains, and saw that those pictures were but shadows of true reality.[10] The same Platonic background was part of the mind-set of Christian Greek writers too; earthly things were for them a terrestrial reflection of heavenly realities.

This naturally affected their interpretation of the Bible. They saw the persons and events of the OT presented as 'types and shadows' prefiguring the 'true reality' to be revealed in the NT, so that the figures and events in the NT are interpreted by reference to figures and events in the OT, and the 'true meaning' of OT figures such as Adam and Melchizedek is 'finally revealed' in the NT. Thus we find references to type and antitype in τύπος τοῦ μέλλοντος (Rom 5.14), or σκιὰ τῶν μελλόντων (Col 2.17; Heb 10.1), and even αὐτὴν τὴν εἰκόνα τῶν πραγμάτων (Heb 10.1). Origen employs this typological method all the time, and on Jn 4.22-23 writes that true worshippers are those who adore the Father 'in spirit and not in the flesh, in truth and not in prefigurative types' (ἐν πνεύματι καὶ μὴ σαρκί, καὶ ἐν ἀληθείᾳ καὶ μὴ τύποις, XIII xviii: *SC* 109). Many other writers, of the patristic, medieval and Renaissance periods interpret Jn 4.22-23 similarly, as a statement advocating and authorizing the employment of typology in Christian preaching and worship, among whom the most concise is Euthymius: οὐκ ἐν σκιαῖς καὶ τύποις, ἀλλ' ἐν ἀληθείᾳ (*PG* 129.1197 A).[11] The ἐν ἀληθείᾳ in Jn 4.22-23, thus understood, highlights the element of covenantal fulfilment in the worship of the new, Christian, era.[12]

With the Enlightenment, the use of typology became in academic theology unfashionable for many generationss. Even the staunchest of conservative exegetes regularly interpreted ἐν ἀληθείᾳ in Jn 4.23-24 solely in terms of a (Classical) Greek background. Zahn and Lagrange, for example, took the phrase to mean *in sincerity, without duplicity* (as in 1 Jn 3.18 and 2 Cor 7.14; 2 Jn 1 and 3 Jn 1), and though this is certainly

---

[10] F. M. Cornford noted that 'a modern Plato would compare his Cave to an underground cinema, where the audience watch the play of shadows thrown by the film passing before a light at their backs' (*The Republic of Plato*, Oxford, 1941, p. 223 fn.1.)

[11] De la Potterie II 677 fn. 98 lists Chrysostom, Theodore of Mopsuestia, Cyril of Alexandria, Ammonius, Theophylactus, and Didymus of Alexandria (*De Spiritu Sancto* 57: *PG* 39.1081 BC); then Thomas Aquinas, Bonaventure, Calvin, Maldonatus, Ribera and Grotius.

[12] It is strange that de la Potterie (II 677) should decline to accept this interpretation of Jn 4.23 on the ground that ἡ ἀλήθεια is never found in the NT with reference to a Christian antitype. It is even more strange that his work contains not a single reference to Jn 6.55 or 15.1.

one possible meaning of the Greek, it can scarcely be the distinguishing
hallmark of the new eschatological form of worship. Bernard's comment
reads (149): 'This is a general statement, and we must not bring in here
thoughts which are peculiar to Christian docrine, because of that fuller
revelation of God which was granted in the Incarnation'. Nowadays, it
would be difficult to propose these last interpretations as satisfactory
exegesis, but it is well to remember that they represent an over-reaction
against the idea that typology is the primary key for unlocking the meaning of the Bible.

ἐν πνεύματι καὶ ἀληθείᾳ

The thrust of Bultmann's commentary (1941) is easy to perceive. Index
IV[13] reveals the preponderance of references to Gnosticism, Hermeticism,
Mandaeans, Mysteries and Neoplatonism over Judaism, Rabbinism and
particularly over the OT. The commentary on Jn 3.1-21 (92-115 = ETr
131-60) illustrates the author's conviction that whereas the Synoptics
reflect in their form and content the world in which Jesus, the Rabbis and
the primitive Church moved, 'in John one feels that one has been
transported into the world of C. Herm. 13 and the Λόγος τέλειος' (93 =
ETr 132). These principles are applied at Jn 4.23. The clue to the ἐν
πνεύματι καὶ ἀληθείᾳ is, he writes, that 'the cultic worship of God is
contrasted, not with a spiritual, inward form of worship, but with the
eschatological worship. The πνεῦμα is God's miraculous dealing with
men which takes place in the revelation.[14] The ἀλήθεια is the reality of
God revealed in Jesus, the 'Word' of God by which the believers are
'sanctified', i.e. are taken out of this worldly existence and set in the
eschatological existence (17.17,19)' (140 = ETr 190-91). Here there is a
cross-reference to the comment on 1.9, which declares that 'the formal
sense of ἀλήθεια in Johannine and in Hellenistic Greek' is *truth* and
reality (32 fn. 1 = ETr 53 fn. 1). For Bultmann, therefore, ἐν πνεύματι
means that God first commands the attention of the human being by the
revelation spoken in Jesus; and ἐν ἀληθείᾳ means that the only genuine
worship, truly worthy of God, is that in which the creature, by acknowledging God's call as divine (πνεῦμα), responds to that call in the manner
in which God intended and so is 'sanctified' and set free.

Dodd's *Interpretation* took shape in the same era as Bultmann's
Commentary. In *Part I: The Background*, after a brief introductory
chapter, the five essays are devoted to the Hermetic Literature, Hellenistic Judaism (Philo), Rabbinic Judaism, Gnosticism and Mandaism.
Though Dodd's style is utterly different from Bultmann's, and though he
argues that there is in John 'a singularly close interweaving of Hebraic

---

[13] On Religio-historical Relations (562-63: ETr 738-40).

[14] Here Bultmann (98 fn. 3 = ETr 139 fn. 1) argues at length that πνεῦμα represents
'the divine power not as it is in itself, but as it impinges on human existence'.

and Hellenistic conceptions [of the Spirit]' (223), his chapter on 'Spirit' (213-27) is replete with references to Philo and the *Corpus Hermeticum*, and gives far more attention to them than to the OT. The statement that God is πνεῦμα means that he is not σάρξ, and does not belong among τὰ κάτω, cf. Jn 3.6 (258). The phrase ἐν πνεύματι καὶ ἀληθείᾳ is for Dodd 'a virtual hendiadys' (223), meaning 'in spirit, that is, in reality' (258) Similarly, in 4.23 οἱ ἀληθινοὶ προσκυνηταί denotes not *'sincere* worshippers' (with reference to their subjective faith) but *'real* worshippers', that is, those whose religious exercises are in fact and in reality an approach to God, and not a ritual which at best merely symbolizes the approach to God (170). It is not unfair (it is meant as a compliment), to say that Dodd's masterpiece presents the Gospel as Philo might have reviewed it.

Both Bultmann and Dodd intended to interpret the Gospel for twentieth-century readers by examining it against the background of the Greek world of its time. Bultmann's commentary was first published in 1941, Dodd's *Interpretation* in 1953 (dedication 1950). Each represents a high point of the Hellenizing schools of interpretation which were dominant in the first half of the twentieth century. But just at that conjuncture, the very foundations of a purely, or even predominantly, Hellenist interpretation of the Fourth Gospel were about to be swept away by the totally unforeseen discovery in 1947 of the great library at Qumran.

One of the early articles based on Qumran texts appeared in 1959, when Schnackenburg published a short essay on Jn 4.23, soon summarized in his commentary (1965). He argued that the association between *spirit* and *truth* is found several times in the writings of the Qumran community, citing first 1QS 4.20-21 ('He will cleanse him of all wicked deeds with the *spirit of holiness*; like purifying waters He will shed upon him *the spirit of truth*'). The Qumran community believed itself to be, in nascent form, the eschatological community of the Lord; so we read, of the postulant entering, that 'he shall be cleansed from all his sins by *the spirit of holiness uniting him to His truth*' (1QS 3.6-7). 'When these become members of the Community in Israel according to all these rules, *they shall establish the spirit of holiness according to everlasting truth*' (1QS 9.3-5). Similar language recurs in the Thanksgiving Hymns, at (for example) 1QH 7.6-7; 12.11-12; and 16.11. The frequency with which the terms *spirit* and *truth* and *holiness* recur in conjunction with one another can now be checked by referring to the *DCH*.

With this in mind, we may turn to the text of Jn 4.23: ἐν πνεύματι καὶ ἀληθείᾳ. The two abstract nouns, both anarthrous and governed by a single preposition, are here so closely linked that they must be considered a pair, and should be understood in terms of Biblical, not Classical, Greek, corresponding to the Hebrew רוּחַ (rūaḥ) and אֱמֶת (ʔɛmet). Taken together as a pair, they mean 'in accordance with the *inspiration* and *teaching* of God as given through the Law, the prophets and the Wisdom literature, and through contemporary preachers such as the Baptist and

Jesus', and the key to their meaning in Jn 4.23-24 is to be found by considering their position in the Fourth Gospel.

The climax of the Prologue is the assertion in Jn 1.14 that the Word made flesh is *full of grace and truth*, a phrase which echoes the ending of Exod 34.6: 'Yahweh, Yahweh, is a God merciful and gracious, slow to anger, and *abounding in merciful love and faithfulness* (רַב־חֶסֶד וֶאֱמֶת: rab-ḥēsēd wᵉʾēmɛt)...'[15] The Word made flesh is also presented in Jn 1.16-17 as the source of a new χάρις ἀντὶ χάριτος, of a grace which supersedes the very greatest blessings imparted in the Law. In place of νόμος, Jesus brings χάρις καὶ ἀλήθεια. This text in 1.17 marks the final occurrence of χάρις in the Fourth Gospel.[16]

Given the importance of χάρις at the conclusion of the Prologue, and given the centrality of the same term in Pauline theology, it is natural to inquire why the word disappears so soon, and so completely, from John. That question makes this an appropriate point at which to ask also why the term *kingdom of God* (or: *of heaven*) which occurs more than 100 times in the Synoptics (Matthew, 55 times; Mark, 20 times, Luke, 46 times), appears only twice in John (3.3, 5),[17] after which it too disappears from the narrative. The word ἀλήθεια supplies a clue to answering both questions. ἀλήθεια is found only seven times in the Synoptics, but not once as a technical 'theological' term.[18] By contrast, it occurs 25 times in John's Gospel and 20 times in the three Johannine Epistles,[19] and always in a sense pregnant with 'theological', that is 'God-related', meaning. Similarly, the noun πνεῦμα occurs 24 times in John's Gospel, referring always to the Spirit of God or the Spirit of Jesus,[20] until it is finally revealed as 'the Spirit of Truth' (14.17; 15.26; 16.13). In John, πνεῦμα and ἀλήθεια take over the roles allotted in other NT books to χάρις and the kingdom.

For if πνεῦμα and ἀλήθεια are linked together as a pair, the grace (χάρις) which supersedes the Law (1.16-17) is the gift of the Spirit which brings into existence upon earth a kingdom that does not originate in this world (3.3-8[21]), and the truth (ἀλήθεια) which supersedes the Law is the revelation that Jesus embodies, and presents to this world, an

---

[15] The same phrase is in mind at Num 14.18; in the two penitential services after the Exile, at Joel 2.13 and at Neh 9.17 (cf. also Jon 4.2); and regularly in the liturgy of the Second Temple: see Pss 25.10; 40.11-12; 57.11; 61.8; 85.11; 89.15; 115.1; 138.2 (nb); cf. 26.3; 117.2. → Jn 1.14e.

[16] In the other 'Johannine' books of the NT, χάρις occurs only in 1 Jn 3.12 (as χάριν τίνος); in 2 Jn 3, Rev 1.4 and 22.21 as an epistolary greeting.

[17] Plus, if you wish, 'my kingdom' in 18.36 (3×), but nowhere in the Johannine Epistles.

[18] Mt 22.16 ‖ Mk 12.14 ‖ Lk 20.21; Mk 5.33; 12.32; Lk 4.25; 22.59. 'As an attribute of God, or a subject of Christ's teaching, it is non-existent in the Three Gospels' (*JV* 1727m).

[19] Out of a NT total of 109 occurrences (none of them in Revelation).

[20] Of 12 instances in 1 John, four refer to deceitful spirits (4.1 [×2], 3, 6).

[21] Compare οὐκ ἔστιν ἐκ τοῦ κόσμου τούτου, 18.36.

entirely new teaching about the Fatherhood of God. It is not therefore surprising that an ancient tradition interprets the Johannine phrase *in spirit and truth* as referring respectively to the Holy Spirit and to Jesus, the Truth Incarnate. This interpretation is first witnessed in the anti-Arian Fathers, Athanasius, Basil, and Hilary,[22] and it is powerfully presented by Cyril of Alexandria.[23]

It lived on through the Middle Ages, where it is in the West most clearly presented by Rupert of Deutz.[24]

On this interpretation, 'Spirit and Truth' in Jn 4.23-24 entail a consciousness of the abiding presence of Jesus' Spirit in the minds and hearts of his followers *after* his (apparent) physical departure. They are inwardly assured that Jesus, though now to human eyes invisible (cf. 'closed

---

[22] Athanasius, *The First Letter to Serapion*, final paragraph (33), in *PG* 26.605-608 = *SC* 15.144; Basil, *De Spiritu Sancto* xxvi 64, in *PG* 32.186 B; Hilary (in very difficult Latin), *De Trinitate* II 31. Origen is disappointing: his long comment in XIII xviii-xxv 109-53 (*SC* 109 pp. 94-115) contains little of exegetical value.

[23] Cyril's comment on Jn 4.23-24 reads: σημαίνει μὲν τῆς ἑαυτοῦ παρουσίας τὸν ἤδη παρόντα καιρὸν, μετασκευασθήσεσθαι δὲ τοὺς τύπους φησὶν εἰς ἀλήθειαν, καὶ τὴν τοῦ νόμου σκιὰν εἰς λατρείαν πνευματικήν. διὰ δὲ τῆς εὐαγγελικῆς παιδεύσεως εἰς εὐάρεστον τῷ Πατρί πολιτείαν χειραγωγηθήσεσθαι λέγει τὸν ἀληθινὸν προσκυνητήν, τὸν ἄνθρωπον δηλονότι τὸν πνευματικὸν ἑτοιμότερόν πως εἰς οἰκειότητα τρέχοντα τὴν πρὸς θεόν. πνεῦμα γὰρ ὁ θεὸς, ὡς πρὸς ἐνσώματον νοεῖται φύσιν. (Pusey I 284[19-26]). 'Referring to the time (now come) of his own Parousia, he asserts that prefigurative types are going to be transformed into truth, and things foreshadowed in the Law will be transposed into spiritual worship. He declares that the genuine worshipper is going to be led by the hand, through that education which the Gospel provides, into a society that is well pleasing to the Father, and by the genuine worshipper is meant, of course, the spiritual person, who is temperamentally better prepared to hasten towards an intimate relationship of kinship (οἰκειότητα) with God. For to an embodied nature, God is understood as Spirit' (Pusey I 284[19-26]). (On οἰκειότης see *PGL* 5a).

This should be read in conjunction with Cyril's comment on Jn 15.1 in Book X 2: ὅνπερ γάρ τρόπον τῆς ἀμπέλου τὸ πρέμνον τῆς ἰδίας καὶ ἐνούσης αὐτῷ ποιότητος φυσικῆς διακονεῖ τε καὶ διανέμει τοῖς κλήμασι τὴν ἀπόλαυσιν, οὕτως ὁ Μονογενὴς τοῦ Θεοῦ Λόγος, τῆς τε τοῦ Θεοῦ καὶ Πατρὸς καὶ τῆς ἑαυτοῦ φύσεως τὴν οἱονεὶ συγγένειαν τοῖς ἁγίοις ἐντίθησι τὸ Πνεῦμα διδοὺς, ἅτε δὴ καὶ συνενωθεῖσιν αὐτῷ διά τε τῆς πιστέως καὶ τῆς εἰσάπαν ὁσιότητος· τρέφει δὲ πρὸς εὐσέβειαν, καὶ ἁπάσης αὐτοῖς ἀρετῆς καὶ ἀγαθιουργίας εἴδησιν ἐνεργάζεται. (Pusey II 535[25-36²]). 'Just as the root of the vine ministers and distributes to the branches the enjoyment of its own natural and inherent qualities, so the Only-begotten Word of God imparts to the Saints as it were an affinity to His own nature and the nature of God the Father, by giving them the Spirit, insomuch as they have been united with him through faith and perfect holiness' (Vol. II, translated by Thomas Randell, p. 364).

[24] 'Adorabitis, inquit, Patrem, Spiritum adoptionis filiorum ab ipso percipientes... Patrem enim in Spiritu adorare quid est, nisi spiritum adoptionis filiorum accepisse in quo clamamus: Abba Pater. ...Quid est adorare Patrem in veritate, nisi in Filio eius manendo (qui dicit, Ego sum veritas) Patrem invocare? Idem ergo est ac si dixisset: Veri adoratores manifesta ac necessaria distinctione personarum adorabunt unum Deum, Patrem et Filium et Spiritum Sanctum' (*PL* 169.363).

doors' in 20.19,26) remains with them. The relevance of Jn 4.10 and 14 then becomes clear. 'The gift of God' (→ 4.10) and 'the spring of living water' (→ 4.14) both refer to that fuller understanding of the word and wisdom of God which will, with the coming of the Spirit of Truth, inaugurate and establish a New Age. Then in 4.21-24, in answer to the Samaritan's entreaties, Jesus discloses, for the first time in this Gospel, that the epicentre of the liturgy of this New Age will be the worshipping of God of Israel as *Father* (4.21).

The verb προσκυνεῖν figures for the first time in this Gospel at 4.20, where it occurs twice, on the lips of the Samaritan; but it now recurs, in vv. 21-24, *seven* times, on the lips of Jesus—seven being a sacral number symbolizing in Hebrew thought, totality.[25] The sevenfold recurrence signals the need for close attention to the use of this verb by Jesus, and the syntactical variations which accompany its use (without object, or followed by the accusative, or followed by the dative: → 4.20, p. 284) are also significant (compare MHT III 245; *JV* 1641-51; *JG* 2019). In the two occurrences on the lips of the Samaritan in 4.20, the verb is absolute, and refers to both past and present, to what we may call 'indeterminate time'.

In strong contrast, the first occurrence on the lips of Jesus (4.21) is emphatically future, and is followed by the dative, the normal construction in the LXX for the liturgy in the OT: ἔρχεται ὥρα ὅτε οὔτε ἐν τῷ ὄρει τούτῳ οὔτε ἐν Ἱεροσολύμοις προσκυνήσετε τῷ πατρί. The mention of the two Temple-mountains calls attention to the liturgical context, and therefore underlines the declaration that authentic adoration will in the future be directed not just τῷ θεῷ but specifically τῷ πατρί. In 4.22 Jesus uses the present tense of προσκυνεῖν twice, followed by the accusative, while declaring that the Samaritans *are unaware*, the Jews *aware* (→ εἰδέναι at 3.2), of *what* (ὅ) is the object of their worship; the difference lies in the fact that the Samaritans are unaware of so many of God's promises. Then in 4.23a comes the central statement of the septenary, the fourth instance. Jesus speaks again, as in 4.21, of the future (ἔρχεται ὥρα), but with a further comment. He repeats that worship will in the future be given to the Father (προσκυνήσουσιν τῷ πατρί), but adds that this genuine worship will be offered ἐν πνεύματι καὶ ἀληθείᾳ. (The reader is also reminded that this hour *is now come*.) The final three occurrences of προσκυνεῖν draw conclusions from this pronouncement in v. 23a. The fifth instance (4.23b) is a present participle (τοὺς προσ-κυνοῦντας αὐτόν) of indeterminate time, applicable to all time—past, present and future—and to all peoples. Here the term ὁ πατήρ appears, for the first time in John, with reference to the human race.[26] καὶ γὰρ ὁ πατὴρ τοιούτους ζητεῖ. *These are the type of people* whom *the Father is seeking out* (ζητεῖ), those *who are* (already) *worshipping him* (τοὺς προσκυνοῦντας αὐτόν) so that they may in the future worship him with

---

[25] Compare Boismard and Lamouille, *Synopse*, 7 1 on p. 61ab.

[26] The only previous reference was at 3.35: ὁ πατήρ ἀγαπᾷ τὸν υἱόν.

a more informed devotion as *Father* (hence the 'liturgical' dative[27]), *in spirit and in truth*. The septenary closes in 4.24 with two references to those who are already worshipping *him*, though not yet as Father (τοὺς προσκυνοῦντας αὐτόν); it reminds them that *God is Spirit*, and therefore, that all who worship *him* (αὐτόν) should do so *in spirit and truth* (ἐν πνεύματι καὶ ἀληθείᾳ δεῖ προσκυνεῖν).

In this sevenfold statement Jesus declares that God wills to be worshipped as Father, by those who already worship him as God. Jesus 'declares that the genuine worshipper is going to be led by the hand, through that education which the Gospel provides…towards an intimate relationship of kinship'[28] with the Father; this 'guiding by the hand' will come to pass by the perception of the uniqueness of Jesus' own Sonship (→ μονογενής at 1.14,18). This journey into perceiving the fullness of the truth about God as Father and about Jesus as his Unique Son begins through the enlightenment of the Spirit (3.3-8), and is brought to completion through him whom this Gospel calls 'the Holy Spirit, the Paraclete' (14.26), 'the Spirit of Truth', who will lead the disciples in all truth (15.26; 16.13, ὁδηγήσει).

This interpretation, by Cyril of Alexandria, of what is meant by adoring the Father in Spirit and Truth, supplies the foundation for worship in the New Age. This scene is set at the place where Abraham built the first altar in the very centre of the Land (Gen 12.7), and where the Samaritans worshipped. The second great statement about the gift of the Spirit will be proclaimed in the Temple at Jerusalem, on the final day of the Feast of Tents (Jn 7.37-39).

---

[27] → 4.20-24 on προσκυνεῖν.
[28] See Cyril, quoted at length above, p. 313.

4. The Officer from Capernaum:
The New Order Presented to the God-fearing among the Gentiles
(4.46-54)

Since it is widely accepted that Jn 4.46-54 is a retelling of the story of the healing of the centurion's servant given in Lk 7.1-10 ‖ Mt 8.5-13, it will be helpful first to recall the points common to those two Synoptic narratives. Both Matthew and Luke state that the entire episode took place in Capernaum, after Jesus had entered that town (Mt 8.5 ‖ Lk 7.1). Both state that a centurion there had a servant (Luke) or a boy (Matthew) who was grievously ill; that he begged Jesus to restore him to health by simply giving a word of command; that Jesus affirmed that nowhere in Israel had he found such great faith (implying that the centurion was not Jewish); and that when Jesus gave the word of command, the servant (or boy) was restored to health, without Jesus ever having set eyes on him.

The principal differences between the two Synoptics and Jn 4.46-54 are that in John the action takes place in Cana, not in Capernaum, and that where Matthew and Luke write of a centurion, John writes of a βασιλικός. βασιλικός is in itself simply an adjective meaning *royal*, and could be applied to any member of a royal family, or of the royal household.[1] In John 4, the word almost certainly denotes an *official in the service of the king*, that is, of Herod Antipas, tetrarch of Galilee, who, though not technically a king, was often given the title.[2] In consequence, βασιλικός is now usually translated *a (royal) official*, or *officer*.[3] It is impossible to be more precise about the man's role.[4]

Exegetes differ over the man's civic status, some preferring to see him as Jewish because of his official position at court, others, to envisage him as a Gentile because of the Synoptic narrative about the centurion. Bultmann writes: 'It is evident that he is a Jew, since nothing is said to

---

[1] For parallels to the first sense, BDAG refers to Lucian, *Dial. Deor.* 20,1; Ps.-Lucian, *De Salt.* 8; Plutarch, *Moralia* 546e. For parallels to the second sense, see the Lexicon to Josephus, *War* II xxi 3 = 597; V II v 2 = 106.

[2] Compare Mt 14.1 ‖ Lk 9.7, 'the tetrarch', with ‖ Mk 6.14 'the king', the term used also in Mt 14.9; Mk 6.22, 25-27. See BDAG 1.

[3] Translators have struggled to render this term. After the AV = KJV and RV had opted for *nobleman*, the RV margin introduced *king's officer*. Then came RSV, *official*, followed by NRSV NIV NAB, *royal official* (so also BDAG); NEB REB, *officer in the royal service*; JB NJB, *court official*. There is no exact equivalent in the ancient world for the modern distinction between the terms *officer* and *official*; I have preferred *officer* in order to reflect the influence of Matthew and Luke's centurion.

[4] As is, for example, Günther Schwarz, '"καὶ ἦν τις βασιλικός..." (Joh 4.46)', *ZNW* 75 (1984), 138, who suggests that perhaps βασιλικός here represents, by retroversion into Aramaic, מְלִיכָא (mālykāʾ) (others read מְלוֹכָא [mālôkāʾ]), meaning counsellor, as in the Targum of 2 Sam 15.12.

the contrary. Also, Jesus' reply in v. 48 in John can have been addressed only to a Jew' (152 Anm. 3 = ETr 206 fn. 7). Schnackenburg is less certain. He writes first: 'The term can mean a court official or—less probably—a military man. In the latter case, he would most likely be a pagan' (I 497 = ETr I 465-66).[5] Then he adds that according to v. 48 Jesus seems to include the man among the Jews of Galilee (though this could be just an impression evoked by the wording of the evangelist), but decides in the end that the evangelist does not seem at all interested in whether he is a Jew or not. See further in Schnackenburg I 504 = ETr I 473.

Bultmann suggests that the Johannine narrative has introduced into the original story a number of variations, among them, changing the heathen officer into a Jewish court official, to illustrate the motif of faith and signs. But when one recalls the generous tribute paid to the centurion by the Jewish elders in Lk 7.4-5 ('he is worthy—he loves our nation and has himself had a synagogue built for us'), it seems likely that Luke (at least) regarded his man as being, in religious terms, not a heathen, but rather one of those God-fearing Gentiles who regularly took part in Jewish worship.[6] See Schürer III 161-73 for the extent of their presence.

If the βασιλικός in John is thus understood, as one of these God-fearers (compare Acts 13.16, 26 and 43[7]), then this fourth and final section of John 3–4 completes the picture of the New Jerusalem by providing within it a prominent place for all who, though not of the Jewish race, shared in the worship of the people of Israel. If this hypothesis is true, some may wonder why John altered the term *centurion*. The most probable explanation is that *centurion* might have seemed to imply positively that the soldier was a Gentile and in no way associated with the people of Israel. John's Gospel is so ordered that Jesus never speaks with a Gentile (not even with the Greeks in 12.20-23) until its climax, when he comes face to face with Pontius Pilate in 18.33-38. The God-fearers (or proselytes), however, were not classed simply as 'Gentiles' without qualification.

4.46 So he came again to Cana in Galilee, where he had made the water wine. Now there was in the service of the king an officer, who had a son that was ill, in Capernaum. 47 This man, having heard that Jesus had come from Judea into Galilee, set off to contact him and started begging him to come down and heal his son, for he was nearly dying. 48 So Jesus said to him, 'Is it the case that, unless you first see signs and wonders, your party will not believe?' 49 The king's officer said to him, 'Sir, come down before my little boy dies.' 50 Jesus said to him, 'Go on your way; your son is going to live.' The man believed the

---

[5] A footnote directs the reader to Josephus, *Ant.* XVII viii 3 = 198, which lists by nationality the guards at the funeral of Herod the Great—Thracians, Germans, Gauls.

[6] See Excursus XIV, 'The Roman Centurion'.

[7] Acts 13.16, ἄνδρες Ἰσραηλῖται καὶ οἱ φοβούμενοι τὸν θεόν, ἀκούσατε; 13.26, ἄνδρες ἀδελφοί, υἱοὶ γένους Ἀβραὰμ καὶ οἱ ἐν ὑμῖν φοβούμενοι τὸν θεόν; and 13.43, πολλοὶ τῶν Ἰουδαίων καὶ τῶν σεβομένων προσηλύτων.

word that Jesus had spoken to him and went his way. [51] While he was still on
his way down, his servants met him and told him that his boy[8] was going to
live. So he inquired of them the hour when he had begun to mend, and they
said to him, 'Yesterday at the seventh hour the fever left him'. [53] The father
knew that was the hour when Jesus had said to him, 'Your son is going to
live'; and he himself believed, and all his household. [54] This was, yet again, a
second sign that Jesus did when he had come from Judea to Galilee.

**4.46. ἦλθεν οὖν πάλιν εἰς τὴν Κανὰ τῆς Γαλιλαίας, ὅπου
ἐποίησεν τὸ ὕδωρ οἶνον. καὶ ἦν τις βασιλικὸς οὗ ὁ υἱὸς
ἠσθένει ἐν Καφαρναούμ.** *Cana in Galilee* has already been identified
with Khirbet Qana (map reference 1787 2478), some 9 miles = 15 km due
north of Nazareth (→ 2.1). It is approximately 25 miles = 40 km distant
from Capernaum, by a road which climbs from more than 600 feet (212
metres) below sea level to some 750 feet (250 metres) above it. On the
word **βασιλικός**, see the introductory paragraphs above to this section.[9]

**47. οὗτος ἀκούσας ὅτι Ἰησοῦς ἥκει ἐκ τῆς Ἰουδαίας εἰς τὴν
Γαλιλαίαν ἀπῆλθεν πρὸς αὐτὸν καὶ ἠρώτα ἵνα καταβῇ καὶ
ἰάσηται αὐτοῦ τὸν υἱόν, ἤμελλεν γὰρ ἀποθνῄσκειν.** To travel
from Capernaum to Cana would normally require an early start and a
midday break for food and rest, both for the travellers and for their
mounts; and a person equivalent in rank to a centurion would not undertake such a journey alone, or on foot (Lagrange). So, where Matthew and
Luke begin their narratives by stating that Jesus had already entered
Capernaum, John begins by telling his readers that the father had already
left his ailing son and undertaken a very arduous journey in order to
present his request to Jesus. The implication is that this man has real
faith. ἀπῆλθεν πρὸς αὐτόν, *set off to contact him*, is aorist, but **ἠρώτα** is
imperfect, therefore *started begging him*, because the petition is held to
be as yet unachieved (BDF 328; MHT III 64-65). καταβῇ is well chosen
for the long descent, and the present tense of ἀποθνῄσκειν brings out
clearly that the boy would soon *be dying*.

48. εἶπεν οὖν ὁ Ἰησοῦς πρὸς αὐτόν. Jesus' words to a single person
are normally introduced not by εἶπε(ν) but by λέγει. In John, εἶπε(ν)
on its own (i.e. without ἀπεκρίθη καί) occurs in nine cases only, each of
considerable importance, six of which concern miracles,[10] as here (thus
JG 2456). Jesus neither consents to nor declines the request, but
addresses to the speaker (πρὸς αὐτόν) a sentence in the plural, implying

---

[8] The only instance of the word παῖς in John, who elsewhere always prefers υἱός:
see *TCGNT*, which rates the reading παις {B}.

[9] The variant βασιλισκος, supported, in Jn 4.46 and 49, by D a and some bohairic
witnesses, is a diminutive, meaning a *petty king*, possibly inserted to correspond with the
rendering *regulus* in the Old Latin and the Vulgate (Lagrange).

[10] Jn 1.42; 12.7; 19.11, and (in the context of a miracle) 4.48; 5.14; 9.7, 35, 37; 11.25.

that the man has not come alone, and that Jesus is speaking to the whole party. Compare the retinue in Lk 7.4-7.

[ἐὰν μὴ] **σημεῖα καὶ τέρατα** [ἴδητε]. In the LXX σημεῖα καὶ τέρατα always translates the Hebrew בְּאֹתֹת וּבְמֹפְתִים (be'otot ubemo-petim), which, whenever it is found in the plural, refers always, with the one exception of Isa 8.18, to the *signs and wonders* worked at the Exodus. In this sense, it occurs 15 times in the HB: Exod 7.3; Deut 4.34; 6.22; 7.19; 26.8; 28.48; 29.2; 34.11; [Isa 8.18;] 20.3; Jer 32.20, 21; Pss 78.43; 105.27; 135.9; Neh 9.10 (HT = LXX Esdras B 19.10, where some codices carry καὶ τέρατα, but not all). The same pair of Hebrew words in the singular occur together in three texts, at Deut 13.2-3 (HT: EVV 13.1-2) and 28.46, but these texts in the singular do not refer to signs worked at the Exodus. Otherwise the two words are not found together in the HB. The same usage, always with reference to the Exodus, is found in the LXX, at Bar 2.11; Wis 8.8; 10.16, and compare Sir 36.5 (σ. καὶ θαυμασια); the phrase occurs also, once only, in the *OTP* (see *CGPAT* 735), in *Ezekiel the Tragedian* at line 226 in the *OTP* II 817. For Philo and Josephus see *TWNT* VII 220-21 and 221-23 respectively (K. H. Rengstorf). In short, σημεῖα καὶ τέρατα (in the plural) always refers to *signs and wonders* comparable to those at the Exodus.

ἐὰν μὴ ... ἴδητε. ἐάν followed by the aorist subjunctive 'represents a definite event as occurring only once in the future and conceived as taking place before the time of the action of the main verb' (MHT III 114 [a] [2]): therefore, *Unless you first see... **οὐ μὴ πιστεύσητε.*** οὐ μή to express emphatic denial is in the NT almost restricted to the book of Revelation (16 times), quotations from the LXX, and the words of Jesus (57/61 occurrences in the gospels): see Zerwick–Smith §444; MHT III 96. οὐ μὴ πιστεύσητε here is consequently taken by many, perhaps most, as an emphatic denial (BDF 365). Another interpretation is, how-ever, possible: the words can, alternatively, be construed as a question (compare Lk 18.7; Jn 18.11; Rev 15.4). Jesus would then be saying, *Is it the case that unless you first see signs and wonders, your party will not begin to believe?* (*your party*, to represent the plural verb). On either interpretation, Jesus deprecates the desire to see signs and wonders as a precondition of believing, but the second interpretation seems to lead more smoothly into v. 49.

49. λέγει πρὸς αὐτὸν ὁ βασιλικός, Κύριε, κατάβηθι. This officer is, after the Samaritan woman (4.11, 15, 19), the second person in the Gospel to address Jesus by the title κύριε. κατάβηθι, *come down* (to Capernaum). **πρὶν ἀποθανεῖν τὸ παιδίον μου.** The diminutive τὸ παιδίον μου (contrast the narrator's formal τὸν υἱόν in v. 47) is as affectionate as it is natural, and is placed, for emphasis, at the end of the sentence. The aorist in πρὶν ἀποθανεῖν contrasts sharply with the present infinitive ἀποθνῄσκειν in v. 47: the aorist ('*does in fact die*') expresses trust in Jesus. *'Sir, come down before my little boy dies'.*

Κύριε, κατάβηθι, shows that the speaker has in a very real sense trust in Jesus as a healer of the sick. Yet this trust cannot be called, without qualification, faith. Indeed, κύριε, κατάβηθι is the very opposite of the centurion's entreaty in Mt 8.8 ‖ Lk 7.6-7, begging Jesus not to come to his house; and Jesus' reply in Jn 4.50 (recalling the centurion's words?) is admirably glossed by Theodore of Mopsuestia as 'It is not necessary for me to come down; for me, it is sufficient that I should simply speak'. **λέγει αὐτῷ ὁ Ἰησοῦς, πορεύου.** Was this first occurrence of πορεύεσθαι in John perhaps inspired by the centurion's use of the same verb as the first example of the type of command that he was accustomed to issue (πορεύθητι, Mt 8.9 ‖ Lk 7.8)? That query is impossible to resolve, but Jesus does tell the officer, quite simply, *Go on your way. Your son is going to live.* **ὁ υἱός σου ζῇ.** ζῇ is a futural present, which we may define as 'differing from the future tense mainly in the tone of assurance which is imparted' (MHT I 120) and which is frequently found in prophecies (BDF 323). Compare 3 Kgdms 17.23: βλέπε, ζῇ ὁ υἱός σου. **ἐπίστευσεν ὁ ἄνθρωπος τῷ λόγῳ ὃν εἶπεν αὐτῷ ὁ Ἰησοῦς καὶ ἐπορεύετο.** This statement represents a clear advance on the simple trust in Jesus as a healer, depicted in v. 49. *To give credence to the word which Jesus had spoken to him,* and to set off without more ado to return to Capernaum unaccompanied by Jesus, was indeed an act of true faith; and it was uninfluenced by any signs or wonders. In these words, the man is presented as having now reached the same level of faith as that portrayed by Matthew and Luke in the story of the centurion.

51. ἤδη δὲ αὐτοῦ καταβαίνοντος is a genitive absolute, common in the Koine, where Classical Greek would have a concordant participle (BDF 423; MHT III 322). Here it denotes an action going on when something else happens: since the participle is in the present tense, ἤδη must be translated not as *already,* but as *still. While he was still on his way down, his servants met him and told him that his boy*[11] *was going to live.*

52. ἐπύθετο οὖν τὴν ὥραν παρ' αὐτῶν. ἐπύθετο is aorist but there is some slight support for the variant ἐπυνθάνετο preferred by Chrysostom and supported by some Old Latin texts (*a d f*) and the Vulgate (*interrogabat*), which would mean *he tried to ascertain* (compare BDF 328; *JG* 2465c). Turner is judiciously cautious about accepting here the imperfect tense and the interpretation which accompanies it; he wisely prefers to see in the aorist ἐπύθετο a most urgent query, to which the answer was already known (MHT III 65). *So he inquired of them the hour when he began to mend.* **εἶπαν οὖν αὐτῷ ὅτι ἐχθὲς ὥραν ἑβδόμην.** For the accusative to denote the point of time, Turner cites Demosthenes

---

[11] The only instance of the word παῖς in John, who elsewhere always prefers υἱός: see *TCGNT*, which rates the reading {B}.

54,10 ἐκείνην τὴν ἑσπέραν *on that evening*, and for the Koine refers to MHT I 63 (MHT III 248). There is no particular symbolism in the fact that the hour was the seventh, though we may deduce that the officer and his party must have set off from Capernaum very early indeed, perhaps before first light, in order to have arrived in Cana just one hour after noon. The customs of hospitality imply that the group spent the night as guests at Cana, and returned the following day.

53. ἔγνω οὖν ὁ πατὴρ ὅτι ἐν ἐκείνῃ τῇ ὥρᾳ ἐν ᾗ εἶπεν αὐτῷ ὁ 'Ιησοῦς, ὁ υἱός σου ζῇ, καὶ ἐπίστευσεν αὐτὸς καὶ ἡ οἰκία αὐτοῦ ὅλη. In the ὅτι clause, some verb such as ἦν must be understood: in John, 'Ellipse is rather frequent after ὅτι, 4.53' (MHT III 304, citing further instances). **ἐπίστευσεν.** This concluding statement, that the officer *believed, and all his household*, can only mean, in Johannine usage, that their new faith in Jesus was complete and absolute. Compare the two statements about the centurion Cornelius in Acts 10.2 ('before'), εὐσεβὴς καὶ φοβούμενος τὸν θεὸν σὺν παντὶ τῷ οἴκῳ αὐτοῦ, and 11.14 ('after'), σωθήσῃ σὺ καὶ πᾶς ὁ οἶκός σου.

54. τοῦτο [δὲ] πάλιν δεύτερον σημεῖον ἐποίησεν ὁ 'Ιησοῦς ἐλθὼν ἐκ τῆς 'Ιουδαίας εἰς τὴν Γαλιλαίαν. As Jn 2.11 marked the ending of the First Week with the first sign at Cana, so this second sign marks the ending of the second section of the Gospel.

This verse is regularly cited in support of the hypothesis that the Gospel writer took this narrative from an earlier source (sometimes called a 'Semeia-Source') which contained also the account of the first 'sign' at Cana (2.1-11). That Jn 4.54 is consonant with that hypothesis cannot be doubted; but it is also compatible with other proposals, such as that John based his narrative on written documents (now lost) which pre-dated the written texts of Matthew and Luke, or even, and perhaps more attractively, on an oral tradition. If this last hypothesis were accepted, Jn 4.46-53 could represent a version that was cherished in the family circle at Khirbet Qana (→ 2.12, on Kaukab), of which a more condensed variant was preached elsewhere (see the comment on ἐπίστευσεν in 4.50), and subsequently incorporated into the Gospels of Matthew and Luke. But in the end, none of the above hypotheses is proved or is, in the absence of first-century literary texts, demonstrable, nor does any one of them appear seriously to affect the meaning of the text.

THE DOUBLE MEANING OF ΠΟΡΕΥΟΥ IN JOHN 4.50

The Greek text of Jn 4.46-53 contains exactly 160 words, the first 80 ending in v. 50 with λέγει αὐτῷ ὁ 'Ιησοῦς, and the second half beginning with πορεύου, ὁ υἱός σου ζῇ. These are the central words of the narrative.

John's normal and preferred word for locomotion is ἔρχεσθαι (157 times) with its compounds (ἀπέρχεσθαι, 21 times; εἰσέρχεσθαι, 15 times; ἐξέρχεσθαι, 30 times; plus 8 others).[12] He uses also ἀναβαίνειν (16 times) and καταβαίνειν (17 times), but always to emphasize the prefix *up* or *down* (the simplex βαίνειν does not occur in the NT). πορεύεσθαι is used less frequently, but, it would seem, with a purpose.

The verb πορεύεσθαι occurs 16 times in John,[13] and ἐκπορεύεσθαι, twice (5.29; 15.26). BDAG gives three meanings: (1) *to proceed, to travel*; (2) *to conduct oneself, to live, to walk*, as in Lk 1.6; Acts 9.31; 14.16; 1 Pet 4.3; 2 Pet 3.3; Jude 11.16; (3) *to go to one's death* (Lk 22.22) as a figurative extension of (1). The first meaning, *to proceed, to travel*, certainly applies to the first two occurrences in John, at 4.50 (πορεύου... καὶ ἐπορεύετο), and to the last one, Jesus' command to Mary Magdalene in 20.17 (πορεύου πρὸς τοὺς ἀδελφούς μου).[14] If we discount the three occurrences in the *pericope de adultera* (7.53–8.11), the remaining ten instances in John all refer to Jesus himself, the first two (in 7.35) being a question by the Jews ('Where is he about to go?'), and the other eight, all statements by Jesus about where he is going (10.4; 11.11; 14.2, 3, 12, 28; 16.7, 28). For this evangelist, there is something special about the verb πορεύεσθαι, which can best be illustrated from its use in the LXX.

In Classical Greek the verb is scarcely ever used in a metaphorical sense (see LSJ: *TWNT* VI 567[18-25]: *Oedipus Tyrannus* 884 is a rare example). In the LXX, by contrast, the verb πορεύεσθαι is regularly used to denote *walking in the paths* set down by Yahweh. The best example is Ps 118(119).1: μακάριοι οἱ ἄμωμοι ἐν ὁδῷ οἱ πορευόμενοι ἐν νόμῳ κυρίου, but there are numerous others (see *TWNT* VI 570[29]-71[38]). In the NT, πορεύεσθαι, when used of the travels of Jesus, is never simply a statement about his movements from one locality to another: it always connotes the concept of his divine mission (*TWNT* VI 574[9-24]). It is to be regretted that the authors of the article in the *TWNT* VI write that the use of πορεύεσθαι 'in a figurative sense' is, by contrast with the LXX, rare in the NT, and with the exception of Lk 1.6, totally absent from the Four Gospels and Paul (*TWNT* VI 575[3-17]). As far as John is concerned, the 'figurative' use so common in the LXX is always there: Jesus' affirmations that he is going to the Father (Jn 14.12, 28; 16.7, 28), and going to prepare a place for his disciples (14.2, 3) can hardly be restricted to an assertion of local separation from the disciples. This journey is to be understood as an action on earth undertaken in perfect harmony with the will of his Father in heaven: *walking in his ways*.

It is logical, therefore, to interpret the three instances of πορεύου in Jn 4.50; 20.17 also as referring to something more than physical travel. In

---

[12] The figures are taken from *NTVoc* 105 and include the *pericope de adultera*.

[13] If we include the three occurrences in 7.53–8.11.

[14] And to the three occurrences in 7.53–8.11.

the LXX, πορεύου or the aorist πορεύθητι is regularly used for the unconditional command of God summoning a person to a mission. So it was with Abraham (Gen 22.2); Nathan (2 Kgdms 7.5); Elijah (3 Kdms 19.15); Isaiah (Isa 6.8-9; 38.5); Jeremiah (Jer 3.12 [LXX]; 42[= Heb. 35].13); Ezekiel (Ezek 3.1); and Hosea (Hos 3.1) (TWNT VI 571³⁴⁻³⁸). So it was with the officer in Jn 4.50: πορεύου, the present imperative, signifies not *Commence*, but *Continue your journey*, first undertaken in faith and hope of healing. *The man believed the word which Jesus had spoken to him, καὶ ἐπορεύετο (imperfect), and continued his journey* back to Capernaum. So ch. 4 concludes with the affirmation of the establishment of a household of followers of Jesus consisting of people not of Jewish blood, in Capernaum.

* * *

Here the part entitled in this commentary 'The New Jerusalem' ends. Its first part, 'The New Temple' (2.13-22) concluded with the statement that after Jesus had risen from the dead, his disciples remembered what he had said, and 'believed in the scripture and the word that Jesus had spoken' (2.22). The second section, here designated 'The New People' (2.23–4.54), was introduced by two somewhat disconcerting statements: that while Jesus was in Jerusalem at the festival of Passover, 'many began to believe (ἐπίστευσαν) in his name', but that Jesus 'would not trust himself to them (οὐκ ἐπίστευεν αὐτὸν αὐτοῖς)' (→ 2.23-24). The two statements in 2.23-24 imply that the meaning of πιστεύειν needs clarification, and it is in chs. 3 and 4 that this clarification begins.

In Jn 3.1-21 (Nicodemus and Judaism), πιστεύειν occurs seven times, four of them in a positive sense (3.12, 15, 16, 18) and three with a negative attached (3.12, 18 [×2]). In the passage addressed to followers of the Baptist, the verb occurs but once, in a very firm and formal positive sense (3.36). In all these texts, seven relating to the Jews and one to the disciples of the Baptist, the 'believing' concerns accepting Jesus as the heaven-sent Son of God, τὸν υἱὸν τὸν μονογενῆ, and perceiving that πᾶς ὁ πιστεύων εἰς αὐτὸν ἔχῃ ζωὴν αἰώνιον (3.16, cf. 36). In John 4 there are again seven occurrences of πιστεύειν, four in vv. 1-45 and three in vv. 46-54, but there is no reference to Jesus as 'Son', and only one short, though significant, passage about worshipping God as Father (4.21, 23). In Samaria, Jesus is presented as a prophet (v. 19), as the Messiah (vv. 25, 26, 29), and finally as the Saviour of the world (v. 42). The four occurrences of the verb πιστεύειν in vv. 21, 39, 41, 42, there-fore always apply to Jesus as a heaven-sent eschatological, but human, figure. In the tale of the official from Capernaum πιστεύειν refers to 'believing' the word of Jesus (vv. 48, 50, 53). At this stage, then, the Gospel asks the Samaritans, and the God-fearers among the Gentiles, simply to accept the teaching of Jesus as a holy man sent from heaven, and to continue to listen to him.

THE ROMAN CENTURION

There is so far no archaeological or epigraphic evidence for the presence of units from the Roman army in Galilee during the years of Jesus' ministry, but that is not proof that there were no individual officers there, perhaps on loan to Herod Antipas, perhaps in retirement.[1] Capernaum was no great distance from Bethsaida Julias to the east of the Jordan, and wherever exactly the latter be located (→ 1.44 fn.), it was certainly close to the border of Philip's territory, and on land which, upon Philip's death childless in A.D. 34, passed by the terms of his will to Tiberius and was thereafter incorporated into the province of Syria (*Ant.* XVIII iv 6 = 106-108). It would not be surprising to find, even before that date, some Roman centurions assisting with the supervising of customs, trade and migration across the borders of the two tetrarchies, the Decapolis and the Province of Syria.

Roman army personnel were employed to do all manner of things, especially in peace-time, notably road-building, bridge-building and tax-collecting; they also served as messengers, interpreters and effectively as a police force, as arbitrators in boundary disputes and as diplomatic envoys. The centurions, who formed the backbone of the army, generally served a life-time in that rank and normally died in service. One striking feature of their rank is the extent to which they were cross-posted from legion to legion, and from province to province, according to need. One man, Petronius Fortunatus, probably by birth an African, served over a period of 46 years in no less than 13 different legions. Given that the Roman army was also deeply religious, even superstitious, and therefore careful to show proper reverence to the *genius loci*, it is not unlikely that some centurions serving in the East should have begun to worship with the Jews, as God-fearing Gentiles. In fact, it would have been more surprising if there had been none.

---

[1] See A. von Domaszewski, *Die Rangordnung des römischen Heeres*, 2nd ed. revised by Brian Dobson, Köln, 1967, 109; Graham Webster, *The Roman Imperial Army of the First and Second Centuries A.D.*, London, 1969, 2nd ed., 1979, especially Chapter VI, 'The Army in Peaceful Activities', 261-80; plus, on the centurion, 117-20, on their pay, 259-60, and on Petronius Fortunatus, 119; G. R. Watson, *The Roman Soldier*, London, 1969, 143-46 (the soldier in peacetime); Benjamin Isaac, *The Limits of Empire: the Roman Army in the East*, rev. ed., Oxford, 1992, 434-45.